Special Edition
Using
Microsoft®
Active
Directory™

Sean Fullerton

James Hudson

201 W. 103rd Street
Indianapolis, Indiana 46290

CONTENTS AT A GL...

SPECIAL EDITION USING MICROSOFT® ACTIVE DIRECTORY™

TRADEMARKS

WARNING AND DISCLAIMER

Development Editor
Victoria Elzey

Technical Editors
Ben Smith
Joanie Rhine
Robert Dring
Steve Judd
Mike Sheketoff
Steve McQuiggen

Managing Editor
Thomas F. Hayes

Project Editor
Tonya Simpson

Copy Editor
Megan Wade

Indexer
Chris Barrick

Proofreader
Jeanne Clark

Team Coordinator
Cindy Teeters

Interior Designer
Ruth Harvey

Cover Designers
Dan Armstrong
Ruth Harvey

Page Layout
Darin Crone
Lizbeth Patterson

CONTENTS

FOREWORD

I joined the Windows NT Server team in early 1995 to work on directory services. My interest in directory services grew out of experiences in developing distributed systems. A distributed system needs a naming service that the elements can use to locate each other. I wanted a naming service that was flexible, secure, and scalable—more than that I wanted a naming service that supported rich query. I saw working on the project that produced Windows 2000 and Active Directory as an opportunity to produce just such a naming service.

Directory services and naming services are often viewed as different animals, but they are in fact the same thing. Many people view a directory service as a store of name and address information about people, like an X.500 directory. In contrast, they view a naming service as a way of getting addresses for computers, given their names, like DNS. In reality, X.500 and DNS provide similar capabilities—given a name, either service can return information associated with that name. Active Directory differs from other directories in that it was designed from the beginning to be a general-purpose repository of information about interesting objects with no particular bias about the kind of objects it will contain. Active Directory combines the rich object model of X.500 with the scalability and simplicity of DNS.

Many contemporary discussions of directory service focus on the Lightweight Directory Access Protocol (LDAP). Ultimately, LDAP is a footnote in the directory service story, not the story itself. A directory service is not useful because it implements a particular protocol; it is useful because it serves the needs of users, administrators, and developers. Active Directory was designed from the beginning to meet the needs of all three communities—this is a key point to remember as you read this book. Users want streamlined access to the resources they need to do their jobs; administrators want a straightforward way to organize and secure those resources; and developers want a programming model that is simple enough to use in small applications and rich enough to use in the largest and most complex jobs.

Active Directory was designed as the hub around which the distributed system is built. It is an integral part of Windows 2000, and understanding Active Directory is the key to a successful Windows 2000 deployment. Future releases of Windows will provide even greater integration with Active Directory. The wide deployment, rich programming model, and ease of integration will encourage developers to integrate their own products with Active Directory.

I hope that readers will strive to learn not just *how* to deploy and manage Windows 2000 using Active Directory, but to understand *why* Active Directory works the way it does and what new capabilities it brings to users, administrators, and developers.

Steve Judd
Redmond, WA
June 2000

ABOUT THE AUTHORS

Sean Fullerton is the President and Principal Consultant for Fullerton Information Services, Inc., in Tulsa, OK. He specializes in Windows 2000, Exchange, and development for both platforms. As a trainer, Sean has delivered Active Directory training to Microsoft Consulting Services consultants throughout the United States and Europe. Sean currently holds the MCSE, MCP+ Site Builder, and MCT certifications.

James Hudson is Senior Instructor for Network Enterprise Technologies in Tulsa, OK. He is an MCSE+I, MCDBA, MCSD, MCP+SB, MCT, CTT, ECNE, MCNI, CCNA, CCDA, and CNX. He has been teaching and consulting on a number of Microsoft products since 1991. He has been a beta tester for Windows 2000 since Beta 1 and has been using and developing exclusively for Windows 2000 since mid-1998.

DEDICATION

This book is dedicated to Jesus Christ, who has provided me with the intellect and support that have made this book possible.

"...And lo I am with you always, even unto the end of the age." Matthew 28:20

—Sean Fullerton

"Who among the gods is like you O LORD, who is like you—majestic in holiness, awesome in glory, working wonders." Exodus 15:11

—James Hudson

SEAN FULLERTON'S ACKNOWLEDGMENTS

First in line is Jim Hudson. What an amazing coauthor. He has encouraged me, challenged me, and been an inspiration to me throughout.

Others who have helped this book to become a reality are Shawn Murray, for getting me involved in the "World Readiness Tour;" Dean Wells (MSETechnology); Joshua Konkle (Digital Knowledge); and all those people who have influenced my life that has led me to this point.

Thanks to both of my parents, for teaching me that the phrase "I can't" does not exist and showing me that there is nothing that I cannot do or achieve if I set my mind to it and for showing me how to think outside the box.

A big thanks goes to Cameron Blake Fullerton for holding down the business while I was buried in my cave working on this book. You made it possible to keep going.

And for the best part of my life, my wife Sharon. She is a trooper to have put up with me while writing this book. She is the light at the end of the tunnel and the song that makes my heart happy. I love you and thank you for loving me!!!

JAMES HUDSON'S ACKNOWLEDGMENTS

There is a huge crowd of people standing behind this book. Thank you Sean for inviting me along; it has been an amazing ride. Thanks to the most important people in my life, Wren, Ian, and Caitlyn, for the times you let me work on the book. Thanks to them and my parents, grandparents, and the rest of my family who encouraged me and gave me the freedom to work hard and to do my best.

To the crowd at Que, who took my poorly expressed rants and made them work.

A big thank you to the folks at Microsoft for making a product I can be passionate about. Thank you for the Tech Weeks, Tech Eds, and conferences where you communicated so much to us early in the beta cycle and through to RTM.

Thanks to the tech editors for improving the book. So many people at Microsoft and the tech editor team worked to get us good information. The mistakes, however, are mine alone.

Proverbs 22:29 says, "Do you see a man skilled in his work? He will stand before Kings, he will not stand before obscure men." Oh, to be that guy someday.

CHAPTER 1

INTRODUCTION TO ACTIVE DIRECTORY

In this chapter

WINDOWS 2000 ACTIVE DIRECTORY

This book is about Windows 2000 Active Directory. Active Directory is a directory service (DS)—a distributed, hierarchical database of objects. Active Directory objects can be users, computers, groups, organizational units, domains, trees, and so on. In addition, Active Directory is fully extensible, and if it does not contain an object type you need, you can simply create one. Active Directory runs on Windows 2000 Domain Controllers and can be accessed by Windows 9x, NT, and 2000 clients. However, to fully take advantage of Active Directory, the client must be Windows 2000.

Active Directory is scalable. A single domain can hold millions of objects. Because it implements multimaster replication, almost any information about an object can be changed on any Active Directory Domain Controller (DC). This eliminates the need to find a central point of modification.

Active Directory is also fault tolerant. An Active Directory domain can (and should) contain more than one Domain Controller. If one DC becomes unavailable, clients can find another DC to authenticate to and use it to search for objects in the Active Directory database.

Windows 2000 and Active Directory are standards based. Active Directory is based on the X.500 standard and includes a myriad of technologies whose implementations are governed by the International Engineering Task Force (IETF) and other standards bodies. These include TCP/IP networking, X.509 public key infrastructures, LDAP v3.0 for finding objects, Kerberos v5 for authentication, and SNTP for keeping time synchronized.

Active Directory implements open APIs, Active Directory Services Interface (ADSI), and Lightweight Directory Access Protocol (LDAP). Information about writing applications to take advantage of Active Directory is freely available on Microsoft's Web site and includes white papers with sample code.

Windows 2000 Active Directory is stable. This is one of the most heavily tested products Microsoft has ever produced. Numerous companies have implemented Windows 2000 and Active Directory in e-commerce sites and massive enterprises and have seen their downtime decrease dramatically.

Active Directory is secure. The Kerberos authentication protocol has been tested and found secure for years. It uses state-of-the-art encryption algorithms. Windows 2000 is much more locked down out of the box than previous versions and includes templates to enable the administrator to customize the computers and Domain Controllers to the desired level of security.

HISTORY OF DIRECTORY SERVICES

Windows 2000 Active Directory is a directory service. Virtually every directory service in the last decade owes its inception to the X.500 standard. Directory services have evolved as the need for them has changed.

X.500

X.500 is an ISO standard for a directory service. It incorporates a very rich, searchable database of information about the objects it represents. It was first produced in 1988 and has been the standard from which most modern directory service implementations have evolved.

Some of the features of X.500, however, are also the reason it has never been fully implemented as a globally accepted product. It is built to run on the OSI protocol stack, which has never been broadly embraced. It also is very data rich and tends to overload the networks on which it runs. Finally, it has a reputation for being very complex to administer. Various implementations of this standard have appeared over the years, but none has ever achieved the kind of market critical mass necessary to become broadly accepted.

LDAP

Lightweight Directory Access Protocol was actually an attempt to "lighten" the overhead required for X.500 and still maintain the base functionality. Work on this standard was begun in 1992, and it was released as an IETF RFC in 1993. Directory Access Protocol (DAP) was a part of X.500, and the new LDAP protocol attempted to make the functionality of X.500 directories available to client computers with the kind of computing horsepower available in the early 1990s.

LDAP has been very successful as a standard; most directory services today, including Active Directory, use LDAP as a part of the DS. Several things have collaborated to make LDAP a success. First is its availability. The overhead is low enough for an LDAP client to actually run quickly enough to be usable. The rising popularity of the public Internet and World Wide Web has increased the need for a publicly available DS and—because LDAP runs over IP—it's a natural for those environments.

BANYAN VINES AND STREETTALK

Streettalk, running on the Banyan VINES product, was the first successful commercial implementation of a DS. Available in the early 1990s, it provided a DS running on UNIX platforms. It could run over IP or IPX. Until the mid-90s it was available only on UNIX operating systems, and even when it was released on other OSs, it never reached saturation.

NOVELL NETWARE DIRECTORY SERVICES

For the mid to late 1990s, NetWare Directory Service has probably been the most widely deployed directory service. First available only on NetWare platforms and only over IPX, in the early 1990s NDS had some growing pains and was not widely implemented until version 4.10 was released in 1995. The current revision is 5.1, and it runs over IP and IPX. Although widely used, until recently the product was hampered by poor integration with IETF standards such as TCP/IP and Domain Name Services (DNS). Earlier versions ran on NetWare only, but recent releases are available for various flavors of UNIX and NT.

ACTIVE DIRECTORY

Active Directory (AD) is the new directory standard for Windows 2000. Windows 2000 was released to manufacturing in mid-December of 1999 and was released on February 17, 2000. Active Directory is included with Windows 2000 Server, Advanced Server, and DataCenter Server. It replaces the flat, nonhierarchical user database available with Windows NT. To view AD as simply a replacement for the NT Security Accounts Manager Database, however, ignores the power and extensibility of Active Directory. Active Directory provides a centralized, globally available repository of information about virtually anything on the network.

WHY A DIRECTORY?

The best analog example of a directory is a phone book. Years ago, a telephone user would pick up the phone, ring the central office, and ask for a particular person or number. This worked fine for small towns with a few phones, but the model failed to scale. We use DSs for the same reason we use a phone book. We cannot possibly remember all the information about every service we will ever need, and the information we had yesterday might not be timely.

Similarly, when our local area networks (LANs) held two or three servers and 100 clients, looking up services and other resources was not a difficult prospect. Now, however, with Enterprise wide area networks (WANs) that comprise thousands to millions of services and objects, a methodology to search for interesting information is critical.

An X.500-based directory service, such as Active Directory, is also *hierarchical*. This means you can create containers such as domains or organizational units to contain objects. This makes searching and managing these objects much faster and more efficient. Rather than having all the users in one container, you can separate them by placing them in various organizational units.

WHAT MAKES A DIRECTORY?

A *directory* is made up of the schema, classes, attributes, and values. Although a multitude of support services exist, such as LDAP and DNS, the directory itself is a database of objects.

SCHEMA

The *schema* is the logical map of the database. The first Domain Controller in the forest creates the default schema from a file used during the installation. This schema is then used to create objects in the domain. The schema includes information about which objects can be created, the attributes of the objects, and the datatypes allowed for those attributes. The schema for any database is the blueprint for that database. The Active Directory schema is extensible—if your enterprise would benefit from an object in the Active Directory that is specific to your industry, you can extend the schema by creating a class for the object. You can also add attributes to the schema.

CLASS

Every object is an instance of a *class*. Therefore, to create any object, a class must exist for that object. An example is a user class. To create a user object named fred, the user class must exist. This class defines the attributes available for the object. It would not make any sense to have an operating system attribute for a user, but it would be perfectly logical to have an operating system attribute for a computer class. A class can be *subclassed*, which means it inherits the available attributes of the parent class, and can even add its own.

ATTRIBUTE

An *attribute* defines information about an object. Examples of attributes are a telephone number, an address, an operating system, a location, and so on. Attributes also have datatypes assigned to an attribute so the information added to an object's attributes is appropriate.

VALUE

An attribute, to be meaningful, must be populated by a *value*. A telephone number attribute is of little use unless it contains a telephone number that is accurate for the user object.

OBJECT

All the architecture of Active Directory work together to create and manage objects. Active Directory, is, after all, a collection of objects. An *object* is a thing, such as a user, computer, printer, or virtually anything that is the end result of a class and its attributes.

ACTIVE DIRECTORY IN A NUTSHELL

In this book, we look at the architecture and implementation of the Active Directory. An emphasis is placed on hands-on demonstrations of common tasks and the architecture behind those tasks. In short, our goal is to make your job as an Active Directory administrator easier. The reason for the architecture is that the AD, similar to all databases, does not respond well to haphazard design and implementation. A thorough knowledge of the implications of choices you make in the design phase of your AD implementation is critical.

PHYSICAL AND LOGICAL STRUCTURE OF THE ACTIVE DIRECTORY

A variety of logical and physical structures collaborate to provide the AD infrastructure.

FORESTS

An Active Directory *forest* consists of one or more AD trees. A forest joins the trees at the top level of the tree with Kerberos transitive trusts. This enables users in one tree of the forest to access objects in another tree. An AD forest shares three things: a common schema; a common Global Catalog, which is a partial copy of every object in the forest; and Kerberos transitive trusts.

TREES

A *tree* consists of one or more domains. These domains are joined to the parent domain and any child domains by Kerberos transitive trust relationships. A trust does not exist between every domain in a tree, but only between parent domains and child domains. Because the trusts are transitive and two-way, a series of trusts can be used for an object to follow from one domain to another to access objects in another domain.

DOMAINS

A *domain* is a partition of the Active Directory database. Objects within a domain are fully replicated to all Domain Controllers that belong to the domain. More than one DC should exist in a domain for fault tolerance, and DCs should be placed near the people who need them in a geographically distributed environment.

ORGANIZATIONAL UNITS

An *organizational unit* is the container object for users, computers, printers, groups, and so on. This enables administrators to segregate users by function rather than have them in a flat structure. Group policy can then be applied to these organizational units based on the users' needs.

USERS, GROUPS, COMPUTERS, AND SO ON

These are the leaf objects managed by the Active Directory. They are instances of a class that hold attributes. Some of the attributes have values; others might not. You can use the Active Directory to search for objects that have a particular value or value range.

DOMAIN CONTROLLERS

A *DC* is a Windows 2000 Server, Advanced Server, or DataCenter Server that has been promoted to a Domain Controller using the Active Directory Installation Wizard. This is a two-way process. A server can be promoted to a DC or demoted from a DC to a member server. Every DC hosts the Kerberos service for authentication, the LDAP service to find objects, and a copy of the AD database for that domain to look up information about the user or computer object as necessary. A DC can also host the Global Catalog.

SITES

A *site* is one or more well-connected subnets. The first site is automatically created when the first DC is created in the forest and is called Default-First-Site-Name. As other DCs and domains are created, it is the administrator's responsibility to create other sites, associate them with IP subnets, and then logically move the DCs into those sites. Site membership then allows a client to select a DC in the same site rather than a DC further away.

SERVICES THAT SUPPORT THE ACTIVE DIRECTORY

A variety of services support the Active Directory. DNS provides IP name resolution, whereas Kerberos provides authentication and works with the security subsystem to provide authorization. The Global Catalog, on the other hand, provides an exhaustive list of every object in the forest, and replication is used to propagate changes from one domain controller to another.

DOMAIN NAME SERVICES

DNS is the default name resolution methodology for Windows 2000 and the Active Directory. Clients and servers use RFC-compliant SRV records to resolve a request for a service or host to an IP address.

KERBEROS

Kerberos is the default authentication mechanism in Active Directory. It is based on the Kerberos V5 standard and is interoperable with other implementations of Kerberos. To authenticate, it relies on a shared secret between the user and Kerberos—usually the user's password.

SECURITY

Every object in the Active Directory is protected by an *access control list (ACL)*, which is a list of who can and cannot touch the object. Before any user, process, or service accesses an Active Directory object, the ACL is checked to authorize that access.

GLOBAL CATALOG

The *Global Catalog (GC)* is hosted on one or more Domain Controllers throughout the forest. The GC is not specific to a domain but holds a copy of every object in the forest and a subset of its attributes. Holding only some information about every object keeps the space requirements for the GC manageable. The information published to the GC is configurable.

REPLICATION

Because Active Directory Domain Controllers all host a writable copy of the domain AD database, updates can occur at any Domain Controller. To keep all DCs up to date on changes, the AD uses a multimaster replication mechanism designed to minimize latency as well as minimize network traffic and duplication of effort.

SUMMARY

Computer network directories have been around for about 15 years. Active Directory is the directory service offering from Microsoft that runs on Windows 2000. It enables administrators to maintain information about objects in the directory and make that information available to authorized users.

CHAPTER **2**

INSTALLING ACTIVE DIRECTORY

In this chapter

AND AWAY WE GO! OR NOT

Installing Active Directory (AD) can be a trivial process. Just go to the run command of any Windows 2000 Server, Advanced Server, or DataCenter Server, and type **dcpromo.exe**, answer a few questions, and you're on your way. Getting married this way is procedurally undemanding also. Both will yield about the same results. Poor or no planning results in a network design that is difficult to extend, modify, and support and does not take advantage of the hierarchical nature of Active Directory.

Installing Active Directory should be a reasoned exercise with about a 10:1 ratio of planning to action for a small company and orders of magnitude more planning for a medium- to large-size company. Although promoting and demoting Domain Controllers (DCs) is a wizard-driven, easy process, the planning and implementation of an Active Directory forest should be a deliberate, orderly process.

You should plan the overall design of your Active Directory first. This includes the number of trees and the domain structure of the trees. *Trees* are made up of domains. Choosing the domain model has a great effect on security, administration, and replication. Your tree and domain structure must integrate with your current or proposed DNS namespace and infrastructure. DNS zone names and Active Directory domain names must match.

BEFORE YOU BEGIN

Running the Active Directory Installation Wizard (dcpromo) is the first step to creating your Active Directory. However, before you lay your hands on the first Windows 2000 Server and begin the Active Directory installation process, you should plan the logical and physical implementation of your forest. Active Directory domains, trees, and forests are discussed at some length in Chapters 11, "Domains, Trees, and Forests," and 12, "Operations Masters." You should read those chapters and Chapters 15, "Site Link Objects and Connection Objects"; 16, "Intra-Site Replication"; and 17, "Inter-Site Replication," as well as Chapters 4, "Installing and Configuring DNS"; 7, "DNS and AD Namespace"; and 9, "Dynamic and Active Directory Integrated DNS," before you begin planning your domains. The Windows 2000 support tools included on the Windows 2000 CD contain some very good documentation on planning, as does the Resource Kit. In an Active Directory forest, everything is connected to everything else, so where you start matters.

Tip

Although we stress the importance of planning in this book, you also should make sure you've modeled your plan, at least to some extent, in a lab environment. Please do not let the first machine you promote to a DC be a production machine. The same goes for upgrades. As much as possible, model your environment in the lab before implementing anything.

PLANNING THE FOREST

The first Active Directory domain you install will set the naming scheme for the tree. You can add other trees to the forest with completely different names, but every child domain of a parent or root domain derives its domain name from the parent. For example, if you choose fis.local as the Active Directory domain name for the first domain, any child domains of fis.local will derive their domain names from fis.local—for example, sales.fis.local or northamerica.fis.local.

CHOOSING THE CORRECT HARDWARE

The first domain controller in the first domain in the first tree in the forest also hosts all five operations master roles and is (by default) the only global catalog (GC) server in the forest. Operations masters are covered in Chapter 12, and global catalog servers are discussed in Chapter 15. These roles can be moved as other DCs come online, but for a while they all will be on the first server you promote.

Although the published minimum for a DC is a P133 with 128MB of RAM, you will find this to be lacking when compared to your actual needs. I have built and tested domain controllers that were P450s with 256MB of RAM that hosted almost a quarter million objects. The machines and Windows 2000 responded very well to the demand. For an Active Directory implementation with thousands or tens of thousands of objects, however, in a real-world scenario you should bring multiple fast processors, a lot of memory, and a very fast SCSI disk array to the table. When you install a DC, you are building a specialized database server, and the hardware should be chosen accordingly. A RAID disk subsystem not only provides fault tolerance but also will spread the I/O necessary to read and update the AD database.

Testing shows that a single-processor XEON 500 server with 512MB of RAM can support up to 30 logons per second, and the same server with four processors can support up to 70 logons per second. The same testing showed that an AD domain with five quad processor servers can support the expected logon traffic of 90,000 users. It also showed that for logon performance, additional processors were the most important feature.

Logon performance is, however, only part of the Active Directory performance picture. Replication and GC performance are also critical and are impacted greatly by your network design as well as server performance.

→ For more information on global catalog servers, **see** "Replicate From," **p. 245**

> **Tip**
>
> Microsoft has an entire white paper on domain controller sizing named DC_Sizing.doc. This (and many other) white paper is available at www.microsoft.com.

Good network connectivity is also required for timely replication. Although much work has gone into making Active Directory replication as efficient as possible, the reality is that the faster, less congested, and more reliable your network is, the fewer replication issues you, the administrator, will encounter.

SOFTWARE YOU WILL NEED

The only software necessary to install Active Directory is a good implementation of Windows 2000 Server, Advanced Server, or DataCenter Server. If you haven't installed DNS on the network or local machine yet, you also need the Windows 2000 CD.

The primary differences between the three flavors of Windows 2000 Server are memory and processor support and support for clustering:

- **Server**—Supports up to four processors and 4GB of RAM, but it has no support for clustering.
- **Advanced Server**—Supports up to eight processors and 8GB of RAM. Supports 2-node clustering and 32-node network load balancing.
- **DataCenter Server**—Supports up to 32 processors and 64GB of RAM. Supports 4-node clustering and 32-node network load balancing.

Note

Although the experience of installing Active Directory is the same for Server, Advanced Server, and DataCenter Server, we will—for the sake of brevity—use the term Windows 2000 Server for the rest of this chapter.

DECISIONS, DECISIONS

The next section walks you through most of the possible scenarios for installing AD servers. Regardless of the scenario, you will encounter several core questions during the dcpromo.exe process, and it is best to have considered and answered those questions in advance.

Those core questions are as follows:

- What are my DNS choices? Will I (can I?) use my current DNS implementation? Where will my DNS be hosted?
- What are my DNS/Active Directory namespace plans?
- What about filesystems? I must have at least one NTFS filesystem on the DC.
- Where will I place the Active Directory database and transaction logs? What about the sysvol volume? (These should be on fast, fault-tolerant drives.)
- What about permissions? Must I water down the permissions structure for any reason?
- What will I set the Directory Services Restore Mode password to? How will I keep track of this?

DNS

The Domain Name Service is critical to the proper functioning of Active Directory. DNS is used to find instances of services such as Kerberos and LDAP running on DCs throughout the enterprise. Installing DNS is covered in Chapter 4. The key point here is that the current DNS infrastructure must be reviewed and compared against the Active Directory DNS requirements—namely, support for SRV records and dynamic updates. Regardless of whether you keep your current DNS or use Microsoft's Windows 2000 DNS, two simple facts must be stressed. First, the DNS you choose *must* support SRV records. If it does not, your clients will not be able to find AD domain controllers. Second, it should support dynamic update. If it does not, I hope you can type. SRV records have a tendency to be verbose, and every adapter on every Windows 2000 computer updates its A and SRV records every time a Plug-and-Play event occurs. Keeping up with this manually will lose its charm very quickly.

During the dcpromo process, the Active Directory Installation Wizard prompts you for a good DNS installation if one is not detected. You must have planned in advance where your DNS is going to be hosted.

CH
2

Note

Although I hate to admit it, if you do not already have a DNS server identified, the easiest way to install and configure DNS for the AD is to ignore the problem until it is raised in the Active Directory Installation Wizard. dcpromo will prompt you to allow it to autoinstall DNS if the promotion process does not detect a serviceable DNS installation that is pointed to by the IP properties on the server. Allowing dcpromo to install and configure DNS is easy and quick and works every time. See Chapter 4 for more details.

NAMESPACES

When DNS is being considered, you are at the same time planning your AD namespace. DNS zone names and Active Directory domain names must match. When you are prompted for the name of your root domain for the forest, you are setting the namespace for the rest of the tree. (See Chapter 7 for more details.) Even if you are only creating a child domain, you must provide the name for that child domain. At this point, however, your only choices are names that extend the current namespace. For example, if your root domain is fis.local, when you create child domains, they must be named domainname.fis.local. If you want to create a domain whose namespace does not match the current root, you must create a new tree in the forest.

FILESYSTEMS

During the dcpromo process for any domain controller, you are required to choose where several files are to be hosted. Although you can move some of these files at a later date, the process is nontrivial. You will be best served by placing the files in their permanent home at the outset. You must plan where to place the database, log, and sysvol shares.

DATABASE

When installing Active Directory, you are prompted for the location of the ntds.dit—the AD database file. This filesystem can be either FAT or NTFS. The default is c:\winnt\ntds (assuming your system root is c:\winnt). In the interests of speed and fault tolerance, this should be placed on a fast redundant disk subsystem, such as a RAID array formatted as NTFS.

LOG

The AD database is transaction logged, and like every other database, the log should be placed on either a fast redundant disk subsystem, such as a RAID array, or at least a physical drive separate from the ntds.dit. Separating these files increases throughput to the database because the I/O streams don't conflict with each other. This also can be either NTFS or FAT.

sysvol

The sysvol share contains the files that represent much of the group policy architecture. This must be on an NTFS drive and should be fast and redundant. Every Windows 2000 client checks for group policy changes every time the computer boots, every time the user logs on, and every 90 minutes thereafter.

PERMISSIONS COMPATIBILITY

Permissions compatibility is one of the most poorly documented decisions. You are asked whether you want to maintain a permissions structure compatible with NT or Windows 2000 only. In a nutshell, if you have routing and remote access servers running on NT, you must say yes to pre–Windows 2000 compatibility. This grants additional permissions that allow down-level RRAS servers to function in an Active Directory domain.

Note

> If the RRAS server is on an NT4 BDC or if you're still in a mixed mode environment and the NT4 RRAS server "happens" to contact an NT4 BDC when checking the user permissions, it works without weakening the permissions. If you have NT 4 RRAS servers, you should choose to weaken the permissions.

DIRECTORY SERVICES RESTORE MODE PASSWORD

Occasionally, you must boot a DC in Directory Services Restore Mode to work directly with some of the AD files. This means that the AD services are not started on the local DC, so the Active Directory database files are not opened and can be manipulated with ntdsutil. An administrative account is held separately from the Active Directory and is used to log on during this process. Saving this password is important, as is realizing that this does not set the password for the Administrator account that is used while the AD is running. They are two separate accounts.

PROMOTING A SERVER TO DOMAIN CONTROLLER

After you have planned your answers to the questions about DNS, namespaces, files and filesystems, permissions, and passwords, which you are asked by the Active Directory Installation Wizard, the rest is just process.

AUTHORIZATION

dcpromo.exe can't be run by just anyone. Creating a new domain or tree requires membership in the Enterprise Administrator group, and creating a new DC in an existing domain requires membership in the Domain Admins global group. An attempt to run dcpromo by a non-Administrator simply returns an error stating that you must be a member of the Administrator group to run dcpromo.

Note

The Enterprise Admins group exists only in the root domain of the forest. In a mixed mode domain, it is a global group; in a native mode domain, it is a universal group.

If you are creating the very first DC in your forest, you must be at least a local administrator to enable the computer on which you are logged to run the dcpromo utility. If you are creating a child domain and are not logged on as an Enterprise Admin, you will have the opportunity to provide other credentials during the promotion process. The easiest way to do this is to log on as the user with sufficient privilege to accomplish the entire task.

CREATING A NEW FOREST

This is the first domain controller in the forest. You have to be logged on as only a local administrator to start this process. You can start the Active Directory Installation Wizard by running dcpromo.exe at the command prompt or with the Run command on the Start menu. Either option displays the Welcome screen shown in Figure 2.1.

Figure 2.1
Using dcpromo.exe to install Active Directory.

Click Next to proceed to the Domain Controller Type page shown in Figure 2.2. Here you have two choices: Domain Controller for a New Domain or Additional Domain Controller for an Existing Domain. Because you are creating a new forest, take the default of Additional Domain Controller for an Existing Domain and click Next.

Figure 2.2
Creating a new domain with dcpromo.

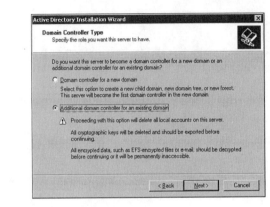

This brings you to the Create Tree or Child Domain screen shown in Figure 2.3. To create a child domain, you must first have a parent domain. Because you are creating the first domain, choose the default of Create a New Domain Tree, and then click Next.

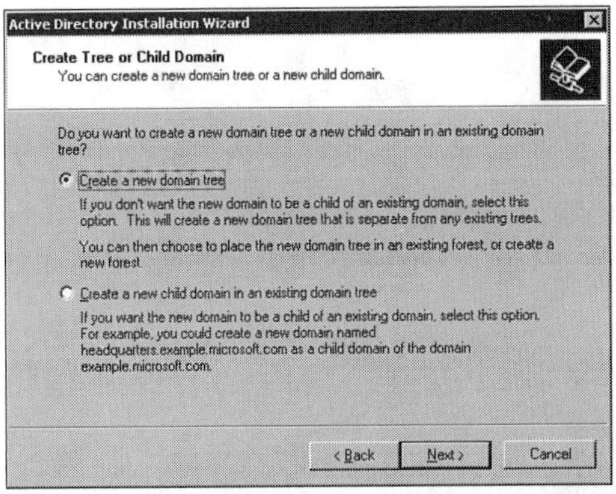

Figure 2.3
You can create a new tree or child domain of an existing tree.

Figure 2.4 shows the Create or Join Forest screen, where you must choose between creating a new forest or a new tree. To review, a new forest implies a completely separate Active Directory from another forest. A new tree has a separate namespace but shares a common schema, global catalog, and Keberos transitive trusts with the other trees in the same forest. Because creating a new forest is your goal, choose the default, and then click Next.

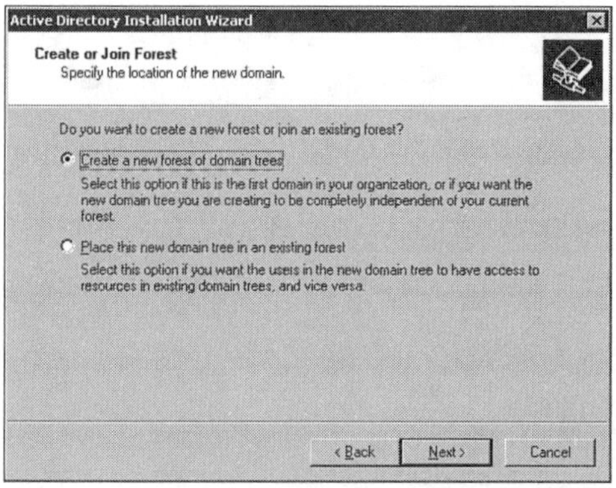

Figure 2.4
Creating a forest creates the first DC in the forest.

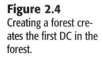

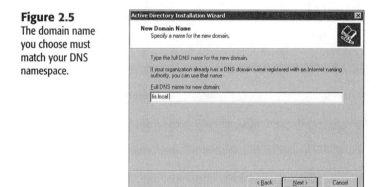

Next, in the New Domain Name page, you must choose the AD domain name that will represent the root of your forest. Because your company name is FIS and you are choosing to use a private, internal DNS namespace, you have chosen `fis.local` as your root domain. Type in the name and click Next. The process will timeout for about a minute while the wizard looks for a domain with the same name on the network. The New Domain Name Page appears in Figure 2.5.

Figure 2.5
The domain name you choose must match your DNS namespace.

After the Active Directory Installation Wizard is confident that you are not creating a domain with a name that already exists on the network, you are presented with the NetBIOS Domain Name page shown in Figure 2.6. This is the domain name that will be used by down-level clients, such as Windows 9x and NT. Generally, this is the leftmost portion of the Active Directory domain name. Click Next.

Tip

The NetBIOS domain name and the Active Directory domain name do not have to match. They should, for simplicity's sake, and by default, they do. The following scenario, however, would require changing one of the NetBIOS domain names. Say, for example, you had a forest with two trees—`fis.local` and `fullertoninfo.com`—and wanted to create a new child domain under each parent domain (`sales.fis.local` and `sales.fullertoninfo.com`). The AD domain names do not collide, but the default NetBIOS names for both domains would be `sales`. This cannot occur, and one of the NetBIOS domain names would have to be changed.

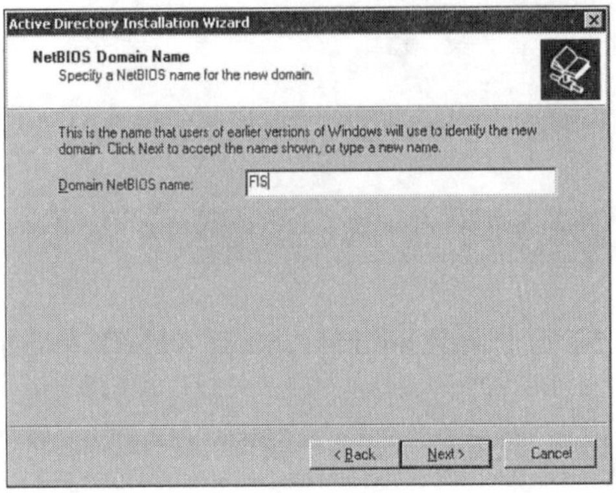

Figure 2.6
By default, the NetBIOS domain name is the first portion of the Active Directory domain name.

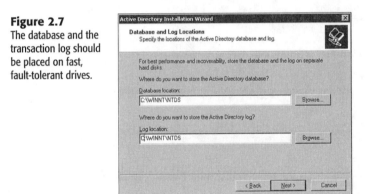

The Database and Log Locations page enables you to choose where to put the files that contain the Active Directory. Hopefully, you have already planned your database and log locations and have fast and redundant disk subsystems for them to reside on. Figure 2.7 shows the default. Choose the drive and subdirectory, and click Next.

Figure 2.7
The database and the transaction log should be placed on fast, fault-tolerant drives.

The Shared System Volume page appears in Figure 2.8. Remember that this is the only folder in this section that must be on an NTFS 5.0 partition. This is where the files that make up group policy will be kept and replicated to other DCs.

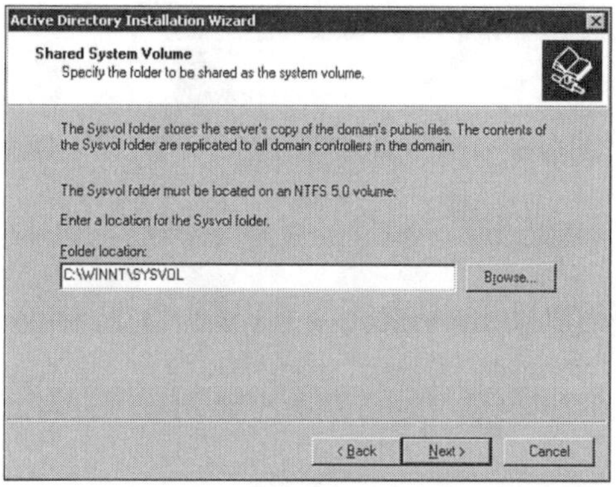

Figure 2.8
The Shared System Volume must be created on an NTFS v5.0 partition.

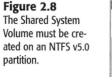

If your Internet protocol properties on the local computer are not set to point to a suitable DNS server, you will see the next two screens. The first screen, shown in Figure 2.9, simply informs you that it has found your DNS configuration to be lacking. This also could mean that it found a good DNS server but did not find a DNS zone created on said DNS server that matched your Active Directory domain name. Either way, the thing to do is to click OK here, and move to the next screen.

Figure 2.9
If dcpromo cannot contact a DNS server, it raises an error message.

You have two choices on the Configure DNS page (see Figure 2.10). You can let the Active Directory Installation Wizard install and configure your DNS, or you can choose to do it yourself after you've installed AD. A lack of a properly configured DNS prevents you from creating child domains or other trees, but it doesn't prevent the installation of the root domain. Installing DNS is covered at great length in Chapter 4. I greatly encourage you to let the Active Directory Installation Wizard install the DNS and then click Next. Allowing dcpromo to install DNS is fast and error-free.

> **Caution**
>
> Please do not let this give you a lackadaisical attitude about DNS. As I make clear in the DNS chapters, for all intents and purposes, no DNS = no AD.

The Permissions page sets the Permissions structure to be either compatible with NT servers or a Windows 2000–only environment (see Figure 2.11). This is discussed in the section "Planning the Forest," earlier in this chapter. If you have NT 4 RRAS servers, you should choose weaker permissions. Choose a setting compliant with your situation, and click Next.

Figure 2.10
You can let dcpromo install DNS for you.

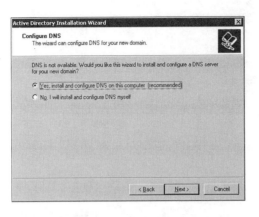

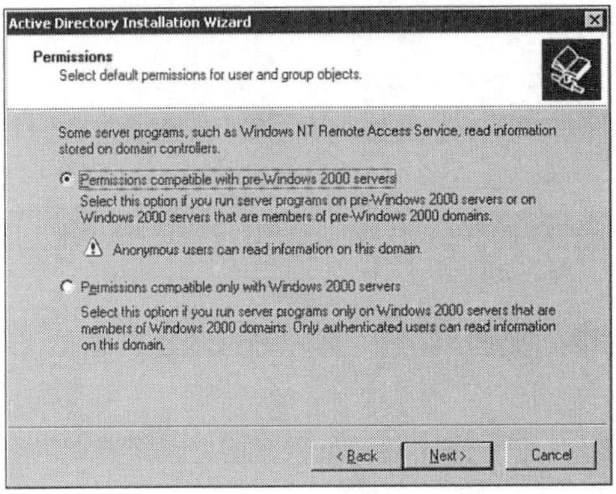

Figure 2.11
You can weaken permissions during the dcpromo process to allow NT 4 RRAS servers.

The Directory Services Restore Mode Administrator Password page, shown in Figure 2.12, sets the password for the local account used to start the domain controller in Directory Services Restore Mode. Set the password and click Next.

Tip

Directory Services Restore Mode is used to start a DC without starting Active Directory. This enables direct manipulation of the database files. For more information on booting in Directory Services Restore Mode, see "Database Maintenance," p. 476.

Figure 2.13 shows the Summary screen. This shows you all the choices you've made in the last few minutes and enables you to review them for typos. In addition, it enables you to, if necessary, go back and change something before committing to the promotion process by clicking Next.

Figure 2.12
The Directory Services Restore Mode password should be documented and stored securely.

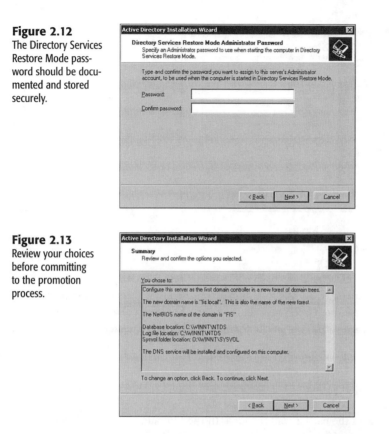

Figure 2.13
Review your choices before committing to the promotion process.

After you have committed to the promotion process, AD is installed in 5–15 minutes, depending on the speed of your computer. During this time, you will see the Configuring Active Directory page.

Tip

If you are upgrading an NT DC with a large SAM, the promotion process might take much longer than if it was a fresh install.

You should be sure not to disturb the server while it is being promoted. If the process is interrupted, the server can be left in an untenable state. In addition, if the process is disturbed, Active Directory can be left in an untenable state and might require reinstallation.

During the promotion process, shares are created and the schema, configuration, and domain portions of Active Directory are created (or replicated if this is not the first DC). If you choose to let the Active Directory Wizard install DNS, you might be prompted to provide a path to the i386 subdirectory of the CD.

When the promotion is complete, the Completing the Active Directory Installation Wizard page appears (see Figure 2.14). After you click OK, you are prompted to reboot. Active Directory will not be started until after the computer is rebooted.

Figure 2.14
dcpromo has completed successfully.

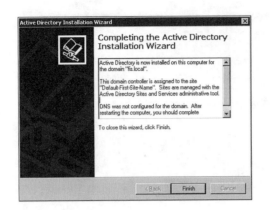

CREATING A NEW TREE

In the previous section, you learned how to create a new forest, which is the beginning of an Active Directory implementation. In this section, you create a new tree in an existing forest. Usually, this is done because the namespaces don't match. The tree you create will still inherit a GC and schema from the root of the forest and will be connected to it by Kerberos transitive trusts.

→ **See** "Trees," **p. 167**

In the previous walkthrough, you created the forest root domain. When you start the Active Directory Installation Wizard by executing dcpromo.exe on another server, you again see the welcome screen you saw in the earlier walkthrough. In the Domain Controller Type screen, choose Domain Controller for a New Domain. In the Create Tree or Child Domain page, choose Create a New Domain Tree.

Figure 2.15 shows the Create or Join Forest page. Select the Place This New Domain Tree in an Existing Forest option and click Next.

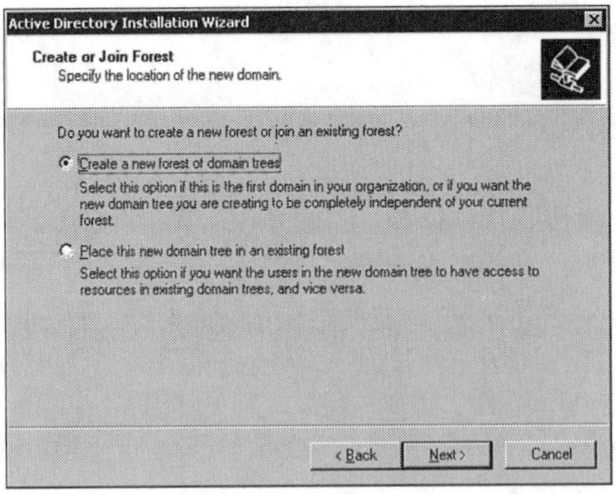

Figure 2.15
Creating a new tree.

When you click Next, you're presented with the Network Credentials page seen in Figure 2.16. Because the root domain of the forest is `fis.local`, you must provide the username, password, and domain of a member of the Enterprise Admins group from the `fis.local` domain.

Figure 2.16
Provide the credentials of an Enterprise Administrator to create a new tree.

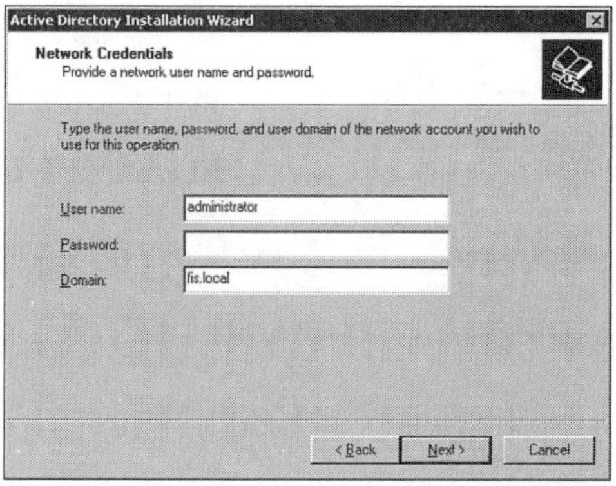

The New Domain Tree page requires you to type in the Active Directory domain name of the root of your new tree, `jmh.local` (see Figure 2.17).

Figure 2.17
Naming the new domain tree.

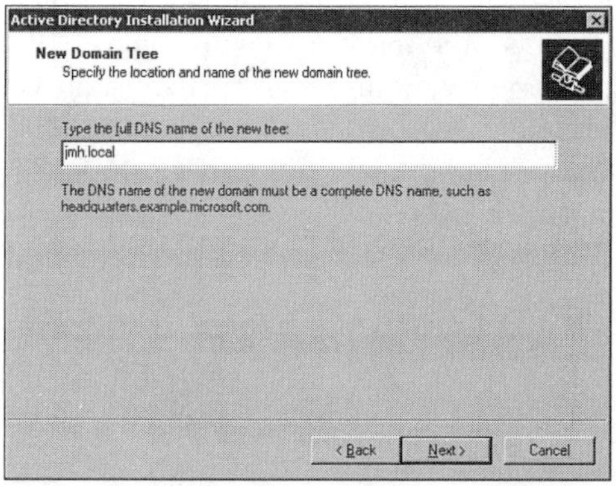

This times out for several seconds while it looks on the network for a name conflict; then the same NetBIOS Domain Name page you saw earlier appears. The next few pages set the database, log, and `sysvol` locations you dealt with in the earlier example. If you do not have a suitable DNS implementation already set up, you get the same two screens you saw earlier prompting you to allow the wizard to install and configure DNS. You also are prompted to set permissions and set the AD Restore Mode password. Finally, you are presented with the Summary page to review your choices and commit to the promotion.

CREATING A CHILD DOMAIN

Creating a child domain is similar to creating a new tree because you still are creating a new AD container inside an existing forest. You start with dcpromo (see the Welcome and Domain Controller Type pages). In the Create Tree or Child Domain page, however, you choose the Create a New Child Domain in an Existing Domain Tree option, as shown in Figure 2.18.

Figure 2.18
Using dcpromo to create a new child domain.

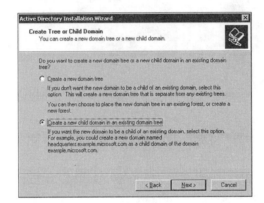

Again, because you are creating objects inside an existing forest, you are prompted for your network credentials. This must be an Enterprise Admin. Figure 2.19 shows the Child Domain Installation page. This automatically populates the Parent Domain text box, and you supply the name of the child domain as shown. So, for sales.fis.local, you simply place sales in the Child Domain text box and the Complete DNS Name of New Domain box concatenates the two together to derive your child domain's Active Directory domain name—sales.fis.local.

Figure 2.19
Naming your new child domain with dcpromo.

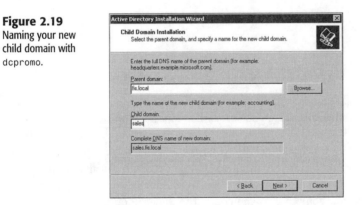

The next few screens are ones you've seen before. Set the NetBIOS domain name; the database, log, and sysvol locations; permissions; and Restore Mode password; and finally review the summary. The promotion process itself is the same as before.

CREATING ADDITIONAL DOMAIN CONTROLLERS

In every Active Directory domain—whether it is a forest root, tree root, or child domain—you should have redundant DCs. These DCs provide fault tolerance and speed. Multiple DCs per domain ensure that, if one goes offline due to hardware failure or a network outage, other DCs still will be online with the exact same information in their databases. Every Windows 2000 domain controller in an AD domain has a writeable copy of the AD database. This means that you can update domain accounts on any DC that is a member of that domain. To create additional DCs, run dcpromo on the member server and click Next on the Welcome page.

The next page you are shown is the Domain Controller Type page, with the Additional Domain Controller for an Existing Domain option selected (see Figure 2.20). This tells the wizard not to create a new domain but to make this a redundant domain controller for the existing domain.

CH

2

Figure 2.20
Adding another
domain controller.

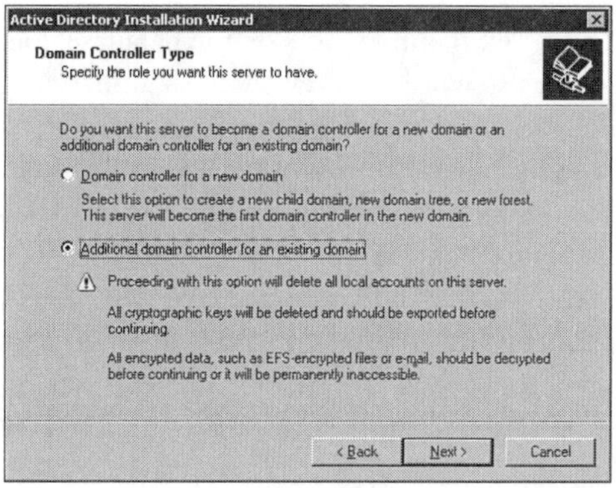

Although NT4 backup DCs can be used in a Windows 2000 Active Directory environment, a native mode domain (which is an AD domain with no NT domain controllers) does not have "backup" domain controllers in the NT4 sense. All Windows 2000 domain controllers are equal, and all Windows 2000 DCs hold a writeable copy of the Active Directory database. This is in contrast to the single-master model of NT4. The exceptions are operations masters, which control very specific modifications to Active Directory. For more information on operations masters, see "Introduction," p. 172.

Next, you will see the Credentials page. The credentials you provide here must be a member of the Domain Admins global group for the domain to which you are trying to add a DC. Clicking Next brings up the Additional Domain Controller page (see Figure 2.21).

Figure 2.21
Entering the name of
the domain you want
to join.

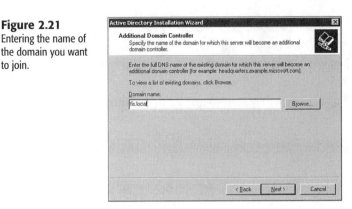

The Additional Domain Controller page simply lets you type in the Active Directory domain name of the domain for which this machine will become a domain controller.

The next few pages are, by now, very familiar. You set the database, log, and `sysvol` locations and the AD Restore Mode password, and review the summary page. The promotion process is the same as before, with one exception. The time necessary to promote the DC also involves replicating the AD database from another DC in the domain to this server. If the database is large, or if the network between this server and the DC is slow, this can take some time. If the time necessary to replicate the DC is lengthy, you will see the option to finish replication later appear in the Active Directory dialog box. This simply enables you to complete the promotion process but continue the replication process when the server reboots.

AUTOMATING dcpromo

Windows 2000 has a broad capability for scripting and automation. Whether it is VBScript logon scripts, Windows Management Instrumentation, or automated setups, Windows 2000 is very scriptable. Virtually everything is available through either a COM interface or simple scripts. You can script the promotion of a server to a domain controller with nothing but dcpromo and a simple text file.

Running dcpromo with an answer file is easy. Simply type **dcpromo /answer:answer.txt** at the command line, and you are on your way. This assumes, of course, that you have a properly configured answer file in the same directory in which you are running dcpromo.

dcpromo answer files follow a very specific syntax, which is documented well (if somewhat tersely) in the file unattend.doc. unattend.doc is a fairly large Word document that is located in \support\tools\deploy.cab. The document can be extracted from the .cab file by using Explorer. unattend.doc mainly documents creating unattended setup files, but it also documents the unattended setup of Active Directory. The following answer file, shown in Listing 2.1, causes the local server to be promoted to a forest root with a domain name of fis.local. Listing 2.1 shows the script in its entirety. Following the listing, we will look at it one line at a time and discuss the impact of each command. This is not an exhaustive list of all commands, but simply a working example. For other parameters, please see unattend.doc.

LISTING 2.1   SAMPLE dcpromo ANSWER FILE

```
[DCInstall]
AutoConfigDNS=YES
CreateOrJoin=Create
DatabasePath="c:\winnt\NTDS"
DomainNetBiosName="fis"
LogPath="c:\winnt\NTDS"
NewDomainDNSName="fis.local"
RebootOnSuccess=Yes
ReplicaOrNewDomain=Domain
SysVolPath="c:\winnt\sysvol"
TreeOrChild=Tree
```

The first line is simply a header that sets up the parameters:

```
[DCInstall]
```

The next line tells dcpromo to automatically install and configure DNS:

```
AutoConfigDNS=YES
```

CreateOrJoin sets whether you are creating a new forest or joining an existing one:

```
CreateOrJoin=Create
```

DatabasePath sets the path to the Active Directory database:

```
DatabasePath="c:\winnt\NTDS"
```

The next line sets the down-level domain name for NT and Windows clients:

```
DomainNetBiosName="fis"
```

LogPath sets the path to the Active Directory:

```
LogPath="c:\winnt\NTDS"
```

The next line sets the AD domain name for the new domain:

```
NewDomainDNSName="fis.local"
```

RebootOnSuccess tells the server to automatically reboot after the promotion process is complete:

```
RebootOnSuccess=Yes
```

ReplicaOrNewDomain sets whether you are creating the first domain controller in a new domain or a domain controller for an existing domain:

```
ReplicaOrNewDomain=Domain
```

CH

2

SysVolPath sets the path to the sysvol folder that holds the SysVol share. This share holds the filesystem objects that make up group policy:

SysVolPath="c:\winnt\sysvol"

TreeOrChild sets whether the domain is the root of a tree or a child domain of an existing tree:

TreeOrChild=Tree

After you have executed the dcpromo /answer:answer.txt command, the promotion proceeds as normal. If you specified the RebootOnSuccess parameter, the system automatically restarts, and when the machine comes back up, the Active Directory is installed.

AFTER dcpromo

Active Directory is created after you have rebooted the domain controller. The new domain controller has several new folders and shares. Additionally, if this is a new domain, you now can see the Active Directory containers created.

NEW SHARES

Two new shares are created on a new domain controller to support its duties in its new role.

sysvol

The SysVol share is where the filesystem objects that comprise group policy are created. Every domain controller has a sysvol folder, and the File Replication Service is used to keep the contents of the sysvol folder synchronized with every other sysvol folder on every other domain controller in the domain. For more information, see Chapter 27, "Active Directory Database Optimization."

netlogon

This share is used to place down-level policies and scripts for Windows and NT clients.

NEW FILES

The majority of the new files created are the database files in the \winnt\ntds folder. These files and their functions are documented in Chapter 27.

DEFAULT CONTAINERS

Figure 2.22 shows the Active Directory Users and Computers (ADUC) Microsoft Management Console (MMC) Snap-in open to domain fis.local. This tool is used repeatedly in this book to demonstrate the functionality of Active Directory. Here you can use it to look at some of the default containers created in AD.

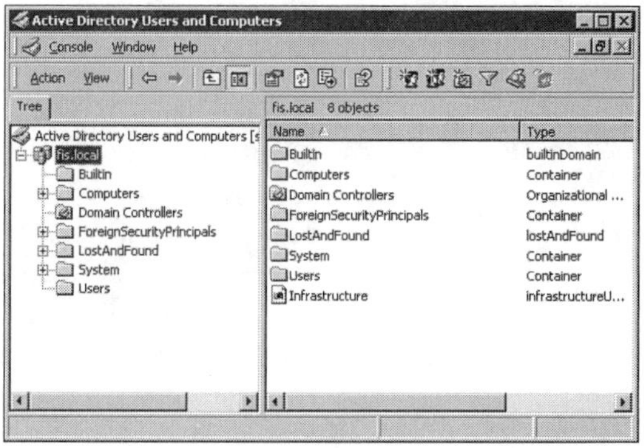

Figure 2.22
The Active Directory Users and Computers MMC Snap-in is your default management tool for your new domain.

BUILTIN

The Builtin container object on a domain controller holds computer local groups.

COMPUTERS

The Computers container is the default home for nondomain controllers that are members of the domain. Computer objects can be moved to organizational units (OU) in the domain, and in many cases they should because group policy can't be attached to a container.

DOMAIN CONTROLLERS

Domain Controllers is the only OU created automatically by Active Directory. It contains all the domain controller computer objects for the domain.

FOREIGNSECURITYPRINCIPALS

This container holds placeholder objects for accounts from various forests you trust. For more information on trust relationships, see Chapter 22, "Managing Group Policy."

USERS

The Users container holds the user accounts, global groups, and domain local groups created when AD is created. Exactly how "local" domain local groups are depends on whether the domain is in mixed or native mode. In mixed mode, the groups are local to the domain controllers; in native mode, they are local to the domain. Every domain is in mixed mode when it is first created, so by default, these are local to the domain. After you have converted to native mode, any of these groups can be converted to virtually any other group type.

→ **See** "Domain Modes," **p. 165**

REMOVING A DOMAIN CONTROLLER

Occasionally, you might want to demote a domain controller to a member server, such as getting new hardware for the DC or in a lab situation in which you want to remove the domain and start fresh. Unlike in NT, which requires a reinstall to change domain membership or demote the domain controller, in Windows 2000 becoming a domain controller is not a one-way trip.

DEMOTION CONSIDERATIONS

The primary issue to consider is that you can add domain controllers to and remove DCs from a domain to your heart's content, but if you remove the last domain controller in a domain, that domain ceases to exist. Granted, a safety mechanism does exist because you must specify that the DC is the last controller in a domain to remove the last DC.

dcpromo IN REVERSE

Oddly enough, you use the same tool to create a DC from a member server that you use to create a member server from a DC. When you execute dcpromo from the Run command or a command prompt, it checks the current state of the local machine. If it is already a DC, it prompts you to remove Active Directory from the local machine, as shown in Figure 2.23.

Figure 2.23
Running dcpromo on a domain controller causes it to demote the server to a member server.

If the machine is a global catalog server, you are prompted to ensure other GCs are available to process user logons. The warning message appears in Figure 2.24.

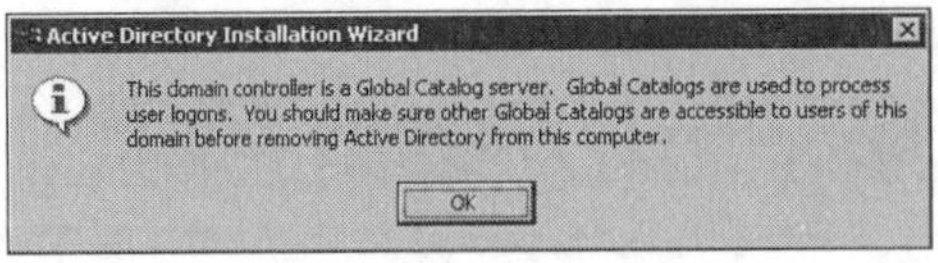

Figure 2.24
Demoting a global catalog server causes a warning message to pop up.

Figure 2.25 shows the Remove Active Directory page. This page asks whether this is the last domain controller for this domain and asks you to select the check box if it is. The informational text in the bottom portion of the page explains the implications of removing the last DC in a domain.

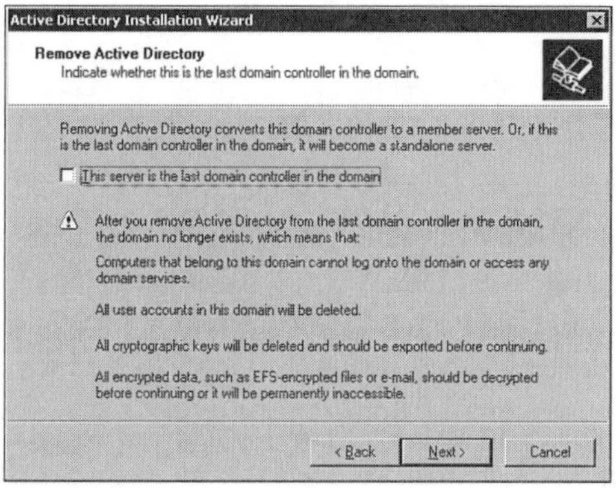

Figure 2.25
If you remove the last DC in the domain, the domain is permanently removed.

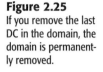

When you click Next, you see the Administrator Password page (see Figure 2.26). Because all computer local accounts on the member server are deleted when it is promoted to a domain controller, local accounts must be re-created when the DC is demoted. This sets the password for the local administrator account.

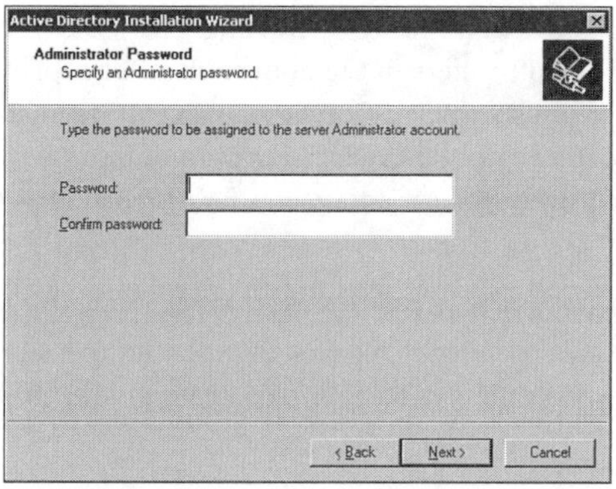

Figure 2.26
Setting the local password on a demoted DC.

Finally, you see the Summary page. This is your last opportunity to click Cancel and abort the process. Clicking Next removes Active Directory, presents the Completion page, and prompts you to reboot.

SUMMARY

Running the Active Directory Installation Wizard is the fourth step in creating a good Active Directory. The first three are planning, planning, and more planning. Running dcpromo is easy, but you can be saddled with the decisions you make with this wizard for years to come. dcpromo creates the first domain in the forest and allows you to create other domains in this and other trees.

TROUBLESHOOTING

BASIC TROUBLESHOOTING

What are some basic rules for troubleshooting dcpromo?

Troubleshooting the Active Directory Installation Wizard really comes in two flavors. I have almost never had a server refuse to create a new forest—for the simple reason that if you have enough memory, disk space, and a good implementation of Windows 2000, not much can go wrong because you are creating almost everything from scratch on the local computer (unless this is an upgrade from an NT domain).

Generally, when I have had problems with dcpromo, it is in creating a child domain, replica server, or new tree. These generally croak because of two things: name resolution and permissions.

TERMINATING CREDENTIALS

I am trying to promote a DC and it is terminating on the Credentials page, saying the domain does not exist or cannot be contacted.

You should keep two main things in mind when creating a new DC. The server you are promoting and the other domain controllers in the domain must be capable of seeing each other. That means the three usual suspects of networking must be in alignment. Routing, addressing, and name resolution must be in place for promotion to occur, and Windows 2000 uses DNS almost exclusively when finding another instance of Active Directory in the domain.

Note

Although you can run many protocols on clients and member servers, domain controllers must have the Internet Protocol installed and properly configured to communicate with other DCs.

Chapters 3, "Domain Name Services," and 10, "Troubleshooting DNS," go into detail on the proper installation, configuration, and troubleshooting of DNS. If you think you might have DNS problems, use the tools in these chapters to resolve those problems.

PERMISSIONS

I am trying to create a child domain, and during the dcpromo process it fails with an access denied error.

Another easy place to make a mistake is permissions. Be sure that you have sufficient privileges to promote the machine to a DC. The privilege level necessary varies based on whether you are creating a new domain; that topic is covered earlier in this chapter. If in doubt, try the process as a member of the Enterprise Admins group—this is the most powerful user in the enterprise.

LOGS

Do any logs exist that I can read to see why my dcpromo process is failing?

A variety of logs are created in the \winnt\debug folders when dcpromo is run. Reading these, particularly dcpromo.log, is highly instructional. If the dcpromo process dies, read these to look for error messages that might provide a clue to the problem.

CHAPTER 3

DOMAIN NAME SERVICES

In this chapter

THE NEED FOR DNS

Domain Name Services (DNS) enable us to use human-friendly names for our computers. Even though the network uses numbers to identify each machine on a network, DNS enables people to think of computers in terms of names; the DNS service then maps those names to numeric addresses. DNS is used only with the Internet Protocol (IP).

DNS is critical to Active Directory (AD) because it is used to find Domain Controllers (DCs) and services on Domain Controllers such as Lightweight Directory Access Protocol (LDAP), Kerberos, and the Global Catalog. When a client needs to authenticate, it issues a DNS request for a nearby Active Directory Domain Controller. The DNS server then replies with the IP address and other information about the DC. In addition, when a DC needs to replicate with other DCs, it uses DNS to find the IP address of the DC. When we use Active Directory tools to add, subtract, or modify an Active Directory object, we use DNS to find an LDAP server running on a DC near us. Without DNS, Active Directory almost completely ceases to function.

The history of DNS began in the early 1980s. For the first few years, the Internet relied on a static text file called a *hosts* file, which was updated frequently and could be downloaded to an Internet-connected machine on a regular basis. Obviously, this did not scale beyond hundreds or thousands of hosts. The first DNS Request for Comments (RFC) appeared in 1984. Since then, DNS has been the standard methodology for name resolution on the Internet.

> **Tip**
>
> An enormous amount of public domain information about DNS can be found at http://www.ietf.org. Internet Request for Comments (RFCs) are considered the authoritative works on any Internet-related protocol or service.

DNS is conceptually a very simple service, akin to a phone directory. Just as a person with a phone directory can translate a name into a phone number, DNS accepts a fully qualified domain name (FQDN) and returns a 32-bit IP address. This is called a *forward lookup*. Or, it can accept an IP address and return an FQDN, which is called a *reverse lookup*. The entire process is known as *name resolution*.

> **Caution**
>
> The first step in installing DNS or Active Directory is planning. Do not begin implementation of production DNS servers until your DNS and Active Directory namespaces have been planned and decided on.

→ For more information about planning DNS namespaces, **see** "Namespaces," **p. 92**

THE FUNCTION OF DNS

The function of DNS is name resolution. When a user tries to access another computer on a network, regardless of the size of the network, an architecture must be in place to map names to addresses. Many name resolution methodologies exist on a Windows 2000 computer, but the default host name resolution methodology is DNS. In this chapter, we discuss DNS as it relates to the Active Directory. DNS is the only name resolution tool that works with the Active Directory. An AD without a properly configured DNS is a standalone AD. You can install the AD on a Windows 2000 server without configuring DNS, but the AD will be almost completely nonfunctional.

Name resolution is the process of mapping a name to an address. This actually happens at several layers of the Open Systems Interconnect (OSI) model.

EXAMPLES OF NAME RESOLUTION

When a network-connected machine begins a conversation with another machine, the first thing it needs to do to contact the target is to map the IP address of the target machine to a Media Access Control (MAC) address. Broadcasting Address Resolution Protocol (ARP) packets so that the two machines can trade MAC addresses and then communicate at the MAC layer of the OSI model accomplishes this. This also enables the two machines to resolve the IP address of their target to a MAC address. Listing 3.1 shows the output of an arp -a command showing the mapping of MAC addresses to IP addresses.

LISTING 3.1   LISTING THE ARP CACHE

```
c:\> arp -a

Interface: 192.168.0.200 on Interface 0x1000003
  Internet Address     Physical Address     Type
  192.168.0.1          00-40-05-1e-30-61    dynamic
  192.168.0.3          00-20-c5-e2-6a-fc    dynamic
  192.168.0.5          00-10-4b-cc-ee-92    dynamic
```

Another type of name resolution is mapping a NetBIOS name to an IP address. This occurs frequently on Windows computers because many Windows computers use NetBIOS over TCP/IP (NetBT) to perform file and print sharing. This occurs through broadcast, Windows Internet Name Service (WINS), or a static lmhosts file. Listing 3.2 shows the output of an nbtstat -c command showing the mapping of IP addresses to NetBIOS names.

LISTING 3.2   DISPLAYING THE NETBIOS NAME CACHE

```
c:\> nbtstat -c

Local Area Connection:
Node IpAddress: [192.168.0.200] Scope Id: []
```

CH

3

LISTING 3.2   CONTINUED

```
              NetBIOS Remote Cache Name Table

      Name              Type      Host Address    Life [sec]
  - - - - - - - - - - - - - - - - - - - - - - - - - - - - - - - - - - - - -
      WOOD          <20>  UNIQUE      192.168.0.1        592
      GOLD          <20>  UNIQUE      192.168.0.5        587
```

The main reason for name resolution, however, that we focus on in this book is the process of finding a Domain Controller. If DCs are incapable of finding each other on the network to communicate, or if clients can't find DCs to log on to, Active Directory becomes useless. Many interrelated services are required for a functioning Active Directory, and all of them can be found on a DC. Kerberos is used for authentication; LDAP is used to find, insert, update, and delete objects; and Global Catalog servers are used to find objects in this and other AD trees in the forest. All these services are automatically installed on an Active Directory DC when the Windows 2000 server is promoted to a DC. These services must be found by a client many times during a session but particularly during the logon process. Additionally, DNS is used not only to find a DC, but also to find a physically close DC that is a member of the client's AD domain—rather than just any DC at random.

➔ For more information on Kerberos, **see** "Kerberos," **p. 290**

➔ For more information on installing Domain Controllers, **see** "Promoting a Server to Domain Controller," **p. 15**

DNS is also one of the first troubleshooting areas that should be addressed when an AD begins to function improperly. DNS is absolutely critical to the location of services and objects within an AD. AD replication and logon use DNS to find other services on the network they need.

➔ For more information on finding services, **see** "Finding a Domain Controller," **p. 94**

Unlike Windows NT, which can use any number of tools and services to locate a DC, Windows 2000 Domain Controllers find each other through DNS and DNS alone. Although other name resolution methodologies can be used by client computers, the default and preferred method is DNS.

USING THE MMC

Virtually every management tool for Active Directory is a Microsoft Management Console (MMC) snap-in. These snap-ins are applications that run in the context of the MMC and are saved with a .msc extension. Although not specifically part of DNS or Active Directory, you will use the MMC throughout this book, so it makes sense to look at it briefly.

DEFAULT CONSOLES

You can open any number of Active Directory and DNS management tools by clicking the following:

- Start
- Programs
- Administrative Tools

You can then use Active Directory Users and Computers to manage Active Directory objects, use DNS to manage your DNS servers, and so on.

CREATING CUSTOM CONSOLES

You also can use mmc.exe to create your own customized MMC consoles. This enables you to group several snap-ins in the same console.

> **Tip**
>
> If you create the console and then save it in the default folder, it ends up in the Administrative Tools folder. This can be handy, but you still must navigate through the Start menus to use it. One of my favorite ways to leverage the MMC is to create a console and save it to the desktop. This enables me to get to the tools I use the most with a double-click.

To create a custom MMC console, open the mmc.exe application, add one or more snap-ins, and then save the console as filename.msc.

To open MMC, type mmc.exe at a command prompt or at the Start, Run menu. This opens the MMC application without any snap-ins loaded. To add snap-ins to the MMC console, click Console, Add/Remove Snap-in. Figure 3.1 shows the empty MMC.

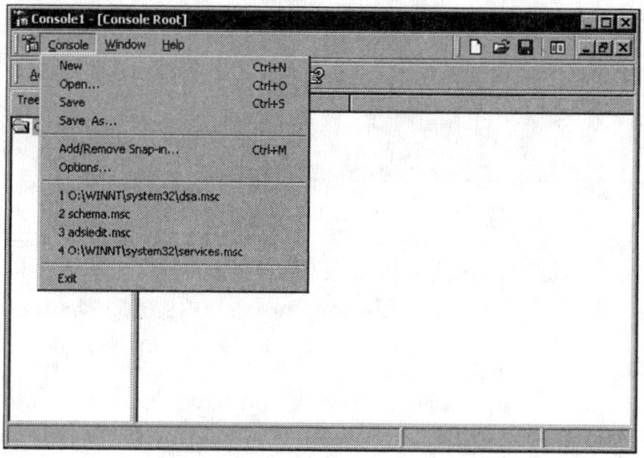

Figure 3.1
The Console menu in the MMC provides all the options to further enhance its use—including the selection to Add/Remove Snap-ins.

Next, you use the menu or Ctrl+M to open the Add/Remove Snap-in property page shown in Figure 3.2.

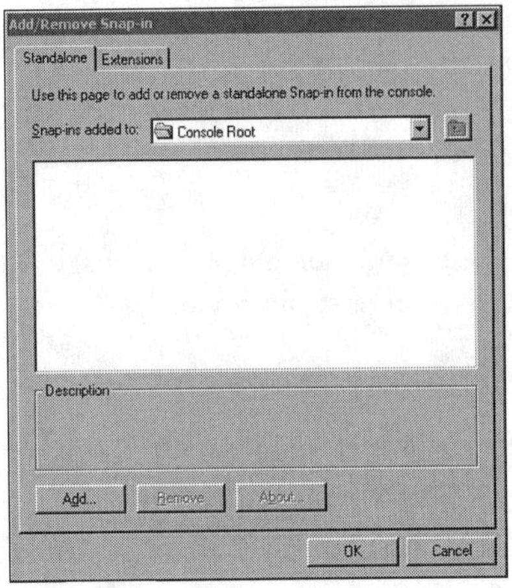

Figure 3.2
The Add/Remove Snap-in property page is where you select which snap-ins to add to which directories.

Clicking Add on the property page opens the Add Standalone Snap-in property page shown in Figure 3.3. Here, you can select the snap-ins you want by either double-clicking them or selecting the name in the Snap-in column and clicking Add.

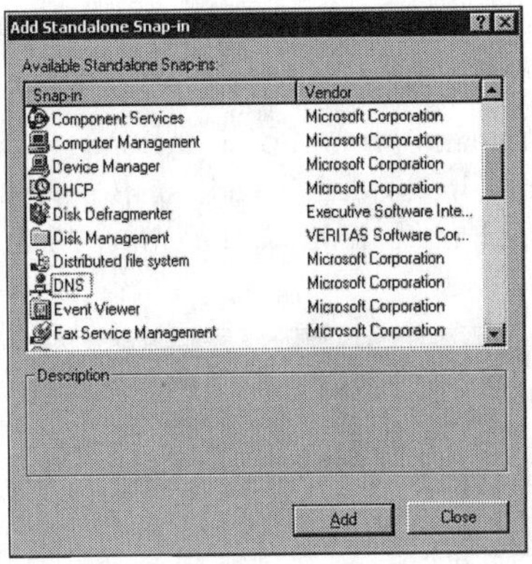

Figure 3.3
You can custom select the snap-ins to add to your MMC.

After you've finished, you can click Close. This returns you to the Add/Remove Snap-in property page shown in Figure 3.4. This page now shows the list of snap-ins that will be in this console.

The last thing you must do to persist the work you have done is to choose Console, Save and decide on a name and location for your new custom MMC console. You can also author and save consoles that cannot be modified for use by junior members of the staff. The MMC online help has more information on this functionality. To access MMC help, choose Help, Help Topics from inside MMC.

Figure 3.4
The console now
shows you the snap-
ins you've selected.

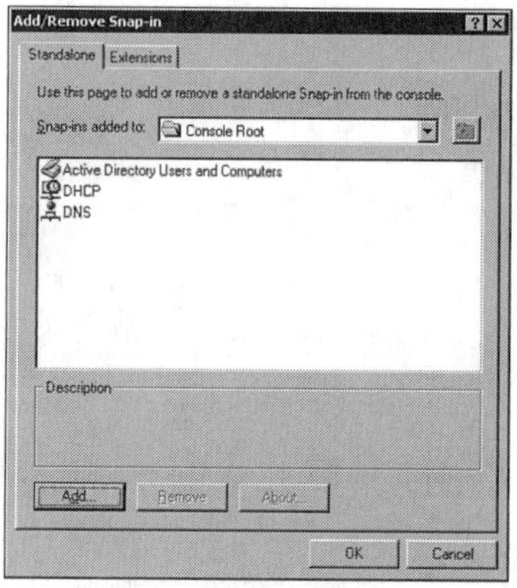

> **Tip**
>
> After you have saved the `.msc` console file, you can email it, copy it, and use it on multiple machines.

CH

3

SUMMARY

DNS is the default name resolution methodology for Windows 2000. It is absolutely necessary for the proper functioning of Active Directory. AD uses DNS to find services throughout the enterprise.

TROUBLESHOOTING

WINDOWS-SPECIFIC DNS

I already have a good DNS; must I use Windows 2000 DNS?

Whichever DNS you use to support Active Directory must support SRV records and should support Dynamic Update. You are not required to use Windows 2000 DNS, but you might find it to be the most straightforward choice. For more information on choosing a DNS implementation, see the section "BIND and the Active Directory" in Chapter 6, "Integrating BIND DNS with Active Directory."

SWAPPING OUT WINS FOR DNS

My company has successfully used WINS for name resolution for years. Do we have to switch to DNS?

You will still need Windows Internet Name Services to support down-level NetBIOS clients such as NT and Windows 9x. However, WINS is not used in any way by Active Directory and does not replace DNS. To install and use Active Directory, you will need a good DNS implementation that supports Active Directory. Windows 2000 DNS is a great choice for supporting Active Directory.

CHAPTER 4

Installing and Configuring DNS

In this chapter

INSTALLING DNS

Three ways to install DNS are available. You can install it through Control Panel, Add/Remove Programs; automatically as a part of the Active Directory install; or through scripting during the unattended installation of the server or by using `sysocmgr.exe` at any time.

Installing DNS is one of the required steps for a good implementation of the Active Directory (AD). Many, if not most, Active Directory installation problems can be traced back to an improperly installed or configured DNS. Most Active Directory/DNS problems occur as the result of not being able to find a Domain Controller (DC) or a service on a DC. If you cannot find a Kerberos KDC, you cannot authenticate. If you can't find an LDAP server, you can't add, delete, or modify AD objects. If your Domain Controllers can't find each other, they can't replicate.

INSTALLING DNS MANUALLY THROUGH CONTROL PANEL

You can install DNS manually on a server either before or after installing the Active Directory or on a non–Domain Controller (any Windows 2000 Server that is not hosting Active Directory). To install manually, from the desktop choose Start, Settings, Control Panel. This presents the Control Panel folder as shown in Figure 4.1.

Figure 4.1
The Windows 2000 Control Panel is the gateway to accessing system configurations and adding and removing new programs.

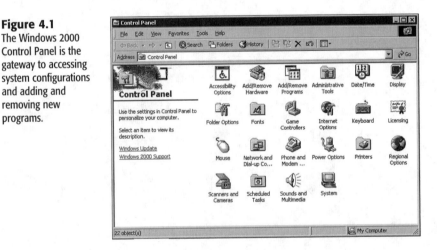

Double-click Add/Remove Programs. This presents the Add/Remove Page (see Figure 4.2).

Click Add/Remove Windows Components. This presents the Windows Components Wizard.

Next, select Networking Services (select the name as you see it in Figure 4.3). Do not click the check box at this level because it will select *all* the Networking Services.

Figure 4.2
Use the Add/Remove Programs page to search on a CD or floppy disk or even to search for updates over the Internet.

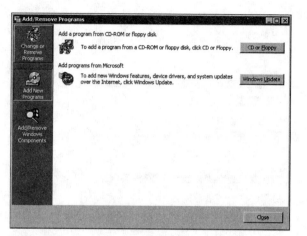

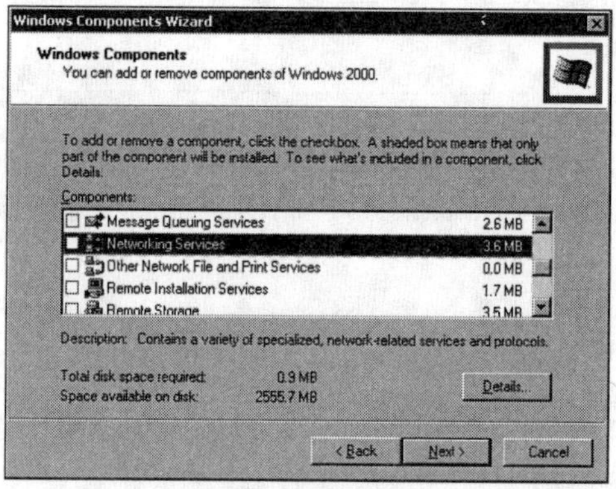

Figure 4.3
Simply click once to highlight the appropriate service in this list.

Next, you should click Details. This brings up the Networking Services page, as shown in Figure 4.4.

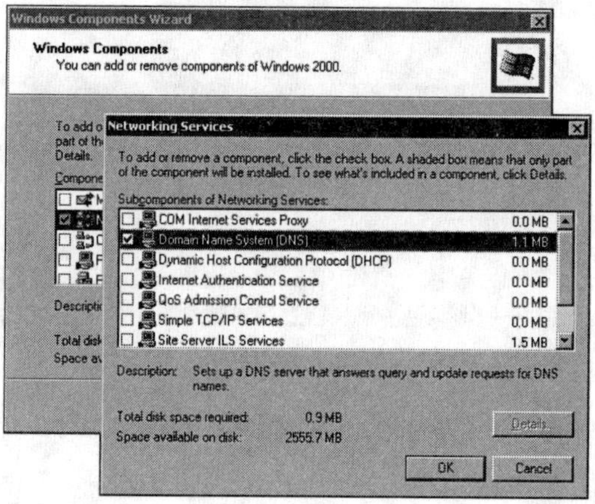

Figure 4.4
The details page for Networking Services enables you to select specific components.

CH

4

From here, click the check box next to Domain Name System (DNS), and then click OK. This returns you to the Windows Components Wizard page, as shown in Figure 4.5. Click Next.

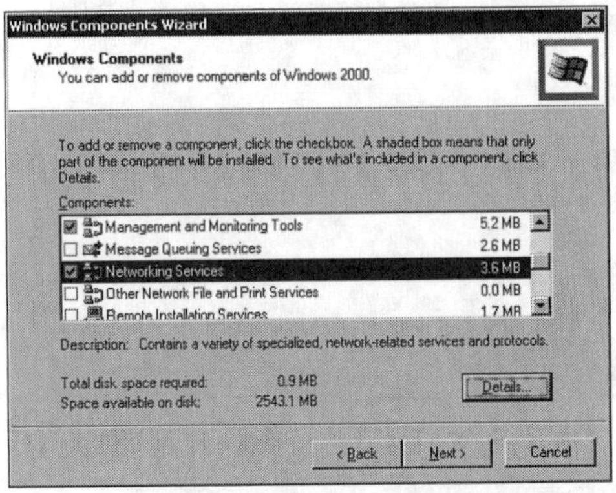

Figure 4.5
The Components Wizard page now shows a check mark next to Networking Services.

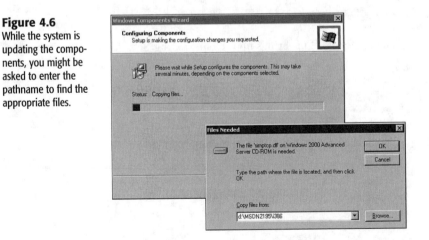

Caution

Notice that the check box next to Networking Services is checked and the box is grayed out. If you accidentally check the Networking Services box without using the Details button to select one service at a time, you will install all eight networking services.

As shown in Figure 4.6, you might be asked to provide a path to the i386 subdirectory of your Windows 2000 CD. If your files are on the hard disk or on a network share, you can provide a UNC or filesystem path to them. Click OK.

Figure 4.6
While the system is updating the compo-nents, you might be asked to enter the pathname to find the appropriate files.

Note

If you have a persistent copy of the i386 source on your hard drive or network and do not want to be prompted for this ever again, you can modify the SourcePath key of `HKLM\Software\Microsoft\Windows\CurrentVersion\Setup`. If this key is correct, any calls to copy files from the source execute automatically without user intervention.

Finally, you see the Completing the Windows Components Wizard page (see Figure 4.7). Click Finish. Note that you no longer have to reboot Windows 2000 like you did on NT before you can configure or use DNS.

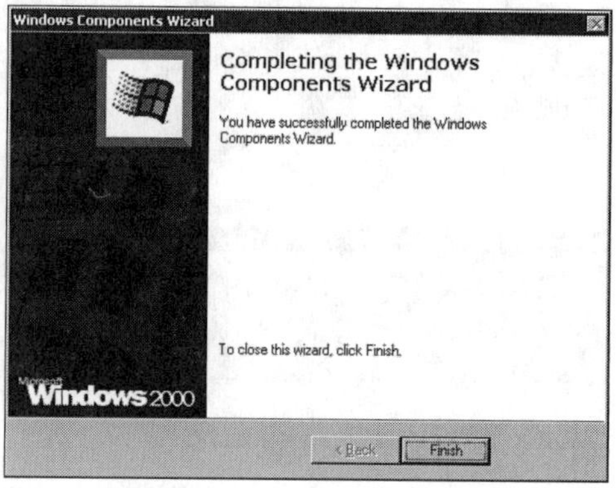

Figure 4.7
Wait for the completion screen before continuing to use the selected components.

At this point, DNS is installed but not configured, and it needs to be configured to support Active Directory. We will look at other ways to install DNS before we move on to configuring DNS in the next section.

INSTALLING DNS AUTOMATICALLY AS A PART OF AD INSTALLATION

When the `dcpromo.exe` AD installation wizard is run, it detects the presence or absence of a running and configured DNS service. It looks for a DNS on the IP address configured as the Preferred DNS Server on the Internet Protocol (TCP/IP) Properties page on the server (see Figure 4.8).

If it does not detect DNS that supports dynamic updates running on the configured DNS server, it pops up a message box to warn you that it cannot contact a DNS server to support your AD domain. It also prompts you to confirm your DNS settings or gives you the option to install and configure the DNS service on the local machine (see Figure 4.9).

Click OK. This takes you to the Active Directory Installation Wizard/Configure DNS page (see Figure 4.10). If you click the radio button next to No, I Will Install and Configure DNS Myself, you are allowed to complete the AD installation wizard. However, until DNS is installed on the configured DNS server, the AD installed on this machine will be incapable of satisfying requests for AD services from other machines and will be only barely functional.

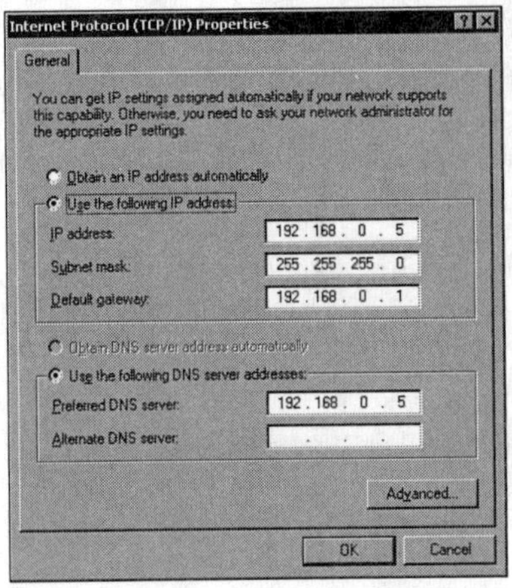

Figure 4.8
Use this screen to set IP and DNS server addresses.

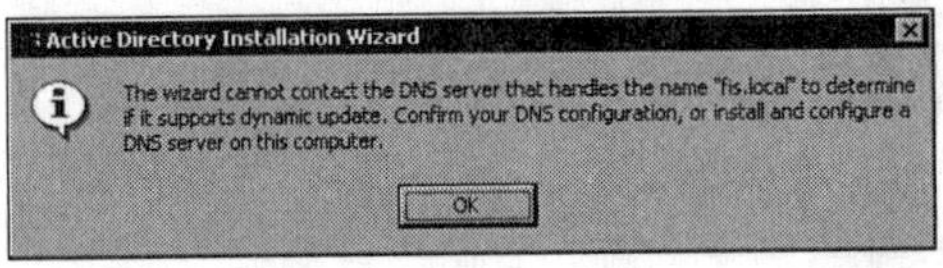

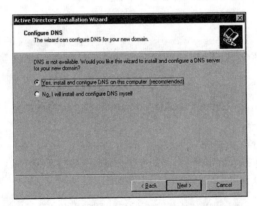

Figure 4.9
The Active Directory Installation Wizard warns you if it can't detect the proper configurations.

Figure 4.10
The Configuration Wizard enables installation and automatic DNS configuration.

The best course of action is always to allow the AD installation wizard to install and configure your DNS, particularly if you are not very experienced with DNS.

Therefore, select Yes, Install and Configure DNS on This Computer (Recommended), as shown in Figure 4.10.

Depending on from where you installed Windows 2000, you might be asked to provide a path to the i386 subdirectory on a Windows 2000 CD (see Figure 4.11).

Figure 4.11
You must provide a
path to the Windows
2000 files.

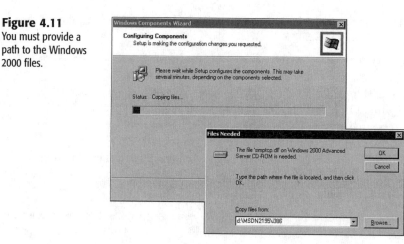

Type the path and click OK. You next see a page showing that the AD Installation Wizard is waiting for the DNS service to start. This, however, does not require any interaction on your part.

When the wizard completes and the new DC is rebooted, you will have an installed DNS service and a forward lookup zone with the same name as your AD domain. It is important to remember that the AD Installation Wizard does not automatically install a reverse lookup zone. Although it is not critical for your DNS to have a reverse lookup zone, two things need to be remembered. The first is that every Windows 2000 client automatically tries to register both its forward (A) and reverse (PTR) records. If a properly configured reverse lookup zone is not available, all your clients will attempt to register their PTR records and will fail. The second is that many network applications will encounter failures as a result of failed reverse lookups on your clients. This includes the DNS troubleshooting tool nslookup.exe.

The default properties of the forward lookup zone created by the AD Installation Wizard are to allow only secure updates. This prevents rogue DNS record updates by unauthorized clients. The default zone type in this scenario is also Active Directory Integrated, which means the zone information is being stored as objects and attributes of the AD rather than in a text file. These settings can, of course, be modified.

The AD Installation Wizard also creates the child domains and records necessary to support the AD.

INSTALLING DNS AUTOMATICALLY THROUGH SCRIPTING

One of my favorite things about Windows 2000 is its scriptability. Whether through unattended setups, Windows Scripting Host, or WBEM, Windows 2000 provides a wealth of opportunities for scripting. In this section, we look at installing DNS using sysocmgr.exe. This executable provides the functionality you see when installing services through Control

CH

4

Panel. Later in this chapter, we look at managing and configuring DNS using dnscmd.exe, which is a part of the Windows 2000 Support Tools.

→ For more information on configuring DNS through scripting, **see** "Manually Installing DNS Zones Using dnscmd.exe," **p. 59**

The online help that ships with Windows 2000 is very well organized and searchable and provides a wealth of technical information for the asking. Many commands and tools are well represented in the Windows 2000 help files. sysocmgr, however, is not one of them. The good news, though, is that it is very easy to use, and after you have seen the functionality, you'll find it helpful for installing virtually any service listed in the [netoptionalcomponents] section of unattend.doc. This document is part of the deploy.cab file in the \support\tools folder of the Windows 2000 CD.

Using sysocmgr.exe to script the install of DNS is very straightforward. First, you must create an answer file. This file can take the following form:

```
[netoptionalcomponents]
dns=1
```

That really is it. This tells sysocmgr to install DNS using the same tools you use to install it manually, only doing so without any user intervention.

You can then use this answer file with the following command, assuming you created it and saved it as c:\scripts\answer.txt:

```
Sysocmgr.exe /i:sysoc.inf /u:c:\scripts\answer.txt
```

When you execute this command from the command prompt, you briefly see some of the same screens you've seen when installing DNS manually. The difference is that these don't require or accept user intervention. You might be asked to provide a path to the i386 subdirectory of your Windows 2000 CD. No other user intervention is required or allowed. This process can take 5–10 seconds depending on the speed of your computer.

The sysoc.inf file referenced in the previous command is automatically installed in \winnt\inf and does not need to be modified for this operation.

CONFIGURING DNS

After the DNS is installed, you must configure one or more forward lookup zones. If you allowed the Active Directory Installation Wizard to install DNS, the forward lookup zone that corresponds to your Windows 2000 domain will be already created and set to allow secure updates. When you open the DNS Microsoft Management Console (MMC) snap-in for DNS from the Administrative Tools folder of your Start menu, you see a screen similar to that shown in Figure 4.12.

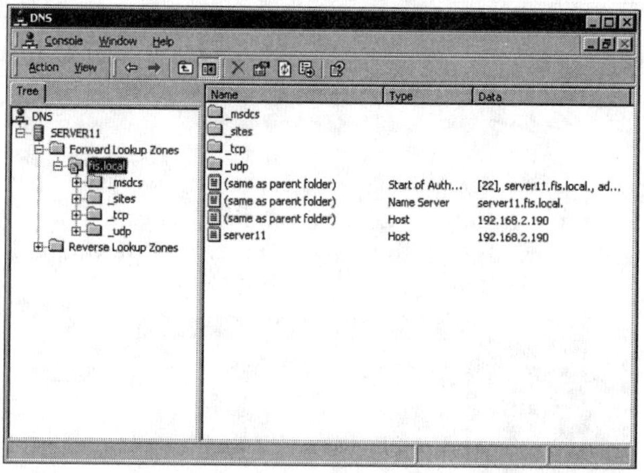

Figure 4.12
The MMC snap-in for DNS presents the current DNS file folder system.

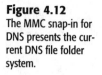

Because the default is to allow secure updates to the DNS zone, many DNS installations don't require any further immediate configuration of this zone. Other AD DCs automatically update their A and SRV records in this zone when they are promoted and the Netlogon service starts. You should remember to create a reverse lookup zone manually for PTR records. This is covered later in this section.

If you have not installed the AD yet, you don't have any autocreated zones. You also might want to create other forward lookup zones manually. Fortunately, a wizard exists to automate much of this.

MANUALLY INSTALLING A FORWARD LOOKUP ZONE

Click Start, Programs, Administrative Tools, DNS. This opens the `dnsmgmt.msc` MMC snap-in shown in Figure 4.13.

Figure 4.13
You can configure a new DNS installation in the MMC.

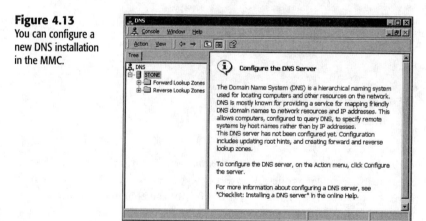

CH
4

Note   You can begin this process in several ways. If you select the server and read the information in the right pane, it tells you to use the Configure the Server command from the Action menu. This simply starts some of the wizards you see in the next few pages.

Select your server and click the plus sign (+) next to your server to open the forward and reverse lookup zone folders on your DNS server. Right-click a forward lookup zone in the tree pane and select a new zone. This brings up the wizard shown in Figure 4.14.

Figure 4.14
Use the New Zone
Wizard to configure
lookup zones.

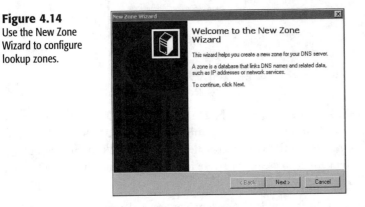

Click Next, and you see the Zone Type page shown in Figure 4.15.

Figure 4.15
Several Zone Type
options are available
in the MMC.

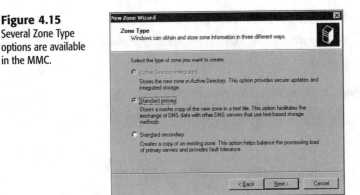

If you don't have the Active Directory installed on this machine, your only options are standard primary and standard secondary zones. A *primary* zone contains a read/write copy of the zone file, whereas a *secondary* zone has a read-only copy of the zone file. An *Active Directory–integrated* zone stores each zone as an object in the Active Directory and provides other features.

Choose the zone type appropriate for your server and click Next. In the Zone Name page shown in Figure 4.16, you must choose a name for your zone. If you are going to use this DNS server with the AD and to resolve requests for AD resources, it is imperative that the AD Domain and the DNS domain name match. If they do not, your Netlogon service will be incapable of registering its SRV records in the proper DNS domain.

Figure 4.16
The DNS zone should match your Active Directory domain name.

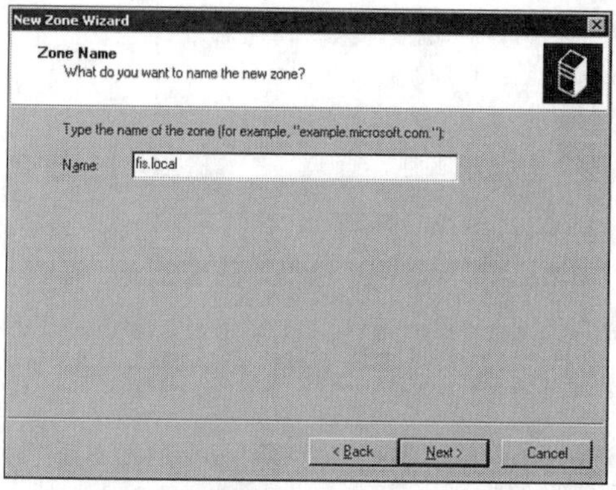

Next, you see the Zone File page, as shown in Figure 4.17. It is almost always best to stick with the defaults here. The default is for the filename to be the zone name followed by .dns. The file is copied to \winnt\system32\dns when it is saved. The Use This Existing File option enables you to recycle DNS configuration files from other DNS servers for this zone. If you have a zone file for a DNS zone already created from a BIND DNS server that holds accurate records, you can reuse this file to keep you from having to reenter your static entries. This file must already be stored in \winnt\system32\dns.

Figure 4.17
You can use an existing zone file or choose to create a new one.

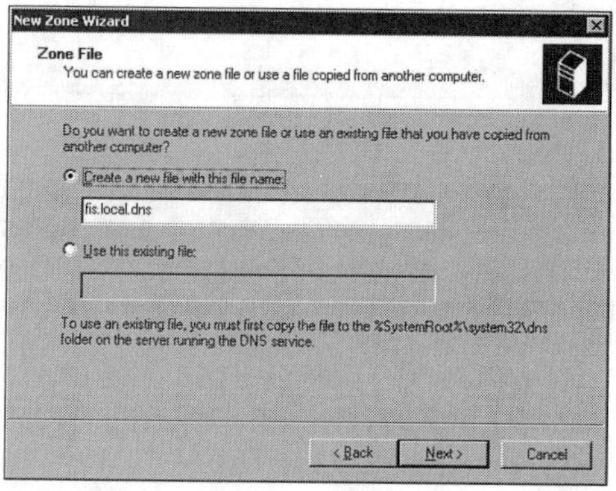

Click Next. Finally, you see the Completing the New Zone Wizard summary page (see Figure 4.18). This just enables you to recheck all your choices before clicking Finish.

Figure 4.18
Click Finish to com-
plete the zone.

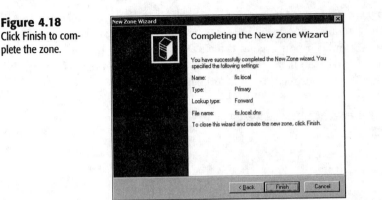

After you have clicked Finish in the summary page, you are returned to the DNS MMC
Snap-in (see Figure 4.19).

Figure 4.19
The newly created
zone in the MMC is
now ready to be
modified.

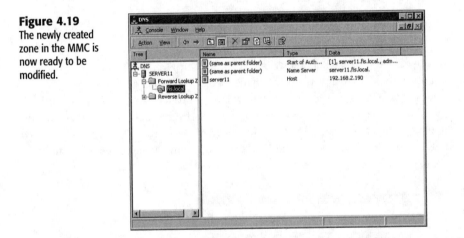

Note

If you create a standard primary zone, the Allow Dynamic Updates option is set to No by
default. This means that all attempts to Dynamic DNS will fail against this zone. You should
change it to Allow Updates if you want it to register A and SRV records for Windows 2000
clients.

MANUALLY INSTALLING A REVERSE LOOKUP ZONE

Although it is not absolutely required, it is certainly best to install and configure one or
more reverse lookup zones for your DNS server. Every Windows 2000 client attempts to
register its A and PTR records upon boot. If no reverse lookup zone exists, the PTR registration fails. Unlike forward lookup zones, whose names are defined based on the AD

domain name, reverse lookup zone names are defined by the network address of the network for which the DNS server is responsible. The format is for the zone name to be the IP network address backward, followed by the `.in-addr.arpa` zone. For example, if your network address is `194.168.4.0`, the reverse lookup zone is named `4.168.194.in-addr.arpa`. However, Windows 2000 DNS provides a wizard to automate the creation of this zone and the formation of a proper name for it. To create a reverse lookup zone, select the reverse lookup zones folder in the tree pane of the DNS MMC Snap-in (see Figure 4.20).

Figure 4.20
Create a reverse lookup zone through the MMC.

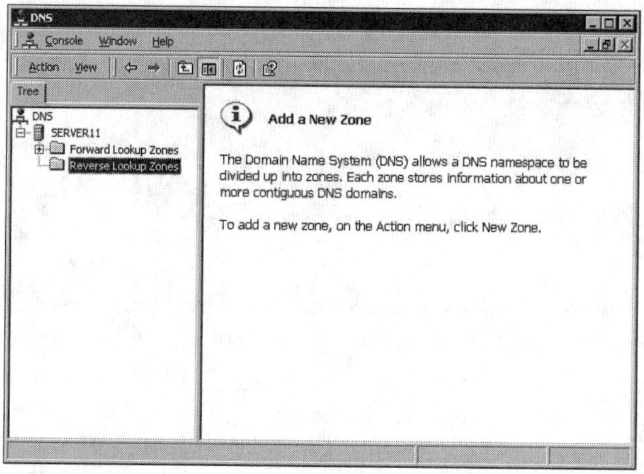

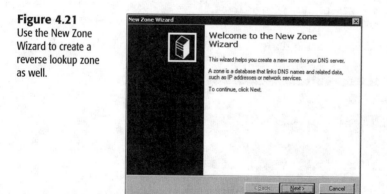

Right-click Reverse Lookup Zones and select New Zone. This opens the New Zone Wizard page shown in Figure 4.21.

Figure 4.21
Use the New Zone Wizard to create a reverse lookup zone as well.

Click Next. This brings us to the same page you saw when you created the forward lookup zone (see Figure 4.22). Again, because this machine is not currently a Domain Controller, Active Directory–integrated zones are not available. Therefore, you must choose Standard

CH

4

Primary or Standard Secondary—remembering that secondary zones are read-only—and click Next.

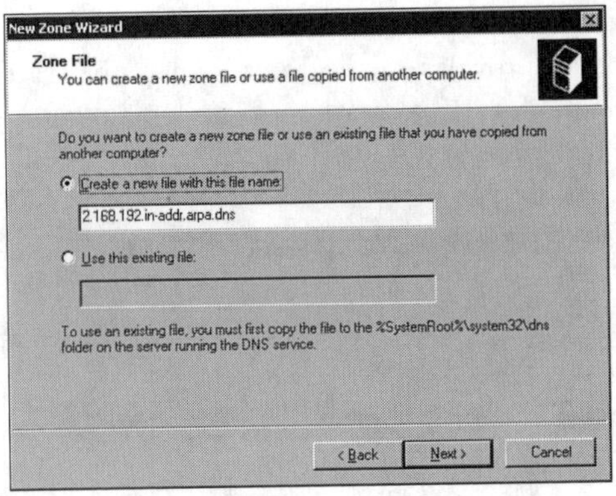

Figure 4.22
Choose a zone type.

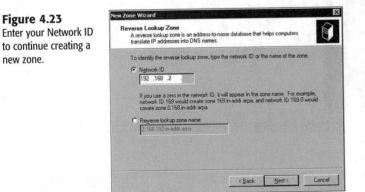

You need to know your network ID to complete the next page (see Figure 4.23). Although this is not a book on TCP/IP addressing, the examples in Table 4.1 should provide some guidance.

TABLE 4.1   NETWORK IDs AND SUBNET MASKS

IP Address	Subnet Mask	Network ID for Page
10.5.1.47	255.0.0.0	10
165.47.53.12	255.255.0.0	165.47
192.168.2.12	255.255.255.0	192.168.2

Note that you do not enter the trailing zeros for the Network ID portion of the page.

Figure 4.23
Enter your Network ID to continue creating a new zone.

You also can enter the reverse lookup zone name manually by selecting the radio button at the bottom of the page.

Click Next. You now can create a new file with the default name or use an existing file (see Figure 4.24). As noted before, reusing an old file enables you to reuse addresses that have already been registered on another DNS server. However, you must manually ensure that the file format adheres to the RFC standards and is properly configured for this server.

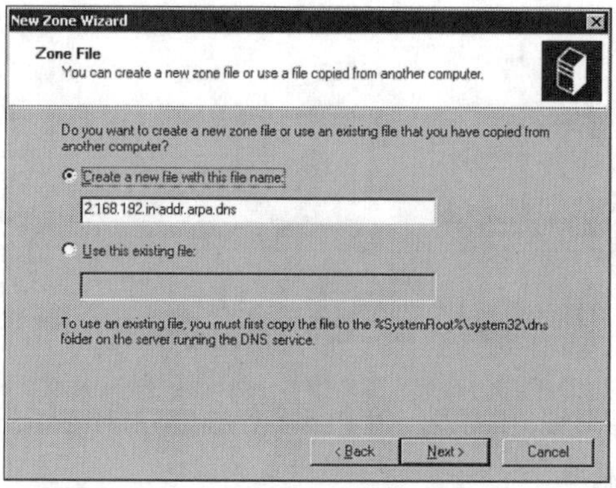

Figure 4.24
Choose the appropriate zone file.

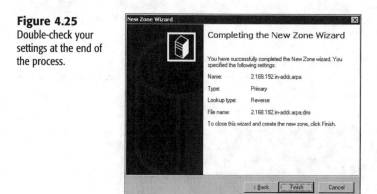

Using the defaults is usually the best policy. These files, similar to other DNS zone files, are saved to `\winnt\system32\dns`. Click Next; finally, you see the summary page (see Figure 4.25).

Figure 4.25
Double-check your settings at the end of the process.

After you click Finish, you are returned to the DNS MMC Snap-in. If you double-click the folder for your new reverse lookup zone, you see the information shown in Figure 4.26.

CH
4

Figure 4.26
The new zone appears in the MMC Snap-in.

Although only Start of Authority (SOA) and Name Server (NS) records are placed automatically, after the zone is configured to allow updates, you'll begin to see PTR records in the reverse lookup zone. You can set the zone to allow dynamic updates by right-clicking the zone and choosing Properties, Allow Dynamic Updates, Yes.

> **Caution**
>
> If you create a standard primary zone, the Allow Dynamic Updates option is set to No by default. This means that all attempts to Dynamic DNS will fail against this zone. You should change it to Allow Updates if you want it to register PTR records for Windows 2000 clients. Windows 2000 clients will attempt to update their PTR records by default. If the zone is set to not allow updates, this operation will fail. Many network operations, such as nslookup, will fail if a reverse lookup is unsuccessful.

After the zone is set to allow dynamic updates, you can register your A and PTR records by opening a command prompt and executing the `ipconfig /registerdns` command, as shown in Figure 4.27.

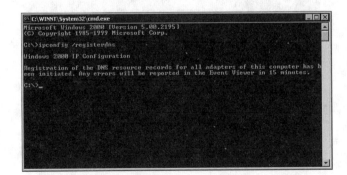

Figure 4.27
You can manually update DNS records with `ipconfig`.

Notice the output from the command in Figure 4.27. If errors are encountered trying to register your records, that information is written to the event log. Most of these errors are caused by pointing the DNS to the wrong place or failing to configure allow updates on the DNS zone.

Note

Don't forget to ensure that the DNS server has the client portion of the IP protocol stack set to use the local DNS. If the local IP settings point to another DNS server, the `ipconfig /registerdns` command attempts to update a remote DNS zone other than the local DNS you just installed.

MANUALLY INSTALLING DNS ZONES USING dnscmd.exe

Just as you can perform a hands-off install of DNS with `sysocmgr.exe`, you can also script the creation and configuration of DNS zones with `dnscmd.exe`. This executable is part of the Windows 2000 Support Tools located on the Windows 2000 CD. To install the tools, double-click `\support\tools\2000RKST.MSI`. This loads the Windows 2000 Support Tools Setup Wizard. This also installs several helpful tools, including `dnscmd.exe`, the Active Directory Replication Monitor, and the `unattend.doc` mentioned earlier in the chapter. These tools are not to be confused with the Resource Kit—another incredible product with a wealth of documentation and specialized tools.

`dnscmd` is well documented in the Tools Help that installs with the Support Tools. This section looks at several examples that enable you to build a working DNS infrastructure from scratch. This tool also can be used in conjunction with `sysocmgr` to create a completely hands-off DNS installation. The basic `dnscmd` syntax is shown here:

```
DnsCmd <ServerName> <Command> [<Command Parameters>]
```

The parameters allowed in `dnscmd` are as varied as DNS itself. We will look at the minimum commands necessary to build a functioning DNS. The following examples assume that you have just finished installing DNS manually through Control Panel or by using `sysocmgr`. In other words, DNS is installed and running but no zones have been created. The DNS MMC Snap-in should look similar to Figure 4.28.

The first thing you must do is create a zone. The code in Listing 4.1 creates a forward lookup zone called `fis.local` with a zone type of standard primary. An interesting feature of `dnscmd` is the capability to use a period (.) to represent the local server rather than hardcoding server names in the scripts. This enables the same script to be used on multiple servers.

LISTING 4.1   CREATING A PRIMARY ZONE

```
dnscmd . /zoneadd fis.local /primary
```

CH

4

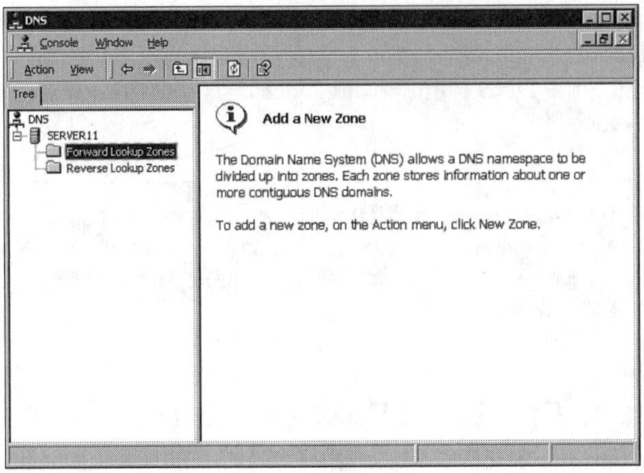

Figure 4.28
Your configured MMC
Snap-in should be
ready to create zones.

Next, you can install a reverse lookup zone by using the same command with different parameters. The following code creates a reverse lookup zone on the local server based on the 194.168.0.0 network address of zone type standard primary:

```
dnscmd . /zoneadd 0.168.194.in-addr.arpa /primary
```

After you have created the zones, you might want to configure them without having to use the DNS MMC Snap-in. To configure zone fis.local (created previously) to allow updates, execute the following code:

```
dnscmd . /config fis.local /AllowUpdate 1
```

Caution

Although the commands to dnscmd are not case sensitive, the command *parameters* are. In the previous examples, config can be cased in any format. AllowUpdate, however, must be cased exactly as shown. The tools Help that ships with the Windows 2000 Support Tools has a listing of all the command parameters and their cases.

Finally, to allow updates to the reverse lookup zone, execute the following:

```
dnscmd . /config 0.168.194.in-addr.arpa /AllowUpdate 1
```

To get help with command-line syntax, you can execute dnsmcd without any parameters and it will fill the screen with online help (see Listing 4.2).

LISTING 4.2 THE ONLINE HELP INFORMATION

```
USAGE:  DnsCmd <ServerName> <Command> [<Command Parameters>]

    <ServerName>:
        .                      -- local machine using LPC
        IP address             -- RPC over TCP/IP
        DNS name               -- RPC over TCP/IP
        other server name      -- RPC over named pipes
    <Command>:
```

LISTING 4.2 CONTINUED

```
         /Info                 -- Get server information
         /Config               -- Reset server or zone configuration
         /EnumZones            -- Enumerate zones
         /Statistics           -- Query/clear server statistics data
         /ClearCache           -- Clear DNS server cache
         /WriteBackFiles       -- Write back all zone or root-hint
                                  ➥datafile(s)
         /StartScavenging      -- Initiates server scavenging
         /ResetListenAddresses -- Select server IP address(es) to serve
                                  ➥DNS requests
/ResetForwarders          -- Set DNS servers to forward recursive
                                  ➥queries to
         /ZoneInfo             -- View zone information
         /ZoneAdd              -- Create a new zone on the DNS server
         /ZoneDelete           -- Delete a zone from DNS server or DS
         /ZonePause            -- Pause a zone
         /ZoneResume           -- Resume a zone
         /ZoneReload           -- Reload zone from its database (file or
                                  ➥DS)
         /ZoneWriteBack        -- Write back zone to file
         /ZoneRefresh          -- Force refresh of secondary zone from
                                  ➥master
         /ZoneUpdateFromDs     -- Update a DS integrated zone by data from
                                  ➥DS
         /ZoneResetType        -- Change zone type
                                  ➥Primary/Secondary/DSintegrated
         /ZoneResetSecondaries -- Reset secondary\notify information for a
                                  ➥zone
         /ZoneResetScavengeServers-- Reset scavenging servers for a zone
         /ZoneResetMasters     -- Reset secondary zone's master servers
         /EnumRecords          -- Enumerate records at a name
         /RecordAdd            -- Create a record in zone or RootHints
         /RecordDelete         -- Delete a record from zone, RootHints or
                                  ➥Cache data
         /NodeDelete           -- Delete all records at a name
         /AgeAllRecords        -- Force aging on node(s) in zone
         <Command Parameters>:
         -- parameters specific to each Command
         dnscmd <CommandName> /? -- For help info on specific Command
```

Notice the last line of Listing 4.2. If you need more specific help with syntax for a command, you can type the specific command with /? to get help with exactly that command. The code in Listing 4.3 shows the output from using this help feature.

LISTING 4.3 HELP FOR A SPECIFIC COMMAND (zoneadd)

```
dnscmd /zoneadd /?

USAGE:  DnsCmd <ServerName> /ZoneAdd <ZoneName> <ZoneType> [<Options>]
        <ZoneName>              -- FQDN of zone
        <ZoneType>:
        /Primary /file <filename>
             -- standard file backed primary;  MUST include filename.
```

CH

4

LISTING 4.3   CONTINUED

```
/Secondary <MasterIPaddress> [<MasterIPaddress>] ..] [/file <filename>]
-- standard secondary, MUST include at least one master IP;
    ➥ filename is optional.
/DsPrimary            -- DS integrated primary zone
<Options>:
[/file <filename>]    -- filename, invalid for DsPrimary
[/load]               -- load existing file;  if not specified,
                         non-DS primary creates default zone records
[/a <AdminName>]      -- zone admin email name; primary zones only
Command completed successfully.
```

SUMMARY

You can install and configure DNS in a variety of ways. The Active Directory Installation Wizard installs the DNS during the AD install; you can install manually through Control Panel; or you can install automatically through scripting. These all achieve the same results: a well-configured name resolution service.

TROUBLESHOOTING

DNS ERRORS

DNS errors show up in the Windows 2000 event viewer.

If your IP protocol stack is set to point to a DNS zone—local or remote—that is not configured to allow updates, you receive errors in the Windows 2000 event viewer stating that dynamic updates were unsuccessful. To address this, make sure your IP stack points to the correct DNS server and that the DNS zone is configured to allow updates.

MISSING SRV RECORDS

DNS and Active Directory are installed, but SRV records are not being created.

Several causes are possible, but the root issue is that the AD is installed but the DNS has not registered the A and SRV records necessary to provide full functionality to the AD. The resolution is simple, though. Make sure the DNS is installed and has a forward lookup zone created and configured whose name exactly matches that of the AD domain installed on this machine. Both the forward and reverse lookup zones must be configured to allow updates or allow secure updates. Use ipconfig /registerdns to ensure that you can update both zones. If you execute this command and it registers both A and PTR records, your DNS service is ready for the next step. Go to a command prompt and issue the following two commands:

```
net stop netlogon
```

```
net start netlogon
```

This causes the Netlogon service to retry writing the `\winnt\system32\config\`
`netlogon.dns` file to the forward lookup zone whose name matches the AD domain name. At that point, other servers and workstations that are configured to use this DNS can join the domain, become DCs of this domain, or authenticate to this domain.

USING A NON-MICROSOFT DNS

I'm using a non-Microsoft DNS and when I install Active Directory, it doesn't function properly.

Regardless of the DNS used with Active Directory, it must support SRV records and should support dynamic update. If the DNS does not, a different DNS must be used. For most installations, Windows 2000 DNS is the best choice for a DNS to support AD.

INTERMITTENT NETWORK SERVICE

After installing additional network services, Active Directory seems to fail intermittently.

If you install any routing and remote access service that modifies the IP configuration on the local machine, your DNS might no longer point to a DNS that can resolve queries for Active Directory services. Use the `ipconfig /all` command and check every DNS-related entry. Use the `nslookup` command to see which DNS server pops up. If it is not the correct DNS, modify the routing and remote access service configuration to point to an appropriate DNS.

CHAPTER 5

DNS Architecture

In this chapter

USING THE DNS MMC SNAP-IN

Now that you have installed and configured your DNS, you need to make sure you understand some of the architecture behind DNS. Although a single DNS server will certainly function in a small network, most DNS servers are configured with the addresses of the root DNS servers that are located all over the world. The true power of DNS becomes apparent when you consider that no DNS server worldwide holds all the DNS information but simply holds information on other DNS servers that enables you to get closer to finding the information you need.

A good understanding of DNS architecture goes a long way when troubleshooting both the Active Directory and DNS. This chapter looks at DNS record types and then dissects a DNS lookup process. A *forward* lookup is the process of finding an IP address from a hostname. A *reverse* lookup is (surprise!) just the opposite—finding a hostname from an IP address.

DNS RECORD TYPES

In the snap-in are several DNS record types. Although this is not an exhaustive list, several types of records are germane to a discussion of DNS and AD. A (address), PTR (pointer), NS (name server), SOA (start of authority), and SRV (service) records are the records this section looks at. In Figure 5.1, you can see several of the record types and some of the information associated with them.

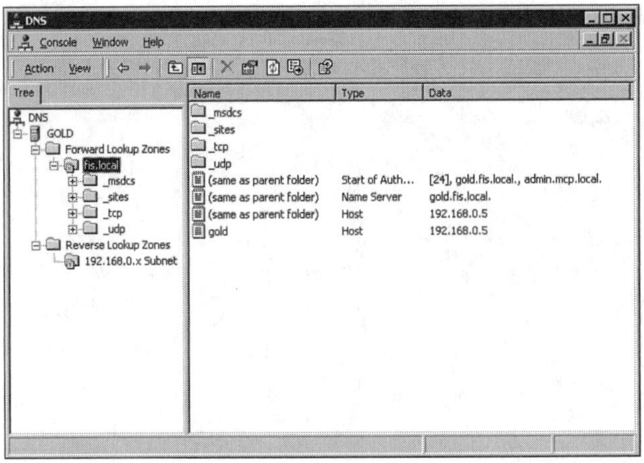

Figure 5.1
Viewing DNS record types.

A RECORDS

Using the MMC, you can double-click any record and see all the information for the record. If you first ensure that you have selected your forward lookup zone (`fis.local` from Figure 5.1), you can double-click the Host or A record for `gold` in Figure 5.1 and get the screen you see in Figure 5.2.

Figure 5.2
A records provide simple IP address-to-DNS name mapping.

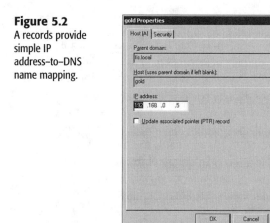

Tip

More information on DNS can be found at www.ietf.org. Some good introductory RFCs are 1034 and 1035.

Here you can see that the A record is one of the simplest yet most essential records in the DNS. It holds the basic name–to–IP address mapping for a particular host.

NS RECORDS

If you click the NS record, you see that Name Server records are simply a listing of all the DNS servers in the zone. An NS record holds a simple fully qualified domain name (FQDN)–to–IP address pair (see Figure 5.3).

Figure 5.3
NS records list all the DNS servers for a zone.

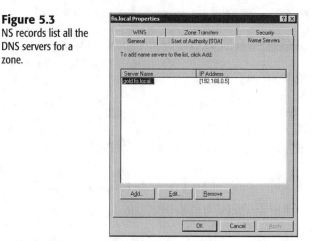

CH

5

SOA RECORDS

The SOA record shown in Figure 5.4 is one of the more detailed records in the zone. It holds the serial number, which is used to keep track of changes to the zone and zone transfers. This number is incremented every time a zone changes. A DNS server configured for standard zones uses the serial number to track which version of the zone database a secondary holds, and if the secondary has an older zone serial number, this triggers a zone transfer. If you are having trouble getting a standard primary zone and standard secondary zone to perform a zone transfer, a good solution to trigger that is to artificially increment the serial number on the primary zone. The SOA record also has information about the responsible person for a zone, which is the person to contact if problems occur.

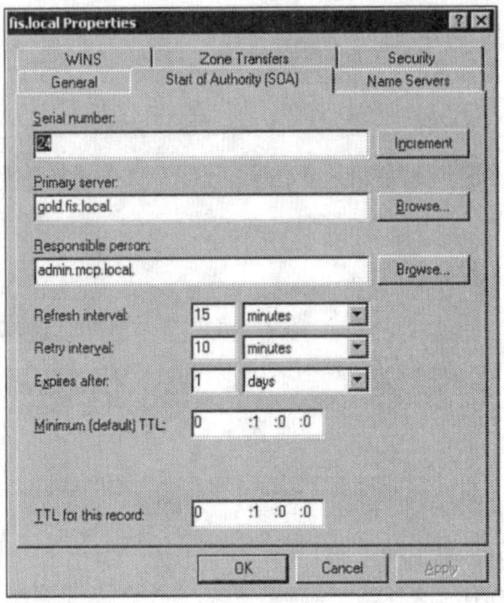

Figure 5.4
SOA records hold zone transfer information about DNS zones.

The Refresh Interval is how often a secondary copy of this zone running on another DNS server checks whether a zone transfer from the primary to the secondary is necessary. The Retry Interval is how often a secondary zone retries a failed zone transfer. The Expires After setting sets how long stale data in a secondary zone will remain if it cannot be verified by contacting the primary server.

PTR RECORDS

To see the next record type, you must go to the reverse lookup zone configured for this server. If you select the reverse lookup zone named 192.168.0.x from Figure 5.5, you see a PTR record for the local DNS server.

This record is similar in structure to the A record, except that it holds its subnet information rather than its parent domain.

Note

The actual format for the records in a zone text file is somewhat different from what you see in the DNS MMC Snap-in. That is, of course, assuming you are using standard zones, which save the information in text files rather than in AD-integrated zones, which store DNS zones as objects in the AD and records as attributes of the zone object.

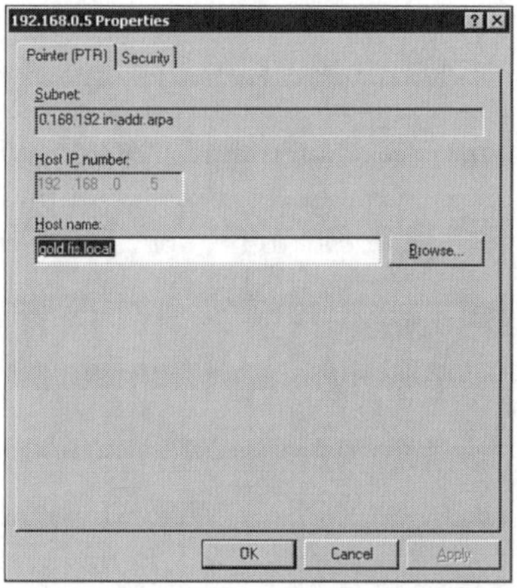

Figure 5.5
PTR records are used
for reverse lookups.

SRV RECORDS

To look at the final record type, you must select one of the subzones in your forward lookup
zone (see Figure 5.6).

Figure 5.6
The _tcp subzone in
DNS.

The zone you have chosen is the Default-First-Site-Name._sites.fis.local zone. We
will discuss the various zones that hold SRV records later in this section, but for the
moment, we are interested in the SRV (service location) record in this zone. It is the function of an SRV record to enable the locating of a computer that hosts a particular service.
You might notice what appear to be redundant instances of the same record in several places
throughout these zones that are autocreated by the AD. This enables finding the same
information based on several criteria—for example, the site in which a service resides or the
domain it belongs to by name (or by its globally unique identifier [GUID]).

CH
5

The SRV record shown in Figure 5.7 is used for the Kerberos service or to enable a client to find an instance of a Kerberos key distribution center (KDC). SRV records are the reason DNS is so crucial to the proper functioning of the AD. In previous versions of NT, you could count on broadcast, lmhosts, WINS, and so on to find a DC. In Windows 2000, however, you must not only find the IP address of the DC, you also must find the port number of one or more services to enable you to authenticate to the domain and then use its services.

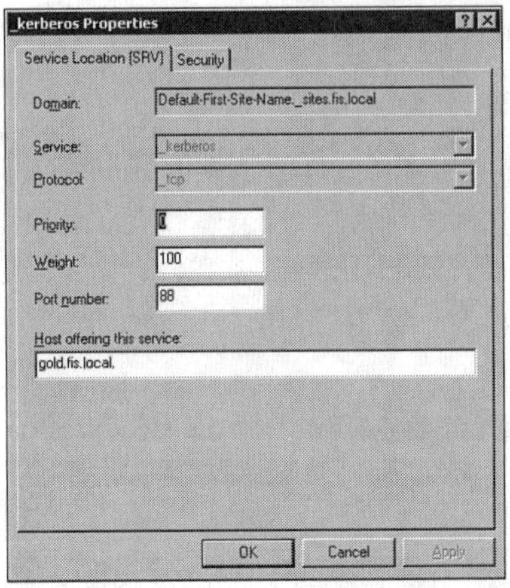

Figure 5.7
Kerberos SRV records are used to find a Kerberos KDC for logon authentication.

The Properties page associated with an SRV record has several settings. The first is simply the FQDN of the domain of which it is a member. Next is the service name, whether it is a global catalog (GC) server, a Kerberos KDC, or Lightweight Directory Access Protocol (LDAP) server. The protocol, either Transmission Control Protocol (TCP) or User Datagram Protocol (UDP), is the next setting.

→ See "Kerberos," **p. 290**

→ See "LDAP," **p. 3**

The next settings are Priority, Weight, and Port Number. Priority enables you to set a level of preference for a particular instance of a service, assuming more than one instance of a service is running in a particular domain. Servers holding a service with a lower priority are offered first; if this does not work, another instance of the same service is offered with a higher priority value. Weight enables you to load balance between two instances of the same service that have the same priority. A higher weight value is returned first if two services tie based on priority, enabling a weighted average to load balance between the records. Port Number is simply the TCP or UDP port assigned to the service. This is crucial because, if the port setting in DNS does not match the port actually used by the service, the client resolves faulty information and then is incapable of contacting the service it needs.

Finally, the host on which the service runs is listed in the Host Offering This Service section. It is important to note that these SRV records are autocreated by the AD when a DC is promoted and usually do not require intervention by the administrator.

ZONES CREATED BY THE ACTIVE DIRECTORY

When you run dcpromo.exe—the Active Directory Installation Wizard—a file called netlogon.dns is created in the \winnt\system32\config directory. When the DC reboots and the netlogon service is started, it writes this file to the DNS zone whose name matches the AD domain this DC hosts. For this to complete, the DNS zone must be set to allow updates or allow secure updates. The zones are named _msdcs, _sites, _tcp, and _udp. Virtually all the records you will find in these zones are SRV records.

Tip

To enable Allow Updates or Allow Only Secure Updates, right-click the zone in the DNS MMC Snap-in, choose Properties, and select the setting from the Allow Dynamic Updates? drop-down box.

Caution

You will rarely modify these records by hand. These records are created and updated by the netlogon service. Whether or not you modify them, every time the netlogon service is started, it rewrites the SRV records. If these records are incorrect or missing, your Active Directory screeches to a halt because these records are used to locate critical services, such as authentication.

_msdcs ZONE

The _msdcs zone holds records for services that might be used by the AD, such as LDAP, but might not be running on Windows 2000 domain controllers. Additionally, SRV records exist that enable you to find instances of a service based on domain GUID rather than domain name. This is useful if a domain has been renamed.

Note

A GUID is a 128-bit globally unique ID—a number that is generated from the time and date stamp at the time of its creation and the MAC address of the machine on which it is created.

Ch
5

_sites ZONE

The _sites zone holds SRV records for services such as Kerberos, LDAP, and global catalog servers, and enables them to be found by site membership. This is very important because a Windows 2000 client always attempts to find a service in its site first. Examples of such services are authentication, DFS, global catalogs, and so on.

_tcp AND _udp ZONES

The _tcp and _udp zones enable SRV records to be grouped based on the OSI transport/session layer protocol they use.

OTHER ZONES IN DNS

If you create child domains of the current AD domain, they automatically create zones in your current DNS zone if they are configured to use this DNS or if you are using AD-integrated zones.

ANATOMY OF A DNS LOOKUP

Now that you understand the architecture and the tools necessary, let's look at a working example. The following example assumes that you have an installed and configured DNS and have access to the Internet. Although the focus of the DNS chapters is how DNS supports the Active Directory, the reality is that most domain name services also support using Internet resources such as the Web and email.

FORWARD LOOKUP EXAMPLE

In this example, you look at the DNS lookups necessary to find a Web site on the Internet. The Web site is www.fullertoninfo.com; the IP address of the client resolver is 192.168.0.200; and its hostname is stone.fis.local. The IP address of the DNS server, on the other hand, is 192.168.0.5, and its hostname is gold.fis.local. The DNS server is configured with the addresses of the root name servers from \winnt\system32\dns\cache.dns. This file is copied to the default DNS directory when you install DNS. You can see that your DNS server is configured with these addresses by right-clicking your server name in the DNS MMC Snap-in and selecting Properties/Root Hints (see Figure 5.8).

Figure 5.8
The Internet root servers.

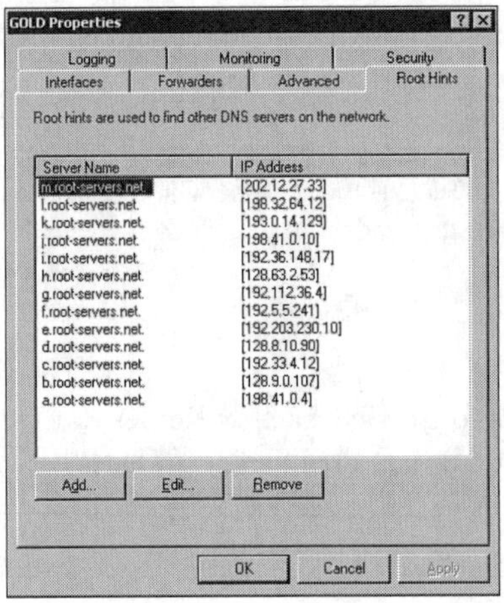

These are the names and addresses of the root servers located around the world. These servers are where you often begin the search for addresses for Internet resources.

You are using the `netmon.exe`, the network monitor tool that ships with Windows 2000 to perform your packet capture. This is a marvelous learning and troubleshooting tool for DNS because all DNS lookups go across the wire as clear text. This means that, if you have a decent packet analyzer and enough free time, you can learn about and troubleshoot virtually anything in DNS. The first frame you see from `netmon` is frame 4: the standard DNS query from `stone` to `gold` for `www.fullertoninfo.com` for a host address. In Figure 5.9, you see that the source is `stone` (the client) and the destination is `gold` (the DNS server).

Tip

You can install Network Monitor from the Control Panel, Add/Remove Programs icon. Choose Add Windows Components and use the Management and Monitoring Tools icon.

Figure 5.9
A DNS standard query in Network Monitor.

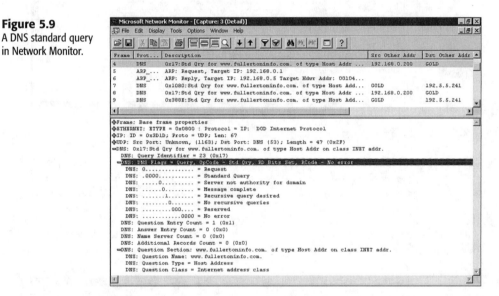

When you look at the DNS flags in Figure 5.9, you see that recursion is desired. This means that, if `gold.fis.local` is not authoritative for `fullertoninfo.com`, the client wants the DNS server to find the information on its behalf.

The next frame of interest is frame 7. Frames 5 and 6 are the DNS server holding an ARP conversation with the default gateway to obtain the MAC address necessary to forward the packet represented by frame 7. Figure 5.10 shows that the destination address is `192.5.5.241`, which is the address of one of the root servers on the Internet.

The other interesting feature of this packet is that the flag is set to request an iterative query. Therefore, if the root server is not authoritative for `fullertoninfo.com`, rather than asking the root server to find it on your behalf, you are asking for a list of DNS server addresses that might have the answer. In human terms, you are saying from your DNS server to the root server, "If you don't know the answer, can you tell me the name (address) of

CH
5

someone who might?" This is where the true beauty of the worldwide DNS system is revealed. Trying to scale a series of servers to keep track of all the addresses on the Internet would be very difficult. An IP address is 32 bits long, which results in the possibility of more than 4 billion addresses on the Internet. If one server tried to keep track of them all, throughput would be abysmal. Every DNS server keeps the portion of the DNS namespace for which it is responsible and looks up the answers it is not required to keep.

Figure 5.10
Querying a root server.

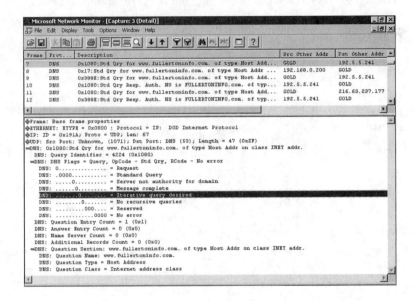

The next frame of interest is frame 10, shown in Figure 5.11. This is the response from the root name server, saying that the authoritative DNS is fullertoninfo.com.

Figure 5.11
The root server response.

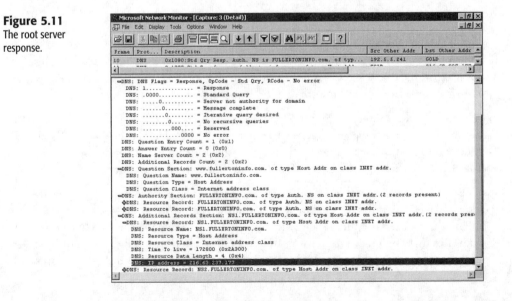

The point of interest in Figure 5.11 is the information in the Additional Records Section of the packet at the bottom of the screen. This is the hostname and IP address of the name server authoritative for fullertoninfo.com.

Frame 11, shown in Figure 5.12, is simply the final iterative request from your DNS server to ns1.fullertoninfo.com for www.fullertoninfo.com.

Figure 5.12
Contacting the authoritative name server.

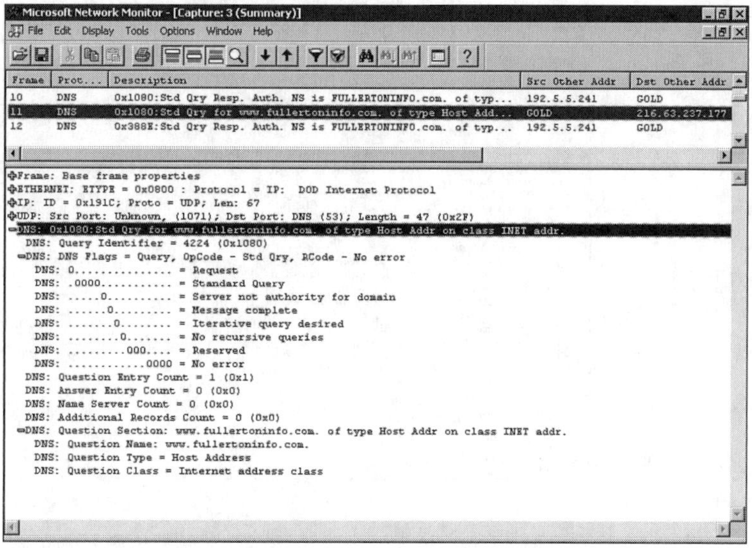

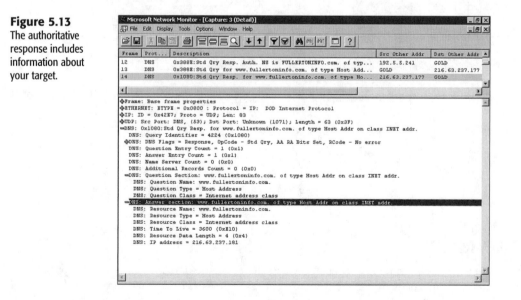

For frame 14, Figure 5.13 shows the response to frame 11. This is the information you requested that started this entire process.

Figure 5.13
The authoritative response includes information about your target.

CH
5

In the answer section of frame 14, you see the IP address of www.fullertoninfo.com.

In frame 18, you see the information being returned to stone, your DNS client (see Figure 5.14).

Figure 5.14
The DNS response to the client.

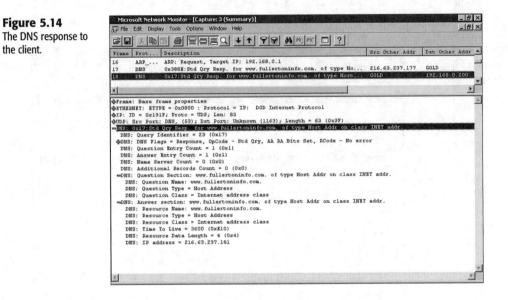

Finally, you can see in the DNS MMC that this information is cached for future use (see Figure 5.15). To view the cache, click View, Advanced from the MMC Snap-in menu.

Figure 5.15
The DNS cache holds recently resolved addresses and names.

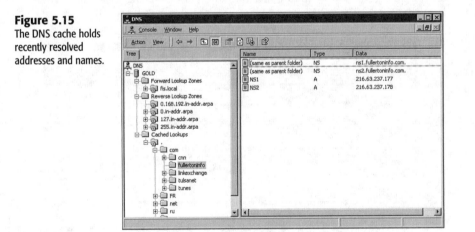

SUMMARY

In this chapter, you looked at components of DNS. You have seen the various types of records and zones. You also have looked at the process of finding a resource on the network.

A variety of DNS record types exist, which all work together to provide name mapping. A and PTR records are the most common records and are used to resolve addresses and names. Other record types identify DNS servers or other services on the network.

Globally, DNS uses an interrelated hierarchy of servers to resolve queries for resources outside the local network. This hierarchy begins with the root name servers and ends with your local DNS.

TROUBLESHOOTING

CAN'T RESOLVE ON THE INTERNET

I've installed DNS but can't resolve anything on the Internet.

If, for whatever reason, you have an empty root zone created, your DNS will not use the root servers described in cache.dns. These root servers are used to find authoritative name servers on the Internet.

CORRUPTED SUBZONES

My subzones that contain SRV records are corrupted.

Delete all the autocreated subzones underneath your forward lookup zones. Stop and restart the netlogon service. This re-creates and repopulates the SRV subzones.

INCORRECT INTERNET ADDRESSES

When I try to go to a Internet address, my resolver uses an old address.

You can flush the DNS client resolver cache with the ipconfig /flushdns command. This forces your client to request a new record from the DNS server.

6

INTEGRATING BIND DNS WITH ACTIVE DIRECTORY

In this chapter

BIND AND THE ACTIVE DIRECTORY

Although Active Directory does require DNS to function properly, it does not require a Windows 2000 DNS. Windows 2000 DNS is the best DNS for the AD because of its ease of use, scalability, and integration with WINS and the Active Directory through AD integrated zones. However, DNS servers exist for virtually every operating system available. DNS runs on Linux, UNIX, NT, and NetWare. Some of these support Active Directory, and some do not. Windows 2000 DNS, however, is specifically designed to support not only the usual task that every DNS server performs—hostname resolution—but also the very important task of providing name resolution for Active Directory.

> **Tip**
>
> This chapter specifically focuses on BIND integration with Active Directory. For more information on BIND and DNS, see Nicolai Langfeldt's book *The Concise Guide to DNS and BIND* (published by Que, ISBN: 0-7897-2273-9).

The requirement for a DNS to function with the AD is very simple. It must support service location (SRV) records. It also should support Dynamic DNS (DDNS) and incremental zone transfers. BIND 8.1.2 and greater support these features. Berkeley Internet Name Domain (BIND) is one of the original implementations of DNS available. Most versions run on UNIX, although some versions do run on other operating systems.

> **Note**
>
> Although dynamic update technically is not a requirement of DNS for supporting Active Directory, because of the amount of information that is modified in the DNS zones, I cannot imagine supporting a nondynamic AD DNS. You should ensure that your DNS supports dynamic update. The good news is that most DNSs that support SRV records also support dynamic update.

→ For more information on dynamic update DNSs, **see** "Dynamic DNS," **p. 116**

WHY USE BIND?

The reasons why a company would choose to use a non–Windows 2000 DNS to support the AD are several. Some companies already have a DNS infrastructure in place and do not want to change it. The company already might have a high level of BIND DNS expertise in-house and wants to exploit that advantage. Whatever the reason, in this section, you look at configuring an existing DNS on a Linux server using BIND 8.1.2. Although you can convert a DNS that has been supporting Active Directory from BIND to Windows 2000 DNS, beginning your AD with the DNS you plan to use already in place is easier.

> **Caution**
>
> Many companies that have been supporting internetworked infrastructures for many years have an investment in UNIX BIND. Be certain that the version of BIND in place supports SRV records. No SRV records means no Active Directory.

BIND CONFIGURATION FILES

Several great books on BIND are available, and this book does not attempt to replace them. This section assumes that named is already installed. Many newer implementations of UNIX/Linux install named by default. Let's just look at the files necessary to support Dynamic DNS and SRV records. This example is taken from a Pentium 75 with 32MB of RAM running Slackware Linux 4.0. The computer's hostname is linux.fis.local, and its IP address is 192.168.0.3. In this section, you look at the files as they exist when you first configure named. Later, you will look at two of the files after you have enabled Dynamic DNS and have allowed a DC to register its A, PTR, and SRV records with named. After you have allowed Active Directory to register its records, you will see a marked increase in the amount of information in your zone files.

> **Tip**
>
> Windows 2000 comes with a great telnet client that is better than many third-party clients. You can use the telnet client to connect to the UNIX server and perform all your management from the Windows 2000 desktop. Some UNIX servers are configured to not allow the root user to connect through telnet. You can, however, connect as an ordinary user and then use the su command to assume the superuser role. This assumes, of course, that you have the credentials to do so.

named.conf

named is the service that runs on most UNIX boxes and provides DNS services. When named starts, it reads a file called named.conf. This file sets the parameters for the service as it boots. Listing 6.1 shows the named.conf file as it exists on your server.

LISTING 6.1   THE BIND named.conf FILE

```
/*
 * A simple BIND 8 configuration
 */

options {
        directory "/etc";
};

logging {
        category lame-servers { null; };
        category cname { null; };
};

zone "fis.local" in {
        type master;
        file "fis.local.dns";
    allow-update { 192.168.0/24; };
};

zone "0.168.192.in-addr.arpa" in {
    type master;
```

CH

6

LISTING 6.1 CONTINUED

```
    file "named.rev";
    allow-update { 192.168.0/24; };
};

zone "." in {
       type hint;
       file "root.cache";
};

zone "0.0.127.in-addr.arpa" in {
       type master;
       file "named.local";
};
```

The options setting shown at the top of Listing 6.1 has one parameter: directory. This simply sets the filesystem directory that will hold all the BIND configuration files. Notice in named.conf that each section begins and ends with curly brackets ({}) and is terminated with a semicolon (;). Each of these files has syntax that is very specific and very rigid. It is not uncommon for the presence or the lack of one character to cause the entire BIND implementation to function erratically or not at all. The logging section redirects logging you do not need to null.

> **Tip**
>
> Because BIND is a publicly supported, open-source product, an enormous amount of free documentation for it is available on the Web. One search on "bind dns" returned 85,500 hits.

The next four sections are configurations for each of the zones that this DNS is maintaining. In the first line of the first zone section, you see that these are parameters for our forward lookup zone fis.local. This is a very important zone because it is where the SRV records for your AD domain, fis.local, will be registered. After BIND is configured and your AD DCs are configured to use this DNS, the next time the netlogon service is started, it updates this zone with all the records for the various services running on that DC. The zone type is *master*, which means it is a primary (read/write) zone as opposed to a slave (read-only) zone. Its file is fis.local.dns. This parameter, coupled with the directory parameter at the beginning of named.conf, causes the /etc/fis.local.dns text file to be read for records for this zone.

The next parameter is one of the most poorly documented and the most critical for Dynamic DNS. The allow-updates section can be set to an IP address or range of addresses. If this section is not included and configured properly, your DNS will function beautifully, but it will be a static DNS. In addition, if you configure this too openly, it will allow dynamic updates from addresses outside the zone, which could—maliciously or accidentally—cause a loss of service due to improperly registered services and servers. The example shown in Listing 6.1 allows any host in the 192.168.0.0 network to add or delete records. Listing 6.2 shows several allow-update parameters and the ranges they allow.

> **Caution**
>
> Case matters; spaces matter; punctuation matters. If it fails, check the documentation. Because the syntax is so very terse, it can be confusing. I spent three days looking for a missing period in my configuration files the first time I set up BIND.

LISTING 6.2   ALLOWING UPDATES TO BIND DNS

```
allow-update { 192.168.0/23; };
```

This setting would allow range 192.168.0.0 - 192.168.1.255 to be updated.

```
allow-update { 172.152.0/16; };
```

This setting would allow range 172.152.0.0 - 172.152.255.255 to be updated.

The next zone section, `0.168.192.in-addr.arpa`, is your reverse lookup zone. This zone allows the registration of reverse lookup (PTR) records. Its type is master, and the file you are using is called `named.rev`. Determining the name of this zone is sometimes difficult. The name is derived from the IP subnet for which it is responsible—only it is written backward and the `.in-addr.arpa` zone is appended to the zone address. This seems odd, except this zone is used for reverse lookups, so naming it seemingly backward is not so strange. Notice that it also has an `allow-updates` section, and it is set to the same range as `fis.local`. This is not always true, but because your AD currently resides on only one subnet for this section, it is the same. If your AD clients are on several subnets, you must create reverse lookup zones that cover the relevant namespace and ensure that `allow-updates` is set properly.

The next section is for zone "`.`". This is the root zone. The file `root.cache` contains the addresses of the root name servers around the world. These authoritative name servers allow you to find name servers anywhere to resolve any name on the Internet.

The final section is for the local reverse lookup zone. The filename is `named.local`, and it contains PTR records for the loopback address.

FORWARD LOOKUP ZONE CONFIGURATION FILES

The next file you look at is easily the most important. `fis.local.dns`, although nearly empty now, will contain your SRV records after you load `named` and begin dynamic updates. Even though your reverse lookup zone also will allow dynamic updates, this file will see most of the action because of all the services that will register themselves multiple times to enable them to be found on several criteria. Listing 6.3 shows this file before dynamic updates begin.

LISTING 6.3   SAMPLE FORWARD LOOKUP ZONE FILE BEFORE DYNAMIC UPDATE

```
@       IN    SOA    linux.fis.local. root.linux.fis.local. (
                     1986020501    ; Serial
                     10800     ; Refresh 3 hours
                     3600    ; Retry   1 hour
                     3600000 ; Expire  1000 hours
```

CH
6

LISTING 6.3 CONTINUED

```
                86400  )    ; Minimum 24 hours

@             NS        linux.fis.local.

localhost      IN    A       127.1
linux         IN    A      192.168.1.3
```

The first line in Listing 6.3 is the start of authority (SOA) record. In Chapter 5, "DNS Architecture," you walked through most of the record types you will see in these files, so we will not repeat that information here. However, you will look briefly at the format of the files and then later contrast their conditions after dynamic updates. Along with the SOA record is an NS record, which lists the name servers authoritative for this zone. Additionally, A records exist for the localhost loopback address and the address of the name server. These are important for startup to ensure that named can check to see where it is running and resolve its own name.

REVERSE LOOKUP ZONE CONFIGURATION FILES

In Listing 6.4, you can see your named.rev file. Your reverse lookup zone, 0.168.192.in-addr.arpa, uses this file.

LISTING 6.4 SAMPLE REVERSE LOOKUP ZONE FILE BEFORE DYNAMIC UPDATE

```
@   IN   SOA    linux.fis.local. root.linux.fis.local. (
          1986020581
          10800
          3600
          3600000
          86400  )
@        NS    linux.fis.local.

3        IN    PTR    linux.fis.local.
```

The format of this file is similar to your forward lookup zone file except for the presence of PTR records. This particular PTR record for the DNS server is important for troubleshooting. When you use the nslookup.exe tool to view and troubleshoot DNS, if it cannot perform a reverse lookup on the current DNS, it freezes for several seconds and is difficult to use.

⚠️ *For more information on how to troubleshoot this, see "nslookup Doesn't Work Properly" in the "Troubleshooting" section at the end of this chapter.*

root.cache

The root.cache file is simple and almost never requires modification. The contents, shown in Listing 6.5, are the name and IP addresses of the root name servers. About the only time you would want to modify this is if you wanted to redirect your DNS to authoritative servers other than the public root servers to concentrate lookups outside the local network on one authoritative server.

LISTING 6.5   root.cache: **THE LIST OF ROOT NAME SERVERS**

```
.                       3600000   IN  NS   A.ROOT-SERVERS.NET.
A.ROOT-SERVERS.NET.     3600000       A    198.41.0.4
;
; formerly NS1.ISI.EDU
;
.                       3600000       NS   B.ROOT-SERVERS.NET.
B.ROOT-SERVERS.NET.     3600000       A    128.9.0.107
;
; formerly C.PSI.NET
;
.                       3600000       NS   C.ROOT-SERVERS.NET.
C.ROOT-SERVERS.NET.     3600000       A    192.33.4.12
;
; formerly TERP.UMD.EDU
;
.                       3600000       NS   D.ROOT-SERVERS.NET.
D.ROOT-SERVERS.NET.     3600000       A    128.8.10.90
;
; formerly NS.NASA.GOV
;
.                       3600000       NS   E.ROOT-SERVERS.NET.
E.ROOT-SERVERS.NET.     3600000       A    192.203.230.10
;
; formerly NS.ISC.ORG
;
.                       3600000       NS   F.ROOT-SERVERS.NET.
F.ROOT-SERVERS.NET.     3600000       A    192.5.5.241
;
; formerly NS.NIC.DDN.MIL
;
.                       3600000       NS   G.ROOT-SERVERS.NET.
G.ROOT-SERVERS.NET.     3600000       A    192.112.36.4
;
; formerly AOS.ARL.ARMY.MIL
;
.                       3600000       NS   H.ROOT-SERVERS.NET.
H.ROOT-SERVERS.NET.     3600000       A    128.63.2.53
;
; formerly NIC.NORDU.NET
;
.                       3600000       NS   I.ROOT-SERVERS.NET.
I.ROOT-SERVERS.NET.     3600000       A    192.36.148.17
;
; temporarily housed at NSI (InterNIC)
;
.                       3600000       NS   J.ROOT-SERVERS.NET.
J.ROOT-SERVERS.NET.     3600000       A    198.41.0.10
;
; housed in LINX, operated by RIPE NCC
;
.                       3600000       NS   K.ROOT-SERVERS.NET.
K.ROOT-SERVERS.NET.     3600000       A    193.0.14.129
;
; temporarily housed at ISI (IANA)
;
```

Cн

6

LISTING 6.5   CONTINUED

```
.                          3600000     NS    L.ROOT-SERVERS.NET.
L.ROOT-SERVERS.NET.        3600000     A     198.32.64.12
;
; housed in Japan, operated by WIDE
;
.                          3600000     NS    M.ROOT-SERVERS.NET.
M.ROOT-SERVERS.NET.        3600000     A     202.12.27.33
; End of File
```

If you are ever concerned that this file needs to be updated, a new one can be obtained from the Internet Network Information Center (InterNIC) at `ftp.rs.internic.net`.

Tip

For the configuration files discussed here to be used by the `named` process, you must stop and start `named`. You can use `ps -x` to get a list of running processes and process ID (PID). If `named` is in the list, you can use the `kill` command to stop it. The syntax is `kill -9 <Process ID>`. To start the process, simply type **named** and press Enter.

Caution

The commands on some flavors of UNIX are close enough to be confusing. If you are using documentation from even a slightly different version of UNIX, the commands and their parameters can vary. Sometimes only the case of the parameter varies from one version to another, but that is enough to mean the difference between success and failure.

named.local

The final file you will look at is the `named.local` file shown in Listing 6.6. This file holds PTR records for the loopback adapter, which is an internal address—`127.0.0.1`—and is used for internal testing and communication.

LISTING 6.6   SAMPLE `named.local` FILE

```
@   IN   SOA   linux.fis.local. root.linux.fis.local.  (
                    1986012101 ; Serial
                            3600     ; Refresh
                            300      ; Retry
                            3600000  ; Expire
                            14400 )  ; Minimum
    IN   NS    linux.fis.local.
0   IN   PTR   loopback.fis.local.
1   IN   PTR   localhost.
```

Now that you have looked at the five files necessary to get `named` running, let's look at the two files that will be updated by dynamic DNS. The following section assumes that you have configured a single Windows 2000 domain controller to use the Linux server, with IP address `192.168.0.3` as its DNS.

ZONE FILES AFTER A DYNAMIC UPDATE

fis.local.dns is your forward lookup zone file and gets the majority of the traffic. Listing 6.7 shows the file after you have configured the DC to use the Linux DNS and have restarted the netlogon service on the DC. This file also is updated with the A records of any Windows 2000 client or server that is configured to use this DNS.

LISTING 6.7 FORWARD LOOKUP ZONE AFTER DYNAMIC UPDATE

```
;BIND DUMP V8
$ORIGIN local.
fis        IN    NS     linux.fis.local.    ;Cl=2
     600    IN    A      192.168.0.5    ;Cl=2
           IN    SOA    linux.fis.local. root.linux.fis.local. (
           1986020527 10800 3600 3600000 86400 )    ;Cl=2
$ORIGIN fis.local.
linux       IN    A    192.168.1.3    ;Cl=2
gold   1200    IN    A     192.168.0.5    ;Cl=2
localhost    IN    A    127.0.0.1    ;Cl=2
$ORIGIN _udp.fis.local.
_kpasswd    600    IN    SRV       0 100 464 gold.fis.local.    ;Cl=2
_kerberos   600    IN    SRV       0 100 88 gold.fis.local.    ;Cl=2
$ORIGIN _msdcs.fis.local.
gc    600    IN    A    192.168.0.5    ;Cl=2
f584ccb8-a9f4-4b4a-b607-a849943b0dde    600    IN    CNAME
➥gold.fis.local.    ;Cl=2
$ORIGIN _tcp.dc._msdcs.fis.local.
_ldap    600    IN    SRV       0 100 389 gold.fis.local.    ;Cl=2
_kerberos   600    IN    SRV       0 100 88 gold.fis.local.    ;Cl=2
$ORIGIN _tcp.Default-First-Site-Name._sites.dc._msdcs.fis.local.
_ldap    600    IN    SRV       0 100 389 gold.fis.local.    ;Cl=2
_kerberos   600    IN    SRV       0 100 88 gold.fis.local.    ;Cl=2
$ORIGIN _tcp.pdc._msdcs.fis.local.
_ldap    600    IN    SRV       0 100 389 gold.fis.local.    ;Cl=2
$ORIGIN _tcp.01f339e8-7fda-4136-8501-869b96be40e5.domains._msdcs.fis.local.
_ldap    600    IN    SRV       0 100 389 gold.fis.local.    ;Cl=2
$ORIGIN _tcp.gc._msdcs.fis.local.
_ldap    600    IN    SRV       0 100 3268 gold.fis.local.    ;Cl=2
$ORIGIN _tcp.Default-First-Site-Name._sites.gc._msdcs.fis.local.
_ldap    600    IN    SRV       0 100 3268 gold.fis.local.    ;Cl=2
$ORIGIN _tcp.onesite._sites.gc._msdcs.fis.local.
_ldap    600    IN    SRV       0 100 3268 gold.fis.local.    ;Cl=2
$ORIGIN _tcp.onesite._sites.fis.local.
_gc    600    IN    SRV       0 100 3268 gold.fis.local.    ;Cl=2
$ORIGIN _tcp.Default-First-Site-Name._sites.fis.local.
_ldap    600    IN    SRV       0 100 389 gold.fis.local.    ;Cl=2
_gc    600    IN    SRV     0 100 3268 gold.fis.local.    ;Cl=2
_kerberos   600    IN    SRV       0 100 88 gold.fis.local.    ;Cl=2
$ORIGIN _tcp.fis.local.
_kpasswd    600    IN    SRV       0 100 464 gold.fis.local.    ;Cl=2
_ldap    600    IN    SRV     0 100 389 gold.fis.local.    ;Cl=2
_gc    600    IN    SRV     0 100 3268 gold.fis.local.    ;Cl=2
_kerberos   600    IN    SRV       0 100 88 gold.fis.local.    ;Cl=2
```

CH

6

The records inserted into the zone file by the `netlogon` process are almost exclusively SRV records. The DC was `gold.fis.local`; therefore, all the records point to that server. These records are used by clients and servers throughout the enterprise to resolve different services.

→ **See** "SRV Records," **p. 69**

> **Tip**
>
> Because of the volume of data added to the zone files by the update process, it is strongly recommended that you back up your zone files before and after you allow them to be dynamically updated. On a small network, at least, replacing the zone files with unsullied originals and stopping and restarting the `netlogon` process on the DCs might be easier than finding and fixing any corruption in the zone files.

Contemplating managing this level of complexity with no tools other than the VI editor can be daunting. One of the main reasons to use a Windows 2000 DNS is ease of use. If you purchase a commercial DNS to run on a UNIX box, you might have a GUI interface to the management software. However, if you choose a freely available BIND, your management interface is a text editor. The good news is that most of the records in this file are updated automatically through Dynamic DNS; however, troubleshooting through these records by hand can be time-consuming.

The other file to be modified by Dynamic DNS is the reverse lookup zone file, `named.rev`, shown in Listing 6.8.

LISTING 6.8 REVERSE LOOKUP ZONE AFTER DYNAMIC UPDATE

```
$ORIGIN 168.192.in-addr.arpa.
0        IN    NS    linux.fis.local.      ;Cl=5
         IN    SOA   linux.fis.local. root.linux.fis.local. (
         1986020582 10800 3600 3600000 86400 )    ;Cl=5
$ORIGIN 0.168.192.in-addr.arpa.
5    1200    IN    PTR    gold.fis.local.       ;Cl=5
3        IN    PTR    linux.fis.local.       ;Cl=5
```

This file is updated with PTR records by all Windows clients or servers configured to use this DNS as well as DCs.

DELEGATING A ZONE

Companies that have an existing investment in BIND are likely to want to retain BIND as their primary name server. One way to do that is simply to configure BIND for dynamic update, as you have seen in this chapter. However, another way will work even if the version of BIND does not support SRV and dynamic update.

You can delegate authority for a zone from one DNS server to another. In the following example, assume that `fis.local` is the root of your DNS namespace and is running on

BIND. You want to create an AD domain called `ad.fis.local`, and you don't want the BIND administrators to be responsible for it.

You can pass the responsibility for the DNS zone, which is necessary for your new Active Directory domain, by delegating authority for that zone from the BIND server to the DNS server running on the AD domain controller. DNS clients configured to use the `fis.local` name server will continue to do so. However, if they request a DNS record from the `ad.fis.local` zone, the record will be retrieved from the DNS server authoritative for the zone.

To delegate a zone from a BIND DNS to another DNS server, you must add two records to the zone file for the parent zone. In this example the parent zone is `fis.local`, and the delegated zone is `ad.fis.local`. To delegate `ad.fis.local`, you add the following two records to the zone file for `fis.local`:

```
ad        IN        NS        ad.fis.local.
ad        IN        A         192.168.1.5
```

The first record is a `name server` record that helps resolve queries about the `ad` zone. The second is sometimes called a *glue* record. It is an A record that points to the IP address of the DNS server that is authoritative for the zone.

SUMMARY

BIND has been around for more than a decade and is one of the most widely used implementations of DNS. It is present in most large companies and will support Active Directory if managed carefully.

The current version supports both SRV records and dynamic updates—the two most critical needs for a DNS to support Active Directory. If you have an investment in BIND, you might want to maintain the current implementation. Remember that a DNS that supports AD must support SRV records and should support dynamic updates.

The minimum recommended version of BIND to work with Active Directory is BIND 8.1.2. As of this writing, the newest release is 8.2.2. Integrating BIND and Active Directory requires a fair amount of expertise but is very manageable.

BIND management is still a very hands-on process, particularly if you choose a publicly available version. Although remarkably stable, current BIND versions require direct management of the zone files if configuration parameters change.

You can mix both Windows 2000 DNS and BIND by using zone delegation. This enables the current BIND implementation to remain in place and places the burden of maintaining the DNS for Active Directory on the AD administrators.

CH
6

TROUBLESHOOTING

NEW BIND CONFIGURATION FILES ARE NOT BEING USED

When you update named.conf *with new configuration files, the changes are not used.*

UNIX is a case-sensitive operating system—everything about UNIX is case sensitive. Check the case of the references in named.conf and the filenames on the filesystem. Every character must match.

nslookup DOESN'T WORK PROPERLY

ping *and other tools might use your DNS, but when you start* nslookup *it fails or issues timeout errors.*

Make sure you have a PTR record in the reverse lookup zone for the DNS server. When nslookup starts, it performs a reverse lookup on the DNS server. If this fails, it causes errors.

named WON'T START

When you try to start the named *process, it fails with little or no errors.*

Every version of UNIX has some kind of system logging. For Linux, the file is /var/adm/ syslog. Very verbose errors and comments on the health of the system and its processes can be found in this file. The following line is from a syslog on my Linux server:

```
Oct 15 23:26:37 linux named[150]: /etc/named.conf:18: syntax error near '}'
```

Let's face it: BIND is not user friendly or intuitive. Therefore, this kind of information is invaluable when looking for errors.

DNS AND AD NAMESPACES

In this chapter

NAMESPACES

When designing the Active Directory, careful planning of the AD namespace is critical. It affects the implementation of both DNS and the AD. One of the first rules of AD/DNS namespace planning is that the AD namespace and the DNS namespace must match. In other words, if you build an AD domain called `fis.local`, you must build a DNS zone named `fis.local`. You can, however, have DNS zones that do not have a corresponding AD domain. In fact, for your external resources, such as Web servers and e-commerce sites, this is preferred. But you *cannot* have AD domains that do not have a corresponding DNS zone.

Tip

You *must* make decisions about the DNS namespace before installing Active Directory. Active Directory naming decisions are forever. See "Namespaces," p. 13.

EXTERNAL NAMESPACES

The *external* DNS namespace is what your customers see from the Internet. This is the DNS domain you already own. In the example from Chapter 5, "DNS Architecture," when you looked up www.fullertoninfo.com, this was an external DNS namespace. This namespace is published in your external DNS servers, is available from the Web, and is used by external customers to resolve your Web and email servers.

INTERNAL NAMESPACES

The *internal* namespace is what you use for your intranet. In the DNS examples, you have used the internal namespace used by Fullerton Information Services, `fis.local`. You do not have to separate your internal and external namespaces. The internal DNS zone name can be the same as your external namespace. In the next section, you look at the pros and cons of separating the internal and external namespaces.

Tip

Several RFCs on DNS naming standards are available, including RFCs 1123, 1034, and 1035. The basics, however, are a–z, A–Z, 0–9, and the hyphen (-). Windows 2000 clients and DNS support many Unicode characters, but this might not be compliant with other systems you need to interoperate with. Windows NT 4 DNS, for example, supports a smaller set of characters than Windows 2000 DNS does.

CHOOSING AN AD NAMESPACE

This section discusses several scenarios for choosing AD domain names. Because you must create DNS zones to match these AD domains, you must integrate your choices with any pre-existing DNS zones.

Caution	Regardless of how you implement the namespace, exercise caution when implementing DNS. Allowing outside users to peruse a DNS that holds information about internal resources is a very serious breach of security. In a dynamic update scenario, it would be even worse if the records or zones were modifiable.

USING THE SAME NAMESPACE INTERNALLY AND EXTERNALLY

This looks at first to be the easiest option. However, on careful perusal, there can be much work to do using this strategy. The foremost danger is security. If, for example, you own `fullertoninfo.com`, you can simply create an AD domain using the `fullertoninfo.com` namespace and point your domain controllers (DCs) to your existing DNS server (assuming it supports SRV records and dynamic updates). The problem here is that the IP addresses of your internal resources, such as DCs, SQL Servers, and so on, are now freely available on the Internet. An intruder could have a field day with this kind of information. You can use the public, external namespace internally, but to do it properly, you must have at least two separate DNS servers. One server would be available externally and have only resource records for external services, such as Web connection and email. The second server would have records for your internal resources and be the DNS provider for your AD domain controllers and clients.

USING A SEPARATE NAMESPACE

In some circumstances, you will need to separate the corporate namespace. You can do this several ways. Your choice depends primarily on what you are trying to accomplish and which DNS resources you already have in place.

SEPARATE EXTERNAL AND INTERNAL NAMESPACES

In the examples throughout this book, you have used a separate internal namespace for the Active Directory. `fullertoninfo.com` has been used for the Web presence, and `fis.local` has been used for the Active Directory. These should be hosted on separate DNS servers on their respective sides of the firewall. `fis.local` is the forest root domain, and every child domain is then derived from the forest root name. For example, if you wanted to create a separate domain in the same tree for the sales department, you could create `sales.fis.local`.

MULTIPLE INTERNAL NAMESPACES

Another way to use a separate internal namespace is handy if you already have an internal DNS infrastructure. Companies with a history of networked UNIX computers are likely candidates for this scenario because of the huge investment of time and expertise in the current DNS namespace.

CH

7

> **Note**
> Even if you have an existing internal DNS infrastructure, you do not have to abandon it as long as it meets the requirements and recommendations for a DNS that will support AD—namely SRV records and dynamic update.

If you already have a functioning DNS infrastructure, you can separate your AD DNS from the current DNS in two ways. One is to create a completely disjointed namespace that has no connection point whatsoever with the current DNS. The downside to this approach is that you now must manage two separate internal DNSs.

Another way to deal with this is to delegate authority for a child DNS zone to the DNS running on the Windows 2000 DCs.

→ **See** "Delegating a Zone," **p. 88**

FINDING A DOMAIN CONTROLLER

Regardless of how you design the namespace, a DNS server is used by an AD client to find a DC. In this section, you look at one of the most important things DNS does for you: finding a domain controller.

SITES

When a client tries to find a DC for its domain, rather than taking one at random, it tries to find a DC in its site. (A *site* is one or more well-connected subnets.) The first site is created by default and is called `Default-First-Site-Name`. This site can be renamed, other sites can be created, and DCs can be moved into sites. A site is always associated with one or more IP subnets.

FINDING A DOMAIN CONTROLLER IN A SITE

A client, whether it is a workstation or server, first performs a lookup for a DC in its site. SRV records are arranged to allow the organizing of services by which site they are a part of. This enables a Windows 2000 client to request a DC "near me" rather than simply request any DC. A client is capable of specifying which site it is a member of and requesting a DC specific to that site. The site name to which a particular client belongs is kept in the Registry at `HKLM\System\CurrentControlSet\Services\NetLogon\Parameters\DynamicSiteName`. Although this information is stored locally in the Registry, if for example, a computer is moved, when it attempts to contact a DC in its original site, the DC compares the current IP address of the client with its site and redirects the client to the appropriate site. This also triggers an update of the Registry information.

Two of the services a client uses when logging on are the LDAP and Kerberos services. Figure 7.1 shows a Network Monitor packet capture of a client booting and logging on to a DC. Frame 12 shows the client requesting an LDAP server for its domain. Notice in the highlighted DNS query section that the client is specifically looking for SRV records for an LDAP server in `Default-First-Site-Name`.

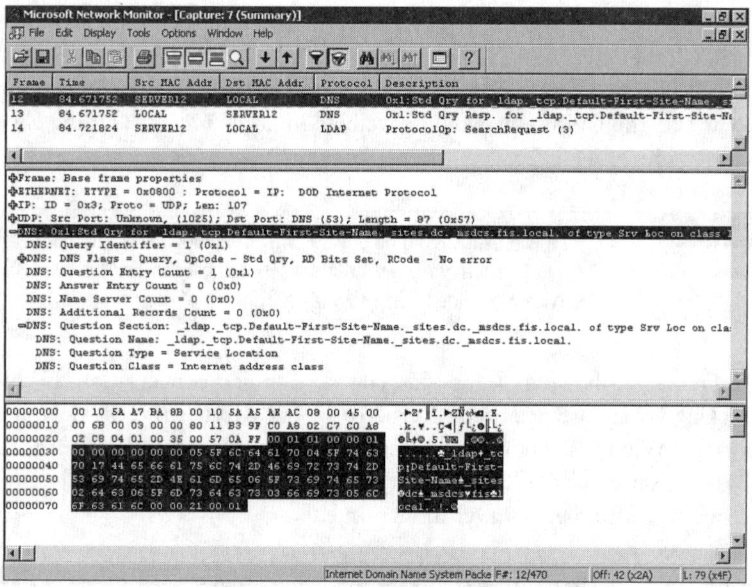

Figure 7.1
Using DNS to find an
LDAP server.

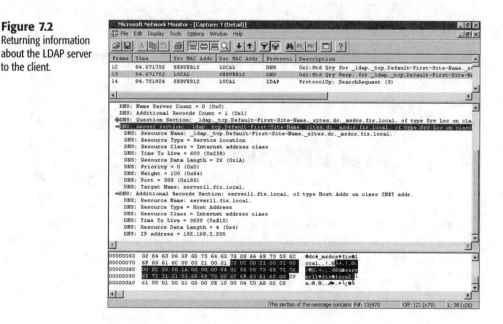

Frame 13 shows the response to Frame 12 (see Figure 7.2). In the highlighted DNS records
section, you can see not only the name of the server providing the service but also the priority, weight, and port number of the service. These are the properties you looked at in the
previous section about record types.

Figure 7.2
Returning information
about the LDAP server
to the client.

Also in Figure 7.2 you can see that the last record in the DNS answer section is the DNS name of the server and the next section. DNS's additional records section helpfully provides the IP address of the server. You should note that, if this domain had multiple DCs in the same site, the DNS reply would have held multiple records and the client would then have chosen one of the DCs.

Note

By this time it should be obvious why designing Active Directory sites is so important. The only opportunity AD has to find a service near the client is by trusting that if the client and service are in the same site, they are "nearby."

In Frame 47, shown in Figure 7.3, you see a similar conversation. In this figure, you are looking for an instance of the Kerberos service. Kerberos is the default authentication service for Windows 2000 and is covered in detail in Chapter 18, "Authentication." Every DC has an instance of the Kerberos service. Notice again that the client is very specific about requesting a Kerberos server in its own site.

Figure 7.3
Using DNS to find a Kerberos server.

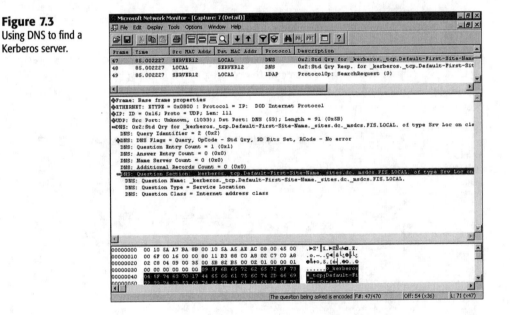

In Figure 7.4, Frame 48 shows the response. In the Answer section of the DNS packet, below the highlighted line, you can see the Priority, Weight, Port, and Target Name of the server. In the Additional Records section, you also can see the IP address of the Kerberos server.

Figure 7.4
Returning information
about the Kerberos
server to the client.

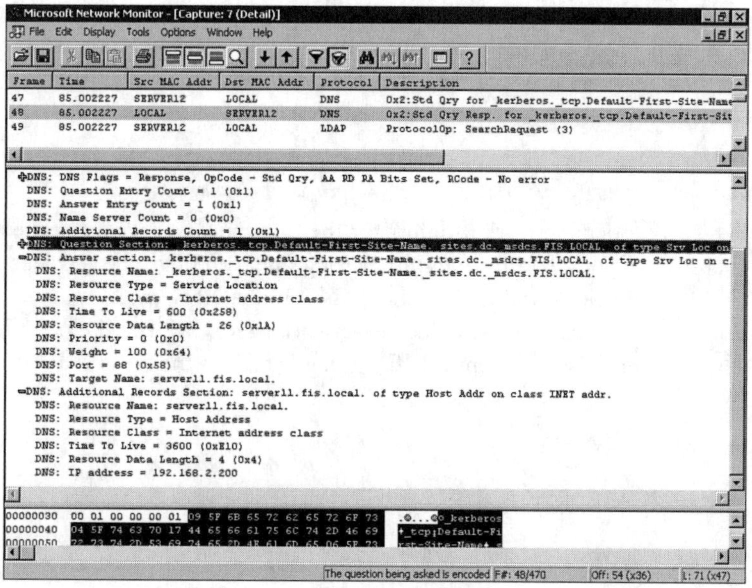

SUMMARY

Designing the AD namespace is an important part of planning your AD. In this chapter, you have looked at some choices for planning the namespace and then followed a client, packet by packet, as it found services on the DC.

You can use the same DNS namespace both internally and externally. You also can choose to separate them into external and internal namespaces.

You also can have multiple internal DNS namespaces; however, the choice to do so must be made based on current DNS infrastructure and projected needs for DNS to support AD.

TROUBLESHOOTING

I CAN'T AUTHENTICATE TO ACTIVE DIRECTORY

You can log on locally but can't authenticate to AD.

If you can get logged on to the Windows 2000 client using a local account but can't authenticate to Active Directory, you have three main suspects to check out. This assumes, of course, that you are sure you have a valid AD user account and you know the password. First, get logged on locally and make sure you can ping a DC. If this fails, you must fix the network before you can log on. Next, check the DNS client using the nslookup command to try to resolve the name of a DC. If your computer's DNS configuration is incorrect, you probably won't be able to find a DC. The third option is the system time. The Kerberos service allows packets to be out of sync plus or minus five minutes. Any more than that and the packets are discarded. This is an unlikely scenario because every client syncs its time with the DC the computer account authenticated to when it booted, but it is possible.

NETWORK MONITOR CAPTURES ARE EMPTY

You are trying to use the netmon tool to troubleshoot network issues, but every time you open the tool and click Capture/Start, the panes and Capture window are empty.

When you open Network Monitor for the first time, you are given the opportunity to choose a network. If you choose the wrong one, you might be accidentally monitoring a virtual connection—rather than the LAN. On the Network Monitor menu bar, choose Capture/Networks. On the Select a Network page, click Local Computer and choose the network whose Dialup Connect BLOB tag is false in the right pane.

CHAPTER 8

WINDOWS 2000 NAME RESOLUTION SERVICES

In this chapter

NAME RESOLUTION IN WINDOWS 2000

Similar to previous versions of NT, Windows 2000 can use a variety of name resolution methodologies. Broadcast, lmhosts, and WINS can be used to find file and print servers, application servers, and so on. These tools, although unnecessary in a NetBIOS-free 2000 environment, provide compatibility with and access to down-level clients. Under limited conditions, you can find a Windows 2000 DC from a Windows 2000 client by using non-DNS name resolution. We must be very clear, however, that although these tools provide down-level name resolution services and limited access to the Windows 2000 domain controllers (DCs), an Active Directory can never be considered fully configured until DNS is in place and properly configured. Trying to resolve Windows 2000 DCs from Windows 2000 clients using broadcast, hosts, lmhosts, or WINS works in a limited fashion, but a high level of unnecessary traffic exists on the wire as a result as the 2000 client tries to resolve using DNS first and then, reluctantly, uses other name resolution methods.

> **Tip**
>
> In a NetBIOS-free environment, WINS, lmhosts, and broadcast are unnecessary. For almost all production environments, however, it will be years before NetBIOS is completely gone.

Because these tools do provide some functionality and will certainly be present in Windows NT/9x environments, it is appropriate to see how they work and are configured in a Windows 2000 environment.

NETBIOS NODE TYPES

The NetBIOS node type determines how Windows performs non-DNS name resolution. Four NetBIOS node types exist: b-node, p-node, m-node, and h-node. The NetBIOS node type is a setting that can be made directly through the Registry, through the Dynamic Host Configuration Protocol (DHCP) or by making the machine a WINS client. These settings are based on RFCs 1001 and 1002.

> **Tip**
>
> An Internet Request for Comments (RFC) is the authoritative work on any Internet Protocol–related subject and is freely available from www.ietf.org.

By default, every Windows 9x/NT/2000 client is b-node. If a client is subsequently configured for WINS, it is automatically set to h-node. You also can set an option in DHCP to modify the NetBIOS node type. The Registry editor, regedit.exe or regedt32.exe, can be used to manually set the node type by modifying or creating the HKLM\System\CurrentControlSet\Services\NetBT\Parameters\NodeType parameter. If you create the new entry, it must be a reg_dword value, and the entries in Listing 8.1 set the following node types:

- **b-node**—Uses broadcast only
- **p-node**—Uses point-to-point (WINS) only

- **m-node**—Uses broadcast first; then if unsuccessful, uses WINS

- **h-node**—Uses WINS first; then if unsuccessful, uses broadcast

LISTING 8.1   HEX VALUES FOR NETBIOS NODE TYPES

```
0x1    -    b-node
0x2    -    p-node
0x4    -    m-node
0x8    -    h-node
```

Note

Setting the NetBIOS node type does not affect a Windows 2000 client's default settings for finding a DC. This always is attempted first through DNS.

BROADCAST/B-NODE

The lowest common denominator for name resolution in any Windows environment is broadcast. b-node, or broadcast, means that a client will attempt to find a server through NetBIOS name broadcast. This has two major problems. First, it places a high number of unnecessary broadcast packets on the network. This causes the network segment to be clogged with useless packets. Because broadcast packets are examined by every instance of a protocol stack, this also can cause unnecessary processor utilization. Second, because, by default, NetBIOS name broadcasts don't cross routers, if the service you are trying to reach is on the other side of a router, you will not be able to resolve the name to an IP address and will not be able to reach the server. The only way to avoid these problems is to ensure that your clients are not set to b-node.

POINT-TO-POINT/P-NODE

The complete opposite of b-node is p-node. This stands for point-to-point and uses a directed datagram to a NetBIOS name server (NBNS), such as WINS, instead of broadcasting to resolve names to IP addresses.

MIXED/M-NODE AND HYBRID/H-NODE

The final two node types are a mixture of b-node and p-node. m-node uses broadcast first and then tries a WINS lookup. h-node, on the other hand, uses WINS first and then tries broadcast. Again, manually configuring a client as a WINS client automatically causes it to become an h-node. If you are configuring a DHCP server and want its clients to also be WINS clients, you not only need to set the DHCP option # 44 to the IP address of the WINS server, but you also must set option # 46 NetBIOS node type to one of the values from Listing 8.1.

Setting the NetBIOS node type is only half the battle if you are supporting WINS, hosts, and lmhosts. The other half of the battle is ensuring that these tools are installed and configured. In the next section, you explore installing and configuring lmhosts and WINS.

THE lmhosts FILE

lmhosts is a static text file used to map IP addresses to NetBIOS computer names. Although its use is discouraged in large environments because managing text files becomes unwieldy, lmhosts is a very useful troubleshooting tool and can be used to find a DC for logging in from Windows 2000 if DNS is not available.

Caution

Although the lmhosts file can be used for troubleshooting, if you leave an lmhosts file on the client, it inevitably becomes stale. DNS and WINS are dynamic and respond to changes in the network; static text files, such as lmhosts, do not. If an entry becomes inaccurate because of changes to the network, the client loses much of its capability to communicate.

Listing 8.2 shows a sample lmhosts file. The file must be named lmhosts and must be in \winnt\system32\drivers\etc. It also must be created and saved in an ASCII text editor, such as Notepad.

LISTING 8.2   USING lmhosts FOR NETBIOS NAME RESOLUTION

```
192.168.2.200    server11    #PRE    #DOM:fis
192.168.2.201    server12    #PRE
```

Caution

The #PRE and #DOM directives in lmhosts are case sensitive.

The format is very simple. Each line begins with the IP address of the server and is followed by the NetBIOS name. Several optional parameters can follow. The #PRE parameter causes the operating system (OS) to preload this line into the NetBIOS name cache, an array in memory of IP address/NetBIOS name pairs. On the other hand, the #DOM:fis parameter tells the OS that this is a DC for the fis domain.

TROUBLESHOOTING lmhosts WITH nbtstat

Inevitably, sometimes you will be unable to "see" a computer. Many times, this is because of a failure to resolve the NetBIOS name to an IP address. Using the nbtstat command to manage your NetBIOS name resolution is an effective troubleshooting methodology for Windows name resolution.

nbtstat.exe enables you to read and purge the NetBIOS name cache. It also can show you open NetBIOS connections.

Several commands are available for using an lmhosts file after it is created. If you are troubleshooting access to a NetBIOS resource on a remote server, you can create the appropriate lmhosts file and reboot the client. When the client starts the network services, it reads the lmhosts file and uses this information to try to locate the remote service. To reload the NetBIOS name cache without rebooting the client, simply execute the following command:

```
C:\> nbtstat -R
     Successful purge and preload of the NBT Remote Cache Name Table.
```

Caution
The parameters for the `nbtstat` command are case sensitive.

To view the current NetBIOS name cache, execute the following code. This is a marvelous way to troubleshoot NetBIOS name mappings. Be careful, however, when using `lmhosts` and leaving them on a client. Some down-level clients use `lmhosts` and the NetBIOS name cache before using WINS, and a bad record in an `lmhosts` file on a client can create a problem that's difficult to troubleshoot. Here's the code to execute:

```
C:\> nbtstat -c

Local Area Connection:
Node IpAddress: [192.168.2.199] Scope Id: []

               NetBIOS Remote Cache Name Table

       Name            Type     Host Address    Life [sec]
    ---------------------------------------------------------
       SERVER12    <03>  UNIQUE     192.168.2.201      -1
       SERVER12    <00>  UNIQUE     192.168.2.201      -1
       SERVER12    <20>  UNIQUE     192.168.2.201      -1
       SERVER11    <03>  UNIQUE     192.168.2.200      -1
       SERVER11    <00>  UNIQUE     192.168.2.200      -1
       SERVER11    <20>  UNIQUE     192.168.2.200      -1
       FIS         <1C>  GROUP      192.168.2.200      -1
```

THE hosts FILE

A `hosts` file provides similar functionality to `lmhosts`. This static text file also must be in `\winnt\system32\drivers\etc`. Although its syntax is similar to `lmhosts`, it is used to map hostnames, whereas `lmhosts` is used to map NetBIOS names. A sample `hosts` file appears in Listing 8.3.

LISTING 8.3   USING A hosts FILE TO MAP DNS NAMES TO IP ADDRESSES

```
C:\WINNT\system32\drivers\etc>type hosts
192.168.2.200    server11.fis.local server11 dc
192.168.2.199    server12.fis.local server12
```

Tip
Make sure your text editor is not automatically appending a file extension to either the `lmhosts` or `hosts` file. If, for example, Notepad saves your `hosts` file as `hosts.txt`, it will not function.

ipconfig

Notice from the lines of the hosts file in Listing 8.3 that you can add not only a fully qualified domain name (FQDN) but also one or more aliases. Aliases can be useful if, for example,
you want to access the host by using the name of the user who normally is logged on to that
machine. You cannot place aliases in an lmhosts, but you can place them in a hosts file. This
can be used to find Web servers, application servers, and so on. You can flush the current
contents of the client resolver cache and read the hosts file into memory with the command
shown here:

```
C:\WINNT\system32\drivers\etc>ipconfig /flushdns

Windows 2000 IP Configuration

Successfully flushed the DNS Resolver Cache.
```

If you want to see the contents of the client resolver cache, you must use the command
shown in Listing 8.4. Listing 8.4 shows the client cache, assuming you have the hosts file
shown in Listing 8.3. Viewing the resolver cache is important for the same reason that viewing the NetBIOS name cache is important. The resolver cache is checked before the hosts
file or DNS are contacted. If bad information exists in the resolver cache, it is used before
any newer, more accurate information is accessed.

LISTING 8.4   USING ipconfig TO VIEW THE RESOLVER CACHE

```
C:\ipconfig /displaydns

Windows 2000 IP Configuration

    server12.
    ----------------------------------------------------------
        Record Name . . . . . : server12
        Record Type . . . . . : 1
        Time To Live  . . . . : 31534949
        Data Length . . . . . : 4
        Section . . . . . . . : Answer
        A (Host) Record . . . :
                        192.168.2.199

    200.2.168.192.in-addr.arpa.
    ----------------------------------------------------------
        Record Name . . . . . : 200.2.168.192.in-addr.arpa
        Record Type . . . . . : 12
        Time To Live  . . . . : 31534949
        Data Length . . . . . : 4
        Section . . . . . . . : Answer
        PTR Record  . . . . . :
                        server11.fis.local

    199.2.168.192.in-addr.arpa.
    ----------------------------------------------------------
        Record Name . . . . . : 199.2.168.192.in-addr.arpa
        Record Type . . . . . : 12
        Time To Live  . . . . : 31534949
```

LISTING 8.4 CONTINUED

```
     Data Length . . . . . : 4
     Section . . . . . . . : Answer
     PTR Record  . . . . . :
                       server12.fis.local

server12.fis.local.
-------------------------------------------------------
     Record Name . . . . . : server12.fis.local
     Record Type . . . . . : 1
     Time To Live  . . . . : 31534949
     Data Length . . . . . : 4
     Section . . . . . . . : Answer
     A (Host) Record . . . :
                       192.168.2.199

server11.fis.local.
-------------------------------------------------------
     Record Name . . . . . : server11.fis.local
     Record Type . . . . . : 1
     Time To Live  . . . . : 31534949
     Data Length . . . . . : 4
     Section . . . . . . . : Answer
     A (Host) Record . . . :
                       192.168.2.200

dc.
-------------------------------------------------------
     Record Name . . . . . : dc
     Record Type . . . . . : 1
     Time To Live  . . . . : 31534949
     Data Length . . . . . : 4
     Section . . . . . . . : Answer
     A (Host) Record . . . :
                       192.168.2.200

server11.
-------------------------------------------------------
     Record Name . . . . . : server11
     Record Type . . . . . : 1
     Time To Live  . . . . : 31534949
     Data Length . . . . . : 4
     Section . . . . . . . : Answer
     A (Host) Record . . . :
                       192.168.2.200
```

ipconfig and nbtstat are important name resolution troubleshooting tools. If you have problems resolving a remote server, this is a good place to look for conflicts. Generally, a good rule of thumb is if you can ping the target by IP address but cannot connect by name, you have a name resolution problem.

→ **See** "General IP Troubleshooting Tools," **p. 151**

Note

Be very careful about referencing your AD domain controllers in the hosts file. Sometimes hosts files are left over from troubleshooting sessions or from when the machine was upgraded. If you have a reference in a hosts file for a DC with the wrong IP address, you will not be able to log on as a domain user. Although the client can be perfectly configured to use DNS, it will always check the client resolver cache for an address before it goes to DNS. If this is wrong in the hosts file, your good record in the DNS will never be used. One way to fix this if you have inadvertently done so is to log on as a local (non-domain) user and fix or remove the hosts file.

WINS

WINS is the last non-DNS name resolution methodology you will look at in this chapter. WINS is a NetBIOS name server (NBNS) used to resolve NetBIOS names to IP addresses. The previous example of NetBIOS name resolution with lmhosts was static. WINS is a dynamic service that stays current with the network and is implemented in most large Windows installations.

A Windows 2000/NT/9x computer that is configured as a WINS client registers itself at boot time with the WINS server, refreshes its entries every three days by default, and unregisters its entry when the system is shut down.

WINS also can be integrated with DNS so that, if the DNS server receives a request for a name it cannot resolve, it can contact the WINS server on behalf of the client and attempt to resolve the computer name using WINS.

INSTALLING AND CONFIGURING WINS

Installing WINS is similar to installing DNS and requires less configuration after it is installed because most of the population of its database is done dynamically by the client. Because it is not hierarchical, you do not have to create zones for the records. You can install it using much of the same methods mentioned in Chapter 4, "Installing and Configuring DNS," for installing DNS. It can be installed by scripting using sysocmgr.exe or through Control Panel, Add/Remove Programs, Add/Remove Windows Components, as shown in Figure 8.1.

CONFIGURING WINS CLIENTS MANUALLY

After you have installed WINS on the server, you must configure the clients to use a WINS server. This accomplishes several things. First, they will register their NetBIOS names, IP addresses, and some services with the WINS server on startup. Second, they will use the WINS server to resolve NetBIOS names. This is done by setting the NetBIOS node type to h-node. WINS provides a dynamic NetBIOS name resolution methodology.

You can set the client to be a WINS client either manually or through DHCP. To do so manually, follow these steps:

1. Open the Network and Dial-up Connections folder from Start, Settings. In this folder, you can double-click the Local Area Connection icon. This brings you to the Local Area Connection Status page.

2. From this page, click Properties and select the Internet Protocol option; then, click Properties.

3. This brings you to the Internet Protocol (TCP/IP) Properties page. Click Advanced and select the WINS tab to get the WINS property page shown in Figure 8.2.

Figure 8.1
Installing WINS through Control Panel.

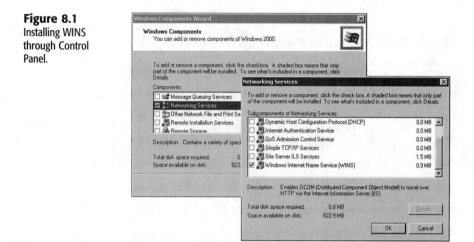

Figure 8.2
Using the WINS property page to add servers.

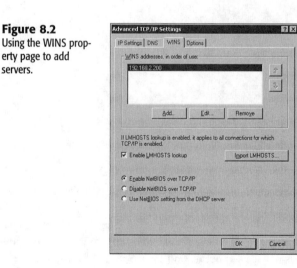

4. After you click Add on the page shown in Figure 8.2, you see the TCP/IP WINS Server page shown in Figure 8.3. Here you can type the IP address of your WINS server and click Add. After you do this, your client is manually configured to be a WINS client.

If you are having trouble getting an lmhosts file to work, make sure the Enable LMHOSTS Lookup check box is selected in the WINS property page.

Figure 8.3
Add IP addresses of
WINS servers using
this input box.

CONFIGURING WINS CLIENTS AUTOMATICALLY THROUGH DHCP

You also can configure clients to use WINS through DHCP. The following section assumes that DHCP is installed and a scope (range of addresses) has been configured. To configure your DHCP clients to use WINS, you must enable and configure Scope Options in the DHCP MMC Snap-in shown in Figure 8.4. Scope option 044 WINS/NBNS Servers must be set to the IP address of the WINS server. If you enter the server name, make sure you click Resolve, and regardless of whether you type in the server name or IP address, make sure you click Add. If you don't and then click OK, the information will not be kept.

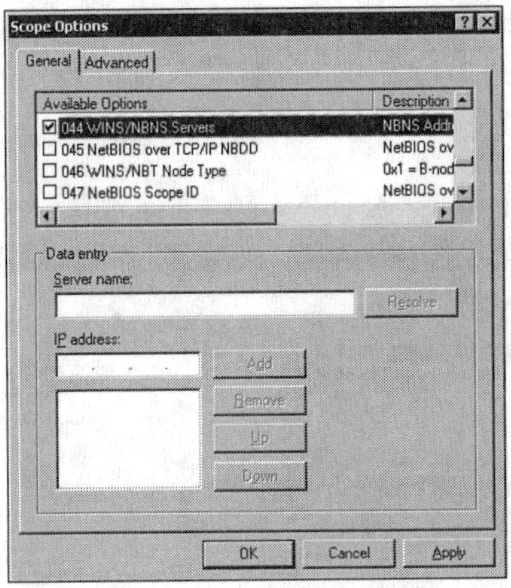

Figure 8.4
Setting the IP address
of the WINS server
using DHCP.

You also must set Scope Option 046 to h-node, p-node, or m-node to use WINS. You can use the information from Listing 8.1, or you can scroll to the right in this window to see the hexadecimal values necessary to set this option to its respective values (see Figure 8.5). If you do not set this last option and your clients are set to the default (b-node), you will have a perfectly functioning WINS server that is never used because all your clients are using b-node.

INTEGRATING WINS WITH DNS

You can configure DNS to use WINS to resolve names that are not in the DNS zone but might be in the WINS database. This is useful in a mixed environment of Windows 9x/NT/2000 clients and servers. Previous versions of Windows relied heavily on WINS to map IP addresses to computer names. Sometimes names were registered in WINS that were not registered in DNS. Because your DNS in 2000 is dynamic and supports live updates similar to WINS, this usually is not necessary in a pure 2000 environment. Indeed, in a pure Windows 2000 environment, WINS is unnecessary because DNS is capable of satisfying all your name resolution needs.

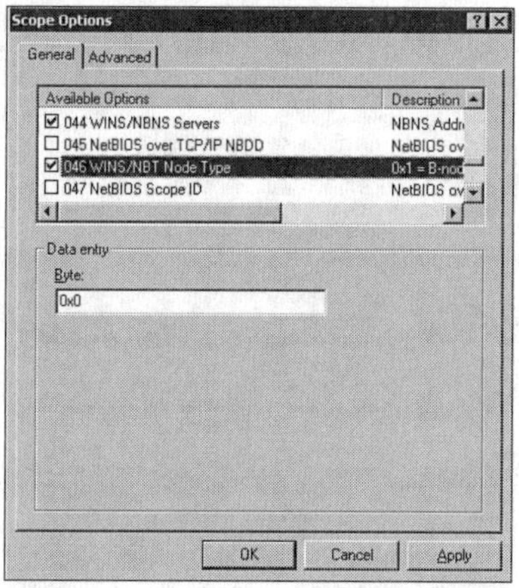

CH
8

Figure 8.5
Setting the NetBIOS node type using DHCP.

To demonstrate this capability and how to enable it, let's use a scenario in which at least one entry exists in the WINS server that does not exist in the DNS server. After you have set the stage, you will configure the DNS server to contact the WINS server if it is incapable of resolving a query for a local machine.

The following scenario assumes that you have the WINS, DNS, and DHCP services running on one Windows 2000 server whose IP address is 192.168.2.200. Additionally, it assumes you have a Windows 2000 client and an NT 4 client, both of which are configured to use DHCP. In addition to the IP address and subnet mask, the DHCP clients are receiving a router address of 192.168.2.201 and a DNS and WINS server on IP address 192.168.2.200. The NetBIOS node type also is set to 0x8, or hybrid, which causes the client to try WINS before broadcast for NetBIOS name resolution.

Windows 2000 clients automatically update their A and PTR records in DNS. Windows NT and Windows 9x clients, however, do not automatically register with DNS. Windows 2000 clients and other Windows clients register with their WINS server if configured to do so by setting the NetBIOS node type and configuring the client with the IP address of one or more WINS servers.

→ **See** "Configuring DHCP for Dynamic Update," **p. 119**

If you are using Windows 2000 DHCP, you can configure the DHCP server to register the A and PTR records for down-level clients because NT and 9x clients can't perform DNS dynamic updates. However, if you are not using Windows 2000 DHCP, your down-level clients can't use the DHCP server to update the DNS. Because Windows 2000 uses DNS by default, there must be some mechanism to allow name resolution.

You will configure the Windows 2000 DNS server to look in the Windows 2000 WINS servers listing for clients it can't resolve, which are assumed to be local. Figure 8.6 shows the current contents of the WINS server. Notice that all three computers—server9, server11, and server12—are listed in the WINS database in the Active Registrations pane.

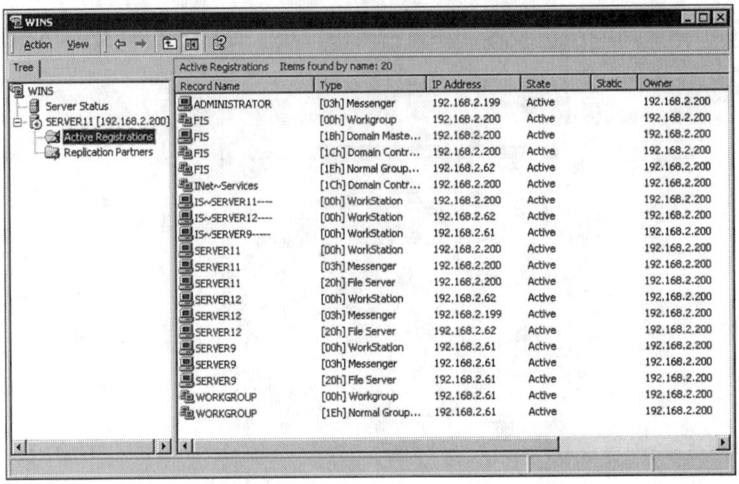

Figure 8.6
Viewing name registrations in WINS.

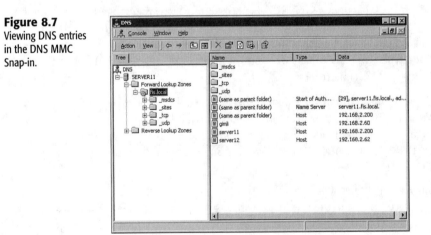

Figure 8.7 shows that the two Windows 2000 computers, server11 and server12, have automatically listed themselves in the DNS. Because server9 is an NT 4 client, its default behavior is not to register in DNS because Microsoft NT 4 DNS servers are static and do not support dynamic updates.

→ **See** "Dynamic DNS," **p. 116**

Figure 8.7
Viewing DNS entries in the DNS MMC Snap-in.

Configuring DNS to Use WINS for Forward Lookups

To allow DNS to use WINS for name lookups, you must configure the DNS server with the IP addresses of one or more WINS servers. This is done on a per-zone basis. Figure 8.8 is the result of right-clicking the `fis.local` forward lookup zone shown in Figure 8.7 and selecting Properties.

→ **See** "Configuring DNS," **p. 50**

CH

8

Figure 8.8
Use the WINS Properties page to configure the DNS zone to use WINS.

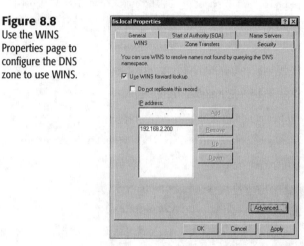

Configuring DNS to Use WINS for Reverse Lookups

For your DNS to use WINS for name lookups, you must configure the DNS server to be fully configured for WINS, you also must configure the reverse lookup zone to use WINS. Figure 8.9 shows the property page that pops up when you right-click your reverse lookup zone and select Properties.

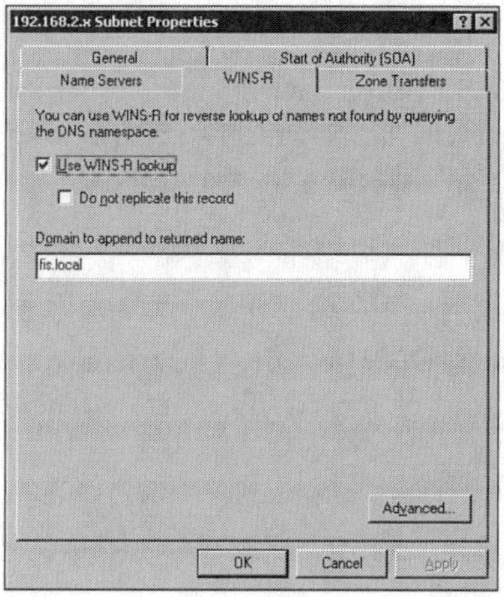

Figure 8.9
Use the WINS-R property page to configure the DNS reverse lookup zone to use WINS.

This enables you to use WINS for both forward and reverse lookups. The Do Not Replicate This Record option is important if you have a mixed Windows 2000 and non–Windows 2000 DNS environment because the WINS and WINS-R records this creates are not compatible with non–Windows DNS and can cause zone transfers to fail.

> **Caution**
>
> If you configure a zone to use WINS and that zone is also configured as a primary zone and has non-Microsoft secondary zones, when the non-Microsoft DNS servers try to perform a zone transfer, that zone transfer can fail. The Do Not Replicate This Record check box keeps WINS-R records from being replicated to other DNS servers.

To test your DNS-to-WINS integration, perform an `nslookup` on `server9` from the Windows 2000 client. Because `nslookup` is purely a DNS tool, this causes the DNS to attempt to resolve an IP address for `server9`; then, because it is not in the DNS zone, it attempts to resolve it from the WINS database. Figure 8.10 shows the `nslookup` command and the response. Even though `server9` was not registered in DNS, your DNS server was capable of contacting the WINS server on your behalf and resolved the query.

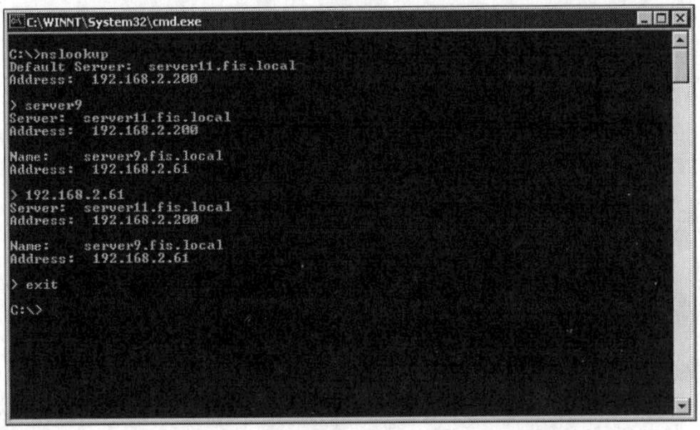

Figure 8.10

`nslookup` can be used to test DNS and WINS integration.

Now, if you use any utility that attempts hostname resolution rather than NetBIOS name resolution, the client resolver contacts the DNS, which—if it does not find the record—contacts its configured WINS server to try to resolve that record.

SUMMARY

In a Windows 2000–only environment, DNS provides all the name resolution necessary for the enterprise. With older clients, however, a need still exists for older, NetBIOS-based tools, such as WINS and `lmhosts`.

TROUBLESHOOTING

PING FAILURE

I can ping the remote host by IP address but cannot ping by name or use the net use *command to mount any of its drives.*

This is a classic example of name resolution failure. Clear the NetBIOS name cache with the nbtstat -R command. Then, clear the DNS resolver cache with the ipconfig /flushdns command. This starts you with a clean slate. Then, try to resolve the DNS name to an IP address with the nslookup <servername> command. Be sure to replace <servername> with the fully qualified domain name (FQDN) of the remote host—for example, nslookup gold.fis.local. If the response is negative, either you are using the wrong name or the server is not registering itself properly in the DNS. You can force the issue by placing the information in a hosts file or an lmhosts file, but the real issue is to find out why the name and address are not updated in the DNS properly. Because the default for Windows 2000 name resolution is DNS, this must be addressed.

CANNOT RESOLVE REMOTE HOSTS

The client is configured to use both WINS and DNS, yet it can't resolve any remote hosts. Is a quick way available to narrow the fault domain for this problem?

The netdiag command (which is included in the Windows 2000 Support Tools on the Windows 2000 CD) runs many common tests, such as whether the client is correctly configured for a DNS and WINS server with one command.

lmhosts IS INCONSISTENT

My lmhosts *file seems to work except for one or two entries.*

Spelling counts, for both the name and the address. As simple as it seems, this is a common error. Also, the #PRE directives are case sensitive.

CANNOT RESOLVE THE WINS SERVER

I can resolve every server using WINS except the WINS server itself.

This is also a very common error. The WINS server must be configured to use itself as a WINS server, just like other WINS clients. Even though you have installed the WINS service, this does not automatically cause the WINS server to use itself for name resolution.

RE-REGISTERING WITHOUT REBOOTING

I want to re-register the WINS client with the WINS server without rebooting.

In Windows 2000, the nbtstat command has a new option. nbtstat -RR causes the WINS client to send a name release followed by a name refresh packet to the WINS server.

CHAPTER 9

DYNAMIC AND ACTIVE DIRECTORY INTEGRATED DNS

In this chapter

DYNAMIC DNS

The only requirements for a DNS to support the Active Directory are support for SRV records, dynamic update, and incremental zone transfers. Windows 2000 supports all these out of the box. This chapter looks at support for Dynamic DNS.

Dynamic DNS (DDNS) is the capability to modify zones on-the-fly. This is a significant departure from previous implementations of DNS, which required not only knowledge to manage them but a fair degree of typing skills. Previous versions of DNS—both on NT and other OSs—required the administrator to manually update zone files every time a machine was added, subtracted, or moved. With Dynamic DNS, when a DDNS-aware client boots, it updates its records with its configured DNS server, and when the netlogon service starts on a DC, it automatically registers the SRV records for its services.

ALLOWING UPDATES

The primary consideration on the DNS server is ensuring, on a per-zone basis, that Allow Updates has been configured. This is set by right-clicking the zone and setting Allow Dynamic Updates? to Yes (see Figure 9.1). If the zone is an AD-integrated zone, you also can choose to allow Only Secure Updates, which means that the updates will be checked against Active Directory Security.

→ **See** "Authorization Step by Step," **p. 320**

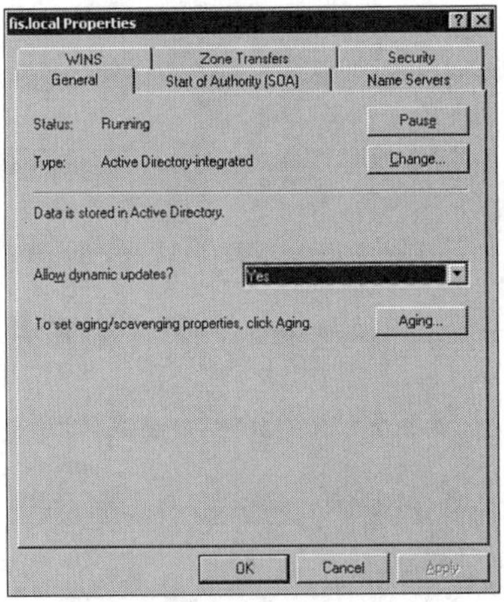

Figure 9.1
Setting the Allow Dynamic Updates option on DNS zones.

Because Windows 2000 clients that have statically assigned addresses automatically update their A and PTR records, very little configuration needs to be done on the client. Later, you will learn how to configure DHCP to dynamically update records, but first let's look at the anatomy of a Dynamic DNS update. It is important to note that the DHCP client service is the service responsible for updating the DNS with the IP address of the client computer, regardless of whether the client computer is configured with a static or DHCP address. In addition, this client runs on any Windows 2000 computer regardless of whether it is using a DHCP server.

→ **See** "DNS Record Types," **p. 66**

→ **See** "DNS Record Types," **p. 66**

Tip

Use `ipconfig /all` to view the IP configuration on the client, including DNS parameters.

DYNAMIC DNS STEP BY STEP

In Figure 9.2, you can see the beginning of a conversation between the DNS client and server before a dynamic update. This Network Monitor capture covers the time from the initial boot of the Windows 2000 client and previous to logon.

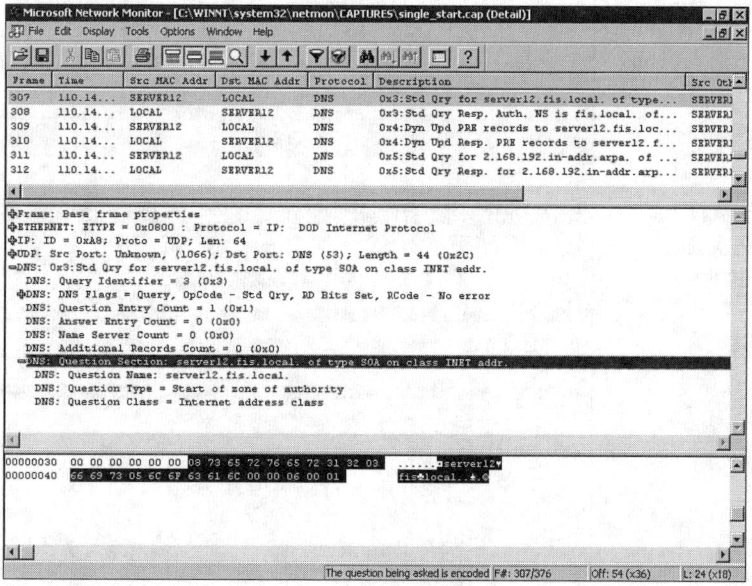

CH

9

Figure 9.2
Query for Start of Authority (SOA).

Frame 307 shows the first DNS packet of the conversation. The client is configured with the IP address of the DNS server and is querying for Start of Authority (SOA) to ensure that this DNS is the appropriate DNS to update.

In Figure 9.3, frame 308 shows the response of the DNS server, claiming to be the authoritative server for this zone and supplying its IP address if necessary.

In Figure 9.4, frame 309 is the actual update request from the client to the DNS server, requesting an update of its A record with its hostname and IP address. In the final DNS resource record section of Figure 9.4, you can see the resource name (`server12.fis.local`), the resource type (`Host Address (A)`), and the IP address (`192.168.2.199`). Frame 310 is the update response telling the client that the record was updated.

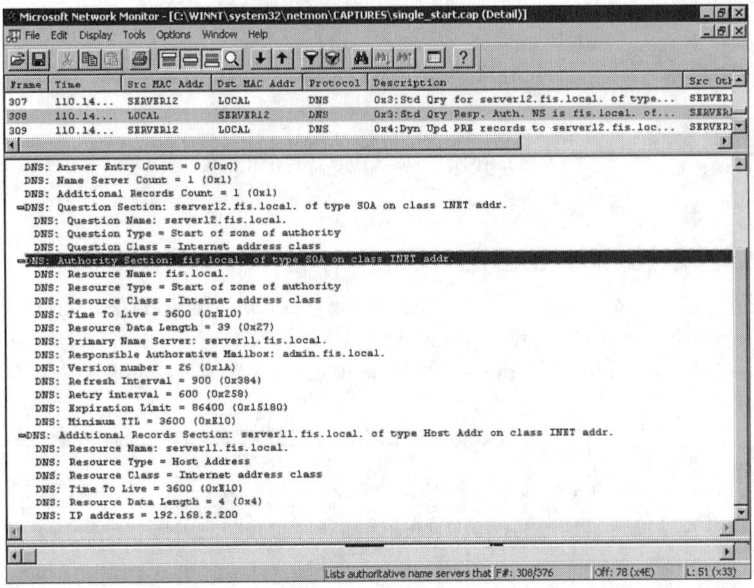

Figure 9.3
The SOA response.

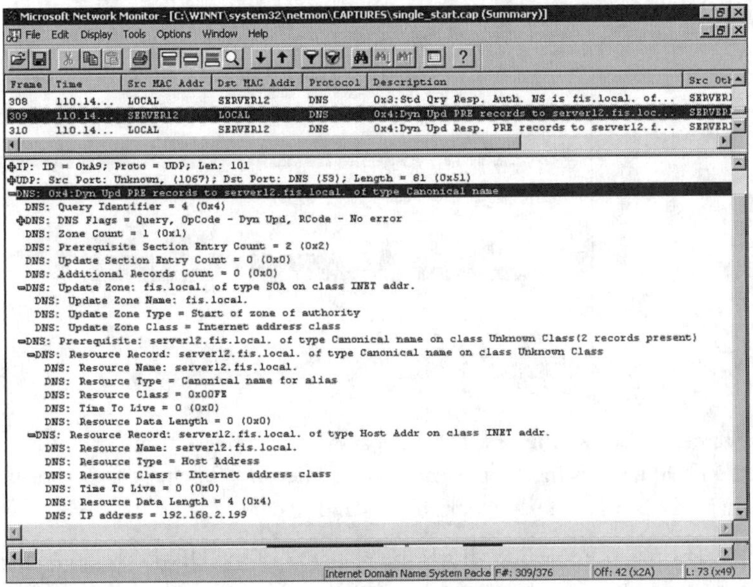

Figure 9.4
The DNS dynamic update request.

The client also attempts to update its reverse lookup address in the DNS server's reverse lookup zone. Similar to updating a forward lookup zone, the client queries for SOA for 2.168.192.in-addr.arpa, the reverse lookup zone. The DNS server then responds that it is authoritative for that zone.

The client then requests the update of its PTR record in the reverse lookup zone.

Configuring DHCP for Dynamic Update

Although the DHCP client service—which runs on every Windows 2000 computer—is responsible for updating the DNS server with the A and PTR records of the client, you can configure the DHCP server to update the DNS on behalf of the client. Figure 9.5 shows the property page that sets these options. This page can be opened by opening the DHCP MMC Snap-in, right-clicking the server name, selecting Properties, and clicking the DNS tab.

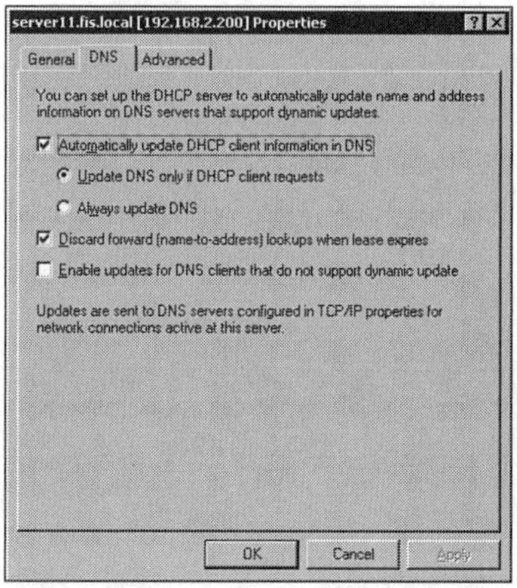

Figure 9.5
DNS DHCP update options.

CH
9

As you can see in Figure 9.5, several options can be set for DHCP and DNS for dynamic update. The default is for the Windows 2000 DHCP client to update its own A record and to request the DHCP server to update the client's PTR record in the appropriate reverse lookup zone. Figure 9.5 shows the default setting for DDNS; this setting does not cause NT DHCP clients to update either the A or PTR record.

Changing the setting to select Always Update DNS is an interesting option because the end result is the same: Both the A and PTR records get updated. The difference is in how they get updated. With this option set, the DHCP server does all the DDNS updating for both the A and PTR records. This setting also does not cause NT DHCP clients to update either the A or PTR record.

The setting that affects NT and other down-level clients is the Enable Updates for DNS Clients That Do Not Support Dynamic Update check box. This causes the DHCP server to always update the PTR record of the client. For the A record to be registered in the DNS by the DHCP server, the client must know its DNS domain name. This can be set either statically in the IP protocol properties of the client or dynamically through DHCP by setting the DHCP scope option #15 to the DNS domain name of the client. In this example, `fis.local.DHCP` can allocate information to clients other than the default of a subnet mask and IP address. DHCP option #15 is defined by RFC 1541 as the DNS domain name that the client should use for DNS name resolution.

> **Note**
>
> A Windows 2000 computer that is a member of an Active Directory domain, by default, derives its DNS domain name from the AD domain of which it is a member.

AD INTEGRATED DNS

For years, Domain Name Services on any OS stored the information about each zone in a text file. This file has a specific format and syntax, but still it is a simple text file easily manipulated by any text editor capable of reading ASCII text. Windows 2000 implements a new feature called Active Directory integrated zones. In this feature, the zone information is not stored in text files; instead, each zone is stored as an Active Directory container object called a DNSZone. Each DNS record in that zone becomes a leaf object called a DNSnode. The properties of the record—the IP address, address type, and so on—become part of a multivalued attribute called a DNSRecord.

→ **See** "Containers," **p. 465**

> **Tip**
>
> Active Directory integrated status is conferred on a per-zone basis rather than per server. A DNS server can have a mixture of standard and AD-integrated zones. If the DNS server is to have any AD-integrated zones, however, it must be running on a domain controller (DC).

VIEWING DNS AS ACTIVE DIRECTORY OBJECTS

To view this DNS information as objects in the Active Directory, you can use the Active Directory Users and Computers (ADUC) MMC Snap-in. To see the DNS objects, you first must open ADUC. Choose Start, Programs, Administrative Tools, Active Directory Users and Computers, and then select View, Advanced Features. Figure 9.6 shows the ADUC open to the proper fis.local DNSZone container object, with the ldap._tcp.dc._msdcs DNSnode highlighted.

To see the DNSRecord attribute, you must use a tool from the Windows 2000 support tools called ADSIEdit. The Windows 2000 support tools are available on the Windows 2000 CD in the \support\tools folder. In Figure 9.7, you can see ADSIEdit open to the exact same DNSZone and DNSRecord that you selected in Figure 9.6.

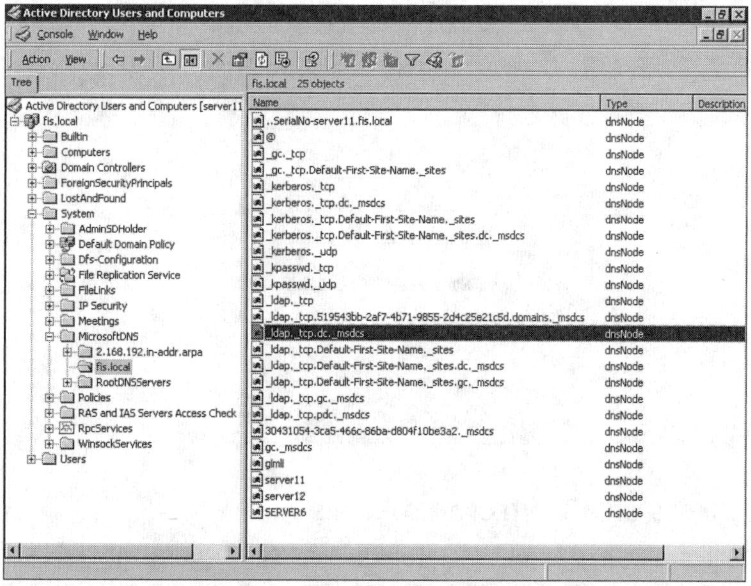

Figure 9.6
DNS objects in AD
Users and Computers.

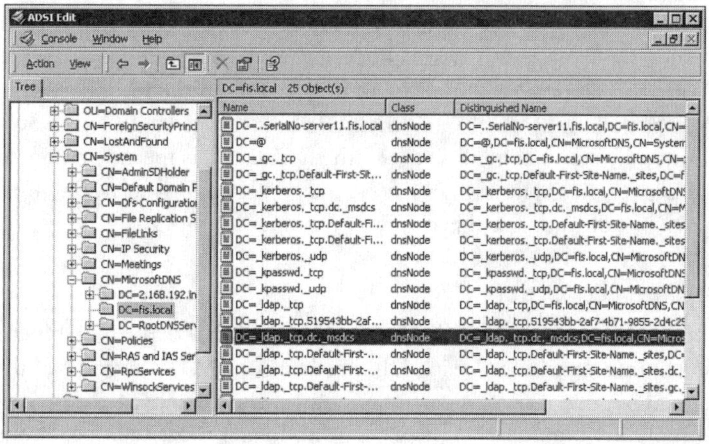

Figure 9.7
DNS objects in
ADSIEdit.

Double-clicking the `ldap._tcp.dc._msdcs` DNSnode object opens the
`DC=_ldap._tcp.dc._msdcs` Properties page (see Figure 9.8). Here you can see the DNSRecord
multivalued attribute that contains all the information about the DNS record, such as its
type, weight, and so on. Although these tools are interesting for looking at the architecture
of the AD-integrated zone and its records, the DNS MMC Snap-in is where you will perform all your management of these records. Converting a zone to AD-integrated does not
particularly change how you manage the DNS, but it does offer some real advantages over
standard primary and secondary zones, such as a much more efficient replication mechanism and the ability to apply security to the DNS records.

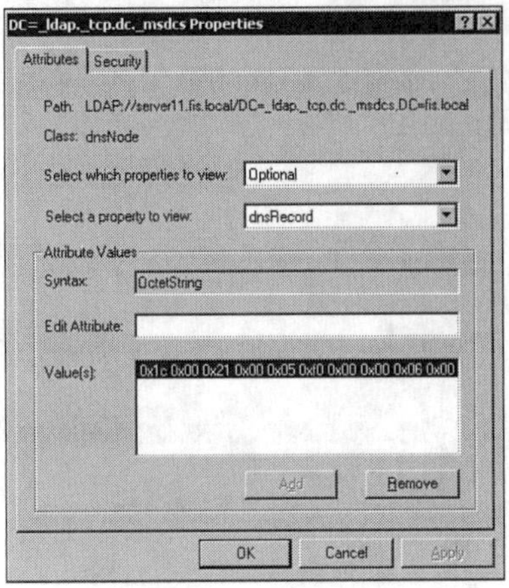

Figure 9.8
A DNSnode object.

ADVANTAGES OF AD-INTEGRATED ZONES

In previous versions of DNS, you were limited to storing your DNS records in static text files. You also were limited to one primary DNS server with zero or more additional secondary servers per DNS zone. This meant that all updates were performed at the primary server. In addition, at a configured interval, the DNS server that held the secondary zone contacted the DNS server that held the primary zone and queried whether any changes to the zone had occurred that needed to be updated on the secondary server. With many DNS servers, including BIND 4.x and the DNS that shipped with NT, when a zone transfer occurred, the entire zone was sent in the update. This meant that one record being changed could trigger the replication of a zone that could conceivably hold hundreds or thousands of records. Needless to say, this could be very inefficient.

REPLICATION EFFICIENCY

Newer versions of BIND and Windows 2000 DNS are capable of incremental transfers, but with AD-integrated DNS, each DNS record is an AD object and all the interesting information about that record is part of a multivalued attribute. Because the AD uses attribute-level replication granularity, one change no longer causes a large amount of redundant data to be replicated.

The Windows 2000 AD uses a multimaster replication model that allows virtually any attribute of an object to be updated on any DC that is a member of that domain. Because every AD-integrated zone is updatable, losing one DNS server does not mean you have lost your only "primary" zone. This removes the central point of failure for updates that was the bane of the old model of a single primary and zero or more secondary zones.

> **Tip**
>
> When planning your DNS placement in large enterprises, make decisions based on update efficiency as well as lookup efficiency. Remember that every Windows 2000 computer will update its A and PTR records periodically to the configured DNS server. If that server is across a slow WAN link, it will be a very slow, very expensive event.

DYNAMIC UPDATE EFFICIENCY

Update efficiency becomes critical in a dynamic update environment. When a client is configured to use a particular DNS server, it queries that DNS for SOA to get the name of the primary DNS server for that zone because, in a primary/secondary standard zone configuration, only primary zones get updated. If the DNS server this Windows 2000 client is configured to use holds a secondary copy of that zone, the secondary DNS then queries the primary for SOA and returns the IP address/hostname information to the client. The client then uses the DNS server that holds the primary zone to update its A and PTR records. The result is that the local DNS (the DNS that the client is configured to use) does not get updated with this new information until a zone transfer occurs. This implies an unacceptable amount of latency and unnecessary network traffic.

This scenario becomes particularly problematic in large, distributed organizations. You would certainly configure your local clients to use the nearest DNS for lookups to minimize round trips across expensive wide area network (WAN) links. However, if the local DNS is configured with secondary zone types for both the forward and reverse lookup zones, your lookups will be local but your updates will always be remote. A statically configured adapter registers itself at boot and every 24 hours thereafter, or when its information changes. A DHCP client updates its information when it obtains, renews, or releases a lease. This can cause a high number of expensive network round trips.

If, in the previous scenario, all the DNS zones involved were AD-integrated zones, this problem could not occur. The reason is simple: Windows 2000 Active Directory uses a multimaster replication model. Every Windows 2000 DC holds a modifiable copy of the Active Directory database. Because, in an AD-integrated zone, every bit of information about the zone is kept in the AD, any client can update its A and PTR records against the DNS server it is configured to use. The AD then replicates this information along with any other AD changes that might have occurred on the DC. This does not mean that you never write information from one zone to another. Quite the contrary. Because the default replication trigger inside a site fires approximately every 5 minutes, and the replication topology inside a site is defined so that changes are replicated to all DCs within a site within 15 minutes, any changes are replicated to all other instances of the zone very quickly. Therefore, this saves inefficient transfers of entire zones, inefficient dynamic updates as described in the previous paragraph, and the update single point of failure.

> **Caution**
>
> With Windows 2000, great care should be taken with DNS zones open to public access, such as DNS servers outside firewalls. Secure updates should be used, or if possible, Allow Updates should be set to No.

SECURE DYNAMIC UPDATES

Another feature of AD-integrated zones is that you no longer leave yourself open to just anyone who wants to update your DNS information. If you are using AD-integrated zones, your DNS information is stored as part of the Active Directory and then is subject to Active Directory security. So if you leave your zones with Allow Updates set to Yes, anyone with a network connection and the proper software can update your zone information. With secure dynamic updates, every modification to the zone information is treated as an AD modification, and as such is subject to AD security—a very robust distributed security model.

In the AD security model, every object in the AD has an access control list (ACL). The ACL is a list of the security identifiers (SIDs) of every user, group, or other AD object that can touch the AD. In the AD, when a process needs to view or modify an object, it must present its SID to authenticate that it has the appropriate permissions to do so.

→ **See** "Authorization Step by Step," **p. 320**

DEFAULT PERMISSIONS ON AD DNS OBJECTS With Allow Updates set to Only Secure Updates, the default is for anyone to be able to see DNS records. However, to create A and PTR records, a user must be a member of the Authenticated Users group.

From an AD security perspective, this means that the group Everyone has read permissions on the DNSZone object. Figure 9.9 shows the default permissions for group Everyone on the zone fis.local. You find this screen by right-clicking the zone name, choosing Properties, and selecting the Security tab. Unlike the AD Users and Computers MMC Snap-in, you do not have to select View, Advanced Features to see security information in the DNS MMC Snap-in. It is important to note that the group Everyone includes anyone with a good network connection. Some network operating systems include only logged-on users in the Everyone group. When Windows 2000 says Everyone, it means every user on the network.

By default, the group Authenticated Users has create child objects permission on the DNSZone object. Figure 9.10 shows the DNS MMC Snap-in still focused on the fis.local DNSZone object but showing the permissions for group Authenticated Users. Although the Security Properties page shows only create child objects for the Authenticated Users group, when you consider that any user who qualifies for Authenticated Users membership is also a member of the group Everyone, the effective permissions for Authenticated Users are create all child objects and read.

Figure 9.9
Group Everyone permissions for DNSZone.

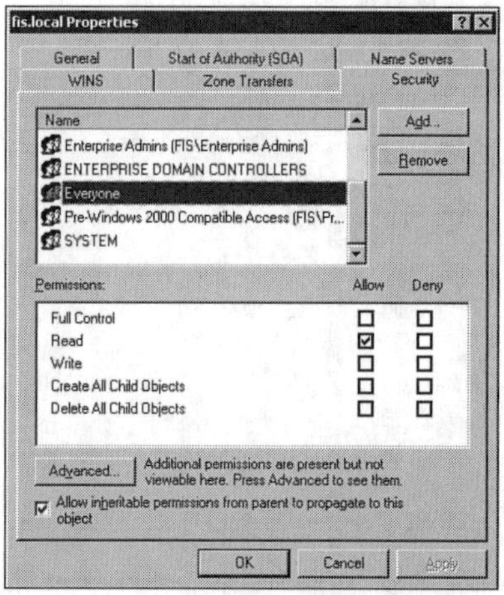

Figure 9.10
Authenticated Users group permissions for DNSZone.

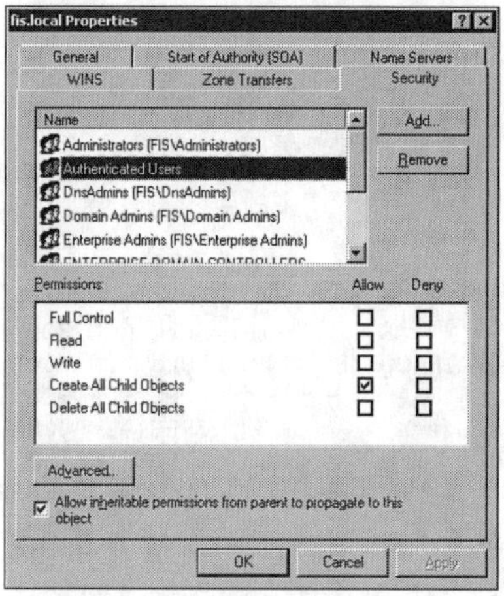

Several groups have full control permissions; among them are Domain Admins, Enterprise Admins, Enterprise Domain Controllers, DNSAdmins, and SYSTEM.

Although any user authenticated to the domain can create DNSnode objects, after they are created, only specified users who have the write permission can modify properties of the object. In Figure 9.11, the DNS record itself has been right-clicked in the DNS MMC Snap-in, and Security has been selected. Here you see the ACL for the DNSnode object for the A record for stone.fis.local. The FIS\STONE user now has full control permission. This enables the computer account to update the properties of its own A record. Other processes will be capable of viewing this record and creating records in this zone, but unless they have write permissions to the DNSnode object, they will not be capable of modifying information about any existing records.

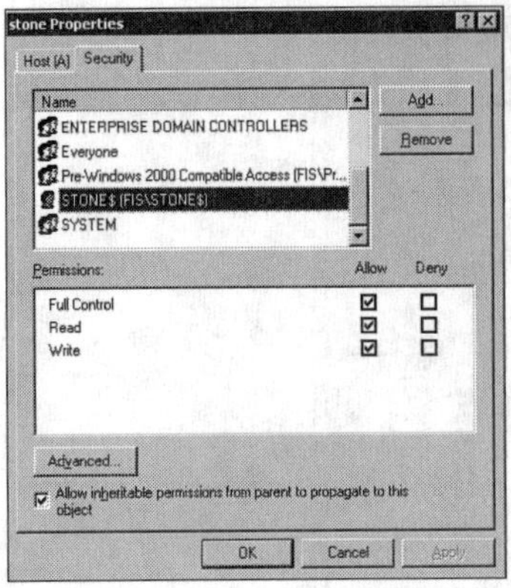

Figure 9.11
AD permissions for the
DNSnode object.

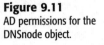

The default permissions on a DNSZone AD object appear in Listing 9.1. These permissions were listed by executing the `dsacls.exe` command from the Windows 2000 Resource Kit.

LISTING 9.1   DEFAULT PERMISSIONS ON A DNSZONE OBJECT

```
O:\>dsacls DC=fis.local,CN=microsoftdns,CN=system,DC=fis,DC=local

Access list:

Effective Permissions on this object are:
Allow FIS\Domain Admins                          FULL CONTROL
Allow NT AUTHORITY\ENTERPRISE DOMAIN CONTROLLERS  FULL CONTROL
Allow NT AUTHORITY\SYSTEM                         FULL CONTROL
Allow NT AUTHORITY\Authenticated Users            SPECIAL ACCESS
                                                  CREATE CHILD
Allow Everyone                                    SPECIAL ACCESS
                                                  READ PERMISSIONS
                                                  LIST CONTENTS
                                                  READ PROPERTY
                                                  LIST OBJECT
Allow FIS\DnsAdmins                               FULL CONTROL
➥   <Inherited from parent>
Allow BUILTIN\Administrators                      SPECIAL ACCESS
➥   <Inherited from parent>

                                                  DELETE
                                                  READ PERMISSIONS
                                                  WRITE PERMISSIONS
                                                  CHANGE OWNERSHIP
                                                  CREATE CHILD
                                                  LIST CONTENTS
                                                  WRITE SELF
                                                  WRITE PROPERTY
                                                  READ PROPERTY
                                                  LIST OBJECT
                                                  CONTROL ACCESS
Allow FIS\Enterprise Admins                       FULL CONTROL
➥   <Inherited from parent>
Allow BUILTIN\Pre-Windows 2000 Compatible Access  SPECIAL ACCESS
➥   <Inherited from parent>

                                                  LIST CONTENTS
```

LISTING 9.1 CONTINUED

```
Permissions inherited to subobjects are:
Inherited to all subobjects
Allow FIS\DnsAdmins                                 FULL CONTROL
➥   <Inherited from parent>
Allow BUILTIN\Administrators                        SPECIAL ACCESS
➥   <Inherited from parent>

                                                    DELETE
                                                    READ PERMISSIONS
                                                    WRITE PERMISSIONS
                                                    CHANGE OWNERSHIP
                                                    CREATE CHILD
                                                    LIST CONTENTS
                                                    WRITE SELF
                                                    WRITE PROPERTY
                                                    READ PROPERTY
                                                    LIST OBJECT
                                                    CONTROL ACCESS
Allow FIS\Enterprise Admins                         FULL CONTROL
➥   <Inherited from parent>
Allow BUILTIN\Pre-Windows 2000 Compatible Access    SPECIAL ACCESS
➥   <Inherited from parent>

                                                    LIST CONTENTS


Inherited to user
Allow BUILTIN\Pre-Windows 2000 Compatible Access    SPECIAL ACCESS
➥   <Inherited from parent>

                                                    READ PERMISSIONS
                                                    LIST CONTENTS
                                                    READ PROPERTY
                                                    LIST OBJECT
Inherited to group
Allow BUILTIN\Pre-Windows 2000 Compatible Access    SPECIAL ACCESS
➥   <Inherited from parent>

                                                    READ PERMISSIONS
                                                    LIST CONTENTS
                                                    READ PROPERTY
                                                    LIST OBJECT
Inherited to user
Allow BUILTIN\Pre-Windows 2000 Compatible Access    SPECIAL ACCESS for Logon
➥ Information    <Inherited from parent>
                                                    READ PROPERTY
Allow BUILTIN\Pre-Windows 2000 Compatible Access    SPECIAL ACCESS for Account
➥ Restrictions    <Inherited from parent>
                                                    READ PROPERTY
Allow BUILTIN\Pre-Windows 2000 Compatible Access    SPECIAL ACCESS for Group
➥ Membership    <Inherited from parent>
                                                    READ PROPERTY
Allow BUILTIN\Pre-Windows 2000 Compatible Access    SPECIAL ACCESS for General
➥ Information    <Inherited from parent>
                                                    READ PROPERTY
Allow BUILTIN\Pre-Windows 2000 Compatible Access    SPECIAL ACCESS for Remote
➥ Access Information    <Inherited from parent>
                                                    READ PROPERTY
The command completed successfully
```

CH
9

The default permissions on a DNSnode object appear in Listing 9.2.

LISTING 9.2   DEFAULT PERMISSIONS ON A DNSNODE OBJECT

```
O:\>dsacls DC=stone,DC=fis.local,CN=microsoftdns,CN=system,DC=fis,DC=local

Access list:

Effective Permissions on this object are:
Allow FIS\Domain Admins                              FULL CONTROL
Allow NT AUTHORITY\ENTERPRISE DOMAIN CONTROLLERS     FULL CONTROL
Allow NT AUTHORITY\SYSTEM                             FULL CONTROL
Allow NT AUTHORITY\Authenticated Users               SPECIAL ACCESS
                                                     CREATE CHILD
Allow Everyone                                        SPECIAL ACCESS
                                                     READ PERMISSIONS
                                                     LIST CONTENTS
                                                     READ PROPERTY
                                                     LIST OBJECT
Allow FIS\STONE$                                      FULL CONTROL
Allow FIS\DnsAdmins                                   FULL CONTROL
➡   <Inherited from parent>
Allow BUILTIN\Administrators                          SPECIAL ACCESS
➡   <Inherited from parent>

                                                     DELETE
                                                     READ PERMISSIONS
                                                     WRITE PERMISSIONS
                                                     CHANGE OWNERSHIP
                                                     CREATE CHILD
                                                     LIST CONTENTS
                                                     WRITE SELF
                                                     WRITE PROPERTY
                                                     READ PROPERTY
                                                     LIST OBJECT
                                                     CONTROL ACCESS
Allow FIS\Enterprise Admins                           FULL CONTROL
➡   <Inherited from parent>
Allow BUILTIN\Pre-Windows 2000 Compatible Access     SPECIAL ACCESS
➡   <Inherited from parent>

                                                     LIST CONTENTS


Permissions inherited to subobjects are:
Inherited to all subobjects
Allow FIS\DnsAdmins                                   FULL CONTROL
➡   <Inherited from parent>
Allow BUILTIN\Administrators                          SPECIAL ACCESS
➡   <Inherited from parent>

                                                     DELETE
                                                     READ PERMISSIONS
                                                     WRITE PERMISSIONS
                                                     CHANGE OWNERSHIP
                                                     CREATE CHILD
                                                     LIST CONTENTS
                                                     WRITE SELF
                                                     WRITE PROPERTY
                                                     READ PROPERTY
                                                     LIST OBJECT
                                                     CONTROL ACCESS
Allow FIS\Enterprise Admins                           FULL CONTROL
```

LISTING 9.2   CONTINUED

```
➡   <Inherited from parent>
Allow BUILTIN\Pre-Windows 2000 Compatible Access   SPECIAL ACCESS
➡   <Inherited from parent>

                                                   LIST CONTENTS


Inherited to user
Allow BUILTIN\Pre-Windows 2000 Compatible Access   SPECIAL ACCESS
➡   <Inherited from parent>

                                                   READ PERMISSIONS
                                                   LIST CONTENTS
                                                   READ PROPERTY
                                                   LIST OBJECT
Inherited to group
Allow BUILTIN\Pre-Windows 2000 Compatible Access   SPECIAL ACCESS
➡   <Inherited from parent>

                                                   READ PERMISSIONS
                                                   LIST CONTENTS
                                                   READ PROPERTY
                                                   LIST OBJECT
Inherited to user
Allow BUILTIN\Pre-Windows 2000 Compatible Access   SPECIAL ACCESS for Logon
➡ Information    <Inherited from parent>

                                                   READ PROPERTY
Allow BUILTIN\Pre-Windows 2000 Compatible Access   SPECIAL ACCESS for Account
➡ Restrictions    <Inherited from parent>

                                                   READ PROPERTY
Allow BUILTIN\Pre-Windows 2000 Compatible Access   SPECIAL ACCESS for Group
➡ Membership    <Inherited from parent>

                                                   READ PROPERTY
Allow BUILTIN\Pre-Windows 2000 Compatible Access   SPECIAL ACCESS for General
➡ Information    <Inherited from parent>

                                                   READ PROPERTY
Allow BUILTIN\Pre-Windows 2000 Compatible Access   SPECIAL ACCESS for Remote
➡ Access Information    <Inherited from parent>

                                                   READ PROPERTY
The command completed successfully
```

The dsacls.exe tool does an excellent job of showing the effective rights for objects in the AD. These listings are helpful for showing the default list of permissions that are created on a zone and records in the zone when the objects are first created. Although these permissions can be modified like permissions on virtually every other AD object are, under most conditions they do not need to be.

ISSUES WITH SECURE DYNAMIC UPDATES   Some scenarios with secure updates bear further examination. Most of them involve secure dynamic updates by a DHCP server. Earlier it was mentioned that, when a DNS record is created, full control rights are automatically assigned to the computer account that created it. In a scenario in which the A and PTR records are being created by the DHCP service, those records are owned by the computer account on the DHCP server. If that server goes down and another DHCP server is used to take its place, the new DHCP server does not own that record and does not have the rights to update the records created by the previous DHCP server, even though it is now leasing addresses previously covered by the old DHCP server.

A solution to this problem does exist, but it must be approached carefully. If the computer on which the DHCP service is running is placed in the DNSUpdateProxy group, all the records it creates will be created without permissions, and the first process that touches that record that is not a member of the DNSUpdateProxy group becomes its owner. This, however, opens some security holes. If you use this fix, you must be sure you don't run your DHCP servers using the DNSUpdateProxy group on the domain controllers. If this is done, all the A and SRV records created by the netlogon service will be insecure. These are the last records in your DNS that you want to be modifiable by anyone.

For example, a simple denial of service attack would be to update the SRV records for the global catalog (GC), Kerberos, or LDAP servers with the incorrect addresses. If your clients were to attempt to use these addresses to log on, they would be unsuccessful at best. At worst, they would be redirected to a server that would record information for further attacks.

ARCHITECTURAL DIFFERENCES IN SECURE DYNAMIC UPDATE   DNS secure updates follow the guidelines in RFC 2078. This specifies the use of the Generic Security Service Application Program Interface (GSS-API). This API enables using security tokens to establish the security context of the update. Additionally, this API, as it is implemented in Windows 2000, uses Kerberos for authentication (as does almost everything else in Windows 2000). You have already looked at the process of dynamic update in this chapter. The basic functions remain the same in secure dynamic update. You still query for SOA, request an update, and receive a response assuring you that the update succeeded. Essentially, the same process occurs with secure updates. The client queries for SOA, receives a response, and then attempts an update. The update is refused, as shown in Figure 9.12.

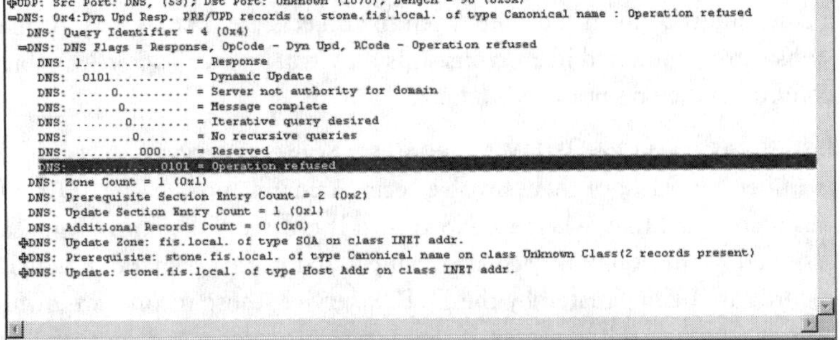

Figure 9.12
A refused dynamic update request.

The client then queries the DNS server to establish a secret key. To do this, you use two new resource record types called TKEY and TSIG. These two record types enable you to provide a security context and are documented in IETF drafts "Secret Key Establishment for DNS (TKEY RR)" and "Secret Key Transaction Signatures for DNS (TSIG)." The TKEY record is used to transfer security tokens and establish secret keys between the DNS client and server. The TSIG record, on the other hand, enables you to transfer and verify messages between the client and server. In Figure 9.13, frame 121 enables you to see the beginning of the secure transmission.

Figure 9.13
A DNS TKEY query.

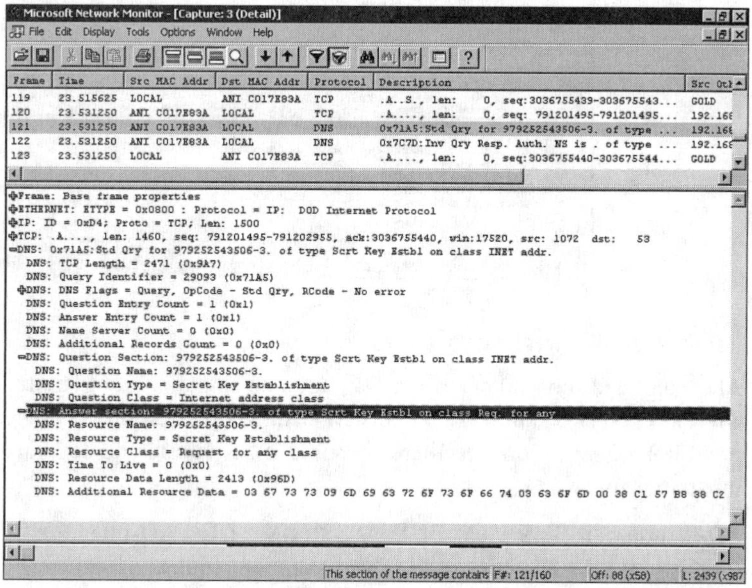

In Figure 9.14, frame 129 shows the second update request along with the additional records section that contains the information necessary to authenticate the update request. Frame 130 is the response from the DNS server showing that the update succeeded.

There is no doubt that configuring zones to require secure updates creates a certain amount of network overhead. Therefore, you must carefully consider how much security you need. Completely accessible networks and secure networks are mutually exclusive concepts. As you move toward one, you move away from the other. It must be clear here, however, that the opportunity for mischief exists. Tools are available to perform dynamic updates, and surely more will become available. When you consider that your AD uses DNS to resolve services and clients, rogue or modified records present a very real denial of service threat. The more you use the AD, the more obvious this will become, because a loss of AD functionality is more often than not traced to a DNS problem. SRV records in particular—because they point to the location of critical services—must be absolutely correct; otherwise, the AD will fail.

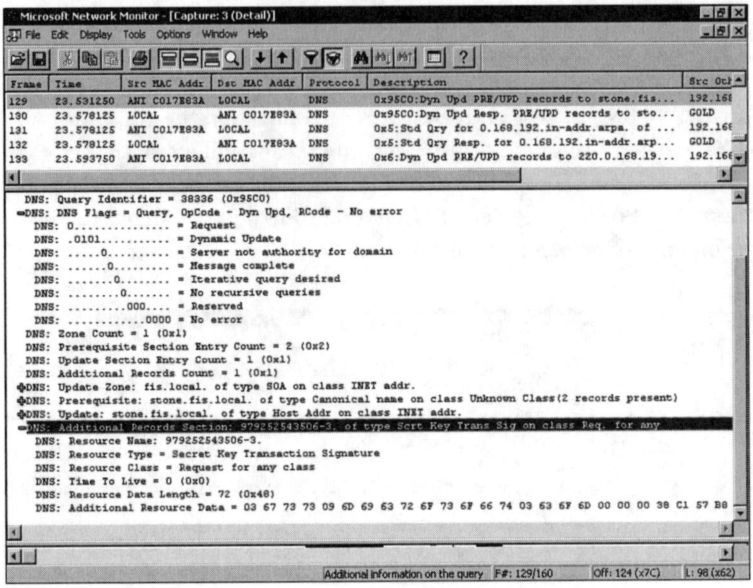

Figure 9.14
An update request
with TKEY and TSIG.

ISSUES WITH AD-INTEGRATED ZONES

AD-integrated zones offer many advantages: no single point of failure, the ability to update anywhere, replacement of zone transfers with AD replication, and security on a per-record basis, if necessary. However, there are some issues you should be aware of when using AD-integrated zones.

AD-INTEGRATED DNS MUST BE INSTALLED ON A DC   AD-integrated zones must be installed on a domain controller. This zone type requires a local instance of the AD database, and the only place that occurs is on an AD DC. If you demote the DC that is running DNS to a member server, all AD-integrated zone information on that server is lost.

> **Tip**
>
> If you are planning, for whatever reason, to demote an AD domain controller that is also a DNS server, don't forget to convert the AD-integrated zones to either standard primary or secondary zones. If you do not, local copies of the zones will be lost. These text copies can be useful for backup or to recreate the zone.

DELETING AD-INTEGRATED ZONES   The other major issue to be aware of surrounds deleting zones from a DNS server. With standard zones, deleting a zone (unless it is the primary with secondaries) is a local issue. Either you want the zone on the local server or you don't. No repercussions occur to other instances of that zone on other DNS servers unless they are secondary to it. AD-integrated zones, however, are really just a certain type of AD object, and when an AD object is deleted, the fact that it was deleted is propagated across the network to all other instances of DCs in the domain.

> If you simply select an AD DNS zone and delete it, it deletes *all* instances of that zone throughout the domain. The only way to get it back is through an authoritative Active Directory restore.

→ **See** "Authoritative Restore," **p. 490**

This has ramifications for deleting an AD zone. If you click an AD-integrated zone in the AD and choose Delete without careful planning, you run the risk of deleting the zone from the AD database and from all the other DNS servers hosting that zone.

To successfully remove an AD zone from a DNS server without deleting it from the AD, carefully complete the following steps:

CH
9

1. Open the DNS MMC Snap-in and select your server.

2. Right-click the server and choose the Advanced tab from the Properties page. As shown in Figure 9.15, set the Load Zone Data on Startup option to From Registry and click OK. If you leave it at From Active Directory and Registry (the default), this will not work.

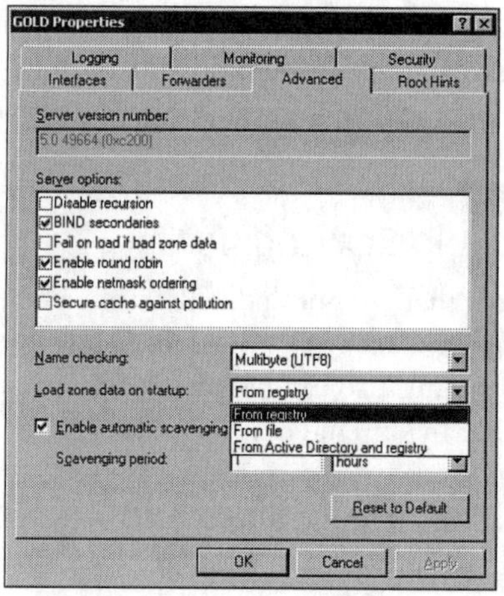

Figure 9.15
DNS startup parameters.

3. Next, select the AD-integrated zone you want to delete, right-click the zone, and select Delete. This causes a message box to pop up, asking if you're sure you want to delete the zone from the server.

4. The next action to take (and the most critical) is the resulting message box shown Figure 9.16. If you click Yes here, your zone will be removed from both the AD and the current DNS server. This will cause a permanent and complete loss of access to the information in this zone. To keep the information in the AD and on other DNS servers but remove the zone from this DNS server alone, click No. As the message box clearly states, this will delete the zone from this server but leave the zone data in the Active Directory.

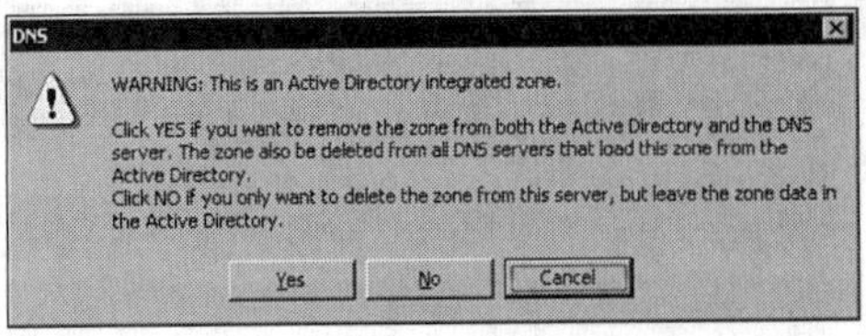

Figure 9.16
AD zone removal
warning.

If you have done all this correctly, the zone should disappear from this server but remain available on other DNS servers. The last thing to check is the NS records in all other instances of this zone on other DNS servers in the domain. This does not remove the NS record in the DNS zone on other DNS servers; those records must be removed manually.

DNS RECORD AGING AND SCAVENGING

Every database must have a mechanism in place to check the validity and sanity of the dataset. The DNS database is no exception. Windows 2000 DNS provides aging and scavenging of records for both AD and standard zones.

Inevitably, some computers will be removed from the network without the opportunity to delete their DNS records. This will, over time, lead to "stale" records in the DNS database. *Aging* enables you and the DNS service to track the time interval since a DNS record has been updated. *Scavenging* is the process of deleting stale records that have been identified by the aging process.

FEATURES OF DNS RECORD AGING AND SCAVENGING

Aging and scavenging enable records that are not updated within a configured interval to be deleted by the DNS server. Scavenging is turned off by default but can be turned on on a per-server and per-zone basis. Scavenging also can be initiated based on elapsed time or manually through the DNS MMC or by dnscmd.exe.

DNS RECORD AGING AND SCAVENGING PARAMETERS AND ARCHITECTURE

To properly configure aging and scavenging, you need to consider several parameters that must be set and understand the interplay of these parameters. You also must understand that although this is a powerful feature for avoiding stale or incorrect records in the AD, misusing it can cause good records to be deleted because they were scavenged too aggressively. For example, if your aging and scavenging parameters were set to one day and a client using DHCP was set to update its adapter only every eight days (the default), a record could be deleted before it had a chance to be updated.

TIMESTAMPS

Records are assigned a timestamp by the DNS service when they are created or updated. In a zone enabled for aging and scavenging, this timestamp is used to keep track of the age of a record and make decisions on whether it counts as a stale record, thus making it a candidate for deletion.

THE NO-REFRESH INTERVAL

The first parameter you will look at is the no-refresh parameter. This is a period of time (by default, seven days) during which a record will accept updates but not refreshes. The difference between an update and a refresh is that an *update* represents a change between the updated data and the data currently on the DNS server. A *refresh*, on the other hand, is simply a dynamic update attempt fired by a configured interval or event in which the data has not changed. During the no-refresh interval, refreshes to records in the zone are not allowed, as shown in frame 15 of Figure 9.17. In this netmon.exe packet capture, this record's information has not been changed but a refresh event has been fired by executing the ipconfig /registerdns command.

Figure 9.17
A refused DNS update request.

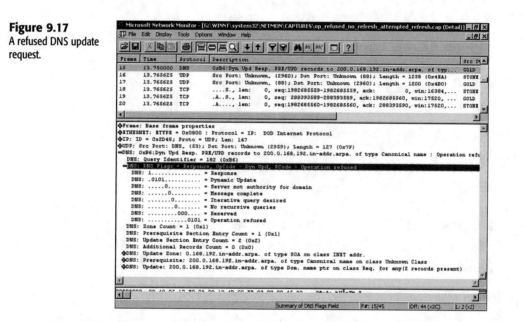

THE REFRESH INTERVAL

The next parameter is the refresh interval parameter. During this time period, which starts at the end of the no-refresh interval, refreshes are accepted for the DNS record. At the end of the refresh interval, if a record has not been updated or refreshed, it is eligible for scavenging.

THE SCAVENGING PERIOD

The scavenging period parameter is how often the DNS server automatically performs scavenging. You also can initiate scavenging manually using the dnscmd.exe or in the DNS MMC Snap-in if View, Advanced is turned on.

VIEWING DNS RECORD AGING AND SCAVENGING OPTIONS IN THE MMC

You can view the timestamp on a particular record by opening the DNS MMC Snap-in and choosing View, Advanced on the MMC menu. After you have turned on Advanced view, you can view when scavenging becomes available for a zone by right-clicking the zone, choosing Properties, and clicking the Aging button. You also can view the update/refresh timestamp for a record by turning on Advanced view, right-clicking the record, and choosing Properties (see Figure 9.18).

Figure 9.18
A DNS timestamp.

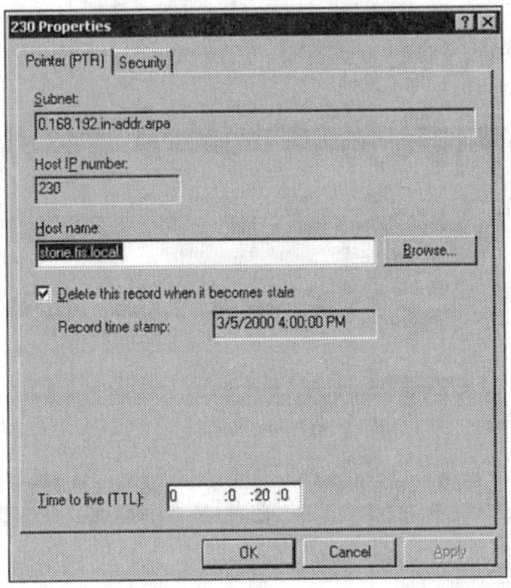

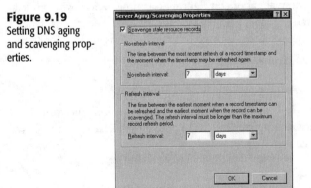

CONFIGURING DNS RECORD AGING AND SCAVENGING OPTIONS

To configure scavenging for all zones on a DNS server, you can right-click the server name in the DNS MMC Snap-in and select Set Aging/Scavenging for all zones.

This displays the Server Aging/Scavenging Properties page shown in Figure 9.19. To enable scavenging for all zones on the server, check the Scavenge Stale Resource Records check box and either accept the defaults or set new values for the no-refresh interval and the refresh interval; then, click OK.

Figure 9.19
Setting DNS aging and scavenging properties.

The zones on the server then inherit the parameters set here.

If any of your zones are AD-integrated zones, you will see the confirmation box shown in Figure 9.20. If you choose Apply These Settings to the Existing Active-Directory Integrated Zones, the scavenging information will be set on all new AD-integrated zones created on this server.

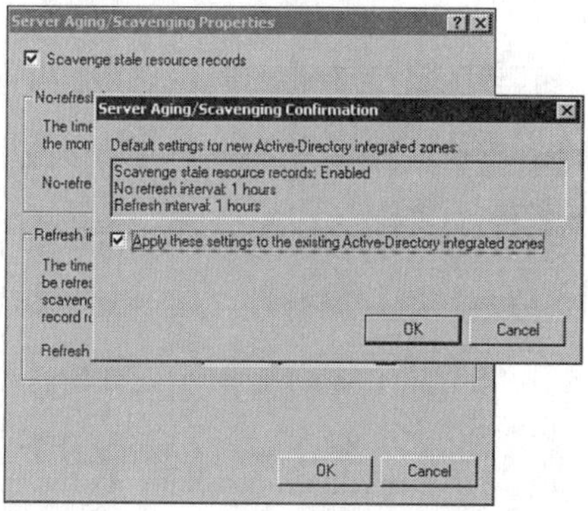

Figure 9.20
Aging and scavenging on AD zones.

To set scavenging on a per-zone basis, right-click the zone, click Properties, and then click the Aging button. This opens the Zone Aging/Scavenging Properties page shown in Figure 9.21. These parameters are the same as the ones you saw in Figure 9.19, but they will impact only the current zone when you click OK.

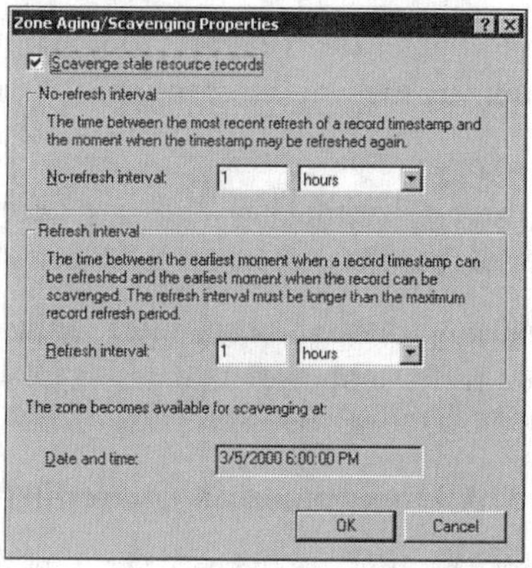

Figure 9.21
Setting aging/scavenging properties on a per-zone basis.

The last parameter to set is the scavenging period. This is set by right-clicking the server in the DNS MMC Snap-in, selecting Properties, and then clicking the Advanced tab (see Figure 9.22). This parameter sets how often the DNS server automatically performs scavenging. This parameter is also propagated throughout the domain for DNS servers in this domain.

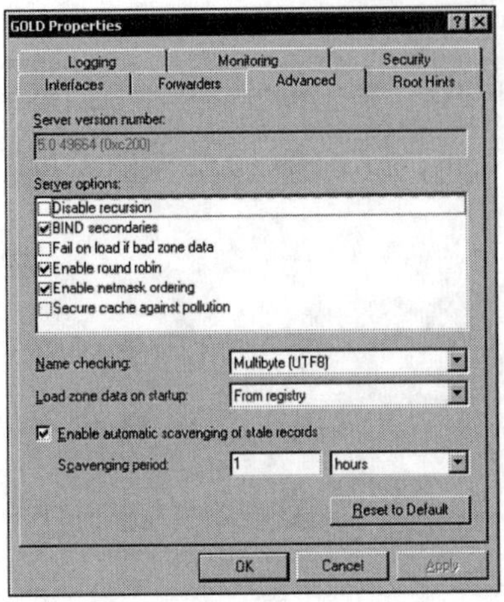

Figure 9.22
Enabling scavenging.

SUMMARY

The only absolute prerequisite for a DNS installation to support the Active Directory is that it support SRV records. However, most users will find it difficult to imagine going back to manually managing DNS zone files after using dynamic updates. Dynamic DNS makes most of the manual support of zones unnecessary, and AD DNS goes one level higher with advanced replication and security on zones and records.

Care must be taken, however, when removing AD zones because removing them improperly can cause the zones to be removed from all Active Directory DNS servers.

Windows 2000 DNS is dynamic. This enables the computer to update its A and PTR records automatically rather than requiring manual intervention.

DNS zones stored in the Active Directory are protected by the same security infrastructure that protects every AD object. Any process that touches an Active Directory DNS record or zone must first be compared to the ACL for the object.

Active Directory DNS zones are replicated through normal AD replication mechanisms, which eliminate redundant replication traffic and cause updates to DNS zones to be replicated throughout the domain quickly.

DHCP can be configured to update DNS zones on behalf of down-level clients.

Windows 2000 DNS can be configured to time out old records in AD-integrated zones. This enables stale records to be removed in a timely fashion.

TROUBLESHOOTING

DNS UPDATES TO A SECURE ZONE ARE FAILING

Your DNS zones are set to allow secure updates, but updates are not occurring in the zone.

Because the default authentication mechanism for Windows 2000 is Kerberos, the TKEY and TSIG records will use Kerberos by default to authenticate between the DNS client and server. If more than a 5-minute time delta occurs between the Kerberos Key Distribution Center (KDC) and the client, the KDC considers the packets to be part of a replay attack and denies authentication, causing your updates to fail. More importantly, however, if the time is misconfigured between the client and the DC, you will have bigger problems— namely, you will not be able to log on. Usually, this is not a problem because in a Windows 2000 domain clients try to synchronize their clocks with that of their domain controller.

CAN'T FIND DNS ZONES IN ACTIVE DIRECTORY USERS AND COMPUTERS

When you open ADUC you do not see any containers that hold the Active Directory DNS information.

Don't forget to turn on the View, Advanced features in the ADUC MMC Snap-in. This causes the System container, which holds the MicrosoftDNS container, to become visible.

> **Tip**
>
> The DNS troubleshooting tool of last resort is Network Monitor. Because almost everything DNS does is in clear text, captures of DNS conversations are usually easy to read.

CAN'T DYNAMICALLY UPDATE ANY DNS ZONES

When you try to update DNS zones set to allow updates, they are not updated.

This could be due to several things. Make sure the client is pointed to the correct server. One way to test this is to make sure the computer on which the DNS server is running is pointed to itself for DNS; then use `ipconfig /registerDNS` to update the A and PTR records. Make sure you are updating the screen inside the DNS console with F5. Use `ipconfig /all` to view the DNS domain name configured for the client. This should match the DNS zone you are trying to update.

CHAPTER 10

TROUBLESHOOTING DNS

In this chapter

DNS TROUBLESHOOTING TOOLS

It would be great to pretend otherwise, but sometimes bad things happen to good DNS servers. Usually, the difficulty is in setting up the DNS, but occasionally DNS servers just need a checkup. It must be very clear that the best troubleshooting tool for virtually anything is a knowledgeable administrator who deeply understands the architecture of the protocols and tools he or she is using.

Years ago, when BIND DNS was the only choice and the DNS management tool was VI (the standard UNIX text editor), most problems came from misconfigured boot and zone files. With the DNS MMC Snap-in and graphical management, a lot of the opportunity for error has been removed. The most common errors for DNS on Windows 2000 center around SRV records that don't get registered, clients that are not pointing to the proper DNS, and simple communication failures between DNS servers.

DNS MONITORING

The first and simplest thing to do appears in Figure 10.1. By right-clicking the server name in the DNS MMC Snap-in and selecting the Monitoring tab, you can either test a simple query and recursive query against the selected DNS server or schedule queries and have them execute automatically.

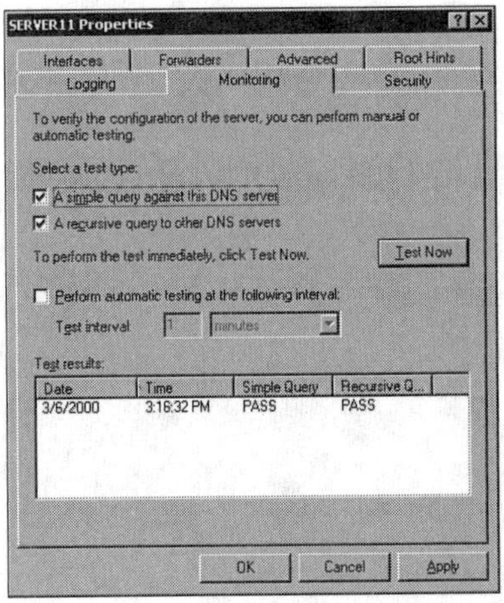

Figure 10.1
Use the Monitoring tab of the SERVER 11 Properties box to test the DNS.

If you schedule the tests, the results pane at the bottom of the property page always shows the results of the last test. You can modify the time interval with the combo box. This is a good way to check the health of the DNS server at a glance. If you stop and start the DNS service and immediately open the DNS MMC Snap-in, you might see an exclamation point next to the server icon and a message saying the tests failed. Simply open the properties page and manually run the test to ensure that the server is indeed working.

DNS LOGGING

Another good troubleshooting tool available in the DNS MMC Snap-in appears in Figure 10.2. This is the Logging tab from the server Properties page. By default, logging is turned off. You can turn on some or all of these options and leave them on for an extended period of time. However, be aware that, depending on how many options you choose to log, the logfile can grow quite large very quickly. In addition, with any logging there is overhead associated with tracking the information. By default, this file is `\winnt\system32\dns\dns.log`.

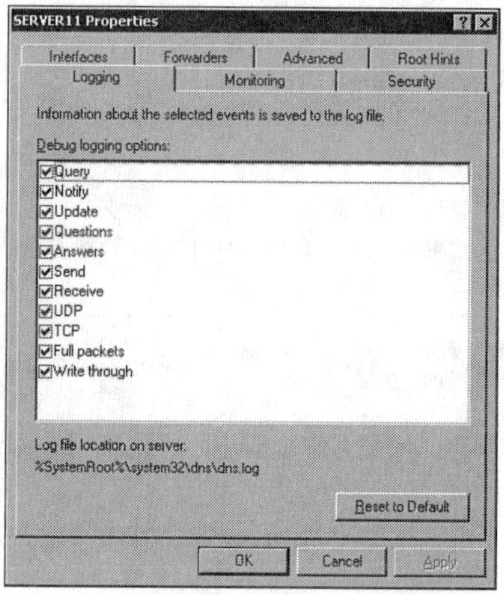

Figure 10.2
Use the Logging tab to choose which options to log during testing.

Listing 10.1 shows the first few lines of a DNS server with all the options turned on. Judicious use of this option makes this a marvelous tool for extended troubleshooting of transient problems. You should find that simply turning this on for an hour and looking through the output is very instructional. Also, along with using the Find command, a good editor enables you to move from one problem area to another. Many times, in these types of scenarios, the problems have a tendency to be repetitive, and seeing the same error repeatedly is often a good first step toward resolving the error.

The first part of the file is information about how long the Windows 2000 server has been up and how long the DNS service has been running. The next section is a key to the output that follows. Again, these files can grow very quickly—keep in mind that Listing 10.1 is only one receive/response pair from one lookup.

LISTING 10.1 DNS TEST LOG

```
DNS Server boot at 3/6/2000.
    610302 seconds since system boot.
Message logging key:
    Field #  Information        Values
    -------  -----------        ------
      1      Send\Receive
      2      Protocol           T == TCP message
                                empty == UDP
```

LISTING 10.1   CONTINUED

```
      3         Remote IP
      4         Xid (hex)
      5         Query\Response      R == Response
                                    empty == Query
      6         Opcode              Q == Standard Query
                                    N == Notify
                                    U == Update
                                    ? == Unknown
      7         [Flags (hex)
      8         Flags (char codes)  A == Authoritative Answer
                                    T == Truncated Response
                                    D == Recursion Desired
                                    R == Recursion Available
      9         ResponseCode]
     10         Question Name

Rcv   192.168.2.59    6000    Q [0000        NOERROR] (3)fis(5)local(0)
UDP question info at 0047158C
  Socket = 456
  Remote addr 192.168.2.59, port 1063
  Time Query=610543, Queued=0, Expire=0
  Buf length = 0x0200 (512)
  Msg length = 0x001b (27)
  Message:
    XID        0x6000
    Flags      0x0000
        QR          0 (question)
        OPCODE      0 (QUERY)
        AA          0
        TC          0
        RD          0
        RA          0
        Z           0
        RCODE       0 (NOERROR)
    QCOUNT    0x1
    ACOUNT    0x0
    NSCOUNT   0x0
    ARCOUNT   0x0
    Offset = 0x000c, RR count = 0
    Name       "(3)fis(5)local(0)"
      QTYPE    SOA (6)
      QCLASS   1
    ANSWER SECTION:
    AUTHORITY SECTION:
    ADDITIONAL SECTION:
```

The logging service logs both forward and reverse lookups, as well as log events such as scavenging.

netdiag.exe

A new network troubleshooting tool, called netdiag.exe, is part of the Support Tools that ship with Windows 2000. This tool does some things that were otherwise difficult to do, such as checking the network card and network bindings, and listing hotfixes that have been applied. Its key facility, however, comes from the fact that with one command you can check a score of parameters and services that an experienced network troubleshooter would investigate, and still have all the information displayed onscreen in a very organized and readable format. Listing 10.2 is the output from a specific DNS test using `netdiag`. `netdiag.exe` entered without any parameters checks virtually everything about the network infrastructure on the local computer and its relationship to the network.

Be aware that some checks involve timeouts, so if you are using this tool to find a problem, `netdiag` might appear to hang. Be patient; let the tests timeout. Then, `netdiag` will return good information, including the tests that failed.

LISTING 10.2   `netdiag.exe` OUTPUT

```
C:\>netdiag /debug /test:dns
    Gathering IPX configuration information.
    Opening \Device\NwlnkIpx failed
    Querying status of the Netcard drivers... Passed
    Testing Domain membership... Passed
    Gathering NetBT configuration information.
    Testing DNS
The DNS registration for server12.fis.local is correct on all DNS servers

    Tests complete.

    Computer Name: SERVER12
    DNS Host Name: server12.fis.local
    DNS Domain Name: fis.local
    System info : Windows 2000 Server (Build 2195)
    Processor : x86 Family 6 Model 5 Stepping 2, GenuineIntel
    Hotfixes :
        Installed?      Name
            Yes         Q147222

Netcard queries test . . . . . . . : Passed

    Information of Netcard drivers:

    - - - - - - - - - - - - - - - - - - - - - - - - - - - - - - - - - - - - - -
    Description: 3Com EtherLink XL 10/100 PCI TX NIC (3C905B-TX)
    Device: \DEVICE\{B16CC3ED-9033-49BA-9F35-E53CD101FBDD}

    Media State:                    Connected
    Device State:                   Connected
    Connect Time:                   3 days, 23:11:04
    Media Speed:                    10Mbps
    Packets Sent:                   109694
    Bytes Sent (Optional):          0
    Packets Received:               308009
    Directed Pkts Recd (Optional):  109848
    Bytes Received (Optional):      0
    Directed Bytes Recd (Optional): 0
```

CH

10

LISTING 10.2 CONTINUED

```
- - - - - - - - - - - - - - - - - - - - - - - - - - - - - - - - - - - - - - - - - -
        [PASS] - At least one netcard is in the 'Connected' state.

Per interface results:

        Adapter : Local Area Connection
Adapter ID . . . . . . . . : {B16CC3ED-9033-49BA-9F35-E53CD101FBDD}

        Netcard queries test . . . : Passed

Global results:


Domain membership test . . . . . . : Passed
    Machine is a . . . . . . . . . : Member Server
    NetBIOS domain name. . . . . . : FIS
    DNS domain name. . . . . . . . : fis.local
    DNS forest name. . . . . . . . : fis.local
    Domain Guid. . . . . . . . . . : {519543BB-2AF7-4B71-9855-2D4C25E21C5D}
    Domain Sid . . . . . . . . . . : S-1-5-21-2517583914-3308934124-110108733
    Logon User . . . . . . . . . . : administrator
    Logon Domain . . . . . . . . . : FIS
    Logon Server . . . . . . . . . : \\SERVER11


NetBT transports test. . . . . . . : Passed
    List of NetBT transports currently configured:
        NetBT_TCPIP_{B16CC3ED-9033-49BA-9F35-E53CD101FBDD}
    1 NetBT transport currently configured.

DNS test . . . . . . . . . . . . . : Passed
        Interface {B16CC3ED-9033-49BA-9F35-E53CD101FBDD}
        DNS Domain: fis.local
        DNS Servers: 192.168.2.59
        IP Address: 192.168.2.62
        Expected registration with PDN (primary DNS domain name):
            Hostname: server12.fis.local.
            Authoritative zone: fis.local.
            Primary DNS server: server11.fis.local 192.168.2.200
            Authoritative NS:192.168.2.200
        Verify DNS registration:
        Name: server12.fis.local
        Expected IP: 192.168.2.62
            Server 192.168.2.200: NO_ERROR
    The DNS registration for server12.fis.local is correct on all DNS servers

The command completed successfully
```

Although netdiag can be used in a very focused manner, as in Listing 10.2, you can also use the /q parameter, which only outputs errors. Listing 10.3 shows the output from a netdiag /q on a machine in which the DNS address was misconfigured on the client.

LISTING 10.3   /q ERROR OUTPUT

```
C:\>netdiag /q
. . . . . . . . . . . . . . . . . . . . . . . . . . . . . . . . . .

        Computer Name: JMHSERVER
        DNS Hostname: jmhserver.fis.local
        System info : Windows 2000 Server (Build 2195)
        Processor : x86 Family 6 Model 5 Stepping 2, GenuineIntel
        List of installed hotfixes :
            Q147222


Per interface results:

        Adapter : Local Area Connection

            Hostname. . . . . . . . . : jmhserver
            IP Address . . . . . . . . : 192.168.2.252
            Subnet Mask. . . . . . . . : 255.255.255.0
            Default Gateway. . . . . . : 192.168.2.201
            DNS Servers. . . . . . . . : 192.168.2.253


            WINS service test. . . . . : Skipped
Global results:
DNS test . . . . . . . . . . . . . : Failed
            [WARNING] Cannot find a primary authoritative DNS server for the name
                'jmhserver.fis.local.'. [ERROR_TIMEOUT]
                The name 'jmhserver.fis.local.' may not be registered in DNS.
        [WARNING] The DNS entries for this DC cannot be verified right now on DNS
    server 192.168.2.253, ERROR_TIMEOUT.
        [FATAL] No DNS servers have the DNS records for this DC registered.
IP Security test . . . . . . . . . : Passed
The command completed successfully
```

When used with the /debug switch, netdiag can also be verbose, generating several pages of information. In many instances, it generates 25 times as much information as is generated without the /debug parameter.

The reason the output in Listing 10.2 is relatively concise even though it uses /debug is because of the /test:dns parameter. This directs netdiag to test only the directed section. The tests available can be seen by using netdiag /q. You can also use the /skip: parameter to skip a test.

REDIRECTING netdaig.exe OUTPUT

As with any command-line tool, you can redirect the output with the > symbol to a text file. You also can pipe the information through any number of filters. The following are some examples:

- netdiag | more—This enables you to view the output from netdiag one page at a time.

- netdiag | <command>—If you have any third-party tools on your workstation, such as Perl, you can easily write scripts into which you can pipe your commands to perform very specific searches. This also can be done with WSH scripts.

- netdiag | findstr—My favorite on Windows 2000 is findstr. This command is the functional equivalent of the grep command in UNIX, which enables very precise searching of a text stream. findstr has several parameters and can be used on files or as a filter through which you can pipe the output from commands. findstr /I causes the search to be case insensitive. Listing 10.4 shows how to find any configuration parameters that contain the word dns.

LISTING 10.4   FINDING CONFIGURATION PARAMETERS

```
C:\>netdiag | findstr /I  dns

    DNS Hostname: jmhserver.fis.local
        DNS Servers. . . . . . . . : 192.168.2.252
        DNS test . . . . . . . . . . . . . : Passed
    PASS - All the DNS entries for DC are registered on DNS
    ↪server '192.168.2.252'.
```

findstr is not exactly intuitive unless you have used grep extensively. If not, the following list should help acclimate you to the more commonly used parameters to findstr:

- /B—Matches the pattern if it's at the beginning of a line.

- /E—Matches the pattern if it's at the end of a line.

- /X—Prints lines that match exactly.

- /V—Prints only lines that do not contain a match.

This is not an exhaustive list, but findstr /? generates a concise list of parameters, and the online help that automatically installs with Windows 2000 has a good section on findstr.

Note   If you are familiar with grep, you will find that virtually every parameter is identical to grep.

ipconfig.exe

ipconfig.exe does exactly what it sounds like. It displays the Internet Protocol configuration of the local computer. Listing 10.5 shows the output of the ipconfig command.

LISTING 10.5   OUTPUT OF ipconfig.exe

```
C:\>ipconfig
Windows 2000 IP Configuration
Ethernet adapter Local Area Connection:
        Connection-specific DNS Suffix  . :
```

LISTING 10.5   CONTINUED

```
      IP Address. . . . . . . . . . . . : 192.168.2.252
      Subnet Mask . . . . . . . . . . . : 255.255.255.0
      Default Gateway . . . . . . . . . : 192.168.2.201
```

By itself, ipconfig lists the bare essentials. ipconfig /all, however, provides a good overview of the IP configuration for the local machine. It is not as verbose as netdiag, nor does it run tests. It simply shows how the IP protocol stack is configured. Because DNS is an integral part of TCP/IP, simply looking at the configuration often highlights any networking problems the machine is having. Listing 10.6 shows the output from the ipconfig /all command.

LISTING 10.6   OUTPUT OF ipconfig /all

```
C:\>ipconfig /all
Windows 2000 IP Configuration
      Hostname . . . . . . . . . . . . : jmhserver
      Primary DNS Suffix . . . . . . . : fis.local
      Node Type . . . . . . . . . . . : Broadcast
      IP Routing Enabled. . . . . . . . : No
      WINS Proxy Enabled. . . . . . . . : No
      DNS Suffix Search List. . . . . . : fis.local
Ethernet adapter Local Area Connection:
      Connection-specific DNS Suffix  . :
      Description . . . . . . . . . . . : 3Com EtherLink XL
➥10/100 PCI TX NIC (3C905B-TX)
      Physical Address. . . . . . . . . : 00-10-5A-A5-AE-AC
      DHCP Enabled. . . . . . . . . . . : No
      IP Address. . . . . . . . . . . . : 192.168.2.252
      Subnet Mask . . . . . . . . . . . : 255.255.255.0
      Default Gateway . . . . . . . . . : 192.168.2.201
      DNS Servers . . . . . . . . . . . : 192.168.2.252
```

The ipconfig.exe command has several new parameters for Windows 2000. Some of these have to do with Dynamic Update, whereas others enable more fine-tuned control of the client name resolution environment. Table 10.1 lists some of the ipconfig parameters and a brief description of their effects.

TABLE 10.1   PARAMETERS FOR THE ipconfig COMMAND

Parameter	Effect
/all	Shows all information about adapters on the computer.
/release	If a DHCP-enabled adapter exists, this causes it to release its DHCP address lease.
/renew	If a DHCP-enabled adapter exists, this causes it to attempt to obtain a DHCP address from the DHCP server.
/flushdns	This purges the DNS resolver cache. It's similar in effect to nbtstat -R for the NetBIOS name cache.

CH

10

TABLE 10.1 CONTINUED

Parameter	Effect
Registerdns	Very important parameter for troubleshooting Dynamic DNS. This parameter causes the client to attempt a Dynamic Update to the Dynamic DNS and attempts to renew a lease with the DHCP server if it is a DHCP adapter.
Displaydns	This dumps the contents of the resolver cache to the screen. This enables you to see what is in memory from a combination of the hosts file and DNS. Very often, it's used in conjunction with /flushdns and /registerdns to troubleshoot Dynamic DNS.

ipconfig /flushdns is useful if you have old or bad records in the client resolver cache. In a distributed database such as DNS, out-of-date information is an occasional but unfortunate reality. ipconfig /displaydns can then be used after /flushdns to show any new records in the cache. An important note to remember here is that records in the hosts file are read and used before the DNS is contacted. Therefore, if you have bad records in the hosts file, your client will never see the good records in the DNS zone. Listing 10.7 shows the output from the ipconfig /displaydns command.

Tip

To completely flush all cached name resolution information, use the ipconfig /flushdns command with nbtstat -R. This flushes all cached DNS records as well as all cached NetBIOS names to IP address mappings.

LISTING 10.7 OUTPUT FROM ipconfig /displaydns

```
C:\WINNT\system32\drivers\etc>ipconfig /displaydns

Windows 2000 IP Configuration

    localhost.
    ----------------------------------------------------
        Record Name . . . . . : localhost
        Record Type . . . . . : 1
        Time To Live  . . . . : 31283730
        Data Length . . . . . : 4
        Section . . . . . . . : Answer
        A (Host) Record . . . :
                        127.0.0.1


    gold.
    ----------------------------------------------------
        Record Name . . . . . : gold.fis.local
        Record Type . . . . . : 1
        Time To Live  . . . . : 3588
        Data Length . . . . . : 4
        Section . . . . . . . : Answer
        A (Host) Record . . . :
                        192.168.0.5
```

LISTING 10.7   CONTINUED

```
1.0.0.127.in-addr.arpa.
       - - - - - - - - - - - - - - - - - - - - - - - - - - - - - - - - - - - - - - - - - - - -
       Record Name . . . . . : 1.0.0.127.in-addr.arpa
       Record Type . . . . . : 12
       Time To Live  . . . . : 31283730
       Data Length . . . . . : 4
       Section . . . . . . . : Answer
       PTR Record  . . . . . :
                        localhost


   silver.
       - - - - - - - - - - - - - - - - - - - - - - - - - - - - - - - - - - - - - - - - - - - -
       Record Name . . . . . : silver.fis.local
       Record Type . . . . . : 1
       Time To Live  . . . . : 3591
       Data Length . . . . . : 4
       Section . . . . . . . : Answer
       A (Host) Record . . . :
                                             192.168.1.4
```

This enables you to view what the resolver sees rather than having to guess. Matching the record names with the IP addresses and looking for bad or out-of-date information can many times resolve any name resolution problems you have.

GENERAL IP TROUBLESHOOTING TOOLS

Although not specifically DNS tools, `ping.exe` and `tracert.exe` are invaluable tools for troubleshooting IP and name resolution.

ping.exe

`ping` simply tests whether you can get an ICMP echo request and echo reply from one host to another, as shown in Listing 10.8.

LISTING 10.8   A GENERAL ping REPLY

```
C:\>ping gold.fis.local

Pinging gold.fis.local [192.168.0.5] with 32 bytes of data:

Reply from 192.168.0.5: bytes=32 time<10ms TTL=128
Reply from 192.168.0.5: bytes=32 time<10ms TTL=128
Reply from 192.168.0.5: bytes=32 time<10ms TTL=128
Reply from 192.168.0.5: bytes=32 time<10ms TTL=128

Ping statistics for 192.168.0.5:
    Packets: Sent = 4, Received = 4, Lost = 0 (0% loss),
Approximate round-trip times in milliseconds:
        Minimum = 0ms, Maximum =  0ms, Average =  0ms
```

CH
10

Generally, output from the ping command is viewed simplistically. If you get a reply, all is well; if not, it's broken. The time information in the output, however, is useful to see how fast and reliable the connection is. If the time varies widely from one request/reply pair to another, it's likely that you are using a very clogged network.

If you can ping the target by IP address but not by name, you have a name resolution problem. If you cannot ping the target by IP address, you have an addressing or routing issue. If you cannot ping the DNS server by IP address, you need to fix the addressing and routing between the client and the DNS server.

> **Tip**
>
> One of the most important things to remember about routing is that the packet must have a path from the source to the target and a path from the target back to the source. In other words, just because the routing is configured properly on the local end doesn't mean you don't have a routing problem.

ping has several parameters that are useful for testing connectivity from point A to point B. Listing 10.9 shows the more commonly used parameters. A full list can be obtained by typing ping /?.

LISTING 10.9   ping PARAMETERS

```
-t              Ping the specified host until stopped.
  -a                Resolve addresses to hostnames.
  -w timeout             Timeout in milliseconds to wait for each reply.
```

The -t parameter is definitely my favorite. Normally, when I simply ping an IP address, it sends three echo requests and that is it. With -t, however, it pings forever. This can be extremely useful when troubleshooting environmental issues such as a loose cable or a downed router. Simply using -t and having someone watch the output while you wiggle cables, change routing tables, or bounce a router can be invaluable.

The -a parameter resolves the IP address you are pinging to a hostname, and -w can shorten or lengthen the timeout value you use when waiting for an ICMP echo reply. This can be useful on a busy network.

tracert.exe

Many times you cannot ping the target, but you are not sure where along all the possible paths the problem lies. tracert.exe is a great tool for finding how far the packets make it between two computers and for pinpointing the failure domain. tracert uses some of the features of the ICMP protocol to dump information about which path a packet takes on a particular trip.

Listing 10.10 shows the output from a tracert command. The -w 5 parameter tells it to wait 5 milliseconds before moving on to the next node, and -d tells it not to try to look up

router names as it passes them. Using these parameters can greatly decrease the time necessary to complete this command. `tracert <target>` without any parameters is a useful, but
somewhat leisurely, command. Because most of us who do this for a living drink way too
much coffee, we generally don't like waiting on slow troubleshooting commands. Besides,
usually when something is broken, you don't have a whole lot of extra time anyway.

LISTING 10.10   A GENERAL tracert OUTPUT

```
C:\>tracert -d -w 5 216.1.73.39

Tracing route to 216.1.73.39 over a maximum of 30 hops

  1   <10 ms   <10 ms   <10 ms   192.168.0.1
  2   140 ms      *      231 ms   38.195.129.110
  3   120 ms   110 ms   110 ms   206.41.128.157
  4   150 ms      *      150 ms   204.6.140.125
  5   151 ms   190 ms      *      38.1.3.13
  6   160 ms   171 ms      *      209.116.50.13
  7      *     150 ms   180 ms   165.117.59.49
  8   181 ms      *      160 ms   165.117.53.29
  9   170 ms   161 ms   160 ms   165.117.48.186
 10      *     251 ms      *      165.117.48.41
 11   250 ms      *      260 ms   165.117.48.133
 12   251 ms      *      250 ms   165.117.56.6
 13   261 ms      *      301 ms   206.181.23.98
 14   330 ms      *      291 ms   209.49.5.2
 15   260 ms      *         *     192.168.1.150
 16   271 ms      *      300 ms   216.1.73.1
 17   281 ms      *      280 ms   216.1.73.39

Trace complete.
```

Sometimes with `tracert`, you will experience hops on the route that are nothing but aster-
isks, yet the trace makes it past that router. Usually, this means the router simply does not
support all the features of ICMP or that the response simply did not make it back to the
source in a timely fashion.

Oddly enough, to get a full listing of the parameters for `tracert`, you do not type `ipconfig`
`/?`. If you do, `ipconfig` tries to `resolve` `/?` to a hostname and then send packets to it. Go
figure. To get a complete list, simply type `tracert`, as shown in Listing 10.11.

LISTING 10.11   USE tracert FOR A PARAMETER LIST

```
C:\>tracert
Usage: tracert [-d] [-h maximum_hops] [-j host-list] [-w timeout] target_name
Options:
    -d                 Do not resolve addresses to hostnames.
    -h maximum_hops    Maximum number of hops to search for target.
    -j host-list       Loose source route along host-list.
    -w timeout         Wait timeout milliseconds for each reply.
```

CH

10

The -d and -w parameters were explained previously. -h is used to set the maximum number of hops (router crossings) before stopping. The -j option, on the other hand, enables you to perform loose source routing, which means you can see the route from your source to a particular target and back. This functionality is detailed in Knowledge Base article #Q169206, available on the Microsoft Web site.

The fault domain is usually wherever the packets stop between your client and the target. Frankly, I use this tool many times to tell simply whether or not the network is broken in an area I have any control over. If I am using the Internet to get to a resource and I find with tracert that the packets stop five hops beyond my ISP, I can't do much to affect that. If your company has a WAN of sufficient size, this can also be useful to allow you to tell which routers or links are down or unavailable and whom to call and yell at.

NETWORK MONITOR

The best tool for serious network troubleshooting always is a packet analyzer. Because the personal version of Network Monitor ships with Windows 2000, you always have a copy of netmon.exe close at hand to help with troubleshooting. Virtually everything DNS puts on the wire is in clear text, so the information is always there for the informed administrator to read.

To install the free version of Network Monitor, follow these steps:

1. Open Control Panel.
2. Double-click Add/Remove Programs.
3. Click Add/Remove Windows Components.
4. Click the down arrow until you see Management and Monitoring Tools.
5. Select that line and click Details.
6. Select the check box next to Network Monitor Tools, and then click OK.
7. This returns you to the Windows Component Wizard. Click Next.
8. You might be prompted to provide the location of the i386 subdirectory on the CD. Click Open.
9. Click Finish.
10. Notice that Windows 2000 does not prompt you to reboot.

You have seen captures from Network Monitor all through the DNS chapters. To use Network Monitor on your own, after you have it installed, simply choose Start, Programs, Administrative Tools, Network Monitor. You might be prompted to choose which network to monitor. Unless you are expressly interested in capturing data from your dial-up, choose the network whose dial-up connection tag is set to false. If you choose the wrong one, you can always change your mind by using the Networks option from the Capture menu.

To start a capture session, simply press F10 or choose Start from the Capture menu. While it is capturing, the various panes give you feedback on how busy the network is and which addresses are active. After you stop the capture (by choosing Capture or Stop or by pressing F11), you can view the captured data by pressing F12 or choosing View Captured Data from the Capture menu. In addition, the toolbar has some buttons that initiate the same actions as the menu.

Choosing to view the data takes you to the Capture Summary page. You can drill down on a particular packet by double-clicking the packet entry.

If you want to know your network and gain a very deep level of understanding about TCP/IP, Network Monitor is your tool.

nslookup.exe

The experienced DNS administrator's tool of choice for testing a DNS will always be nslookup. It is not pretty or terribly easy to use. It is, however, extremely well documented because it has been in use for more than a decade. nslookup.exe is a command-line tool that can be used in interactive or noninteractive mode. Listing 10.12 shows nslookup being used in noninteractive mode. The syntax is simple: nslookup <hostname> <servername>.

CH

10

LISTING 10.12   nslookup IN NONINTERACTIVE MODE

```
O:\>nslookup silver.fis.local 192.168.0.5
Server:  gold.fis.local
Address:  192.168.0.5

Name:    silver.fis.local
Address:  192.168.1.4
```

The <servername> is optional. If it is omitted, nslookup simply uses the configured DNS server for that computer.

nslookup can also be used in interactive mode. Listing 10.13 shows a session using nslookup with some of the more common commands, such as ls.

LISTING 10.13   A BASIC nslookup EXAMPLE

```
C:\>nslookup
Default Server:  gold.fis.local
Address:  192.168.0.5

> stone.fis.local
Server:  gold.fis.local
Address:  192.168.0.5

Name:    stone.fis.local
Address:  192.168.0.230

> 192.168.1.4
Server:  gold.fis.local
Address:  192.168.0.5
```

LISTING 10.13 CONTINUED

```
Name:      silver.fis.local
Address:   192.168.1.4

> ls fis.local
[gold.fis.local]
 fis.local.                 A        192.168.0.5
 fis.local.                 A        192.168.1.4
 fis.local.                 NS       server = silver.fis.local
 fis.local.                 NS       server = gold.fis.local
 gc._msdcs                  A        192.168.0.5
 gold                       A        192.168.0.5
 silver                     A        192.168.1.4
 stone                      A        192.168.0.230
> exit

C:\>
```

In addition, you can use the server command inside nslookup to change the focus of the current session to a different DNS server. For example, the following starts with the focus on the local DNS server and then changes to another DNS server:

```
C:\>nslookup
Default Server:  jmhserver.fis.local
Address:   192.168.2.252

> server 192.168.2.200
Default Server:  [192.168.2.200]
Address:   192.168.2.200
```

One of the most common mistakes made with DNS is forgetting to create a PTR record in the reverse lookup zone for the DNS server. When nslookup starts, it performs a reverse lookup on the DNS server. If no PTR record exists for the DNS server, nslookup hangs for several seconds trying to resolve the DNS. To fix this, either explicitly create a PTR record for the DNS server or simply create a reverse lookup zone and turn on dynamic updates for the zone. Then, either reboot the server or execute the ipconfig /registerdns command to update both the A and PTR records.

Because this is where most common errors occur, I have provided the following example of how to list PTR records in a reverse lookup zone. It's important to include in-addr.arpa.

```
C:\>nslookup
Default Server:  gold.fis.local
Address:   192.168.0.5
>ls -t PTR 0.168.192.in-addr.arpa
>[gold.fis.local]
>125
5                              PTR    host = gold.fis.local
```

Even though nslookup is very terse, you can get help inside the console. Listing 10.14 shows the output of typing help at the nslookup prompt.

LISTING 10.14 nslookup OUTPUT

```
C:\>nslookup
Default Server:  gold.fis.local
Address:  192.168.0.5

> help
Commands:    (identifiers are shown in uppercase, [] means optional)
NAME            - print info about the host/domain NAME using default server
NAME1 NAME2     - as above, but use NAME2 as server
help or ?       - print info on common commands
set OPTION      - set an option
    all             - print options, current server and host
    [no]debug       - print debugging information
    [no]d2          - print exhaustive debugging information
    [no]defname     - append domain name to each query
    [no]recurse     - ask for recursive answer to query
    [no]search      - use domain search list
    [no]vc          - always use a virtual circuit
    domain=NAME     - set default domain name to NAME
    srchlist=N1[/N2/.../N6] - set domain to N1 and search list to N1,N2, etc.
    root=NAME       - set root server to NAME
    retry=X         - set number of retries to X
    timeout=X       - set initial time-out interval to X seconds
    type=X          - set query type (ex. A,ANY,CNAME,MX,NS,PTR,SOA,SRV)
    querytype=X     - same as type
    class=X         - set query class (ex. IN (Internet), ANY)
    [no]msxfr       - use MS fast zone transfer
    ixfrver=X       - current version to use in IXFR transfer request
server NAME     - set default server to NAME, using current default server
lserver NAME    - set default server to NAME, using initial server
finger [USER]   - finger the optional NAME at the current default host
root            - set current default server to the root
ls [opt] DOMAIN [> FILE] - list addresses in DOMAIN (optional: output to FILE)
    -a              - list canonical names and aliases
    -d              - list all records
    -t TYPE         - list records of the given type (e.g. A,CNAME,MX,NS,PTR etc.)
view FILE           - sort an 'ls' output file and view it with pg
exit                - exit the program
```

To increase how much information you get with each query, you can set the debug level and then execute the query, as shown in Listing 10.15.

LISTING 10.15 EXECUTING AN nslookup QUERY

```
C:\>nslookup
Default Server:  gold.fis.local
Address:  192.168.0.5

> set d2
> silver.fis.local
Server:  gold.fis.local
Address:  192.168.0.5

-----------
SendRequest(), len 44
```

CH

10

LISTING 10.15 CONTINUED

```
      HEADER:
          opcode = QUERY, id = 2, rcode = NOERROR
          header flags:  query, want recursion
          questions = 1,  answers = 0,  authority records = 0,  additional = 0

      QUESTIONS:
          silver.fis.local.fis.local, type = A, class = IN

- - - - - - - - - - - -
- - - - - - - - - - - -
Got answer (104 bytes):
      HEADER:
          opcode = QUERY, id = 2, rcode = NXDOMAIN
          header flags:  response, auth. answer, want recursion, recursion avail.
          questions = 1,  answers = 0,  authority records = 1,  additional = 0

      QUESTIONS:
          silver.fis.local.fis.local, type = A, class = IN
      AUTHORITY RECORDS:
      -> fis.local
          type = SOA, class = IN, dlen = 39
          ttl = 3600 (1 hour)
          primary name server = gold.fis.local
          responsible mail addr = admin.mcp.local
          serial  = 77
          refresh = 900 (15 mins)
          retry   = 600 (10 mins)
          expire  = 86400 (1 day)
          default TTL = 3600 (1 hour)

- - - - - - - - - - - -
- - - - - - - - - - - -
SendRequest(), len 34
      HEADER:
          opcode = QUERY, id = 3, rcode = NOERROR
          header flags:  query, want recursion
          questions = 1,  answers = 0,  authority records = 0,  additional = 0

      QUESTIONS:
          silver.fis.local, type = A, class = IN

- - - - - - - - - - - -
- - - - - - - - - - - -
Got answer (50 bytes):
      HEADER:
          opcode = QUERY, id = 3, rcode = NOERROR
          header flags:  response, auth. answer, want recursion, recursion avail.
          questions = 1,  answers = 1,  authority records = 0,  additional = 0

      QUESTIONS:
          silver.fis.local, type = A, class = IN
      ANSWERS:
      -> silver.fis.local
          type = A, class = IN, dlen = 4
```

LISTING 10.15   CONTINUED

```
        internet address = 192.168.1.4
        ttl = 3600 (1 hour)

-----------
Name:    silver.fis.local
Address:  192.168.1.4

> exit
```

nslookup is not an intuitive tool. It is, however, invaluable for troubleshooting DNS on any platform.

SUMMARY

Domain name services can be complex to install, maintain, and troubleshoot. It is a distributed database that can be updated, under some circumstances, virtually anywhere by virtually anyone. It is absolutely critical in maintaining the proper functioning of the Active Directory. Because the original RFCs were written in 1984, it has been around—in some form—longer than most tools in use today. It is well documented in the Online Books, in the Resource Kit, and freely on the Web. In addition, because it is RFC compliant, Microsoft's version of DNS interoperates very well with other implementations of DNS. The best thing to do to prepare for DNS is to understand IP and DNS architecture and how the Microsoft Windows 2000 Active Directory uses it.

Cн
10

TROUBLESHOOTING

NEW RECORDS AREN'T IN THE DNS ZONE

When you check your DNS zone, you find that clients are not updating their A and PTR records in the zones.

When you install DNS, by default, Allow Updates is turned off. Open the DNS console, right-click your zone, and choose Properties. Make sure Allow Updates is set to Yes. Then, either reboot the computer or use `ipconfig /registerdns` to cause the records to be updated. Don't forget to update the display in the DNS console by either pressing F5 or clicking the Refresh button on the toolbar.

RUNNING nslookup FAILS

When you go to a command prompt and attempt to use nslookup in interactive mode, the interface hangs.

Several issues can actually cause this: a misconfigured DNS address, no PTR record on the DNS server, or routing issues between the client and DNS.

The first and most obvious thing to check is that the client is configured with the proper address. Use `ipconfig /all` and look closely at the address for the DNS server.

If the DNS server does not have a reverse lookup zone configured, this can cause `nslookup` to hang. Make sure the `.in-addr.arpa` zone is configured for the DNS server and that it has a PTR record. If it does not, make sure Allow Updates is turned on and use the `ipconfig /registerdns` command to update the A and PTR records.

Check to see whether the client can `ping` the IP address of the DNS server. If not, check the subnet mask and default gateway of the client and use `netdiag /q` and check the default gateway tests or use `tracert` to see where communication fails from the client to the DNS server.

CHAPTER 11

DOMAINS, TREES, AND FORESTS

In this chapter

INTRODUCTION

Domains, trees, and forests are important concepts to understand when exploring Active Directory. So much of what you interact with is directly related to how early decisions were made with regard to the domain structure. But before you can really design an Active Directory implementation for your company or any other entity, you must get a firm grip on what exactly a domain is, what its relationship to a tree is, and why a forest exists.

This chapter looks at these items and discusses where they are used. However, because this whole discussion is based on logical concepts versus physical realities, there will be as many variations to the scenarios presented here as there are grains of sand in the Mojave Desert.

DOMAINS

A *domain* is a boundary for security, administration, and replication. A domain holds a distinct group of objects (users, computers, groups, and so on) that are related in some way. When you install the first Active Directory domain controller (DC), you are creating the first domain in your enterprise. This domain will hold users, computers, groups, organizational units (OU), printers, and a wide variety of other object types that have been previously defined by the schema.

→ **See** "Schema Components," **p. 189**

These domains are ordered in a hierarchy. If you have only one domain in your enterprise, you have a *flat* domain hierarchy. However, as your network grows, you might find yourself creating child domains. Figure 11.1 shows a simple parent-child domain model. The domain `fis.local` is the root of the domain and the parent, whereas `na.fis.local` and `sa.fis.local` are child domains.

Figure 11.1
A single tree forest
with three domains.

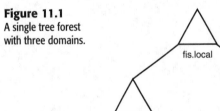

fis.local

na.fis.local   sa.fis.local

BOUNDARIES

As mentioned previously, a domain serves as a boundary of sorts. The boundaries are for security, administration, and replication. One of the keys to a forest is that all the domains in that forest—regardless of their locations—are connected in some way to all the other domains in the forest. However, limits do exist, and those limits are enforced through domains.

Security

So just how is a domain a security boundary? In Figure 11.1 you would have separate security policies for each domain. A security policy applies to all security principals within a single domain. All the settings under Account Policies and Public Key Polices are part of this security policy. An example of a security policy is when you set items such as minimum password length, enforce password history, account lockout duration, account lockout threshold, and so on. These policies are global for the domain. In other words, you can enforce them only at the domain level—not the OU level.

→ **See** "Introduction to Group Policy," **p. 334**

Note

> Although you can set these policies at the organizational unit level, they will have no effect. Only if they are modified at the domain level are they processed and enforced. When they are enforced, however, they have domain-wide scope.

These security policies affect only the domain in which they are set. This enables you to design your domains, to some extent, based on security. Also, the policies can be adapted over time as the needs of the organization change.

Administration

From an administrative point of view, the boundary for a domain administrator is that it has no inherent authority in any other domain. Therefore, if you add a user to the Domain Admins global group in the `fis.local` domain, that user can administer only the `fis.local` domain. (The assumption is made that the `fis.local` Domain Admins group is the only group to which this user belongs.) As it might seem, each Domain Admin group in each domain can manage only its own domain. The only group that has *global* permissions is the Enterprise Admin group, which can manage the entire forest.

However, you can give users from other domains the permissions necessary to manage a domain. For example, you could add a user from the `sa.fis.local` domain to the local administrators group in the `fis.local` domain. This would give the user many administrative-level permissions in the domain. Cross-domain administration is possible but is not enabled by default.

Caution

> Although, by default, the administrator user in a given domain has no authority in another domain, an exception to this rule does exist. The Enterprise Admins group in the forest root domain has, by default, one member: the administrator for that domain. Therefore, any member of the Enterprise Admins group has authority throughout the forest. So access to this group should be closely guarded.

Caution

> The Enterprise Admin can be locked out of a child domain. Essentially, you remove the inheritable full-control access control entry (ACE) from the access control list (ACL) on the domain object; then, you remove the Enterprise Admins from the built-in administrators group.

CH
11

> The Enterprise Admins group in the forest root domain, by default, has one member: the administrator for that domain. Any member of the Enterprise Admins group has authority throughout the forest; therefore, access to this group should be closely guarded.

REPLICATION

When dealing with replication, a user created in `fis.local` does not get replicated to any other domain in the enterprise. Each domain controller for the `fis.local` domain is the only instance of that object in the directory.

Note

> The one exception to the concept of replication boundaries is a global catalog (GC) server. A GC holds a copy of every object in the forest, except a subset of its attributes. For more information on GC servers, see the section "Replicate From," in Chapter 15, "Site Link Objects and Connection Objects."

Because a domain is a distinct namespace within Active Directory, you are ensured that objects from one domain will not "automagically" appear in other domains. This distinct namespace (partition) is a vital aspect of understanding Active Directory. The domain partition is different for each domain in the enterprise. Figure 11.2 shows the default domain partition for the domain `fis.local`.

Note

> Although a domain is a replication boundary for the domain naming context, you should note that the other two naming contexts—configuration and schema—are replicated to every DC in the forest. These two replication NCs, however, should be relatively static and should cause a minimum of replication traffic compared to the domain NC. For more information on naming contexts, see the section "Naming Contexts" in Chapter 16, "Intra-Site Replication."

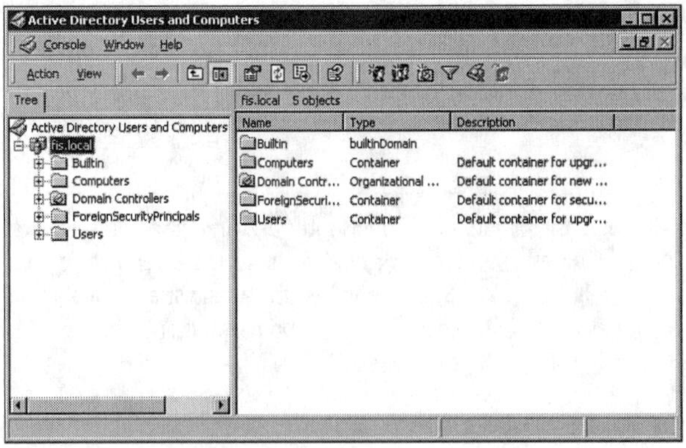

Figure 11.2
Viewing the domain partition for the current domain.

DOMAIN MODES

Many features of AD behave differently based on whether the domain is in mixed or native mode. A Windows 2000 domain in mixed mode can have NT backup domain controllers (BDCs) present in the domain and can even add NT BDCs to the domain. On the other hand, a Windows 2000 domain in native mode has no NT BDCs and has been explicitly converted to native mode.

> **Tip**
>
> Even in mixed mode, Active Directory provides almost innumerable advantages over NT domains. Kerberos authentication, hierarchical management, delegation of authority, and group policy are still available to Windows 2000 clients and servers that belong to an Active Directory domain, even in mixed mode.

MIXED MODE

Every Windows 2000 domain is in mixed mode when it is first installed. Even if it has only one Windows 2000 domain controller, it still is in mixed mode until the administrator explicitly converts it to native mode. No action is necessary or possible for the domain to be in mixed mode.

→ For more information on converting to native mode, **see** "Native Mode," **p. 166**

CH **11**

> **Tip**
>
> The presence or absence of Windows 9x clients or NT clients or member servers is an absolute nonissue when considering converting to native mode. The only rule on whether you can convert to native mode is the presence or absence of NT BDCs. If you have even one NT BDC still in your domain, the domain must remain in mixed mode.

A domain must remain in mixed mode if it has any NT BDCs. The domain must remain in mixed mode until the last remaining BDC has been upgraded or retired.

> **Note**
>
> A BDC is a domain controller from NT 4.0 that contains a read-only copy of the directory database. BDCs were used to add resilience to the directory. In addition, they were placed at remote locations to prevent logon traffic from having to cross the WAN links.

ADVANTAGES OF MIXED MODE

Even though the goal of every Windows 2000 domain is to be converted to native mode, mixed mode does have some advantages:

- **Support for NT BDCs**—Mixed mode can have NT BDCs. This enables a gradual, measured movement from NT domains to Active Directory.

- **Scalability**—Even in mixed mode, an Active Directory domain can have up to 40,000 objects. The 40,000-object limit is a limit of the NT BDCs you are replicating to in mixed mode. In native mode, AD domains that hold millions of objects have been built.

- **Security**—Although a mixed mode domain is not necessarily more secure than a native mode domain, if you are unsure about the physical security of some of your BDCs, mixed mode has the advantage that the BDC holds a read-only copy of the database. Modifying the SAM database on the BDC is not possible.

Note

Although the NT BDC in mixed mode has a read-only copy of the SAM database, using the User Manager for Domains to perform basic user management is possible, even in a Windows 2000 Active Directory domain. However, realize that, even though the User Manager for Domains interface is open and running on the NT BDC, the focus of the interface is on the PDC Emulator Operations Master for the domain.

NATIVE MODE

To reap all the benefits of Active Directory, a domain must be in native mode. In native mode, all NT BDCs have been upgraded or retired. Simply removing all the NT BDCs, however, does not automatically convert a domain to native mode.

CONVERTING TO NATIVE MODE

Converting to native mode is essentially a two-step process. First, you must double-check that no NT BDCs are in the domain. Then, you use the following steps to convert to native mode (the following steps assume your domain is `fis.local`):

1. Open the Active Directory Users and Computers MMC Snap-in by choosing Start, Programs, Administrative Tools.
2. Select the domain and right-click Properties.
3. At the bottom of the `fis.local` properties page in the Domain Mode frame, click the Change Mode button.
4. Select OK and close the MMC.

Tip

If no Change Mode button exists, your domain has already been converted to native mode. You only need to do this once per domain—not on each DC.

ADVANTAGES OF NATIVE MODE

Windows 2000 Active Directory native mode has numerous advantages. The availability of universal groups alone is worth the effort. Some of the advantages are more subtle, however. The advantages are as follows:

- **Universal Groups**—Universal groups can contain users and groups from any domain in the forest and can be used to assign permissions to any object in the forest. Universal groups are available only in native mode.

- **Group Conversion**—In native mode you can convert any group type to any other group type and back.

- **Group Nesting**—Although you can perform limited group nesting in mixed mode, this capability is greatly enhanced in native mode.

- **Movetree**—You can use `movetree.exe` from the Windows 2000 Support Tools to move organizational units and their contents from one domain to another. However, the target domain must be in native mode.

- **Remote Access Policies**—Controlling access to the network using remote access policies is available only for users on standalone routing and remote access servers or users in a native mode domain.

> **Caution**
>
> Universal groups are a marvelous, powerful feature of Windows 2000 Active Directory. They do come with a price, though. The membership of every universal group in the forest is held on every global catalog server in the forest. This means that every time you modify the membership of any global group in the forest, you are causing replication to every GC in the forest. This information is held on the GC because, during logon, the membership of universal groups is parsed to see whether the authenticating user is a member of any universal group. This enables the authorization data field of the Kerberos packet to be properly populated. For more information on Kerberos authentication, see "Authenticating to the Domain" in Chapter 18, "Authentication."

> **Tip**
>
> In native mode, a GC server is required for logon for every user except the administrator account. This is provided so that in a crisis the administrator can log on and configure a GC server. However, in a single-domain environment, a user can be authenticated without a GC.

TREES

When you add another domain to your enterprise and it is a child domain of the first domain, you are essentially creating a *tree*. These domains are connected through a Kerberos transitive trust. The tree model is such that the name of the tree is always the name of the root of the tree. In Figure 11.1, for example, the tree name is `fis.local`.

> **Tip**
>
> The namespace you choose for your tree must match your DNS namespace. If you want to create a tree namespace and use a namespace that does not currently exist in your DNS, you can create a new DNS namespace with Windows 2000 DNS. For more information on DNS namespaces, see Chapter 7, "DNS and AD Namespaces."

One of the characteristics of a tree is that it shares a contiguous namespace with other domains in the same tree regardless of the number of domains the tree contains. Figure 11.3 shows a deep domain tree structure, but the name of the tree is still `fis.local` and all child and grandchild domains share that namespace.

Tip

You can use the Active Directory Domains and Trusts MMC Snap-in (`domain.msc`) to view your tree and forest structure.

Figure 11.3
Planning a naming
structure for the tree.

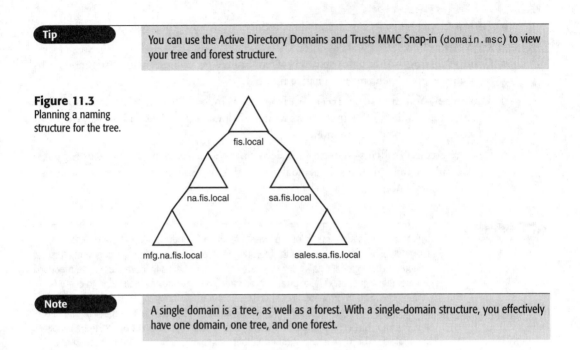

Note

A single domain is a tree, as well as a forest. With a single-domain structure, you effectively have one domain, one tree, and one forest.

FORESTS

A *forest* is a collection of trees that do not share the same contiguous namespace. Figure 11.4 shows just such an entity. Because `fis.local` was the first domain in the forest, it retains the title of forest root. The `fullertoninfo.com` domain is a member of the `fis.local` forest but is the root of its own tree.

Figure 11.4
Building a forest with
multiple trees.

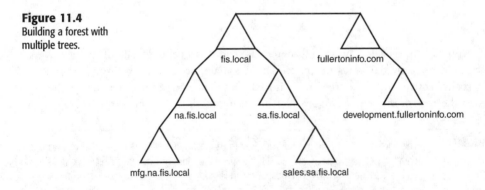

Caution

Although `fis.local` and `fullertoninfo.com` appear to be at the same level in the forest because they are both roots of their own trees, a forest has only one forest root domain, and that is the first domain created in the forest. By default, this is the home of two groups that exist only in the forest root domain—Enterprise Admins and Schema Admins.

The two trees are connected through a two-way transitive trust. This trust enables users in the `mfg.na.fis.local` domain to gain access to resources in the `fullertoninfo.com` domain. This is achieved by the administrator in the `fullertoninfo.com` domain granting permissions to the appropriate resources in the domain. In NT 4, the administrator had to create these trusts manually. With Windows 2000, however, these trusts are automatic and transitive.

In addition, all domains in a forest share the following:

- **Configuration naming context**—The configuration NC contains such data as the various sites, site links, services, and partitions that are in your Active Directory.

- **Schema naming context**—This naming context contains the actual schema used in your instance of the Active Directory.

- **Global catalog**—A GC server is a domain controller that holds, along with a complete copy of its own domain naming context, a full copy of the schema and configuration naming contexts (just like every other DC) and a complete list of every other object in every other domain naming context, but an incomplete list of the attributes for the objects.

Caution

Although you can join two forests at the forest root domain with a trust relationship, do not assume that this makes the two forests one. You cannot merge forests in Windows 2000 Active Directory. You can create trusts between Active Directory domains in the forests, but they still will maintain separate schema and configuration naming contexts and will not share GC servers. Additionally, that trust at the top of the forest will not provide access from any domain in the first forest to any domain in the second. Doing so requires explicit trust relationships between all the source and target domains. These trusts do not use Kerberos but rather the NTLM style of trust found in NT 4.0.

Сн
11

One very important thing to remember is that the forest root is worth protecting. The forest root is the first domain in the enterprise. Because of this, it is highly recommended that you install at least two domain controllers in the forest root. If you ever experience a failure of the last DC in the forest root, hope that your rèsumè is on a floppy in your pocket. The best thing you can hope for is a recent backup of that DC and a big pot of coffee because it's going to be a long night. Essentially, losing the forest root equates to losing your forest.

SUMMARY

Domains, trees, and forests are the basic building blocks of Active Directory. Even if you have only one domain, you still have a single-domain tree and a single-tree forest.

Although a domain serves as a boundary for replication, security, and administration, you must have at least one domain to have Active Directory. In many cases, you will find that you will create more than one domain for security purposes, as well as an additional level of control for replication.

A tree is a collection of domains with a contiguous namespace that are connected by Kerberos transitive trusts. The top-level domain in the tree is known as the tree root.

A forest is a collection of one or more domains in one or more trees that are connected by Kerberos transitive trusts and that share a common GC and schema. The forest really defines the absolute boundary for your instance of AD.

TROUBLESHOOTING

I'M UNABLE TO ADD A BDC TO A MIXED MODE DOMAIN

My domain is in mixed mode, but I am unable to add an NT BDC to the Active Directory domain.

You can add NT BDCs to the domain while the Active Directory domain is in mixed mode; however, doing so is not intuitive. Before you install the NT BDC, use the srvmgr.exe tool on the Windows 2000 domain controller to create the DC account for the new BDC. Be sure to add it as a Windows NT BDC when prompted. Then, when you are prompted to create a BDC during the NT installation, you will be able to join the domain. If you don't do this, you will get an error message stating that the computer account does not exist or is inaccessible.

I AM RECEIVING NAME CONFLICT ERRORS WHEN ADDING A CHILD DOMAIN

I have created a forest with several trees. I'm trying to add a child domain in one of the trees and when I try to name it, dcpromo *complains about a name conflict.*

Even if you have implemented several trees in your forest to avoid naming conflicts and to provide contiguous namespaces, naming collisions with down-level domain names can still occur. For example, if you have a domain called sales.fis.local and try to create a domain in another tree in the same forest with a name of sales.fullertoninfo.com, the NetBIOS domain name for both domains will be sales. If you insist on doing this, you will need to modify the NetBIOS domain name for the second domain.

CHAPTER 12

OPERATIONS MASTERS

In this chapter

INTRODUCTION

Active Directory is a distributed directory whereby each Domain Controller (DC) in the forest has a writeable copy of the directory database. As a result, certain operations must be performed on only one DC. Each of these domain controllers is referred to as an *operations master* or *flexible singe-master operation (FSMO)*.

Caution	By default, the first Domain Controller, in the first domain, in the first tree in the forest, holds all five operations master roles and is the only Global Catalog (GC) Server. This should be addressed early in the forest's life by moving some of the OM roles to other DCs and creating more GC Servers, preferably one GC per site.

Active Directory performs a variety of operations that are replicated to every DC in the forest or domain depending on the operation being performed. For example, creating a new user is replicated to only other DCs in the domain, whereas adding a new attribute to the user class in the schema affects all DCs in the forest and therefore is replicated to all DCs in the forest. If a conflict occurs while performing these operations, the process of conflict resolution occurs. However, some instances exist in which it makes more sense to actually not have a conflict or to simply prevent the conflict. That's where the operations masters come in.

Five operations master roles exist: domain naming master, schema master, RID master, infrastructure master, and PDC emulator master.

The owner of each role is recorded in the AD Configuration partition using the `fsmoRoleOwner` attribute. The attribute is populated with the DN of the NTDS Settings object of the computer it represents—in other words, CN=NTDS Settings, CN=TULDC01, CN=Servers, CN=Tulsa, CN=Sites, CN=Configuration, DC=adbook, and DC=local.

You can determine the placement of these roles pretty easily. The first DC in the forest initially holds all the FSMO roles. You should move or transfer these roles to other DCs after they are in place.

Follow these steps to determine who holds the roles for RID Master, PDC Emulator, and infrastructure master (IM):

1. Open Active Directory Users and Computers.
2. Right-click Active Directory Users and Computers [`hostname.domain.local`] and click Operations Masters.

Figure 12.1 displays the tabs you see, each displaying the various roles that are domain-wide roles.

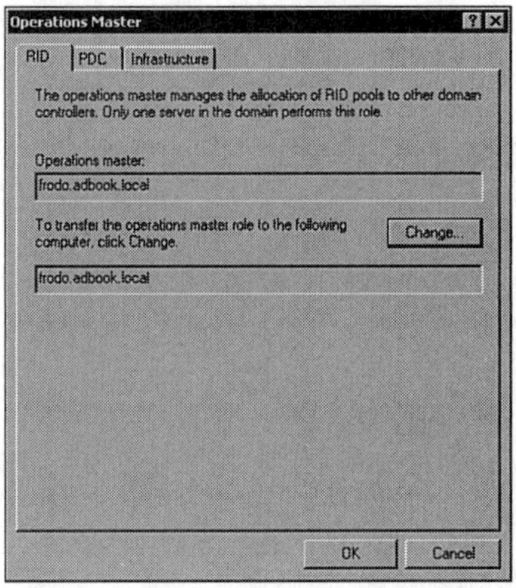

Figure 12.1
The Operations Master window gives you three tabs of selections.

To locate the server holding the Domain Naming master role, perform these steps:

1. Open Active Directory Domains and Trusts.
2. Right-click Active Directory Domains and Trusts and click Operations Master.

Figure 12.2 displays the dialog box for the domain naming FSMO.

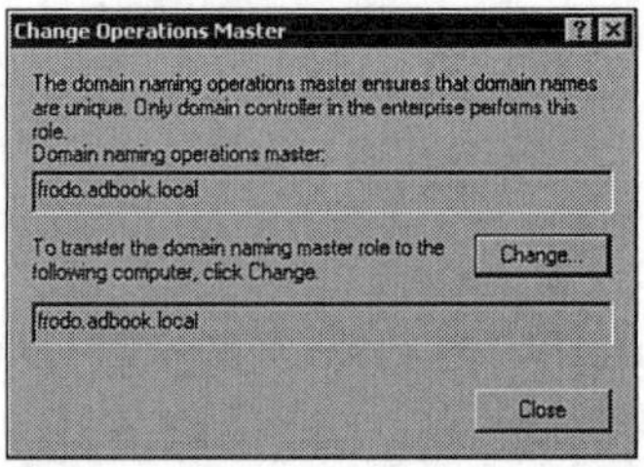

Figure 12.2
Transfer or change the domain naming master role with the Change Operations Master window.

CH

12

Before being able to locate the schema master, you must register the schmmgmt.dll. Then, you must create a custom MMC for the schema snap-in. You do so by performing the following steps:

1. Open a command prompt.
2. Type **regsvr32.exe schmmgmt.dll** and press Enter.
3. Type **MMC** and press Enter.
4. In the MMC console that appears, click Console, and then click Add/Remove Snap-in.
5. Click Add on the Standalone tab.
6. Select Active Directory Schema from the list and click Add; then click Close.
7. Click OK.
8. Click Console, Save As and name the console Schema Manager.

To locate the server holding the schema master role, perform these steps:

1. Open the Schema Manager.
2. Click Active Directory Schema for the snap-in to connect to the schema master.
3. Right-click Active Directory Schema and select Operations Master.

Figure 12.3 displays the server name holding the schema master role for the `adbook.local` domain.

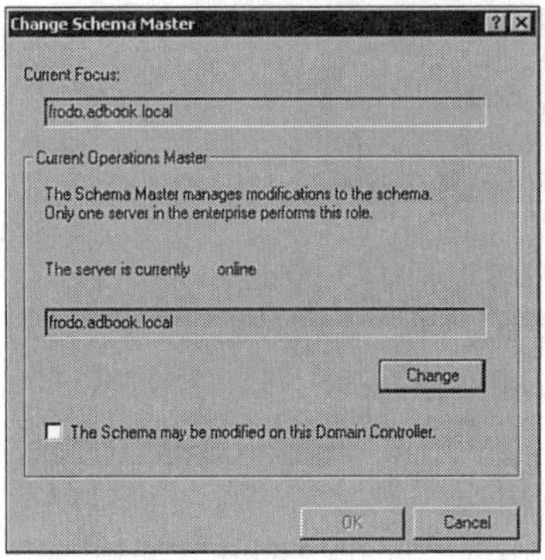

Figure 12.3
Use this window to change schema masters.

→ For more information on modifying the schema, **see** "Modifying the Schema," **p. 193**

FOREST-WIDE ROLES

Within a single forest are two FSMOs that operate as per-forest roles: schema master and domain naming master. Each of these FSMOs performs tasks that must be completed at a single DC for proper operation of Active Directory. Either of these two roles can exist on any DC in the forest. These roles are capable of being held on only a Windows 2000 Domain Controller.

SCHEMA MASTER

The schema master initially is located on the first DC installed in the forest. Because only one schema is shared between all DCs in the forest, only one schema master exists. Any time a change is made to the schema, the change is performed at the schema master. You can transfer the schema master role to any DC in the forest. The owner of each role is recorded in the Active Directory Configuration partition using the `fsmoRoleOwner` attribute, which is written at

```
LDAP://CN=Schema,CN=Configuration,DC=adbook,DC=local.
```

→ For more information on transferring roles, **see** "Transferring Roles," **p. 181**
→ For more information about the schema, **see** "Schema Components," **p. 189**

DOMAIN NAMING MASTER

By default, the domain naming master is also located on the first DC installed in the forest. Whenever you add a new domain or remove existing domains from the forest, the domain naming master is the one that performs these functions. If the domain naming master is unavailable, you are not able to add a new domain or remove any domains.

Another point that we will explore later is that the domain naming master must be also a Global Catalog Server. Because the GC has a partial replica of all objects in the enterprise, it is capable of handling the request to determine whether the new domain has a unique name. For further details on FSMO placement, see the section "FSMO Placement," later in this chapter.

The `fsmoRoleOwner` attribute for the domain naming master is written at

`LDAP://CN=Partitions,CN=Configuration,DC=adbook,DC=local`

DOMAIN ROLES

The schema master and the domain naming master are *forest-wide* roles. This means that no matter how many or how few domains you have, you still have only one each of these operations masters. The next (and last) three operations masters we will look at are specific to the domain. If you have one domain, you have one each of the infrastructure master, PDC emulator, and RID master. If you have 10 domains, you have 10 each of the infrastructure master, PDC emulator, and RID master. There is always one per domain.

These roles can all be one machine and, by default, are located on the first Domain Controller in the domain. However, as we will see in the next sections, moving them to different machines is wise unless you have a very small network.

INFRASTRUCTURE MASTER

The infrastructure master is responsible for updating the cross-domain group to user references. This means that when a user is moved from one group to another, or even when the user object is renamed, the infrastructure master facilitates updating the changes and replicating them out through normal replication. It does this to maintain an up-to-date and accurate Active Directory database.

In a distributed directory environment, this role is important because sometimes when the name of an object is changed, a delay occurs in viewing the new name in the group membership list.

This is also important if you move an object from its current location when the object belongs to a group in another domain. The group will show a temporary absence of the user even though the group membership has not changed. The infrastructure master is the DC that alters the group object to reflect the new location of the object.

The infrastructure master discovers changes by periodically querying the GC for updates. In a multidomain forest, the infrastructure master cannot be located on a GC Server. If it is, cross-domain object references are never recognized. In addition, if the IM is a GC, it never looks for objects it doesn't have. The infrastructure master should be located near a GC Server, preferably in the same site.

The owner of each role is recorded in the Active Directory Configuration partition using the fsmoRoleOwner attribute, which is written at

```
LDAP://CN=Infrastructure,DC=adbook,DC=local
```

RID MASTER

The relative identifier (RID) master is responsible for handing out RIDs to DCs for the purpose of security principal creation. A RID is a portion of the Security Identifier (SID). Specifically, it is considered a sub-authority when looking at the structure of a SID. A SID always is unique because it identifies a security principal.

The domain SID is the first portion of the SID of any object in the AD; the RID, on the other hand, is the last part of a SID. In fact, the RID is what makes a SID unique—the RID is a unique identifier that is relative to the domain. The RID master is the server responsible for delivering a pool of RIDs to each DC in the domain.

→ For more information on SIDs and RIDs, **see** "Security Identifiers," **p. 312**

After this pool reaches 80% depletion of RIDs, it will make a request to the RID master for another pool. As each DC uses a RID, it will not use that RID again. The same goes for the RID master when it issues a pool of RIDs. Domain Controllers are assigned RID allocation pools of 500 by the RID master in a sequential order. Every time the Domain Controller assigns an object a SID, it uses the next available RID in its allocation pool. This continues until 80% of the RID pool has been depleted.

You will note Event ID 16647 in the System log as depicted in Figure 12.4 whenever a DC makes a request for more RIDs.

Figure 12.4
The Event Properties window logs when the DC requests more RIDs.

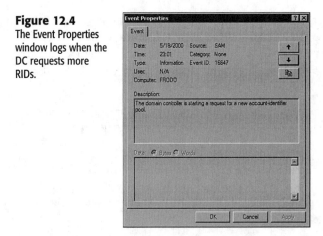

You also will note Event ID 16648 as well whenever a RID pool request is successful, as seen in Figure 12.5.

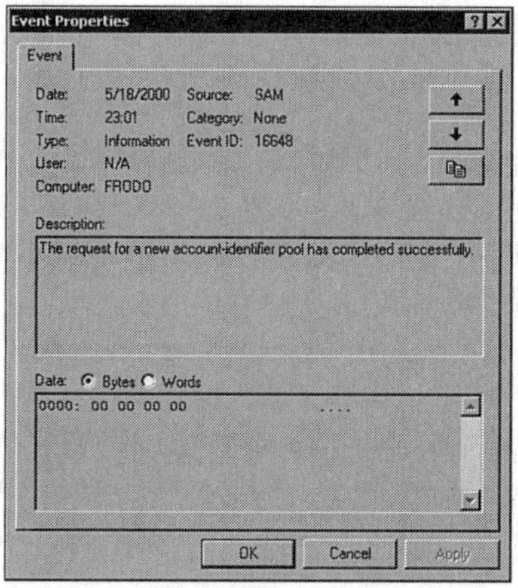

Figure 12.5
The next logged event shows that the RID pool request was successful.

If the RID master is unavailable when a DC issues a request for more RIDs, the DC no longer is capable of creating accounts. However, you can change the focus of Active Directory users and computers to another DC in the domain to create the account. This is assuming that this DC has not also depleted its pool of RIDs. A DC that has no available RIDs to allocate and that cannot contact the RID master for a new pool writes NT event error 16645 to the system log.

> **Note**
> The RID master is also the specific DC that handles the reception and addition of objects being migrated to the domain from other domains. It does this by using the movetree command.

→ For more information on movetree, **see** "movetree," **p. 504**

CH
12

The owner of each role is recorded in the Active Directory Configuration partition using the fsmoRoleOwner attribute, which is written at the following:

LDAP://CN=Rid Manager$,CN=System,DC=adbook,DC=local

PDC EMULATOR

The primary domain controller (PDC) emulator has almost a split personality. The functions it performs depend on whether it is operating in mixed or native mode.

→ For more information on domain modes, **see** "Domain Modes," **p. 165**

In *mixed* mode, the PDC emulator is responsible for replicating changes from Windows 2000 DCs to the NT 4 backup Domain Controllers (BDCs). The process is the same as in Windows NT 4.0 Server. A change is made at the PDC, and it then announces it has changes. Then, the BDC requests those changes. Also, if an administrator attempts to use User Manager for Domains from a down-level client, it attempts to contact the PDC emulator.

The owner of each role is recorded in the Active Directory Configuration partition using the `fsmoRoleOwner` attribute, which is written at

`LDAP://DC=adbook,DC=local.`

Some functions are the same regardless of the mode of the domain. The PDC emulator acts as the domain master browser and processes password changes from other DCs. This last function is worth looking at in more detail.

PASSWORD CHANGES

In a distributed directory environment, in which all directory servers are capable of making changes to the directory, a variety of challenges must be handled. One of those is how to handle a user changing her password. Password changes can occur at any DC in the domain to which the user belongs.

The issue that presents itself is if the user attempts to log on and is authenticated by another DC (other than the one that received the password change initially) before the password change has been replicated. Inside a site, this could take up to 15 minutes; between sites the time required is entirely dependent on the replication schedule.

The process of a password change is fairly straightforward. Whenever a user makes a password change, the change occurs at the DC from which the user is currently authenticated. That DC then attempts to replicate on a best-effort basis the password change to the PDC emulator. The PDC emulator then updates its copy of the AD database. I say "best effort" because the DC attempts to send the change, but if the replication attempt is unsuccessful, the password change occurs during the next normal replication cycle.

If the PDC emulator is not in the same site as other DCs, you might find it helpful to turn off the urgent replication by changing the `AvoidPdcOnWan` parameter in the Registry key `HKEY_LOCAL_MACHINE \CurrentControlSet \Services \Netlogon \Parameters` to a 1. After this change, the DC that receives the initial password change replicates the change only during normal replication.

→ For more information on the PDC emulator's role in replication, **see** "Password Changes," **p. 264**

MAINTAINING SYNCHRONIZED TIME

The PDC emulator is also responsible as the authoritative time server for the domain, and the PDC emulator in the forest root is authoritative for the forest. It is important that all Domain Controllers in the domain agree on what time it is within a five-minute window. The default authentication mechanism in Windows 2000 is Kerberos. By default, if the Kerberos service receives a packet that has a timestamp that is more than five minutes out of sync with the local computer time on the DC, the packet is discarded.

➔ For more information on Kerberos and time, **see** "Maximum Tolerance for Computer Clock Synchronization," **p. 309**

The timekeeping responsibilities are shared as follows:

■ The PDC emulator in the forest root domain sets the time for the forest. It can be set to use an external time source with the `net time` command.

➔ For more information on the `net time` command, **see** "Maximum Tolerance for Computer Clock Synchronization," **p. 309**

■ All other PDC emulators in all the other domains in the forest use the PDC emulator in the forest root as their authoritative time server.

■ All other Domain Controllers use the PDC emulator for their domain as the authoritative time server.

■ All Windows 2000 clients, either workstations or member servers, then use the Domain Controller to which they are authenticating as their time server.

> **Tip**
>
> Down-level and NT clients that are not using the Active Directory client always change their passwords at the PDC emulator. Because of this, the PDC emulator should be near the "center" of the network and should be very well connected.

TRANSFERRING AND SEIZING ROLES

It is possible to transfer the FSMO roles from one DC to another. This might be done because of planned maintenance or outage on a Domain Controller or for performance issues. We now take a look at transferring and seizing the roles. Both will occur some time during your career as a Windows 2000 Active Directory administrator, and understanding the differences between the two will make your life a little easier. Transferring a role is fairly straightforward and can be done with the GUI. Seizing a role is somewhat invasive and requires `Ntdsutil`.

To transfer the roles, you must have the appropriate permissions. The exact group membership varies based on the specific role you want to manage.

The Domain Admins group and the Enterprise Admins group have the change RID master, change PDC, and change infrastructure master permissions by default.

The Schema Admins group has the change schema master permission, and the Enterprise Admins group has the change domain naming master permission.

You can further control who has permissions by assigning the appropriate permission to a new group. To assign permissions, you must use ADSI Edit, a tool that comes with the Windows 2000 Support Tools.

CH

12

Follow these steps to install ADSI Edit:

1. Insert either the Windows 2000 Server or Windows 2000 Advanced Server CD and navigate to the Support\Tools directory.

2. Double-click the 2000RKST file. This file is an MSI file and invokes the Windows Installer server to install the application.

3. Select the Typical Installation mode, and it will install ADSI Edit as a part of the default install.

ADSI Edit appears in Programs, Windows 2000 Support Tools, Tools. Another idea is to use group policies to either assign or publish the Support Tools to members of an IT OU or even a child OU called AD Admins. I have the software installed on all DCs in our organization and administrative workstations.

To assign another user or group the ability to transfer the role of the infrastructure master, do the following:

1. Open ADSI Edit and right-click the ADSI Edit node in the Tree view and select Connect to.

2. In the Name field, type **Infrastructure Master**. (You could type anything you want in this box.)

3. Select Distinguished Name, as shown in Figure 12.6.

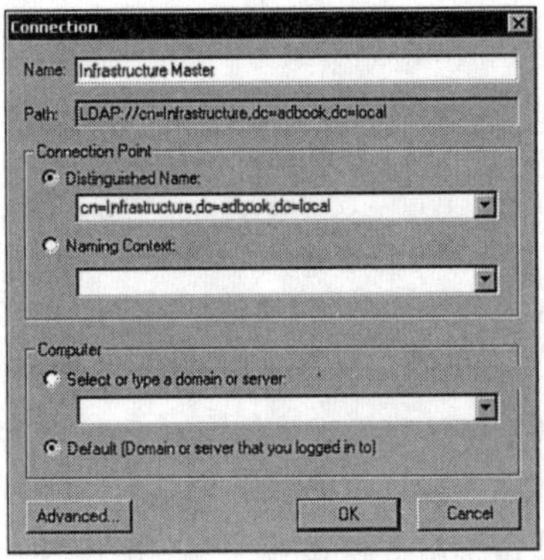

Figure 12.6
Use the Connection window to connect ADSI Edit to a different context.

4. Type the DN of the object appropriate role—in other words, **cn=Infrastructure,dc=adbook,dc=local**.

5. Click OK.

6. Right-click the new node and select Properties.

7. Click the Security Tab and assign the change infrastructure master permission to the appropriate account.

These steps vary depending on the role you want to modify. For example, you only need to expand the Domain NC node and navigate to the System node to view the RID Manager$ attribute (see Figure 12.7).

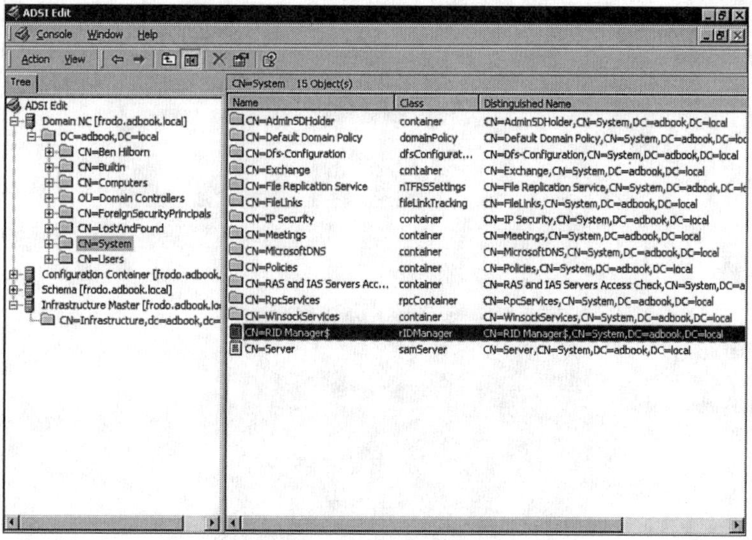

Figure 12.7
By expanding the Domain NC node, you can view the RID Manager$ attribute of the System container.

TRANSFERRING ROLES

Transferring the role of a FSMO role to another DC is not a daunting task. However, a transfer assumes that you have access to the original FSMO role owner. To transfer roles, the tools vary depending on the role you need to move.

The first tool we will look at is the MMC Snap-in for the appropriate role.

To transfer the role for the PDC emulator, RID master, and infrastructure master, you use Active Directory Users and Computers:

1. Open the Active Directory Users and Computers console.
2. Change the focus of the MMC to the DC that will be the new FSMO role owner by right-clicking Active Directory Users and Computers and selecting Connect to Domain Controller.
3. Select the DC that will hold the new role, as shown in Figure 12.8, and click OK.
4. Right-click Active Directory Users and Computers again and select Operations Master.
5. Select the appropriate tab for the role you want to transfer.
6. Click the Change button to transfer the role to the current DC. Notice that in Figure 12.9, the current operations master is frodo.adbook.local. If you click the Change button, the role transfers to the DC listed in the lower text box.

CH

12

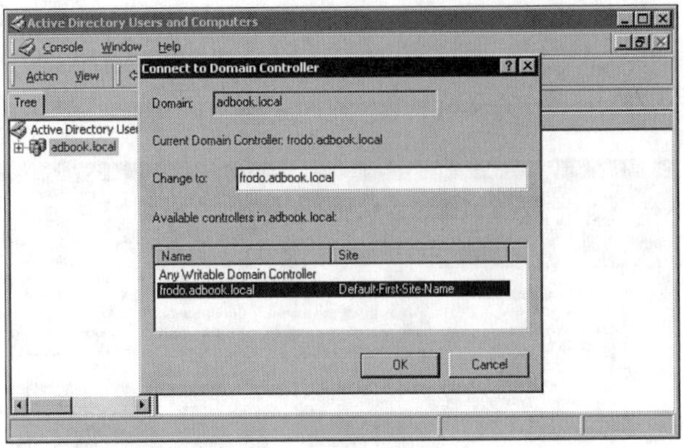

Figure 12.8
Focus Active Directory Users and Computers on the DC that will receive the FSMO role.

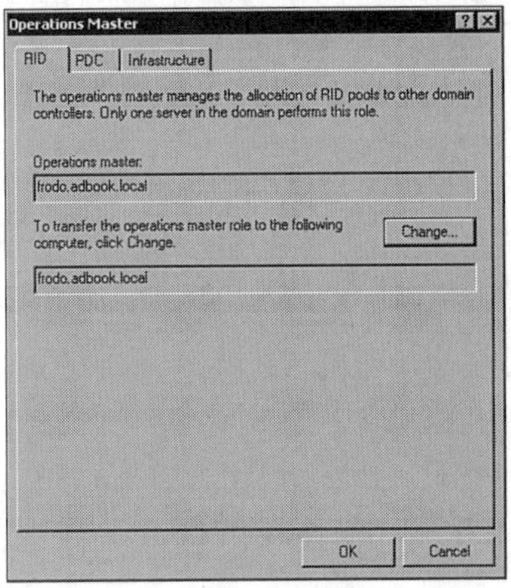

Figure 12.9
The current operations master is noted in the RID tab of the Operations Master pane.

To transfer the role for the domain naming master, you must use the Active Directory Domains and Trusts console. Follow these steps:

1. Open the Active Directory Domains and Trusts console.

2. Change the focus of the MMC to the DC that will hold the domain naming master role by right-clicking Active Directory Domains and Trusts and selecting Connect to Domain Controller.

3. Select the DC that will hold the new role, and click OK.

4. Right-click Active Directory Domains and Trusts and select Operations Master.

5. Click the Change button to transfer the role to the current DC.

The schema master role requires a few extra steps:

1. You will need to add the Active Directory Schema snap-in by installing the `adminpak.msi` file and selecting Install All of the Administrative Tools. The `adminpak.msi` file is located in the `winnt\system32` directory.

2. Click Start, Run and type **MMC**. This starts the MMC console.

3. Click Console, Add/Remove Snap-in, and then click Add.

4. Select Active Directory Schema and click Add; then click OK.

5. Change the focus of the MMC to the DC that will hold the Schema Master role by right-clicking Active Directory Schema and selecting Change Domain Controller.

6. Select the DC that will hold the new role, and click OK.

7. Right-click Active Directory Schema and select Operations Master.

8. Click Change to transfer the role to the new DC.

TRANSFERRING ROLES WITH Ntdsutil

Another method of transferring roles is by using Ntdsutil. Ntdsutil has many uses, but this section focuses just on transferring roles.

→ For more information on Ntdsutil, **see** "Other Maintenance Tasks," **p. 477**

NTDSUTIL.EXE is a powerful command-line utility used to directly manipulate the Active Directory. Certain operations on the AD necessitate the use of Ntdsutil—seizing FSMO roles is one of those operations. You can also use Ntdsutil to gracefully transfer any of the FSMO roles. The transferring of roles works essentially the same way as using the MMC Snap-ins, but the actions are performed in a command window.

You can invoke the utility either by typing **ntdsutil** at a command prompt or by typing **ntdsutil** in the Run dialog box, as shown in Figure 12.10.

Figure 12.10
The initial Ntdsutil interface is reached from the command prompt.

To prepare to transfer roles with Ntdsutil, you must first type **roles** at the prompt. Figure 12.11 displays what you see after typing **roles** and then **help**.

The first step in using Ntdsutil is to make a connection to the DC that will receive the role. After you make the connection, you must use credentials of a user who has permission to perform the transfer.

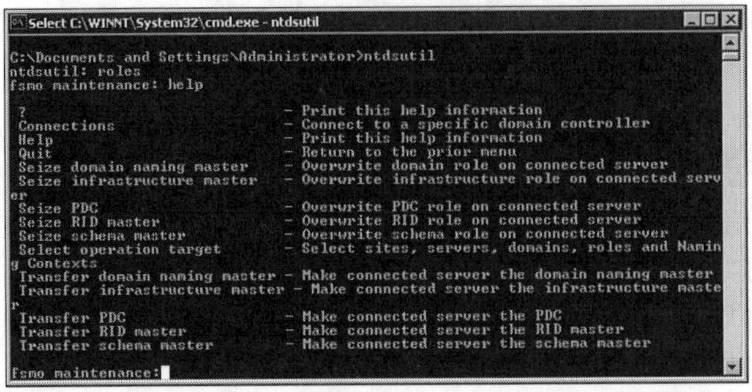

Figure 12.11
Descriptions for
Roles commands
can be found by
typing **help**.

The following steps outline how to transfer a role:

1. Type **ntdsutil** at a command prompt.

2. Type **roles** at the ntdsutil prompt.

3. Type **connections**. This takes you to the area for establishing the connection to the appropriate DC.

4. If you are not logged in as a user with the permission to transfer roles, you must type **set creds** *domain username password*—for example, set creds adbook.local administrator password.

Note   If the password is blank, type **NULL** for the password.

---

5. You now must connect to the server that will receive the role. Type **connect to server** *servername*—for example, connect to server frodo.

6. To return to the FSMO maintenance options, type **quit**.

7. Depending on the role you want to transfer, type the appropriate role transfer command:

   - transfer PDC

   - transfer RID master

   - transfer schema master

   - transfer infrastructure master

   - transfer domain naming master

8. You then are prompted with a dialog box that asks you to confirm your selection. This is an ideal time to verify that the DC listed in the dialog box is the one you want to transfer the role. By answering Yes, you transfer the role to the connected server.

SEIZING ROLES

A more tragic method of moving the role to a new DC is known as a *seize*. It's tragic because it assumes that the existing role owner is no longer functioning and has no plans of functioning any time soon.

Seizing the role is in essence the same as transferring the role, but it assumes the original role holder is incapable of being contacted.

To seize the role, you must use `Ntdsutil`. The steps are essentially the same as mentioned previously in transferring roles, but in step 7, you use any of the following commands (depending on the role you want to seize):

- ■ seize domain naming master
- ■ seize infrastructure master
- ■ seize PDC
- ■ seize RID master
- ■ seize schema master

Just to make sure I have made the point, you want to be really sure that the current FSMO role owner is unavailable and has no plans to reappear in the network at any time. For example, if you seize the schema master role and then bring the old schema master back online, you might corrupt the schema irretrievably.

FSMO PLACEMENT

Determining optimum placement for your role owners is easy—as long as only one DC is in the enterprise! If not, you'll face a few challenges.

Initially, the first DC in the enterprise holds all the FSMO roles. Each additional DC in the domain and in the enterprise requires additional planning. Some basic guidelines can be followed regardless of other conditions.

The domain naming master should be located on a Global Catalog Server. Because the domain naming master must ensure that no other domains exist with the same name during the addition of a domain to the enterprise, it uses the GC for this function. However, if you have only one domain in your forest, this is not required because all DCs have complete knowledge of all objects in the directory.

Do not place the infrastructure master on a GC. Instead, place it within the same site as a GC. The infrastructure master must periodically check references for objects that it does not have. It also must be capable of communicating with a GC to determine whether the objects to which it does have references have changed—and if so, it can replicate those.

It is also advantageous to plan for a current FSMO and a standby FSMO for each domain. These two DCs should be direct replication partners.

→ For more information on replication partners, **see** "Topology Generation," **p. 261**

For forest roles, place the domain naming master and the schema master on the same DC. Microsoft recommends this as an always.

SUMMARY

Operations masters roles can be an arcane subject. They are assigned by default, and when they're working, they're invisible. However, in any situation except a tiny domain, it pays to assign the roles manually to different computers. Many performance problems can be addressed by properly placing operations masters.

The two forest-wide roles are the schema master and domain naming master. The remaining three—the PDC emulator, RID master, and infrastructure master—are specific to the domain.

TROUBLESHOOTING

SLOW PASSWORD CHANGES

Password changes for my 2000 clients and down-level clients running the Active Directory client are fast, but when other clients change their passwords, it is very slow.

Down-level clients that do not have the AD client software can change their passwords only at the PDC emulator. Make sure that the PDC emulator is online and has fast connections to the rest of the network.

NEW USER CREATION ERRORS

When I try to create a new user, I am unable to and receive an error message that says The directory service has exhausted the pool of relative identifiers.

Make sure the RID master is online and functional. Also, ensure that the Domain Controller you are using can reach the RID master.

W32TIM ERROR #62

I am getting W32Time error #62 in my event viewer system log.

This means that the forest root PDC emulator is not configured with the address of an external authoritative time server. This might not be a huge issue, but you can put it to rest with the `net time /setsntp:<ip address>` command. Microsoft TechNet article Q216734 describes how to use a network time source in Windows 2000 and lists the IP addresses of the official network time sources.

CHAPTER 13

ACTIVE DIRECTORY SCHEMA

In this chapter

INTRODUCTION

The Active Directory schema is the forest-wide definition of objects that exist by default in the directory. It is analogous to the blueprint used to build a house. The schema defines which objects can exist and which attributes exist for those objects. The ability to extend the schema is, in my opinion, one of the most powerful features of Active Directory. This chapter looks first at the architecture of the schema and then at how and why to modify it.

Caution

Although the ability to extend the schema and therefore Active Directory is a very big advantage to Windows 2000, schema modifications are forever. A company policy should be in place that specifies who modifies the schema and under what conditions.

Most companies are deluged with data, much of which is redundant. Active Directory allows for a single repository of globally interesting data. Contact lists, configuration information, and so on can now be added to AD and then used by any application that is written to use the AD database.

Application developers soon will be able to use Active Directory through this feature. One of the best examples of this will be Exchange 2000. Exchange no longer has its own directory service. Instead, it will extend the schema with new classes and attributes that will enable new objects to be available in the directory. This is merely the first of many applications that will leverage the power inherent in the schema and the Windows 2000 Active Directory.

Note

Active Directory is not designed to replace your SQL databases. Information placed in AD should be concise, globally interesting, and reasonably static.

The schema contains definitions for all objects available to Active Directory. For an object to exist, it must have been defined by a template, or what is referred to as a *class*.

A class is a template that defines the characteristics of objects. If you were to build a house, you would use a set of blueprints that defines the characteristics of the house. Another individual could build another house using the same set of blueprints, but the house would not necessarily be the same—hopefully, it would at least have an address different from yours.

The characteristics are referred to as *attributes*. Attributes define unique characteristics of the object. Using the house analogy again, the house can have a color attribute and that attribute can contain a value of either red or green. A *user* is a class of object that has a variety of attributes ranging from name to phone number.

Classes and attributes are independent of each other. Although a class needs attributes to exist, attributes can be implemented in zero or more classes.

Every class, however, has both mandatory and optional attributes. *Mandatory* attributes must be populated before an instance of a class can be created. *Optional* attributes are exactly that—optional.

Schema Location

The Active Directory schema is initially defined at the installation of the first DC in the enterprise. The actual schema is initially defined in NTDS.dit. This file is used during the dcpromo process for the creation of the directory. The schema.ini file contains the information to create the default objects in the directory as well as information about security and Active Directory display specifiers.

The directory is installed by default to the %SystemRoot%\NTDS directory. This can be changed during the installation of each DC and is covered in detail in Chapter 2, "Installing Active Directory."

Schema Components

You must understand several pieces of the schema to be able to make informed decisions about modifying it. Even if you have no plans to modify your schema, bear in mind that many applications you install in the future will modify the schema during their install processes. Therefore, it is important that you understand the schema, its components, and the implications of schema modifications.

Classes

As mentioned before, a class is essentially a blueprint, a template. Several classes exist: user classes, computer classes, printer classes, and so on. Any given object in the Active Directory is an *instance* of a class. As I type this paragraph, the user I am logged on as is an instance of the user class. Just as a manufacturing company can use a template of a widget to make widgets, a class is used to create objects. What kind of object you get when you create one is completely dependent on the class.

Some examples of information contained in a class definition are the Lightweight Directory Access Protocol (LDAP) name, the globally unique identifier (GUID), and the object identifier (OID) for the class.

To describe the object that will be created from the class, the class definition holds information about mandatory attributes, optional attributes, and rules regarding which possible classes can be parents of the class. This brings us to the subject of subclassing and inheritance.

Subclassing and Inheritance

Every class in the schema is a subclass of the top class. The schema is hierarchical, so if a class is derived from a parent class, the child class inherits all the attributes of the parent class. You therefore can add attributes to the new class and further derive child classes from this parent class which, in turn, inherits the attributes of its parent class.

For example, if you subclass the user class by creating class mechanic, class mechanic will inherit all the attributes of class user. You then can add attributes to class mechanic, such as toolset. If you then subclass the mechanic class by creating class APmechanic, class APmechanic will inherit all the attributes of both class user and class mechanic.

ATTRIBUTES

Attributes are simply characteristics. You recognize people because of their physical and mental attributes. In that same way, a class is recognized by the arrangement of attributes that make up the class. If a class has an operatingSystem attribute, you can assume that it is some type of computer. An attribute definition is stored separately from the class definition, which enables you to apply a single attribute to more than one class.

An example of an attribute is the Common-Name attribute that is assigned to every object. This attribute not only is used to identify the object, but it is frequently used in searches.

By default, 863 attributes and 142 classes are contained in the schema, and because you can create your own classes and attributes, the sky is the limit. We will not discuss all the possible attributes here, but we'll instead focus on architecture, how to maintain the schema, and how and why to modify the schema. An exhaustive list of all the syntaxes and attributes is found at http://msdn.microsoft.com/certification/schema/syntaxes.asp.

> **Note**
>
> Although modifying the schema is comparatively easy, it would be a mistake to approach such modifications with a cavalier attitude in a production environment. We will discuss how and why to modify the schema later in this chapter.

SYNTAXES

Every attribute also has a syntax associated with it that defines its datatype, byte ordering, and so on. Although you can create new classes and attributes, because syntaxes are predefined, you cannot create new syntaxes. Twenty-three predefined syntaxes exist. Table 13.1 shows syntaxes that can be used to create attributes in Active Directory.

TABLE 13.1   ATTRIBUTE SYNTAXES IN AD

Name	Description
Distinguished Name	Fully qualified distinguished name of an AD object
Object Identifier	ISO OID
Case Sensitive String	Case-aware string of characters
Case Insensitive String	Character string; case is not checked
Print Case String	Case-sensitive, printable string
IA5-String	Case-sensitive, printable string
Numerical String	Digit string
OR Name	X.400 oMObjectClass
DN Binary	Distinguished name and binary large object (BLOB)
Boolean	True or False
Integer	32-bit number

TABLE 13.1   CONTINUED

Name	Description
Enumeration	32-bit enumeration
Octet String	Byte string
Replica Link	System only
UTC Time	Universal time coordinated time as a string
Generalized Time	Generalized time as a string
Unicode String	String using 16-bit Unicode storage
Address	Presentation address
Access Point	X.400 `oMObjectClass`
DN with String	Distinguished name and Unicode string
NT Security Descriptor	Octet string used by NT/2000 security mechanisms
Large Integer	64-bit number
SID	Security identifier, used to uniquely identify security principals

OBJECT IDENTIFIERS

An *object identifier (OID)* identifies every class in the schema. An OID is simply a dotted decimal number that looks suspiciously like an IP address with delusions of grandeur. You have probably seen OIDs if you have worked with SNMP.

An example of an OID is `1.2.840.113556.1.4.757`. This number provides a universally unambiguous numeric identifier for a class. Because it is hierarchical, you can also trace the parentage of the class all the way to the root. In this example, `1` refers to the ISO, `2` to ANSI, `840` to the U.S.A., `113556` to Microsoft, `1` to the Active Directory, and so on.

The International Standards Organization (ISO) is responsible for organizing and maintaining this numeric namespace, but—in most instances—it passes local authority to a governing body specific to a country. In the United States that body is the American National Standards Institute (ANSI). You can obtain information on requesting an OID from the ANSI by going to `http://web.ansi.org/public/services/reg_org.html`. A substantial fee is associated with obtaining an OID, but in a production environment, this is critical. If you decide to make up your OID out of whole cloth (like you did 5–10 years ago with IP addresses), you run the risk of colliding with an official OID when you install software from another vendor. When you get an OID for your organization, you should take the same care to use the namespace wisely as you would to plan IP address allocation.

TOOLS FOR EXPLORING THE SCHEMA

Several tools are available on a Windows 2000 server to look at the schema. Because these tools are capable of direct modification, be sure you use them with at least as much respect and fear as you show the Registry Editor. One mistake here could be forever.

It also is important to remember that even appropriate schema modification triggers replication to every domain controller in the forest. Unnecessary modifications should be avoided.

> **Caution**
>
> If you do extend the schema to install an application, make sure that the schema update has had time to replicate throughout the forest before installing the application; otherwise, installation can fail because the attributes and classes needed to support the application have not been replicated to all domain controllers in the forest. If you (or anyone else) goes to a computer in the forest and attempts to install the application, and that computer holds an old copy of the schema, your installation will fail.

You also should keep good records about which attributes and classes have been added. If you deactivate an attribute that is still in use by a class, you can invalidate that object.

ACTIVE DIRECTORY SCHEMA

If you want to see the schema, it can be viewed with the Active Directory Schema MMC Snap-in. This MMC Snap-in is not available by default. To make it available, you can simply run the `adminpak.msi`. This gives you access to several management interfaces that are not installed by default. You also can simply register the `%SystemRoot%\system32\schmmgmt.dll` by running the command in Listing 13.1. Be sure to use the correct drive letter for your system.

LISTING 13.1 REGISTERING schmmgmt.dll

```
O:\>regsvr32 o:\winnt\system32\schmmgmt.dll
```

If the registration is successful, you will see the output window shown in Figure 13.1.

Figure 13.1
Registering
schmmgmt.dll.

After you have loaded the Active Directory Schema MMC add-in by using the Add/Remove Snap-in command on the Console menu in MMC, you will see a window similar to Figure 13.2. You will use this tool later in the chapter to modify the schema, but for now it is useful for browsing the schema and getting a picture of what we have discussed so far.

ADSIEDIT

Another useful tool is `adsiEdit.msc`. This MMC Snap-in does not show the schema per se, but it does enable you to look at the attributes for a particular object, as well as many of the values assigned to those attributes. It is useful for understanding how the attributes relate to each object as well as for performing low-level editing of the Active Directory. This tool is added when the Windows 2000 support tools are installed from the `support/tools` folder on the installation CD. adsiEdit appears in Figure 13.3.

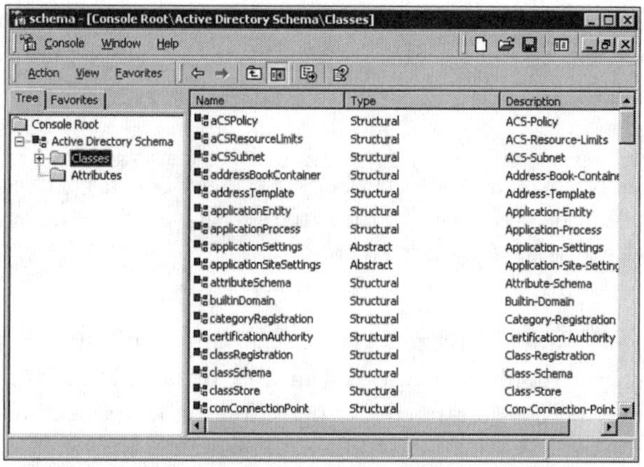

Figure 13.2
The AD schema snap-in.

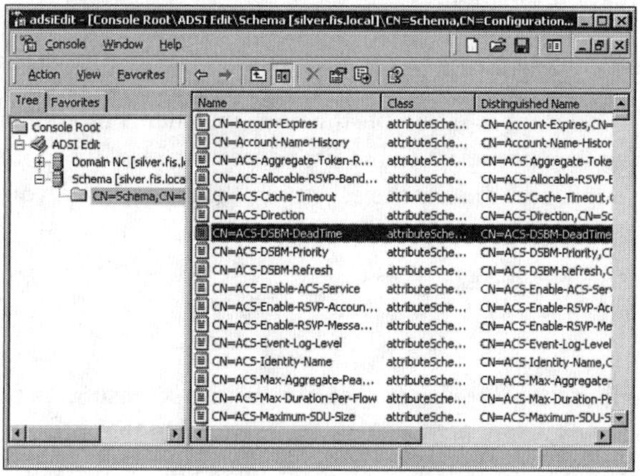

Figure 13.3
A schema container in adsiEdit.

If you select an object in the right pane and right-click Properties, you will see many of the properties.

MODIFYING THE SCHEMA

The bottom line is that, sooner or later, you or an application you install will modify the schema. Perhaps the single biggest issue to keep in mind is that schema modifications are not unique to the computer, the domain, or the tree. They are global to the *forest*. Every member of a forest has three things in common with every other member: Kerberos transitive trusts, a common global catalog (GC), and a common schema. Modifications you make to the schema are replicated to every domain controller in the forest.

REASONS FOR SCHEMA MODIFICATION

Several reasons exist to modify the schema, but generally they all boil down to a need to store information in the Active Directory. If classes and attributes are already defined to store the information you need, schema modification is not necessary. However, if you need classes or attributes that do not yet exist, you must use the Active Directory schema snap-in to make your changes.

> **Note**
> You also can use `ldifde.exe` and ADSI through COM to modify the schema programmatically. Some very good information and sample code for this is available at this Web site address: `msdn.Microsoft.com`.

One good reason to modify the schema is to take advantage of the globally available AD database. Virtually every application uses a data store of some kind, and having that data store available everywhere is an attractive proposition for an application developer. If, for example, your application needs to save information about a user that is available from anywhere in the domain (or the forest, if replicated to the GC), the Active Directory is the perfect place to store that information.

PLANNING FOR SCHEMA MODIFICATION

After deciding what you want to accomplish with your schema modification, you must decide whether to create a new class or modify an existing class by adding existing or new attributes. Unless you plan to modify the schema programmatically, you also must make the Active Directory schema tool available.

→ **See** "Active Directory Schema," **p. 192**

SCHEMA ADMINS

In addition to installing the AD schema tool, you must also ensure that you are logged on as a member of the Schema Admins group that is contained in the forest root domain. This group is a global group in a mixed mode domain and a universal group in a native mode domain. Additionally, by default, it has only one member—the Administrator account from the forest root domain. Other members can be added to the group, but by its nature, this should be an exclusive club.

ENABLING SCHEMA MODIFICATION

You also must ensure that schema modification is turned on. By default, schema modification is turned off to disallow casual changes to the schema. To enable schema modifications, open the Active Directory Schema MMC Snap-in and right-click the Active Directory Schema entry, as shown in Figure 13.4; then, choose Operations Master.

This opens the Change Schema Master dialog box shown in Figure 13.5. Make sure the check box next to The Schema May Be Modified on This Domain Controller is selected. You also can use this dialog box to change the Schema Operations Master to a different machine, if necessary.

→ **See** "Seizing Roles," **p. 185**

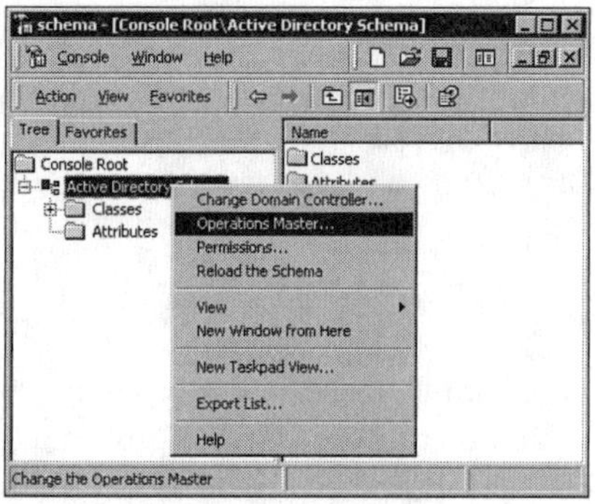

Figure 13.4
Using the AD schema snap-in to enable schema modification.

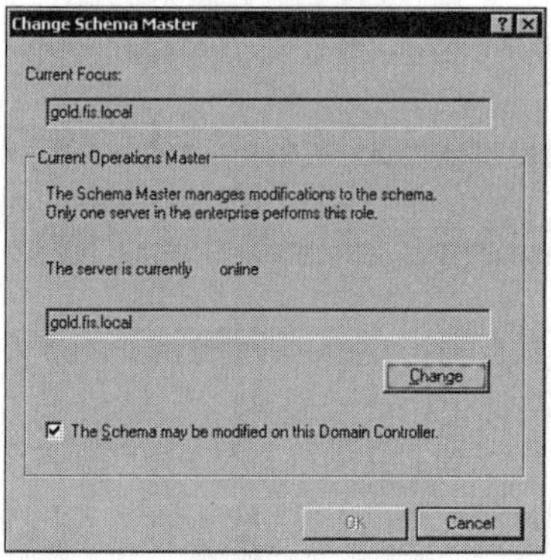

Figure 13.5
The schema Operations Master property page.

ADDING CLASSES AND ATTRIBUTES

Now that you have made your preparations, you can modify the schema. Although you can modify the schema by changing or adding attributes and classes, in this demonstration you will add attributes and then use the new attributes to create a new class. For example, you will create a class called fIS-Appserver (which is a subclass of computer) and a new attribute called fIS-Apptype-Description (which you will add to class fIS-Appserver to describe the type of application it is hosting).

→ **See** "Indexing Attributes," **p. 202**

Caution

New classes and attributes in the Active Directory schema are permanent. They cannot be deleted; they can only be deactivated.

→ **See** "Deactivating Classes and Attributes," **p. 201**

CH

13

Note

Although you can add classes and attributes to the schema, they will not automatically show up in your management tools, such as the Active Directory Users and Computers MMC Snap-in. You must have an application to take advantage of these new objects that will be created from your new class and attributes.

CREATING AN ATTRIBUTE

To add an attribute to the schema, you simply open the Active Directory schema tool, select and right-click the Attributes folder, and then choose Create Attribute (see Figure 13.6). It is important to note that you can perform this procedure from any Windows 2000 computer that has the Active Directory schema tool available; however, the focus of the tool must be on the schema Operations Master and the actual changes occur on the server currently holding the Operations Master role.

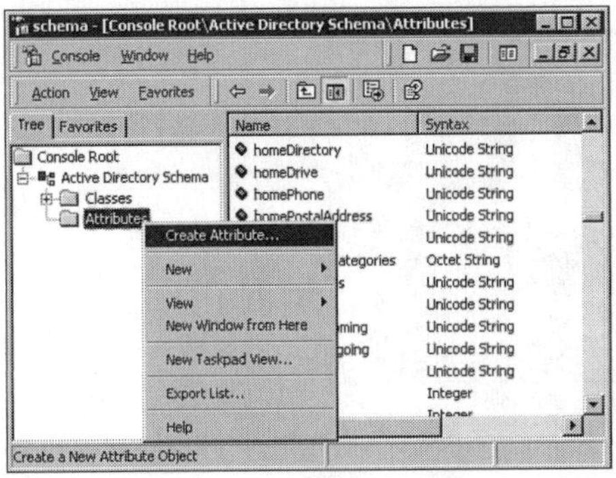

Figure 13.6
Creating an attribute with the AD schema.

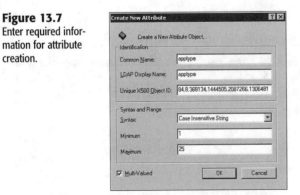

When you do this, you will see the Schema Object Creation dialog box, reminding you of the seriousness and permanence of modifying the schema. Click Continue.

Next, you see the Create New Attribute property page, shown in Figure 13.7. Here you must provide information about the attribute, such as its name and datatype.

Figure 13.7
Enter required information for attribute creation.

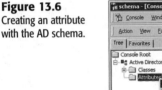

The Common Name is the relative distinguished name in the Active Directory. This value must be unique among all the attribute and schema objects in the Schema container and is a Unicode string. Several guidelines for creating a common name must be followed:

- **Use the first section for a company prefix**—This prefix should then become the standard. The company's stock symbol would be a good choice. This will keep all the company-specific additions easily sorted. This should be followed by a hyphen.

- **The next section should describe the product**—Each section should be separated by a hyphen.

- **The next section should describe the attribute**—Be as short and to the point as possible.

The LDAP Display Name is the name LDAP uses to search and modify values for this attribute. Although you can leave the LDAP Display Name field blank, it is good practice to explicitly declare this property. If you leave it blank, the system will derive the name from the common name of the object, but this can cause collisions. The rules for an LDAP Display Name are as follows:

- Always derive the LDAP Display Name from the common name (cn).

- Make sure the first character is lowercase.

- Capitalize the first character after each hyphen.

- Remove all hyphens except those immediately after the company and product sections of the name.

The Unique X500 Object ID must be entered as a valid OID. Again, in a production environment, you should register an OID from the ANSI. If this is a test environment, you can use the `oidgen.exe` tool provided in the Windows 2000 Server Resource Kit to create an OID.

`oidgen.exe` creates a base OID pair: one for use if you are creating a class and the second for creating an attribute. You should use the value created as the root of the numeric namespace. This means that if `oidgen` generates
`1.2.840.113556.1.4.7000.233.28688.28684.8.441552.1179789.1195496.1590404` as your base, you should use
`1.2.840.113556.1.4.7000.233.28688.28684.8.441552.1179789.1195496.1590404.1` as your first value. `oidgen` is easy to use and requires no parameters. You might want to set the window size to 100 or larger to accommodate the length of the value generated.

The Syntax determines the datatype for the attribute, and you can add a minimum and a maximum value for the attribute. Because you are creating and making the decisions about this attribute, reasonable minimum and maximum values are up to you.

→ **See** "Syntaxes," **p. 190**

Because, in this sample plan for the new fIS-Appserver class, it can have more than one application placed on it, the Multi-Valued check box has been checked. This simply enables you to store more than one value per attribute on an object. This is appropriate for storing

CH

13

information such as telephone numbers, IP addresses, and email addresses, in which more than one correct value potentially could exist.

The attribute is created when you click OK.

CREATING A CLASS

The process of creating a new class in the Active Directory schema is similar to the last section's process. With the AD schema tool open, select and right-click the Classes folder. Then, choose Create Class, as shown in Figure 13.8.

Figure 13.8
Creating a new class with the AD schema.

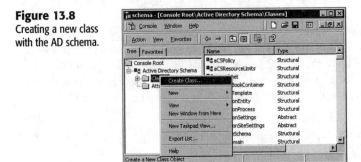

You once again see the Schema Object Creation Warning dialog box; click Continue.

In Figure 13.9, you can see the Create New Schema Class property page. Once again, fill in the values you have chosen for Common Name, LDAP Display Name, and Unique X500 Object ID using the naming rules from the previous section "Creating an Attribute." You set the Parent Class as type computer so that it will inherit the properties of the parent class. In addition, leave the Class Type at its default—Structural. This is the only class type that can have an instance in the Active Directory. Abstract and auxiliary classes are used to create instances of other classes. Structural classes, however, are used to create AD objects, which is your goal here. The various types of classes are explained in Table 13.2.

Figure 13.9
Naming the new class.

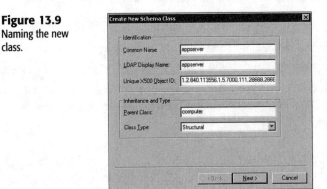

TABLE 13.2 ACTIVE DIRECTORY CLASSES

Class Type	Use
Structural	Structural classes are used to create objects in Active Directory and are derived from either other structural classes or an abstract class. They also can contain auxiliary classes in their definitions.
Abstract	Abstract classes can't be used to create objects in Active Directory. They are used as templates to create other classes.
Auxiliary	Auxiliary classes contain lists of attributes and are used similarly to an include file to add attributes en masse to a structural class.

When you click Next, you see the Create New Schema Class dialog box shown in Figure 13.10. Here you use the Add button to add your new attribute, fIS-Apptype-Description, as a mandatory attribute. Remember that because your new fIS-Appserver class is a subclass of the computer class, it inherits many mandatory and optional attributes, as well as the one you have added here. When you click Finish, your class is created.

Figure 13.10
Adding attributes to a new class.

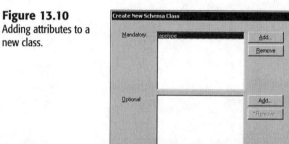

When designing the new class, remember to use mandatory attributes to define information that must be available at creation time. Optional attributes can then be used to define information that is useful but not critical.

Figure 13.11 shows your new class in the Classes folder. It is now ready for use in an application or with the adsiEdit tool.

USING YOUR NEW CLASS

To test your new class, you can use the adsiEdit tool. Figure 13.12 shows that the tool has been opened from the Support Tools folder and the domain naming context for your domain (fis.local) has been expanded. Because fIS-Appserver is a subclass of computers, you can create fIS-Appserver in any organizational unit (OU) or other container. Here, you will create it in the Computers container because it is a special type of computer object.

CH
13

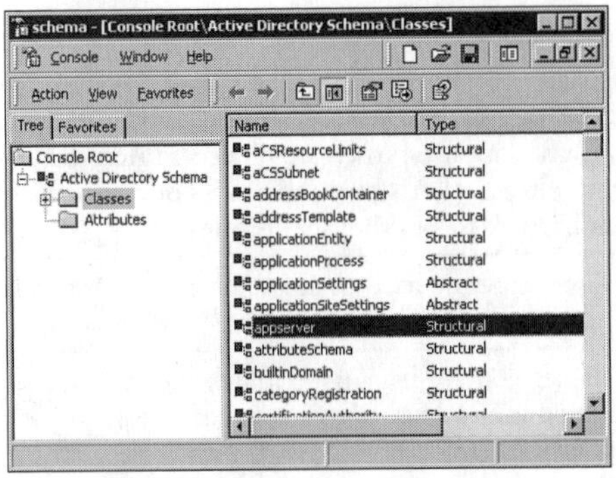

Figure 13.11
The new class in the
AD schema.

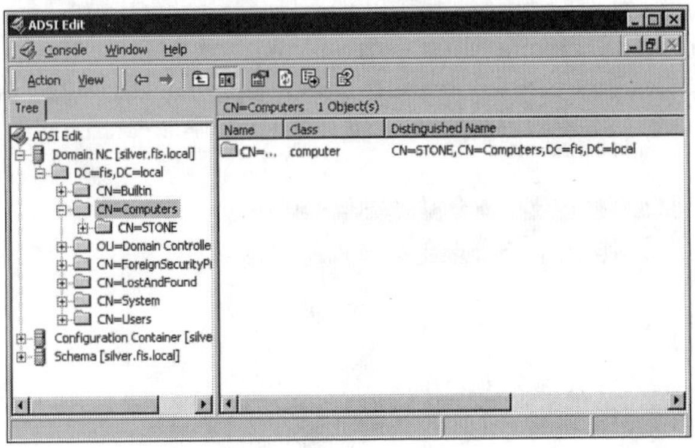

Figure 13.12
The Computers con-
tainer in adsiEdit.

To use your new class, you must create an instance of the class: an object. This enables you
to see that your work has been successful, and it also enables you to use the new class and
attribute you have created. To create a new instance of an fIS-Appserver object from your
new class, simply right-click the container and choose New, Object (see Figure 13.13). This
starts the Create Object Wizard.

Figure 13.13
Creating a new
instance of a class—
an object.

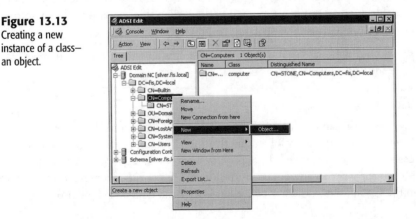

On the Create Object page, choose your class from the list available, and then click Next.

In the next three dialog boxes, you choose the cn, sAMAccountName, and fIS-Apptype-Description parameters for your new object. This is obviously a subset of the attributes available for this class. If you need to set more attributes for the object, you can click the More Attributes button on the last dialog box of the wizard.

When you click Finish, your new object is created and you see adsiEdit (see Figure 13.14). If you open the Active Directory Users and Computers tool, you will also see it there.

Figure 13.14
The new object in adsiEdit.

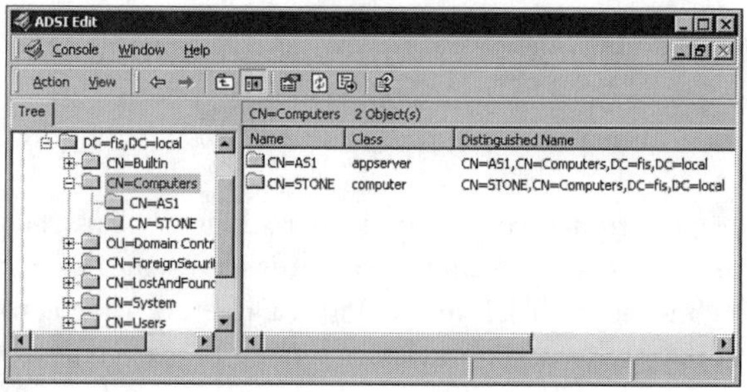

SCHEMA REPLICATION

When modifying the schema, it is important to consider replication. Again, the schema is replicated to all domain controllers in the forest. This means that your new classes and attributes are replicated to every DC in the forest.

Two copies of the schema actually exist: one in memory and one on disk. The copy in memory, called the schema *cache*, is checked to validate any changes made to the Active Directory. When performing schema modifications, the copy on disk is actually modified, and, over the next five minutes, is used to create a new copy of the schema cache. The schema partition of the AD is replicated to all DCs in the domain, but for increased responsiveness, the schema partition is loaded into memory. Every five minutes the cached copy of the schema is verified against the schema partition of the AD. If the schema has been modified, the new schema automatically is reloaded into memory.

When you have modified the schema, be aware that until the changes have replicated throughout the forest, you might encounter problems using the new classes and attributes. Inside a site, the changes should replicate within 15 minutes; however, in a highly disconnected, multisite environment, this could take several hours. It just depends on the intersite replication topology and schedule.

CH
13

DEACTIVATING CLASSES AND ATTRIBUTES

All schema extensions (adding classes, subclasses, or attributes) are irreversible and permanent. After they're added, objects can never be removed from the schema. However, they can be deactivated, if they were not part of the default schema and are not currently in use in the schema. If you want to deactivate an attribute you have added, you must make sure you have first deactivated any classes that use that attribute. If you do not, you will receive the error message shown in Figure 13.15. To deactivate an attribute, follow these steps:

1. Open the AD Schema MMC Snap-in.
2. Double-click the attribute.
3. Select the Deactivate This Attribute check box and click OK.

Figure 13.15
The error message.

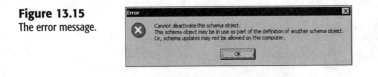

After you deactivate an attribute, you can no longer add it to a class, and after you deactivate a class, you can no longer create an object that is an instance of that class. To deactivate a class, simply select and right-click it in the Active Directory schema tool; then, choose Properties. The interface to deactivate a class is located on the General tab, shown in Figure 13.16.

Figure 13.16
Deactivating a class.

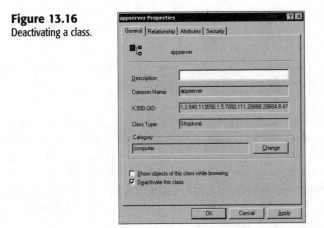

Simply check the Deactivate This Class check box and click OK. This is a reversible process, but until the class or attribute is reactivated, no other changes can be made to it.

The Relationship tab enables you to add auxiliary classes to the class. The Attributes tab, on the other hand, enables the addition of mandatory and optional attributes to the class. Finally, the Security tab sets the access control list (ACL) for the Active Directory object.

INDEXING ATTRIBUTES

You can modify the schema by configuring an attribute to be indexed. Just like any database, indexing a column makes searches for that information faster and more efficient. Indexing an attribute can make lookups in the Active Directory faster for that attribute. However, the same rules apply here that apply when choosing columns to index in an enterprise database. Four guidelines should be kept in mind when deciding whether or not to index an attribute.

First, the attribute should be a good candidate for an index. It should be reasonably narrow and the value in the attribute should be unique with an even range of values. An example of a good choice is indexing based on state, assuming you have users all over the United States. A bad example is indexing based on gender—with only two possible values, it is not exactly unique.

Second, although indexes can speed up reads, they also can negatively impact the performance of writes. If you have too many indexed attributes, updating an object can take longer because of the need to update the associated indexes.

Third, an attribute set to be indexed will be indexed on every instance of a class that uses the attribute. You cannot selectively choose to index an attribute for a particular class. If the attribute exists on more than one class and is indexed, it will be indexed on all instances of the class that use the index.

Fourth, indexes take up space. Indexing a wide attribute can take up a lot of space, so factor this into your capacity planning when making decisions in this area. You should index only attributes that might be frequently queried because indexing does increase the use of system resources.

Procedurally, indexing an attribute is not challenging. After you have enabled schema modifications and logged on as a member of the Schema Admins group, you can simply load the AD schema tool, right-click an attribute, and index away. The interface is shown in Figure 13.17. To index the attribute, select the Index This Attribute in the Active Directory check box.

Figure 13.17
Indexing an attribute.

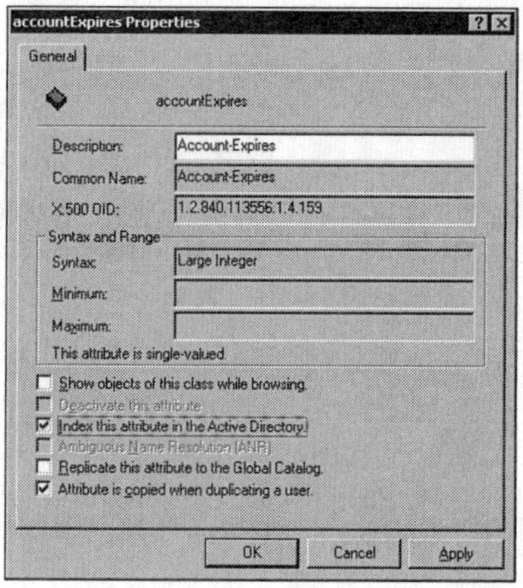

After you have checked the Index This Attribute in the Active Directory check box and clicked OK, you are finished. The schema change will trigger a schema update on each DC and the DSA will create the index.

CH
13

Several other options are available in this dialog box. Although they aren't directly related to indexing, they are explained in Table 13.3.

TABLE 13.3 MORE INDEXING PROPERTIES

Option	Explanation
Show Objects of This Class While Browsing	Allows objects to be visible while browsing.
Deactivate This Attribute	Makes the attribute unavailable to new classes.
Index This Attribute in the Active Directory	Creates an index for this attribute in AD to speed searches.
Ambiguous Name Resolution (ANR)	Aids in "fuzzy" searches.
Replicate This Attribute to the Global Catalog	Replicates the attribute to every GC server in the forest to aid in searches.
Attribute Is Copied when Duplicating a User	You can copy user objects in AD Users and Computers. If this option is checked, the attribute is copied from the source user object to the target user object. It's applicable only to user objects.

REPLICATING ATTRIBUTES TO THE GLOBAL CATALOG

You also can modify the schema by replicating attributes to the global catalog. The advantage is that your applications can perform fast searches for objects in other domains without having to refer to DCs authoritative for that domain—that is, if the attributes for the object they are searching for exist in the GC and the searches are initiated as GC searches. Many attributes are marked for replication to the GC by default, but you can add to the list. Some examples are c (country-name), CA-Certificate, and cn(common-name).

Remember that the entire forest shares a common GC. Although only one GC is installed by default—on the first domain controller in the forest root domain—other Active Directory DCs should be configured as GC servers. A GC server holds (along with full copies of its own domain database, the schema, and configuration partitions) a copy of every object in every domain in every tree in the forest, but only a subset of the attributes of each object. Exactly what comprises this subset is up to you.

Marking an attribute for replication to the global catalog is almost as simple as indexing an attribute. However, realize that when you mark an attribute for replication to the GC, you are setting it to be copied to every GC server in the forest. This can have far-reaching implications for replication traffic. Any attribute that is replicated to the GC can cause unnecessary GC replication if updated frequently.

An attribute marked for replication to the global catalog should have three characteristics.

First, it should be globally interesting. If the attribute you choose to replicate to the GC is never searched for outside the domain to which the object belongs, its availability in the GC is wasted.

Second, it should be reasonably static. In an enterprise environment, replication to all the GC servers in the forest can be expensive. To avoid unnecessary replication, the attribute should be one that does not change very often.

Third, it should be fairly small. The value stored in the attributes replicated to the GC should be relatively small so as not to unnecessarily increase the size of the global catalog or the amount of data being replicated among GC servers. If it is not small, you must take into account the additional size requirements when you are sizing your GC servers.

Refer to Figure 13.17 for the dialog box used to mark an attribute for GC replication. Simply checking the Replicate This Attribute to the Global Catalog check box and clicking OK accomplishes the task.

Summary

The globally available database that comprises much of the Windows 2000 Active Directory is fully extensible and is rife with possibilities for all kinds of applications. It can be modified and extended by tools available in the operating system or programmatically through COM interfaces and script. It is an interesting exercise because, although it is not demanding from a procedural point of view, doing it properly and for the right reasons can be somewhat abstract and nontrivial.

You can modify the schema in many ways. One way is to create a new attribute. This enables that attribute to be used by other classes to track information that is important to you.

You also can add classes. After a class has been added, instances of that class (objects) can be created in Active Directory.

You can modify the schema by modifying existing attributes or classes. Indexing an attribute to speed searches is an example of this.

Much of the schema modification that takes place will be performed by software written to take advantage of the schema. This software will modify the schema as it is installed and use the schema as a lightweight globally available database.

Troubleshooting

Can't Modify the Schema

When you open the AD schema tool and try to make any modification or extension to the schema, the options are grayed out or don't work.

This is generally due to one of two things, or both. First, make sure you are logged on as a member of the Schema Admins group. Then, make sure that the schema has been marked for modification.

→ **See** "Schema Admins," **p. 194**

→ **See** "Enabling Schema Modification," **p. 194**

UNAVAILABLE OM

You can't connect to the schema Operations Master.

If the schema Operations Master is temporarily unavailable, you can fix the network problem or wait for it to come back online. If it is permanently unavailable, you will need to seize the Operations Master role.

→ **See** "Seizing Roles," **p. 185**

VARIOUS TROUBLESHOOTING ISSUES

You can use the Registry to increase the amount and verbosity of the error messages written to the event log. To raise the Directory Services logging level, set the Registry key `hkey_local_machine\system\currentcontrolset\services\ntds\diagnostics\ internal processing` to 3.

CHAPTER 14

ACTIVE DIRECTORY SITES

In this chapter

INTRODUCTION TO SITES

Active Directory is truly an enterprise-scale directory service, and sites help provide this scalability. As discussed in earlier chapters, sites enable the administrator to control Active Directory replication traffic.

A *site* is a collection of IP subnets that share high-speed, reliable connectivity between DCs. I say domain controllers in this case because we are focusing on Active Directory and, in particular, replication. However, sites are also used for controlling client authentication traffic and the application of group policy objects. This chapter focuses on the replication aspect of sites and how they are utilized with regard to Active Directory replication.

> **Note**
>
> A high-speed connection is defined as 10Mbps or greater, so essentially, servers connected within a LAN define your sites with regard to site design. However, many times you will find that what is "good" network connectivity for one is not for another. This determination will be largely left to you, but 10Mbps is a good starting point from which to work.

An important thing to keep in mind as you think about sites is that no relationship exists between sites and the domain structure of your organization. Sites typically reflect your network's physical connectivity instead of the more logical design of your domain structure, which often reflects the logical structure of your company. Therefore, you're likely to need more than one domain within the confines of a single site or even need a single domain spanning multiple sites.

Because sites are not related to domains, the site configuration information is stored in the configuration naming context (NC). This particular naming context is replicated to all DCs in the forest, regardless of their domain membership.

→ **See** "Intra-Site Replication," **p. 249**

ARCHITECTURE

This section's goal is to help you understand the architecture of the site object and the role it plays in replication and authentication. If you already understand site architecture and concepts and just want to know how to create and configure them, you can probably skip this section. But I do feel that in order to understand when and why you should create sites, you must know how they function.

As mentioned previously, sites are defined by areas of good network connectivity. For some, "good" is subjective. One group might define 10Mbps as "good," whereas another will not accept anything less than 100Mbps. So, in an attempt to clear the air for purposes of replication and site design issues, we will define "good" as 10Mbps or greater.

HOW ARE SITES USED?

Sites are used to control replication traffic between DCs through scheduling and to control authentication requests from a client by having the client attempt to locate and contact a DC in its site.

WHERE DO SITES LIVE?

Sites reside in the configuration NC. This means that site information is global throughout the enterprise and is completely independent of the domain structure.

HOW ARE DOMAIN CONTROLLERS ADDED TO A SITE?

During the process of becoming a domain controller (DC), the dcpromo process must determine with which site to deposit the new DC. This is accomplished by dcpromo attempting to locate the site of which the server is a member. This assumes that the site and subnet have been previously configured. If dcpromo is incapable of finding a site, it selects the site from which the source information for the directory is being retrieved.

HOW IS SITE MEMBERSHIP DETERMINED?

Site membership is determined by the client's subnet. However, after the client has determined its membership, it performs a query using Domain Name Service (DNS) to find the service for which it is looking. The following list shows a series of entries that are maintained in the DNS zone, which represent specific DCs with regard to their site memberships in Active Directory:

```
_gc._tcp.Default-First-Site-Name._sites.adbook.local
```

```
_ldap.tcp.Default-First-Site-Name._sites.adbook.local
```

```
_ldap.tcp.Default-First-Site-Name._sites.dc._msdcs.adbook.local
```

This information is obtained for the client by the first authenticating DC; the client then stores this information and queries appropriately for a domain controller/global catalog in its site. If the client is moved to another site, it still continues to query a DC in the old site until it gets an updated site referral from the old DC.

Note

Remember that the purpose of DNS is to resolve a hostname to an IP address. The configuration NC stores the references to the directory objects.

REQUIREMENTS

Before getting into creating sites, we need to look at a few of the requirements for sites to function as designed.

SUBNET

Because a site is an area of well-connected computers within a subnet and also is a collection of subnets, subnets are a requirement. By default, Active Directory does not have a subnet defined. It is up to you, the administrator, to define each subnet on your network.

Сн
14

Note

An IP subnet is a numeric range of addresses usually associated with a physical LAN segment. The IP specification provides for Class A addresses with more than 16 million addresses in one network, Class B addresses with 65,536 addresses in one network, and Class C addresses with 254 addresses in one network. These ranges frequently do not match up well with the current physical layout of the network. An A, B, or C network can be separated into several numerically contiguous ranges to enable the address range to more closely match the physical layout of the network.

An example is a Class C network, 192.168.2.0, that provides a single range of 254 usable addresses. You could separate it into 8 ranges of 32 addresses each, using a subnet mask of 255.255.255.224 rather than the default subnet mask of 255.255.255.0.

When determining which subnets to define in Active Directory, take an inventory of each subnet on the network. After you have your subnets, assess which ones will contain directory-enabled machines. Then, create a subnet object for each subnet in your network.

To create a subnet, follow these steps:

1. Open Active Directory Sites and Services.

2. Right-click Subnet, and then click New Subnet (see Figure 14.1).

Figure 14.1
Creating a new subnet using Active Directory Sites and Services.

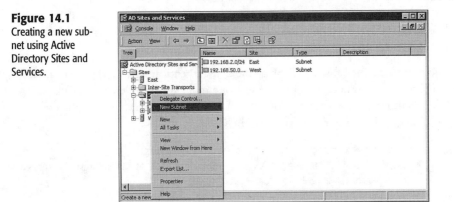

3. Then enter the address for your network and the subnet mask used to designate your network. For example, if your network is using the private 10.1.x.x range of IPs, your configuration for one subnet would look similar to Figure 14.2.

    You also must select the site to associate the new subnet to. This might seem a little backward because you must create a site to create a subnet. However, you can create the sites first and then associate them with the appropriate subnets. Either way, the end result is the same. Regardless, select the site you want to associate with this particular subnet.

4. The final result will look similar to Figure 14.3.

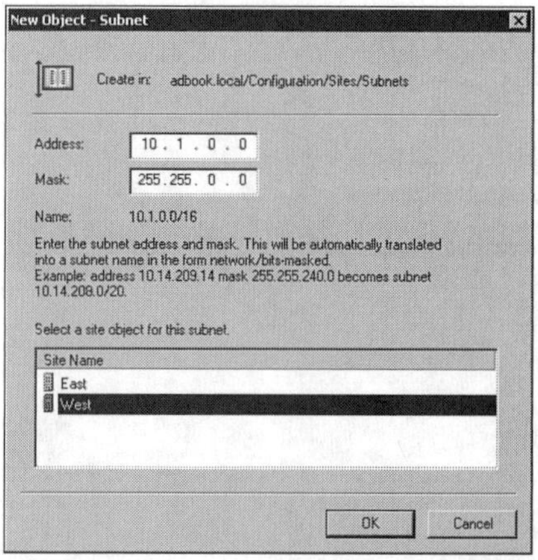

Figure 14.2
Assign the appropriate network ID for the subnet.

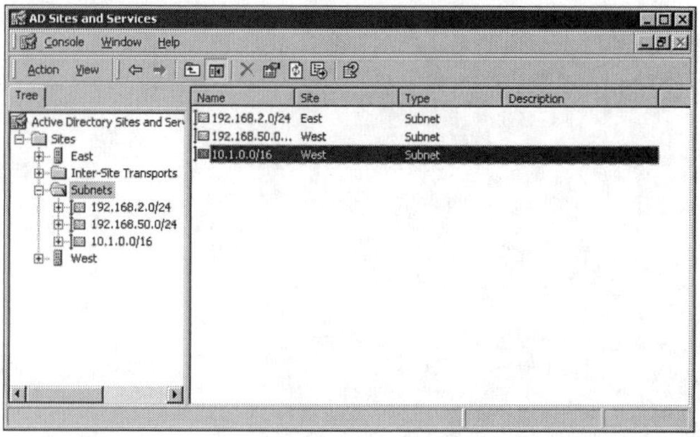

Figure 14.3
The Sites and Services tool helps you see the subnet and the site to which it belongs.

CONFIGURING THE SUBNET

The subnet object that is created does not have many configuration options. You can change the site association of the particular subnet at a later time by opening the subnet object's Properties dialog box and changing the site in the Site drop-down box, as shown in Figure 14.4.

Notice that you have the option to select no site association. This enables you to create a subnet ahead of time and then, when you are ready to bring servers online in that particular subnet, you can change the site association.

The next tab is the Location tab (see Figure 14.5). Location is used with the location tracking feature for printing. To use this feature, you must first enter the location in this tab.

The remaining two tabs are Security and Object. The Security tab is used to designate who can manage this object in Active Directory. By default, Enterprise Admins, Domain Admins (for that domain), and the System account all have full control permissions to the subnet object. Notice that Authenticated Users has read permissions only (see Figure 14.6).

CH

14

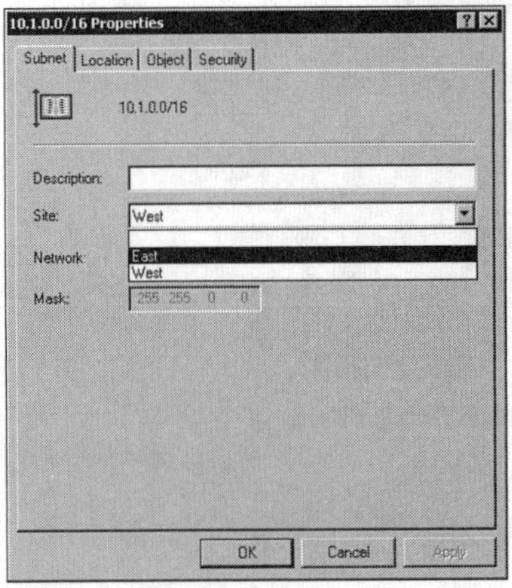

Figure 14.4
You can change the site association of a subnet at a later time.

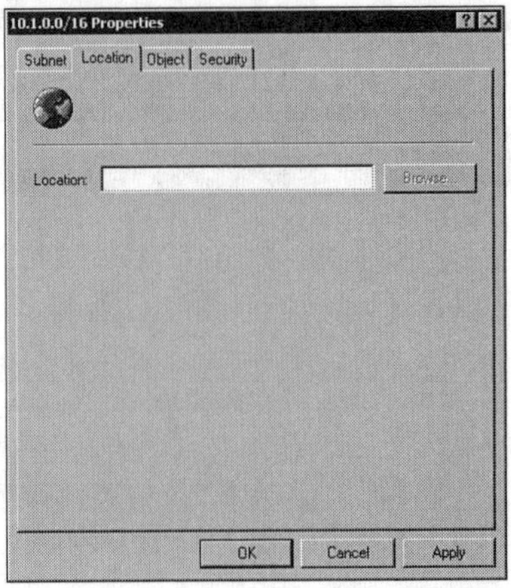

Figure 14.5
For the printer location feature to function correctly, you must add a location to the subnet.

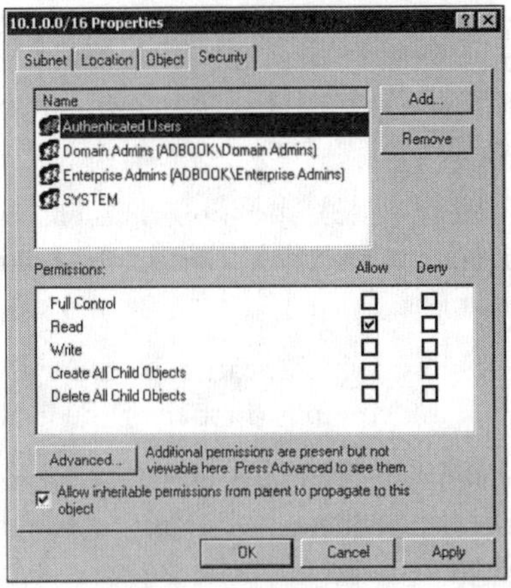

Figure 14.6
Setting security on objects in Active Directory enables true delegation of control.

The Object tab has specific information about this instance of the object (see Figure 14.7). "This instance" refers to when the object is replicated to other DCs and the USN is different. The Object tab also displays the fully qualified domain name (FQDN) of the subnet object, such as in the following code line:

```
Adbook.local/Configuration/Sites/Subnets/192.168.2.0\/24
```

Figure 14.7
By looking at the Object tab, you can determine when the object was created as well as the USN values.

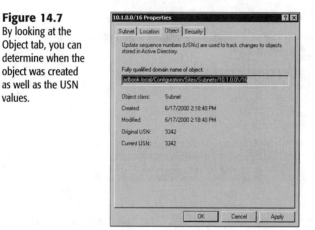

CREATING SITES

The first site you will encounter is known as Default-First-Site-Name. This site is created by the dcpromo process and includes the first domain controller for the domain and forest. If you never create any other sites or subnets, all subsequent DCs will be located in the default site container.

If you have precreated your sites and associated the appropriate subnets with those sites, each DC you install after that time will be placed in the appropriate site container. This assumes that each DC is configured with the appropriate IP address for the subnet.

Note

DCs that are already installed must be moved manually if a site is created and associated with an existing subnet.

The process of creating a site is simple. As mentioned in the previous section, you must have a subnet first. Now, you've probably realized that you can create a site without first creating a subnet. However, if you do so, the site will not function as a method of controlling user authentication.

You also must create a site link with which to associate your site.

→ **See** "Site Link Objects," **p. 231**

Сн
14

To create the site object, follow these steps:

1. Open Active Directory Sites and Services.

2. Right-click the Sites container (as shown in Figure 14.8), and then select New Site.

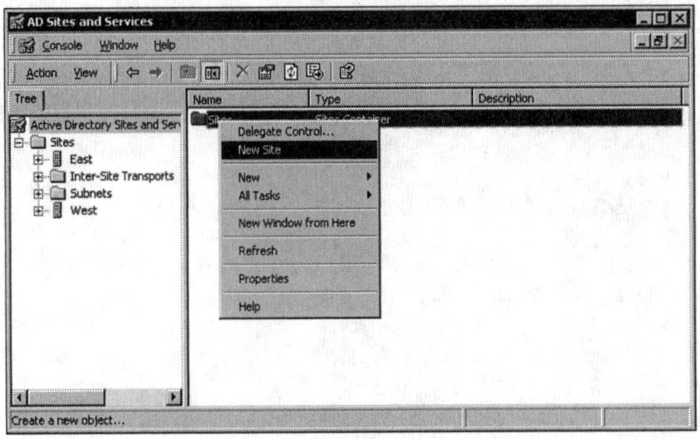

Figure 14.8
Creating a new site for
Active Directory helps
control replication and
authentication.

3. Type a name for the Site object in the Name field. This name has to adhere to the following rules:

   • It must be no greater than 63 characters.

   • It can contain only alpha characters, numeric characters, and hyphens.

   • It can contain *no* spaces or periods.

   • It *can't* be comprised of only numbers.

Tip

A common practice is to name sites based on their geographical locations.

4. Select the appropriate Site Link object and click OK (see Figure 14.9).

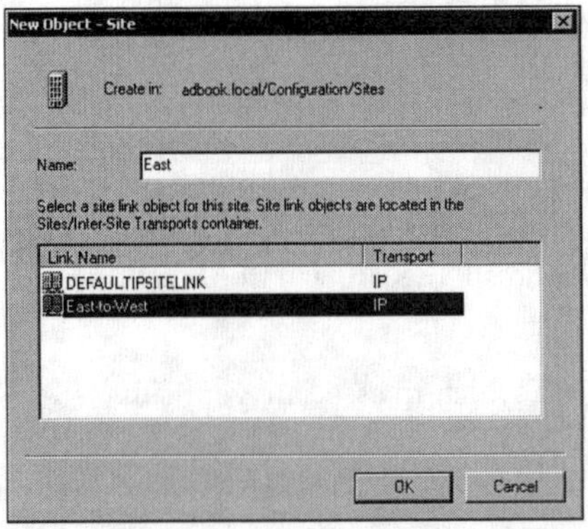

Figure 14.9
Adding the name of
the site and selecting
a site link.

You will receive a dialog box outlining the additional steps necessary to make the new site function correctly, as shown in Figure 14.10.

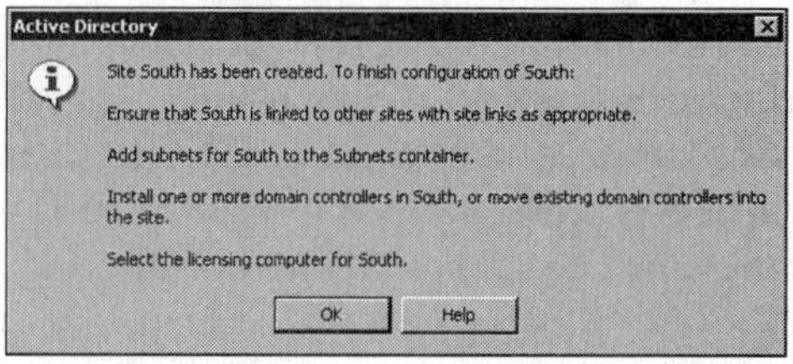

Figure 14.10
You still will need to make sure site links are created between the sites, as well as move any existing DCs that belong in this site.

SERVER OBJECTS

The server object is a child object of the site, so let's look at some of the issues surrounding the server object.

The server object is different from the computer object representation you will find for the DC in the Domain Controllers organizational unit (OU). The server object is a representation of the DC in the configuration NC, whereas the computer object is a representation of the DC in the domain NC. The computer object is a security principal. The server object, on the other hand, is used for the purposes of replication and site membership.

Figure 14.11 shows the server object for the West site. You will also notice that the server object has a child object as well, NTDS Settings. We will discuss that object later in this chapter.

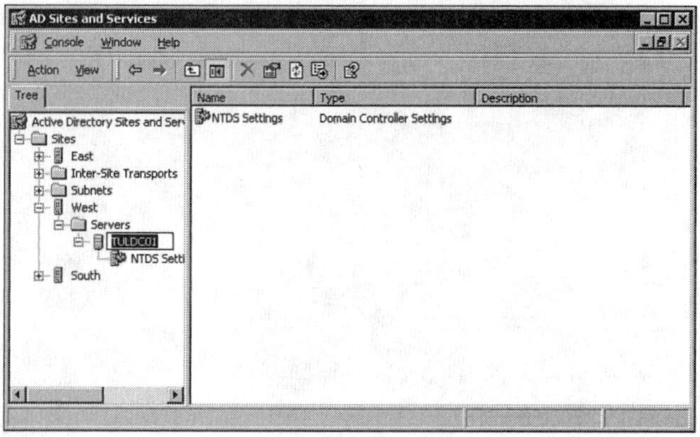

Figure 14.11
The server object is a representation of a DC and is located in the site container.

Only three operations can be performed on the server object: moving the object to a new site (which is covered in the section "Moving a DC to a New Site"), deleting the object, and renaming the object. If you choose to delete the object, you must ensure that the actual computer represented by the object is no longer on the network. When an object is deleted from the directory but the physical object still exists—in this case, the server object—the server

CH

14

will no longer be capable of functioning in Active Directory. If you rename the object, you will be unable to successfully replicate. This option, therefore, should not be used.

The properties on the server object are used to determine which server will be the preferred bridgehead server for the transports in this site. The concept behind a bridgehead server is that all connections from this site to another site go through the bridgehead server. By default, the Knowledge Consistency Checker (KCC) is responsible for selecting the bridgehead servers when it creates the connection objects between servers in separate sites. (Connection objects are covered in Chapter 15, "Site Link Objects and Connection Objects.") However, as the administrator, you can choose to override what the KCC wants to do by selecting servers to be *preferred* bridgehead servers. It is important to note that the inter-site topology generator (ISTG) is the actual server that performs the selection of bridgehead servers. The ISTG is a specific DC in a site that is responsible for creating connection objects between sites. The KCC is the actual process that runs while the ISTG is a role.

To select a preferred bridgehead server, perform the following steps:

1. Open Active Directory Sites and Services.
2. Expand the site object and then the Servers container, in which the server object is located.
3. Right-click the server object and select Properties.
4. Select the transport (IP or SMTP) for which you want this server to act as a bridgehead server, and then click Add (see Figure 14.12). Then, click OK.

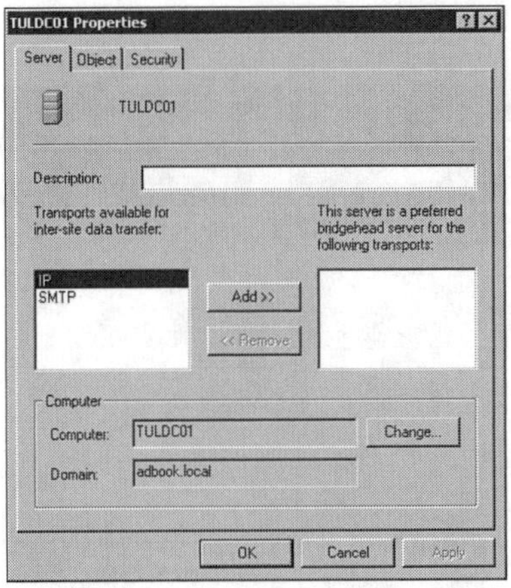

Figure 14.12
Select the transport to designate this server as a bridgehead server for this site.

If you choose to designate a server as a preferred bridgehead server, you will have taken control away from the KCC. In addition, you will need to designate a bridgehead server for each domain in each site.

Consider Figure 14.13, which shows three sites and two domains (na.adbook.local and adbook.local). You would need to designate one DC from the adbook.local domain in each site as a bridgehead server and one DC from the `na.adbook.local` domain in Sites B and C for replication to work correctly.

Figure 14.13
A sample site configu-
ration.

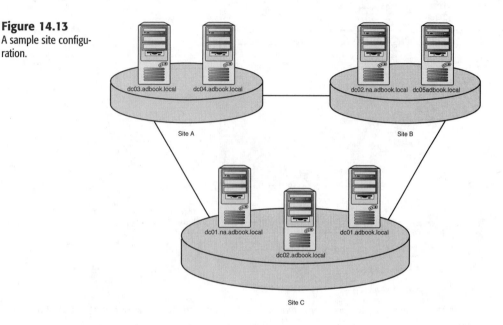

If of the DCs that have been designated as bridgehead servers are unavailable, the KCC will be incapable of creating connection objects using the other servers because they have not been designated as preferred bridgehead servers.

THE NTDS Settings OBJECT

The NTDS Settings object has only two configuration options available, as shown on its Properties page in Figure 14.14. You can either set the query policy or designate the server that is the parent to the NTDS Settings object as a global catalog. The NTDS Settings object serves as a connection point for connection objects.

The Query Policy settings enable you to customize LDAP administrative limits. This enables you to determine the amount of resources this particular server will consume when performing LDAP functions.

The object that is referenced in Figure 14.14, with regard to the query policy, is the queryPolicy object. The queryPolicy object is located in the directory at

```
Cn=Query-Policies,CN=Directory Service,CN=Windows NT,CN=Services,
➥CN=Configuration,DC=domain,DC=domain
```

You can Settings define limits for various settings using NTDSUtil. You should be careful with these settings, however, because they can have adverse effects if they're not tested prior to implementation.

CH

14

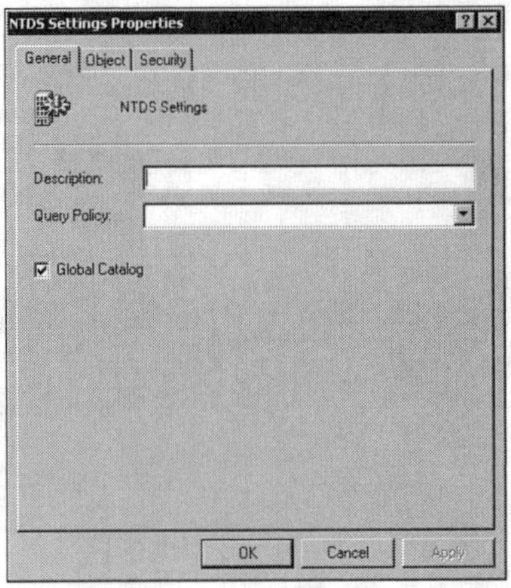

Figure 14.14
You can make a DC a
global catalog server
by selecting the Global
Catalog check box.

To view default settings for the default query policy, follow these steps:

1. At a command prompt, type **ntdsutil**.

2. Type **LDAP policies**.

3. Type **Connections**.

4. Type **Connect to Server** *servername* (where *servername* is the name of the AD server from which you want to read the settings).

5. Type **Show Values**.

The default Settings settings are shown in Table 14.1.

TABLE 14.1   DEFAULT QUERY POLICY SETTINGS

Attribute	Default Value
MaxPoolThreads	4
MaxDatagramRecv	1,024
MaxReceiveBuffer	10,485,760 (bytes)
InitRecvTimeout	120 (seconds)
MaxConnections	5,000
MaxConnIdleTime	900
MaxActiveQueries	20
MaxPageSize	1,000
MaxQueryDuration	120 (seconds)
MaxTempTableSize	10,000
MaxResultSetSize	262,144
MaxNotificationPerConn	5

To change any of these settings, you must type the following:

```
Set policyname to newvalue
Ex. Set MaxPoolThreads to 10
```

After you have made the changes, you must type **Commit Changes** for the settings to take effect. You also can cancel any uncommitted changes you have made by typing **Cancel Changes**.

You can create a new query policy by using adsiEdit, writing your own script using ADSI, or using the modifyldap.vbs script included with the Windows 2000 Resource Kit. The easiest method, in my opinion, is using adsiEdit.

Here's how to use adsiEdit to create a custom query policy:

1. Open the adsiEdit tool.

2. Expand the configuration container object and navigate to CN=Services,CN=Windows NT,CN=Directory Service, CN=Query-Policies (see Figure 14.15).

Figure 14.15
The queryPolicy object can be modified by using adsiEdit.

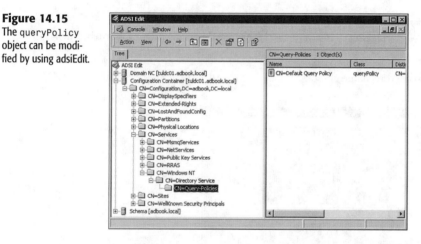

3. Right-click CN=Query-Policies; select New, and then select Object (see Figure 14.16).

Figure 14.16
You must create a new object that will represent your settings for a new query policy.

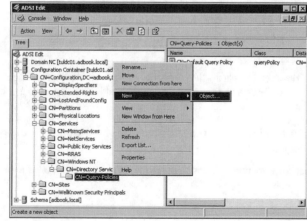

CH
14

4. Select the `queryPolicy` object class, as shown in Figure 14.17.

Figure 14.17
Using adsiEdit to create an object requires you to select the appropriate object class.

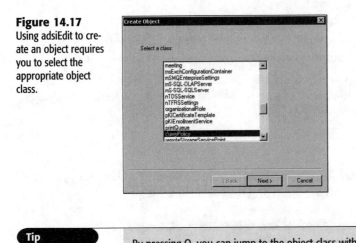

By pressing Q, you can jump to the object class without having to scroll down the list.

5. You now need to name the object (see Figure 14.18).

Figure 14.18
Name the object something that references the type of settings it will contain.

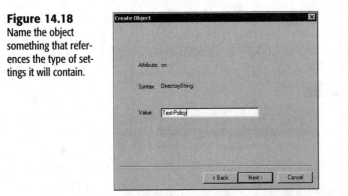

6. If you want to add other attributes to this object, you can (see Figure 14.19).

However, by defining the `class` object, the attributes that are specifically needed are added by default. Click More Attributes to add additional attributes, or click Finish.

7. Now, you must add values to the `lDAPAdminLimits` attribute for the policy. Right-click the new policy object and select Properties.

8. In the Select a Property to View drop-down box, select lDAPAdminLimits (see Figure 14.20).

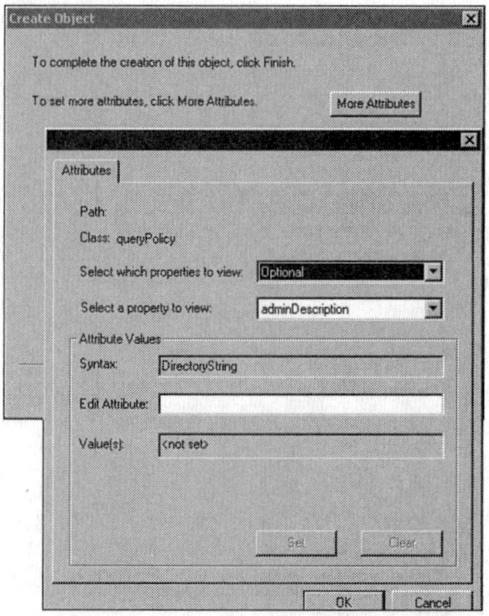

Figure 14.19
Adding additional attributes is possible but not always recommended.

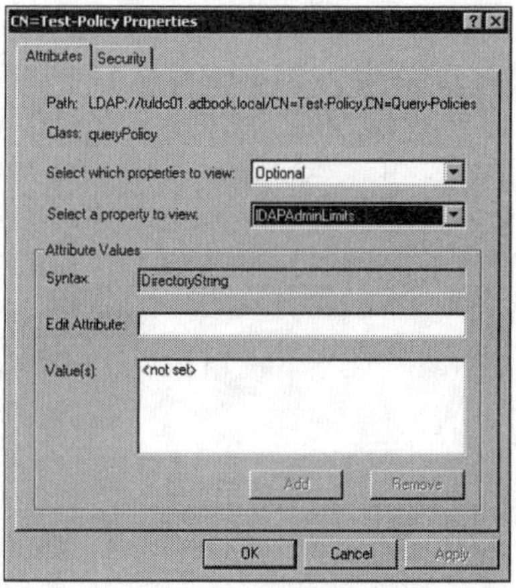

Figure 14.20
Select which property to edit.

9. Refer to Table 14.1 for the values to populate the lDAPAdminLimits attribute. You must add each value individually by typing in the value in the Edit Attribute text box and clicking Add (see Figure 14.21).

Note

The default settings are adequate for most installations, and you should thoroughly test any settings that you change in a lab before implementing them in a production environment.

CH

14

Assigning query policies is accomplished on a server-by-server basis in each site. This is useful in scenarios in which you want to control how the DC can respond to outside requests. It also can be used to protect against denial of service attacks by tuning the DC to handle only a small amount of requests. Additionally, you can tune a DC to handle only certain functions by configuring the settings.

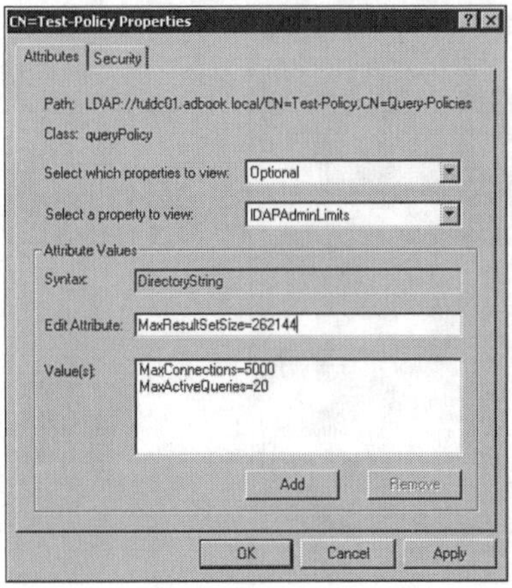

Figure 14.21
Adding the setting name and the value is important to correctly configure a new query policy.

Another unique feature of the `queryPolicy` object is its capability to add an IP deny list, which enables you to disallow certain DCs from answering LDAP queries from any IP in the IP deny list. You can edit this list by using NTDSUtil or adsiEdit; however, using NTDSUtil is the easiest method by far because the value is stored in the directory as an octet string. The one limitation when using NTDSUtil is that you can edit only the current policy in effect on the server to which you connect. Changing other policies requires using either adsiEdit or a script using ADSI.

To add an IP address to the current IP deny list using NTDSUtil, follow these steps:

1. At a command prompt, type **ntdsutil**.

2. Type **IPDeny List**.

3. Type **Connections**.

4. Type **Connect to server *servername*** (where *servername* is the DC for which you want to edit the IP deny list).

5. Type **quit**.

6. To add a single IP address by typing **Add *x.x.x.x* Node**—for example, Add 10.1.1.1 Node.

7. To add a range of addresses, type **Add *x.x.x.x* Mask**—for example, Add 10.1.1.0 255.255.255.0.

8. After you have finished adding entries to the list, type **Commit**.

You can view the list of entries by typing **Show**. Any entry that has not been committed to the list will show an asterisk (*) next to its index number (see Figure 14.22).

Figure 14.22
Uncommitted entries to the IP deny list.

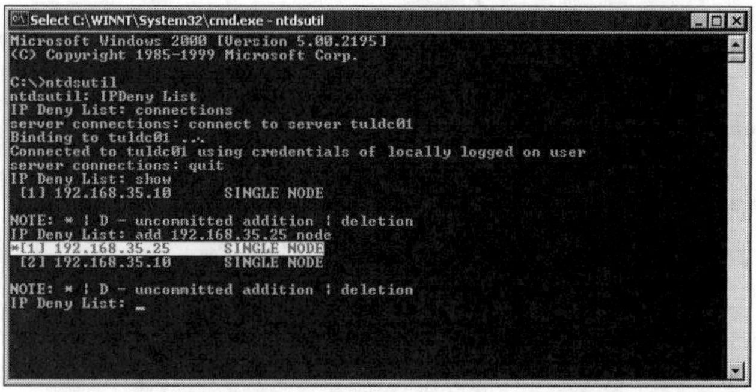

As mentioned earlier, to change other query policies you have created, you must use adsiEdit and edit the LDAPIPDenyList property. Figure 14.23 displays the attribute and the value for the entry of 192.168.35.10 255.255.255.255.

Figure 14.23
To change the IP deny list, you must use adsiEdit.

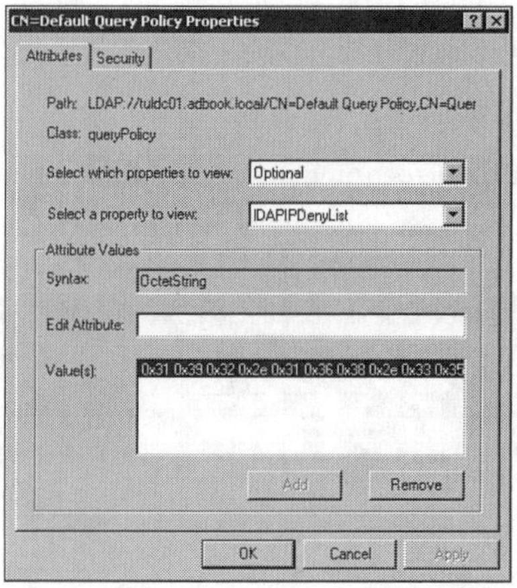

MOVING A DC TO A NEW SITE

After creating the site object and associating the site with the appropriate subnet, you must move the domain controller into the new site.

> **Note**
>
> When moving a DC into a new site, verify that the network card for the DC is configured with the correct IP address and subnet mask for the site.

To move a DC to a new site, perform the following steps:

1. Open Active Directory Sites and Services.
2. Expand the site in which the DC currently resides. The default location for each new DC added to the enterprise is either in Default-First-Site-Name or the site of the source DC.

CH
14

3. Expand the Server container and select the DC you want to move.

4. Right-click the DC, and then click Move.

5. You will see the Move Server dialog box. Select the name of the new site to which you want to move the DC, and click OK.

The server will now be moved to the new Site container object you specified.

SITE LICENSING SERVER

The last step in creating a site is selecting the licensing computer for the new site. The licensing computer for the site is used to control replication of licenses from the license logging service. Each site must have a specific server designated as the site licensing server. This server, however, does not have to be a domain controller. Licensing information is replicated through the license logging service to the site licensing server in each site. This provides the administrator with one location at which to view license information for each site in the enterprise.

To create or change the site licensing server, follow these steps:

1. Open Active Directory Sites and Services.

2. Click the site object and select the Licensing Site Settings object for the site (see Figure 14.24).

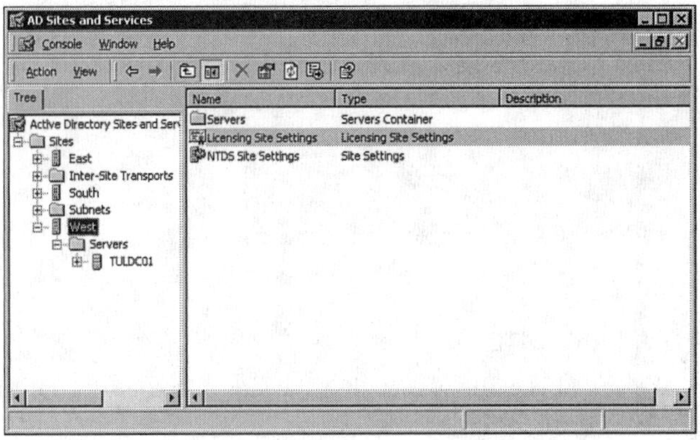

Figure 14.24
The Licensing Site Settings object is located in the root of the Sites container.

3. Right-click the Licensing Site Settings object and select Properties.

4. In the lower portion of the Properties dialog box, you will see the current computer name that is handling the licensing for this particular site. In addition, you will see the particular domain (see Figure 14.25).

5. Click the Change button, and you will be presented with the Select Computer dialog box, from which you can select another server in this site to assume the role of site licensing server (see Figure 14.26). Click OK.

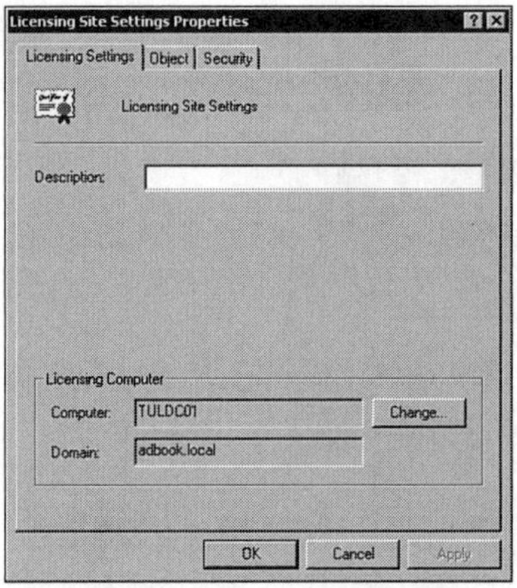

Figure 14.25
The Licensing Settings tab displays the current licensing server and allows it to be changed.

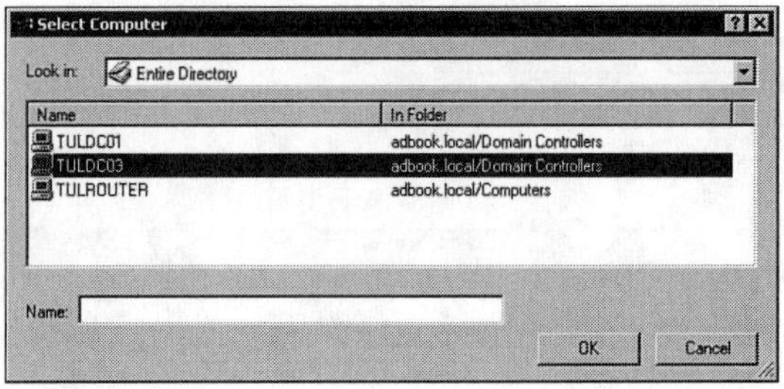

Figure 14.26
You can select any server in the directory to take the role of the licensing computer.

6. Verify that the correct server is displayed in the Computer text box, and then click OK.

THE NTDS Site Settings OBJECT

The NTDS Site Settings object is a child of the site object. This object sets the default schedule all connection objects receive when the KCC creates each connection object—by default this is set to 1 hour. You also can determine which server is the ISTG for this site.

→ See "Intra-Site Replication," **p. 249**
→ See "Inter-Site Replication," **p. 273**

To change the default schedule for replication with a site, follow these steps:

1. Open Active Directory Sites and Services.

2. Expand the Sites container and the site on which you want to change the schedule.

3. Highlight the site object and right-click the NTDS Site Settings object in the left pane; then, select Properties (see Figure 14.27).

4. Click the Change Schedule button on the Site Settings tab.

5. Select any of the following options (see Figure 14.28):

   • None (No replication will occur)

   • Once per Hour (Default)

- Twice per Hour
- Four Times per Hour

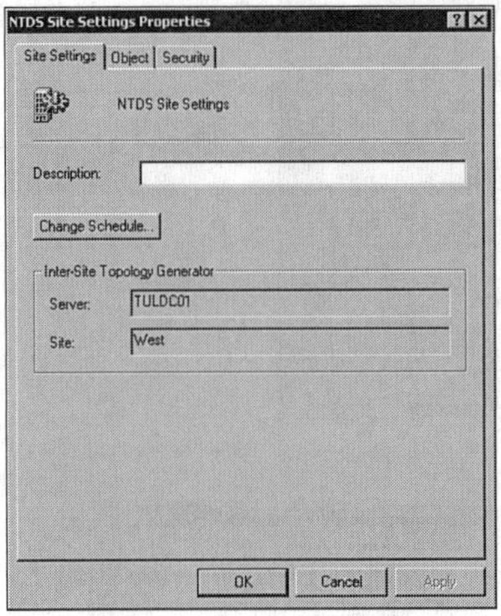

Figure 14.27
The Site Settings tab of the NTDS Site Settings Properties dialog box displays the current ISTG owner for the current site.

Note

This setting affects the defaults for any new connection objects created after the setting is configured.

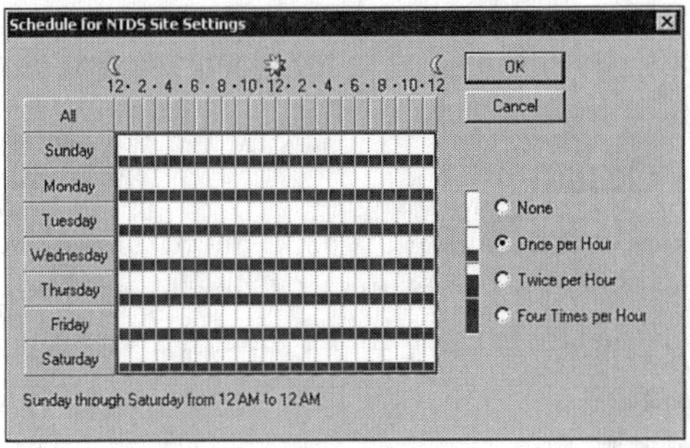

Figure 14.28
This schedule affects any future connection objects.

6. Click OK on the Site Settings tab, and then click OK in the NTDS Site Settings Properties dialog box.

Every connection object created by the KCC from this point forward will reflect this new schedule.

SUMMARY

Sites are just the beginning of understanding and configuring replication with Active Directory. They are the basis for how you will establish replication any time you have slow links between locations and you want to control replication traffic and authentication traffic. Remember to place a global catalog and DNS server in each site to further optimize your network. This alleviates clients traversing the WAN to issues queries against the GC and also lessens the traffic generated by DNS lookups.

CHAPTER 15

SITE LINK OBJECTS AND CONNECTION OBJECTS

In this chapter

INTRODUCTION

This chapter discusses site link objects and connection objects. These two types of objects play an extremely important role in how your replication will or will not work—so much so that if they are not configured correctly, you can pretty much guarantee that replication will flat out not work. Another possible outcome of not wisely understanding and implementing connection objects and site links is replication inefficiency.

Site link objects play a role in inter-site replication, whereas connection objects exist in both inter-site and intra-site replication. This chapter focuses on the configuration parameters. Chapters 16, "Intra-Site Replication," and 17, "Inter-Site Replication," look at intra- and inter-site replication, respectively.

Site links are used to connect two separate Active Directory sites to enable you to control the schedule and the interval for replication, as well as assign cost values for each site link.

Site links also enable a specific Knowledge Consistency Checker (KCC)—the Intersite Topology Generator (ISTG)—to create connection objects between sites. However, connection objects between domain controllers (DCs) in a site automatically are created by KCC whether or not site links are present. We will discuss, in more detail, the process of how this happens in later chapters.

Two types of site links exist in Active Directory: The first is RPC over IP, and the second is SMTP over IP (as if it had a choice).

For the purpose of this chapter, I have created a virtual network design I will use throughout the next few chapters. Figure 15.1 diagrams the domain structure, and Figure 15.2 diagrams the site topology.

Figure 15.1
Domain structure.

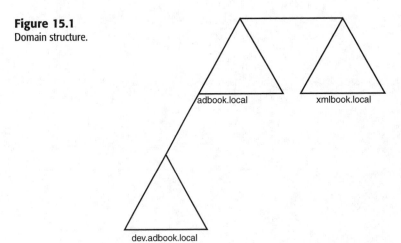

adbook.local

xmlbook.local

dev.adbook.local

Figure 15.2
Site topology.

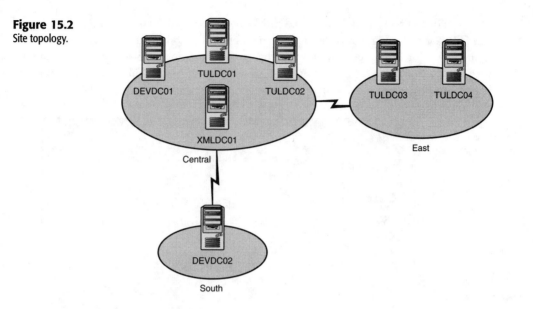

SITE LINK OBJECTS

Site links are manually created by an administrator who wants to connect to Active Directory sites for the purpose of replicating objects. Site links enable the administrator to create a schedule, during which replication can occur; establish the frequency at which replication will occur within the confines of the schedule; determine the transport protocol that will be used by the site link; and establish a cost to provide a level of fault tolerance to the replication topology. When an administrator creates a site link between two sites, a KCC with the ISTG role creates the connection objects between the bridgehead servers in each site. In addition, these servers are selected by the ISTG, unless manually overridden.

Site links are located by using Active Directory Sites and Services. You must navigate to the Inter-Site Transports container, as shown in Figure 15.3. Then, you select a transport for the appropriate site link.

The DEFAULTIPSITELINK object is the default site link object created by the installation of Active Directory and is the site link associated with the Default-First-Site-Name site object. It is safe to rename this site link.

INTER-SITE TRANSPORTS

Whenever you create a site link, you must determine which type of site link to create: either IP or SMTP. A variety of reasons exist to choose one over the other, and this chapter looks at some of those before venturing into the configuration details for each.

An *IP* site link assumes a reliable connection, even if it's a slow one. *SMTP*, on the other hand, can be used in environments in which the connection might not be reliable. This is because of the nature of the two types. IP site links are *synchronous* in nature. A DC in one site sends out its replication request and then waits to hear a response from the receiving side. Therefore, having more than one outstanding replication request at a time for that DC is impossible. In an environment in which connections are not reliable, this is not desirable. Instead, you would use the SMTP site link, which is *asynchronous*. This enables multiple requests to be outstanding at one time.

Figure 15.3
The Inter-Site Transports container.

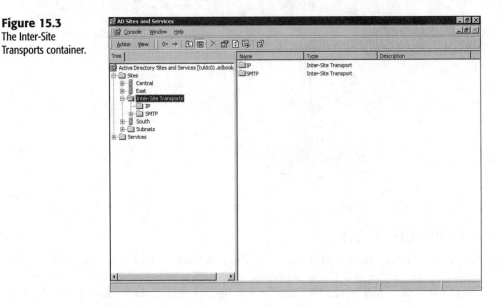

An example of when an SMTP site link might be warranted is when the quality of the physical link is seriously in question—for example, the PSTN connection to the branch office deep in the interior of Brazil.

SMTP site links do have one very large limiting factor. They are capable of replicating only the configuration naming context and the schema naming context. Therefore, SMTP site links can only be used between sites between AD domains. However, you can replicate global catalog information using SMTP site links.

When choosing between IP and SMTP links, you also must consider the physical location of your domain controllers with regard to your network firewall. If a DC is located behind the firewall, you most likely will encounter problems with IP because IP site links use dynamic port mappings. If you need to assign a fixed port for use by the RPC endpoint mapper, you must insert the value TCP/IP Port as REG_DWORD and assign any available port you want to use to the following Registry key:

```
HKEY_LOCAL_MACHINE\SYSTEM\CurrentControlSet\Services\NTDS\Parameters
```

However, per Microsoft Knowledge Base articles, replication through a firewall is not supported because a variety of ports must be opened for replication to work correctly. Instead, Microsoft recommends using a virtual private network (VPN).

IP SITE LINKS

The IP site link is really RPC over TCP/IP, but for simplicity's sake, it's referred to as an IP site link. Because of the way it is implemented, this type of site link enables point-to-point, low-speed connectivity between all domain controllers in a forest, whether it be the domain NC, the configuration NC, the schema NC, or the GC information. It also happens to be the only site link transport that can be used to replicate the domain naming context from one site to another.

If you have two DCs that belong to the same domain but are in different sites, you must create an IP site link.

To create an IP site link, follow these steps:

1. Open Active Directory Sites and Services and expand the Inter-Site Transports container.
2. Right-click the IP container and select New Site Link to create the site link, as shown in Figure 15.4. (We discuss site link bridges later in this chapter.)

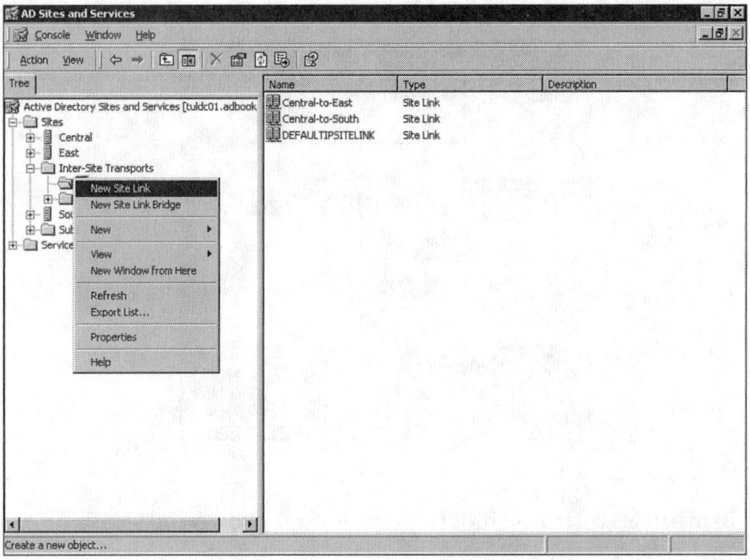

Figure 15.4
Selecting New Site Link.

3. You now need to name the site link; I recommend an intuitive name that will help you identify the site link at a later date—for example, TUL-to-OKC (see Figure 15.5).
4. Select at least two sites to include in the site link by selecting the two sites and clicking Add; then, click OK (see Figure 15.6).

SMTP SITE LINKS

Configuring SMTP site links is a bit more involved than creating IP site links because a certificate authority (CA) is required. This is essential because each DC in the enterprise requires a certificate to digitally sign and encrypt the SMTP replication messages. I have included the steps to install an enterprise root CA here, but the configuration and implications of setting up a PKI infrastructure is beyond the scope of this book.

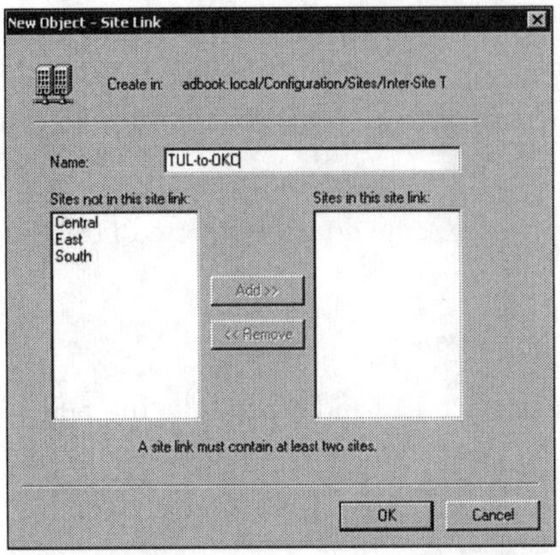

Figure 15.5
Naming the new site link.

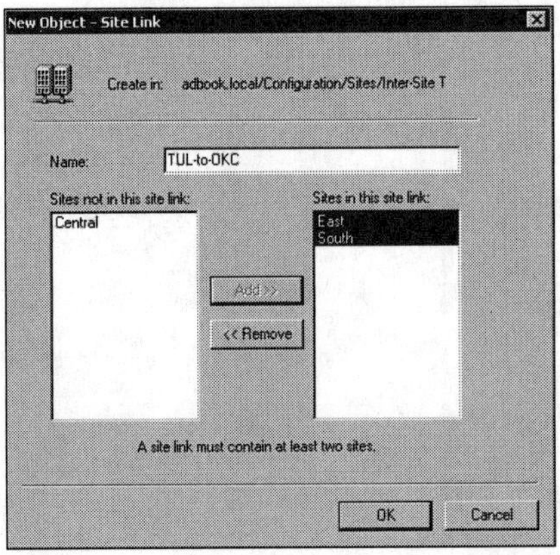

Figure 15.6
Adding sites to the site link.

To install an enterprise root (CA), perform the following steps:

1. Open Control Panel and double-click Add/Remove Programs.

2. Click Add/Remove Windows Components to launch the Windows Components Wizard.

3. Select Certificate Services and click OK (see Figure 15.7).

4. If this is the first certificate service in the enterprise, click the radio button next to Enterprise Root CA; then, click Next (see Figure 15.8).

5. You now need to fill in the empty fields in the CA Identifying Information dialog box, as appropriate (see Figure 15.9). Click Next when you're finished.

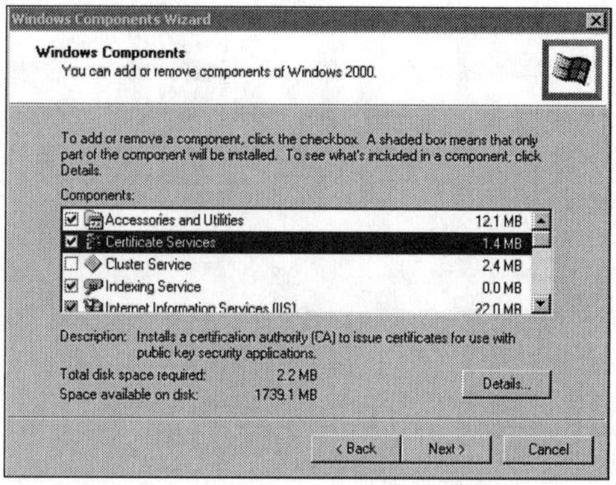

Figure 15.7
Adding certificate services.

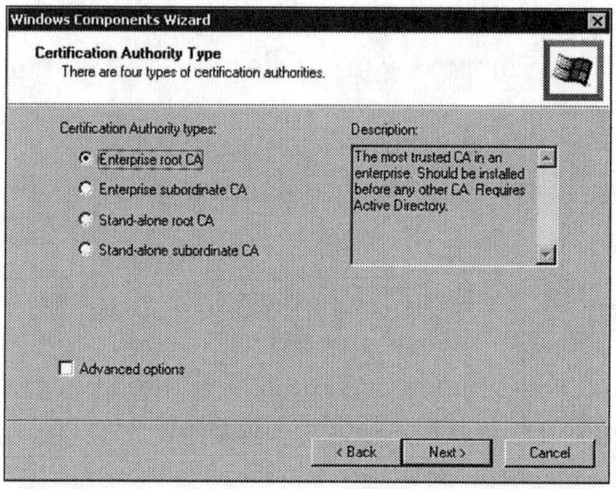

Figure 15.8
Selecting the certificate authority type.

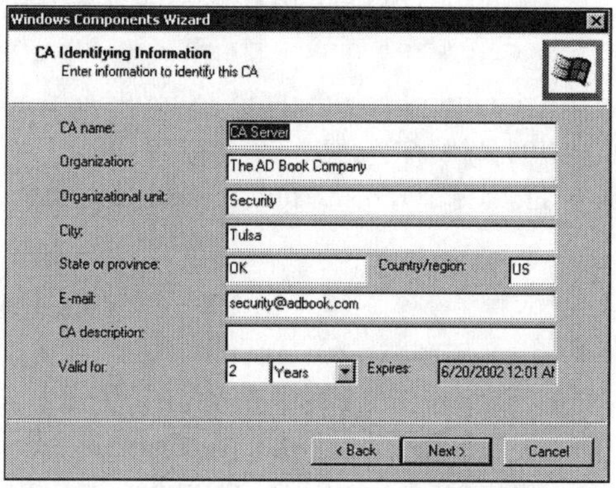

Figure 15.9
Entering CA identifying information.

6. Select the location for the certificate database and the database log (see Figure 15.10). Then, click Next.

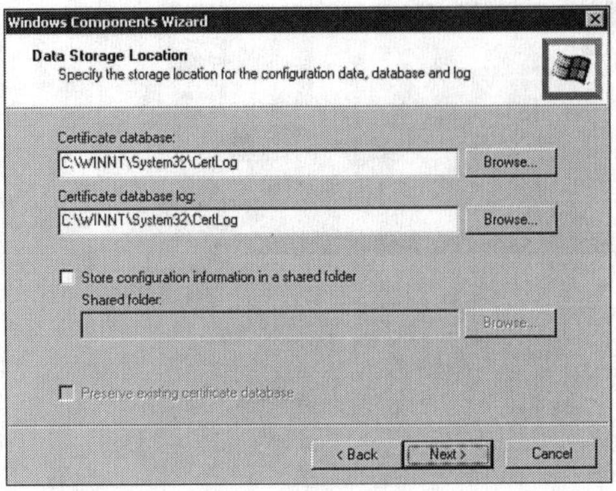

Figure 15.10
Database and log
locations for the cer-
tificate database.

7. If Internet Information Server is installed on the server on which you are attempting to install the CA, you will be prompted with a dialog box that states it will temporarily stop the IIS service.

The DC requests a certificate from the CA. If you need to speed up this process, you can force it by rebooting the DC.

After you have installed the CA and verified that the DC in the other domain and site has received a certificate from the CA, you can proceed with setting up SMTP replication. Creating the SMTP site link is the same as creating an IP site link, except it is created in the SMTP container under the Inter-Site Transports container.

To create an SMTP site link, follow these steps:

1. Open Active Directory Sites and Services and expand the Inter-Site Transports node.

2. Right-click SMTP and select New Site Link.

3. You now need to name the site link; I recommend an intuitive name that will help you identify the site link at a later date—for example, DFW-to-TUL.

4. Select at least two sites to include in the site link by selecting the two sites and clicking Add; then, click OK.

SCHEDULES

Each site link you create will have a schedule you can control. This is one of the advantages of site links. The schedule for a site link defines when replication *can* occur—not necessarily when it will occur. This is an important factor when planning your inter-site replication model. Figure 15.11 shows the default schedule for a site link, and as you can see, replication is available 24 hours a day, 7 days a week.

When you set this schedule, the KCC uses it to create the schedule that shows up on the automatically generated connection objects.

Figure 15.11
The default site link schedule.

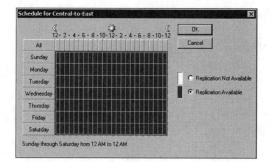

When you are creating your site links and assigning schedules between them, it is vital that, when you have a topology similar to that shown in Figure 15.12, the two site links have an overlapping schedule. Otherwise, domain replication will fail between DC01 and DC02 for the adbook.local domain. The actual time during which replication can occur is directly related to the time that overlaps. For example, if the site link connecting Dallas to Tulsa is scheduled for 8 p.m.–12 a.m. and the site link connecting Tulsa to St. Louis is 11 p.m.–3 a.m., the only opportunity for replication to occur is between 11 p.m. and 12 a.m.

Figure 15.12
Sample schedule scenario.

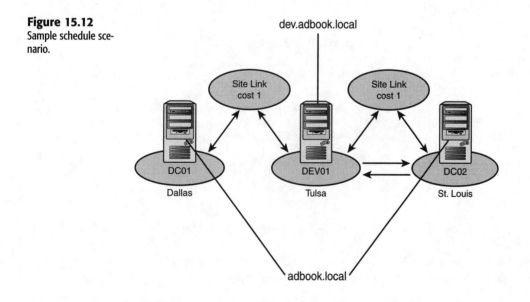

To change the schedule for a site link object, follow these steps:

1. Right-click the site link object on which you want to change the schedule, and click Properties.

2. Click the Change Schedule button shown in Figure 15.13.

Figure 15.13
Site link properties.

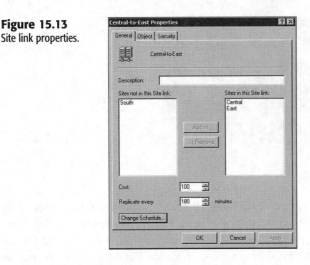

3. The blue area defines when replication is available. To change the schedule, select an area of the schedule and make a selection as to whether replication should or should not be available. For example, Figure 15.14 displays that replication is not available on Sunday or Monday.

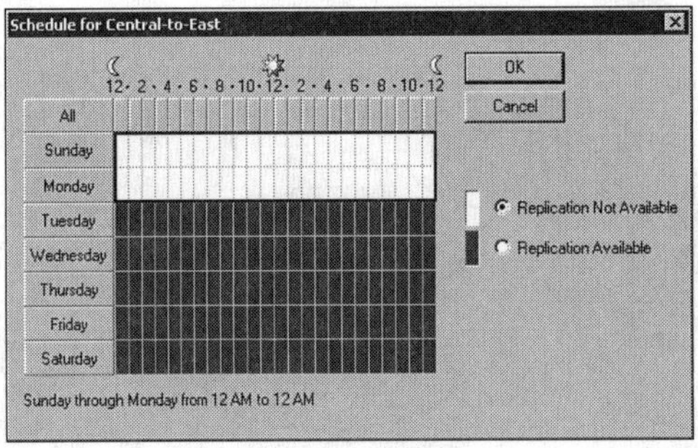

Figure 15.14
Create a schedule for
the site link.

4. Click OK twice to close the site link Properties dialog box.

SMTP site links ignore the schedules set on the site link properties and instead focus on using the interval for determining when to replicate.

Changing the schedule is not enough when you are configuring when replication will occur because it defines only when replication *can* occur and not necessarily when it *will* occur.

REPLICATION INTERVALS

Intervals define how often during the allotted schedule replication actually will occur. By default, this is set to once every three hours. Remember that this affects how the KCC creates and adjusts connection objects. You can adjust the intervals through the properties of the site link object.

Follow these steps to adjust the frequency at which replication occurs:

1. Right-click the site link and select Properties.

2. On the General tab, in the box labeled Replicate Every, change the value to how often during the defined schedule you want replication to occur (see Figure 15.15).

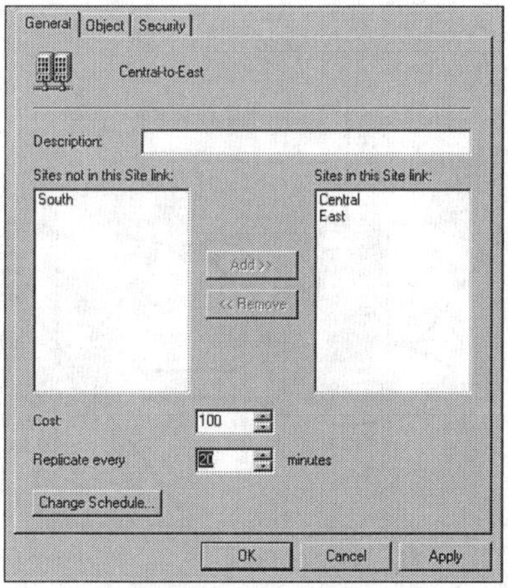

Figure 15.15
Changing the interval at which replication occurs.

When more than two sites are involved to complete replication, the replication interval will be the maximum of the intervals that were set. For example, if the replication interval is set to once every three hours on the site link connecting Sites A and B, and the site link connecting B and C is set to once every two hours, replication will occur once every three hours along that path. This essentially means that any DC replicating from Site A to Site C will occur in those timeframes.

> **Note**
>
> Replication times are not precise: The actual replication takes place within 15 minutes of the replication interval time. For example, if replication is set to occur at 02:00, replication will occur sometime between 02:00:00 and 02:14:59.

COSTS

You can assign costs to site links in an attempt to build a more resilient replication topology. *Costs* are arbitrarily assigned values ranging from 1 to 32,767. You assign these costs based on the monetary cost, availability, and performance of the connection between the sites. For example, say you have a T1 connection between Dallas and Tulsa, a connection between Dallas and Oklahoma City, and another link between Tulsa and Oklahoma City. You would be able to create a site link between Tulsa and Dallas with a low cost and then create a site link between Dallas and Oklahoma City and Tulsa with a higher cost. If the link between Dallas and Tulsa failed, the KCC could create temporary connection objects through the Oklahoma City site to regain the connectivity necessary to complete replication.

Note The actual path of the IP packets is determined by the routers on your network, not by the AD.

Costs are cumulative in nature. So in Figure 15.16, the cost to replicate from the Dallas site to the St. Louis site is 2.

Figure 15.16
Cumulative cost.

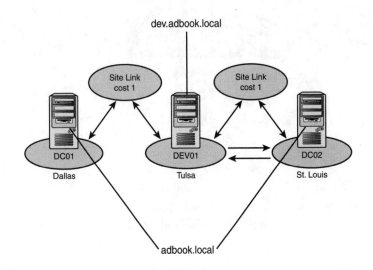

One thing to keep in mind when assigning cost is that you must allow some room to grow. Determine in advance a cost structure based on the amount of bandwidth available. You could assign a T1 link a cost of 100 and a 256KB Frame Relay circuit a cost of 400. Whichever site link is the lowest cost is the one replication will use.

SITE LINK BRIDGES

Another object used in the process of Active Directory replication is the site link bridge object. Site link bridges are used when you have a network that is not fully routed and is representative of a set of site links.

To create a site link bridge, perform the following steps:

1. Open Active Directory Sites and Services and expand the Inter-Site Transports container.

2. Right-click the appropriate transport and click New Site Link Bridge. If you attempt to create a site link bridge and you do not have at least two site links of that transport type created, you will receive an error (see Figure 15.17).

Figure 15.17
You get an error if you don't have at least two site links available.

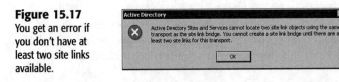

3. Enter the name of the site link bridge and select two site links to be a part of the bridge; then, click OK (see Figure 15.18).

Figure 15.18
Adding site links to a site link bridge.

Site links are transitive by nature, and in most cases you will not need to create site link bridges. But if you ever want to turn off the transitive nature of all site links, you can.

Here are the steps to turn off site link transitivity:

1. Open Active Directory Sites and Services and expand the Inter-Site Transports node.

2. Right-click the appropriate transport and select Properties.

3. Clear the Bridge All Site Links check box and click OK (see Figure 15.19).

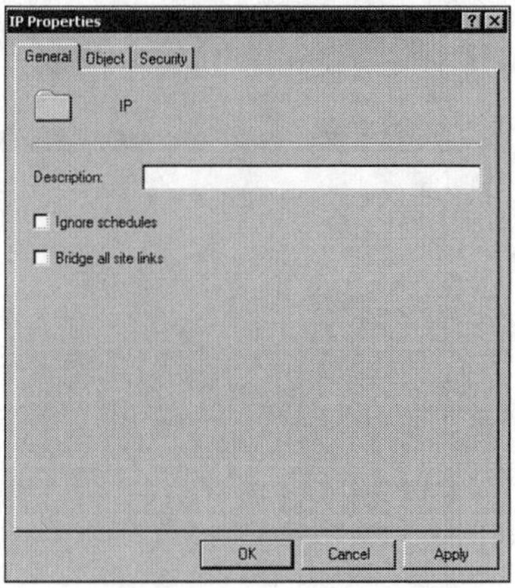

Figure 15.19
Turn off automatic bridging of all site links.

You also might notice that you can enable site links to ignore schedules. This is available to both IP site links and SMTP site links. However, as mentioned earlier, the SMTP site link ignores any schedule settings.

CONNECTION OBJECTS

Connection objects are directory representations of a connection from one DC to another and are the most important objects with regard to replication. They are of the class nTDSConnection, as defined in the schema, and have six mandatory attributes (see Table 15.1).

TABLE 15.1   MANDATORY ATTRIBUTES FOR nTDSConnection OBJECTS

Attribute Name	Datatype
enableConnection	Boolean
fromServer	DN
instanceType	Integer
objectCategory	DN
objectClass	OID
options	Integer

The key thing to note about connection objects is that they are unidirectional in nature but are always created in pairs so that replication consists of two one-way connections. Therefore, when viewing connection objects in AD Sites and Services, look at them from the perspective that they are coming *from* a server *to* the server you are viewing. In Figure 15.20, you can see that the TULDC01 domain controller has four connection objects from various DCs in other sites and its own site—Central.

Figure 15.20
Connection objects.

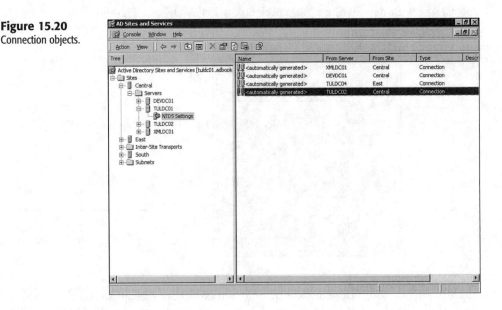

Connection objects are automatically created by the KCC both within the site and between sites. The KCC automatically creates connection objects between DCs in different sites if a site link connects the two sites.

You can create your own connection objects to create your own replication topology both for intra- and inter-site replication. If you choose this method, the KCC will not make any changes to the manually created connection objects. Not only will KCC not alter manually created connection objects, but it will not take them into account when calculating the replication topology. The KCC is capable of determining which connection objects it owns based on the options attribute of the connection object. The value must be equal to 1 for the KCC to manage the object. If you create your own connection object, the options value is set to 0.

CONNECTION OBJECT PROPERTIES

Connection object properties enable you to change everything from the transport to the schedule at which it performs replication. Figure 15.21 shows the properties for a connection object that represents a connection object from one DC in the Central site to a DC in the South site.

Figure 15.21
Connection object properties.

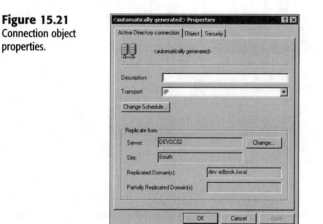

Next, you take a look at each option available in the Properties dialog box.

TRANSPORT

The Transport drop-down box lists the type of site link this connection object uses. Referring to Figure 15.21, you can see that the selected transport is IP. Table 15.2 displays the three options available in this list. For more information on how these transports are used, refer to the "Inter-Site Transports" section earlier in this chapter.

TABLE 15.2   TRANSPORT OPTIONS

Transport Type	Description
IP	This reflects inter-site communication using low-speed RPC over IP for replication.
RPC	This also is RPC over IP, but it assumes a high-speed connection for intra-site replication.
SMTP	This uses asynchronous Simple Mail Transport Protocol to communicate over slow-speed links.

SCHEDULE

Clicking the Change Schedule button on the Properties page brings up a schedule you can set for when replication can occur across this connection object. Figure 15.22 displays a schedule set by the site link schedule to be available once every three hours and to replicate once during that hour. This is the default setting for inter-site connection objects as defined by the site link that is associated with this connection object.

Figure 15.22
Schedule for an inter-site connection object.

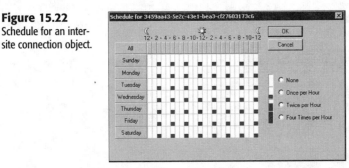

Figure 15.23 displays the default schedule for a connection object used for intra-site replication. This shows that replication is currently scheduled to occur once every hour. This is set based on the schedule set on the NTDS Site Settings object.

Figure 15.23
Schedule for an intra-site connection object.

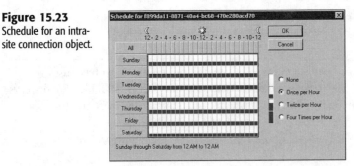

Within a site, the schedule defines when replication occurs if no changes have occurred to the directory. For details on intra-site replication, see Chapter 16. By default, when a change occurs within a site, a change notification is sent to the DC's replication partners five minutes after the change has occurred. However, when a change occurs between sites, this differs, in that the schedule defines when replication can occur.

REPLICATE FROM

The Replicate From option enables you to change an automatically created connection object's source server. However, when you do this, you are again changing the ownership of the connection object. Consequently, the KCC will ignore this object and not adjust the settings. When you change the source server, you should note which directory partition this connection object was replicating.

Figure 15.24 shows an <Enterprise Configuration only> connection object. Connection objects must determine which directory partition they are responsible for replicating.

Figure 15.24
Enterprise configuration replication.

Four areas of replication exist: domain, configuration, schema, and global catalog. For more details on the replication topology, see Chapter 16.

Figure 15.25 displays the properties of a connection object that replicates the configuration and schema NCs through the <Enterprise Configuration only> tag. Then, in the Partially Replicated Domain(s) field you can see that it is also replicating information about the dev.adbook.local domain to the TULDC01 server. The TULDC01 domain controller is also acting as a GC server.

> **Note**
>
> The GC server is a domain controller that receives a copy of all the objects in a forest but only a partial attribute list for each object. A set of default attributes is predefined, but you can add more attributes to the list. The GC server is designed to facilitate deep searches of the directory. It operates on port 3268, and there should be at least one GC server per site.

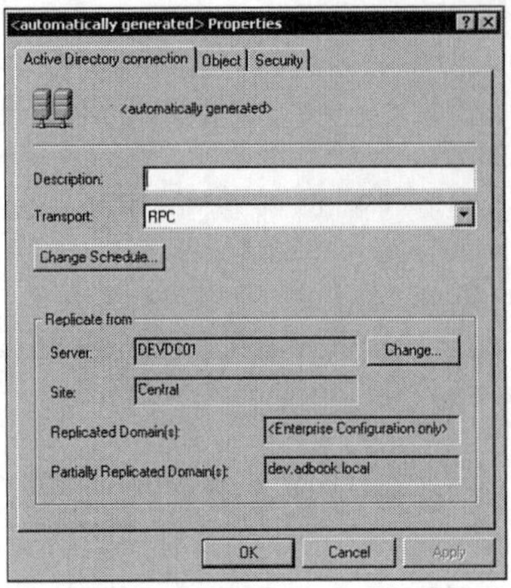

Figure 15.25
GC and enterprise data replication.

CREATING CONNECTION OBJECTS

By default, connection objects are created automatically by the KCC both for intra-site and inter-site replication. You can create your own connection objects if you feel that the KCC did not select an adequate replication topology.

To manually create connection objects, follow these steps:

1. Open Active Directory Sites and Services.

2. Expand the site object and locate the NTDS Settings object on the server on which you want to create connection objects (see Figure 15.26).

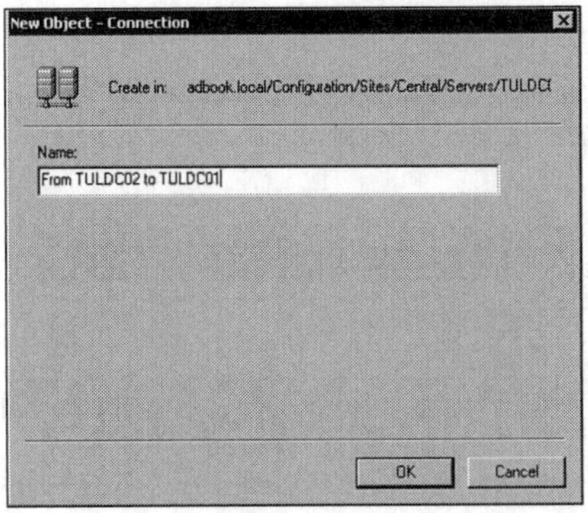

Figure 15.26
Naming the new connection object.

3. Right-click the NTDS Settings object and select New Active Directory Connection.

4. In the Find Domain Controllers dialog box, select the DC from which you want to create a connection, and click OK.

5. Type the name for the connection object and click OK.

6. Right-click the new connection object and select Properties.

7. Click Change Schedule and create a new replication schedule for the connection. The default schedule is to replicate four times per hour, 24 hours a day.

8. If the connection object is for intra-site replication, leave the transport set to RPC. However, if the connection object is to be used for inter-site replication, select IP.

9. Click OK to finish creating the first connection object. You will need to repeat steps 4–8 to create the other side of the connection.

CH
15

Manually created objects are not managed by the KCC. Therefore, if replication fails using the current replication topology and manually created connection objects, the KCC creates new connection objects and ignores the others.

You can turn off the KCC for the purposes of creating replication topologies for both intra-site and inter-site; however, that's not advisable. You must use the Active Directory Administration Tool (LDP) to perform this operation. LDP can be installed by running Setup from the Support\Tools folder of the Windows 2000 CD.

SUMMARY

Site links are one of the most important aspects of inter-site replication. As you begin to design your Active Directory replication topology, you will need to pay close attention to the network traffic that currently exists in order to properly tune the schedules and costs for these objects. By carefully understanding the current traffic and the impact of changes to the directory, you will be able to better create and maintain a robust replication topology.

CHAPTER 16

INTRA-SITE REPLICATION

In this chapter

INTRODUCTION TO REPLICATION

Intra-site replication is the process by which domain controllers (DCs) within a single site replicate directory information to one another. However, before we get into how intra-site replication works, let's look at the concepts behind replication in Active Directory.

So what exactly is replication? Essentially, it is nothing more than making sure that changes, when you create, modify, or delete a user or any other object in Active Directory, get copied to the domain controllers. (Deletes are handled a little differently, but you will look at that process in more detail later.) Any network of any size must deal with replication. About the only way to not deal with replication is to maintain only one domain controller in a single domain environment. One thing to note is that replication takes place at the attribute level and not at the object level. For example, if the phone number of a user object is changed on one DC, the phone number attribute is what gets replicated—not the entire user object.

Replication occurred in NT 4, but not to the extent it does in Windows 2000. So, to be able to really manage a Windows 2000 network, a thorough understanding of replication is a must.

Replication in Windows 2000 is now peer-to-peer replication, which is more properly referred to as *multimaster* replication. In fact, Microsoft is referring to the replication model as "multimaster, loose consistency with convergence." This chapter looks at each of these terms to help you get better familiarized with just how Windows 2000 handles replication.

MULTIMASTER

Every domain controller in a Windows 2000 domain maintains a writable copy of Active Directory for the domain. This enables any change to the directory to be introduced at any DC in the domain. Every DC is considered an equal as far as the directory is concerned. Differences do exist when you start looking at Operations Master roles. This gives network clients the capability to not only locate any DC for logon authentication, but also to process changes to object attributes. This greatly distributes the system load across all the DCs in the domain.

This differs dramatically from the NT 4 model of PDC/BDC, in which only the PDC has a writable copy of the SAM and each BDC maintains only a read-only copy to ease authentication.

LOOSE CONSISTENCY

Although every DC has a complete copy of the Active Directory database, each DC must receive updates through replication from the DC on which the change took place—which is also referred to as an *originating write/update*. Instead of updates being made to every DC as soon as the origination write takes place, a pause of five minutes occurs, which is called the *change notification interval*. This results in what is referred to as *loose consistency*. Loose consistency occurs when one or more DCs has more recent information than any other DC in the domain. For example, you create a user on DC1 and after five minutes, the user object is replicated to DC2.

WITH CONVERGENCE

With convergence is the idea that at some point in the distant future, when either no changes have occurred or replication has completed, all databases will reach a point of convergence. At that point, all databases will contain the same objects with all the same values for each property. Now, this will not always be the case, as noted by the use of the phrase loose consistency. The key is that this can occur but might or might not, depending on how often objects in the AD are updated or added.

Now that you know the concept behind replication, let's look at how it actually happens; then we'll talk about some more concepts.

In this example, you look at a simple network with only two domain controllers, DC1 and DC2, all in one site. (A *site* is a collection of IP subnets that share "good" network connectivity: 10Mbps.) Open up Active Directory Users and Computers and create a new user, called Blake.

When you create a user, the object is created on the DC on which Active Directory Users and Computers is currently focused.

Therefore, the object is created on that DC first. Five minutes after the creation of the new user account, DC1 sends out a change notification to its replication partners. In this example, it has only one partner—DC2. Therefore, DC2 initiates replication and asks for the changes. DC1 then sends over the new object, completing the replication.

NAMING CONTEXTS

Three partitions exist in the AD database that are referred to as *naming contexts (NCs)*. Each NC contains specific information that is self-contained in the AD database. The three NCs are the domain NC, schema NC, and configuration NC. Each NC resides in the file NTDS.DIT, and each NC maintains its own replication topology. Let's take a look at each one.

THE DOMAIN NC

The domain NC contains the information that you, as the administrator, will most likely experience on a day-to-day basis. The domain NC contains all the objects and all the attributes for the given domain, such as user objects, organizational unit (OU) objects, group objects, and computer objects. Figure 16.1 shows the domain NC for the adbook.local domain and the various types of objects available in the domain NC.

The domain NC is replicated to every DC in a domain. However, the domain NC does not replicate to other DCs for other domains. For example, only the DCs for adbook.local receive replication updates for the adbook.local domain, and they don't receive updates for the dev.adbook.local domain.

THE SCHEMA NC

Just as its name suggests, the schema NC is the partition that contains the actual schema used in your instance of the AD (see Figure 16.2). I say "your" instance because every enterprise has the potential to have a schema different from the enterprise a floor below it or across the city. This largely depends on the types of applications each company installs on its servers.

Figure 16.1
The domain NC and its objects.

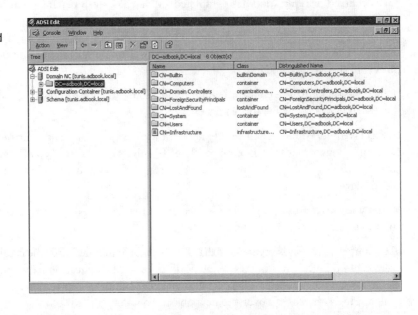

Figure 16.2
The schema NC.

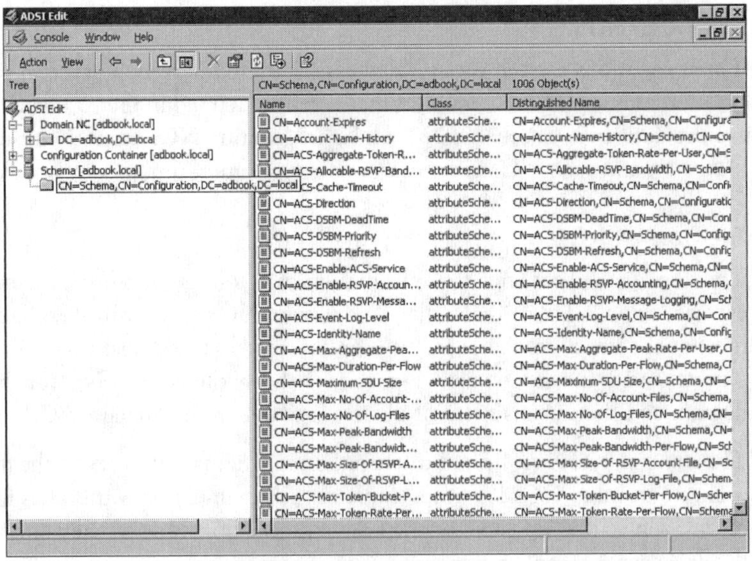

Applications such as Exchange 2000 alter the schema to provide certain functionality and to extend the use of the Active Directory. Even though changes to the schema might be rare initially, as developers begin to see the power of using the AD for their applications, an increase in applications extending the schema should occur.

A member of the Schema Admin group using the AD schema snap-in for the MMC performs each change to the schema. The actual change itself is performed at a DC known as the Schema Operations Master. This is a particular role managed by the first DC in the forest. You can transfer the role to another DC in the forest, but only one Schema Operations Master can exist in a forest.

Because the schema is the same across all domains in the forest, the replication of the schema is forest wide.

THE CONFIGURATION NC

The configuration NC contains such data as the various sites, site links, services, and partitions that are in your AD. Looking at the adsiEdit tool, shown in Figure 16.3, gives you a good sense of the types of data found in the configuration NC.

Figure 16.3
The configuration NC.

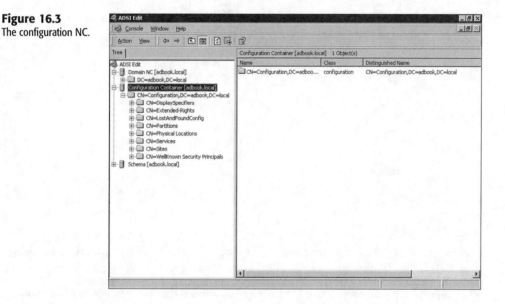

The configuration NC is also global to the entire forest; therefore, it is replicated to all the DCs in the forest.

UPDATES

Replication occurs when one of the following four updates has occurred:

- Add
- Delete
- Modify
- Change

An *add* occurs whenever an object is first created in the directory structure. A *delete* occurs when that object is requested to be removed from the directory. Deletes are handled differently from other directory modifications and are covered later in this chapter, in the section "Deleted Objects." A *modify* occurs when an attribute is changed on the object, such as the address of a user. Finally, a *change* differs from the other three in that it occurs when an object has its distinguished name (DN) changed. This typically occurs when an object is moved from one container to another. In addition, changing the name of the object or the name of its parent object is considered a change.

These changes occur either as a result of an originating write or a replicated write. An *originating* write occurs when some process modifies some aspect of objects in the directory at its point of origin. Figure 16.4 demonstrates this with four DCs in the same domain.

Figure 16.4
Originating writes.

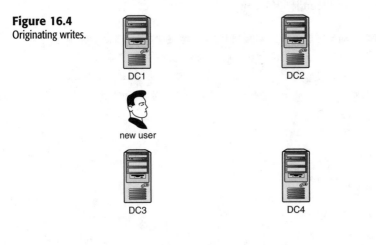

A new user object is created on DC1; then the originating write takes place on DC1. When replication occurs, the creation of the new user object on each subsequent DC is considered a *replicated* write. This is an important distinction that we will discuss later.

One important note about Active Directory replication is that it replicates at the attribute level. So when you change a phone number, an address, or some other attribute on an object, the attribute is the only thing that is replicated.

UPDATE SEQUENCE NUMBERS

Whenever the directory is modified on a DC, a value known as the *update sequence number (USN)* is modified. The USN is used to determine the current status of this instance of the directory. The USN value is a 64-bit value assigned to the DC. Every update that occurs to this instance of the directory causes the USN value to be incremented by one.

The USN is a transactional number that assists with the replication process by tracking when a change to an instance of the directory takes place. When an update occurs on a DC, this number is incremented by one. However, this value is incremented only if the update is successful. By using USNs instead of time-based replication, the AD is more resilient than other forms of replication. As an administrator, you can't change a USN value manually. They are referenced only for conceptual purposes.

> **Note**
>
> Active Directory does not use timestamps as the primary method to determine which updates are the most recent. Timestamps are used in the conflict-resolution process.

You can view the most recent USN value for an object by looking at the Object tab for properties of the object. Figure 16.5 shows the original USN and the current USN for the user object Cameron Blake.

Figure 16.5
Original and current USNs.

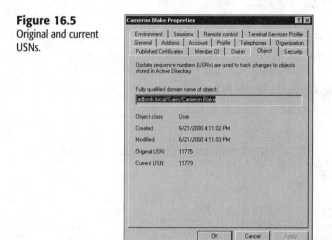

The current USN value is the highest USN from among all the attributes for that particular object. Each modification of the directory causes the USN to get incremented, and that USN is then stored with the attribute for the purposes of replication. You can view the USN of a single attribute by using the AD Replication Monitor tool.

> **Note**
>
> The Active Directory Replication Monitor is installed from the Support/Tools directory of the Windows 2000 CD.

To view the current USNs for an object, follow these steps:

1. Open Active Directory Replication Monitor.

2. Right-click the Monitored Servers node, and then click Add Monitored Server.

3. You can either search the directory for a server to monitor or type the name explicitly. In this example, you will add the server explicitly, so click Next (see Figure 16.6).

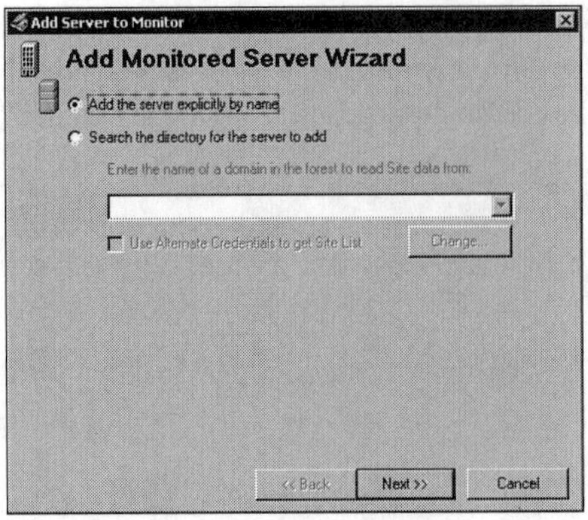

Figure 16.6
Adding a monitored
server.

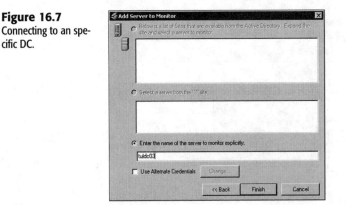

4. In the bottom text box, type the name of a DC in the domain that contains the object; then click Finish (see Figure 16.7).

Figure 16.7
Connecting to an spe-
cific DC.

5. Right-click the server object and select Show Attribute Meta-Data for Active Directory Object (see Figure 16.8).

Figure 16.8
The option for seeing
the metadata about
an object in the direc-
tory.

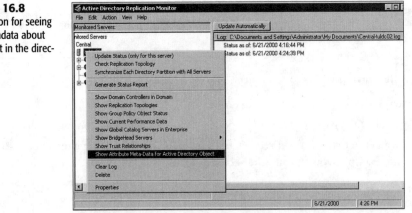

6. If you are currently logged on as someone other than administrator, you can supply a different user name and password to enumerate the objects; then click OK.

7. Type the DN of the object for which you want to view the USN list (see Figure 16.9).

Figure 16.9
The DN of the object.

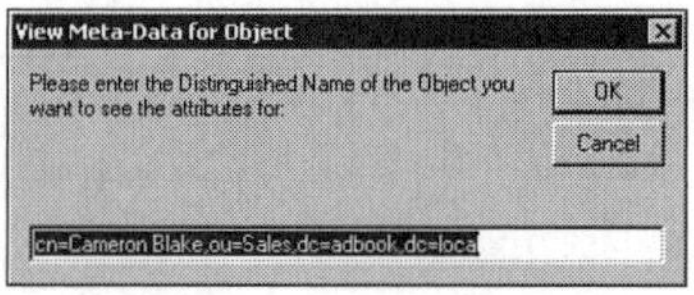

The list you get is a list of all the populated attributes on this DC. In Figure 16.10, notice that the attribute 1 has a higher USN value than the other attributes. Figure 16.11 shows the current USN for the same object. This is the highest USN value on any of the attributes for that particular object.

Figure 16.10
Metadata on an object.

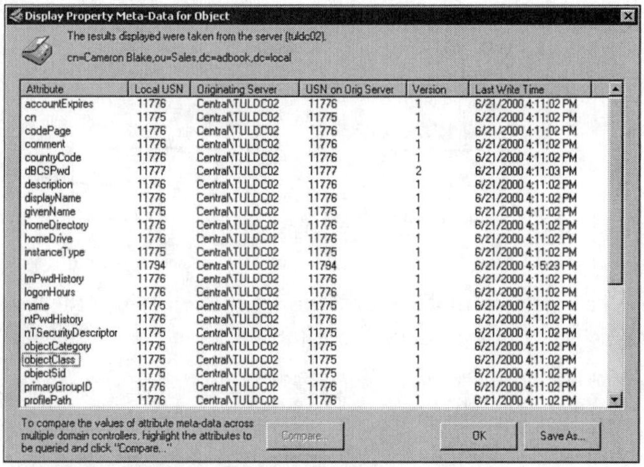

Figure 16.11
The current USN.

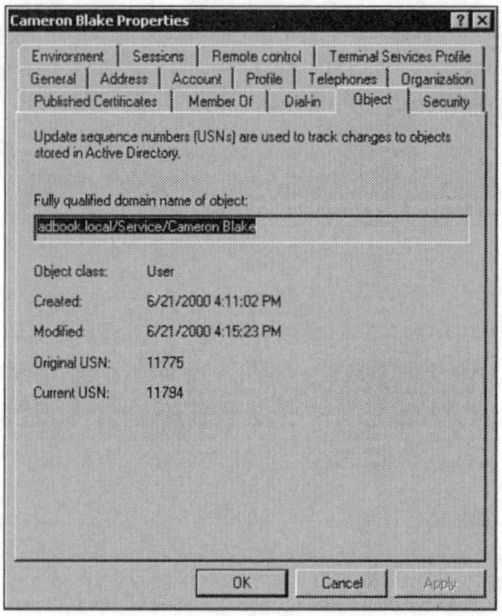

The USN value is used in two other areas: the high-watermark and the up-to-dateness vector.

THE HIGH-WATERMARK

The high-watermark is the last USN value received from a DC during replication. It is stored on the receiving DC and reflects the most recent change it has received from the sending DC. The last USN received is stored with the database GUID from which it received the update. In Figure 16.12, the receiving DC is DC2, and you can see that replication is complete at this stage because the last update it received from DC1 is the current USN value for DC1.

Figure 16.12
An example of a completed replication.

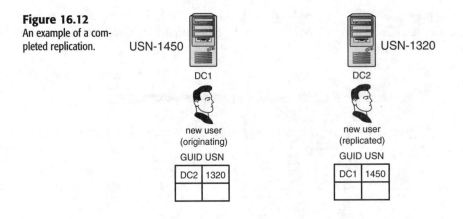

You can use the repadmin tool and the following code to show the high-watermark value (replace *naming context* with the correct domain, as in the example on the second line):

```
repadmin /showreps naming context /Verbose
ex. repadmin /showreps adbook.local /Verbose
```

Figure 16.13 shows the output and highlights the high-watermark.

Note

The repadmin tool is a command-line tool that enables you to view current values and also manage portions of the replication process manually. This is helpful if you need to verify replication results or test various scenarios during a pilot. It's also useful for general troubleshooting options.

THE UP-TO-DATENESS VECTOR

The up-to-dateness vector is very important because it is used to inhibit the same replicating write from being written to an instance of the directory from more than one source. The up-to-dateness vector is stored by every DC and reflects the USN of every DC that has ever had an originating write.

This is best explained through an example.

Figure 16.13
repadmin output of
high-watermark.

Figure 16.14 shows that all DCs have received the new user object that was created on DC1. The high-watermark value for DC3 shows that it is not up to date with DC2. Therefore, it sends a replication request that contains the up-to-dateness vector for DC1 to DC2. DC2, however, notices that DC3 has already received the update from another source and does not send the change.

Figure 16.14
Up-to-dateness vector
example.

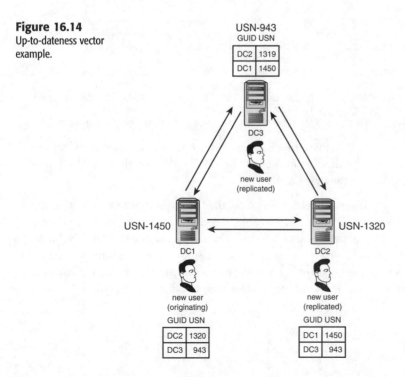

You can view the up-to-dateness vector by using the repadmin tool and the following code:

```
repadmin /showvector naming context servername
ex. repadmin /showvector dc=adbook,dc=local tuldc02.adbook.local
```

CONFLICT RESOLUTION

You might be wondering how conflicts are handled if Active Directory does not use timestamps for objects. The answer to that is through the use of *stamps*. These stamps are composed of three parts: the version number, the originating time, and the origination DSA.

The version number is assigned and incremented at the originating write. So, when you change the address of a user, the current version number for that attribute is increased by one and the date and originating DSA are stored.

The following code shows the stamps for the Sales OU for the adbook.local domain:

```
Loc.USN   Originating DSA Org.USN        Org.Time/Date  Ver Attribute
=======   =============== =======        =============  === =========
  11773   Central\TULDC02   11773 2000-06-21 16:10.28    1 objectClass
  11773   Central\TULDC02   11773 2000-06-21 16:10.28    1 ou
  11773   Central\TULDC02   11773 2000-06-21 16:10.28    1 instanceType
  11773   Central\TULDC02   11773 2000-06-21 16:10.28    1 whenCreated
  11773   Central\TULDC02   11773 2000-06-21 16:10.28    1 nTSecurityDescriptor
  11773   Central\TULDC02   11773 2000-06-21 16:10.28    1 name
  11773   Central\TULDC02   11773 2000-06-21 16:10.28    1 objectCategory
```

After changing the name of the OU from Sales to Service, the stamps reflect the change as follows:

```
Loc.USN   Originating DSA Org.USN        Org.Time/Date  Ver Attribute
=======   =============== =======        =============  === =========
  11773   Central\TULDC02   11773 2000-06-21 16:10.28    1 objectClass
  12029   Central\TULDC02   12029 2000-06-21 18:48.49    2 ou
  11773   Central\TULDC02   11773 2000-06-21 16:10.28    1 instanceType
  11773   Central\TULDC02   11773 2000-06-21 16:10.28    1 whenCreated
  11773   Central\TULDC02   11773 2000-06-21 16:10.28    1 nTSecurityDescriptor
  12029   Central\TULDC02   12029 2000-06-21 18:48.49    2 name
  11773   Central\TULDC02   11773 2000-06-21 16:10.28    1 objectCategory
```

The version number is the first thing that is compared if you receive a conflict. If the version number is the same, the time is followed by the GUID. Because the GUID is guaranteed to be unique, it creates the tiebreaker.

For example, say an administrator creates and edits the Cameron Blake user account by adding a home phone number to the user account. Another administrator attached to a different DC also adds a home phone number value. The user account never had a value for home phone number, so when the phone number is added to the account, the version number on both DCs is now 2. And assuming that the two administrators added the attribute at the exact same moment in time, the DSA GUID is used to determine the winner.

DELETED OBJECTS

It was previously mentioned that deleted objects are handled differently. This is due to the fact that, in a distributed directory structure such as Active Directory, you can't just delete an object from a instance of the directory and have it automatically removed without some other assistance—a tombstone.

Whenever an object is deleted, the lack of its existence is not what is replicated. Instead, a *tombstone* is set, which signifies that the object has been marked for deletion. The tombstone has a lifetime (by default) of 60 days, at which time the garbage collection process actually deletes the object from the directory.

Although changing the tombstone lifetime is not recommended, it is possible.

To change the tombstone lifetime, perform the following steps:

1. Open adsiEdit.
2. On the Configuration Container, navigate to CN=Windows NT,CN=Services.
3. Right-click CN=Directory Service and select Properties.
4. In the Select a Property to View box, select tombstoneLifetime.
5. In the Edit Attribute box, type the desired value and click the Set button.

> **Note**
>
> Do not change the Edit Attribute value to anything less than 60 days. In fact, this value should be left as the default.

The tombstone is what is replicated to all DCs that reference this object. By setting the tombstone lifetime to such an extended period of time, the tombstone can be completely replicated throughout the domain. The garbage collection process runs every 12 hours on each DC and is the one responsible for physically removing the object from the directory.

TOPOLOGY GENERATION

Active Directory replication within a single site consists of ring topology that is generated by the Knowledge Consistency Checker (KCC). By default, the KCC runs every 15 minutes and goes through a two-step process as it prepares to create connection objects.

The KCC is the sole replication topology generator within the confines of a site, and it performs this task automatically. The topology it generates is a bidirectional ring between DCs, generated by using the MEMCMP function to put the DSA GUIDs in order. It then creates connection objects to create replication partners. It creates these connection objects in such a manner that, statistically, no hops greater than three exist for any one DC in the ring. It also creates the objects in such a way that the ring can survive the failure of any one connection object.

So, from any point in this ring, a modification can reach any DC in the ring within three hops. However, this changes after eight or more DCs exist within the same site. At that point, the KCC creates what is known as *optimizing edges*. These are additional connection objects that enable replication to continue to function in three hops or less.

When the KCC creates connection objects, it doesn't delete or modify any manually created connection objects. It also doesn't create any additional connection objects if the manually created connection objects meet the current replication needs of the site. However, if at any time replication no longer functions with the manually created connection objects, the KCC creates temporary connection objects to enable replication to occur with minimal interruption.

Because more than one directory partition exists in a site, the KCC must manage each connection object to determine which connection objects will replicate what data. If only one domain and one site exist, the KCC creates enough connection objects to replicate all the directory partition information. If, on the other hand, separate domains exist within a site, the KCC must create separate connection objects to replicate the configuration and schema NCs.

THE KNOWLEDGE CONSISTENCY CHECKER

The KCC is mentioned often in the preceding sections, so we should spend at least a little time looking at what it does.

The KCC is a process that operates all DCs in the enterprise. You can manage the KCC indirectly through tools such as the Active Directory Sites and Services tool and the Active Directory Replication Monitor.

As mentioned earlier, the KCC performs a two-step process to determine replication topologies. The first phases consists of three steps:

1. Evaluate the current topology.
2. Check to see whether any failures using the existing connection objects have occurred.
3. Create any new connection objects necessary to maintain the no-greater-than-three-hops replication topology.

The second phase is using the information discovered and processed during phase one to create replication links that Active Directory can use to replicate and track which NC replicates from which servers.

You can modify the intervals during which the KCC performs its operations. To do so, you must modify the following Registry key:

```
HKEY_LOCAL_MACHINE\SYSTEM\CurrentControlSet\Services\NTDS\Parameters
Repl topology update period(secs)
```

The default setting is 900 seconds, or 15 minutes.

In addition, you can change the value for when the KCC first starts, as shown in the following code (by default, it starts five minutes after Active Directory starts—which is reported by Event ID 100 in the Directory Service event log):

```
HKEY_LOCAL_MACHINE\SYSTEM\CurrentControlSet\Services\NTDS\Parameters
Repl topology update delay(secs)
```

THE INTRA-SITE REPLICATION PROCESS

We have spent a lot of time discussing replication, but now we need to look specifically at how intra-site replication works. This section looks at intra-site replication by walking through a scenario, using Figure 16.15 as the base example.

Figure 16.15
The intra-site replication process.

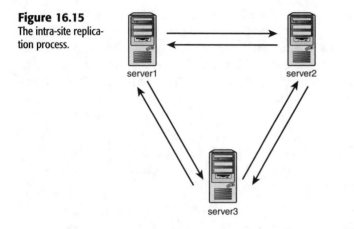

server1, server2, and server3 are all within the same domain, adbook.local, and are completely up to date at the moment.

The administrator for the adbook.local domain creates a new OU in the directory while focused on server1. A timer is initiated on server1 that will kick off replication within five minutes. During this time, the directory continues to batch changes to the directory. This is set in the Registry under the following key (the default setting is 300 seconds, or five minutes):

```
HKEY_LOCAL_MACHINE\SYSTEM\CurrentControlSet\Services\NTDS\Parameters
Replicator notify pause after modify(secs)
```

A change notification is sent to one of server1's replication partners—server2 in this example. At this time, server1 pauses for 30 seconds before sending a change notification to server3. The pause between change notifications is also configurable through the Registry by editing the following entry:

```
HKEY_LOCAL_MACHINE\SYSTEM\CurrentControlSet\Services\NTDS\Parameters
Replication notify pause between DSAs(secs)
```

After the user has been created, the USN for server1 is incremented by one. Thus, after server2 receives the change notification from server1, it requests the changes by sending its high-watermark to server1. server1 then assesses which changes it needs to send based on the high-watermark received from server2.

server2 then incorporates those changes into the directory and subsequently updates its high-watermark for server1 and its up-to-dateness vector for server1.

server3 goes through the same process as server2. Because the directory has changed on server2, it sends out a change notification to its replication partners, and server3 sends its high-watermark and up-to-dateness vector to server2. Next, server2 evaluates those values and determines that server3 is up to date; therefore, server2 does not send any changes to server3.

At this stage, the directory has reached a point of convergence.

URGENT REPLICATION

An additional level of replication occurs, by default, within a site. Three events cause an immediate change notification to be sent to replication partners. The first is account lockout, the second is change of an LSA secret, and the third is change in the RID Master. The Knowledge Base article Q232690, found at the Microsoft Web site, provides an excellent discussion on the differences in how this is handled with regard to Windows 2000 DCs and NT 4 BDCs in the same domain.

ACCOUNT LOCKOUT

If you have configured user accounts to be locked out after a specific number of logon attempts, the locked status is urgently replicated to the PDC Emulator and then urgently replicated to all DCs in the same domain and the same site.

Urgent replication is the sending of the change notification without waiting the default five minutes. If this sending of the change notification fails, the account lockout replicates during the course of normal replication.

CHANGE OF AN LSA SECRET

LSA secrets are the passwords for the trusts that are established between domains and the passwords used for computer accounts in the domain. By default, these passwords change every seven days.

PASSWORD CHANGES

Replication of password changes is urgently replicated but does not occur in the same way as the other urgently replicated items.

When a user changes a password, that change is urgently replicated to the PDC Emulator for that domain. So any time a user changes her password, that change is immediately sent to the PDC Emulator for the domain. This enables the user to log on even if she attempts to authenticate to a DC that might not have received the directory change. Instead of denying the user, the DC attempts to authenticate her at the PDC Emulator for that domain.

One thing worth noting with regard to all urgent replication notifications is that urgent replication occurs on a "best effort" basis. Essentially, if the urgent replication fails, the change replicates during the course of normal replication.

INTRA-SITE REPLICATION MANAGEMENT TASKS

You, as the administrator, can manually initiate many of the processes you have looked at in this chapter through the use of Active Directory Sites and Services. You also can check on the status of replication within a site fairly easily by using either repadmin or the Active Directory Replication Monitor.

USING ACTIVE DIRECTORY SITES AND SERVICES TO MANAGE INTRA-SITE REPLICATION

Here are the steps to force replication between DCs:

1. Open Active Directory Sites and Services.

2. Expand the Sites node and locate the site within which you want to initiate replication (see Figure 16.16).

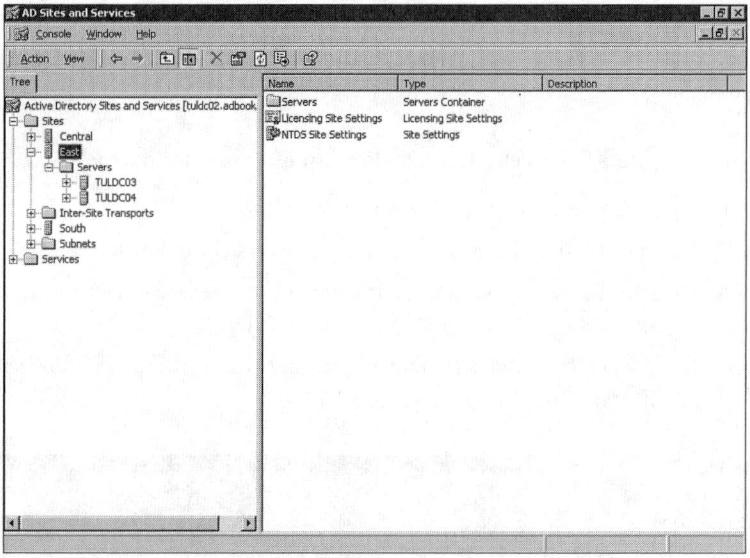

Figure 16.16
Locate the site within which to initiate replication.

3. Expand one of the server objects to locate the connection objects below the NTDS Settings object, and then select the connection object that is from another server within this site (see Figure 16.17).

4. Right-click the connection object and select Replicate Now.

5. Repeat step 4 for each connection object on this server that represents a connection from another DC in this site.

6. Repeats steps 3–5 for each server in this site.

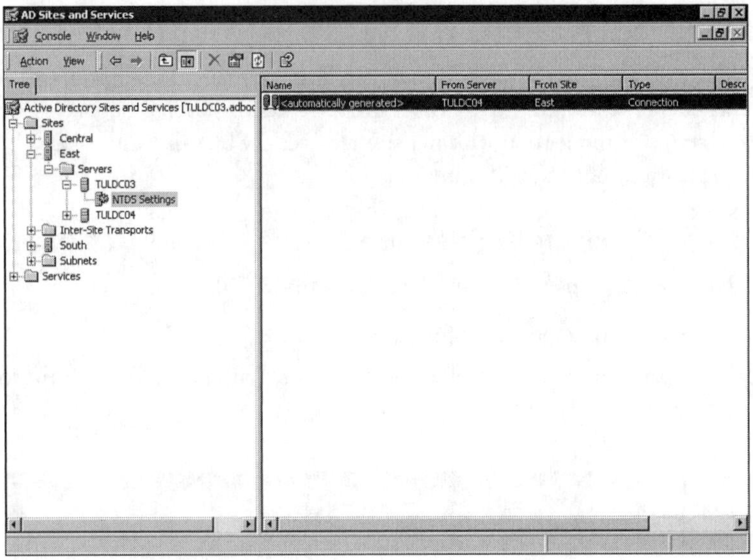

Figure 16.17
Select the connection object.

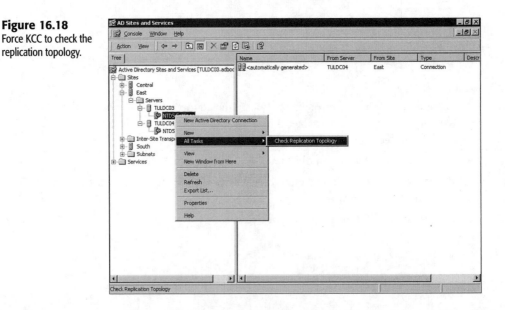

To force the KCC to check the replication topology, follow these steps:

1. Open Active Directory Sites and Services.

2. Expand the site object to display the Servers container for the appropriate site.

3. Expand the Servers container and expand the server object to display the NTDS Settings object.

4. Right-click the NTDS Settings object and select All Tasks. Then select Check Replication Topology (see Figure 16.18).

Figure 16.18
Force KCC to check the replication topology.

USING ACTIVE DIRECTORY REPLICATION MONITOR TO MANAGE INTRA-SITE REPLICATION

To use the AD Replication Monitor to force the KCC to check the replication topology, follow these steps:

1. Open the Active Directory Replication Monitor.

2. Right-click the Monitored Servers node, and then select Add Monitored Server.

3. Click Next to add the server name explicitly (see Figure 16.19).

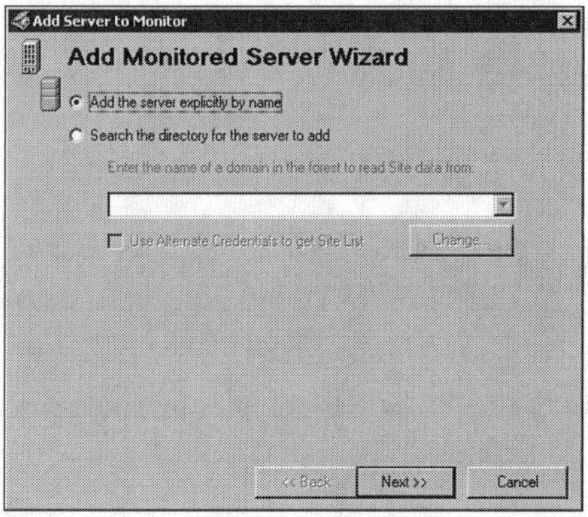

Figure 16.19
Defining which server to connect to.

4. Type the name of the server in the site you want to manage and click Finish (see Figure 16.20).

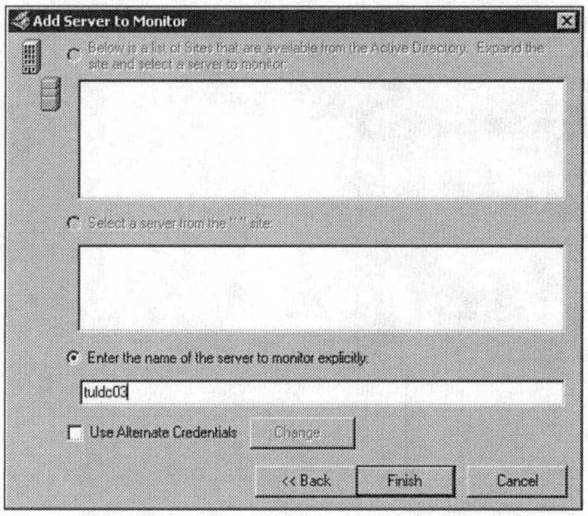

Figure 16.20
Connect to the server explicitly.

5. Right-click the server node and select Check Replication Topology (see Figure 16.21).

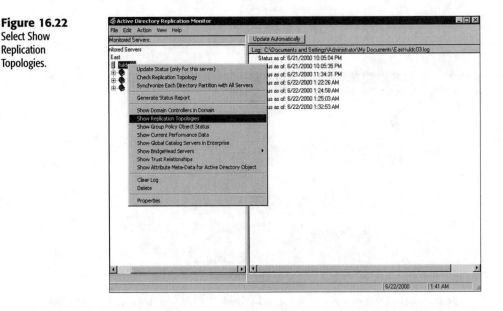

Here are the steps for showing the replication topologies for intra-site replication:

1. Perform steps 1–4 in the previous section.

2. Right-click the server object; then select Show Replication Topologies (see Figure 16.22).

Figure 16.22
Select Show
Replication
Topologies.

3. Click View, and then select Connections Objects Only.

4. Right-click each server that appears in the View Replication Topology window; then select Show Intra-Site Connections (see Figure 16.23).

Figure 16.23
Show intra-site connection objects visually.

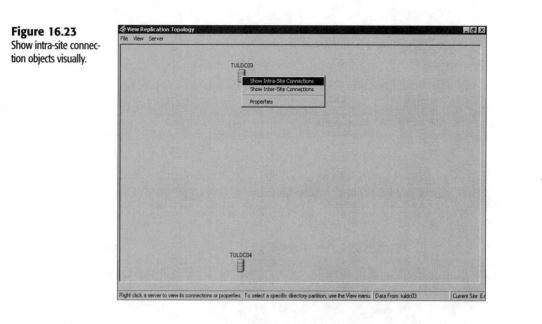

This tool displays the connection objects in a color-coded manner that enables you to see who are direct-replication partners. This is helpful when you have a large number of servers in the same site and have a complex ring.

To view replication status information, perform the following steps:

1. Expand the domain NC for the domain, and then select the icon that denotes a direct replication partner (see Figure 16.24).

Figure 16.24
Select the direct replication partner.

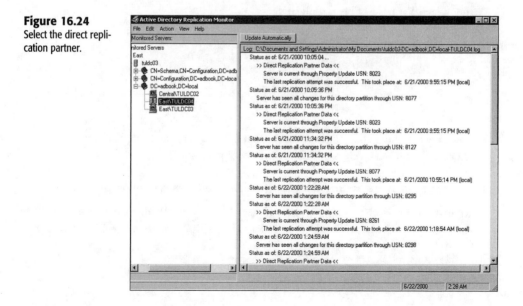

2. View the log in the Log pane to find out when replication occurred last and the last USN replicated.

3. Click View, and then select Refresh or press F5 to refresh the view. You also can set the view to update automatically by clicking the Update Automatically button at the top of the Log pane.

To determine the current USN value for a server and view any unreplicated objects, follow these steps:

1. Right-click the icon representing a direct replication partner; then select Check Current USN and Unreplicated Objects.

2. Click OK to use your existing credentials (see Figure 16.25).

Figure 16.25
Use your existing cre-
dentials.

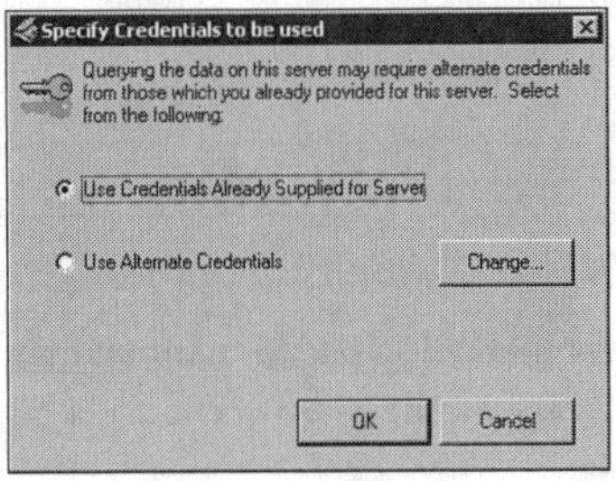

3. If this instance of the directory is up to date, you receive a dialog box similar to the one shown in Figure 16.26. On the other hand, if the instance is not up to date, you get a dialog box similar to that shown in Figure 16.27, which displays the current USN and the object that has not been replicated.

Figure 16.26
Up to date.

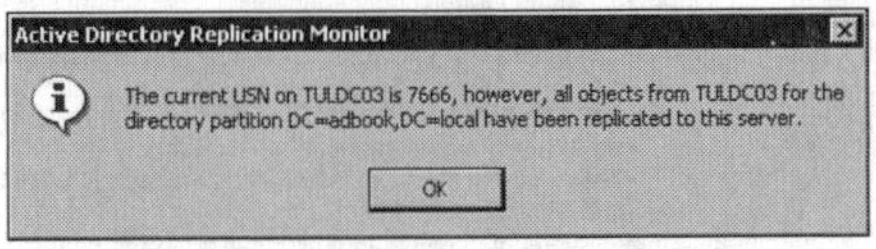

4. You can view the metadata of the object that has not been replicated yet by double-clicking the line that refers to that object (see Figure 16.28).

To synchronize an entire naming context with replication partners, follow these steps:

1. Right-click any of the naming context objects listed in the Monitored Servers pane, and then select Synchronize This Directory Partition with All Servers (see Figure 16.29).

Figure 16.27
Not up to date.

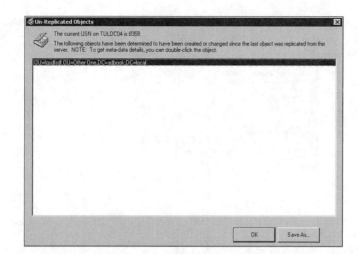

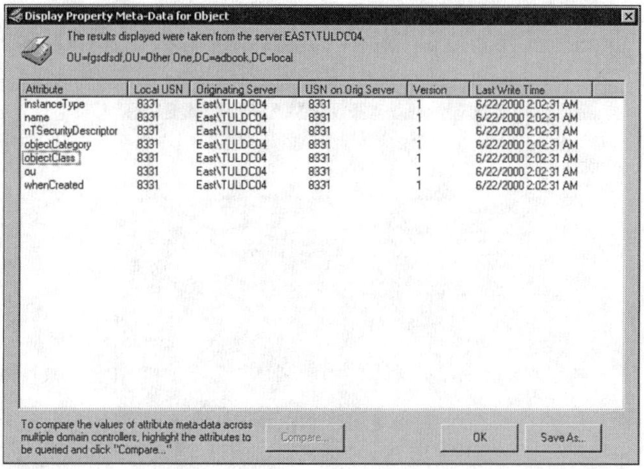

Figure 16.28
Metadata for an
object that has not
been replicated.

2. You next are presented with three options (see Figure 16.30):

- **Disable Transitive Replication**—Only servers that are direct replication partners receive the updates.

- **Push Mode**—Instead of the normal pull-based replication, this server now pushes all the updates to all its replication partners.

- **Cross Site Boundaries**—All servers connected through an IP site link receive these updates.

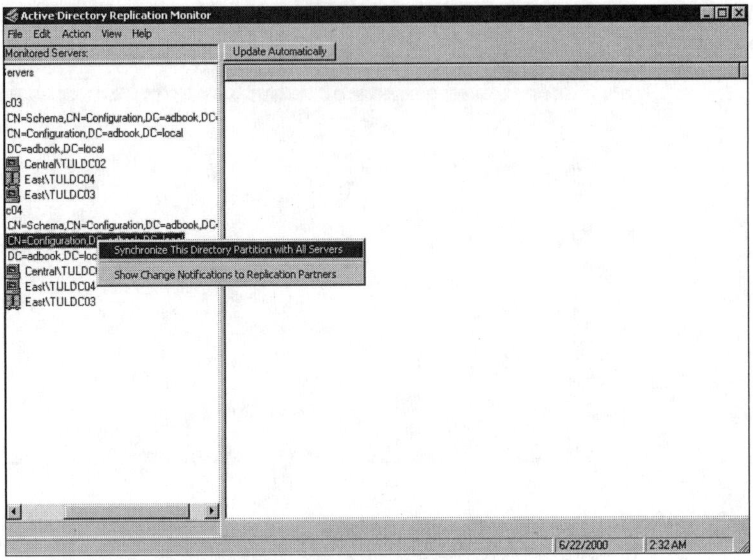

Figure 16.29
Make the synchronization request for this directory partition.

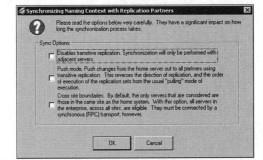

Figure 16.30
Select the method of synchronization.

3. Click OK.

4. Click Yes if you are sure you want to perform this replication.

5. After synchronization is complete (actually the request has completed), you receive a dialog box confirming completion.

CHAPTER 17

INTER-SITE REPLICATION

In this chapter

INTRODUCTION

Inter-site replication differs from intra-site replication not only because it occurs between sites instead of within a site. The primary distinguishing features are that replication between sites is compressed, can be scheduled, and is not based on a change notification.

As you look at inter-site replication, you might need to refer to Chapters 14, "Active Directory Sites," and 15, "Site Link Objects and Connection Objects," for reference.

→ **See** "Active Directory Sites," **p. 207** and "Site Link Objects and Connection Objects," **p. 229**

TOPOLOGY

The inter-site replication topology is not created the same way as intra-site. Remember that in intra-site it is a bidirectional ring, whereas in inter-site replication it is referred to as a *spanning tree model*. An example appears in Figure 17.1.

Figure 17.1
Spanning tree replica-
tion topology.

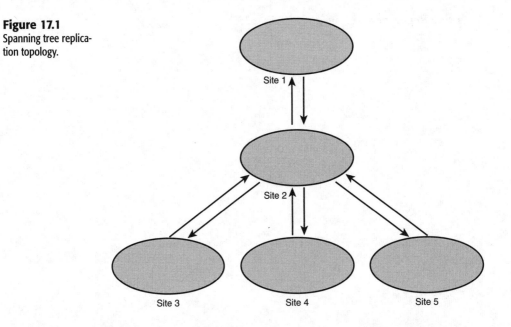

This topology is largely affected by the manner in which you create the site links connecting the sites. So in comparison to the automatic nature of intra-site topology generation, the inter-site topology generation requires a little more manual intervention.

Assuming you have three sites connected with equal speed connections, you need three site links—or perhaps only two, depending on how your network is connected. Based on this scenario, the KCC will generate an inter-site topology.

The actual machine within each site that is responsible for the creation of the topology is known as the *inter-site topology generator*.

INTER-SITE TOPOLOGY GENERATOR

The inter-site topology generator (ISTG) is any DC within the site (irrespective of the domain) that assumes the ISTG role. This is typically the first DC in the site, and it retains this role unless a server failure occurs.

The role is determined by the existence of the `interSiteTopologyGenerator` attribute that lives on the `NTDS Site Settings` object.

To determine the DC acting as the ISTG, follow these steps:

1. Open Active Directory Administration Tool (LDP).
2. Click Connection and select Connect.
3. Type the name of a server in the site you want to investigate (shown in Figure 17.2) and click OK.

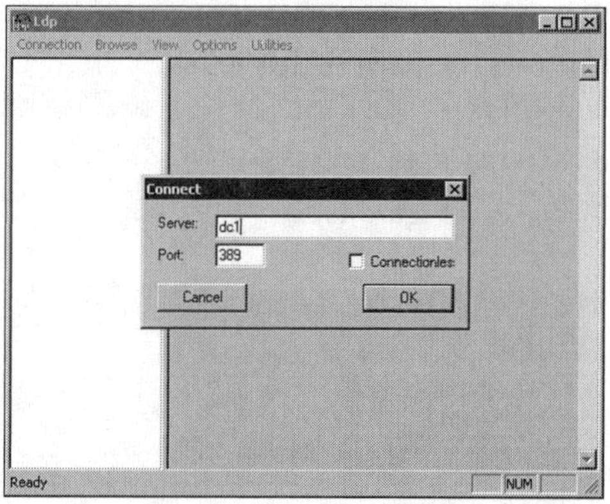

Figure 17.2
The server name.

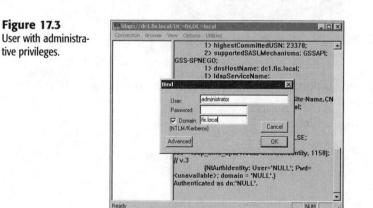

4. Click Connection, and then click Bind. Enter the username and password with administrative privileges, as shown in Figure 17.3. Then click OK.

Figure 17.3
User with administrative privileges.

5. Click Browse, and then select Search (see Figure 17.4).

Figure 17.4
Perform a search of
the directory.

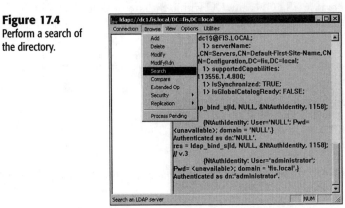

6. In the Base Dn field, type `cn=Sites,cn=configuration,`
   `dc=`*rootdomain*`,dc=`*domainsuffix*.

7. In the Filter field, type `(cn=NTDS Site Settings)`.

8. Select Subtree for the Scope (see Figure 17.5).

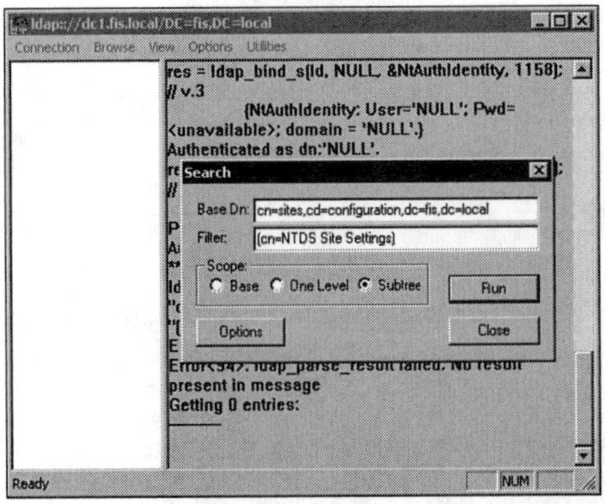

Figure 17.5
Restrict the search to
just the nodes and
depth for which you
are looking.

9. Click Options and type `interSiteTopologyGenerator` in the Attributes field, and then
   click OK (see Figure 17.6).

10. Click Run, and then click Close.

Figure 17.7 displays the results of the search. Notice that the attribute returns the DN for
the NTDS Settings object on the server that holds the ISTG role.

Figure 17.6
Search for the ISTG attribute.

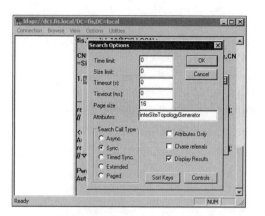

Figure 17.7
Search results and the ISTG.

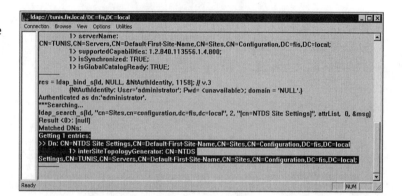

You also can use the Active Directory Sites and Services snap-in to locate the ISTG by selecting the properties of the NTDS Site Settings object.

Each DC in the site is notified of this attribute's existence through replication. The current ISTG then writes this attribute every 30 minutes to its directory. You can change this value through editing the following Registry entry:

```
HKEY_LOCAL_MACHINE\System\CurrentControlSet\Services\NTDS\Parameters
KCC site generator renewal interval (minutes)
```

If the ISTG is unavailable for 60 minutes, another DC assumes the role. The process by which the ISTG is determined to no longer be available is based on the modifications ISTG makes to the interSiteTopologyGenerator attribute. Each DC monitors the times for these modifications, and if it does not fall within a certain time frame (60 minutes), another DC assumes the role by ordering the DSA GUIDs in ascending order and selecting the next one in line. You also can modify a Registry key to change the fail-over value like so:

```
HKEY_LOCAL_MACHINE\System\CurrentControlSet\Services\NTDS\Parameters
KCC site generator fail-over(minutes)
```

The ISTG creates in-bound connection objects after reviewing the lay of the land and creates these connection objects on its own instance of the directory from the bridgehead servers in other sites. These are replicated to the actual bridgehead server in the site through the normal course of intra-site replication. For example, in Figure 17.8, Site A and Site B have a site link connecting the two sites. Within each site, the KCC has already generated the connection object's connection on the DCs in a bidirectional ring.

Figure 17.8
An example of ISTG.

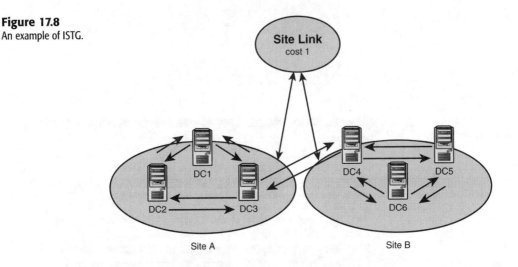

DC3 and DC4 are the bridgehead servers for the two sites. (See the next section, "Bridgehead Servers," for more information.) Assume that DC1 and DC5 are the current ISTG owners. The KCC running on the ISTG creates two connection objects on its own replica connection: DC3 and DC4. The KCC also creates the connection objects with the same parameters as defined by the site link schedule and interval.

BRIDGEHEAD SERVERS

Bridgehead servers are DCs that have been designated by the ISTG to act as such. By creating a list of DSA GUIDs and selecting the DC at the bottom of the list, the bridgehead server is selected for a site. The number of bridgehead servers created by the ITSG is one per transport per site and per domain.

All replication traffic from one site to another travels through the bridgehead server. You will find connection objects from other sites to the bridgehead server in your site and vice versa.

You can assign your own preferred bridgehead servers. (See Chapter 14 for more information.) However, when you decide to designate your own bridgehead servers, remember that if replication fails, the KCC will *not* select any other DC to act as a bridgehead server if that DC is not a part of your designated list of preferred bridgehead servers.

THE REPLICATION PROCESS

As mentioned previously, intra-site replication is initiated based on change notification. However, inter-site replication, by default, is not. Instead, replication occurs between sites based on the schedule set on site links and the frequency at which replication will occur. This serves to give administrators the ability to control replication between locations that might not have connections with a lot of available bandwidth.

Essentially, three items control the replication process between sites: the cost assigned to the site link, the schedule, and the interval associated with the site link.

COST

In the "Costs" section of Chapter 15, you looked at cost as an arbitrary value assigned to a site link for the purpose of reflecting the lowest cost path across which replication will occur. The higher the number, the more expensive the link.

Figure 17.9 shows a sample network diagram of four cities connected through a variety of network connections. When creating sites and associating cost to each site link, you must consider all the links together.

CH
17

Figure 17.9
A sample network.

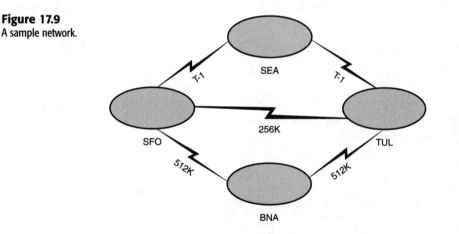

Figure 17.10 shows the site links connecting these sites and their associated costs. As long as the links between SFO and SEA and between SEA and TUL are active, any replication traffic destined to TUL from SFO takes the least expensive cost route, which is SFOtoSEA and SEAtoTUL. (This example assumes a single domain.) However, if either of these links goes down, replication can continue but would travel through the SFOtoTUL site link because its total cost is less than the combined cost of SFOtoBNA and BNAtoTUL (110). This does not imply that this is the actual path the packets take when delivering the replication data.

Figure 17.10
Site links and costs.

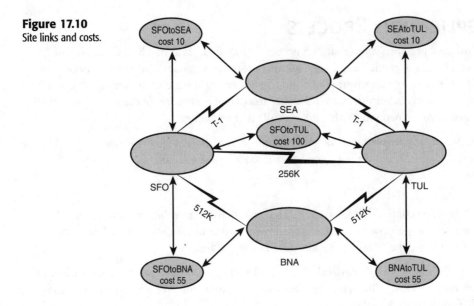

Schedule and interval are covered in Chapter 15, but the following is mentioned for your current scenario.

Continuing on with the sample network, let's broaden the picture a little and add DCs and bridgehead servers to the picture.

SCHEDULING

The basic inter-site replication process is illustrated in Figure 17.11. The particulars are described in the following steps:

1. A user object is modified on DC1.

Figure 17.11
The inter-site replica-tion process.

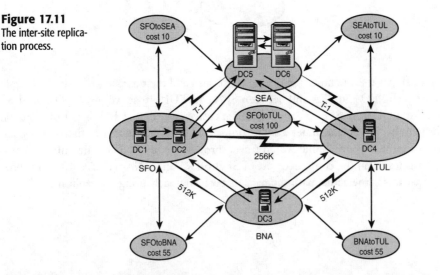

2. DC1 waits five minutes before sending out a change notification to DC2. At that time, DC2 then asks for the modification.

3. DC2, being the bridgehead server, waits for the site link to become available (9 p.m.–12 a.m.).

4. DC2 replicates its changes based on the interval, assuming the defaults (somewhere between 9 p.m. and 9:15 p.m.).

5. DC5 receives the modification and sends out a change notification to DC6 five minutes after the modification.

6. DC6 requests the modification and incorporates the modification into its replica of the directory.

7. DC5 also waits for its window of opportunity for replication to occur to the TUL site, and the circle continues until all DCs are current.

In the previous example, inter-site replication occurred only during the window of opportunity. If you want to maintain a change-based replication topology for not only intra-site but also inter-site replication, here's how:

1. Open ADSI Edit.

2. Expand the Configuration container and navigate to Inter-Site Transports.

3. Right-click the CN=IP node and select Properties (see Figure 17.12).

Figure 17.12
Select the IP transport object.

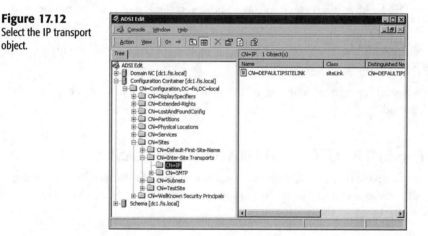

4. Change the Select a Property to View drop-down to Options.

5. Change the value for the attribute by typing 1 in the Edit Attribute text box if the Value(s) field is <not set>, as shown in Figure 17.13.

Note

If the value in the Value(s) field is anything other than <not set>, you must perform a Boolean BITWISE-OR calculation. A BITWISE-OR takes two values and compares them. If either of the values is 1, the result is 1. Only if both the values is 0 does it return 0.

CH

17

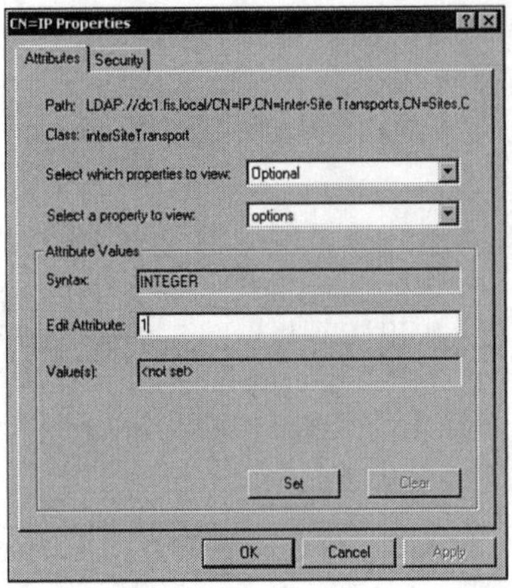

Figure 17.13
Change the option's attributes to enable change notification based on replication.

6. Click Set.

RECIPROCAL REPLICATION

Another issue involves sites that are not always available, such as a dial-up connection. You can implement what is known as *reciprocal* replication. The result of enabling this feature is that when DC-A in Site A dials DC-B in Site B, DC-A initiates replication by requesting changes from DC-B. After it has received those updates, it sends out a change notification to DC-B. DC-B then requests changes from DC-A, resulting in a two-way replication link.

In a branch office situation in which you have a dial-up connection, this is extremely useful, particularly if you're using a VPN to get to the site.

To enable reciprocal replication, repeat steps 1–5 from the previous process but change the value to a 2 instead.

INTER-SITE REPLICATION MANAGEMENT TASKS

When trying to manage replication, a variety of tools are available that can be used, along with some optimizations that can be set to improve performance for replication. Most of the time, settings vary based on the environment.

REPADMIN

The repadmin tool provides a lot of functionality for the management of replication. The Windows 2000 online help provides an explanation of the switches used with the tool. This chapter discusses only the switches that help you initiate replication and view the status of replication.

The following is a list of some of the switches that can be used with the repadmin tool. It is not meant to be a complete list but only to show some of the more useful switches. For a complete list, please refer to the online help on Windows 2000 Server:

- /u:*username*—Used to pass an alternative username; can also be used with the domain as a prefix to the username if the account is in a different domain.

- /pw:*password*—Specifies the password for the referenced user. For example
  `repadmin /u:adbook\administrator /pw:password`

- /sync *naming context DestinationDSA SourceDSA UUID*—Forces replication to occur between two DCs for a specific naming context. Here's an example:
  `repadmin /sync dc=adbook,dc=local tuldc01.adbook.local`
  `➥46332206-76ae-4cb9-85e2-96e91c3bcf1b`

- /syncall *DestinationDSA namingcontext*—Forces replication between all replication partners of the Destination DSA. For example
  `repadmin /syncall tuldc01.adbook.local dc=adbook,dc=local`

- /getchanges *namingcontext* /verbose /statistics—Using the verbose and statistics switches shows a great amount of information with regard to which objects have been added, deleted, modified, or moved. For example
  `repadmin /getchanges adbook.local /verbose /statistics`

To initiate replication successfully using the repadmin tool, you must determine the DSA UUID for the DC from which you want to replicate. To do so, follow these steps:

1. At a command prompt, type **repadmin /showreps *FQDN of server*** (where *FQDN of server* might be dc1.fis.local).

2. Look for the replication partner DSA UUID from which you want to initiate replication. Highlight it and copy it to the Clipboard (see Figure 17.14).

Figure 17.14
Copy from the command prompt.

3. Type **repadmin /sync *namingcontext destination DSA sourceDSA UUID*** (for example, you might type repadmin /sync dc=fis,dc=local 46332206-76ae-4cb9-85e2-96e91c3bcf1b).

After you press Enter, be prepared to wait before you see results. The length of the wait depends on the number of objects to be replicated. To ignore any schedules, use /force with the syntax in step 3. Figure 17.15 displays the results of the sync request.

CH

17

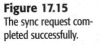

Figure 17.15
The sync request completed successfully.

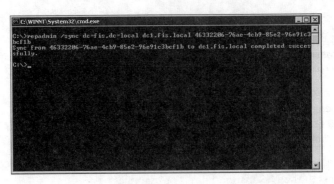

If you want to just fire off the command and not wait for the results, you can use the switch /async instead of /sync. Also, if you want to force replication with all the DC's replication partners, use /syncall instead of /sync.

TUNING

In some instances, you will want to tune replication or even diagnose certain aspects of the process, which is what this section discusses.

As your network grows, you might find yourself in a position where the CPU cycles on your DCs are experiencing moments when they're pegged at 100%. This can be caused by having a large number of domains and sites in your enterprise. If the number of domains plus one times the number of sites squared is greater than 100,000, you should consider some of the recommendations outlined in a Knowledge Base article from Microsoft (Q244368). This can involve everything from disabling the KCC and manually creating all the connection objects between sites to disabling automatic site link bridges and manually creating site link bridges only where appropriate. This is really only appropriate when a site has a domain controller but no adjacent site has a DC in the same domain.

If you want to be able to determine just how long the KCC process is taking on individual DCs, change the value of the following Registry entry to a 3 or greater:

```
HKEY_LOCAL_MACHINE\System\CurrentControlSet\Services\NTDS\Diagnostics\
➥Knowledge Consistency Checker
```

Along those same lines, you can change the replication events value to 3 or greater, which will enable you to see the actual replication events in the Directory Service Event Log. You also will be able to see such things as when the inbound request is made for each of the NCs as well as the updates to the up-to-dateness vectors (see Figure 17.16). The values for enabling diagnostics logging are as follows:

```
0=None
1=Minimum
3=Medium
5=Maximum
```

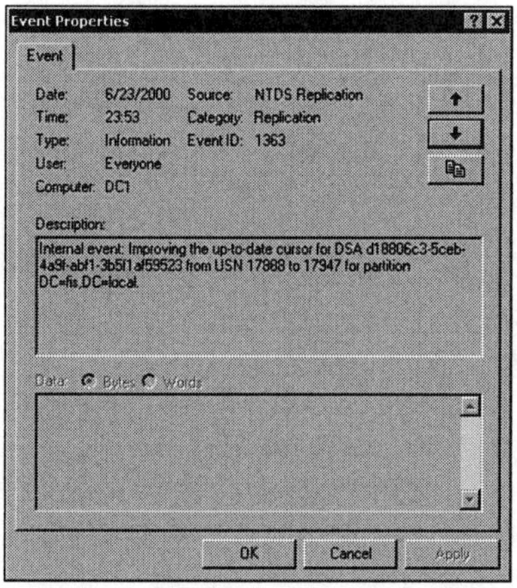

Figure 17.16
Event ID 1363—an up-to-date vector event.

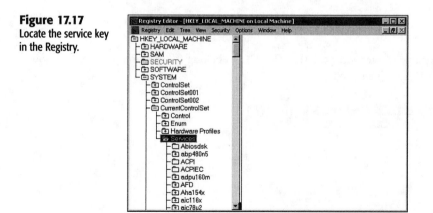

> **Note**
>
> Use diagnostic logging only for troubleshooting and on non-production DCs because this can have an adverse effect on performance and can fill the logs very quickly.

Although this isn't directly related to inter-site replication, you can configure a DC to have membership in multiple sites. This enables a DC to publish its services in more than one site so that those services are more readily available to clients in those sites.

To publish a DC in more than one site, follow these steps:

1. Type **regedt32.exe** from the Start menu Run dialog box.

2. Navigate to HKEY_LOCAL_MACHINE\System\CurrentControlSet\Services\Netlogon\ Parameters (see Figure 17.17).

Figure 17.17
Locate the service key in the Registry.

3. Click Edit and select Add Value, as shown in Figure 17.18.

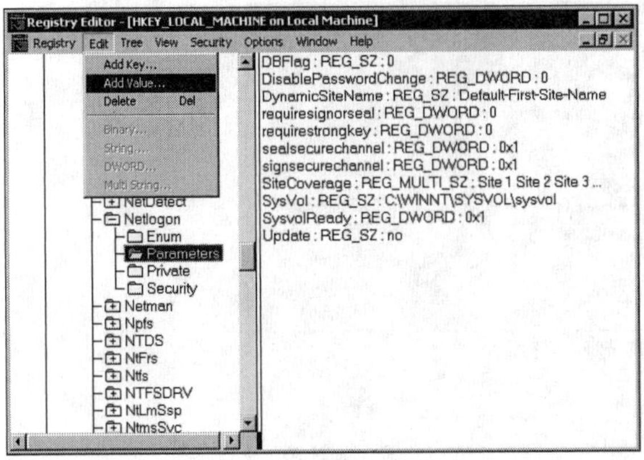

Figure 17.18
Add a new value to
the Registry for
`SiteCoverage`.

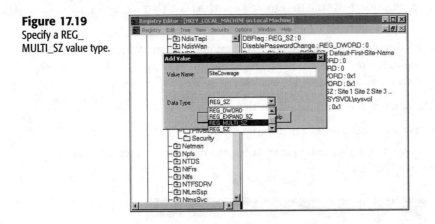

4. In the Value Name field, type **SiteCoverage**.

5. In the Data Type combo box, select REG_MULTI_SZ and click OK (see Figure 17.19).

Figure 17.19
Specify a REG_
MULTI_SZ value type.

6. Type the name of each site you want this DC to belong to (one line per site), as shown
in Figure 17.20. Then click OK.

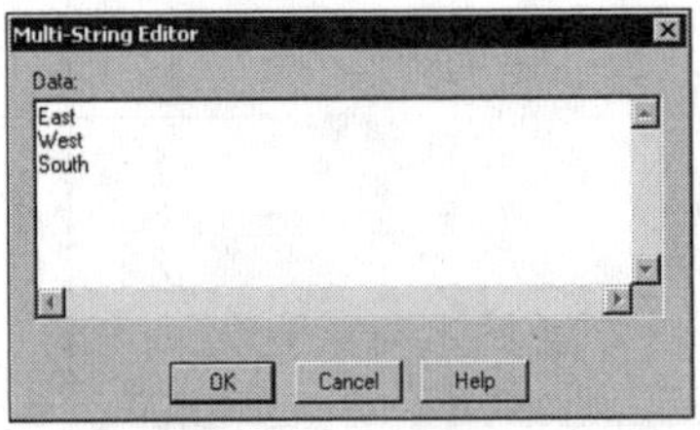

Figure 17.20
Add each site for
`SiteCoverage`.

7. Finally, to enable clients to look up the site membership of this DC, see Chapter 5, "DNS
Architecture," which discusses how to add SRV records with the appropriate syntax.

Whenever the KCC evaluates the topology and determines that certain DCs are no longer available, it creates new connection objects to enable replication to continue. For replication between sites, the requesting DC must have made at least one attempt before the KCC determines that a failure has occurred. In addition, at least two hours must have expired since the last successful replication. You can modify these limits by editing the Registry to include two values: `IntersiteFailuresAllowed` (the default value is 1) and `MaxFailureTimeForIntersiteLink (secs)` (the default value is 7200).

> **Tip**
>
> Add each new value for each option you want to change as a `REG_DWORD` type to the `HKEY_LOCAL_MACHINE\System\CurrentControlSet\Services\NTDS\Parameters` section of the Registry.

MONITORING REPLICATION

During the course of learning about replication, Performance Monitor is one of the most helpful tools. Because replication occurs via RPC or SMTP (which are digitally signed and encrypted), using Network Monitor just does not do the trick.

CH

17

To monitor replication, you must select a variety of counters from the NTDS object, as shown in Figure 17.21.

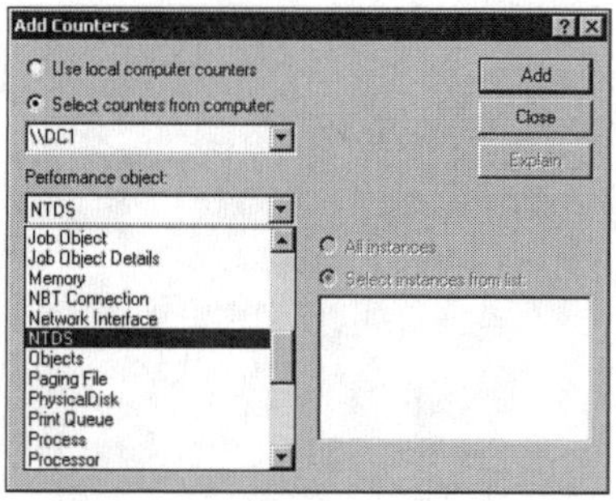

Figure 17.21
Select the NTDS performance object.

The following counters are directly related to replication (an asterisk has been added to the most important ones):

```
DRA Highest USN Committed (High part)
DRA Highest USN Committed (Low part)
DRA Highest USN Issued (High part)
DRA Highest USN Issued (Low part)
DRA Inbound Bytes Compressed (Between Sites, After Compression) Since Boot
DRA Inbound Bytes Compressed (Between Sites, After Compression)/sec
DRA Inbound Bytes Compressed (Between Sites, Before Compression) Since Boot
DRA Inbound Bytes Compressed (Between Sites, Before Compression)/sec
DRA Inbound Bytes Not Compressed (Within Site) Since Boot
DRA Inbound Bytes Not Compressed (Within Site)/sec
DRA Inbound Bytes Total Since Boot
DRA Inbound Bytes Total/sec
DRA Inbound Full Sync Objects Remaining *
```

```
DRA Inbound Object Updates Remaining in Packet *
DRA Inbound Objects Applied/sec
DRA Inbound Objects Filtered/sec
DRA Inbound Objects/sec
DRA Inbound Properties Applied/sec
DRA Inbound Properties Filtered/sec
DRA Inbound Properties Total/sec
DRA Inbound Values (DNs only)/sec
DRA Inbound Values Total/sec
DRA Outbound Bytes Compressed (Between Sites, After Compression) Since Boot
DRA Outbound Bytes Compressed (Between Sites, After Compression)/sec
DRA Outbound Bytes Compressed (Between Sites, Before Compression) Since Boot
DRA Outbound Bytes Compressed (Between Sites, Before Compression)/sec
DRA Outbound Bytes Not Compressed (Within Site) Since Boot
DRA Outbound Bytes Not Compressed (Within Site)/sec
DRA Outbound Bytes Total Since Boot
DRA Outbound Bytes Total/sec
DRA Outbound Objects Filtered/sec
DRA Outbound Objects/sec
DRA Outbound Properties/sec
DRA Outbound Values (DNs only)/sec
DRA Outbound Values Total/sec
DRA Pending Replication Synchronizations *
DRA Sync Failures on Schema Mismatch *
DRA Sync Requests Made *
DRA Sync Requests Successful
DS % Reads from DRA *
DS % Reads from KCC *
DS % Searches from DRA *
DS % Searches from KCC *
DS % Writes from DRA *
DS % Writes from KCC *
```

CHAPTER 18

AUTHENTICATION

In this chapter

ENTERPRISE SECURITY

Security is of paramount importance in an enterprise environment. Every operating system that is designed to run in a multiuser environment has a security scheme. This chapter looks at two basic issues in security: authentication and authorization.

Authentication asks the question, "Who are you?" Several methods are available for identifying users, computers, and processes in Windows 2000. In most situations, you'll require the authenticating user to provide a password using an authentication protocol. The default is Kerberos v5, but you also can use NTLM v1 and v2 for backward compatibility with down-level clients. You also can use X.509 certificates through a public key infrastructure (PKI) to authenticate with smart cards or through certificate mapping.

After you have authenticated a user, the next process is that of authorization. *Authorization* is primarily interested in your level of authority or permission on the network. It asks, "What can you do?" In Windows 2000, this is satisfied primarily through the use of security identifiers (SIDs). A SID uniquely identifies you, and as you move through the network using different services, you are authorized to use each service by presenting your SID and the SID of every group of which you're a member. This list of SIDs is called an *access token*. That service, file, or Active Directory object then looks at your list of SIDs and compares it with its own discretionary access control list (DACL). If it finds a match, you are allowed to use that service.

Authentication is the process of identifying a user. We humans do this based on physical characteristics if we personally know someone, or based on credentials from a trusted authority if we do not. The default authentication protocol for Windows 2000 is Kerberos, and the trusted authority is a Kerberos Key Distribution Center (KDC).

KERBEROS

Kerberos authentication in Windows 2000 uses a shared secret, the password, to identify the user, and then grants him a ticket containing information about who he is. This ticket can then be used to obtain access to services throughout the forest.

HISTORY OF KERBEROS

Kerberos was created as part of project Athena at MIT in the 1980s. It is a mature, tested authentication protocol that has been implemented on thousands of servers over several decades. Kerberos was chosen as the default authentication protocol for Windows 2000 for its robustness, availability, and proven track record.

ADVANTAGES OF KERBEROS

Kerberos has several advantages over previous authentication protocols. It is interoperable with Kerberos implementations on other operating systems, is faster, and provides a much simpler trust model for Windows 2000 domains. Specifically, its advantages are as follows:

- **Interoperability**—Kerberos is not a proprietary standard; it is based on an IETF standard, RFC 1510. Kerberos on Windows 2000 integrates with Kerberos realms on other operating systems. Tools in the Windows 2000 support tools, such as `ksetup` and `ktpass`, facilitate that interaction.

- **Simpler Trusts**—Because Kerberos trusts are transitive and are built automatically as child domains are added to the Active Directory tree, managing trusts is much simpler.

- **Mutual Authentication**—Using Kerberos, you can verify the identity of parties on both ends of the network connection. This was not possible with previous versions of Windows NT.

- **Impersonation**—This is critical in a multitier development environment. Impersonation enables a process to authenticate and work on the behalf of another process using the first process's credentials. This means that a COM+ DLL can authenticate to a remote SQL server using the Kerberos credentials of the user who called the DLL rather than a fixed user/password pair.

- **Faster Authentication**—Kerberos grants a ticket to an authenticated user that is good, by default, for 10 hours. This means that after you have a ticket for a particular server, you can open and close connections to that server for 10 hours without having to recommunicate with the Kerberos service. After you have authenticated and received a ticket for that service, your ticket is good for 10 hours. This setting can be altered by modifying the Default Domain group policy.

Note

The Windows 2000 support tools are available on the Windows 2000 CD in the `\support\tools` folder.

CH

18

KERBEROS ROLES IN WINDOWS 2000

Every Windows 2000 domain controller (DC) hosts an instance of the Kerberos service called the Kerberos Key Distribution Center. This means that a client can authenticate to any DC in its own domain. Although Kerberos on Windows 2000 is implemented as a single service, conceptually a Kerberos Authentication Architecture contains several roles. We will discuss the process of using these services in more detail later in the chapter.

KEY DISTRIBUTION CENTER

The Key Distribution Center is the actual service that runs on every Windows 2000 domain controller. It is started by the local security authority (LSA) and runs in the process space of the LSA. The KDC uses the Active Directory database as its account database. Because each DC in the domain runs the KDC, your Kerberos implementation is fault tolerant, assuming you have two or more DCs per domain.

The KDC is associated with an automatically created user account named `krbtgt`. This account can't be deleted or renamed. Its password is changed periodically by the system and is used to create the secret key for encrypting and decrypting ticket-granting tickets (TGTs) issued by the authentication service.

AUTHENTICATION SERVICE

The authentication service is the portion of Kerberos that is responsible for the initial authentication of clients. After you have proven that the client is indeed who she claims to be by comparing your shared secret (a hash generated from the password), you issue the client a ticket-granting ticket. This TGT can then be used to obtain tickets from this KDC for admission to other services throughout the domain and forest.

TICKET-GRANTING SERVICE

The ticket-granting service (TGS) issues tickets to other services. After a client has used the AS to authenticate to the KDC and has received a TGT, it can present this TGT to the KDC as many times as necessary to obtain tickets to other services, such as file and print, email, SQL servers, and so on. A ticket to one of these services is called a *session* ticket because, by default, it is good for opening sessions with the service for the next 10 hours.

Note

This discussion of Kerberos authentication assumes that the IP protocol is installed and running on both the DC and the client. If both parties cannot use IP to communicate, no Kerberos authentication will occur. You can use IPX to authenticate to a Windows 2000 domain controller, but the authentication mechanism used will be NTLM.

KERBEROS KEY DISTRIBUTION

The process of authenticating to a Windows 2000 domain is basically that of obtaining one or more Kerberos keys. These keys contain information about who the client is and who issued the ticket (the KDC), and a list of the SIDs for the client and any groups of which the client is a member. The list of SIDs then provides authorization for the client.

Note

Kerberos authentication is the default for Windows 2000. If a Windows 2000 client is authenticating to an NT domain controller, it uses NTLM. Windows 9x and NT computers cannot use Kerberos, so even if they are authenticating to a Windows 2000 DC, they use NTLM (the default authentication protocol for Windows NT).

KERBEROS TOOLS

One of the disadvantages of trying to understand the Kerberos protocol using a network protocol analyzer, such as Microsoft Network Monitor, is that virtually everything that goes over the wire between the client and the KDC is encrypted. Some tools are available, however, that enable you to see which tickets have been issued to the client and where they came from. The two tools you will use in this section are from the Windows 2000 Server Resource Kit and are called `kerbtray` and `klist`.

kerbtray

kerbtray is a graphical tool that runs in the status area of the desktop next to the time and date icon. kerbtray enables you to list and purge tickets for the current logon session. This is a useful tool for viewing the current Kerberos architecture and troubleshooting Kerberos. kerbtray can be loaded by double-clicking its icon in the default installation path for the Resource Kit, c:\program files\resource kit. After you have loaded it, you can view the current list of tickets by double-clicking its icon in the lower-right corner of your screen. Figure 18.1 shows the default interface for kerbtray.

Figure 18.1
The kerbtray tool.

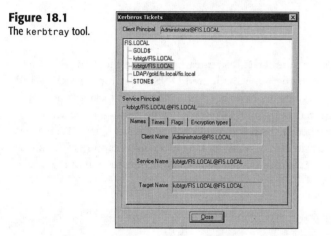

> **Note**
>
> Although you can use klist and kerbtray to purge the Kerberos tickets held by the currently logged-on user, you can accomplish the same thing by simply logging off.

klist

klist shows much of the same information that kerbtray does but in a textual format. You also can use klist to view or purge Kerberos tickets. Listing 18.1 shows the parameters output by entering the klist command at the command prompt. You will use kerbtray and klist in the next section as you look at various options for Kerberos and the process of getting a ticket.

LISTING 18.1 klist.exe PARAMETERS

```
C:\>klist
Usage: klist <tickets | tgt | purge>
```

AUTHENTICATING TO THE DOMAIN

Getting a Kerberos TGT is the first step in authenticating to the domain and using services on the network. The Kerberos KDC on the domain controller and the Kerberos security support provider (SSP) on the client collaborate to authenticate and authorize the user so he can then take advantage of services throughout the network.

> **Note** The process of obtaining a TGT and a session key to the computer to which you are logging on completes successfully before you ever see the desktop.

FINDING THE KDC

Before you can trade credentials with the KDC, you must find one on the network. The client uses the local DNS resolver to query the configured DNS server for the SRV record for a DNS server in its site. This ensures that you are authenticating as locally as possible. Listing 18.2 shows the partial contents of the DNS resolver cache on the local machine. This shows the entry for the instance of the Kerberos KDC for this site. gold.fis.local is the DNS name for the DC in this site. If you were looking at a packet capture for this, you would see the IP address for gold.fis.local in the additional records section of the standard query response for this record.

LISTING 18.2   DNS INFORMATION FOR THE KDC

```
_kerberos._tcp.default-first-site-name._sites.dc._msdcs.fis.local.
    --------------------------------------------------------
Record Name . . . . . : _kerberos._tcp.Default-First-Site-Name._sites.dc.
➡_msdcs.FIS.LOCAL
        Record Type . . . . . : 33
        Time To Live  . . . . : 517
        Data Length . . . . . : 12
        Section . . . . . . . : Answer
        SRV Record  . . . . . :
                        gold.fis.local
                        0
                        100
                        88
                        0
```

LOGGING ON

The first part of this section involves getting the credentials and preparing them to cross the unsecured network.

OBTAINING THE PASSWORD

When the user presses Ctrl+Alt+Delete at the Welcome to Windows dialog box, she is presented with the Log On to Windows dialog box. When she enters her username and password, this information is passed to the winlogon process, which in turn passes it to the local security authority.

ENCRYPTING THE PASSWORD

Before this information is passed across the network, however, the LSA uses a one-way hash algorithm to create a secret key from the user's password. This secret key then is saved to the credentials cache—a portion of volatile memory that is never paged to disk—so that it can be retrieved and used again if necessary, if the TGT expires and requires renewal or if you need to perform NTLM authentication. This cache is destroyed when the user logs off.

OBTAINING A TGT FROM THE KDC

The next components of this process are the LSA and Kerberos SSP on the client and the Kerberos KDC, AS, and TGS on the domain controller. The TGT that they collaborate to obtain is used throughout the logon session to obtain session tickets to other services.

CLIENT REQUEST FOR A TGT

The client sends a message to the KDC using the IP protocol to port 88 that includes the username, the user's account domain, and preauthentication data (usually a timestamp) that is encrypted with the client's secret key.

THE KDC'S RESPONSE

When the KDC receives the message from the client, the username is in clear text. The KDC then uses the Active Directory database to look up the user and the user's password property. This property does not hold the password itself, but instead holds the same secret key derived from the password that was created on the client when the user began the logon process. The KDC uses the stored secret key to decrypt the preauthentication information located in the message. If it matches what the KDC expects, the KDC then assumes that this is a good logon attempt and prepares a response.

The response includes a session key that the client and KDC share and a TGT for the user's domain. Listing 18.3 shows the TGT for a logon session using the `klist` command.

LISTING 18.3   TGT FOR A LOGON SESSION USING `klist`

```
C:\> klist tgt
Cached TGT:
ServiceName: krbtgt
TargetName: krbtgt
FullServiceName: Administrator
DomainName: FIS.LOCAL
TargetDomainName: FIS.LOCAL
AltTargetDomainName: FIS.LOCAL
TicketFlags: 0x40e00000
KeyExpirationTime: 256/0/29920 0:100:8048
StartTime: 4/15/2000 11:27:41
EndTime: 4/15/2000 21:27:41
RenewUntil: 4/22/2000 11:27:41
TimeSkew: 4/22/2000 11:27:41
```

The TGT is used by the client to obtain tickets to other services during this logon session. It contains a session key that the client and KDC share and authorization data that is a list of SIDs for groups of which the user is a member. This list of SIDs includes all groups in the logon domain of which the user is a member and all Universal groups of which the user is a member. This information is digitally signed so that the client cannot modify the list of SIDs in her token and change her level of access.

GETTING A SESSION TICKET FOR THE LOCAL COMPUTER

At this point, the user is well on her way to logging on. She has been identified by the KDC and has a TGT. The desktop still has not appeared onscreen, however, because she does not yet have a session ticket for her local computer.

REQUESTING A SESSION TICKET

The LSA on the client sends a message to the KDC, requesting a ticket good for admission to the local computer. This message includes the computer's name, the computer's domain, the TGT, and an authenticator encrypted with the client's session key that was obtained in the previous conversation with the KDC. Kerberos does not assume a secure network, and portions of any messages that are sent between the security services on the client and server are encrypted with the session key the client and server share to ensure that every message is secure.

THE KDC'S RESPONSE

After the KDC has established that the client's request is good—by checking the authenticator in the previous message—it issues a ticket to the local computer. This ticket includes a session key for the user and computer to share. Interestingly, the message also includes information for the local computer. However, this information is encrypted with the session key the computer shares with the KDC so the user cannot modify it, see it, or change its security context to the local computer. During the boot of the local computer, it authenticated to the KDC using its computer account and obtained a session key for just this purpose.

COMPLETING THE LOGON PROCESS

At this point, the user has proven both to the domain and to the local computer that she is who she says she is. This information is passed to the `winlogon` process, which creates the desktop and passes on the user's logon token. Any processes created from this point will inherit the security context of the user.

Listing 18.4 shows the tickets received by the logged-on user at the beginning of the logon session. These tickets include the ticket to the local computer, the session ticket with the KDC, and the TGT.

LISTING 18.4   USING `klist` TO VIEW TICKETS FROM THE KDC

```
C:\klist tickets
Cached Tickets: (5)
  Server: krbtgt/SALES.FIS.LOCAL@SALES.FIS.LOCAL
```

LISTING 18.4   CONTINUED

```
        KerbTicket Encryption Type: RSADSI RC4-HMAC(NT)
        End Time: 4/15/2000 2:32:13
        Renew Time: 4/21/2000 16:32:13


    Server: krbtgt/SALES.FIS.LOCAL@SALES.FIS.LOCAL
        KerbTicket Encryption Type: RSADSI RC4-HMAC(NT)
        End Time: 4/15/2000 2:32:13
        Renew Time: 4/21/2000 16:32:13


    Server: SERVER9$@SALES.FIS.LOCAL
        KerbTicket Encryption Type: RSADSI RC4-HMAC(NT)
        End Time: 4/15/2000 2:32:13
        Renew Time: 4/21/2000 16:32:13


    Server: LDAP/server9.sales.fis.local/sales.fis.local@SALES.FIS.LOCAL
        KerbTicket Encryption Type: RSADSI RC4-HMAC(NT)
        End Time: 4/15/2000 2:32:13
        Renew Time: 4/21/2000 16:32:13


    Server: SERVER5$@SALES.FIS.LOCAL
        KerbTicket Encryption Type: RSADSI RC4-HMAC(NT)
        End Time: 4/15/2000 2:32:13
        Renew Time: 4/21/2000 16:32:13
```

CH

18

AUTHENTICATING TO OTHER DOMAINS IN THE TREE

The previous example showed how a user becomes authenticated in her home domain and receives a list of her credentials. In a multidomain environment, users will need to access services in other domains in the forest. In previous versions of NT, this required a complex web of non-transitive trusts that stretched explicitly from every domain that contained users to every domain that contained services. Because Kerberos trusts are transitive, you are no longer required to maintain these explicit trusts. The trust relationships that are automatically created when a child domain is created are sufficient for authentication throughout the forest. In addition, they are mandatory, and therefore cannot be disabled under any circumstances.

AUTOMATIC KERBEROS TRANSITIVE TRUSTS

When an Directory tree or forest is built, as domains are added to the tree, transitive, two-way trust relationships are created between parent and child domains. Figure 18.2 shows three domains in a single tree. The domain names are a.com, b.a.com, and c.a.com. Domain names are, of course, contiguous with the parent DNS domain name.

Figure 18.2
Automatically created
trusts in a forest.

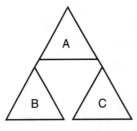

A two-way trust relationship exists between domain A and domain B. Also, a two-way trust relationship exists between domain A and domain C. However, an explicit trust relationship does *not* exist between domain B and domain C, but that does not mean they do not trust each other. They *do* trust each other because the trust relationships between the respective domains and the parent domain are transitive. B trusts A and A trusts C; therefore, B trusts C. This is completely the reverse of one-way, non-transitive trust relationships in NT. You can use the Active Directory Domains and Trusts MMC Snap-in to add explicit trusts to NT 4 domains, MIT Kerberos v5 realms, and other Windows 2000 forests. But inside your own forests, explicit trusts are unnecessary.

> **Note**
>
> Adding trust relationships inside a forest is unnecessary. However, in the next section when we discuss Kerberos referrals, you will see why in some circumstances, adding these relationships is appropriate to help speed up authentication.

MANAGING TRUSTS

You can use the Active Directory Domains and Trusts MMC Snap-in, `domain.msc`, to view and add trusts. Figure 18.3 shows the snap-in open to the `fis.local` domain. The basic interface for this tool shows the top-level domain `fis.local` and its child domain.

Figure 18.3
The AD Domains and
Trusts tool.

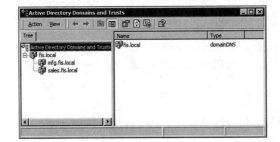

You can't do much from here except right-click one of the domains and choose either Manage or Properties. If you choose Manage, the Active Directory Users and Computers MMC Snap-in (`dsa.msc`) opens, with the focus on the selected domain. On the other hand, if you choose Properties, the `fis.local` Properties dialog box shown in Figure 18.4 pops up.

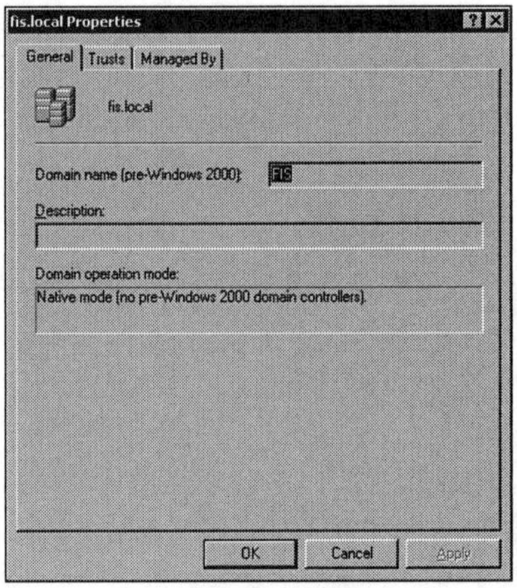

Figure 18.4
The domain properties page.

The General tab of the `fis.local` Properties page is mostly informational, except for the option that enables you to change the domain mode from mixed to native. A *mixed mode* domain—which is the default when Windows 2000 is installed—allows the presence of NT backup DCs (BDCs). A *native mode* domain, in contrast, is made up of Windows 2000 DCs. Both modes support a mixture of clients and servers, but a native mode domain supports only Windows 2000 DCs.

The Trusts tab of the `fis.local` Properties dialog box is where you view existing and create new trust relationships (see Figure 18.5). Here you can create one-way, transitive, shortcut trusts with other domains in your forest, or you can create one-way, non-transitive trusts with NT domains or other Windows 2000 forests. You will use this tab later in this section to create and demonstrate shortcut trusts. In Figure 18.5, you also can see the trust structure between `fis.local` and `sales.fis.local`, and `fis.local` and `mfg.fis.local`.

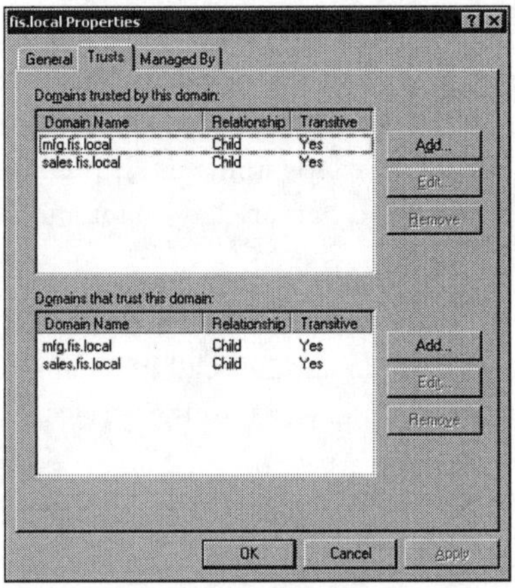

CH
18

Figure 18.5
Viewing trusts with AD Domains and Trusts.

Figure 18.6 shows the Managed By tab of the `fis.local` Properties page. This is where you can embed contact information about the domain. To add the information, simply click the

Change button and select a domain user. This interface will then inherit any information about that user that is already present in the Active Directory database. The View button provides a shortcut to view the property page for the selected user and update it if necessary.

Figure 18.6
Management infor-
mation in AD
Domains and Trusts.

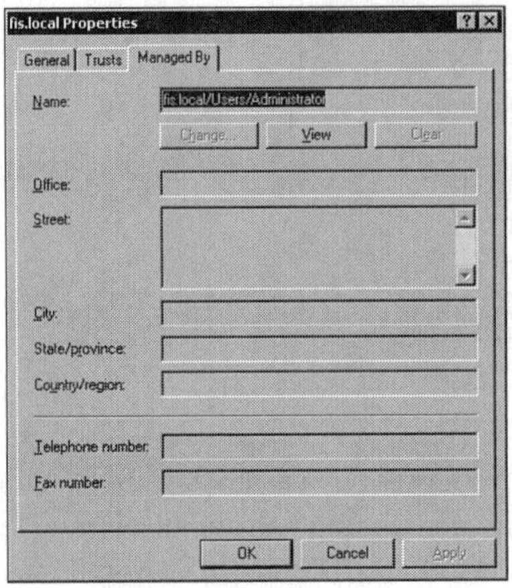

HOW TRANSITIVE TRUSTS WORK

The reason transitive trusts work is very simple: Kerberos. Referring to Figure 18.2, domains B and C both trust domain A. Each domain has at least one DC, which means it has at least one Kerberos KDC. When a child domain is added to the tree, the TGSs in the parent and child become security principals in each other's domain and create and share a session key. When a user needs access to a service in another domain, the KDCs can collaborate and build an authentication referral path from the client to the server.

CROSS-DOMAIN AUTHENTICATION EXAMPLE

Figure 18.7 shows the `fis.local` domain with two child domains: `sales.fis.local` and `mfg.fis.local`. In this example, `client.sales.fis.local` wants to connect to `server.mfg.fis.local`. Which kind of server it is is immaterial. It could be anything from the server service hosting a file share to a SQL Server. Any client and service that can use Kerberos will follow this example.

Each domain has a single domain controller hosting a Kerberos KDC. The client is in one child domain and needs access to the service in another child domain. The Kerberos referrals follow a trail from the client up the tree and down to the service.

CLIENT REQUEST TO THE SALES KDC

This example assumes that the user at the client has already logged on and has a TGT to the local KDC. When the client begins its attempt to connect to the server, the connection attempt is the same as if the server were in the same domain. The client contacts the TGS of the KDC on the local domain controller and asks for a ticket to the server. It includes the following in the message: the name of the target (Server), the target domain (mfg.fis.local), the TGT for the local domain (sales.fis.local), and the authenticator that is part of every Kerberos message to prove its identity.

Figure 18.7
A sample domain structure.

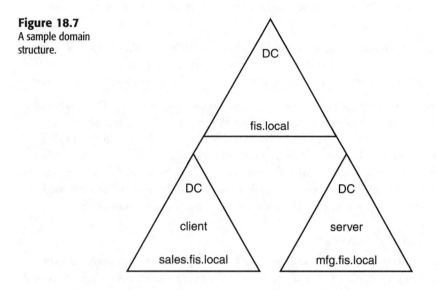

SALES KDC RESPONSE TO THE CLIENT

Because your KDC is not authoritative for the mfg domain, it must either refer your client to a KDC that is authoritative or refer it up the tree. Because no shortcut trust exists between the KDC in sales and the KDC in mfg, the KDC in sales responds with a session key and a TGT to the TGS on the KDC in fis.local. The TGT is encrypted with the secret key that is created when the trust relationship is established.

CLIENT REQUEST TO KDC IN fis.local

The client then sends a message to the KDC in fis.local. This message is almost identical to the one you sent to your own KDC except, of course, the TGT and session key are for the fis.local KDC.

fis.local KDC RESPONSE TO THE CLIENT

The KDC in fis.local is not authoritative for the mfg domain. However, because it does have a trust relationship with the mfg domain, it responds with a message that is almost identical to the message your client received from its KDC, except that the information is focused on the mfg domain.

CLIENT REQUEST TO THE KDC IN mfg

The client then sends a TGS request for a session ticket to the KDC in mfg. This contains information about the requested target and credentials from the KDC in fis.local.

mfg KDC RESPONSE TO THE CLIENT

The KDC is authoritative for the mfg domain and responds with a session ticket for the client to present to the server and the client's copy of the session key for the client and server to share. This copy of the session key is encrypted with the session key the client and KDC share.

It is interesting to note that some of the information in the ticket the client will present to the server in mfg is intended for the server but is given to the client to pass to the server. This information, however, is encrypted with the secret key the KDC in mfg and the server share.

The session ticket not only includes the server's copy of the session key for the client and server to share, but also includes the client's authorization data. This authorization data includes the SID for the user logged on at the client, SIDs for the groups in the user's account domain (sales), SIDs for universal groups of which the user or one of her groups in the sales domain is a member, and SIDs for groups in the target domain (mfg) of which the user or one of her groups is a member. Remember that this authorization data is signed to prevent the client from modifying it before it passes the information on to the server.

CLIENT REQUEST TO THE SERVER

The client, having traversed the Active Directory tree and gained the necessary introduction to the server, then presents its credentials to the server. These credentials include its name, the ticket to the server, and authentication data encrypted with the session key it shares with the server.

SERVER RESPONSE TO THE CLIENT

The server responds with its own authenticator encrypted with the session key it shares with the client.

Listing 18.5 shows the output from the klist.exe tool at the end of this demonstration. Here you can see tickets to all the KDCs in the scenario and the ticket to the server.

LISTING 18.5 LISTING THE TICKETS FROM CROSS-DOMAIN AUTHENTICATION

```
C:\>klist tickets

Cached Tickets: (8)

    Server: krbtgt/MFG.FIS.LOCAL@FIS.LOCAL
        KerbTicket Encryption Type: RSADSI RC4-HMAC(NT)
        End Time: 4/15/2000 2:10:23
        Renew Time: 4/21/2000 16:10:23


    Server: krbtgt/FIS.LOCAL@SALES.FIS.LOCAL
        KerbTicket Encryption Type: RSADSI RC4-HMAC(NT)
        End Time: 4/15/2000 2:10:23
        Renew Time: 4/21/2000 16:10:23
```

LISTING 18.5   CONTINUED

```
Server: krbtgt/SALES.FIS.LOCAL@SALES.FIS.LOCAL
   KerbTicket Encryption Type: RSADSI RC4-HMAC(NT)
   End Time: 4/15/2000 2:10:23
   Renew Time: 4/21/2000 16:10:23


Server: krbtgt/SALES.FIS.LOCAL@SALES.FIS.LOCAL
   KerbTicket Encryption Type: RSADSI RC4-HMAC(NT)
   End Time: 4/15/2000 2:10:23
   Renew Time: 4/21/2000 16:10:23


Server: SERVER12$@MFG.FIS.LOCAL
   KerbTicket Encryption Type: RSADSI RC4-HMAC(NT)
   End Time: 4/15/2000 2:10:23
   Renew Time: 4/21/2000 16:10:23


Server: SERVER9$@SALES.FIS.LOCAL
   KerbTicket Encryption Type: RSADSI RC4-HMAC(NT)
   End Time: 4/15/2000 2:10:23
   Renew Time: 4/21/2000 16:10:23


Server: LDAP/server9.sales.fis.local/sales.fis.local@SALES.FIS.LOCAL
   KerbTicket Encryption Type: RSADSI RC4-HMAC(NT)
   End Time: 4/15/2000 2:10:23
   Renew Time: 4/21/2000 16:10:23


Server: SERVER5$@SALES.FIS.LOCAL
   KerbTicket Encryption Type: RSADSI RC4-HMAC(NT)
   End Time: 4/15/2000 2:10:23
   Renew Time: 4/21/2000 16:10:23
```

CH

18

ADVANTAGES TO THE PREVIOUS SCENARIO

Now that the client and server have been formally introduced, they can open and close connections for the next 10 hours without contacting any of the KDCs involved in this scenario. This is one of the key advantages of Kerberos from an application scalability perspective. NTLM must authenticate every open connection. Therefore, in an NTLM scenario, if the client and server were to open and close a connection in the next 10 hours, you would have to authenticate every open connection to a DC. With Kerberos, as in the previous example, the client and server have all the authentication data they need for the next 10-hour session, regardless of the number of open connections.

EXPLICIT TRUSTS

As you have seen in the previous section, Kerberos trusts are transitive. This means that every domain in a forest does not require an explicit trust with every other domain in the forest to be capable of passing credentials between security principals in the forest. Because of this—and because Kerberos trusts are automatically created when you add domains to the forest—administrators are relieved of much of the burden of managing explicit trust relationships that was present in NT.

If, however, you want to create trusts with other forests or NT domains, or if you want to create shortcut trusts, you must use the Active Directory Domains and Trusts MMC Snap-in (ADDT). This section demonstrates the use of the ADDT snap-in by creating a shortcut trust between sales.fis.local and mfg.fis.local. A *shortcut* trust is an explicit, transitive Kerberos trust created with the intention of shortening the Kerberos referral path that was demonstrated in the last section.

SHORTCUT TRUSTS

As was demonstrated in the previous section, to use services in another domain, the client is referred up the tree by the KDC until it reaches a point at which the referral process can run down the tree to the desired domain. If you have one domain that often uses resources in another domain, it might be worth the management overhead to create a shortcut trust. In this demonstration, you will create a shortcut trust between the sales and mfg domains to shorten the Kerberos referral path. Then, you'll look at the process of a client in sales accessing a server in mfg to see how much shorter the Kerberos path is.

CREATING A SHORTCUT TRUST

To create a shortcut trust, load the Active Directory Domains and Trusts MMC Snap-in and select the domain that holds the servers you are interested in (mfg). Right-click the domain and choose Properties, Trusts. This opens the Trusts tab of the mfg.fis.local Properties page (see Figure 18.8). For users in sales to be able to access services in mfg, you must set the trust relationships so that mfg trusts sales.

Figure 18.8
The Trusts Properties page.

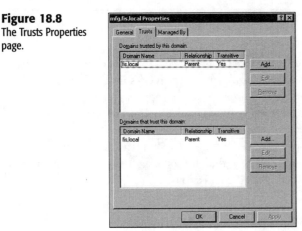

CONFIGURING mfg TO TRUST sales

The first thing you must do is set mfg.fis.local to trust sales.fis.local. Click the Add button next to the Domains Trusted by This Domain section of the Trusts tab. This pops up the Add Trusted Domain dialog box, shown in Figure 18.9. In the Trusted Domain text box, type **sales.fis.local**, which is the domain that holds the users who need shortcut access to this domain. The password you set here will be needed when you set the other side of the trust relationship on the sales domain. After you have entered the information, click OK.

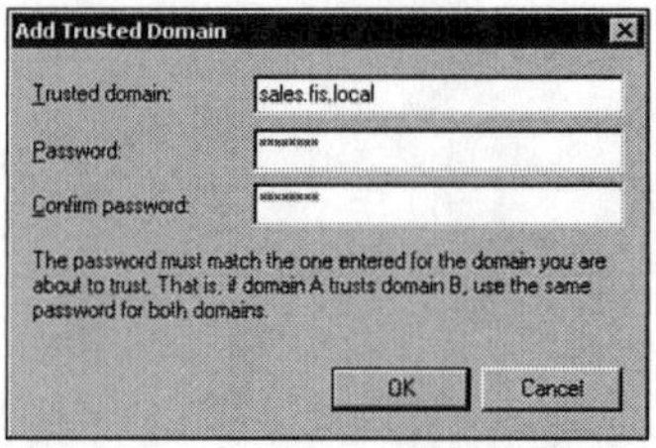

Figure 18.9
Entering the trust password.

The informational dialog box shown in Figure 18.10 reads like an error message, but it is primarily informational. The message appears regardless of which side of the trust you set up first. Click OK.

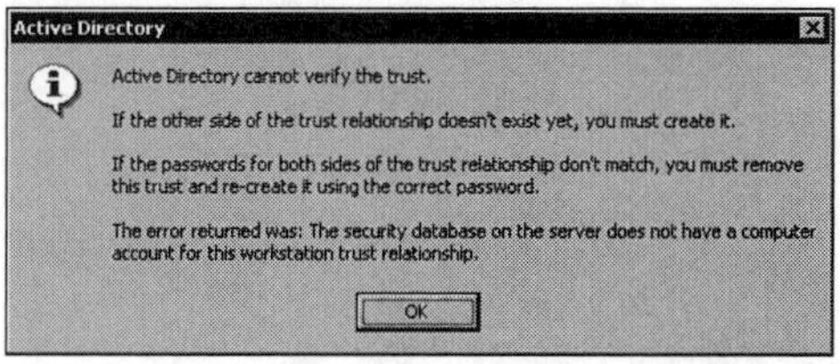

Figure 18.10
Trust verification information.

CH
18

The results appear in Figure 18.11. Active Directory identifies this as a shortcut trust automatically and also flags it as transitive. This means that, if you create other domains underneath sales, they will be capable of using this shortcut, rather than having to traverse the tree to the root. After you click OK on this page to close it, you are ready to configure the sales domain.

ALLOWING mfg TO TRUST sales

The other side of the relationship must be set at the sales domain. This can be performed physically anywhere you can create an authenticated connection to the Active Directory, but the focus of modification is now the sales.fis.local domain (see Figure 18.12). Figure 18.12 shows the default settings for the sales.fis.local domain, with Kerberos transitive trusts to the parent domain fis.local. Click the Add button next to the Domains That Trust This Domain window.

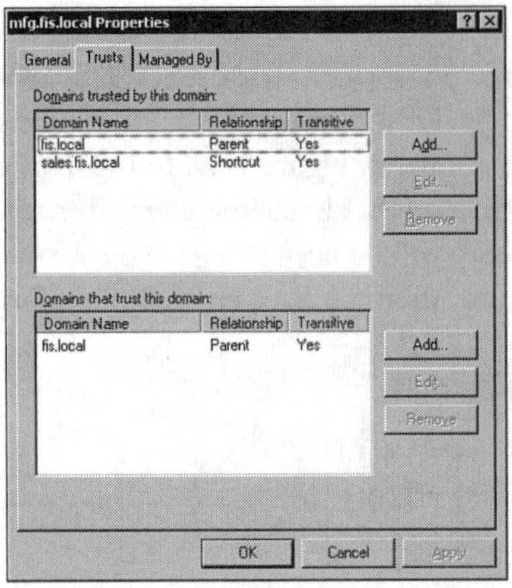

Figure 18.11
Finished shortcut trust.

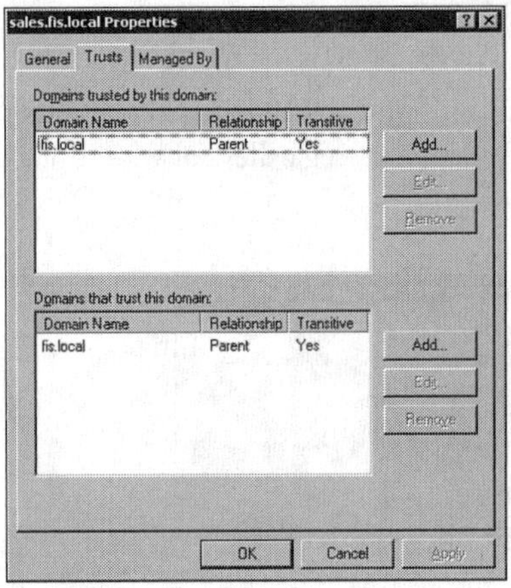

Figure 18.12
Sales domain default trusts.

Here you are presented with the Add Trusting Domain dialog box, shown in Figure 18.13. Enter the name of the trusting domain, `mfg.fis.local`, and the password you used in the Add Trusted Domain dialog box. Adding a domain trust requires an overt act by Domain Admins on both sides of the trust. You must know the password used when the other side of the trust was initiated.

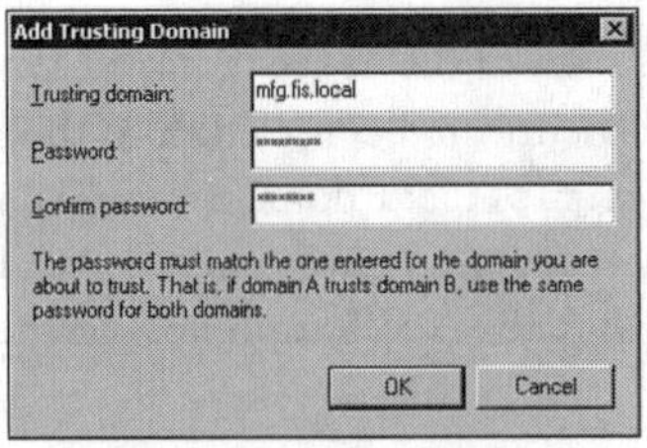

Figure 18.13
Entering the trust password.

Because, in this example, you are setting up both sides of the trust while logged on as administrator@mfg.fis.local, you are presented with the Active Directory dialog box shown in Figure 18.14. It requires the username and password of a domain administrator for the sales.fis.local domain. Enter this information and click OK.

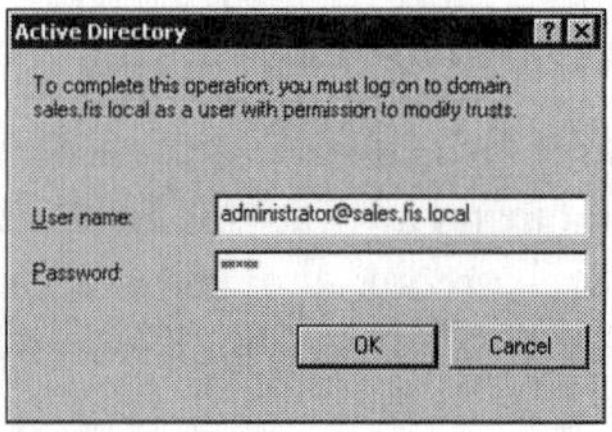

Figure 18.14
Authenticating as a different user.

The Active Directory dialog box shown in Figure 18.15 enables you to verify the trust. This simply checks the settings on both ends of the trust and verifies its utility. Click Yes.

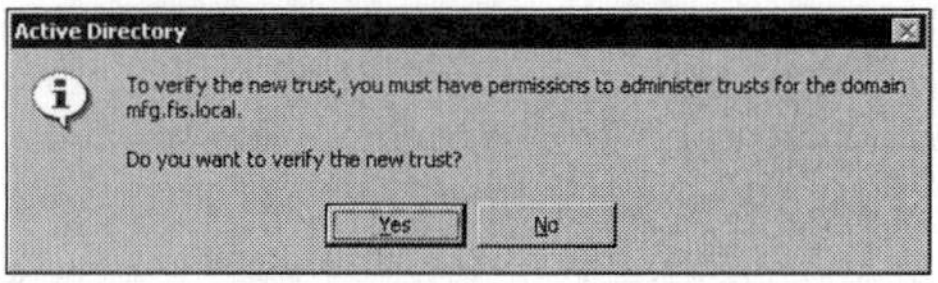

Figure 18.5
Verifying the trust.

Upon success, you will see a message box indicating that the trusting domain has been added and the trust verified.

The result appears in Figure 18.16. This also has been automatically identified as a transitive shortcut trust. Click OK to close the properties page.

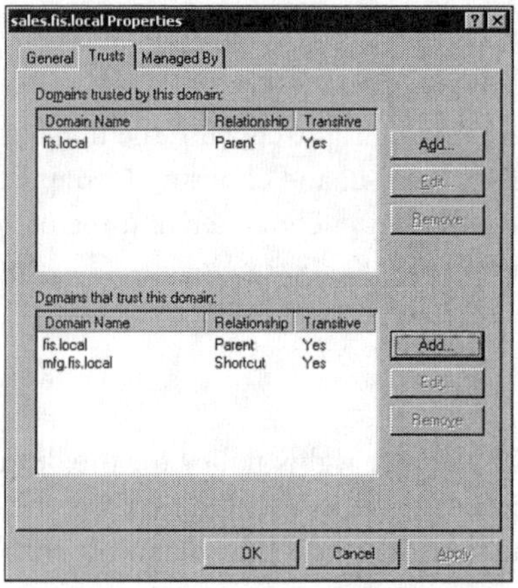

Figure 18.16
The finished shortcut trust.

TESTING THE SHORTCUT TRUST

After you have configured the trust architecture so that mfg trusts sales, you can test the trust using the klist and kerbtray tools. Remember, the shortcut trust you created is not designed to enable you to use services in another domain in the tree. You can already do that because of Kerberos transitive trusts. The shortcut trust is simply to shorten the Kerberos referral process, speed authentication, and reduce network use.

In Listing 18.5, after you had logged on to the client in sales and used the service in mfg, you had eight tickets. When you run the same command after setting up the shortcut trust, you have only seven tickets. This is because you aren't required to get a referral to the fis.local domain and are shortcutting across an explicit trust relationship between sales and mfg.

> **Note**
>
> In this example, you configured mfg to trust sales. This allows shortcut access by clients in sales to services in mfg. If you want clients in mfg to access servers in sales using a shortcut trust, you must configure another trust in the other direction.

TO TRUST OR NOT TO TRUST

Shortcut trusts are an important capability from an application scalability perspective; however, remember that you are trading speed for complexity. One of the advantages of Windows 2000 is the automatic creation of transitive, two-way, Kerberos trusts. Adding shortcut trusts is a step back in time toward managing explicit trusts on NT. When you consider that a client usually uses Kerberos referrals to authenticate to a server once per logon session, in many situations the time saved will not outweigh the additional complexity of shortcut trusts.

KERBEROS POLICY

Many of the settings for Kerberos are intrinsic. However, some settings can be changed. They are set through group policy and are defined at the domain level.

Five settings can be modified for Kerberos group policy. By default, they are part of the default domain policy, which can be found by right-clicking the domain in the Active Directory Users and Computers MMC Snap-in and choosing Group Policy, Edit. Kerberos settings are part of the Computer Configuration container, and the path is Windows Settings, Security Settings, Account Policies, Kerberos Policies. The following section discusses each setting, its impact, and its defaults.

ENFORCE USER LOGON RESTRICTIONS

This policy causes the KDC to check the user rights policy for the destination computer during every request for a session ticket. It checks that the user has either the logon locally or the access this computer from the network right. The default is enabled.

MAXIMUM LIFETIME FOR A SERVICE TICKET

This policy sets the maximum duration for a session ticket and is expressed in minutes. The default is 600 minutes, or 10 hours.

MAXIMUM LIFETIME FOR A USER TICKET

This policy sets the maximum duration for a TGT and is expressed in hours. The default is 10 hours.

MAXIMUM LIFETIME FOR USER TICKET RENEWAL

Because Kerberos tickets can be renewed, this sets the maximum lifetime for a renewed ticket. The value is expressed in days, and the default is seven days.

MAXIMUM TOLERANCE FOR COMPUTER CLOCK SYNCHRONIZATION

This group policy setting determines how skewed the time can be between the client and the Kerberos KDC. If the timestamp on a message from the client is more than the configured interval, the message is considered to be part of a replay attack and is discarded. The setting is expressed in minutes, and the default is five minutes.

> **Tip**
>
> A time skew issue is reported in the Event Viewer System Log as a `Failure to connect to a domain controller`, error code 1938.

CH
18

Allowing the time to become unsynchronized beyond the time skew setting causes authentication attempts by services as well as users to fail. This is an easily overlooked troubleshooting tool. By default, every workstation and server considers its logon DC to be authoritative for the time; the DCs consider the PDC emulator FSMO role authoritative; and each PDC emulator looks to the PDC emulator of its parent domain, all the way up to the forest root. The PDC emulator in the forest root domain can be set to use an external time source by using the command shown here:

```
C:\> net time /setsntp:192.5.41.209
```

This command causes the server to use one of the clocks at the U.S. Naval Observatory as an authoritative timeserver.

> **Note**
>
> Microsoft TechNet article Q216734 describes how to use a network time source in Windows 2000 and lists the IP addresses of the official network time sources.

Every machine checks its authoritative timeserver at boot and then every eight hours to ensure that time remains in sync.

Note

The Windows 32 Time Service (w32time) does not use a set interval for the period at which it synchronizes the computer's clock with a network time source or PDC emulator. Instead, it uses a dynamic process of time synchronization beginning at five minutes. The more accurate the local computer's system clock is, the less often the period of synchronization—until reaching the maximum of every logon and every eight hours thereafter. This information is stored in the Registry under the path `Hkey_Local_Machine\System\CurrentControlSet\Services\W32Time\Parameters` and can be altered using the command-line utility `w32tm.exe`.

SUMMARY

Every logon session requires authentication, whether it is an interactive logon session for a user, a network session between a user and a service, or the service itself. The Kerberos protocol is the default authentication protocol for Windows 2000. It uses information in the Active Directory database to identify each security principal as it requests credentials from the Kerberos KDC. Along with information that uniquely identifies each user, the KDC returns authorization data that enables Windows 2000 to determine the level of privilege for a user. This authorization process is what Chapter 19, "Authorization," discusses.

TROUBLESHOOTING

CREATING TRUSTS FAILS

I can't create a trust between two domains.

When you are trying to create an explicit shortcut trust or an NTLM trust to an NT domain, the process might fail. Here are several issues to look for:

- **Network**—Look for the obvious. Routing, addressing, and name resolution must be in place for trusts to work. Also, Kerberos trusts require an IP connection. If you can't ping the target domain controller by name, you probably won't be able to create a trust to it.
- **Permissions**—Although, as shown in this chapter's example of creating a shortcut trust, you do not have to be logged on as a member of the Enterprise Admins group; doing so will cancel a number of permissions issues.
- **Time**—Kerberos is time sensitive. If the time skew between any of the DCs exceeds five minutes, you will have authentication issues.

CAN'T USE AD DOMAINS AND TRUSTS

When I open Active Directory Domains and Trusts, I am unable to use it.

Make sure that DNS is configured properly. Many of the administrative tools will not operate properly if the DNS is not running or is misconfigured.

CHAPTER 19

AUTHORIZATION

In this chapter

AUTHORIZING ACCESS TO ACTIVE DIRECTORY

Every object in the Active Directory has a list of who can and cannot touch the object. This list and the services that use the list comprise the authorization component of the Windows 2000 security architecture. Every attempt to access a resource must pass through this component to receive permission to use the resource. This chapter discusses the architecture of authorization and then looks at some examples of using that architecture to both grant and deny access to Active Directory objects.

RIGHTS VERSUS PERMISSIONS

A user's overall level of privilege is determined by user rights and permissions. *User rights* are computer wide and are set by local and Active Directory group policy. An example is the log-on locally right. This chapter focuses on specific object-level permissions, such as the create child objects permission.

SECURITY COMPONENTS OF THE ACTIVE DIRECTORY

An understanding of the architecture of Active Directory security is necessary to properly administer Active Directory objects. This section identifies the major players in security and describes how they work together to provide an orderly access mechanism based on levels of privilege. Understanding the architecture is also an important component of successful troubleshooting. In this section, you also look at the security components of the Active Directory.

GLOBALLY UNIQUE IDENTIFIERS

Every object in the Active Directory is identified by a globally unique identifier (GUID) and a security identifier (SID). A *GUID* is a 128-bit number that uniquely identifies an object and is immutable. Even if you move the object to another domain in the tree, its GUID remains the same.

> **Note**
>
> An object's GUID is stored in the `objectGUID` attribute and must be unique within the forest and time. Regardless of what changes occur to an object, the GUID never changes. GUIDs are never recycled; that is to say, after they're created, they are unique within a forest forever.

SECURITY IDENTIFIERS

From a security perspective, an Active Directory object's permissions are determined by looking at a list of the SIDs of the object and the SIDs of every group of which the object is a member. Although the bit-level structure of a SID is beyond the scope of this book, a *SID* is made up primarily of a number that identifies the domain to which the object belongs and a numeric relative identifier (RID) that is unique to that object and is never reused.

Note A SID in Windows 2000 is primarily composed of two parts: the SID of the domain, which is guaranteed to be unique within the forest and never reused, and the RID, which is unique within the domain and never reused. From a security perspective, a SID is a unit to which a level of permission can be applied. Each security principal has its own SID.

RELATIVE IDENTIFIERS

Every Windows 2000 domain controller (DC) is assigned a RID pool by the RID Master Operations Master. This pool of numbers is unique and is never reused. Windows 2000 Active Directory uses a multimaster model, which means (among other things) that an AD object can be created on any Windows 2000 domain controller. When a DC creates an object, it assigns a SID, which is made up—in part—of the domain identifier and a RID from the RID pool on the local DC.

SECURITY DESCRIPTOR

Every Active Directory object also has a security descriptor that contains information about who can and cannot touch the object. Along with structural information in the header, the security descriptor holds the following information.

OWNER

Every object has an owner, and in most situations that owner can do virtually anything with the object. Even if the owner does not have explicit permissions to an object, in most situations, it can give itself the necessary permissions to perform an action.

Note The owner of an object is identified by the SID of the owner's user object, with the exception of objects owned by members of the domain group Administrators and Domain Admins (by way of membership in the Administrators group). Ownership of objects owned by members of these groups is recorded with the SID of the Administrators group.

CH
19

PRIMARY GROUP

This entry is used by the POSIX subsystem to support the POSIX implementation of groups and by Services for Macintosh.

Note POSIX is an attempt by UNIX vendors to specify a level of interoperability with various UNIX vendors. Windows 2000 supports a basic level of POSIX compliance.

ACCESS CONTROL ENTRIES

An *access control entry (ACE)* is simply information about a particular user or group and its permissions. An ACE is made up of information about whether it is an allow or deny ACE, the SID of the user or group on the ACE, and an access mask. This mask is a list of operations that is allowed or denied on the object.

When a user attempts to access an object, the SIDs contained in the user's access token are used to compile the user's effective permission on the object. All ACEs that apply to the user are cumulative, with the exception of deny permissions, which always override allow permissions.

DISCRETIONARY ACCESS CONTROL LIST

The *discretionary access control list (DACL)* contains a list of access control entries. When the user tries to access an object, security checks the DACL to see whether she is listed. In a nutshell, Active Directory security can be reduced to the following statement: If your SID—or the SID of a group to which you belong—is in one or more of the ACEs on the DACL for the object you want to use, and it is not a deny ACE, you will be granted access.

> **Note**
>
> Both positive and negative permissions exist. When you look at the DACL for an object, both explicit allow and deny ACEs exist. Because deny ACEs take precedence over allow ACEs, you can *lower* someone's level of privilege by adding him to a group, if that group has an explicit deny to an object for which he also has an explicit or implicit allow. This is demonstrated later in the chapter.

INHERITANCE   When you set security on an object by specifying who can and cannot access the object, you can set the permissions to be inherited by objects lower in the tree. This is the default behavior in Active Directory. Child objects inherit the DACL of the parent object. If no parent object exists, the child object inherits the DACL of the object's class from the schema.

ACEs usually are added to a DACL in canonical order. This means that explicit ACEs are listed before inherited ACEs, deny ACEs are listed before allow ACEs, and inherited ACEs are listed in the order in which they are inherited. This helps enforce the rule that deny permissions override allow permissions, and that explicit permissions override inherited permissions.

SYSTEM ACCESS CONTROL LIST

The *system access control list (SACL)* is conceptually similar to the DACL, except that it is used for auditing rather than for determining access. Group policy is used to enable auditing. Audit policies are defined in the local security policy.

→ **See** "Local Policies," **p. 348**

ACCESS TOKENS

An *access token* is created by the Local Security Authority (LSA) and is essentially a combination of a list of SIDs for the user and his groups, and a list of privileges granted to the user and groups by the local security policy. Every process created by the user has a copy of this access token.

GROUPS

Two basic group types are available in the Active Directory: security and distribution. Because distribution groups are used primarily by email and are not used for access control, let's focus on security groups.

Security groups are used to centralize access to objects. If a security group has an access permission and a user is a member of that group, he inherits that permission. This is a function of virtually every modern operating system and greatly reduces the amount of time spent managing permissions. Three group scopes exist in Active Directory—domain local, global, and universal.

→ **See** "Groups," **p. 432**

NATIVE VERSUS MIXED MODE

Group behavior differs based on whether the domain is in native or mixed mode. When a domain is created or upgraded, by default, it is in mixed mode. After any NT backup domain controllers (BDCs) are eliminated, the domain can be set to native mode using the domain Properties page shown in Figure 19.1. To use this page, open the Active Directory Users and Computers MMC Snap-in, right-click the domain, and choose Properties. A domain in native mode has many more options for group nesting, as well as other advantages. Your goal should be to convert your domain to native mode as soon as possible.

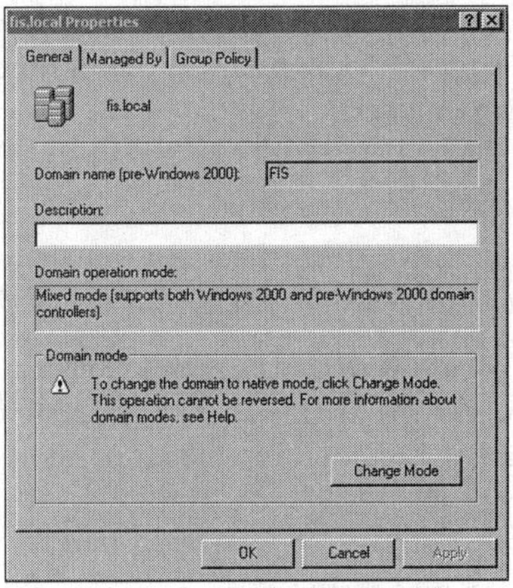

Figure 19.1
Changing from mixed mode to native mode.

CH 19

→ **See** "Domain Modes," **p. 165**

Note
By default, all domains in Windows 2000 operate in mixed mode. A domain should be changed to native mode only when no NT 4.0 BDCs are present and no NT 4.0 BDCs will ever be needed in the Windows 2000 domain. The conversion from mixed mode to native mode is a one-way, irreversible switch.

> **Note**
>
> The presence or absence of Windows 9x or NT clients or member servers is a nonissue in the decision to move to native mode. Only the presence of NT BDCs in the domain, applications that require local access to an NT 4.0 SAM, or a clear path back to NT 4.0 domains require a domain to remain in mixed mode.

DOMAIN LOCAL GROUPS

In native mode, domain local groups can contain users, domain local groups, global groups, and universal groups. The global groups and universal groups can be from any domain in the forest and can be used to assign permissions to any local object, such as a printer or file share. The common wisdom among NT administrators has always been to place users in global groups, place global groups in local groups, and then assign permissions to the local group. Although the landscape gets a little more complex with Windows 2000 and the advent of universal groups, this is still a good rule of thumb and is the only way to go in a single-domain environment. In native mode, a domain local group can be used to assign permissions to any object in the local domain. In mixed mode, you can still use domain local groups, but only on DCs.

GLOBAL GROUPS

Global groups can contain users from the current domain, and in native mode, they can contain global groups from the current domain. In addition, global groups can be used to assign access permissions to any object in the forest. However, they usually are used to contain users and are then placed inside domain local groups in this or other domains. This makes for a very scalable access control model.

UNIVERSAL GROUPS

Universal groups are available only in native mode. They can contain users and groups from any domain in the forest and can be used to assign permissions to any object in the forest.

The approved way to use universal groups is to restrict their membership to global groups from domains throughout the forest and manage membership by adding and removing users from the global groups. This dramatically reduces the amount of Active Directory replication associated with using global groups.

UNIVERSAL GROUPS AND GLOBAL CATALOG SERVERS

Because universal group membership is replicated to every global catalog (GC) server in the forest, replication is an important consideration. Modifying the membership on a global group causes replication traffic to every domain controller in the domain, but it does not trigger replication traffic in all other domains in the forest. Universal groups can contain members from any domain in the forest, and their membership list is held on every GC server in the forest. Their possible effect on replication traffic should be considered when designing the group structure for the domain, tree, and forest.

COMPUTER LOCAL GROUPS

Although not actually a part of the Active Directory, computer local groups are present both in mixed and native modes. These are the computer-specific local groups you used in Windows NT to place global groups in. This model still works, and in mixed mode it is still a usable strategy. In native mode, however, the use of domain local groups instead of computer local groups is encouraged.

To modify computer local groups on a workstation or member server, you must load the Local Users and Groups MMC Snap-in (`lusrmgr.msc`), shown in Figure 19.2. You also can manage Local Users and Groups in the Computer Management MMC.

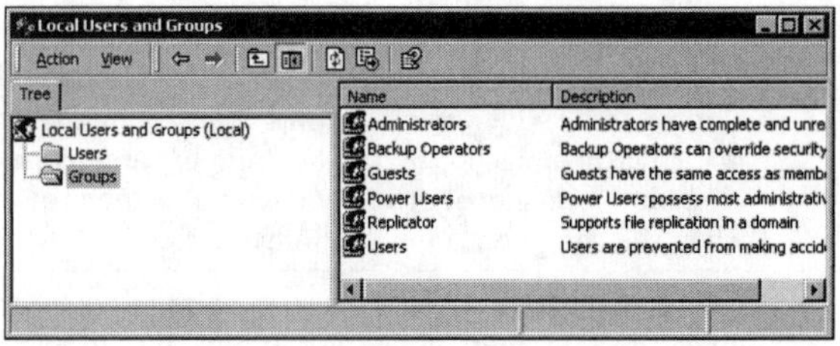

Figure 19.2
Using the Local Users and Groups MMC Snap-in.

NESTING GROUPS

An important administrative concept for Windows 2000 is nesting groups. Although limited group nesting is available in mixed mode, this is greatly enhanced in native mode. Examples include placing global groups into domain local groups, domain local groups into other domain local groups, global groups into other global groups, and global groups into universal groups. This enables you to modify the level of privilege for a user without touching the ACL on a single object, by simply adding or removing the user from one or more groups. Remember also that you can create groups that have explicit deny permissions on one or more objects and add users to them temporarily or permanently to ensure that the user does not have permissions.

CH
19

SYSTEM-CREATED GROUPS

A variety of groups of all types are created by default both when the operating system is installed and when an Active Directory domain is created. The following is not an exhaustive list, but it does cover those that are most commonly used.

GROUPS ON THE LOCAL COMPUTER

These are groups created on every computer when the Windows 2000 operating system is installed. Table 19.1 lists some of the groups and their uses.

TABLE 19.1   SYSTEM-CREATED GROUPS ON THE NON-DOMAIN CONTROLLERS

Group Name	Description
Administrators	This computer local group has unrestricted access to the local computer. The Domain Admins global group is automatically added to this group when the computer joins the domain. This provides members of the Domain Admins global group the ability to manage the local computer without having to know the local administrator password.
Backup Operators	This group can bypass normal restrictions by using the backup software to access the entire filesystem. The Backup Operators local group possesses the user right to back up files and directories, restore files and directories, log on locally, and shut down the system.
Users	This group primarily has read permissions to much of the computer and read/write to their home directories. The Domain Users global group is automatically added to this group. This enables you to set certain automatic permissions on the local computer for anyone who logs on. The Domain Users global group becomes a member of the Local Users group when the computer joins the domain.
Power Users	This group has all the Users group permissions and read/write access to much of the system, including the capability to install applications. Members of this group also can create and delete shares and printers, create local users, and delete and manage local users they have created.

DOMAIN GROUPS

These groups are created when the first domain controller is installed and are used throughout the domain. Table 19.2 shows some of these groups.

TABLE 19.2   AUTOMATICALLY CREATED GROUPS IN ACTIVE DIRECTORY

Group Name	Description
Domain Admins	This group has unrestricted access to the domain.
Domain Users	This group contains every user in the domain.
Domain Guests	This group contains all users who are currently accessing the domain using the guest account.
Schema Admins	This group exists only in the forest root domain. Members are authorized to modify the Active Directory Schema.
Enterprise Admins	Enterprise Admins are used to create trees and domains. This group also exists only in the forest root domain. In mixed mode, it's a global group, and in native mode, it's a universal group. By default, only the Administrator account in the forest root domain is a member. This group has far-reaching permissions, so its membership should be closely guarded. Some operations can be carried out only by the EA, such as creating new domains and trees and authorizing DHCP and RIS servers in the Active Directory.

BUILT-IN GROUPS

The computer local groups shown in Table 19.1 do not exist on DCs. Similar groups, called built-in local groups, are explained in Table 19.3. The computer local groups that existed on the DC before it was promoted using the dcpromo.exe tool are destroyed. These built-in local groups are local to all domain controllers rather than to the local computer.

TABLE 19.3   BUILT-IN LOCAL GROUPS

Group Name	Description
Administrators	This built-in local group has unrestricted access to domain controllers.
Backup Operators	This group can bypass normal restrictions by using the backup software to access the entire filesystem. The Backup Operators local group possesses the user right to back up files and directories, restore files and directories, log on locally, and shut down the system.
Account Operators	Account Operators can create and delete accounts and manage accounts. This group is empty by default and cannot manage administrator accounts.
Print Operators	Members can manage printers and queues. The Print Operators have full control over all printer objects.
Server Operators	Members can log on interactively to the DC, format drives, create and delete shares, and shut down the DC.

SPECIAL GROUPS

Several groups do not show up in the GUI user management tools. These groups do, however, appear on the Security tab of an object's Properties page and can be used to assign permissions to users who are fulfilling a particular role. Table 19.4 shows some of these groups.

TABLE 19.4   SPECIAL WINDOWS 2000 GROUPS

Group Name	Description
Interactive	This group includes any user currently logged on to the local computer through the console.
Network	Members include any user accessing the computer through the network.
Creator/Owner	This group is populated by whomever owns the object and by default is granted a full control allow ACE for an Active Directory object.
Authenticated Users	This group includes any user currently authenticated to the forest.
Everyone	This group includes anyone currently on the network, including users authenticated under the guest account and anonymous users. This group should be handled with care. If you grant permissions to the Everyone group, you are essentially giving permissions to anyone with a network path to your system. When trying to give lowest-common-denominator access, consider the Authenticated Users group instead.

> **Note**
>
> Membership in these special groups is automatic and is not configurable.

AUTHORIZATION STEP BY STEP

Now that you have a handle on the components of Active Directory security, let's take a look at authenticating, getting your authorization data, and accessing an object. This process essentially involves acquiring a list of who you are (user and group SIDs) and then presenting that list to whomever you are interested in accessing.

GATHERING THE USER'S CREDENTIALS

In Chapter 18, "Authentication," you looked at the logon process from a Kerberos perspective. In that chapter, you saw how a Kerberos key distribution center (KDC) uses a secret key created from your password to prove your identity when you first request a ticket granting ticket (TGT).

AUTHORIZATION DATA IN THE TGT

When the KDC creates the TGT, it uses the user's Active Directory object to retrieve her SID and a list of all the SIDs of the domain local and global groups of which the user is a member. The AD also contacts a global catalog server to retrieve a list of universal groups of which the user is a member. This information is placed in the authorization data field of the TGT and is signed by the KDC using its secret key.

> **Note**
>
> In a single-domain forest, no need exists to contact a GC server to determine the user's universal group membership because all domain controllers have the full information from the forest.

AUTHORIZATION DATA IN THE SESSION TICKET

When you request access to a particular server on the network, your client computer sends a message to the KDC that presents your TGT as your credentials and asks for a session ticket to the requested server. The KDC uses its secret key to unpack the authorization data from the TGT and places it in the authorization data field of the session ticket. Also, if the KDC is in a domain different from the client, it checks to see whether any security groups exist in this domain to which the user or any of his groups belong. If so, it adds the SIDs of those groups to the authentication data field.

SECURING THE AUTHORIZATION DATA

This time, the information is signed with the session key the KDC shares with the target server. The client's session key for the server is then returned to the client to present to the server. The authorization data is signed to prevent tampering. If it is modified at all, the digital signature is invalid and the information is discarded.

Now that you have your list of credentials and a session ticket to a server, you can open a connection to a service on the server and present your credentials.

GETTING AN ACCESS TOKEN

When you send the session ticket to your target server and connect to a service, the service passes the session ticket to the Kerberos Security Support Provider (SSP). The SSP validates the session ticket, unpacks the authentication data using the session key it shares with the KDC, and passes the information to the LSA. The LSA checks whether any computer local groups hold as members the user or any group the user belongs to. This information is used to build an access token. The LSA then returns the access token and assurances that the user's identity is valid to the service the user is trying to access.

The service then completes the connection to the client and attaches the client's token to a thread.

USING THE ACCESS TOKEN

When your thread accesses an object using your authenticated connection and access token, the object manager compares your list of requested access permissions with the DACL on the object. It checks one permission at a time, looking for ACEs on the DACL that contain SIDs that match a SID in the user's access token. As it finds matches that are allow ACEs, a mask that contains all the granted permissions is built to return to the object manager. If it finds any deny ACEs that match any SIDs in the user's token, access is denied. During this process, information also is returned on whether auditing is desired for the object. Whether an event is audited or not is determined by the SACL. When the list of required permissions has been fully checked and authorized, the granted access mask is returned to the calling process and the access is allowed.

Note	The object manager in this scenario is simply the service that controls the type of object you are accessing—in other words, the Active Directory for AD objects and the NTFS Filesystem for filesystem objects.

CH
19

MODIFYING PERMISSIONS

The default permission structure of Active Directory is a great start to a secure network. However, day-to-day maintenance of the enterprise requires modifying permissions by creating and deleting groups, adding and subtracting members from groups, and adding and subtracting permissions from objects. This section looks at some examples of modifying permissions.

Let's first look at modifying permissions by using the Security tab of the Properties page of the object in the Active Directory Users and Computers MMC Snap-in. This allows a *very* granular approach to maintaining levels of privilege. Then, you will use a new tool in the Active Directory—the Delegation of Control Wizard—to allow en masse granting of permissions to an organizational unit (OU).

USING THE SECURITY TAB

The Security tab of many objects is not visible by default in the Active Directory Users and Computers MMC Snap-in (ADUC). To see the Security tab, use the View menu and select Advanced Features.

You then use the acctg OU, which currently holds only two users, ian and caitlyn, as your target. You will grant members of the acctg_admins domain local group various permissions to enable them to manage acctg users. Currently, your acctg_admins group has only one user: caitlyn. The users and groups appear in Figure 19.3.

Figure 19.3
Using the Active Directory Users and Computers MMC Snap-in to manage security.

For members of acctg_admins to manage certain properties of users in the acctg OU, right-click the organizational unit and select Properties. This opens the acctg Properties dialog box. Then, click the Security tab (see Figure 19.4).

Figure 19.4
The acctg Properties page shows the currently assigned permissions for the OU.

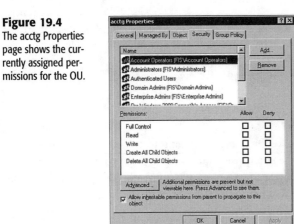

You can use this property page to set broad permissions. The Name box enables you to add security principals (usually users or groups) to the DACL on this object and also remove them. The Permissions box lists five basic permissions with corresponding check boxes to allow or deny those permissions. The permissions are briefly discussed in Table 19.5.

TABLE 19.5 SETTING ACTIVE DIRECTORY PERMISSIONS

Permission	Description
Full Control	A security principal that has full control permissions is capable of taking virtually any action with the object.
Read	Read all properties of the object.
Write	Write all properties of the object.
Create All Child Objects	This permission is applicable to container objects, such as organizational units, and allows the creation of objects within the container. If this permission is not set to This Object and All Subobjects on the Advanced page, you can create an OU in this container, but you can't create objects in the OU.
Delete All Child Objects	This permission enables the deletion of objects within the container.

Note

A *security principal* is simply anything that has an account in the Active Directory and to which authentication and authorization is applied. Usually this is a user, group, or computer.

To set permissions with the granularity that you need, click the Advanced button. This loads the Access Control Settings for acctg dialog box (see Figure 19.5). Here you can set whether the permission is assigned just to this object or is inherited to child objects. In addition, you can set very specific permissions at the per-attribute level.

Note

Much of what you see in the Access Control Settings for acctg dialog box is identical to the permissions structure for NTFS filesystems. Active Directory objects, however, have a much more granular permission structure.

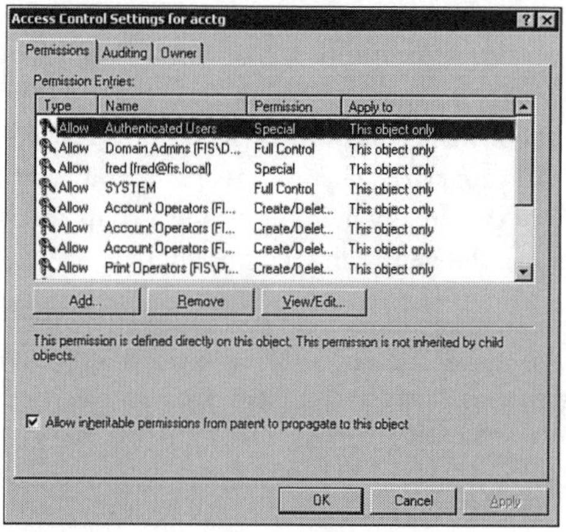

CH

19

Figure 19.5
Setting permissions for the acctg OU.

To add the acctg_admins group to the DACL for this object, click Add. The Select User, Computer, or Group page appears in Figure 19.6.

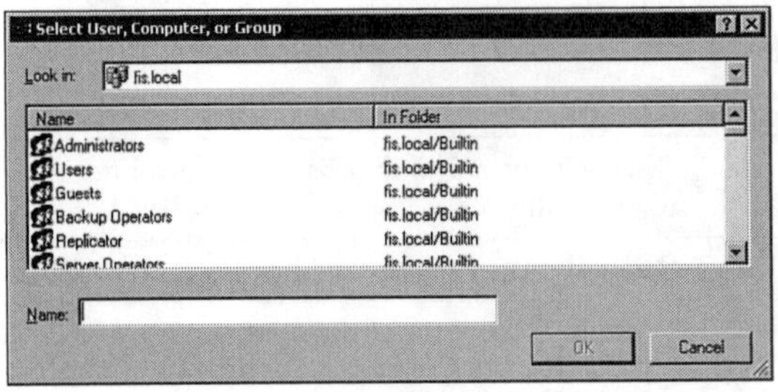

Figure 19.6
Adding users and groups to the acctg OU access control list.

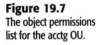

After you have clicked the Name heading to sort the list, clicked the group you want to add, and clicked OK, you see the Permission Entry for acctg dialog box shown in Figure 19.7.

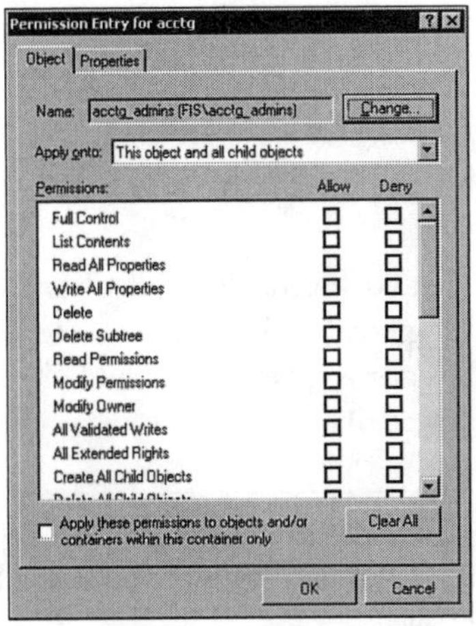

Figure 19.7
The object permissions list for the acctg OU.

Because you want to grant only user-specific access permissions to the acctg_admins group, use the Apply Onto drop-down list to set it to User Objects. This displays a list of permissions for user objects. In this example, you will give the acctg_admins group permissions to look at users' properties and modify their passwords (see Figure 19.8). You have given the acctg_admins group the read all properties, change password, and reset password allow permissions. It is important to note that, if any member of this group receives the deny permission for any of these permissions, the deny will take precedence.

Note

Many times the permissions you need will not appear when you first open the page simply because the list is so long that you must scroll down or up to find all the permissions you want to change.

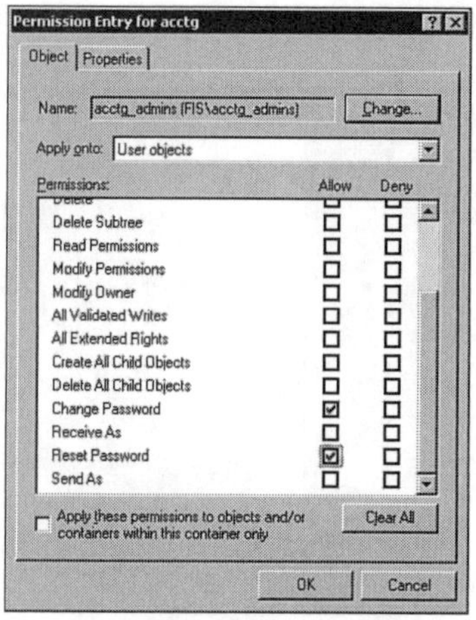

Figure 19.8
Adding new permissions to the access control entry for acctg_admins.

After you click OK to apply the changes and dismiss the two properties pages, acctg_admins appears in the acctg Properties page (see Figure 19.9). Notice that the Permissions box is empty for the entry. If the permissions structure is too granular to appear properly in this box, the entry appears with an empty Permissions list. If you need to modify this list at a later date, you can use the Advanced button to do so.

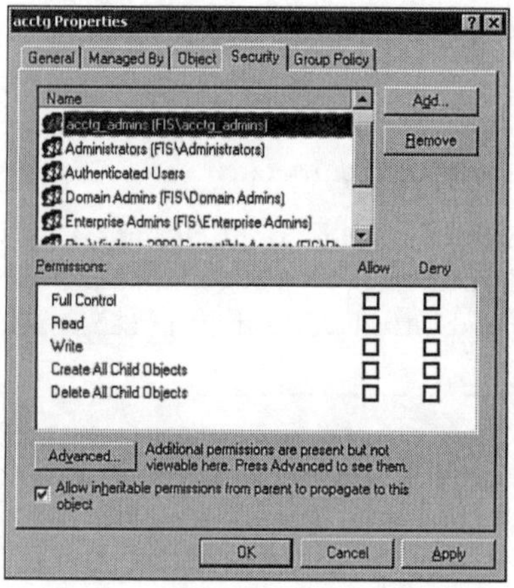

Figure 19.9
The acctg_admins group has been added to the access control list for the acctg OU.

To see the effect of the permissions you applied to the acctg OU, look at the Security tab of the Properties page for the ian user object in the OU. Because ian is a user in the OU, you see that acctg_admins has the inherited permission to change and reset his password and read his object properties. Also, because the check boxes for these permissions are checked and grayed out, you know that these are inherited permissions (see Figure 19.10).

CH
19

Figure 19.10
The end result:
Members of the
acctg_admins group
now have permis-
sions to the acctg OU.

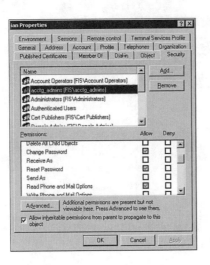

USING THE DELEGATION OF CONTROL WIZARD

Although managing permissions manually is very powerful and is necessary in some cases, it also is sometimes a trial-and-error process. Many permissions interact with each other, and understanding that interaction is a subtle art.

Fortunately, a tool is available that makes much of the drudgery of assigning permissions a simple point-and-click event. You can use the Delegation of Control Wizard to assign permissions on organizational units. To demonstrate the Delegation of Control Wizard, let's use the same OU and users from the previous exercise. You have removed the permissions that you previously assigned and are starting from scratch.

You can start the Delegation of Control Wizard by right-clicking the OU and selecting Delegate Control from the Active Directory Users and Computers MMC Snap-in. This loads the Delegation of Control Wizard introduction shown in Figure 19.11.

Note

You can delegate authority using the Delegation of Authority Wizard at the domain or OU level, but authority can't be delegated over the system containers, such as Users, Computers, and Builtin.

When you click Next, you see the Users or Groups page. Figure 19.12 shows that the Add button has been clicked to add the acctg_admins group to the list. Click Next.

Figure 19.11
Starting the Delegation of Control Wizard.

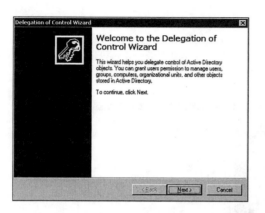

Figure 19.12
Allowing a group to manage the acctg OU.

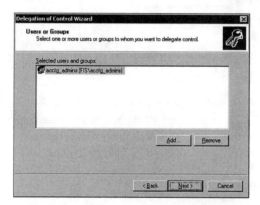

The Tasks to Delegate page shown in Figure 19.13 enables you to decide to set very general or very granular permissions. You have given the acctg_admins group all the permissions in the Delegate the Following Common Tasks box. This enables them to perform most of the day-to-day tasks of managing a group of users.

CH
19

Figure 19.13
Choosing tasks to delegate.

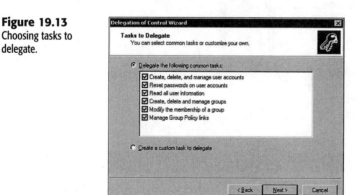

If you select the Create a Custom Task to Delegate option, you are given granular access to the permissions granted. Because you have chosen the easy way out, after you click Next, you see the Completing the Delegation of Control Wizard page shown in Figure 19.14. This page has summary information about your choices.

Figure 19.14
Finishing the Delegation of Control Wizard.

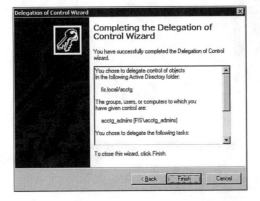

The Delegation of Control Wizard is a powerful tool. Figure 19.15 shows the same Security tab for user ian that you looked at in Figure 19.10. You now see that the acctg_admins group has inherited full control permissions to the ian user. This enables members of this group to manage the users in this OU without having to be Domain Admins.

Figure 19.15
The end result: Members of the acctg group have almost complete control over the acctg OU.

TROUBLESHOOTING PERMISSIONS

Permissions problems usually come in two flavors. Either the user can do something he shouldn't, or he can't do something he should. This section looks at some techniques and tools for troubleshooting permissions.

THE BASICS

The basics of troubleshooting permissions are not glamorous. A certain amount of simply poking around, trying various tasks, and looking for patterns is involved. An organized approach to this, however, follows a certain pattern. The following list is a good place to start when trying to resolve why a user can or can't touch certain objects.

The first thing to do when troubleshooting a user's permissions is to make a list of all the groups of which he is a member. This might not be trivial in an enterprise environment. A user can be a member of every group type you have seen listed in this chapter. The following are some good points to remember:

- **Don't forget about the special groups, such as interactive and network**—Users enter and leave group membership on these as their activities change.

- **Log on as the user and make sure that what he is reporting is indeed what is happening**—Many times users are simply confused about what they can and can't do.

- **Use the Security tab of the object your user is trying to access and look for both explicit and inherited permissions.**

- **Always remember that deny permissions override allow permissions**—If your user is a member of 99 groups with the allow permission and 1 group with the deny permission, his effective permission is deny.

- **Make sure you understand the permissions necessary to accomplish a task**—Some tasks require a combination of permissions. This is why the Delegation of Control Wizard is such a marvelous tool.

TOOLS

Some tools from the Windows 2000 Resource Kit and support tools make this easier and faster. All these tools come with a handful of command-line parameters. These parameters are documented at the command line with the /? parameter and in the Tools Help. The following sections discuss some of the more useful options.

dsacls.exe

dsacls is a command-line tool from the Windows 2000 support tools that enables you to view or change the DACL on an object. Listing 19.1 shows partial output from viewing the caitlyn object in the acctg OU from the previous section. Note that the object you are interested in is described using X.500 syntax.

LISTING 19.1   DISPLAYING ACLs USING dsacls.exe

```
C:\>dsacls cn=caitlyn,ou=acctg,dc=fis,dc=local
Access list:
Effective Permissions on this object are:
Allow FIS\Domain Admins                    FULL CONTROL
Allow NT AUTHORITY\SYSTEM                   FULL CONTROL
Allow BUILTIN\Account Operators            FULL CONTROL
```

CH

19

LISTING 19.1   CONTINUED

```
Allow NT AUTHORITY\SELF                          SPECIAL ACCESS
                                                 READ PERMISSIONS
                                                 LIST CONTENTS
                                                 READ PROPERTY
                                                 LIST OBJECT
Allow NT AUTHORITY\Authenticated Users           SPECIAL ACCESS
                                                 READ PERMISSIONS
Allow FIS\acctg_admins                           FULL CONTROL
➥<Inherited from parent>
```

The advantage of dsacls is that you can print this off, look at the list of ACEs, and compare them with the groups of which your user is a member.

Tip

You can pipe the output of a command-line utility to a file by appending the command with >*filename*.txt. Here's an example:

```
C:\>dsacls cn=caitlyn,ou=acctg,dc=fis,dc=local >caitlyn.txt
```

After executing the preceding command, a file appears in the root of c:\ called caitlyn.txt, which contains the output of the command.

acldiags.exe

acldiags is also from the Windows 2000 support tools. It can be used to check effective permissions and to send the output as tab-delimited to import it into a database. In an enterprise environment, this enables the importing of the information to an industrial-strength database, such as SQL Server, and complex querying of the structure. Listing 19.2 shows partial output of the acldiags command against the acctg OU.

LISTING 19.2   USING acldiags TO SEE EFFECTIVE PERMISSIONS FOR AN OU

```
C:\>acldiag "ou=acctg,dc=fis,dc=local" /geteffective:user /tdo

ou=acctg,dc=fis,dc=local
Owner    FIS\Domain Admins
Permissions Not Protected, Auditing Not Protected

This object     Allow    FIS\acctg_admins     Read gPOptions property
This object     Allow    FIS\acctg_admins     Write gPOptions property
This object     Allow    FIS\acctg_admins     Read gPLink property
This object     Allow    FIS\acctg_admins     Write gPLink property
This object     Allow    FIS\acctg_admins     Create Group objects
This object     Allow    FIS\acctg_admins     Delete Group objects
This object     Allow    FIS\acctg_admins     Create User objects
This object     Allow    FIS\acctg_admins     Delete User objects
```

Tip

The Windows 2000 Resource Kit also ships with a Tools Help file that explains the use of the tools in greater detail.

`enumprop.exe`

The `enumprop.exe` Windows 2000 Resource Kit tool enumerates the properties of an object, including its group membership. This can be a faster way of finding a user's group membership than looking it up in the Active Directory Users and Computers MMC Snap-in. This information also could be used through scripting. A variety of interesting information is available here, but from an authorization troubleshooting perspective, the capability to dump the group membership quickly and at the command line is probably the most pertinent. Listing 19.3 shows the use of `enumprop.exe` to view a user's security information.

LISTING 19.3   USING enumprop TO VIEW SECURITY INFORMATION FOR A USER

```
C:\>enumprop "LDAP://cn=caitlyn,ou=acctg,dc=fis,dc=local"

LDAP://cn=caitlyn,ou=acctg,dc=fis,dc=local: 31 set properties.

 1: memberOf: CN=acctg_admins,OU=acctg,DC=fis,DC=local
 2: accountExpires: 9223372036854775807
 3: badPasswordTime: 0
 4: badPwdCount: 0
 5: codePage: 0
 6: cn: caitlyn
 7: countryCode: 0
 8: displayName: caitlyn
 9: dSCorePropagationData:
        4/20/2000 4:36:05 PM
        4/20/2000 4:15:19 PM
        4/20/2000 3:44:29 PM
        4/20/2000 3:33:54 PM
        7/14/1601 10:36:49 PM
10: givenName: caitlyn
11: instanceType: 4
12: lastLogoff: 0
13: lastLogon: 126007586826935000
14: logonCount: 4
15: nTSecurityDescriptor:
16: distinguishedName: CN=caitlyn,OU=acctg,DC=fis,DC=local
17: objectCategory: CN=Person,CN=Schema,CN=Configuration,DC=fis,DC=local
18: objectClass:
        top
        person
        organizationalPerson
        user
19: objectGUID: {E04AE8D5-1A71-4641-84AE-4D58051BC042}
20: objectSid: S-1-5-21-1935655697-1409082233-1801674531-1145
21: primaryGroupID: 513
22: pwdLastSet: 126006491559503750
23: name: caitlyn
24: sAMAccountName: caitlyn
25: sAMAccountType: 805306368
26: userAccountControl: 512
27: userPrincipalName: caitlyn@fis.local
28: uSNChanged: 71137
29: uSNCreated: 71133
30: whenChanged: 4/19/2000 8:19:16 PM
31: whenCreated: 4/19/2000 8:19:15 PM
```

CH

19

runas

The runas command is built into the Windows 2000 operating system and will soon become your favorite permissions troubleshooting tool. It fixes nothing in and of itself, but enables you to start commands under the credentials of another user. You can use the runas option to start a GUI tool by pressing the Shift key and right-clicking the icon, or you can start a command session by using the command shown in Listing 19.4. Any commands started from the command window created from the runas command inherit the access token of the specified user.

LISTING 19.4 USING runas TO AUTHENTICATE AS A DIFFERENT USER

```
O:\WINNT>runas /user:ian@fis.local cmd
Enter password for ian@fis.local:
Attempting to start "cmd" as user "ian@fis.local"...
```

SUMMARY

Every object in the Active Directory is protected by an access control list. The ACL is a list of who can and can't access the object. Users are granted access to objects by directly adding their users or groups of which they are members to the ACL for the object.

TROUBLESHOOTING

MISSING SECURITY PAGE

When I select an object in the Active Directory Users and Computers MMC Snap-in, I don't have a security page.

Make sure Advanced Features is selected on the View menu in the MMC.

DENIED PERMISSION FOR AN OBJECT

When I try to change permissions for an object, I get a message box that says You only have permission to view the current security information on <object>.

You are not authenticated with sufficient permissions to change the permission structure for that object. Log off and log back on as a more powerful user or use the runas command to authenticate with more permissions.

NEW USERS AREN'T PERMITTED

I have added a user to a group, but she isn't experiencing the new permissions she should receive.

Because much of the information about which groups a user is a member of is gathered during the authentication process, your user might need to log off and log back on to the new group membership added to her user token.

CHAPTER 20

GROUP POLICY

In this chapter

INTRODUCTION TO GROUP POLICY

The Active Directory has many features and facets, including Kerberos authentication, multimaster replication, and transitive trusts. The most visible feature of the AD, however, is the functionality provided by group policy. Group policy provides the capability to give the user a consistent desktop experience no matter where he logs in. Group policy can be used to set mundane features, such as whether the user gets the Run command; it also can be used to enforce arcane features, such as the Kerberos ticket lifetime. Virtually anything can be set by group policy. Although literally hundreds of predefined settings exist in the AD, group policy—like many other facets of the Active Directory—is fully extensible. You can extend group policy using administrative templates.

> **Tip**
>
> If you are an NT administrator contemplating upgrading to Windows 2000 and Active Directory, include group policy in your planning. The structure of your AD has an enormous effect on how you implement group policy because users and computers inherit group policy based on where their accounts reside in AD.

It is important to define what group policy is and what it is not. *Group policy* is a series of settings that affect the Registry, security, application installation and configuration, services, logon and logoff scripts, startup and shutdown scripts, and folder redirection. Group policy is not NT system policy. Although they can do some of the same things, architecturally they are dissimilar.

Like NT system policy, group policy can modify the Registry, but NT system policy many times "tattoos" the Registry. This is because, although you could use system policy to modify the Registry, no automatic undo feature is available if you remove a policy setting or a user or computer from being impacted by that setting. Settings made by system policy remain in effect unless you somehow explicitly undo them.

Group policy, on the other hand, rewrites the appropriate portion of the Registry every time a change is made, whether that change is to add or remove an item from management by group policy. For example, if you were to create a group policy that removed the Internet Explorer icon from the desktop, the next time any user affected by that group policy logged on, she would no longer have an Internet Explorer icon on her desktop. Unlike system policy, however, if you remove that group policy, the next time she logs on, her IE icon would be back (unless, of course, it was impacted by yet another group policy). Active Directory group policy can be applied to sites, domains, or organizational units (OU). Assigning group policy at the domain level can paint change with a very broad brush; assigning at the OU level can provide very granular control.

An understanding of the architecture and use of group policy is critical if you want to take full advantage of the Active Directory. So much of the functionality, power, and ease of use is dependent on group policy. Before we dive off deeply into the architecture and minutiae of group policy, however, let's look at a simple, visual example.

A SIMPLE GROUP POLICY EXAMPLE

In Figure 20.1, you can see that we have created an OU called GPTest that holds one user named Joe. When Joe logs on at this point, he gets the standard Windows 2000 desktop. You will change this through group policy, which will impact Joe no matter where he logs on in the domain.

Figure 20.1
The GPTest OU appears under `fis.local` in the AD.

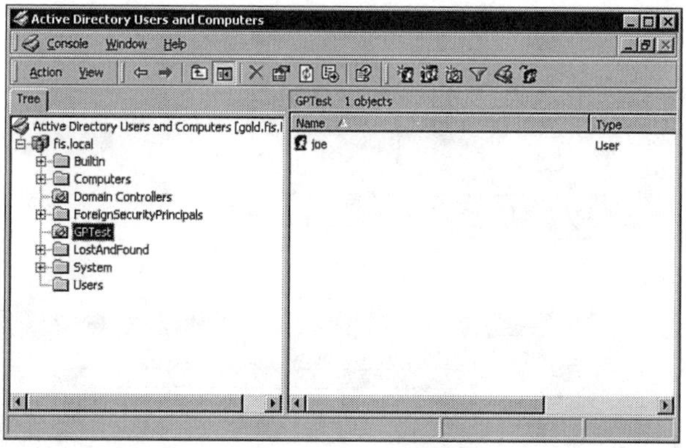

In this demonstration, you will create a group policy for the GPTest organizational unit and then make some simple, easy-to-observe changes. Even though Joe is currently the only member of the GPTest OU, anyone or any computer you create or move in to this OU inherits and is affected by this group policy.

> **Tip**
> If you are going to test this in a production environment (which is probably not a good idea to begin with), create a throwaway OU and user. After you have tested the group policy, you can delete the group policy and then delete the OU and user en masse.

> **Caution**
> Deleting an OU that holds a group policy does NOT delete the group policy.

You display the group policy property page shown in Figure 20.2 by right-clicking the organizational unit and selecting Properties. You create a new group policy for the GPTest OU by clicking New and—if you choose—renaming the group policy object.

When you click Edit in the tab shown in Figure 20.2, the group policy editor opens (see Figure 20.3). Here, you can set options that will affect both user and computer. Because this is a simple walkthrough to demonstrate exactly what a group policy is, we'll stick with changing several settings under Start Menu & Taskbar and Desktop.

CH
20

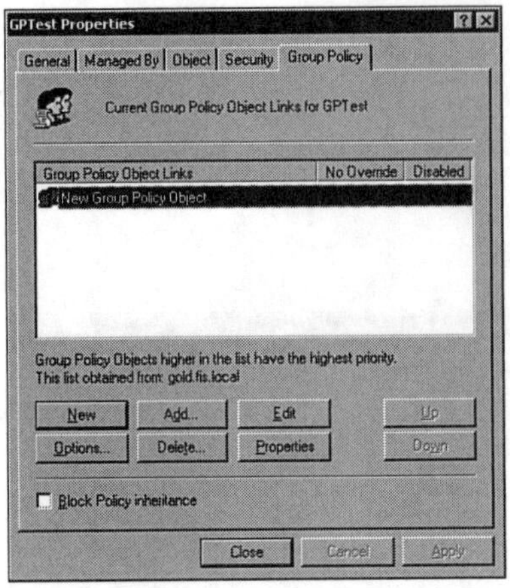

Figure 20.2
Create a new group policy from the Group Policy tab of the GPTest Properties window.

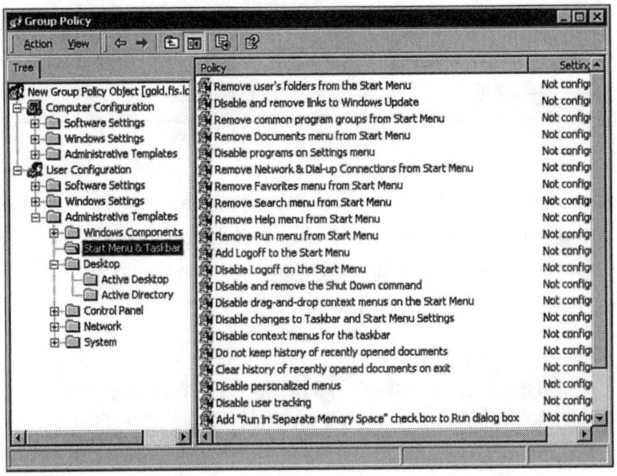

Figure 20.3
The group policy editor provides useful demonstrations for group policy options.

When you double-click Remove Run Menu from Start Menu, you see the property page in Figure 20.4. When you enable this setting and click OK, you are specifying that you want to remove the Run command from the Start menu.

Note

Note that no Edit/Undo command or Save command exists in the group policy editor. Every edit implies a save. If you modify it in the editor, it is saved to the group policy the moment you modify it. However, this does not mean that the group policy is applied to the client. Group policy application occurs at startup, logon, and every 90 minutes +/- 30 minutes at the client.

To further demonstrate group policy, let's set Remove Documents Menu from Start Menu. In addition, under the Desktop folder, you will enable the Hide Internet Explorer Icon on Desktop setting.

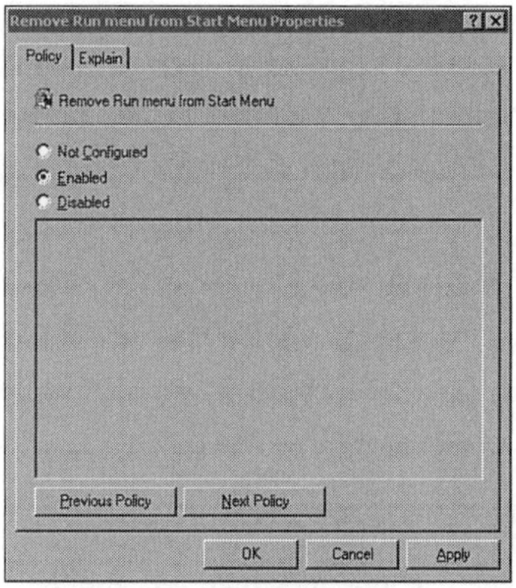

Figure 20.4
Use policy choices to
modify the Start
menu.

When you are finished, close the group policy editor and GPTest property page and log off. Then, log on as Joe.

Figure 20.5 shows that your group policy has taken effect for Joe. Set three settings in the group policy for the GPTest organizational unit. You have removed the IE icon and Run and Documents from the Start menu. Any user you add to the GPTest OU will also receive these settings the next time he logs on. Additionally, if you removed the group policy or the settings you've made, the desktop reverts to its former state automatically.

> **Tip**
>
> A good, quick way to test whether a group policy that implements no user elements is working and being applied to the user or computer is to add a visible element such as removing an icon from the desktop or an element from the Start menu. If the modification is innocuous, it will have little effect on current users, can be used to see whether the group policy is being processed at all, and then can be reset after the troubleshooting is complete.

Figure 20.5
The result of group
policy for user Joe
means the Start menu
has fewer options
than before.

WHY GROUP POLICY?

Okay, it's fair to say that I think group policy is neat. That is probably not enough reason, though, to read several chapters on the subject. How about this reason: Group policy enables you to enforce sameness, and when I say *enforce*, I mean it. If a computer or user is configured to receive group policy, there is no escape. The administrator for that site, domain, or OU is completely in control of who receives what group policy. Virtually any configuration setting can be set through group policy, and it requires no more administrative effort to assign group policy to 1,000 computers than it does to 10 computers.

TYPES OF GROUP POLICY

The two main areas in group policy are user and computer. This is not to say that they are different group policies; indeed, every group policy has a user and a computer section.

COMPUTER GROUP POLICY

The computer portion of a group policy modifies the HKEY_LOCAL_MACHINE (HKLM) subtree of the Registry of the machine on which it is applied. This section can be seen in Figure 20.6, which is a snapshot of the Default Domain Controllers group policy. This group policy is automatically created when you install the Active Directory and is applied to every DC in the domain. The hostname that shows in the top line in the tree pane, [gold.fis.local], shows the DC on which the group policy editor is focused. This DC is where changes will be made and then automatically replicated to other DCs.

Figure 20.6
The group policy editor shows the default options.

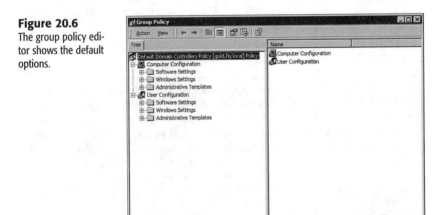

Computer group policy is applied at system startup. The settings in the computer portion of any group policy are designed to be applied to the computer regardless of who logs on, or even whether anyone logs on.

Note   Assigning group policy involves more than just modifying the Registry, such as logon scripts, and installing software.

USER GROUP POLICY

The User portion of any group policy modifies the HKEY_CURRENT_USER (HKCU) subtree of the Registry. This portion of group policy is designed to change the user's experience through logon scripts, modifying the Start menu, and enforcing a common desktop. User group policy is applied at logon.

The difference between the two sections is important for several reasons. Computer group policy is applied when the machine starts up and before the Ctrl+Alt+Delete box is displayed. User group policy, on the other hand, is applied at logon and before the desktop is displayed. Say, for example, you've configured the group policy to install software automatically using the Windows Installer Service. If you assign it to the computer, it will be installed at startup; however, if you assign it to the user, it will be installed whenever that user logs on. Both computer and user group policy are also assigned during a periodic refresh cycle, every 90 minutes (plus or minus 30) on computers, and every 5 minutes on DCs.

APPLYING GROUP POLICY

Group policy can be applied to three Active Directory container objects: sites, domains, and organizational units. In addition, every local computer has one local group policy that impacts it whether or not it is a member of a domain (by default, almost nothing is enabled in it). Although much of what you see in this book is available in local group policy, we will concentrate on Active Directory group policy.

CHOOSING WHERE TO ASSIGN GROUP POLICY

Assigning group policy is not operationally difficult. Planning an appropriate group policy infrastructure, however, is a non-trivial event. You can place a few monolithic group policy objects at the domain level and they will trickle down to every user and computer in the domain. Conversely, you can choose a very granular approach by assigning group policy to OU. The following lists several good rules of thumb for designing group policy:

- **For performance, choose fewer policies rather than many**—This obviously must be balanced against your need for granularity, but it is faster for your clients to parse and assign a few large group policy objects rather than many group policy objects with just a few modifications each.

- **Resist the temptation to create a complex web of conflicting group policies, permissions, modifications, and group policy inheritance overrides**—You can accomplish your goals this way, but it will be a nightmare to troubleshoot and maintain.

- **Start with a few group policy objects assigned at the OU level**—Test them, and if they provide long-term value, you can link them to the domain, and in effect "promote" them to impacting the entire domain.

CH
20

- **Keep a log of your changes**—Create a database (either textual or electronic) of changes made through group policy and where they were applied. This can be used to re-create or troubleshoot group policy.

- **Remember that the higher in the directory structure the group policy is assigned, the more users and computers it will affect.**

- **Keep group policy in mind when designing your OU structure**—Where a computer and user account reside in the domain completely affects what group policies they inherit.

- **Fully use the new logon script functionality available with Windows Scripting Host**—You can do virtually anything with these VBScript or JavaScript files. Remember that you can apply startup and shutdown scripts to computers and logon and logoff scripts to users.

- **Group users and computers with common application needs and desktop needs together in the same OU or OU tree**—This enables you to organize your group policy more effectively.

- **Leverage the capability of group policy to install, upgrade, and delete applications on the client PC**—This can reduce the TCO for your client computers.

ASSIGNING GROUP POLICY

You use different tools to assign group policy depending on where you are assigning it. Active Directory Sites and Services is used to assign group policy to sites. Active Directory Users and Computers, on the other hand, is used to assign group policy to domains and organizational units. The processes of assigning group policy to sites, domains, and OU differ slightly:

- **Sites**—Open the AD Sites and Services MMC Snap-in (`dssite.msc`) and select the site. Right-click the site and choose Properties/Group Policy.

- **Domains**—Open the AD Users and Computers MMC Snap-in (`dsa.msc`) and select the domain. Right-click the domain and choose Properties/Group Policy.

- **OU**—Open the AD Users and Computers MMC Snap-in (`dsa.msc`) and select the OU. Right-click the OU and choose Properties/Group Policy.

Group policy is implemented only on Windows 2000 computers. Although support does exist for Windows 9x and NT clients to participate in the AD, this does not extend to group policy. Even if the down-level client is a member of the domain and logs on to the Active Directory, it is not impacted by group policy.

GROUP POLICY AND SECURITY GROUPS

The term *group policy* does not mean that the policies are somehow attached to security groups. You cannot assign group policy to security groups. As a member of various security groups, you receive group policy, but the presence or absence of your user object in a particular group does not determine whether you receive group policy. You and your computer receive group policy based on where your user and computer accounts are located in the Active Directory. If you are a member of a site, domain, or OU that has a group policy assigned to it, you receive the effect of the group policy. Where security groups of which you are a member are defined does not affect your receiving group policy. However, you can escape the effects of group policy by assigning a particular set of permissions to a security group.

SUMMARY

Group policy is used to do everything from configuring desktops to setting Kerberos policy. It is a very visible feature of the Active Directory. With group policy, you can leverage scripting, automatic application installation, public key infrastructure key management, and IP security. It is an enormous advantage in a large, distributed environment because it enables the modification of the user's environment without physically visiting the client PC.

TROUBLESHOOTING

MISSING GROUP POLICY

I have created a group policy, but one of my field offices is not receiving it.

Group policy is automatically replicated to every DC in the domain. This can take some time, however. Therefore, until the filesystem objects that represent most of group policy arrive at the DC to which your clients are logging on, they will not receive that group policy.

PROBLEMS WITH CHILD OU

My top-level OU are applying a new group policy, but several of the child OU are not.

It is possible to set block inheritance on a particular OU. If this happens, group policy inheritance is blocked until the setting is removed or No Override is set.

USERS AREN'T APPLYING GROUP POLICY

A subset of users is not applying a group policy.

By default, the Authenticated Users group has the read and apply group policy permission to every group policy. If a user or group is explicitly denied one or both of those permissions, they can't apply group policy.

SETTINGS AREN'T BEING APPLIED

My users are not getting some of the settings I anticipated from my group policy.

The effective group policy a user or computer receives is the result of ALL the group policies assigned to ALL the containers of which it is a member. If a group policy conflicts with yours, it might override it based on its proximity to the user or computer or its override settings.

CHAPTER 21

GROUP POLICY SECTIONS

In this chapter

OVERVIEW OF GROUP POLICY SECTIONS

This chapter looks at the basic use and meaning of many of the folders and nodes in the group policy object. Literally hundreds of settings exist in group policy, so this is not an exhaustive list, but rather a primer on where to start in group policy to configure your domain to meet the needs of your organization. You will revisit many of the group policy sections discussed here and see how to modify and use them, but for the moment let's take a leisurely tour of some of the options presented in group policy. The computer and user sections this chapter discusses appear in Figure 21.1. You'll look at the default domain policy because several group policy sections, such as Kerberos, exist that can be applied only at this level. Any modifications made to the default domain policy are applied to every user or computer throughout the entire domain, unless they're overridden by another group policy.

Figure 21.1
The computer and user group policies.

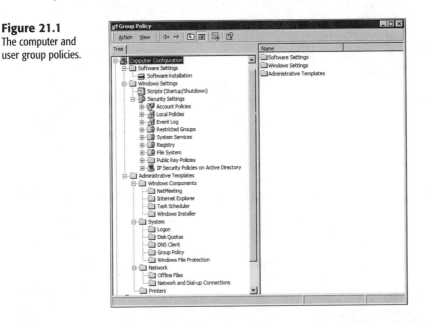

> **Caution**
>
> You can't open the Group Policy Editor in read-only mode. In a production environment, be very careful when viewing group policy. No File/Save option is available here—every edit implies a save.

COMPUTER CONFIGURATION

The Computer Configuration section is applied to each computer that is a member of the site, domain, or organizational unit (OU). These settings are applied at startup, regardless of who logs on or whether anyone logs on at all.

Tip

You can configure some group policy settings to not be applied if the computer detects that group policy is being applied over a slow link.

➔ **See** "Group Policy," **p. 360**

SOFTWARE SETTINGS

The Software Settings section has one child node—Software Installation—and is very straightforward. It appears in Figure 21.2 with one application set up as assigned, which means it will be installed on startup.

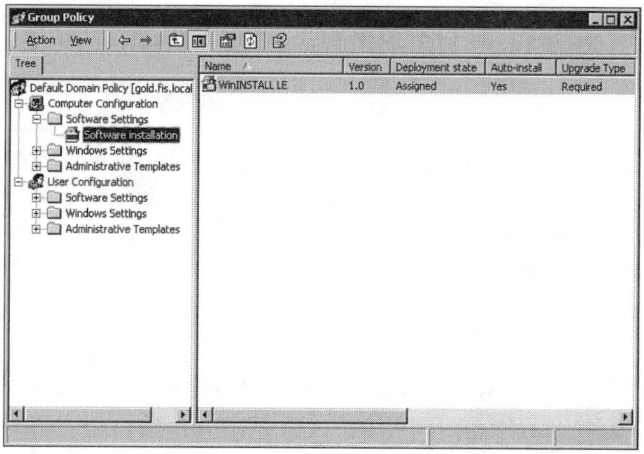

Figure 21.2
The software installation node.

SOFTWARE INSTALLATION

Any software assigned to the computer through this group policy setting is installed before anyone logs on. This enables you to assign software to the computer regardless of who uses it. This is a detailed process and is covered in more detail in Chapter 22, "Managing Group Policy." Software that is assigned to computers will be fully installed the next time the computer boots. In contrast, software that is assigned to users is pre-installed at the next logon, but the files are not actually copied to the local drive until the user tries to use the application.

Caution

Software can be installed and uninstalled through group policy. Be careful when removing assigned or published applications from group policy.

➔ **See** "Assigning and Publishing Software Through Group Policy," **p. 388**

WINDOWS SETTINGS

The Windows Settings section has several subsections and nodes, from startup scripts to public key polices. Much of the security settings you choose to apply through group policy is set in this section.

SCRIPTS

The addition of a robust scripting architecture is an exciting feature of Windows 2000. Every Windows 2000 computer—whether Professional, Server, Advanced Server, or Datacenter Server—implements Windows Scripting Host (WSH) 2.0. This means you can write scripts in VBScript or JavaScript and they will run on any Windows 2000 computer without any further configuration. The possibilities here are endless.

> **Caution**
>
> Logon scripts are similar to any other power tool. Be very careful. Test your scripts in a small situation before applying them en masse.

WSH also supports COM+, which means you can write Component Object Model (COM) dynamic link libraries (DLL), distribute them through the software installation feature of group policy, and then call them from inside your WSH scripts. You can assign scripts to run either at startup, shutdown, or both. This is another detailed feature that is covered in detail in Chapter 22. Figure 21.3 shows the interface for setting startup and shutdown scripts.

> **Note**
>
> Embedding scripts that require user input is rarely useful here. If you do embed scripts, such as message boxes, that require the user to click OK, the script will hang until the user interacts with the system.

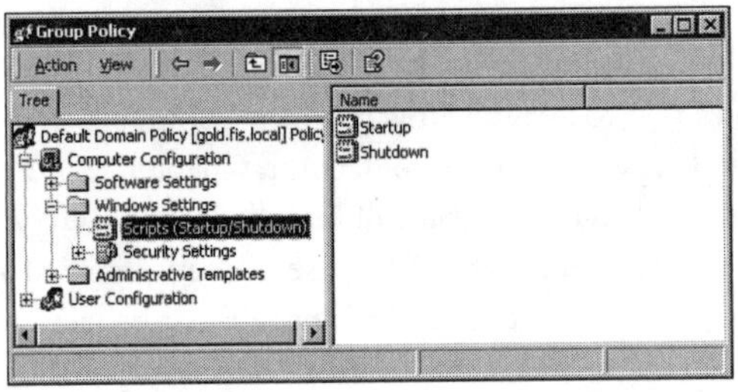

Figure 21.3
Startup and shutdown scripts.

SECURITY SETTINGS

The Security Settings section could (and probably will) fill at least one book. But not this book. A massive amount of detail and strategy must be considered here. We'll take a look at the basics and defer some of the minutiae. If you are an experienced Windows NT administrator, you have seen many of these settings in the User Manager for Domains.

ACCOUNT POLICIES This section you to set password policy, account lockout policy, and Kerberos policy. These settings are not to be set lightly or without due thought. If you set them too loosely, your system can be less secure that it needs to be. If you set them too tightly, you raise the level of administrative overhead. Usability and security are mutually exclusive goals. As you move toward one, you move away from the other.

Password policy settings affect password age, affect whether or not you enforce password history, and set password complexity requirements. This can have a major effect on your security. People will use no password, the same password, or short, easy-to-guess passwords. My favorite is the password on the sticky note affixed to the monitor. My grandfather used to have a safe in his shop, with the combination written in pencil on the wall above the safe. Go figure. This section enables you to set criteria on the use of passwords and enforce this across the affected site, domain, or OU. One of the advantages of group policy and your ability to assign it to sites, domains, and organizational units is that you can group together computers and people that require greater security and more finely tune security. The Password Policy interface appears in Figure 21.4, with the domain default settings.

> **Tip**
>
> Account policy and public key policy can be set at only the domain level and have domain-wide scope.

Figure 21.4
Defining maximum password age.

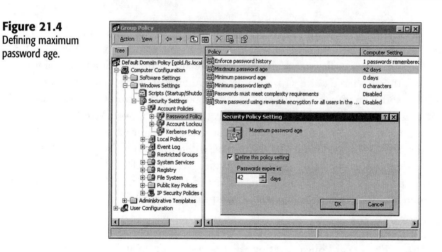

Account lockout policy affects what happens when a threshold is reached on bad logon attempts. This is where you protect yourself from brute-force password attacks, simple guessing, and dictionary attacks. If the settings in this section are set properly after the threshold of misspelled passwords is reached, the account is locked out until it is unlocked by an administrator (or someone with that permission). Although this is a great place to lock down your domain, be aware that setting this too rigidly can cause you to spend much more time than you planned simply resetting accounts because your users can't type. Figure 21.5 shows the domain account lockout policy default settings.

Ch
21

Figure 21.5
Setting account lock-out policy.

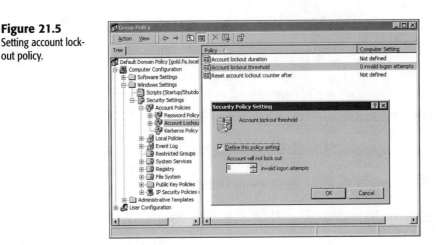

> **Caution**
>
> Locking down security can have unintended consequences. If you make password restrictions too onerous, your users might write their passwords on the bottom of their keyboards. If you set lockout policy too stringently, you might spend more time unlocking accounts than you planned.

Kerberos policy is one of the settings that is available only at the domain policy level. This is rarely modified. Windows 2000 clients will be unable to authenticate using Kerberos if this setting is improperly configured. Kerberos is the default authentication protocol for Windows 2000. It uses shared secrets (passwords) to authenticate users and services for Windows 2000, and then gives them tickets that are good for admission to domain controllers (DCs) and other computers and services throughout the network. Kerberos is extremely robust and has been an IETF standard for decades. Figure 21.6 shows the default settings for domain Kerberos policy. The settings here determine how long the tickets are valid and how skewed the clocks between two computers can be before the Kerberos service considers packets from the other computer to be part of a replay attack. The defaults in the Kerberos group policy section are adequate for most installations.

→ **See** "Kerberos Policy," **p. 308**

LOCAL POLICIES　The Local Policies section enables you to set up auditing, user rights assignment, and security options.

Auditing enables you to create a trail of events that is rich with information. You can audit logon events, file access, and so on. You also can choose to audit both success and failure. This information is written to the event logs, which can be viewed with eventvwr.exe, the Event Viewer. This tool appears in Figure 21.7 with the focus on the security log where much of the auditing information will be stored.

Figure 21.6
Kerberos time skew.

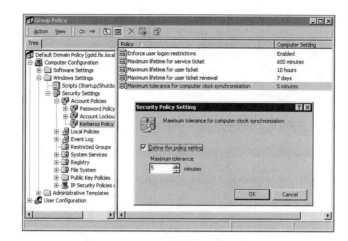

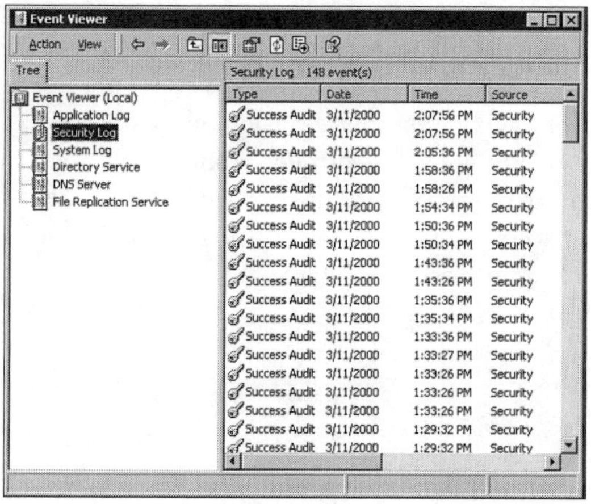

Figure 21.7
The Event Viewer
security log.

This information is kept in several files with the `.evt` extension in `\winnt\system32\config`. The key mistake not to make here is making the logging too verbose. It is acceptable to audit many events for a short period of time as long as you understand the cost. If you choose to audit too many events, you can cause high levels of processor utilization and disk writes as the information is written to the logs. The logs themselves are by default only 512KB and are set to overwrite every seven days. This is too small for many verbose logging environments. These settings can be changed on a per-log basis in the Event Viewer. You can see the list of auditable events in Figure 21.8.

Tip

Creating a schedule for reviewing logs is an excellent practice. You are spending processor cycles and disk space to log the information, yet it is of little use if it is not reviewed regularly.

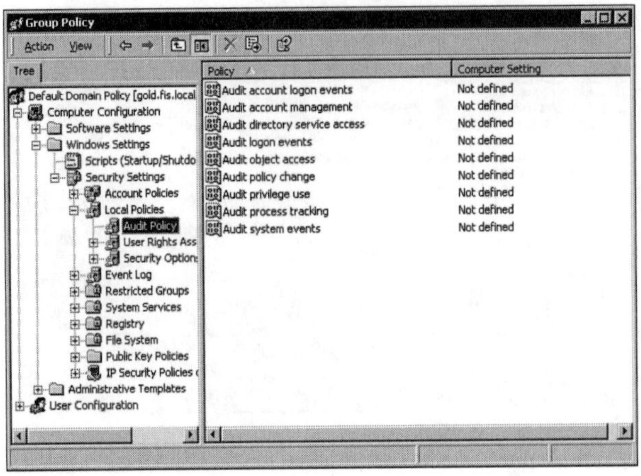

Figure 21.8
Audit policy options in Windows 2000.

User rights assignment enables you to set which rights any user or group has. These are separate from filesystem or Active Directory permissions. Examples of user rights are log on locally, change the system time, or log on as a service. Several of these rights are extremely important. By default, everyone does not have the log on locally right to a domain controller. This is set in the default domain controller group policy. You can add or subtract who can log on at the console to a DC with this right. If you have set a service to log on as a particular account, if that account does not have the log on as a service right, the service will not load. A lengthy list of rights exists. In Figure 21.9, you see the deny logon locally right set to group `tempusers`.

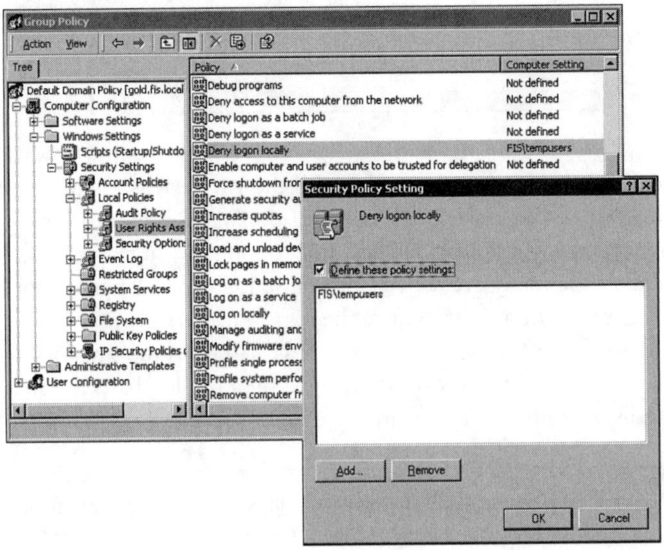

Figure 21.9
Setting security policy.

Security options enable you to configure security for many situations. In this section, you can make decisions about whether to display a legal message at logon and whether to allow drivers that are not digitally signed to be installed; you also can set some smart card behaviors. A very secure system has many of these turned on. Figure 21.10 shows some of the configurable options, with the Clear Virtual Memory Pagefile When System Shuts Down option configured.

Figure 21.10
Group policy security options.

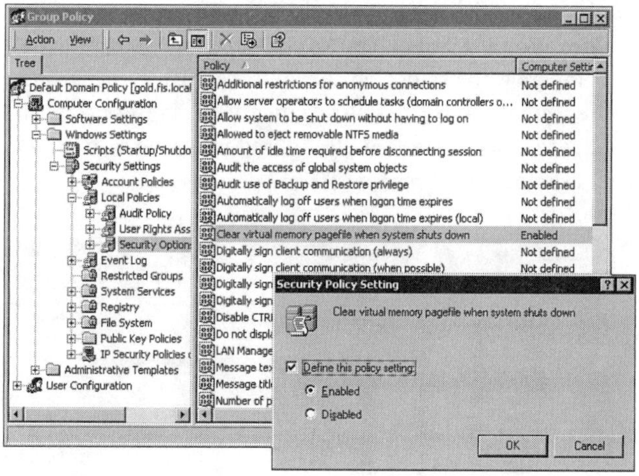

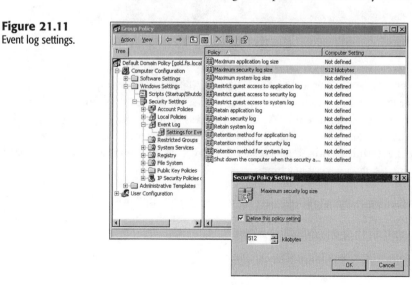

EVENT LOG The Event Log section is simple: It holds one node, Settings for Event Logs (see Figure 21.11). Here you make default settings for all the event viewer logs in the domain. This is much more efficient than setting these parameters manually for each machine.

Figure 21.11
Event log settings.

The Settings for Event Logs node enables you to set the default size, retention behaviors, and security on the Windows 2000 event logs. These files are located in \winnt\system32\config. One of these is potentially very invasive. The Shut Down the Computer When the Security Audit Log Is Full setting might be necessary for a secure computer, but it will cause problems that are difficult to predict if it's accidentally set.

RESTRICTED GROUPS The Restricted Groups section of the Security Settings folder has the potential for confusion if used improperly. To use restricted groups, you add one or more groups to the folder and then add an approved list of members. The next time group policy is applied, any members who are not on the approved list in this group policy are removed. Even if they are repeatedly added, the list of members is reset every time group policy is applied. Figure 21.12 shows this folder configured with one restricted group, salesadmins, which has one allowed member, fred.

Figure 21.12
Configuring restricted groups.

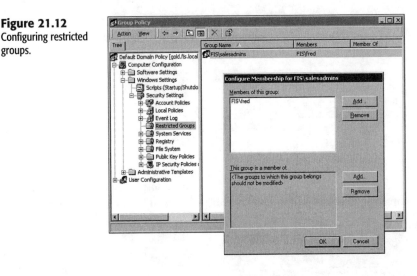

SYSTEM SERVICES This section enables you to set the default startup as disabled, manual, or automatic for each of the system services present on a Windows 2000 computer. If, for example, you wanted to make sure the SMTP service was running on every computer in the domain, you could set the service to start here without having to touch each computer. You also can define the default security on each service. Figure 21.13 shows the Indexing Service set to start automatically on every machine.

REGISTRY The Registry folder enables you to configure security on Registry keys. This sets access control, auditing, and ownership. Figure 21.14 shows the HKEY_CLASSES_ROOT\ai key set with permissions to flow down to child keys.

Figure 21.13
System Services group policy.

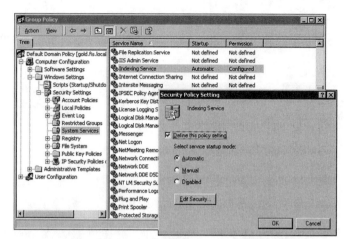

Figure 21.14
Setting security on Registry keys.

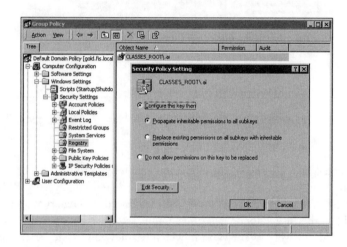

FILE SYSTEM This folder enables you to configure security on files or folders, including access control, auditing, and ownership. Figure 21.15 shows the file `c:\softinstall\SWIADMLE.MSI` set with inheritable permissions.

PUBLIC KEY POLICIES This is an area that requires much planning and expertise to properly configure. Failure to plan well when modifying these settings can cause computers to be almost unusable. Managed well, however, these settings will enable your computers to interoperate with other computers in a Windows 2000 environment and even with services outside the domain.

Trust is the basis for a public key infrastructure (PKI). When you present a certificate from an X.509 certificate server, it must be from a CA that you trust; otherwise, the certificate is worthless. In this folder you can set who your trusted certification authorities (CA) are and also keep a certificate revocation list. To receive the full benefit of this section, you should have a root CA installed somewhere in the forest. This root CA can then issue certificates

CH

21

throughout the forest to computers, users, and services, and they in turn can use them to prove their identity to each other with digital signatures as well as use them as the basis for encryption.

Figure 21.15
Configuring filesystem permissions through group policy.

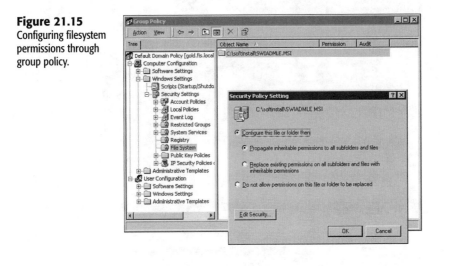

> **Tip**
>
> Using public key policy requires access to an X.509 certificate server. You can install certificate services on any Windows 2000 server.

The Encrypted Data Recovery Agents section enables you to set a list of users you trust to recover files that have been encrypted with the Encrypted File System (EFS) feature of Windows 2000. A *recovery agent* is a user who is allowed to unencrypt a file that has been encrypted by other users. By default, the administrator is listed in this folder. Figure 21.16 shows the Add Recovery Agent Wizard, which enables you to add other users as recovery agents.

Figure 21.16
The Add Recovery Agent Wizard.

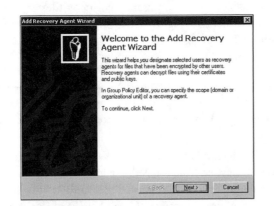

The Automatic Certificate Request settings set parameters for automatically giving certificates to computer accounts in the domain. This sets which types of certificates are automatically granted to an authenticated computer account in the domain the next time it logs on.

The Trusted Root Certification Authorities is a list of all trusted root CAs. This means if you receive a digital certificate signed by a CA on this list, you can assume that it is a good certificate. This section also enables you to import a file that contains a certificate trust list (CTL). This file can be of several file types.

Enterprise trust is where you create new certificate trust lists for a particular purpose and populate them with a list of CAs.

IP SECURITY POLICIES ON ACTIVE DIRECTORY   This is another section that must be approached with planning and knowledge. Internet Protocol Security (IPSec) is a host authentication, data integrity, and data encryption methodology for protecting information as it moves from one computer to another across the network. This protocol functions below the protocols in the TCP/IP protocol stack and as such is invisible to the user and the applications. Many good methodologies are available for encrypting information on the network, but many of them are application specific and require special support in the application. IPSec is completely abstracted from the applications that are being used and is a robust feature for protecting your network communications.

You can create new IPSec policies using the IP Security Policy Wizard, or you can use one of the three default predefined policies. These policies can be specific about the subnets with which they communicate, the port numbers, and the protocols. In most situations, the three default policies should suffice. Figure 21.17 shows the IP Security Policy Wizard, which is used to create new IP security policies.

Figure 21.17
The IPSec Policy
Wizard.

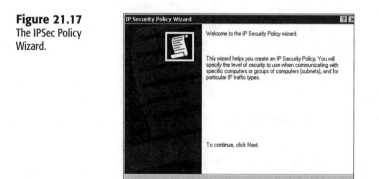

Note

IPSec is not currently implemented on Windows NT or 9x. If you set these policies to *require* IPSec, you will not be able to communicate with down-level clients.

The client (respond only) IPSec policy defines that the client never initiates IPSec communications. However, the client can respond to a request for secure communications and negotiate the appropriate parameters for the connection.

With the server (request security) IPSec policy, the server always tries to negotiate security with the requesting client. However, if the client doesn't support IPSec or is not configured to use IPSec, the server allows unsecure connections.

The secure server IPSec policy simply communicates through IPSec or not at all. Be careful implementing this on DCs. If any of your clients are incapable of using IPSec, they will also be incapable of logging on.

Caution

The default authentication used by IPSec is Kerberos. Because of the default Keberos time delta of five minutes, time skew issues can cause communication failures between two machines. This can be difficult to track down and troubleshoot.

Note

Encrypting the data before it is sent across the wire and unencrypting it on the other end is a computationally intensive process. Be aware of the costs when implementing IPSec and choosing the encryption method. Both 3Com and Intel have good, low-cost NICs that implement IPSec on the card.

ADMINISTRATIVE TEMPLATES

Administrative Templates is a section of group policy that deals with Registry-based policy settings. The templates you see in the Group Policy Editor are built based on three template files that, by default, exist in \winnt\inf. The three templates loaded by default are conf.adm, inetres.adm, and system.adm. You can modify what is contained in this section by loading and unloading .adm template files. You also can create your own template files and then load them here. Figure 21.18 shows the Add/Remove Templates interface. You can load this page by right-clicking the Administrative Templates folder and selecting Add/Remove Templates.

When you load new templates, you see the interface update immediately with new options specified by the template.

Note

Although Windows 2000 .adm templates resemble system policy templates from Windows NT 4, they are not the same thing. The syntax is subtly different, and they should not be mixed.

Figure 21.19 shows another important, useful feature of administrative templates. With the Show Configured Policies Only option set, when you are troubleshooting group policy (notice I didn't say *if*), you can modify the interface to show only those group policy folders that hold configured options. Note, however, that this option does not persist from one editing session to another.

Figure 21.18
Adding templates to
group policy.

Figure 21.18
Adding templates to
group policy.

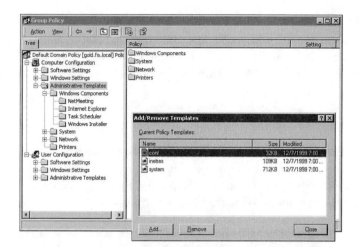

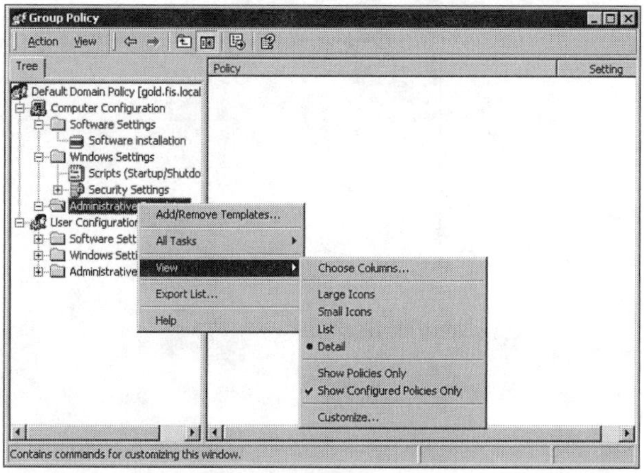

Figure 21.19
Viewing only config-
ured policies.

GROUP POLICY SETTINGS IN ADMINISTRATIVE TEMPLATES

All the policy settings in the Administrative Templates section have essentially the same format. Unlike the previous group policy settings you have looked at that had extensive wizards
and property pages associated with them, these pages simply are set one of three ways: not
configured, enabled, or disabled. Enabled means that the policy will be enforced; disabled
means that the policy will not be enforced; and not configured means that the policy will
not be affected one way or the other. This third setting is necessary because group policy is
inherited from the site, domain, or OU to which it is linked. You could very likely have conflicting policies set on a particular configuration. The not configured option enables a group
policy setting that is configured on a site, domain, or OU above the group policy in the
Active Directory to fall through this group policy and still take effect.

CH
21

WINDOWS COMPONENTS

This folder holds folders for configuring NetMeeting, Internet Explorer, Task Scheduler, and the Windows Installer Service. These folders hold many configurable options that make administering a Windows 2000 Active Directory much simpler and more organized.

NETMEETING This folder has only one option, which can be enabled or disabled: Disable Remote Desktop Sharing.

INTERNET EXPLORER This section enables you to set options that affect Internet Explorer security, proxy, update, and interface settings. Figure 21.20 shows one of my favorite features of the settings in the Windows Components folder. This is the Explain tab that is on every policy setting in the Windows Components folder.

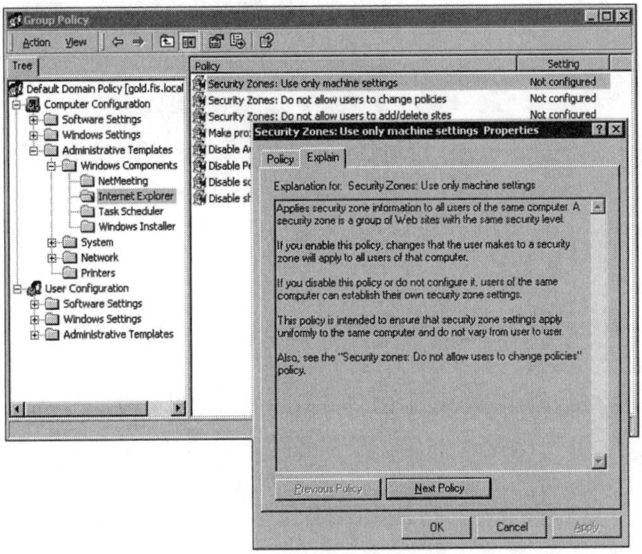

Figure 21.20
Using help text in group policy.

This is a marvelous feature because so many policy settings exist, which makes keeping track of them all difficult.

Note

Some of the computer group policy settings in the Administrative Templates folder either interact interestingly with or require the presence of a corresponding setting in the user group policy settings. Judicious use of the Explain tab can save you section a lot of time when troubleshooting these issues.

TASK SCHEDULER The Task Scheduler folder of group policy settings enables you to lock down a user's ability to modify scheduled tasks on his client workstation. Here, you can set whether or not he can stop or start tasks, add new tasks, or even look at tasks that are scheduled. The Task Scheduler icon is located in Control Panel.

WINDOWS INSTALLER   The Windows Installer folder enables you to configure the parameters under which the Windows Installer service will run. This is the service that runs on the client, enabling you to install software through group policy. It also can be used at the client to install any native or repackaged Windows Installer file. A *native* Windows Installer file is one that is packaged by the developer and holds a variety of information about the application itself. Native Windows Installer files can be self-healing, which means they can enable a missing or corrupt file and, in the background, replace that file from the original source without user or administrator intervention. The Windows Installer service is what manages this kind of functionality. Repackaged Windows Installer applications can be assigned through group policy but do not self-repair.

This folder enables you to set Windows Installer files to install with elevated privileges, determine which options are available to the user while the installation is occurring, and allow the administrator to install software while connected through Terminal Server. Figure 21.21 shows the Always Install with Elevated Privileges Properties dialog box. This is an interesting policy setting because it must be enabled in both the computer and user settings for it to take effect. This is a security-sensitive setting and should be used with caution.

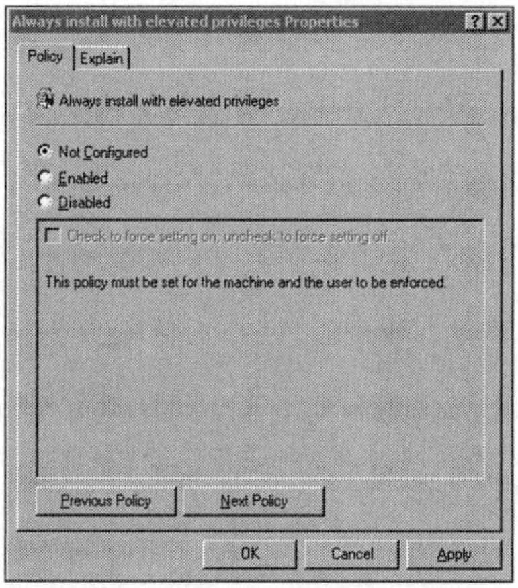

Figure 21.21
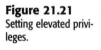
Setting elevated privileges.

SYSTEM

The System folder of Administrative Templates enables you to set system-level group policies, such as slow link detection, parameters for loading roaming profiles, and so on. Figure 21.22 shows a policy that enables you to run local programs at startup. These programs should reside in the \winnt folder of the client or should be registered here with a fully qualified pathname.

LOGON   The Logon folder holds policy settings that configure whether logon scripts run synchronously or asynchronously, whether startup/shutdown scripts are visible at runtime, and slow link detection.

CH
21

Figure 21.22
Running programs at
logon.

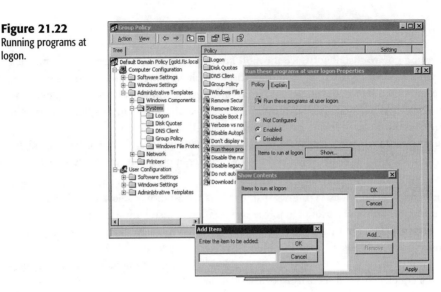

DISK QUOTAS   Disk quotas are a long-awaited feature of Windows 2000. With this group policy folder, you can choose the severity of the event when a user exceeds her storage limits on a drive. You can log an event when the limit is approached or when it is exceeded, and you can choose to enforce the limit by denying additional disk space to the user.

DNS CLIENT   The DNS Client folder contains one policy setting, which enables you to set the primary DNS suffix: `fis.local`.

GROUP POLICY   The Group Policy folder enables you to configure how group policy is applied and how it is refreshed. Additionally, policies are available to configure slow link detection. When a group policy is applied, the system pings the server to check the throughput of the link. If a slow link is detected, you can use the policies in this folder to determine which portions of the group policy are applied. In addition, a process exists even if the group policy objects have not changed. By default, when a group policy is being processed, it checks the current version of the group policy modifications on the client and the current version of the group policy on the server. If they are the same, group policy is not applied. This is done to speed group policy processing. With this option, you can be certain that group policy is being updated at every startup.

WINDOWS FILE PROTECTION   The Windows File Protection group policy is used to set the size and location of the Windows file protection cache and the scanning frequency of the service. Windows file protection protects files in system folders from being replaced. If a file in a protected folder is replaced, the Windows File Protection service checks whether it's the correct version, and if it's not, replaces it with the correct version from the `\winnt\` `system32\dllcache`.

NETWORK

The Network group policy section hosts two folders. These are used to configure offline files and network dial-up connections.

OFFLINE FILES   The Offline Files section of group policy is particularly useful to mobile users. Offline files keep a copy of the user's file both on the local computer and on a share on the network. This enables the user to work on files even when he's disconnected from the network; then, when he is reconnected, the synchronization manager is used to replace older files with the newest versions of the file. A multitude of options are available here to configure whether offline files are turned on, the presence of reminder balloons to show the user he has lost his network connection, and the cache size. Figure 21.23 shows the files not cached group policy configured for .exe and .bmp files.

Figure 21.23
Configuring offline files.

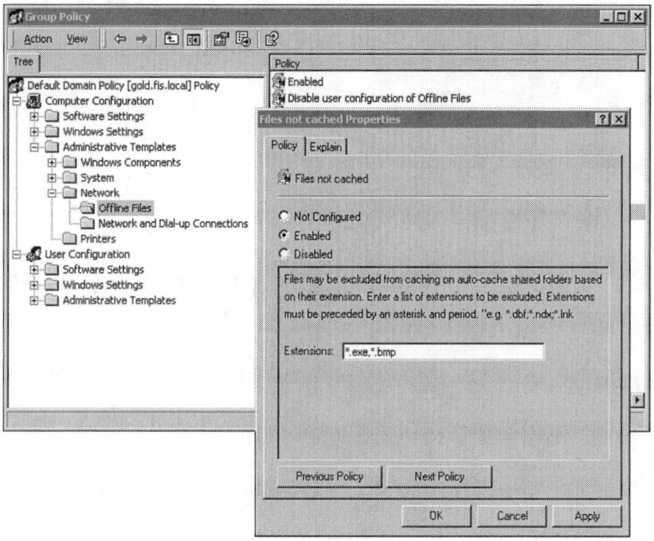

NETWORK AND DIAL-UP CONNECTIONS   The Network and Dial-Up Connections group policy setting simply allows or disallows the capability to enable the built-in network address translation feature of dial-up connections. Network address translation enables you to aggregate one or more internal IP addresses behind one valid connection, usually a dial-up connection to the Internet. This enables multiple internal clients to access an external network using one valid connection.

PRINTERS

The final section of computer group policy enables the configuration of printers (whether they are automatically published in the Active Directory), the default location when searching for printers, and the enabling or disabling of Web printing, which enables printers to be displayed in a Web page and connected to through the Web page.

CH
21

USER CONFIGURATION

The User Configuration section of group policy holds configuration options for much of the same areas that are affected by computer configuration group policy. However, these are applied per user, at logon, rather than the computer configuration default of per machine at startup. Much of this material has already been covered, so this section looks only at the user policies that differ from computer policies. Figure 21.24 shows the group policy sections available in User Configuration.

Figure 21.24
User group policies.

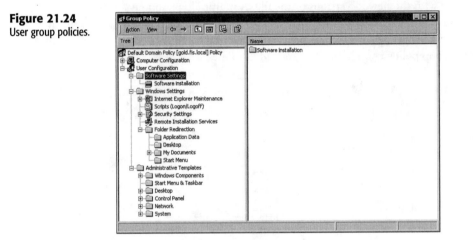

SOFTWARE SETTINGS

The Software Settings group policy sets options for software installation. It contains one child section: Software Installation.

SOFTWARE INSTALLATION

This area has an identical interface to the matching section in Computer Configuration. The difference, although architectural, is important. When you assign software to a computer through group policy, the software installs completely at the next startup. If you want the software completely installed on a computer, regardless of who logs on and when, this is the option you want. The disadvantage is that, if your organization turns on many of your computers at the same time, your network bandwidth use will be very high. If, however, you assign it to a user through this group policy setting, the desktop is updated when the user logs on, but the files of the application itself are not installed until the first use. This means that if a feature of a particular application is never used, it is never installed—which saves bandwidth, disk space, and time.

> **Note** You can assign or publish software to users. Software assigned to a user installs the next time the user logs on, without user interaction. Published software is available but is not automatic.

→ **See** "Assigning and Publishing Software Through Group Policy," **p. 388**

WINDOWS SETTINGS

Although much of the Windows Settings area in User Configuration is identical to the same area in Computer Configuration, some differences do exist. These folders configure IE, logon scripts, RIS, security, and folder redirection.

INTERNET EXPLORER MAINTENANCE

Although an Internet Explorer section exists under Administrative Templates both in the Computer and User Configuration areas, the computer section enables you to set many administrative options for IE. The section under User Configuration, on the other hand, enables you to set much of the user interface for the browser, configure channels, and set Internet security. As the browser becomes more and more the default container for enterprise applications, this is a very powerful feature.

BROWSER USER INTERFACE   The Browser User Interface section of group policy sets the browser title, bitmaps, and logo for Internet Explorer. This is useful for companies that want to enforce a consistent look for IE. The property pages for these settings are interesting because they are almost miniprograms that provide an intuitive interface for setting options for IE. Figure 21.25 shows the Custom Logo dialog box for this section. Here, you can set your company logo and choose its size. Notice that these pages do not have an explain section like the Administrative Templates section does. Therefore, you should make good use of the ToolTip help available here. You can use ToolTip help by clicking the question mark icon in the upper-right corner of the page shown in Figure 21.25 and then clicking the area you are curious about.

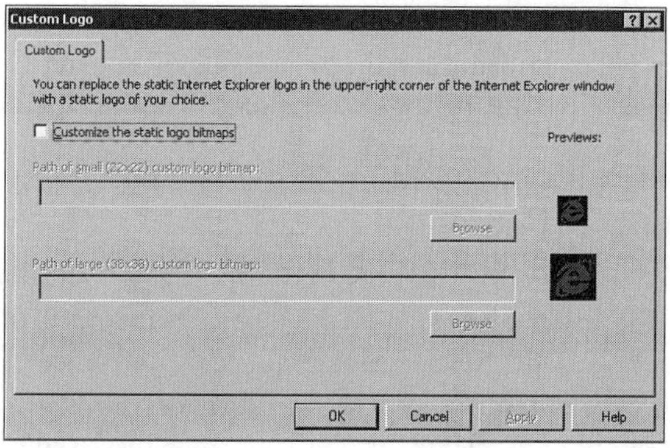

Figure 21.25
Setting custom logos for IE.

CONNECTION   The Connection area of group policy is used to modify the Internet Explorer connection settings. This enables you to set dial-up connection settings, proxy server settings, and automatic browser configuration (which enables you to refresh the customization information on the local browser at configured intervals). In addition, one other interesting setting is available here: the user agent string. This is part of the information

CH
21

that is sent in an HTTP header to a Web server. This information could be used in several situations to keep browsing statistics on an intranet because this information can be parsed by software on the Web server and logged for later evaluation.

URLs The Uniform Resource Locator section of group policy sets up the favorites list; settings for home, search, and help; and channels for the browser. This enables a company to decide which pages are automatically offered to the user, and it can be a great tool for focusing IE as a productivity tool rather than a plaything. The home page could be set to a particular intranet Web application, the company home page, and so on. The help page also could be set to the company help desk's home page with a FAQ for IE users and links to other help areas.

SECURITY The Security section sets options on security zones in IE and trusted publishers. This is similar to the Security Settings/Public Key policy area, except that it is focused on IE. You can use this area not only to distribute a list of trusted certificate authorities, but also to prevent users from modifying this setting locally.

PROGRAMS The Programs section configures which programs will be launched automatically when a user chooses an Internet service. This enables you to choose the default mail client, HTML editor, and so on that the user will use from inside IE.

SCRIPTS (LOGON/LOGOFF)

These settings are almost identical to the startup/shutdown scripts in the Computer Configuration section of group policy. The obvious difference is that because these are user configuration settings, they are applied when the user logs on or off rather than at the start-up and shutdown of the machine. Chapter 22 covers the syntax and use of scripts.

SECURITY SETTINGS

This section of group policy is identical to its namesake in Computer Configuration, except that it holds only one configurable option—Enterprise Trust, which also is present in Computer Configuration.

REMOTE INSTALLATION SERVICES

Remote Installation Services (RIS) is part of Microsoft's change and configuration management infrastructure. RIS enables you to build a reference Windows 2000 PRO computer and then use the `riprep.exe` tool to make a snapshot of the reference PC. This snapshot is then copied to a disk image on the RIS server and is made available to users and administrators so they can reinstall it on new computers or computers that need to be reset to a known good state. Using RIS and a RIS boot disk, this can be done over the network with a minimum of OS expertise and administrative rights.

CHOICE OPTIONS Figure 21.26 shows the group policy interface to configure RIS client installation options. These options affect how much choice the user has inside the RIS client application, whether or not she can restart a failed setup, and whether or not troubleshooting tools are available to her while she rebuilds the PC. You also set the name of the computer automatically and where its computer account will be created in the Active Directory namespace.

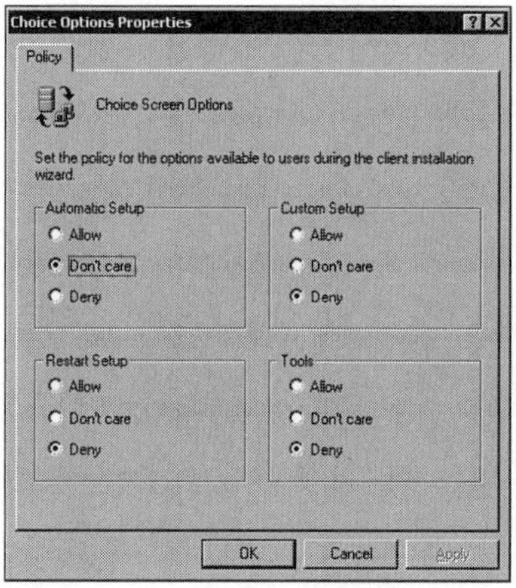

Figure 21.26
Setting RIS group policy.

FOLDER REDIRECTION

You can use the Folder Redirection group policy to cause users' folders that are normally stored on the local machine to be stored remotely on a server. This has several advantages. If the user roams from computer to computer, this enables his documents to move with him. Storing user files centrally also greatly increases the chance of their being backed up consistently. This section has many options, and because they impact the location, security, and availability of user data, we'll look at the options in some detail. You can see the configuration property pages by right-clicking a folder and selecting Properties.

> **Note**
>
> Roaming user profiles are copied across the network from the server to the client every time the user logs on. In contrast, this is not true of redirected folders. They are located on the server; they simply appear to be located locally on the client, but they are not.

The following folders can be redirected to a server location through group policy: Application Data, Desktop, My Documents, My Pictures, and Start Menu. You can choose to redirect some, all, or none of these folders. You also can choose to redirect all users to a central location, or you can separate the users by group. Figure 21.27 shows the Desktop folder redirected for everyone to the redir share on server gold.

When specifying the target setting for the folder, you have three options: No Policy, Basic, and Advanced. Choosing No Policy means the folder will not be redirected. Choosing Basic causes everyone's folder to be redirected to the same location. This is somewhat misleading, though, because you can still specify a unique home folder for each user with the %username% variable. Choosing Advanced enables you to specify a different top-level folder for each

Ch
21

group. You also could separate groups not only by folder but also by server because the interface enables you to specify servername/sharename pairs.

Figure 21.27
Configuring desktop redirection.

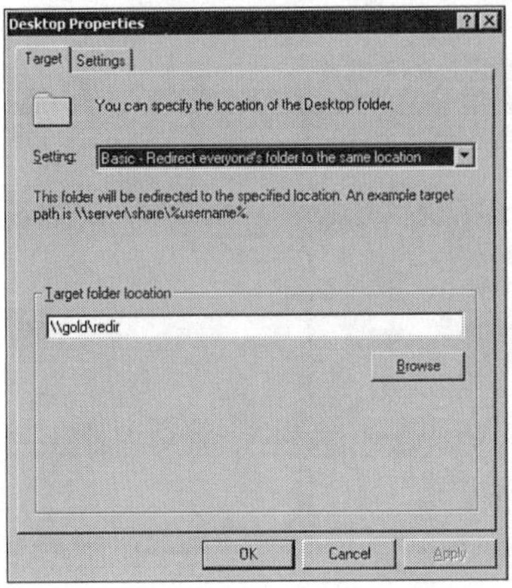

The Settings tab of the group policy property page sets the security of the redirected folder, whether to move contents of the current folder to the redirected folder, and behavior when the group policy is removed. Figure 21.28 shows the Settings tab with the default options set.

Figure 21.28
Desktop redirection settings.

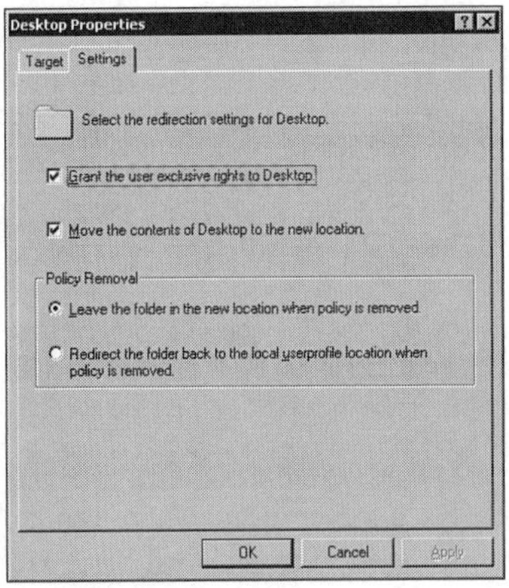

The Grant the User Exclusive Rights to Desktop option sets the permissions so that only the user has any permissions on the redirected folder. Even administrators will not have any permissions here (although they can still take ownership).

Note

> This is similar to the behavior of an autocreated home directory from Windows NT 4 and 2000. Although the user and the system are the objects on the access control list for the folder, the administrator always has take ownership permissions for any filesystem on a Windows 2000 computer. The administrator initially is denied access to the folder, but using the Explorer interface and the Advanced Settings option of the Security tab, the administrator can take ownership of a file or folder and then grant permissions as necessary.

The Move the Contents of Desktop to the New Location option enables the current contents of the folder to be redirected to the new location rather than starting with empty folders.

The final section of this property page configures behavior when the group policy is removed. The default option of Leave the Folder in the New Location When Policy Is Removed causes the folder to remain on the redirected server when the group policy no longer applies. The other option copies the redirected folders to the current location of the user profile—either local or remote—when the group policy is no longer in effect.

ADMINISTRATIVE TEMPLATES

Similar to the Administrative Templates section in the Computer Configuration group policy, these settings are Registry-based policies that are built from the three default administrative templates: system.adm, inetres.adm, and conf.adm. Several common group policy settings exist in the Administrative Templates area, but several policies also exist that are unique to this area.

You can export the group policy from Administrative Templates. Figure 21.29 shows a neat trick you can perform with any group policy folder in the Administrative Templates area. If you right-click any group policy folder and choose Export List, the contents of the folder are copied to the text file you choose in a tab-delimited format. This means you can export the configuration names and settings to a format that can be imported by virtually any database. This is a useful tool in a large enterprise for troubleshooting group policy conflicts.

Figure 21.29
Exporting administrative templates settings.

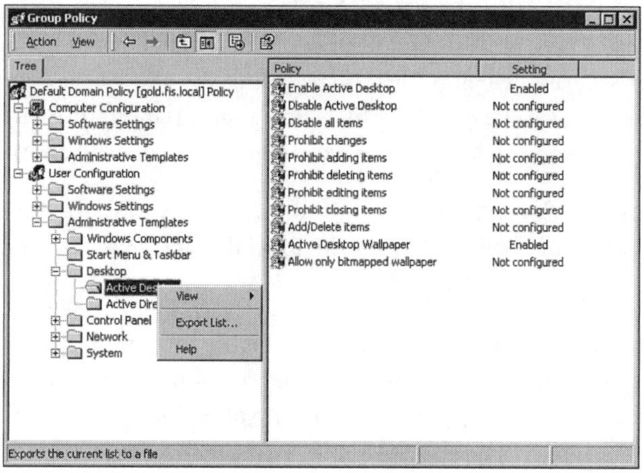

In Figure 21.29, User Configuration, Administrative Templates, Desktop, and Active Desktop were right-clicked. When you select Export List, you are given the opportunity to select a text file and folder in which to save the information. The output appears in Listing 21.1.

LISTING 21.1   CONTENT OUTPUT FOR GROUP POLICY SETTINGS

```
Policy                          Setting
Enable Active Desktop            Enabled
Disable Active Desktop            Not configured
Disable all items               Not configured
Prohibit changes               Not configured
Prohibit adding items           Not configured
Prohibit deleting items           Not configured
Prohibit editing items           Not configured
Prohibit closing items           Not configured
Add/Delete items               Not configured
Active Desktop Wallpaper          Enabled
Allow only bitmapped wallpaper    Not configured
```

> **Note**
>
> When you save this information and then display it in a text editor such as Notepad, the text might not be as well formatted as shown here. When you attempt to import it into a database, however, it will import smoothly because it is a tab-separated format, which is easily readable by most database import tools, such as BCP or Data Transformation Services on Microsoft SQL Server 7.

WINDOWS COMPONENTS

The Windows Components group policy has many sections in common with its namesake in Computer Configuration. In addition, several new sections exist that do not appear in the Computer Configuration version.

NETMEETING   The most obvious difference you will notice between the computer and user NetMeeting group policies is the former has 1 configurable option, whereas the latter has 32. NetMeeting is a very powerful application. The options in this group policy node generally affect either security or bandwidth. NetMeeting can allow other users to control your desktop, and this needs to be enabled only when appropriate. It also enables the sending and receiving of video streams, which can be demanding on network bandwidth.

INTERNET EXPLORER   Several group policy nodes enable you to modify Internet Explorer. This section is primarily focused on locking down the user interface and disallowing any changes to the corporate standard for IE.

WINDOWS EXPLORER   If you want to present a highly focused desktop environment to your users, the Windows Explorer group policy is an area of particular interest. Here, you can hide drives or most of the network and even control the navigation of the Common Open File dialog box.

MICROSOFT MANAGEMENT CONSOLE   The MMC is the default container for virtually every management snap-in on a Windows 2000 computer. With this group policy, you can limit which snap-ins are available to users and whether or not the MMC can be used in author mode. In author mode, users can create their own customized collections of loaded MMC snap-ins.

TASK SCHEDULER   This group policy node is identical to the Computer Configuration version. Refer to "Task Scheduler" in "Computer Configuration."

WINDOWS INSTALLER   Although the Windows Installer group policy in User Configuration is smaller than the same node in Computer Configuration, some new settings are available here. One of the most interesting is the Disable Media Source for Any Install setting. With this enabled, you can prevent users from installing any software that is not provided by group policy and the Windows Installer service.

START MENU AND TASKBAR

This group policy node enables you to make highly visible changes to the desktop configuration for the user. This provides more opportunity to provide a highly focused environment for users. With these options, and other options available in the Administrative Templates group policy, you can greatly constrict the choices a user has on her desktop.

DESKTOP

This is another group policy with many configurable options that immediately impact users. Most of the icons that normally appear on a standard Windows 2000 desktop can be removed here. Even though a particular icon is removed from the desktop, it does not mean it is not available by other means. You therefore must make sure you have removed all access to a particular feature if that is your goal.

ACTIVE DESKTOP   The Active Desktop enables you to set HTML wallpapers and add Web-based content to the desktop. Here, you also can enable or disable Active Desktop and also restrict the users' ability to remove or edit HTML content on the desktop.

ACTIVE DIRECTORY   The Active Directory group policy enables you to configure and restrict Active Directory searches. Active Directory can consume many resources on remote servers. Here you can restrict the size of the resultset from an AD search and control the availability of the Active Directory folder in My Network Places.

CONTROL PANEL

The Control Panel group policy enables you to lock down access to tools and options in the Windows 2000 Control Panel. You can completely disable Control Panel or just certain applets.

ADD/REMOVE PROGRAMS   This group policy sets the behavior of the Add/Remove Programs Control Panel applet. You can completely remove it, remove the ability to use the applet to install software from removable media, or hide certain portions of the applet.

DISPLAY   This group policy sets the user's level of control over modifying the display properties and the screensaver. You can require the screensaver to be password protected or completely disable screensavers.

PRINTERS   The Printers group policy can be used to restrict the addition and deletion of printers from the local computer and set the default search path for network printers.

REGIONAL OPTIONS   This group policy can set the required language to be used for Windows 2000 menus and dialog boxes.

NETWORK

The user Network group policy, similar to the computer Network group policy, has two nodes—Offline Files, and Network and Dial-Up Connections.

OFFLINE FILES   Similar to the same area in Computer Configuration, this sets the behavior for offline files. This setting enables you to keep a copy of files on both the local computer and a shared network server. Files can be modified while disconnected from the network and then synchronized with the server version the next time you connect.

NETWORK AND DIAL-UP CONNECTIONS   This group policy sets the level of user choice over network connections. It determines a user's ability to create and modify network settings and connect LAN and RAS sessions. Because network configuration rarely should be attempted by desktop users, this is a good folder to restrict to avoid unnecessary reconfiguration.

SYSTEM

The System area enables you to disable the command prompt, require code signing for device drivers, and download missing COM components. It also has two subfolders: Logon/Logoff and Group Policy.

LOGON/LOGOFF   This group policy sets the environment at logon and logoff. Here you can decide whether the user can change his password with the Ctrl+Alt+Delete security dialog box, set the behavior of logon/logoff scripts, and run executable programs at logon.

GROUP POLICY   The Group Policy section sets options for configuring and applying group policy. You can set the default refresh rate for group policy, values for slow link detection, and the behavior for .adm template files.

SUMMARY

Literally hundreds of options are available in group policy. Group policy can be applied to computers or users. The options range from the mundane, such as logon scripts, to the arcane, such as Kerberos and PKI.

TROUBLESHOOTING

CHANGES AREN'T BEING SAVED

I've made changes to group policy, and the changes have disappeared.

If multiple administrators are using the group policy interface, the last writer wins. A good policy is to identify a particular console or administrator to modify group policy.

ASSIGNED SOFTWARE DOESN'T INSTALL

I have assigned software to an OU, but the software is not automatically installed.

Check the group policy and make sure the software was assigned rather than published. If it is published, the user still has to use Add/Remove Programs to install the software.

LOGON SCRIPTS AREN'T RUNNING

I have created a group policy to assign logon scripts to users, but the scripts are not running.

Make sure you can resolve the share that the scripts are on. If you can't "see" it, you can't execute it.

PROBLEMS WITH GROUP POLICY AND 98 AND NT CLIENTS

Group policy is not being applied to my 98 or NT clients.

Group policy currently has no effect on non–Windows 2000 clients. Group policy is processed by Windows 2000 clients only.

CHAPTER 22

MANAGING GROUP POLICY

In this chapter

OVERVIEW OF GROUP POLICY ADMINISTRATION

Chapter 21, "Group Policy Sections," discussed every node in the computer and user group policies to familiarize you with their possibilities. By now it should be obvious that virtually anything can be set by group policy. Indeed, many extremely important, domain-wide options are set in group policy and nowhere else.

This chapter looks at the day-to-day creation, application, and management of group policy. A series of rules surround applying group policy to users and computers and how an object's location in Active Directory can affect which group policy is applied to that object.

The last chapter focused on the Group Policy Editor. Here you look at many of the options you have for creating properties, modifying properties, and linking group policy. This chapter uses the same organizational unit (OU) used in Chapter 20, "Group Policy," to demonstrate group policy.

THE GROUP POLICY TAB

The Group Policy tab of the OU Properties page can be seen in Figure 22.1. You can reach this page by right-clicking your OU and choosing Properties. Almost all your management of group policy begins with this page. Because group policy can be linked to a site, a domain, or an organizational unit, you will find this tab available from the Properties page of any of those objects.

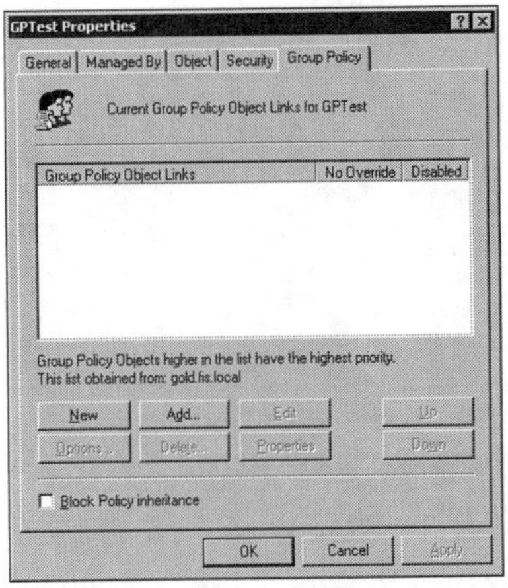

Figure 22.1
Using the Group Policy tab on the GPTest Properties page.

NEW

When you click the New button, a new group policy is created, called (by default) New Group Policy Object. It is created in the Group Policy Object Links window shown in Figure 22.1. This can and should be renamed to something more descriptive. One of the most common group policy troubleshooting issues is the collision of configured settings. If you organize and name your group policy by effect, keeping track of changes is easier.

ADD

If you click the Add button on the Group Policy tab shown in Figure 22.1, you see the Add a Group Policy Object Link dialog box shown in Figure 22.2. The difference between New and Add is that you can use group policy objects located in other areas of the Active Directory and link them to sites, domains, or organizational units. You can even reach across the forest and link to group policy in other domains.

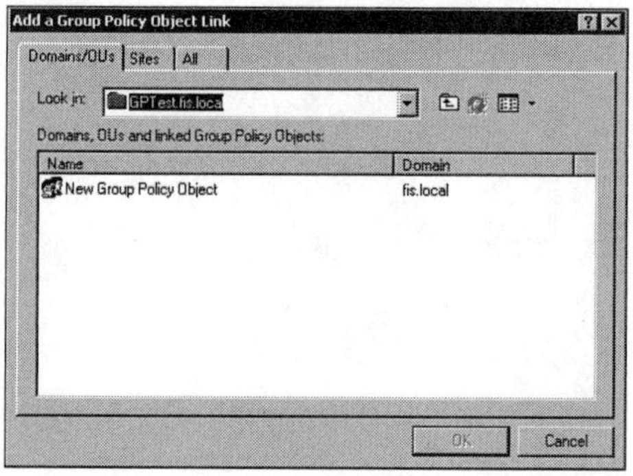

Figure 22.2
Using the Add button to link an existing group policy.

The Domains/OUs, Sites, and All tabs enable you to search the Active Directory for group policy objects linked to other containers in the AD and use them, rather than start from scratch with a new group policy. Figure 22.3 shows the All tab of the Add a Group Policy Object Link dialog box. On this page, by default, you see all the group policy objects currently available in this domain.

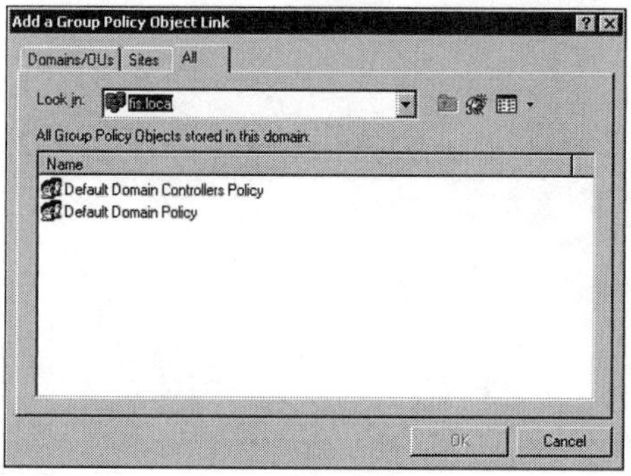

Figure 22.3
Searching the domain for group policy.

You can search by site, domains, or organizational units. Although the group policies shown in Figure 22.3 are the default group policies created when a domain is installed, a large enterprise will have many group policies. To read information about the group policy, right-click the group policy name and choose Properties. This opens the Policy Properties page shown in Figure 22.4. The section "Properties," later in this chapter, discusses the Policy Properties page in more detail.

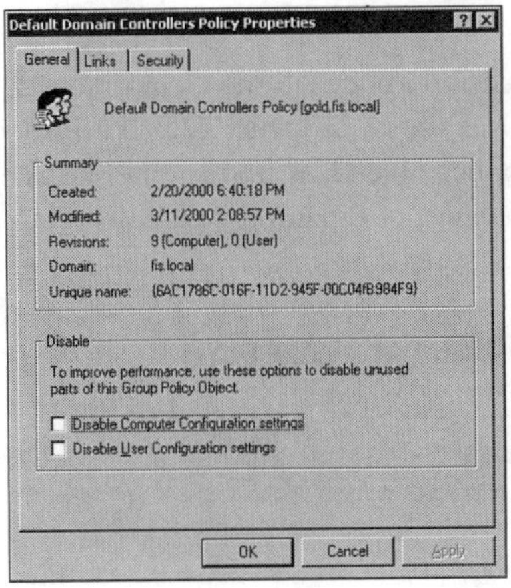

Figure 22.4
Viewing the proper-
ties of a group policy.

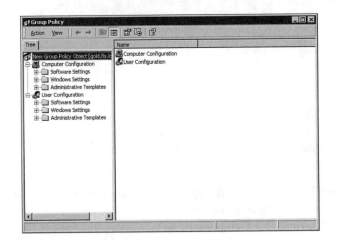

EDIT

When you select a group policy and click Edit, you see the screen shown in Figure 22.5. Because Chapter 21 discussed the Group Policy Editor in detail, we will not revisit this tool here.

Note When the Group Policy Editor is opened, its focus is on the domain controller (DC) that currently holds the PDC Emulator Operations Master. If you override this and set the focus to another DC, you increase the risk of having your modifications to the group policy over-written through replication. The best environment has a high degree of cooperation among the administrators when modifying group policy.

Figure 22.5
Using the Group
Policy Editor.

OPTIONS

Clicking the Options button pops up the New Group Policy Object Options dialog box you see in Figure 22.6. Here you can set No Override, which prevents group policy lower in the

Active Directory hierarchy from overriding settings in this group policy. On the Group Policy tab, you can see the Block Policy Inheritance option (refer to Figure 22.1). This is the opposite of No Override. Selecting Block Policy Inheritance means that you do not want any configuration from higher-level group policy to be inherited by objects in this container or any child container. If a conflict occurs between Block Policy Inheritance and No Override, No Override wins, which means the group policy set higher in the Active Directory hierarchy takes effect.

Figure 22.6
Setting group policy options.

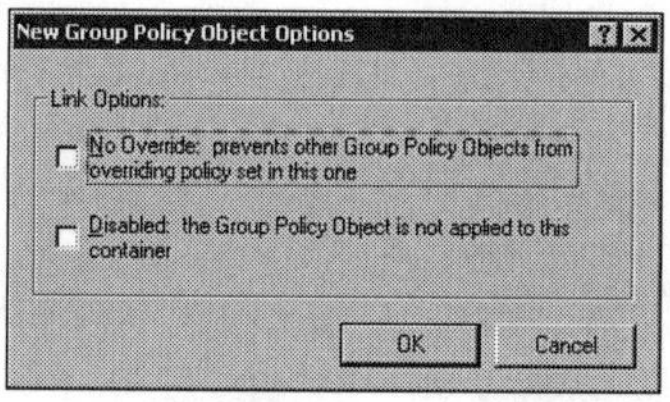

Note

You should use the Block Policy Inheritance and No Override settings very sparingly. Tracking down why a group policy does or does not take effect the way you expected is complex enough without adding these two variables.

Selecting the Disabled check box causes the selected group policy to not be applied to the OU. This is especially useful if you are in a long editing session and do not want interim changes to the group policy to be propagated to clients until you finish and enable the group policy.

DELETE

The Delete option is not as obvious as it seems. When you click the Delete button, you are presented with the choices shown in Figure 22.7. You can choose to permanently delete the group policy or simply unlink it from the current container. Removing the link is conceptually the opposite of clicking the Add button. If you choose to unlink the group policy, you can link it to other container objects or relink it to this one using the Add button.

Figure 22.7
Managing group policy links.

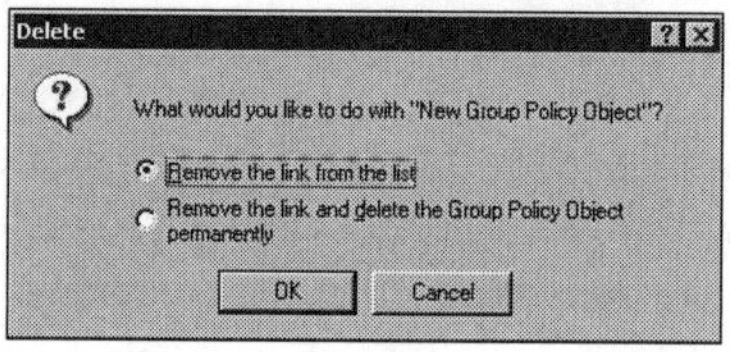

PROPERTIES

Clicking the Properties button opens the New Group Policy Object Properties page shown in Figure 22.8. This page has three tabs: General, Links, and Security.

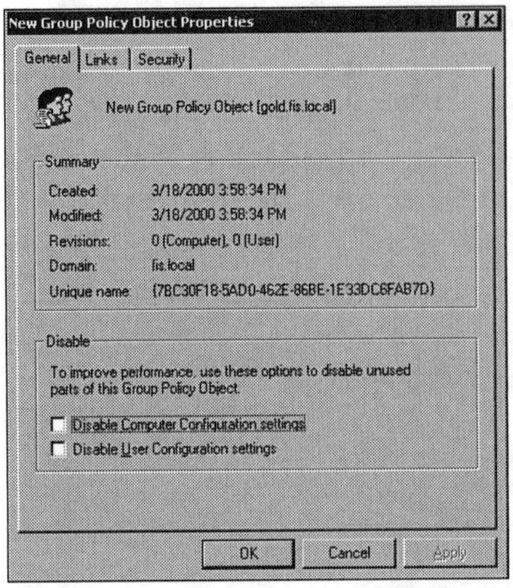

Figure 22.8
Managing group policy properties.

The General tab has summary information about when the group policy was created and modified and information used by the Active Directory to invoke the group policy. The Created and Modified values are timestamps. Revisions is an integer that is incremented every time the group policy is modified. When a user logs on, Active Directory checks the revision numbers of the group policy before it was parsed and applied. If the group policy revision numbers are the same as the last time it was applied, the group policy has not been modified since the last time the user logged on and does not need to be reapplied. This significantly speeds up the logon process for the user and saves network bandwidth.

The Domain information in the Summary area is the location of the group policy. The Unique Name is a globally unique identifier (GUID), a system-generated number used to track objects in the Active Directory. Because part of the information about a group policy is kept in the Active Directory and part is kept on the filesystem, this GUID becomes the connection point for keeping this information synchronized.

The Disable section of the New Group Policy Object Properties page enables you to selectively disable either the computer or user section of a group policy. If the user or computer section has no configured options, you can disable it. This causes the Active Directory to ignore that section when group policy is being applied, speeding the group policy application and logon process.

The Links tab of the New Group Policy Object Properties page shows any other container objects that might be linked to this group policy. If you work in a large enterprise, you probably should check this before you modify or delete a group policy because it could be used by sites, domains, or organizational units other than the currently selected ones. Figure 22.9 shows the Links tab after the Find Now button has been clicked, which causes a search of the domain for other containers linked to this group policy.

The Security tab of the New Group Policy Object Properties page is an important section because, for any user to be impacted by group policy, he must have the read and apply group policy permissions for the group policy object. Later, this chapter covers various security issues surrounding group policy. Figure 22.10 shows the Security tab with the default permissions.

Figure 22.9
Using the Links tab to search for domains or organizational units that are linked to this group policy.

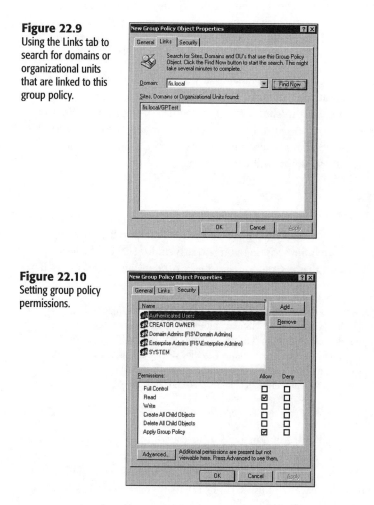

Figure 22.10
Setting group policy permissions.

The Authenticated Users global group is, by default, everyone who is authenticated to the domain. This group has read and apply group policy permissions for the group policy. This allows anyone who is logged on to the domain and whose user object is a member of a container object that inherits this group policy to apply this group policy.

FEATURES OF GROUP POLICY

In the next few sections of this chapter, you look at several technologies that are most commonly used with group policy. These are not completely exclusive to group policy. For example, you can use logon scripts outside group policy, but their true power becomes evident when they are used in conjunction with group policy.

LOGON SCRIPTS

This section discusses logon scripts and software installation through group policy. Although group policy has other features, such as the capability to manage the public key infrastructure (PKI), Kerberos, and IPSec, these technologies are covered in later chapters— or in the case of IPSec, other books.

Naming this section "Logon Scripts" is really a misnomer because you actually can take virtually any .vbs file and execute it at the command line. You also can attach it to a computer through group policy and run it at startup/shutdown or attach it to user group policy and run it as a logon/logon script. They are referred to as *logon scripts* in this section, however, for two reasons. First, until now, attaching a script to a user could be done only at logon. Second, that is probably where these scripts will continue to be used the most.

WINDOWS SCRIPTING HOST

The Windows Scripting Host (WSH) 2.0 is the underlying scripting architecture that makes logon scripts in group policy possible. It is difficult to overstate the importance of scripting in Windows 2000. This is not the batch file scripting you had in Windows NT. This is a full-featured, 32-bit, scripting language that is Component Object Model Plus (COM+) based.

> **Note**
>
> Although this is not a book about COM+, writing about WSH without mentioning COM+ is difficult. In a nutshell, COM+ is a programming technology that defines a contract between applications and discreet units of functionality called *COM+ servers*. This contract states not what it will do or how it will do it, but simply how they will communicate. These COM+ servers are dynamic link libraries (DLLs). You can do virtually anything with a COM+ DLL. Much of the functionality with WSH this chapter exposes is through system-supplied COM DLLs, but you also can (usually easily) write your own.

With no additional tools other than the components supplied with the Windows 2000 operating system, you can map drives, connect to printers, load applications in memory, check for the existence of files and folders, and (if necessary) create files and folders. You can use WSH to send mail and update databases and use COM+ DLLs that are hosted. Anyone who has professionally managed a UNIX server will tell you that much of the work he does is encapsulated in scripts. The emphasis in this chapter is on the use of WSH for logon scripts, but their functionality as management scripts should not be ignored.

Let's first look at how to write and execute some simple WSH scripts; then we'll take a brief look at VBScript syntax. Finally, you will write a useful logon script and attach it to a group policy.

> **Note**
>
> Although you will use VBScript for the following examples, the default allows both VBScript and JScript. In addition, WSH is extensible to other scripting engines, such as Perl.

VBSCRIPT SYNTAX

One of the best things about learning to use Visual Basic Scripting is how flexible it is. The same code you write here can be used almost without modification in an Active Server page, in client-side VBScript functions in a Web page, inside Office 2000 as VB for Applications, or in a regular forms-based Visual Basic application. Literally hundreds of good books on VB are available, and this will not attempt to be another. But let's take a look at some basics.

A SIMPLE VBSCRIPT EXAMPLE

In the time-honored tradition of programming books everywhere, the first example simply writes "hello world" to the screen. Setting this up requires no extra programming tools. You can write it in Notepad or use Copy Con to create a text file. Creating a basic program is easy: Simply create a text file with the filename `hello.vbs` and add the following text:

```
msgbox "hello world"
```

Wow. Everyone still with me? I know that was tough. Now it is time to execute the program. This is almost as demanding as writing it. Simply type the fully qualified pathname of the program—for example, `c:\hello.vbs`—or find it in Windows Explorer and double-click it. Either method causes the output you see in Figure 22.11.

Figure 22.11
Executing a simple script.

The simplicity inherent in trivial VBScript programs sometimes belies the power. Just because creating simple programs is easy doesn't mean you can't do any real work with them.

SAMPLE LOGON SCRIPT

This next example does some actual work. In it, you use scripting to help set the environment for a user. You map a network drive, connect to a printer, and load Internet Explorer into memory on the desktop. At the end of this chapter, you will take the examples of the features of group policy and pull them together to create a group policy that would be very useful in a real-world environment. The logon script appears in Listing 22.1.

> **Note**
>
> The ' character is simply one of the ways you can document your scripts.

LISTING 22.1 SAMPLE VBSCRIPT LOGON SCRIPT

```
'   declare variables
dim wshnetwork
dim ie

'   suppress error messages
on error resume next
```

LISTING 22.1   CONTINUED

```
'   set reference to WSH network object
set wshnetwork=wscript.createobject("wscript.network")

'   remove network drive in case it is already in use
wshnetwork.removenetworkdrive "z:"

'   add network drive
wshnetwork.mapnetworkdrive "z:","\\gold\dl"

'   add connection to a network printer
wshnetwork.addwindowsprinterconnection "\\gold\hp5"

'   set new printer as default printer
wshnetwork.setdefaultprinter "\\gold\hp5"

'   set reference to Internet Explorer object
set ie=createobject("internetexplorer.application")

'   load microsoft home page
ie.navigate"http://www.microsoft.com"

'   make application visible
ie.visible=true
```

THE LOGON SCRIPT LINE BY LINE

This logon script does three things. It maps the z: drive to the dl share on server gold; it maps to and sets as the default printer the hp5 printer on server gold; and it loads the Internet Explorer application with the www.microsoft.com page loaded. Let's walk through the script one line at a time and talk about what happens.

In the 'declare variables section, you set aside space in memory for your two variables: wshnetwork and ie. Notice that you do not declare the variables as a particular data type. That is because in VBScript you get only one datatype—variant. Therefore, you don't have to declare the datatype.

The 'suppress error messages section is really quite interesting. The on error resume next command tells the script that, rather than halting on any error (the default behavior), it will suppress error messages and continue the script.

Note

Do not enable the on error resume next command during the creation and debugging of the scripts. If you do and you have problems with your script, it simply dies and you will never receive any error output of any kind. If you have this command in your script, comment it out with a ', and then enable it when you are ready to distribute the script.

You need the on error resume next command because if you try to add a network drive that is already mapped to z:, you receive an error and the script terminates. Additionally, if you do not have z: mapped and you try to remove it, you receive an error and the script terminates.

(That seems perversely predictable, doesn't it?) This command enables you to set the commands and recover from inevitable errors.

The `'set reference to WSH network object` section loads the `wscript.network` object into memory. When you call this code, what actually happens is the `wscript.network` progID is used to find `clsid` (`HKEY_CLASSES_ROOT\CLSID\{F935DC26-1CF0-11D0-ADB9-00C04FD58A0B}`). One of the properties of `clsid` is the `inprocserver32` key. This is a fully qualified pathname to the DLL `\WINNT\System32\wshom.ocx`. This DLL then is loaded into memory, and the methods of this COM object are now available to you. Conceptually, the same thing happens when you load the `InternetExplorer.Application` object. The process you are causing here is called *instantiation*. It is simply loading a COM object into memory and establishing a relationship with it so you can use its functionality.

The `'remove network drive` section ensures that another network connection is not using the `z:` drive you want to use. The command is simple and takes one parameter: the drive letter you want to free. Part of the point of this logon script is to provide the same environment every time you log on. Because creating persistent network connections is possible either at the command line or with Internet Explorer, you use this command to ensure that another network connection is not currently attached to this drive letter.

The `'add network drive` section takes two parameters, the letter to which you want to attach this and the sharename you want to attach. You must make sure beforehand that the share is available and that the intended user has sufficient permissions to use the share. The effects of this line of code can be seen in Figure 22.12.

Figure 22.12
Using Explorer to see that your network drive has been added.

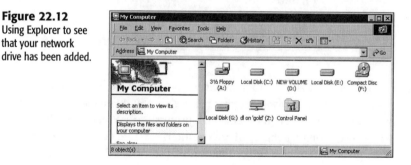

The `'add connection to a network printer` section takes one parameter—the Universal Naming Convention (UNC) of the printer share. Make sure you use the `addwindowsprinterconnection` method rather than the old WSH 1.0 `addprinterconnection` method. The old version does not work well with Windows 2000. The effect of this line of code can be seen in Figure 22.13.

The `'set reference to Internet Explorer object` section of code instantiates the IE application object and makes it available.

The `'load microsoft home page` section uses the `navigate` method of the IE object to load the Microsoft home page or any page you choose. A good choice for this parameter is an

informational page on your corporate intranet that is updated daily with information your
users need.

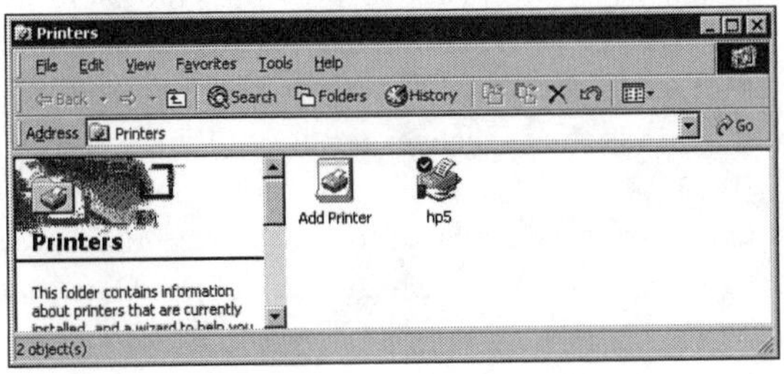

Figure 22.13
The network printer
has been added by
your logon script.

Because many COM objects run without a visible component, you must explicitly make the
application visible. The `make application visible` section of code enables you to see the
final effect of your logon script, the loading of IE (see Figure 22.14).

Figure 22.14
Internet Explorer is
opened and a specific
page is loaded via
script.

You don't have to become a Visual Basic programmer to take advantage of group policy.
Hundreds of configurable options are available that require absolutely no coding. I believe,
however, that in the future the mark of an experienced, professional Windows 2000 manager will be a facility with a scripting language. Many situations respond very well to scripting,
whether it is logon scripts as shown here or the multitude of scenarios that can be answered
through administrative scripting.

You have just grazed the surface of what is possible with logon scripts. The entire Windows
2000, Office 2000, and Windows Management Instrumentation (WMI) object models are
open to you using the Windows Scripting Host. The WSH programming environment is
very well documented on the Microsoft Developer Network site, as well as on many other
third-party sites throughout the Internet.

ATTACHING A LOGON SCRIPT THROUGH GROUP POLICY

After you have written or identified your WSH script, you can attach it to a site, a domain,
or an OU through group policy. First, you must choose the container object you want to
receive the logon script. For this example, you have identified an OU called support, which

will use your logon script. These are desktop support people for one of your business units, and you want to configure the desktop when they log on, so that certain tools and features will always be available to them.

First, you must open the Group Policy Editor. Because you are applying this script to users, you must choose the User Configuration, Windows Settings, Scripts node of group policy (see Figure 22.15).

Figure 22.15
Using the Scripts node under User Configuration to attach a logon script.

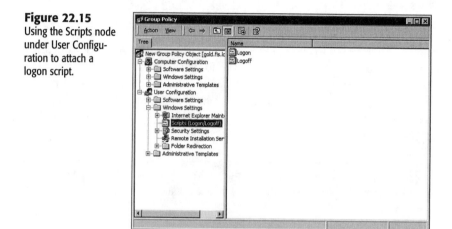

To apply a logon script here, you must double-click the Logon icon in the Name pane of the Group Policy Editor. This opens the Logon Properties page shown in Figure 22.16. Here you can assign and configure one or more logon scripts for this group policy.

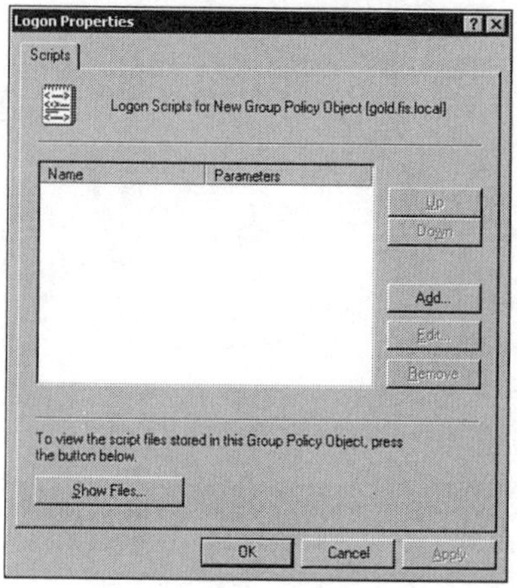

Figure 22.16
The Logon Properties page is where you add the path to your logon script.

At this point, to understand what you are going to do next, you need to understand a little bit about group policy architecture. A group policy object is really made up of two things: a group policy container, which is information about the group policy stored in the Active

Directory, and a group policy template, which is a series of filesystem objects (files and folders). The group policy identifier is the GUID, which is a system-generated hexadecimal number used to synchronize the information in the AD with the filesystem. The group policy container is replicated to other domain controllers through normal AD replication, but the group policy template is replicated to other DCs through the File Replication Service (FRS).

If you want your logon script to be universally available, you must copy it to the scripts subdirectory of your group policy template. To do so, simply use Explorer and right-click and copy your file; then click the Show Files button (refer to Figure 22.16). This opens the Logon page shown in Figure 22.17. You can then paste the file into this page. After you have done so, this file is replicated to all the other domain controllers in your domain. You don't have to copy the logon script to the Logon folder for your logon script to work. For this group policy to function predictably on all DCs, however, you must make sure that the logon script is available on all DCs in your domain. Placing the script so that it will be automatically replicated by the File Replication Service is the easiest way to accomplish this.

➔ **See** "File Replication Service," **p. 409**

Note

Notice the path at the top of Figure 22.17. This is the filesystem path to the SysVol share on the local domain controller. Because the GUID is the name of the group policy, the folder is named using the GUID.

Figure 22.17
The Logon folder on the SysVol share.

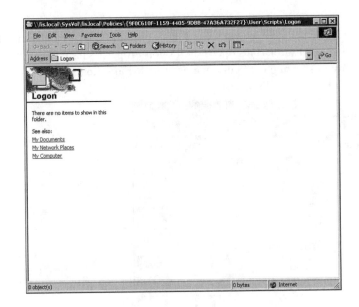

When you close the Logon page, you can click the Add button on the Logon Properties page to add your logon script. This opens the Add a Script dialog box shown in Figure 22.18.

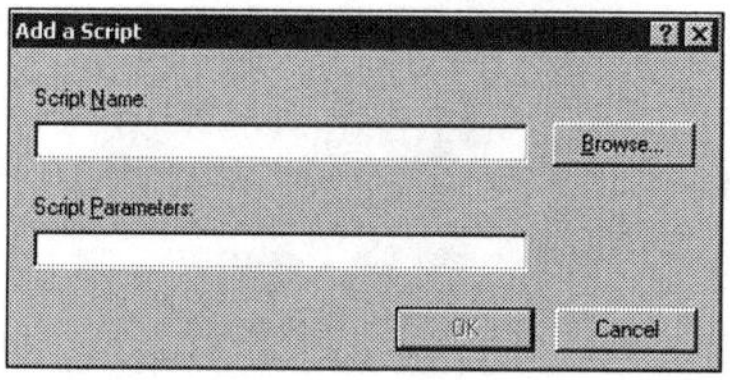

Figure 22.18
Providing a pathname
and parameters for
your logon script.

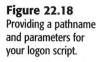

You can either type in the name of your script or use the Browse button. If you have added your script to the Logon folder, it will appear in the Browse page shown in Figure 22.19. You can simply select it and click Open. This returns you to the Add a Script page, where you can click OK. Doing so causes your script to be applied as a logon script to this group policy. Remember that every edit is an implied save in the Group Policy Editor.

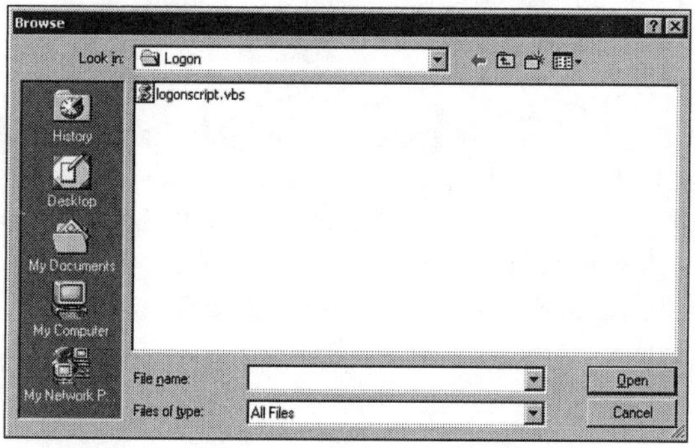

Figure 22.19
Browsing for your
logon script.

Although we have demonstrated applying a script to the logon event for a user, remember that you can apply scripts at the startup/shutdown of a computer and the logon/logoff of a user using group policy.

INSTALLING SOFTWARE THROUGH GROUP POLICY

This is another feature of group policy that is not completely limited to group policy. You can use the Windows Installer Service to install software at the command line or through the Explorer, but the true power of this architecture becomes evident through group policy. With group policy, you can leverage the functionality of the Windows Installer Service to apply software en masse to as many clients as you choose. And you can do so with the same management investment it takes you to set up group policy for one machine or user.

WINDOWS INSTALLER SERVICE

The Windows Installer Service is responsible for installing, maintaining, and repairing software on a Windows 2000 computer. Proper use of the Windows Installer Service requires that software installation packages be in a Windows Installer or .msi format. The .msi file is a database of Registry settings, desktop and Start menu shortcuts, and the files that make up an application. The Windows Installer Service also enables transactional installation of software.

FEATURES OF NATIVE WINDOWS INSTALLER PACKAGES

Two kinds of Windows Installer packages exist, native and repackaged. A *native* package is created by the developer who wrote the application and requires a high degree of knowledge about the files, shortcuts, Registry entries, and so on that comprise the application. A *repackaged* application, on the other hand, can be created by anyone who has access to the appropriate software. The Winstall LE software that ships on the Windows 2000 CD can be used to create repackaged applications.

SELF-REPAIRING

Upon startup, an installed native Windows Installer package checks to see whether the requested files for the feature of the application are available. If they are not—or if they are corrupted—the Windows Installer Service attempts to reinstall only the files necessary to restore functionality to the application.

ON DEMAND INSTALL

Windows Installer packaged applications are frequently separated into features. For example, if you use group policy to install Office 2000 and you use only Word and Excel, these are the only features of that product that will ever be installed. All the other features will not take up hard drive space or the bandwidth necessary to install. However, if a user ever tries to use them, if the source files are still available in their original location on the network, the feature will be installed.

ELEVATED PRIVILEGES

You also can set a native application to install with *elevated* privileges. This means the application does not install using the credentials of the currently logged on user, but rather uses a separate set of credentials with the authority to install software. This can be controlled through group policy.

ASSIGNING AND PUBLISHING SOFTWARE THROUGH GROUP POLICY

You can assign software through group policy—both to users and computers. In contrast, however, you can publish software only to users. The difference is important, as you will see in this chapter. Assigned software is installed without user intervention the next time either the computer is booted or the user logs on, depending on whether the software was assigned to the user or computer. Published software is available through the Add/Remove Programs icon in Control Panel and is easy to install, but the user must choose to install. With assigned software, however, the software is installed regardless of the desires of the user.

The subtleties of assigned software can be confusing. If software is assigned to the computer, the files that comprise the software are copied to the local computer during the boot process. On the other hand, if the software is assigned to the user, the files are copied when the user invokes the software either by opening a data file associated with the application or by choosing the application from the Start menu. In either case, the Start menu is updated to show the new application before the desktop is displayed, and a brief configuration process occurs, which runs the first time the software is used.

AN EXAMPLE OF ASSIGN AND PUBLISH

In this example, you use two Windows Installer files that ship on the Windows 2000 CD: adminpak.msi and 2000rkst.msi. adminpak.msi contains many of the Windows 2000 management tools, and 2000rkst.msi contains the Windows 2000 support tools.

You will assign the support tools to the computer and publish the management tools to the user. This will cause the support tools to be fully installed before the Ctrl+Alt+Delete Logon box is displayed. The management tools require an overt act on the part of the user to be installed. But if she decides to install them, they will be easily available and the installation, upgrade, and removal will be completely guided by the Windows Installer Service.

To begin, you must create or identify a group policy object. You then use the Support OU you used in the earlier section "Logon Scripts." Next, along with the logon script, you set every computer in its OU to automatically receive the support tools. You also make the management tools a mouse click away. Figure 22.20 shows the Group Policy Editor open to the Software Installation Group Policy nodes you will modify.

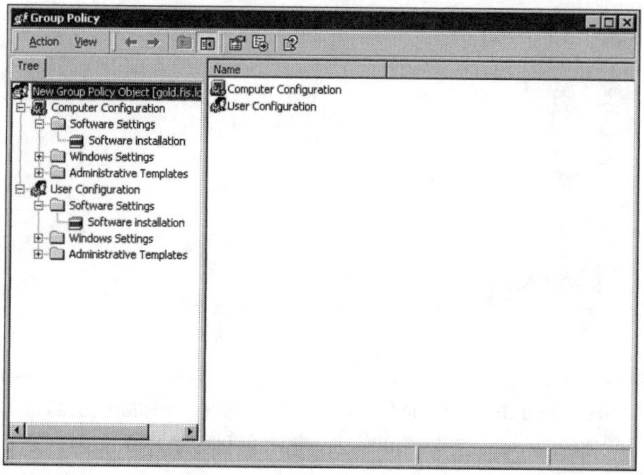

Figure 22.20
Using the Software Installation nodes for both computers and users.

To assign the support tools to the computers in the Support OU, select the Software Installation node under Computer Configuration, Software Settings (see Figure 22.21). Then, right-click the node and select New, Package.

This pops up the Open dialog box shown in Figure 22.22, enabling you to type the name of the network share that hosts your installation source. This can be a distributed filesystem (DFS) share or a simple network share. Your Windows Installer Service package, 2000rkst.msi, is available on \\gold\softinstall\support\2000RKST.MSI.

After you have entered the UNC path and filename of your installation source and clicked OK, you are presented with the Deploy Software dialog box shown in Figure 22.23. This page lets you select a deployment method: Published, Assigned, or Advanced Published or Assigned.

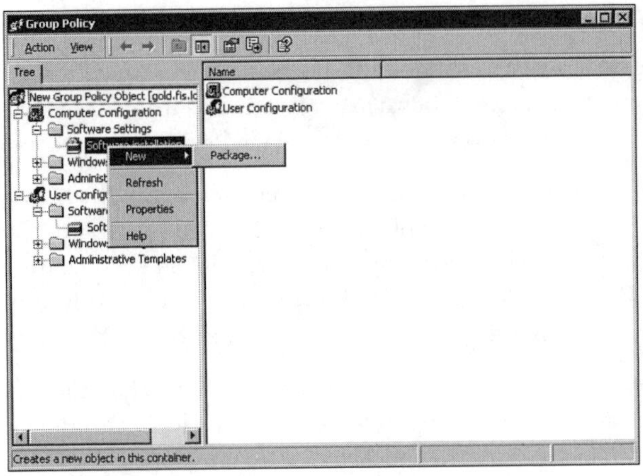

Figure 22.21
Adding a new MSI package to be installed.

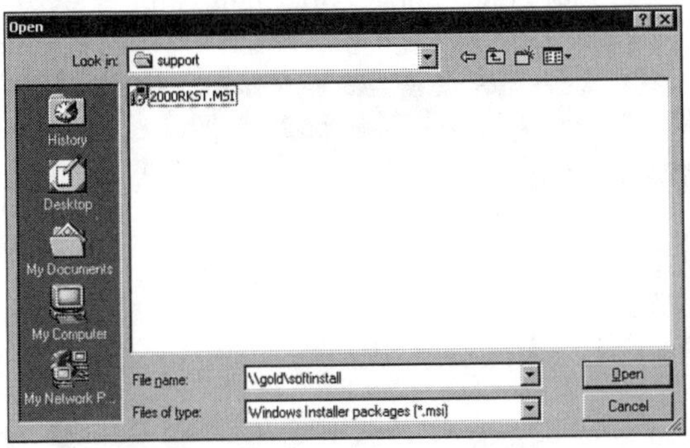

Figure 22.22
Browsing for your package.

> **Note**   The reason the Published option is not enabled in Figure 22.23 is that publishing software to a computer is not possible; it can be published only to a user.

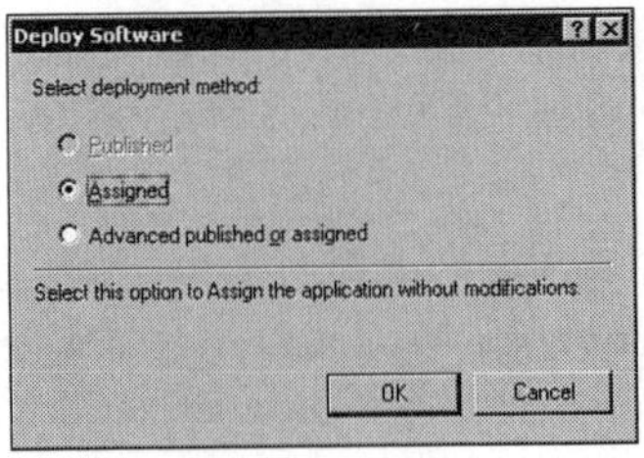

Figure 22.23
Choosing a deployment method: Published or Assigned.

If you choose Assigned, your group policy is configured with the default deployment options for this software package. The result appears in Figure 22.24. This is really all that is required for a basic assignment: Choose the group policy, assign or publish the package, and document where the package is located.

Figure 22.24
Your package is successfully assigned.

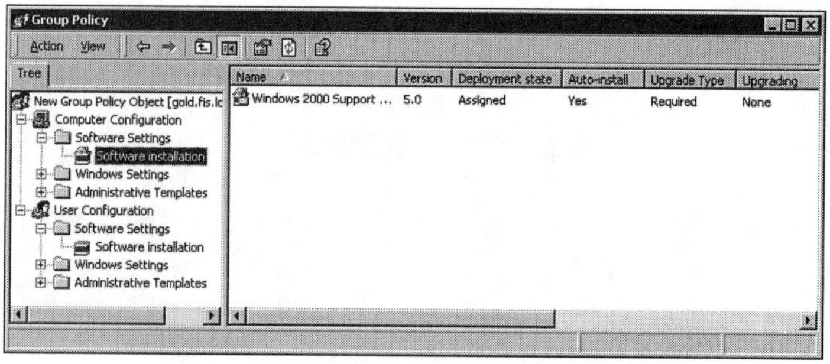

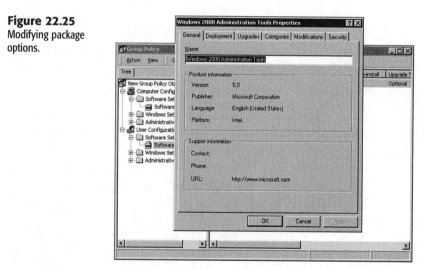

Publishing the `adminpak.msi` administrative tools is similar to the previously described process. We will take the time, however, in this section to document some of the options that are available when you assign or publish software. To publish the Administrative Tools Windows Installer package to all the users affected by this group policy, you must begin on the User Configuration, Software Settings, Software Installation node. After you have right-clicked the node and chosen New Package, you are presented with the same options you saw in the previous section. Here, you have chosen Advanced Published or Assigned and clicked OK. This opens the Windows 2000 Administration Tools Properties page shown in Figure 22.25.

Figure 22.25
Modifying package options.

Note

If you choose Published or Assigned, you are not presented with the Properties page. To display the Properties page for an application package, simply right-click the package and select Properties.

The General tab shown in Figure 22.25 is primarily an informational page. You can see product information, version numbers, and support information.

The Deployment Tab, shown in Figure 22.26, enables you to configure the package deployment options. Figure 22.26 shows the default settings.

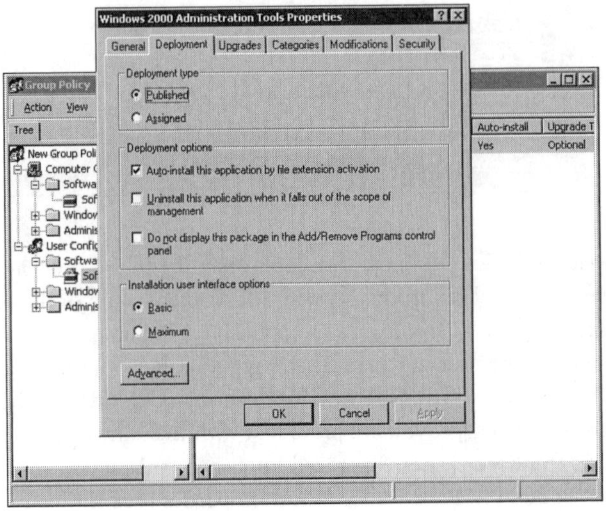

Figure 22.26
Modifying deployment and uninstall options.

The Deployment Type simply enables you to choose Published or Assigned. Published has been chosen for this package. It might not be automatically installed, but it will appear in the Control Panel, Add/Remove Programs icon.

Deployment Options has three configurable settings:

- **Auto-Install This Application by File Extension Activation**—This option causes the application to be automatically installed through document invocation. If you execute a document whose file extension is registered to this application, the application is installed using the Windows Installer.

- **Uninstall This Application When It Falls Out of the Scope of Management**— Although you can use group policy to install and uninstall software, this setting causes the software to uninstall even if you move the user from this OU.

- **Do Not Display This Package in the Add/Remove Programs Control Panel**—The application, if published, does not appear in Control Panel. But it can still be installed through document invocation.

The Installation User Interface Options section configures how much control the user will have during the install process.

The Upgrades tab, shown in Figure 22.27, enables you to deploy upgrades to your applications. You need the required .msi package location to configure these options. You can also flag these as mandatory upgrades.

Figure 22.27
Adding upgrades to published or assigned packages.

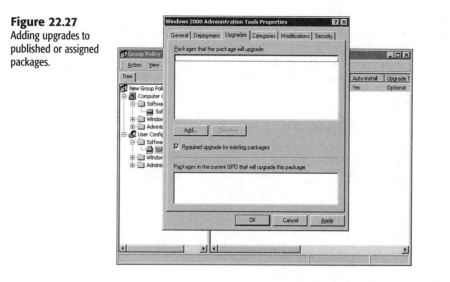

The Categories tab enables you to select in which categories this application will be displayed, in the Add/Remove Programs applet (see Figure 22.28). You can use the Properties page of the Software Installation group policy node to create categories. You will look at configuring the Software Installation node itself at the end of this section.

Figure 22.28
Creating application categories.

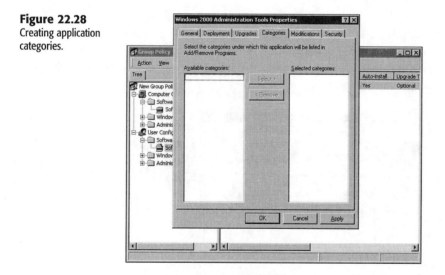

The Modifications tab, shown in Figure 22.29, enables you to assign transforms to the package. A *transform* is a script that modifies the default installation properties for a Windows Installer package.

Caution

Because every edit implies a save in the Group Policy Editor, you should not click OK on this property page until the list is fully populated with the transforms you want to apply. Software could be deployed with an incomplete list of transforms, which could cause a problematic install.

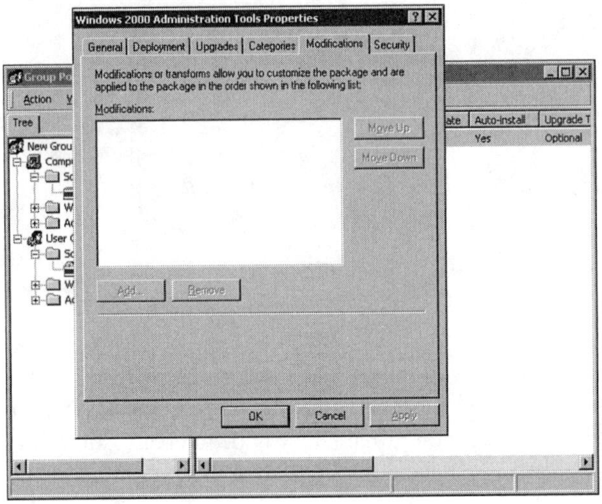

Figure 22.29
Transforming MSI packages.

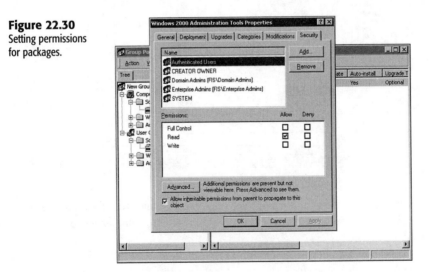

The Security tab sets the access control list (ACL) for the package (see Figure 22.30). You should remember that everything has an ACL in Active Directory. Figure 22.30 shows the default permissions for the group Authenticated Users. The read permission allows the user to read and install the package.

Figure 22.30
Setting permissions for packages.

> **Note**
>
> Along with Active Directory permissions, the package file must have the appropriate filesystem permissions set for the user to be able to install the package. Some native packaging software saves the finished package with highly restrictive permissions set. If the user can't read the package, she can't install it.

When you click OK, your administrative tools are published to this group policy.

TESTING YOUR GROUP POLICY

You can test your group policy by making sure that your client computer account and user account are in the OU that is linked to this group policy. The default container for a non-DC is the Computers container. This container is not really an OU and as such can't directly have a group policy applied to it. For this example, you have moved your computer account to the Desktop OU and made sure you have a test user account named `Joe` in the OU. The setup is shown in Figure 22.31.

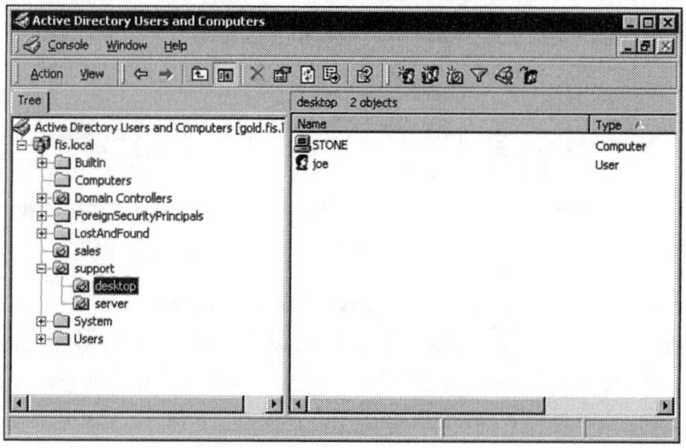

Figure 22.31
Viewing your test OU setup.

Because you have assigned software to your computer, you must reboot the test computer to test your software installation group policy. When you do so, you notice that the boot process takes longer than normal and that the status message box sticks at `Applying Software Installation Settings`. This is because, if you assign software to computers, the software is completely installed and configured before you see the Ctrl+Alt+Delete logon box. After you log on as any user, you see that the support tools have been installed, without any user intervention. Figure 22.32 shows the Start menu updated with the new tools.

> **Note**
>
> Although group policy is refreshed on clients every 90 minutes (plus or minus 30 minutes), software assigned through group policy is not installed unless the computer reboots (if assigned to the computer) or the user logs on (if assigned to the user).

Figure 22.32
Your assigned software is now installed.

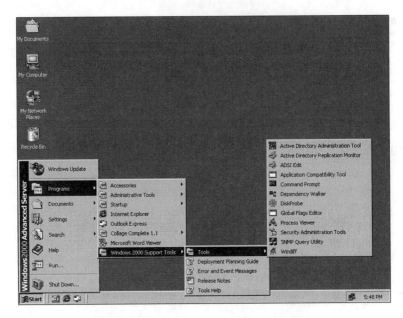

To test the software you published to the user, you must log on as user Joe. After you have done so, you can see from looking at the Start menu that no additional software has been applied. To receive the benefit of the published software, you could invoke an application that is assigned to your specific application or use Control Panel.

When you open Control Panel, Add/Remove Programs, you see three options: Change or Remove Programs, Add New Programs, and Add/Remove Windows Components. You are interested in Add New Programs. When you select this icon, you see the detail pane flash to Searching for programs on the network; then it shows your published application (see Figure 22.33).

Figure 22.33
Viewing your published software package in Add/Remove Programs.

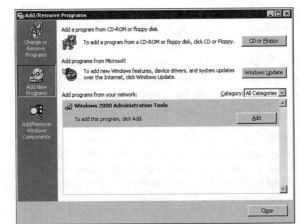

When you select your published application in the Add Programs from Your Network pane, the Windows Installer Service loads and installs your administrative tools .msi package.

CONFIGURING THE SOFTWARE INSTALLATION NODE

Most of the software installation configuration you have done so far has been specific to a particular package. You can set defaults for all packages assigned to the computer or user through this group policy. You do this by configuring the software installation group policy node. Figure 22.34 shows the Software Installation Properties page, which is opened by right-clicking User Configuration, Software Settings, Software Installation and choosing Properties. This opens with the General tab displayed.

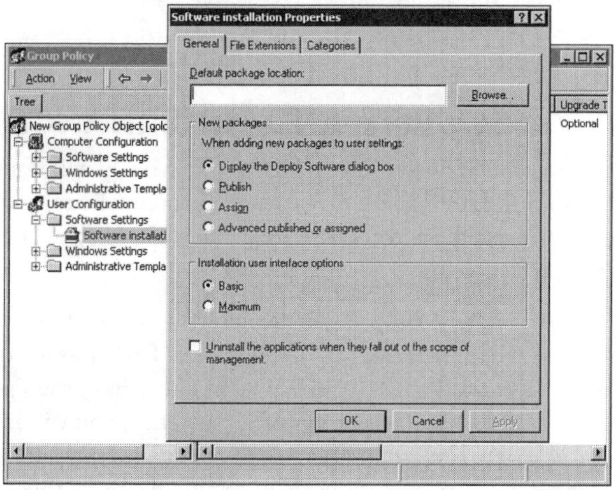

Figure 22.34
Modifying default software installation properties through group policy.

The Default Package Location text box lets you configure a network share that will, by default, host your Windows Installer packages. This can be overridden, but when you create a new package with this option set, this is the share your Open dialog box displays. If you centralize your software installation shares, this option can save you a lot of time.

The New Packages section of the Software Installation Properties page sets the default deployment option—Publish, Assign, or Advanced Published or Assigned.

The Installation User Interface Options section sets the Basic (the default) or Maximum option. This sets how much input a user has when an application is automatically installed on the local computer.

Selecting the check box next to Uninstall the Applications When They Fall Out of the Scope of Management sets whether a Windows Installer package is automatically uninstalled when a particular group policy no longer impacts the user.

The File Extensions tab of the Software Installation Properties page enables you to set the precedence of applications that use the same file extensions. If you have several applications that will open when you double-click a certain file extension, you can set which application is opened.

The Categories tab is a great tool if you are publishing a large number of applications. If you do not create software categories and then assign packages to them as you publish, our users will simply see a list of applications in the Control Panel Add/Remove Programs applet. With categories, you can at least enforce some order on the way in which the applications are categorized.

> **Note**   Regardless of which group policy or OU you create software categories for, the list is domain wide. Modifications can be made to the software categories list on any group policy, but the changes are reflected throughout the domain.

GROUP POLICY SECURITY AND INHERITANCE

After you have created and applied group policy, you inevitably will want to delegate management to other administrators, make exceptions to group policies, and troubleshoot group policy application. In this section, you take a look at group policy security and how it is inherited throughout the domain.

The first and most basic rule is that group policy flows down the tree. The second is that any group policy close to you overrides any group policy farther away. If you are a member of a container object, a site, a domain, or an OU that either has group policy assigned to it or is below a container object that has group policy assigned, you will inherit that group policy. If conflicts exist between group policy settings, the nearest setting will apply. Like most rules, however, these have exceptions. This section discusses those exceptions because they form the heart of managing group policy.

GROUP POLICY INHERITANCE

Figure 22.31 shows the fis.local domain with one of the OU subtrees fully open. User joe and his computer are members of the Desktop OU, which is a child of the Support OU. joe also is a member of the fis.local domain and the Default-First-Site-Name site. All these containers can hold group policy, and if they do, joe and his computer will process that group policy. It is important to note that joe will not be affected by group policy set on the Server OU because he is not a member of it nor is it above him in the Active Directory hierarchy.

Group Policy inheritance is usually additive. In other words, if one group policy above joe configures a setting and a different group policy above joe configures a different setting, joe receives both. If the two group policies set the same parameter, by default, the closest writer wins.

AN INHERITANCE EXAMPLE

For example, suppose the Support OU had a group policy assigned to it that enabled the following settings:

- User Configuration, Administrative Templates, Start Menu and Taskbar, Remove Run from Start Menu.
- User Configuration, Administrative Templates, Start Menu and Taskbar, Remove Search Menu from Start Menu ENABLED.

Also, suppose the Desktop OU has a group policy with the following settings:

- User Configuration, Administrative Templates, Start Menu and Taskbar, Add logoff to the Start Menu.
- User Configuration, Administrative Templates, Start Menu and Taskbar, Remove Run from Start Menu DISABLED.

The next time joe logs on, he will have logoff added and search removed from his Start menu. The logoff and search settings did not collide; therefore, they collaborate to provide an environment for joe. The Remove Run setting did collide, however, and the default behavior is that the last writer wins. This is a large part of the power of group policy. You set general group policies high in the Active Directory structure and let them flow down by default.

Overriding Group Policy Inheritance

You can, however, override the default behaviors for group policy inheritance. The settings No Override and Block Inheritance provide this functionality.

Block Inheritance   Block Inheritance means exactly what its name implies. If you set Block Inheritance on an OU, it will not allow group policy to flow down from any containers above it in the Active Directory tree. Block Inheritance acts like an umbrella, shielding you from whichever group policy settings might be flowing down from above. The Block Inheritance option is set per OU and can be set at the domain level to prevent group policy applied at the site level from flowing down to the domain.

No Override   No Override is the exact opposite of Block Inheritance. No Override forces group policy inheritance. If a higher group policy is set to No Override and a lower group policy is set to Block Inheritance, No Override wins. If several group policies are set with the No Override option, the highest No Override wins. The No Override option is set per group policy.

Inheritance Example Revisited

In the previousexample, you had some settings that did not collide; therefore, they were inherited. The settings that did collide applied the default rule of closest group policy, or last writer wins. Let's perform the test again, with one setting changed. You will set the group policy for the Support OU to No Override. If you do so, when Joe logs on, he has no Run or Search on his Start menu and Logoff has been added. Even though the closer group policy specified that Run should be enabled, it was overruled by the higher group policy with Run removed and No Override set.

> **Note**
>
> No Override does not cause all group policies below it to lose effect. It simply means that in case of a collision, the higher group policy setting wins. This is the exact opposite of default behavior.

The previous example and discussion explored the collision of dueling group policy settings and the No Override option. In this example, you have No Override set in the higher group policy. If you also have Block Inheritance set in the lower group policy, it would have no effect because No Override defeats Block Inheritance. In addition, if you have multiple No Overrides set, the highest one wins.

GROUP POLICY SECURITY

Every object in the Active Directory has an access control list, and group policies are no exception. Your ability to process a group policy and to create and modify group policy is a direct result of the ACL. The group policy security interface is shown in Figure 22.35, with the default permissions set for the Authenticated Users group.

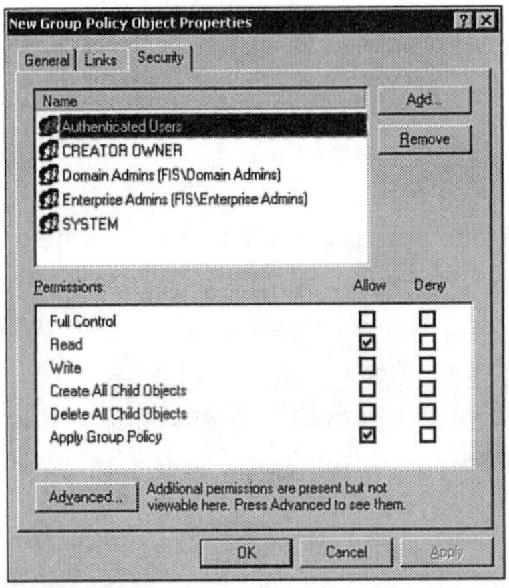

Figure 22.35
Viewing the default permissions on a group policy.

APPLYING GROUP POLICY

The basic rule of group policy security is that to be affected by group policy, you—or a group of which you are a member—must have the read and apply group policy permissions to the group policy. By default, the Authenticated Users group has these permissions.

MODIFYING GROUP POLICY

To modify an existing group policy, the user must have the write permission to the group policy. By default, the System, Enterprise Admins, Domain Admins, and Creator Owner groups have this permission.

CREATING AND LINKING GROUP POLICY

The best way to grant someone the permission to create group policy involves two steps. First, you must make her a member of the group policy Creator Owner group. This can be done by using the Member Of tab on the Users Properties page in AD Users and Computers. Then, you must use the Delegation of Control Wizard for the OU you want her to create and manage group policy for and give her (at a minimum) the manage group policy links permission to the OU. This will allow her to create group policy. Additionally, because she has created it, she is now the owner, and as such, will be able to modify it. The Delegation of Control Wizard's Tasks to Delegate dialog box is shown in Figure 22.36. This also enables you to link and unlink group policy from the current OU.

Figure 22.36
Delegating control of group policy for an OU with the Delegation of Control Wizard.

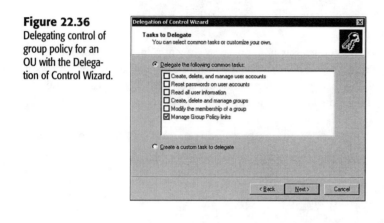

> **Note**
>
> Although the previously mentioned rules hold true for most group policies, to apply group policy to a site, you must be a member of the Enterprise Admins Global group. This group should have a highly restricted membership.

CREATING EXCEPTIONS TO GROUP POLICY APPLICATION

Sometimes you might want to create exceptions to group policy processing and application, and the good news is you can. To allow a user to be invisible to group policy, you need only to give him explicit deny access to the apply group policy permission. Two simple rules make this work. First, deny always wins over allow. Second, a user must have read and apply group policy to process that group policy.

GROUP POLICY EXCEPTION DEMONSTRATION

The next section illustrates a likely scenario for many medium- to large-size companies. You will use the permission modifications to allow a user in the Support OU to bypass group policy. This will allow him to be a member of the OU without receiving the security limitations of the group policy. You will use the Support OU and the supportadmin user shown in Figure 22.37.

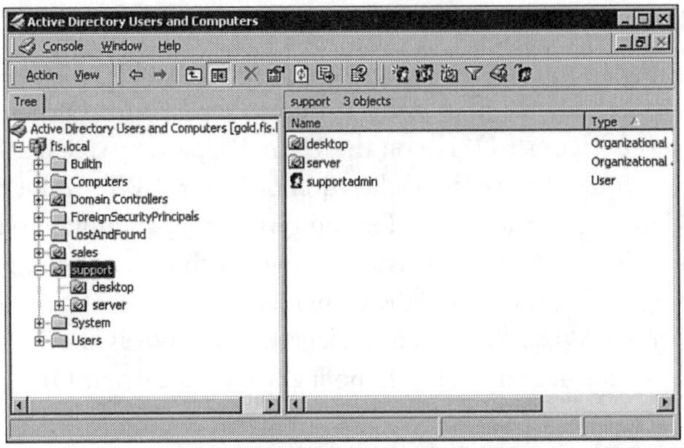

Figure 22.37
Viewing the setup for
the example.

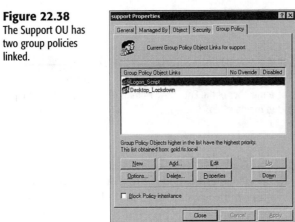

The Support OU has two group policies assigned to it, as shown in Figure 22.38. The logon_script group policy applies the logon script you wrote earlier in the chapter. You want the supportadmin user to apply this group policy because it maps drives and printers and opens the IE browser. The desktop_lockdown group policy, however, removes Run from the Start menu and removes several desktop icons. It is designed to create a very focused desktop environment for your telephone support users. You do not want this group policy to be applied to supportadmin.

Figure 22.38
The Support OU has
two group policies
linked.

To ensure that supportadmin receives the appropriate group policy, select the logon_script group policy shown in Figure 22.38 and click Properties; then click the Security tab. This loads the Logon_Script Properties page shown in Figure 22.39. Here you see that the Authenticated Users group has read and apply group policy permissions for the logon_script group policy. These permissions allow Authenticated Users (supportadmin) to process group policy. Clicking Cancel returns you to the Support Properties page.

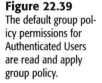

Figure 22.39
The default group policy permissions for Authenticated Users are read and apply group policy.

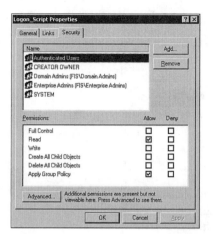

Next, select the desktop_lockdown group policy from the Support Properties page and click Properties; then click the Security tab on the Desktop_Lockdown Properties page. Next, you must explicitly add supportadmin to the ACL for this object and then give him the deny access control entry (ACE) for the apply group policy permission. Click Add on the Desktop_Lockdown Security tab and add supportadmin to the ACL. After you have added him to the ACL for this object, you can then give him the deny ACE for apply group policy. When you click Apply, you see the Security message box shown in Figure 22.40, informing you that the deny entries take precedence over allow. Because that is exactly what you are counting on, click Yes.

Figure 22.40
Setting deny ACEs causes a warning to be displayed.

The result appears in Figure 22.41. Authenticated Users (of which supportadmin is a member) still has read and apply group policy. supportadmin, however, now has an explicit deny for apply group policy, which will override his allow from Authenticated Users, causing the desktop_lockdown group policy to have no effect on him.

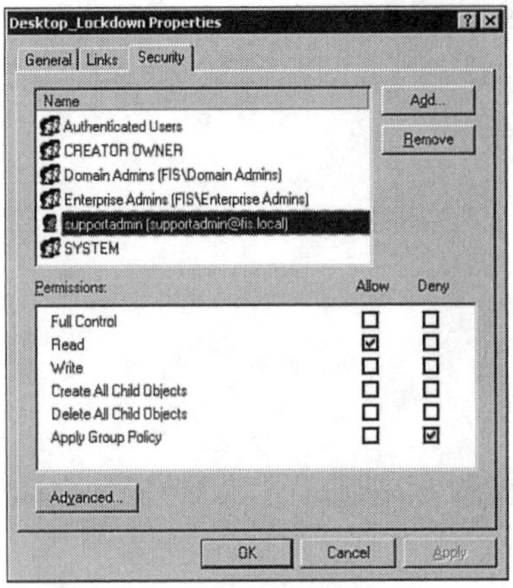

Figure 22.41
Setting a deny ACE
for `supportadmin`
makes him immune
to that group policy.

If you also wanted the `supportadmin` user to be able to edit the desktop_lockdown group policy, you could simply allow him the write ACE for this group policy. This would not allow him to create new group policy, but it would let him modify this one.

SUMMARY

Proper management of group policy can make administering a Windows 2000 domain much easier and can really enable your users to benefit from many of the enhancements in Windows 2000.

Group policy is one of the most powerful tools in the Active Directory toolbox, but as such, it should be implemented only after very careful testing. Group policy in itself is not dangerous, but because it allows such sweeping changes to be made to 1 user or 1,000 users with the same amount of effort, caution should be exercised when implementing it in a production environment.

Group policy can be applied to sites, domains, and organizational units. It is processed by users and computers. Where a user or computer account resides in Active Directory determines which group policies it inherits.

TROUBLESHOOTING

INTERMITTENT LOGON SCRIPTS

My logon scripts execute for some users and not for others, even when they are in the same OU.

Make sure the logon scripts are being replicated to all DCs. Copy the logon scripts to the Logon folder for the group policy. The group policy folders are located on the SysVol share of any DC for your domain.

→ **See** "Group Policy Template," **p. 408**

This enables the File Replication Service to automatically copy the logon scripts to every other DC in the domain.

SELF-REPAIR DOESN'T ALWAYS WORK

Some of my applications that have been installed through group policy self repair and some do not.

Native Windows Installer packages are capable of self repair. Repackaged applications are not.

→ **See** "Windows Installer Service," **p. 387**

CHAPTER 23

GROUP POLICY ARCHITECTURE

In this chapter

OVERVIEW OF GROUP POLICY ARCHITECTURE

This chapter looks at group policy architecture and troubleshooting. The best troubleshooting tool in the world is a solid understanding of the architecture you are using, so we will look at that first. We also look at how group policy is stored, applied, and replicated. In addition, troubleshooting common group policy issues is discussed.

GROUP POLICY STORAGE

A group policy object is really made up of two things, a group policy container and a group policy template. The *container* is stored in the Active Directory and is identified by a globally unique identifier (GUID). The *template* is a collection of filesystem objects that are stored in the sysvol share on every Domain Controller. It is also identified by a GUID. The GUID is used to keep the two parts of the group policy object synchronized.

GROUP POLICY CONTAINER

The information kept in the Active Directory is basically configuration information about the group policy itself—version numbers, policy settings, and so on. This information is replicated as a part of normal AD replication. This means that any changes are replicated to its direct replication partners in the same site within 5 minutes, to other domain controllers in the same domain and site within an average of 15 minutes, and to DCs in the same domain in other sites based on the intersite replication schedule. This information is replicated as part of the domain replication partition.

GROUP POLICY TEMPLATE

The group policy template contains logon scripts, Registry files, administrative templates, and virtually all the information that is actually applied to users and computers as a part of group policy. This information is kept under the sysvol share on every DC and is replicated by the file replication service. Each group policy template is kept in a series of folders whose top-level folder name is the group policy GUID of the group policy. Listing 23.1 shows a snapshot of the sysvol share on a brand new DC. The two group policies shown are the autocreated default domain and default DC group policies. The sysvol share and folders and files underneath that share are created by dcpromo.exe when the computer is promoted to a DC.

LISTING 23.1   THE sysvol SHARE

```
----fis.local
    +---Policies
    |   +---{31B2F340-016D-11D2-945F-00C04FB984F9}
    |   |   +---MACHINE
    |   |   |   +---Microsoft
    |   |   |       +---Windows NT
    |   |   |           +---SecEdit
    |   |   +---USER
```

LISTING 23.1   CONTINUED

```
|   |           +---Microsoft
|   |               +---RemoteInstall
|   +---{6AC1786C-016F-11D2-945F-00C04fB984F9}
|       +---MACHINE
|       |   +---Microsoft
|       |       +---Windows NT
|       |           +---SecEdit
|       +---USER
+---scripts
```

Note

Although looking at the filesystem structure of a group policy is architecturally very interesting, the management interface remains the Active Directory Users and Computers MMC Snap-in.

GROUP POLICY REPLICATION

As mentioned earlier, the Active Directory portion of the group policy is replicated using normal AD replication mechanisms. On the other hand, the file-based portion—the group policy template—is replicated using the file replication service.

FILE REPLICATION SERVICE

The file replication service (FRS) is automatically installed and configured on every Domain Controller. No management console exists for FRS. The FRS replicates changes to group policy templates to all other DCs in the domain. One example of this is a change to an administrative templates setting in the group policy, which would cause a change in the registry.pol file. This change then would be replicated to all other DCs in the domain so that, when a user or computer processed group policy, they would receive the same settings regardless of which DC they logged in to.

→ For more information on administrative templates, **see** "Administrative Templates," **p. 356**

The replication granularity for FRS is the file. This means that if you change one byte of a file, it is replicated to all the other DCs in your domain.

The FRS uses the same connection objects and replication schedule that the AD replication uses, but it does not compress information when it crosses site boundaries. The reason the sysvol folder must be installed on a drive formatted with the NTFS filesystem is because FRS uses features of the NTFS filesystem to track changes to files on the sysvol folder and then replicate those changes. FRS keeps information about replication partners and so on in a JET database: \winnt\ntfrs\jet\ntfrs.jdb.

FRS does not have a readily available console snap-in to manage the service; however, a utility is included in the Windows 2000 Resource Kit called ntfrsutl.exe that allows you to dump information to the screen about FRS configuration. We will use `ntfrsutl` in the "Troubleshooting" section at the end of this chapter.

GROUP POLICY PROCESSING

Group policy is processed in the following order: the local group policy, followed by any group policy assigned to the site, domain, and OU of which the user and computer are members.

Most of the information processed by the client is kept in a series of files and scripts located on the `sysvol` share of the DC authenticated to. Conversely, much of the executable code necessary to use this information is stored on the client. Examples of this include the Windows Installer Service that is responsible for installing software packages and the client-side extension DLLs that process various portions of the group policy.

Listings 23.2–23.8 have been abbreviated for clarity. They are from the file `\winnt\debug\usermode\userenv.log`, which is created when you turn on verbose group policy logging by modifying the Registry on the local computer. To create this file, do the following:

1. Open `regedt32.exe` or `regedit.exe`.

2. Navigate to `HKLM/Software/Microsoft/Windows NT/CurrentVersion/Winlogon`; make sure you have the Winlogon key selected.

3. Create a new value in the `HKLM/Software/Microsoft/Windows NT/CurrentVersion/Winlogon`.

4. The value name is `UserEnvDebugLevel`.

5. The value datatype is `Reg_Dword`.

6. The value is 30002 hex.

7. Log off and log on.

8. Because computer policy is applied to a large degree at startup, to view computer policy being processed, you must restart the local computer.

Listing 23.2 is a portion of the file `userenv.log` that shows group policy being applied at computer startup.

LISTING 23.2   APPLYING GROUP POLICY

```
ApplyGroupPolicy: Entering. Flags = 7
ProcessGPOs:
ProcessGPOs:  Starting computer Group Policy processing...
ProcessGPOs:
EnterCriticalPolicySection: Machine critical section has been
➥claimed.  Handle = 0x3b4
```

Several portions of this file are very interesting. From a troubleshooting perspective, this kind of verbose logging is absolutely invaluable. This type of log serves as almost a packet analyzer for group policy processing. You do not have to guess what is happening; you can follow the game play by play.

The first interesting section is the PingComputer, shown in Listing 23.3. This is where the client computer uses an ICMP echo request/reply pair to assess the link speed to the Domain Controller. If the reply comes back in less than 10ms, the link is assumed to be fast. If not, it sends several arbitrary-length messages to the server and measures the round-trip time. By default, the link is assumed to be fast if it measures out at 500Kbps or faster. This threshold can be modified through group policy at \Computer Configuration\ Administrative Templates\System\Group Policy\Group Policy Slow Link Detection.

LISTING 23.3 PingComputer **EXECUTION**

```
PingComputer:  First time:  0
PingComputer:  Fast link.  Exiting.
```

The User name section shown in Listing 23.4 refers to the computer account. In the next line, you can track which DC you are getting your group policy from.

LISTING 23.4 **IDENTIFYING THE COMPUTER ACCOUNT**

```
ProcessGPOs:  User name is:  CN=TUNIS,OU=gptest,DC=fis,
➥DC=local, Domain name is:  FIS
ProcessGPOs: Domain controller is:  \\bangalore.fis.local
➥Domain DN is fis.local
```

Next, Listing 23.5 uses LDAP to find any and all group policies bound to containers of which you are a member. Listing 23.5 shows only one OU being searched.

LISTING 23.5 **SEARCHING OU**

```
SearchDSObject:  Searching <OU=gptest,DC=fis,DC=local>
SearchDSObject:  Found GPO(s):  <[LDAP://CN={D9860BD5-4653-4930-8754-
➥80D2BE5CC417},CN=Policies,CN=System,DC=fis,DC=local;0]>
```

The following code compares the version numbers of the group policy container with the group policy template. If these match, the version of the group policy in the AD matches the version of the group policy on the sysvol share. Because these are replicated separately, it is possible for them to be temporarily out of sync. Here's the code:

```
ProcessGPO:  Found machine version of:  GPC is 3, GPT is 3
```

The next section of interest shows the client finding the appropriate file path for the group policy. This is shown in the following:

```
ProcessGPO:  Found file system path of:  <\\fis.local\
➥SysVol\fis.local\Policies\{D9860BD5-4653-4930-8754-80D2BE5CC417}>
```

Another feature of group policy is that if no changes are to be applied since the last boot, you do not needlessly apply group policy. The following code snippet shows this occurring for one of the group policies applied to this computer:

```
ProcessGPOs: Processing extension Registry
CompareGPOLists:  The lists are the same.
CheckGPOs: No GPO changes and no security group
➥membership change and extension Registry has NoGPOChanges set.
```

Although several redundant entries have been left out in the interest of brevity, this section shows much of the rich information that can be gleaned from group policy verbose logging. The User section is much the same as the computer policy you saw earlier. Finally, the computer group policy processing ends with the lines shown here:

```
LeaveCriticalPolicySection: Critical section 0x3b4 has been released.
ProcessGPOs: Computer Group Policy has been applied.
ProcessGPOs: Leaving with 1.
ApplyGroupPolicy: Leaving successfully.
```

PROBLEMS WITH GROUP POLICY

The best tool for troubleshooting is knowledge of the architecture. This section looks at some tools and techniques to apply that knowledge.

The group policy problems most people face are not system failures, but rather an unintended consequence of group policy application and inheritance. The problems can be broken down into the following areas:

- Replication issues
- Inheritance issues
- Permissions issues

REPLICATION ISSUES

The first set of issues usually resolve themselves in a few minutes. Because AD replication and FRS replication are not exactly the same thing, the group policy template and the group policy container can be temporarily out of sync. When this happens, simply allowing the two replication services to catch up with each other should fix the problem. Although it is unlikely that the AD and FRS will become out of sync in respect to group policy, it is possible. If, for example, the FRS is incapable of starting on a Domain Controller, changes to group policy will not be applied on that DC until the FRS service is started.

The tool that shows you whether you have a version mismatch between the group policy container and the group policy template is gpotool.exe, which is part of the Windows 2000 Resource Kit. Listing 23.6 shows the partial output of running gpotool when the newest version of the group policy container has replicated to a DC but the group policy template has not.

LISTING 23.6   RUNNING gptool

```
Policy {A19929BA-54C7-410A-BE7B-9320E0022CF8}
Error: Version mismatch on silver.fis.local, DS=196608, sysvol=131072
Details:
-------------------------------------------------------------
DC: gold.fis.local
Friendly name: frs_gpo
Created: 3/25/2000 2:56:36 PM
Changed: 3/25/2000 3:20:12 PM
DS version:     3(user) 0(machine)
Sysvol version: 3(user) 0(machine)
Flags: 0
User extensions: [{35378EAC-683F-11D2-A89A-00C04FBBCFA2}
➥{0F6B957E-509E-11D1-A7CC-0000F87571E3}]
Machine extensions: not found
Functionality version: 2
-------------------------------------------------------------
-------------------------------------------------------------
DC: silver.fis.local
Friendly name: frs_gpo
Created: 3/25/2000 2:56:36 PM
Changed: 3/25/2000 3:20:44 PM
DS version:     3(user) 0(machine)
Sysvol version: 2(user) 0(machine)
Flags: 0
User extensions: [{35378EAC-683F-11D2-A89A-00C04FBBCFA2}
➥{0F6B957E-509E-11D1-A7CC-0000F87571E3}]
Machine extensions: not found
Functionality version: 2
```

CH
23

Generally, the fix for this is time. You should also make sure that you can "see" the PDC emulator and your replication partners. Check the usual network suspects: routing, addressing, and name resolution. Ping your replication partners by name and by IP address. Make sure the FRS is running on both DCs, and check the event log for errors. An interesting trick for checking file replication is to create a test file in the sysvol folder in the group policy template folder for the group policy in question and see whether the file is being replicated to the target server.

Note

Because, by default, the focus of the group policy editor is on the PDC emulator, if you load the Active Directory Users and Computers on the computer whose group policy application you are troubleshooting, you will see the newest version of the group policy. The problem is that the focus of modification is on the PDC emulator and the focus of the application is at the DC to which the client is authenticated. If the versions are different, you see the newest version in the group policy editor, but the current version on the DC you are logging on to is what is applied to your user and computer. This can be very confusing.

INHERITANCE ISSUES

Inheritance issues usually are not a system failure. They usually are the result of poor planning or a lack of understanding of the implications of group policy inheritance. If a group policy is above a user or computer in the Active Directory tree, by default the user or computer receives that group policy. Chapter 22, "Managing Group Policy," looked at the no override and block policy inheritance options. These should be used sparingly.

Group policy inheritance problems generally fall into two basic categories. Either the user is getting settings you don't want her to have or the user is not getting settings you do want her to have.

This kind of troubleshooting can be tedious. In its most basic form, you must start at the root of group policy processing and traverse the tree down to the area you are interested in. Group policy processing starts with the local group policy and then checks for and applies group policy for site, domain, and OU. A useful tool is to create a test user at each level from the domain down the tree and log on and document which group policy settings that user received.

Another Resource Kit tool that can make this kind of troubleshooting simpler and faster is gpresult.exe. Listing 23.7 shows the output from running gpresult at the command line.

LISTING 23.7   gpresult **COMMAND-LINE OUTPUT**

```
Microsoft (R) Windows (R) 2000 Operating System Group Policy Result tool
Copyright (C) Microsoft Corp. 1981-1999

Created on Saturday, March 25, 2000 at 10:12:39 AM

Operating System Information:

Operating System Type:      Server
Operating System Version:   5.0.2195
Terminal Server Mode:       None


############################################################

  User Group Policy results for:

  CN=Administrator,CN=Users,DC=fis,DC=local

  Domain Name:      FIS
  Domain Type:      Windows 2000
  Site Name:        Default-First-Site-Name

  Roaming profile:    (None)
  Local profile:      O:\Documents and Settings\Administrator.FIS

  The user is a member of the following security groups:

    FIS\Domain Users
    \Everyone
    BUILTIN\Users
    BUILTIN\Administrators
    FIS\Domain Admins
    FIS\Schema Admins
    FIS\Enterprise Admins
    FIS\Group Policy Creator Owners
```

LISTING 23.7 CONTINUED

```
\LOCAL
NT AUTHORITY\INTERACTIVE
NT AUTHORITY\Authenticated Users

############################################################

Last time Group Policy was applied: Saturday, March 25, 2000 at 9:59:12 AM
Group Policy was applied from: gold.fis.local

============================================================

The user received "Registry" settings from these GPOs:

    Default Domain Policy

############################################################

    Computer Group Policy results for:

    CN=STONE,OU=desktop,OU=support,DC=fis,DC=local

    Domain Name:        FIS
    Domain Type:        Windows 2000
    Site Name:          Default-First-Site-Name

    The computer is a member of the following security groups:

        BUILTIN\Administrators
        \Everyone
        BUILTIN\Users
        FIS\STONE$
        FIS\Domain Computers
        NT AUTHORITY\NETWORK
        NT AUTHORITY\Authenticated Users

############################################################

Last time Group Policy was applied: Saturday, March 25, 2000 at 9:53:39 AM
Group Policy was applied from: gold.fis.local

============================================================

The computer received "Registry" settings from these GPOs:

    Local Group Policy
    Default Domain Policy

============================================================
The computer received "Security" settings from these GPOs:

    Default Domain Policy
```

CH
23

LISTING 23.7   CONTINUED

```
============================================================
The computer received "EFS recovery" settings from these GPOs:

    Local Group Policy
    Default Domain Policy


============================================================
The computer received "Application Management" settings from these GPOs:

    Default Domain Policy
    Logon_Script
```

This tool can check user settings only, computer settings only, or both. In addition, it can be used in verbose mode. This tool also does much of the documentation for you when you need to see why group policy is not being applied as you expected.

PERMISSIONS ISSUES

You should remember the basics of group policy permissions here. For group policy processing to take place for a user or computer, they must have the read and apply group policy permission set for them or a group of which they are a member. Also, if the user (or computer) or a group of which the user's a member has an explicit deny for a particular group policy, he will not process that group policy. gpresult.exe is useful here, too, because it shows at the beginning of its output which security groups the user's a member of and which group policy is being applied.

SUMMARY

Group policy is a highly visible part of the Active Directory. You can use it to set virtually anything. Your users see the effects of group policy before virtually anything else in the Active Directory. Used properly, it is one of the best new features of Windows 2000.

A solid knowledge of architecture is the best troubleshooting tool. In this chapter, we have looked at how group policy works and some tools to enable you to observe it in action and to correct common problems.

TROUBLESHOOTING

CHANGES AREN'T BEING EFFECTED

Changes made to the group policy are not being replicated to a Domain Controller.

The File replication service, which is responsible for copying changes made to the group policy from one DC to another, rarely breaks. Generally, if the network and Active Directory are healthy enough to replicate changes to the AD from one DC to another, FRS works also. However, if it does fail, the first things to check are the usual suspects on the network—routing, addressing, and name resolution. FRS can't replicate to what it can't see. Use ping and tracert to ensure that the respective DCs can communicate. Also, use the following checks to help you troubleshoot:

- **Make sure the FRS service is started**—If you change the startup account for the service in the service's MMC Snap-in, the service can fail on startup.

- **Use the event viewer to view the FRS container for error or warning messages.**

- **Check the drive that hosts the sysvol share and make sure it has enough free space**—Because, by default, this is the same drive that hosts the ntds.dit AD database, this should never even approach being full.

- **Use Active Directory Sites and Services to see whether a replication connection object is linking the Domain Controllers in question**—Because of the transitivity of replication, a direct path does not have to exist, but if you are troubleshooting, creating a replication connection object between the two DCs speeds things up. Because connection objects are unidirectional, make sure one is pointing from the source to the target and one is pointing from the target to the source.

- **Finally, use the ntfrsutl.exe tool from the Windows 2000 Resource Kit**—This tool can be used to check the configuration for the service, its memory use, and history of replication with other DCs. One good use for this tool appears in Listing 23.8. This is a highly abbreviated version of the output from the ntfrsutl command.

LISTING 23.8   USING ntfrsutl.exe FOR TROUBLESHOOTING

```
C:\ntfrsutl ds lisbon
NTFRS CONFIGURATION IN THE DS
SUBSTITUTE DCINFO FOR DC
   FRS  DomainControllerName: (null)
   Computer Name          : LISBON
   Computer DNS Name       : lisbon.fis.local

BINDING TO THE DS:
   ldap_open  : lisbon.fis.local
   DsBind     : lisbon.fis.local

COMPUTER: LISBON
   DN   : cn=lisbon,ou=domain controllers,dc=fis,dc=local

      MEMBER: LISBON
         DN   : cn=lisbon,cn=domain system volume
      MEMBER: TUNIS
         DN   : cn=tunis,cn=domain system volume
```

Although Listing 23.8 leaves out 98% of the output from the ntfrsutl command, it is important to note the inclusion of the Lisbon and Tunis Domain Controllers in the replica set. If they are not part of the replica set, they will not replicate.

Tip

An excellent Knowledge Base article (#Q257338) on troubleshooting FRS can be found at www.microsoft.com.

GP CHANGES ARE BEING LOST

Changes made to group policy by several administrators are being lost after replication.

FRS uses a "last writer wins" mentality. The best practice is to set aside a single administrative PC to make changes to group policy. Otherwise, if two administrators modify the same group policy at two different PCs, the last one to save wins.

USER, GROUP, AND CONTACT OBJECTS

In this chapter

USER OBJECTS

At this stage we will look at user and group objects from an administrative and a management perspective—essentially, what you can do with these objects and how you create, delete, and modify them.

The user object is the best place to start because it is what you are probably most familiar with, from an administrative point of view. A user object can be created anywhere inside the domain. The user can exist in an organizational unit (OU), inside a container, or even at the root of the domain.

You will notice that initially the built-in user objects are located in the User container. Containers are different from organizational units, in that they are a separate class of object. The User container exists primarily to provide a default location for NT 4 user accounts to reside in after an upgrade. More specifically, whenever you create a user with the NT 4 User Manager for Domains, it places the user in the User container.

Four ways are available for creating a user object. You can click the icon on the menu bar for creating a new user, as shown in Figure 24.1. You also can right-click an object in the tree pane and select New, User from the menu. The third method, which you look at in Chapter 30, "Scripting the Active Directory," is to write a script using VBScript or any other scripting language supported by Windows 2000. The fourth method is to copy an existing account to a new one. We discuss this last method later in this chapter.

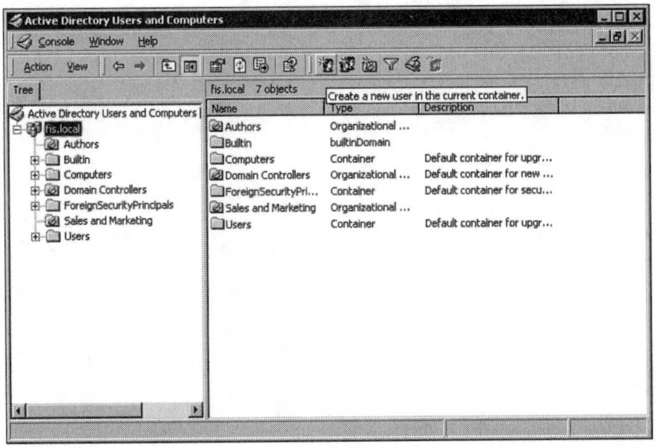

Figure 24.1
Creating a new user can be accomplished numerous ways. One of the fastest is to use the toolbar options.

CREATING A USER OBJECT

To create a user object, first click the Create a New User button. You are presented with the New Object - User dialog box, as shown in Figure 24.2.

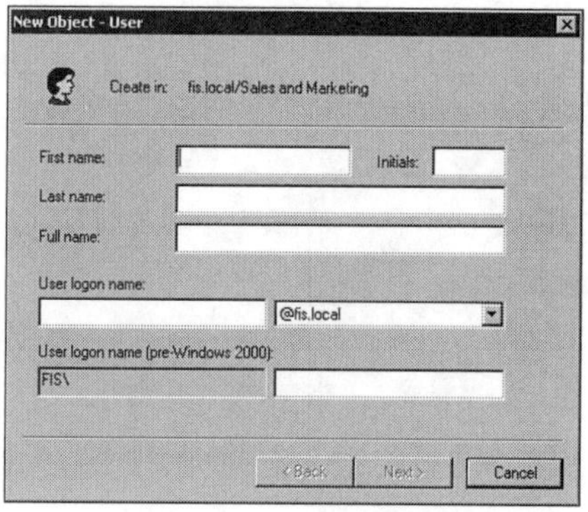

Figure 24.2
The Create a New User Wizard presents some of the options necessary for creating a user object. You must further edit the object after creation.

Notice that the dialog box tells you where the new object will be created—in this case, in the Sales and Marketing OU.

After you fill out the user's first name, initial, and last name, you must fill in the User Logon Name field. You have two options here: The first is a text box in which you can type the user logon name for Windows 2000. This name is also referred to as the user principal name (UPN). This name is in the format of an email address. Whenever a user logs on to a Windows 2000 Server or Windows 2000 Professional, the preferred method is to use the UPN in the format of *username@domainname*—for example, `sean@fis.local`.

A few rules are worth noting with regard to creating user accounts:

- The UPN must be unique within the forest.
- The pre–Windows 2000 logon name must be unique within the domain.
- The display name must be unique to the domain and must be no longer than 64 characters.
- The username can be up to 104 characters.
- The username cannot contain the following characters: <, >, :, ;, [,], /, \, |, ?, *, +, =, ", and ,.

However, you can have more than one domain suffix; thus, you could have one user whose name is `sean@fis.local` and another whose name is `sean@tulsa.fis.local`. This does not have to map to your domain name either. To add another UPN suffix, open the Active Directory Domains and Trusts MMC. Then, right-click the Active Directory Domains and Trusts node (not the domain), and select Properties. You will see the Active Directory Domains and Trusts Properties dialog box, as shown in Figure 24.3.

The next text box in the New Object - User dialog box is for another user logon name, but this time it's used for pre–Windows 2000 clients or down-level logons. So, if a user is logging on at a Windows 9x or NT 4 client, he would log on as normal.

The user logon names in the two separate text boxes do not have to match, but for simplicity, it is recommended that you keep the user logon names the same.

CH

24

Figure 24.3
The use of UPNs enables the creation of unique names within a large organi-zation in a manner that's easy for users to understand.

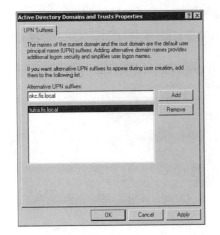

After you click Next, you are presented with the dialog box for defining the password options (see Figure 24.4).

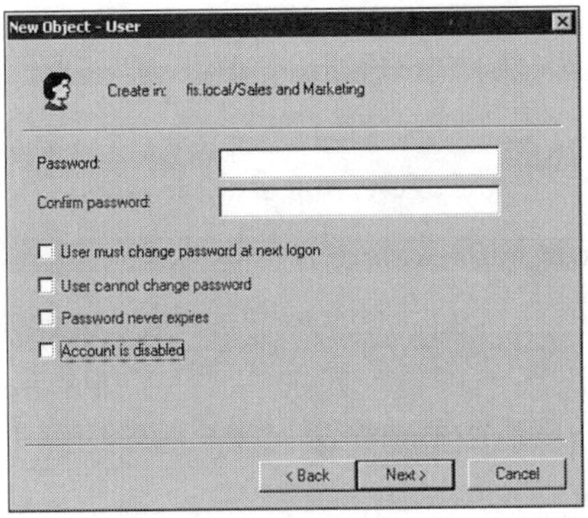

Figure 24.4
Password options for a user account.

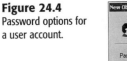

The four check boxes are exclusive. You can't select both User Must Change Password at Next Logon and User Cannot Change Password. If you attempt to do so, a dialog box appears, stating that is not allowed and it subsequently clears the User Cannot Change Password check box.

If you have selected User Must Change Password at Next Logon and then select Password Never Expires, a dialog box similar to the one shown in Figure 24.5 appears. After that warning box pops up, it clears the User Must Change Password at Next Logon check box.

You also can create a user account that is initially disabled. This could be used whenever you get a change request to create a user account for a new employee but the employee does not start for another week.

After you click Next, you see a summary screen that summarizes the settings you specified for the new user account. This has completed the creation of the new user object. However, at this point, you still have more options you can configure for the user.

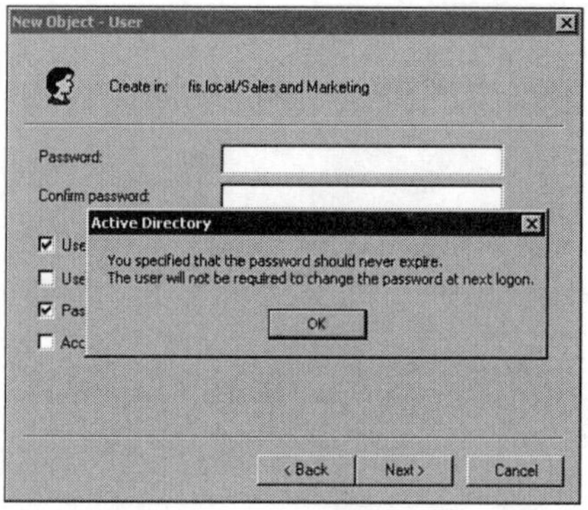

Figure 24.5
Be careful when setting the password options to never expire and to require the user to change her password at the next logon.

To continue configuring the user account, either double-click the object or right-click the object and select Properties. This displays the Properties dialog box.

The number of tabs you see depends on how your Active Directory has been extended. When Exchange 2000 is released, you will see even more tabs because user accounts are mail-enabled through the Active Directory Users and Computers MMC Snap-in. You also will see the tabs if you have installed the Active Directory Connector.

THE GENERAL TAB

The General tab is where the basic information about the object is entered. Each of these text boxes is an attribute stored on the object in Active Directory. However, one of the characteristics of Active Directory is that an attribute that does not have a value does not take up physical space in the database. The database increases in size only when you enter a value for the attribute.

Notice in Figure 24.6 that two Other buttons are available next to the Telephone Number and Web Page fields. These buttons enable you to add multiple phone numbers and multiple Web addresses for a single user. The phone number field you see in Figure 24.6 is stored in the attribute telephoneNumber and is a single-valued attribute. The Other button, however, stores the phone numbers in a multivalued attribute called otherTelephone. The Web page attribute is stored in the attribute WWHomePage and is a single-valued attribute. The additional Web page addresses are stored in the attribute url, which is multivalued.

By storing this kind of information in the directory, it can be used to eliminate other directories that might be storing similar information. By using either Visual Basic or Visual C++, developers can create applications that can read and modify this information and also create some very robust human resource applications.

THE ADDRESS TAB

The Address tab, obviously enough, is where you enter the user address information.

CH
24

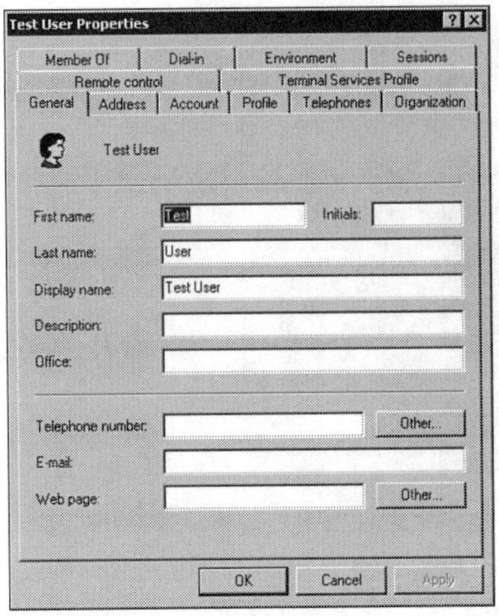

Figure 24.6
The General tab lists a
lot of information
about the user.

THE ACCOUNT TAB

Figure 24.7 shows the Account tab for the user object. You can change the UPN and the
down-level logon name.

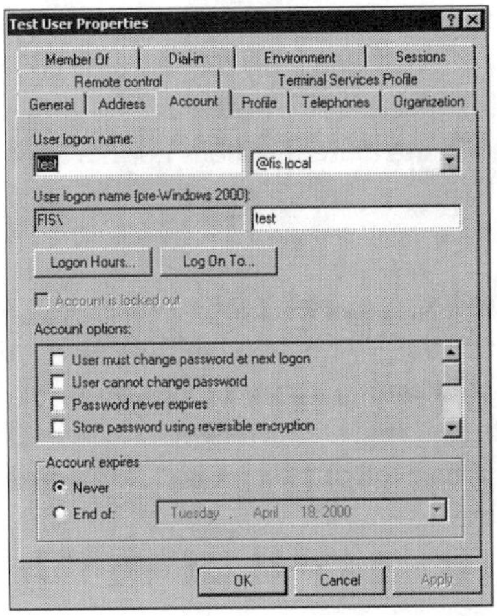

Figure 24.7
Use the Account tab
to modify the user
account options.

LOGON HOURS   The Logon Hours button displays the dialog box shown in Figure 24.8.
On this screen, you can specify the hours and days during which a user is allowed to log on
and specify the days and hours during which the user is not allowed to log on. The default
setting is to allow a user to log on at all times.

By default, a user does not get kicked off the network if the time passes for which she is able
to log on. However, the user is no longer able to make any new connections to network
resources.

Figure 24.8
The Logon Hours option can be extremely useful in an environment in which users work shifts.

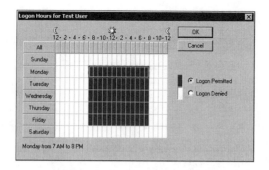

You can forcibly disconnect users from the network after their logon hours have expired by creating a group policy. (See Chapter 20, "Group Policy," for more information.)

LOG ON TO   The Log On To button enables you to specify to which workstations a user can log on. This attribute is limited to 60 workstation names. Some additional options are available that pertain to security for user accounts, such as the following:

- **Store Password Using Reversible Encryption**—You can enable this option to enable the recovery of passwords in case of an emergency.

- **Smart Card Is Required for Interactive Authentication**—With Windows 2000 now providing support for smart cards, you can require all or only some of your user accounts to use smart cards to log on locally.

- **Account Is Trusted for Delegation**—An account can be created for a particular service. In NT 4, services either run under the security context of the local system or as a domain account on that computer. However, in Windows 2000, services can now access resources on other computers on the network through delegation of authentication. You must enable this option if the service is going to run under its own account and not the local system.

- **Account Is Sensitive and Cannot Be Delegated**—You might have some accounts that should not have delegation enabled for them. In those cases, enable this option.

- **Use DES Encryption Types for This Account**—If you need to use DES encryption types in your networks, enable this option.

- **Do Not Require Kerberos Pre-Authentication**—If this account is using some other implementation of the Kerberos protocol, you can enable this option to provide support.

    You also can set an account to expire at a particular time. This option is useful for temporary employees.

THE PROFILE TAB

Figure 24.9 displays the Profile tab. Under User Profile are two text boxes: one for the profile path and one for the logon script path. To create a roaming profile for a user, type the UNC pathname to the share in which you want the profile to be stored—for example, *servername**sharename*. This server does not have to be a domain controller; it could be any server the user is able to access.

CH

24

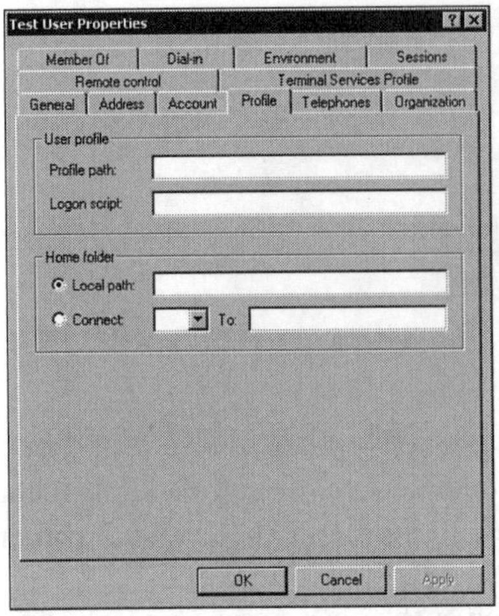

Figure 24.9
The Profile tab is where you can set the profiles for the user as well as his home directory.

To specify a logon script for a particular user, type the name of the script in the Logon Script text box. However, using group policies is a better method for implementing logon scripts as well as logoff scripts.

In the Home Folder options, you can specify one of two locations for a user's home folder. One method enables the home folder to point to a local path on the user's workstation, whereas the other method enables a network path to be mapped using the Connect To option (see Figure 24.10).

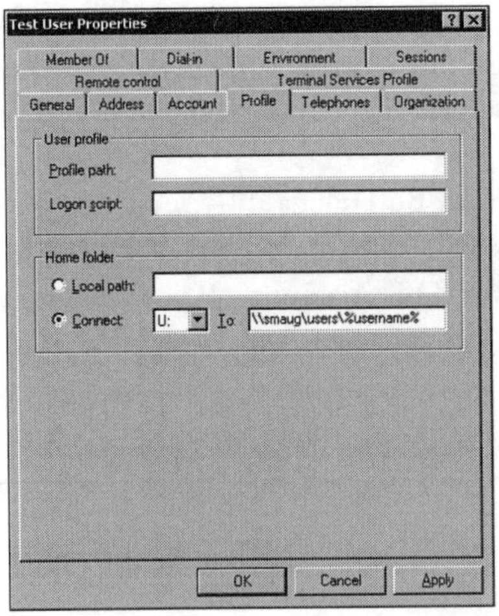

Figure 24.10
This option enables a mapped network drive for the user's home directory.

By using the %username% variable, the system creates a folder named after the username and assigns the user full control and the Administrators group full control.

Although this feature is nice to have and most readers probably have used this in NT 4, folder redirection with My Documents is a better solution.

→ **See** "Group Policy," **p. 333**

THE TELEPHONES TAB

The Telephones tab is not a complex tab, but as Figure 24.11 shows, the options are extensive. Not only can you store any assortment of numbers for a user, but you also can store multiple values for these fields. The key thing that really makes this powerful is when developers begin to see its potential.

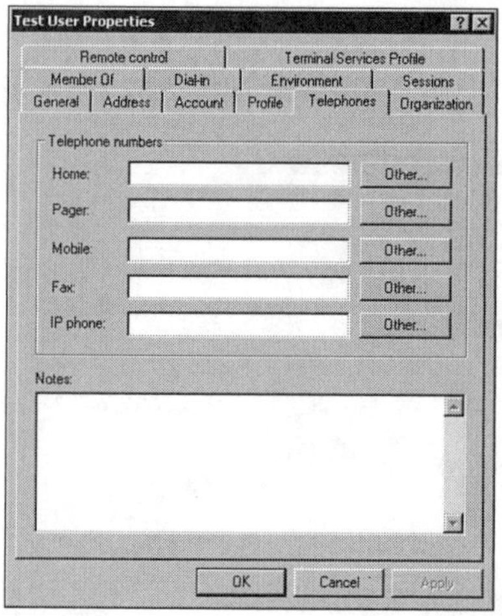

Figure 24.11
You can store way too many numbers here, but it does provide a convenient place for Active Directory–enabled applications to store and retrieve this type of information, creating a single directory.

CH 24

THE ORGANIZATION TAB

The Organization tab also is not a very complex tab, but here is where you can begin to see some influence from Exchange (see Figure 24.12). The Manager and Direct Reports options are straight from Exchange. With this kind of information now being stored in one central location, developers can create robust HR applications.

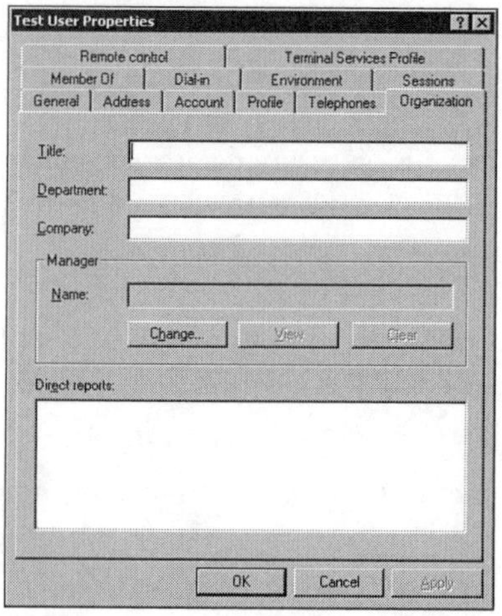

Figure 24.12
By adding organizational information to the user object, Active Directory–enabled applications can further leverage this data.

You can select only user objects when you click the Change button on this tab. Additionally, by clicking the View button, you can see the properties of the manager for this user. The Clear button removes any value from the Manager field.

THE MEMBER OF TAB

By adding users to groups, administration becomes much easier. On the Member Of tab, you can add a user object to any group in the forest. This attribute is stored as a multivalued attribute in Active Directory. Again, enabling a rich set of potential applications to be built can really streamline the administration of AD objects. You also can see the location of the group object of which the user is a member (see Figure 24.13).

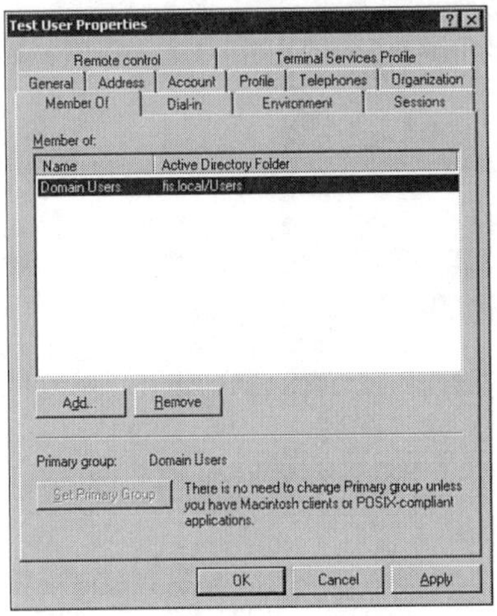

Figure 24.13
Determining the groups to which a user belongs is easy using the Member Of tab.

Much like the Manager button in the Organization tab, the Add button enables you to select only groups in which to place the user.

You can set a Primary Group for a user, but this is only for users who are logging on from Apple clients.

THE DIAL-IN TAB

The appearance of the Dial-in tab depends on the mode of your domain. If your domain is in mixed mode, certain limitations exist to what is enabled (see Figure 24.14).

MIXED MODE OPTIONS   The default option is to deny access for newly created user accounts. This applies to both dial-in and VPN access. The only other options you can configure in mixed mode are the Callback Options. The value for Always Callback To is limited to 48 characters during mixed mode.

NATIVE MODE OPTIONS   In native mode, the tab changes to allow more configuration options (see Figure 24.15).

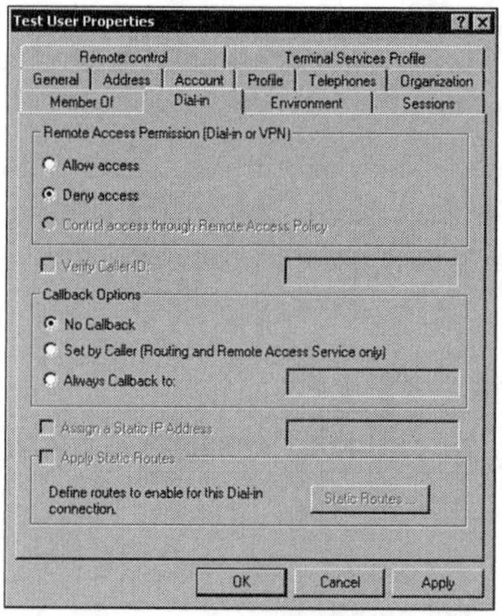

Figure 24.14
Various options are available, depending on the mode of the domain. This is maintained for compatibility for NT 4 users.

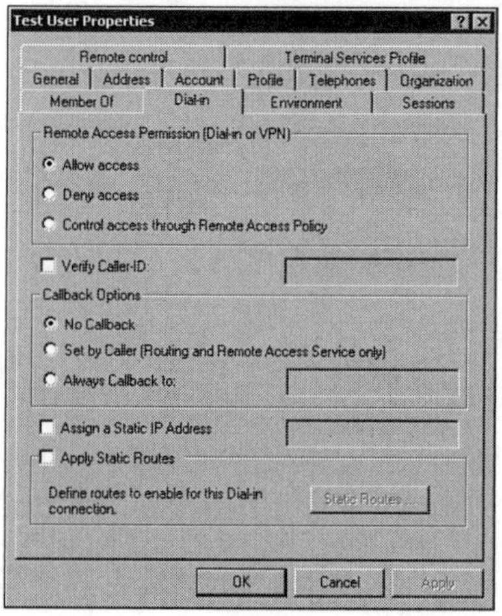

Figure 24.15
Native mode enables administrators even more control over how their users access the network via dial-in.

You now can verify the number from which the remote access was initiated. This is useful as long as the number from which the user will be dialing is known, such as a remote office. But to fully support this functionality, both sides of the call must support caller ID. If caller ID is not supported, the user is denied access, regardless of the number. If you are allowing access to your network via a VPN, this number is the IP address of the client. Again, this is a useful feature if you are sure of the IP address of the client. If your remote users are using any of the national ISPs, such as MSN, AOL, and so on, the clients are most likely being passed a DHCP-assigned IP. If this is the case, this feature will not allow access. This option could be useful in a remote office situation in which you have dedicated access or are working with a local ISP and can be assigned a static IP address.

Whenever a new user is created in native mode, the default setting is to control access through Remote Access Policy (RAP). This is a policy that is set at the routing and remote access server.

You can assign a static IP address for a particular user for remote access. A computer is still configured for either static or DHCP addressing, but this option enables you to specify an address for the remote connection. As a part of this, you also can set static routes for remote users.

This covers the major tabs you will see as an administrator for user objects. You might see more tabs that are specific to your installation. You definitely will see more tabs if you are using Exchange 2000. Also, if you have the Advanced Features option turned on, you will see even more—namely, Object and Security (see Figure 24.16).

Figure 24.16
When the MMC enables advanced features to be viewed, the Object, Security, and Published Certificates tabs appear.

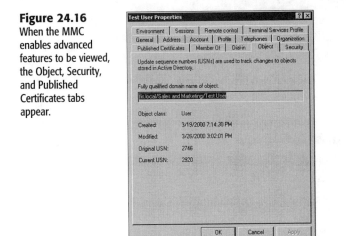

COPYING AN EXISTING USER ACCOUNT

Another method for creating user objects is to create a template account with some basic settings. For example, you could create a template account for all members of the Accounting department. When a new employee is hired to work in the Accounting department, all you have to do is right-click the template account and select Copy.

Table 24.1 shows what is and what is not copied for a copied user account.

TABLE 24.1 PROPERTIES FOR USER ACCOUNTS			
Tab	**Property**	**Copied**	**Not Copied**
Address	Street address		X
	P.O. box	X	
	City	X	
	State	X	
	ZIP Code	X	
	Country	X	
Account	User logon name		X

TABLE 24.1   CONTINUED

Tab	Property	Copied	Not Copied
	Logon hours	X	
	Log on to	X	
	Account options	X (This can be changed with the Copy Object-User Wizard)	
	Account expires	X	
Profile	Profile path	Modified to show new user's name	
	Logon script	X	
	Local path	X	
	Connect	Modified to show new user's name	
Telephone	Home		X
	Pager		X
	Mobile		X
	Fax		X
	IP phone		X
	Notes		X
	Other		X
Organization	Title		X
	Department	X	
	Company	X	
	Manager	X	
Dial-in	None of the options for dial-in are copied.		
Member of	All memberships are retained.		

It is important to note that when the user is assigned permissions and rights individually, those will not be copied to the new user account. This is another good example of why administering based on group memberships is much easier to manage than administering based on individual accounts.

When you create a template user account, set the option to disable the account; otherwise, a potential security risk exists.

GROUPS

Groups are designed to make life easier for an administrator. Instead of assigning users permissions on a individual basis, you can create groups and add various user accounts as members. When you create groups, you should create them based on the types of tasks their members will perform. In Windows 2000, groups can contain computer objects, user accounts, contacts, and other groups.

In NT 4, the Backup Operators group can back up, restore, and overwrite files for the purpose of backing up and restoring data. The same concept applies when you create groups in Windows 2000.

For example, I have a group of graphic artists who are working on our company Web site. I could create a group called "Web Artists," add each graphic artist's user account to the group, and then assign the group the appropriate permissions to a folder on the Web server that contains images. By virtue of their membership in the group, the users would have the permissions assigned to the group.

GROUP TYPES

Two types of groups are found in Windows 2000: security and distribution. The type of group is defined when you create the group, but more specifically, it is stored in Active Directory as the attribute groupType on the Class group.

Security groups are used primarily for the purpose of assigning permissions and denying permissions to the members of the group. You also can send email to a security group, whereby each member of the group would receive the message.

Distribution groups are used to group users together for sending email. This group type will reach its full potential with applications such as Exchange 2000. If you have a specific need to group objects together, but the group will not be used for assigning permissions, this is the group type to select.

GROUP SCOPE

In addition to group types, group scopes are also available. The group scopes are domain local, global, and universal. Each group scope functions differently based on the mode of the domain in which it exists.

DOMAIN LOCAL GROUPS

Domain local groups in a mixed mode domain can hold user accounts, contacts, and global groups from any domain in the forest. In native mode, they can have user accounts, computers, contacts, global groups, and universal groups as members from any domain in the forest. In addition, other domain local groups from the same domain can be nested into domain local groups. However, when it comes to assigning permissions, domain local groups can be assigned only to resources within the same domain, regardless of the mode.

GLOBAL GROUPS

Global groups, in mixed mode, can contain only users from the same domain to which the global group belongs. In native mode, global groups can have users, contacts, computers, and global groups as members.

Global groups can be assigned permissions to any resource within the forest, regardless of the domain.

UNIVERSAL GROUPS

Universal groups are new to Windows 2000. Universal security groups are available only in a domain operating in native mode. And like the name suggests, they can have accounts, global groups, and other universal groups from any domain in the forest as members.

Universal security groups can be assigned permissions to any resource in the forest.

Because the global catalog (GC) contains the *membership* of each universal group, you should keep the number of members to a minimum. The key point here is not really the fact that the membership is stored in the GC, but instead that whenever you make any change to the membership of a universal group, that change is then replicated across your network. One of the recommended methods for alleviating this excess network traffic is to limit the membership of universal groups to only other groups. Then, you add or remove accounts from these other groups because the membership of domain local and global groups is not replicated to the GC.

CREATING GROUPS

Creating a group in Windows 2000 is not difficult. Figure 24.17 shows the New Object - Group dialog box from a native mode domain. The universal group scope option would be unavailable in a mixed mode domain.

Figure 24.17
Create a group using the Create a Group Wizard.

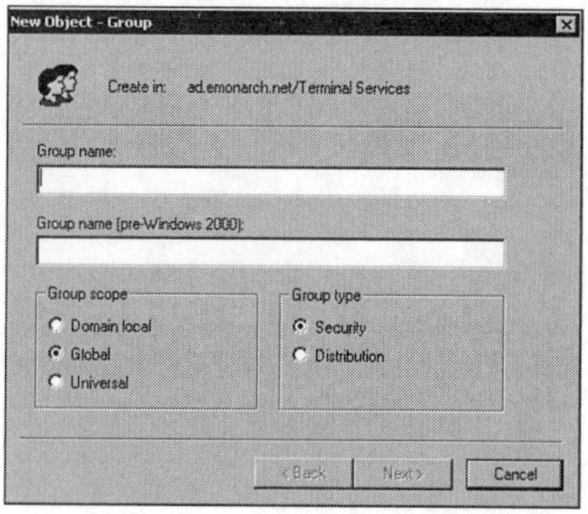

You should watch out for a few items as you name this group. The value you enter in the Group Name text box must be unique to the container in which the group will reside. The Group Name (Pre–Windows 2000) value must be unique within the domain. My recommendation is to use names that help reflect the purpose and scope of the group. A good example is Global Web Developers for a global group containing Web developers or

DL-Color Printer for a domain local group that is used to assign permissions to the color printer. If you have multiple color printers, use some other distinguishing value to designate the appropriate printer—for example, floor, cube address, and so on.

MODIFYING GROUPS

After the group has been created, you will need to add members to it. Figure 24.18 shows the Members tab of the My Group Properties page.

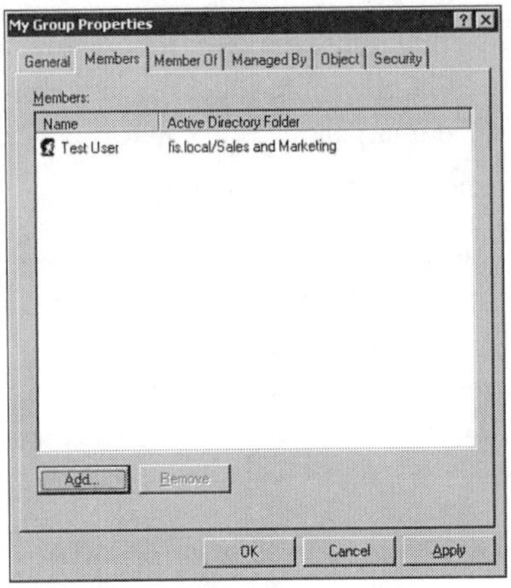

Figure 24.18
When in native mode, you can add groups of the same type to the group as well as other user objects. In mixed mode, group nesting is not allowed.

Adding members to a group is straightforward. Click Add, and then select the accounts you want as members. One of the nicest features is that Windows 2000 presents you with only the accounts that are capable of being members, with one exception: It shows the group you are working with as a potential member. However, after you add it and then click OK, an error appears stating that you can't add a group to itself.

To select accounts from other domains, click the Look In option and either select the specific domain in which you want to find the accounts or select The Entire Directory to get a complete list from which to choose.

You also can type the names of the members separated by a semicolon. If more than one name matches what you typed, a dialog box similar to that shown in Figure 24.19 appears.

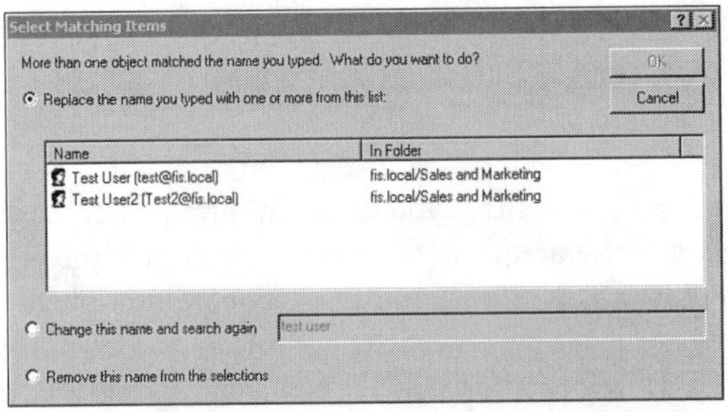

Figure 24.19
Select matching items.

You can the select one of the accounts from the list, perform the search again, or just remove the name from the list.

CHANGING GROUP SCOPE

You also can change the group scope after you create the groups, but some restrictions do exist.

A global group can be changed to a universal group, but only if the group is not a member of another global group.

A domain local group can be changed to a universal group, but only if it is not a member of another domain local group.

When it comes to universal groups, you cannot change their scopes.

PLANNING GROUP USAGE

When it comes to using groups, it is widely accepted that using them is much better than not using them. However, you can use groups incorrectly and end up causing yourself more work instead of easing the administrative load, as is their intended use.

In NT 4, the common acronym used for correct group usage is AGLP—accounts go into global groups, global groups go into local groups, and then you assign permissions to the local groups. In Windows 2000, this acronym has been slightly modified to reflect the new groups, AGDLP. But where is the universal group in this acronym? Well, it is recommended that you limit the membership of universal groups to global groups.

Universal groups can be useful when you have groups of users throughout your company who are on teams working together. By placing global groups from the various departments into the universal group, you can centrally manage the resource permissions.

GROUP NESTING

Another feature of Active Directory is the capability to nest groups. The extent to which you can nest groups is determined by the mode of your domain.

In native mode, universal groups can contain other universal groups and global groups. Domain local groups can contain other domain local groups from the same domain and universal and global groups from any domain. Global groups, on the other hand, can have other global groups as its members.

Mixed mode restricts the amount of nesting you can use. Local groups (member server and Windows 2000 Professional only) can have global groups as members.

The reason group nesting is important is that the number of members of a group has been tested up to 5,000. So the best practice is to create smaller subgroups and then populate the broader groups with these subgroups. For example, you could create one group called Accounting, and then create smaller groups called Accounts Payable, Accounts Receivable, Payroll, and so on. You then could place the appropriate users in the correct subgroup, with the Accounting group having the smaller subgroups as members.

CH

24

CONTACTS

Contacts are unique objects in that they do not serve a distinct purpose without Exchange 2000. These objects cannot be assigned permissions, although they can be members of a group.

With Exchange 2000, the contact object takes on a whole new role. For those familiar with Exchange prior to Exchange 2000, a custom recipient was an object in the Exchange directory that represented an outside email address. For example, as a consultant, I want my contact information to be readily available to my clients. So, I create a custom recipient with all my contact information; now users can see me in their global address lists. In addition, when performing directory synchronization between Exchange and some other email system— such as Microsoft Mail, Lotus Notes, cc:Mail, and so on—the "foreign" email address shows up as a custom recipient in the Exchange global address list.

With Exchange 2000 no longer supporting its own directory, Windows 2000 Active Directory provides the same functionality.

Another use I can see for the contact object comes from a development standpoint. If you are creating an HR application that will pull information from the directory, it is highly likely that you could publish contractors as contact objects in your directory. This would facilitate searching the directory for vital information. Instead of having two databases to search to find information on staff and consultants, you can now search one.

SUMMARY

Users, groups, and contacts are three of the most commonly used objects in Active Directory because they represent one of the most numerous resources in a company network. You now have a great amount of information about users that you can store. Through leveraging this information, companies will be able to streamline the number of directories they must support and truly make Active Directory the repository for resources.

TROUBLESHOOTING

UNABLE TO CREATE A NEW USER

I am trying to create a new user account in an OU that has no users, but I keep getting a message saying a user already exists with this name.

Remember the name restrictions that are in place when creating users in the directory. The UPN must be unique within the forest, and the pre–Windows 2000 user logon name must be unique within the domain. Another restriction is that the display name must be unique within the container. You should add the user's middle initial to help ensure you have unique names. This also applies to creating any type of object in the directory—the display name must be unique.

UNABLE TO CREATE A UNIVERSAL SECURITY GROUP

When I try to create a universal security group, the universal option is grayed out. But when I select Distribution, the option becomes available.

The only time you can create a universal security group is when the domain is in native mode.

UNABLE TO START A PROGRAM AT LOGON

I have set the option to start an application at logon on the Environment tab, but when the user logs on, the application does not start.

This tab is specifically for the terminal server. When a user logs on to a terminal session, that application will start, but not when they log on locally.

CHAPTER 25

PRINTER, COMPUTER, AND SHARED FOLDER OBJECTS

In this chapter

PRINTER OBJECTS

Adding a printer to the directory has to be one of Active Directory's most impressive features. This is due largely to the fact that, in the past, users had to browse for printers on the network, which generated an unnecessary amount of network traffic.

When publishing a shared printer to Active Directory, users now are able to search the directory for a specific printer based on their printing needs. No longer do they have to go around and ask other people where to find a printer that prints double-sided, collates, staples, and delivers to your desk. (Okay, that last feature is a wish, but it would be useful!) Now a user can search the directory for that information.

ACTIVE DIRECTORY AND PRINTERS

Printing in Active Directory is the responsibility of the *print server*, the computer to which the printer is physically attached. When a printer is first shared, it is automatically published in the directory. The print server is not linked to a specific domain controller, but instead randomly selects a domain controller (DC) to publish the printer. It publishes the printer only to its own domain—for example, if the print server is a member of east.fis.local, the printer is published in the east.fis.local domain and not the fis.local domain.

The printer is published as a child object of the computer to which it is attached. To view the printer as an object in Active Directory Users and Computers, you must enable the View Computers and Groups as Containers option in Active Directory Users and Computers, under the View menu.

Note

Although the default option is to list the printer in Active Directory, you as the administrator can determine which printers you want listed by disabling the specific printers, thus preventing them from being published in the directory. However, this must be done on a printer-by-printer basis.

More specifically, the printer is published as a printQueue object. Table 25.1 shows some of the attributes that are published to Active Directory.

TABLE 25.1   PUBLISHED ACTIVE DIRECTORY ATTRIBUTES

Attribute	Friendly Name	Description
cn	Directory service name	Object name.
uNCName	Network name	UNC path.
assetNumber	Asset number	Many companies assign asset tags to physical devices.
description	Comment	An administrator can add a description to describe what this particular printer is used for.
driverName	Model	Model of printer.

TABLE 25.1   CONTINUED

Attribute	Friendly Name	Description
location	Location	Used by printer location tracking.
portName	Port	Designates which port is supported by this printer.
printBinNames	Input trays	The names for each paper tray.
printCollate	Supports collation	Tells whether the printer supports collation.
printColor	Supports color printing	Tells whether the printer supports color.
printDuplex Supported	Supports double-sided printing	Tells whether the printer supports double-sided printing.
printerName	Name	
printLanguage	Printer language	PDL used by the printer.
printMax Resolution Supported	Maximum resolution	DPI supported.
printMediaReady	Paper available	Which paper is currently loaded.
printMediaSupported	Paper types supported	Which types of paper are supported.
printMemory	Installed memory	How much memory is currently installed in this printer.
printOwner	Owner name	The owner's name.
printRate	Speed	The overall speed of the printer.
printRateUnit	Speed units	How speed is measured.
printPagesPerMinute	Pages per minute	How many pages per minute the printer can print.
printShareName	Share name	The share name.
printStapling Supported	Supports stapling	Whether the printer supports stapling.
serverName	Server name	The name of the print server.
url	Web page address	The URL of the printer's Web page.
versionNumber	Object version	Used for replication and object changes.

Users can search for a printer that matches each of these attributes. This enables users to locate a printer that meets their needs for a particular print job. As the administrator, you can further control which printer users are able to find and their ability to use that printer.

Note

One thing to consider is that, although these options are available to be used for searching for printers, only some of them are truly useful. Some of the attributes, such as portName, are not useful to the user performing a search.

CH

25

With this automatic publishing of printers to Active Directory come some further automatic processes that run with respect to printers—namely, the pruning process.

Pruning printers from the directory is fairly simple: You just turn off the computer to which the printer is attached for at least 24 hours. The object is then removed from the directory. The pruning interval, by default, is eight hours. The pruning service attempts to contact the print servers that belong to the same site as the DC running the service. It attempts to contact the print server two subsequent times before removing the object. This in turn translates into three attempts before the object is pruned from the directory.

If a print server is down for a couple of days, the printers are automatically deleted from the directory by the pruning service. However, upon the start of the spooler service, the print server verifies that any printers that are shared and published are "republished" in the directory.

As with almost anything, you can control this behavior with group policies. The following policies are for controlling the pruning process (all are found under `Computer Configuration\Administrative Templates\Printers`):

- **Allow pruning of published printers**—If this policy is disabled, any printer published by the affected computer is not pruned from the directory if a domain controller cannot contact the print server. If you have a computer that is frequently removed from the network, this could be a useful policy to eliminate the extra traffic from republishing and replication of "new" objects.

- **Prune printers that are not automatically republished**—You can publish printers that are not connected to a Windows 2000 computer. Because these computers are not capable of republishing their printers to the directory and the pruner does not remove their objects by default, these printers are not published. Instead, the object is created either by using Active Directory Users and Computers or by using the script `pubprn.vbs` (see the section "Adding Printers to the Directory from Non–Windows 2000 Print Servers," later in this chapter, for more details).

→ To publish a non–Windows 2000 printer to the directory, **see** "Adding Printers to the Directory from Non–Windows 2000 Print Servers," **p. 448**

- **Directory pruning intervals**—This policy applies only to domain controllers and enables you to control the frequency at which the pruner contacts print servers.

- **Directory pruning retry**—The pruner attempts two retries for a total of three attempts before removing the printer object from the directory. You can further control that behavior with this policy.

- **Directory pruning priority**—You can enable the pruner thread to run at a higher thread priority. By default, the pruner runs at normal.

- **Check published state**—A computer with published printers attached checks the status of the published object when the spooler service starts. However, you can configure the server to periodically check the state of published printers.

PRINTER LOCATION TRACKING

One of the great features of Active Directory is when a user performs a search of the directory; the user is returned a result that shows the closest objects by looking at the IP address and subnet. (This is discussed in more detail in Chapter 14, "Active Directory Sites.") However, in the case of printers, this might not be the "closest" printer. You might have a local printer on the same subnet as your computer but that is located three floors down. This is where the Printer Location Tracking feature fits in.

The Printer Location Tracking feature enables an administrator to designate a location for each device on a network. When you try to find a printer, a Browse button appears next to the Location text box when you search for a printer (see Figure 25.1). This enables your users to search for a printer without knowing to which computer to connect but instead which printer is closest to them.

Figure 25.1
Use the Find Printers dialog box with Location Tracking enabled to find the printer nearest to your physical location.

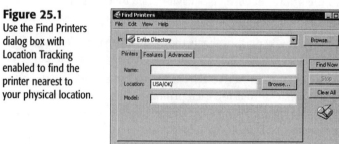

You can narrow down your location choices by browsing the network in a particular location (see Figure 25.2).

Figure 25.2
Continue to select a location in the choices provided to finally choose your desired print location.

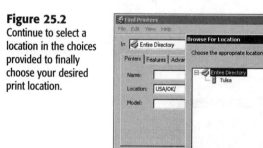

Configuring a computer group policy enables this feature. The two specific policies are pre-populate printer search location text and computer location. These two policies can be found under a computer policy in the Printers node. For more information on how to configure group policy, see Chapter 22, "Managing Group Policy."

CH
25

Note When configuring a group policy, remember that being a computer policy causes these set-tings to be applied to all computers in the organizational unit (OU) or domain where you have applied the policy.

Computer location sets the location for all computers in the OU for which the group policy is implemented, whereas the prepopulate printer policy places the default location in the search text box. This feature also is responsive to the permissions set on the printer object. If users do not have at least read permissions on the print object, they are not able to display the printer, even through a search.

MANAGING PUBLISHED PRINTERS

Other policies are available that enable you as the administrator to further control both the Location Tracking feature and the printer publishing behavior. The following list explains each policy:

- **Allow printers to be published**—By default, this is the normal behavior. You can dis-able this feature, which causes users to be unable to publish printers to the directory.

- **Automatically publish new printers in Active Directory**—This is also the default behavior. You can disable this behavior to cause each printer to have to be manually added to the directory (if you consider clicking a check box manual labor). This policy is ignored if Allow Printers to Be Published is disabled.

ADDING A PRINTER

Adding a printer attached to a Windows 2000 network requires nothing more than sharing the printer. But, for those new to Windows printing, the following steps explain how to add and share a printer:

1. Click Start, Settings, Printers.

2. Double-click Add Printer. Figure 25.3 shows the Add Printer Wizard. Click Next to continue.

Figure 25.3
The Add Printer Wizard walks through the adding process, ensuring that you select and choose all items necessary for the task.

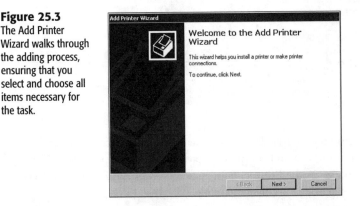

3. You must determine whether this is a local printer or a network printer (see Figure 25.4). This example assumes a local printer, so you can see the process of preparing a printer to be shared on a network. The option exists to have Windows 2000 automatically detect the printer as long as it is Plug-and-Play. If the printer driver exists in the `driver.cab` file, you do not need to provide any additional disks for your printer.

> **Note**
>
> The options are a little different if you will be connecting to a network printer. After selecting the Network Printer option, you can either search the directory for a printer, type the name of the printer, and even browse for the printer, or type the URL for a printer on the Internet or your corporate intranet.

Figure 25.4
Select either Local Printer or Network Printer.

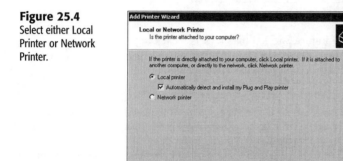

4. If your printer is not Plug-and-Play, a list of port options appears (see Figure 25.5). You must select to which port your printer is attached before continuing. Otherwise, Windows 2000 installs the printer without any other intervention from you.

Figure 25.5
The system must know on which port to look for the print device.

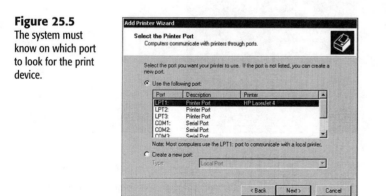

5. Next, you must select the type of printer you have attached to the server. The wizard provides several companies and hardware devices from which to choose (see Figure 25.6).

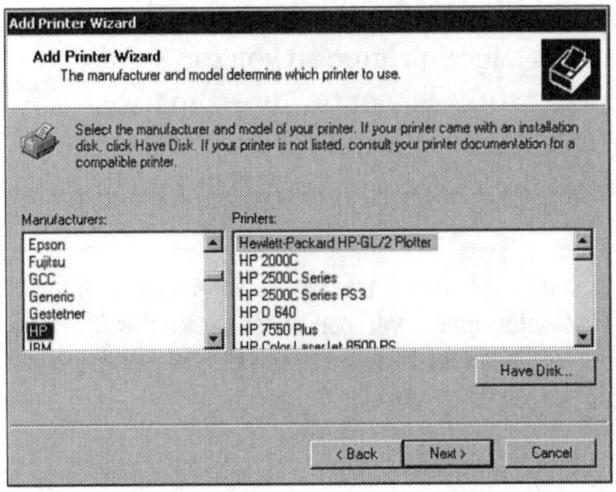

Figure 25.6
Be sure to select the correct printer manufacturer and model.

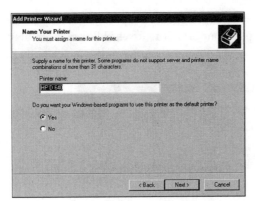

6. Now name your printer (see Figure 25.7). This name is what the printer will be referred to locally—not from the network. You also can set this printer to be the default printer if you want.

> **Note**
>
> If you intend to share this printer in the future, you must take into consideration the type of client that will be connecting to it. Do not use any name greater than eight characters long if you will be sharing this printer with DOS clients. In Windows 2000, you are allowed to include spaces and even special characters in the name of the printer. However, you should test the name with other applications and clients before settling on a naming convention for printers.

Figure 25.7
Choose a unique and yet appropriate name for your printer while remembering any restrictions that might affect clients connecting to a shared printer.

7. Figure 25.8 illustrates the option to share your printer. By default, if you decide to share this printer, it becomes listed in Active Directory as a child object of the computer to which it is attached. You can move the printer after you have finished the installation. The printer is stored as an object class of printQueue.

→ To move a printer, **see** "Modifying a Printer," **p. 447**

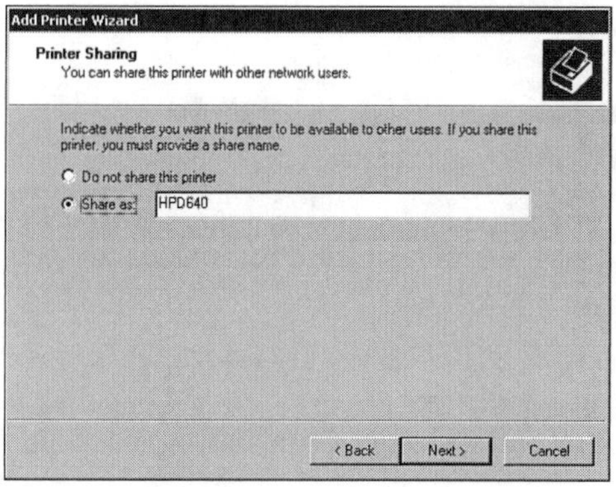

Figure 25.8
To enable other users on the network to use your printer, select the Share As radio button.

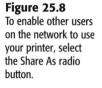

8. The Location and Comment screen enables you to add more detail for the users' information, such as 2nd Floor Room 125 (see Figure 25.9). This information is stored in Active Directory, and a user can search on it. The same applies to comments, except comments are actually stored in the attribute description.

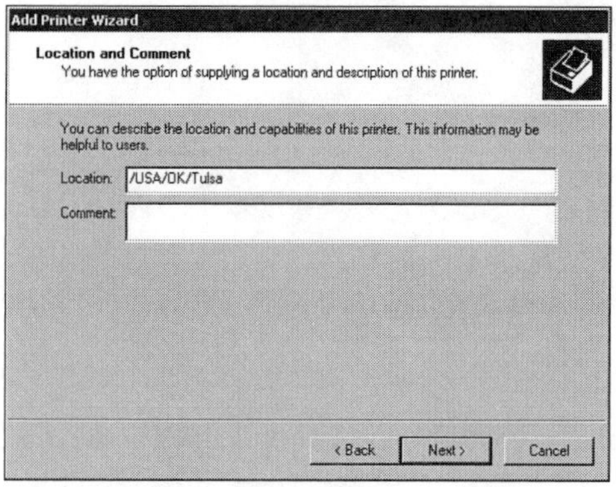

Figure 25.9
Use the Location and Comment boxes to define your printer and its location for searchability on the network.

9. After filling in the Location and Comment fields, you are asked whether you want to print a test page. This is normally a good idea, just to see whether the printer is actually the one you specified.

10. Finally, you are shown a summary page that details all the choices you made during the installation process (see Figure 25.10). You can change any of these items before finishing the installation by clicking the Back button.

MODIFYING A PRINTER

After you have installed a printer, you can modify certain items with respect to Active Directory. If you no longer want the printer to be published in the directory, right-click the printer from inside the Printer dialog box and select Sharing. Then, clear the List in the Directory check box (see Figure 25.11).

Figure 25.10
Study the printer summary page carefully to ensure everything is exactly as you intend before finishing the process.

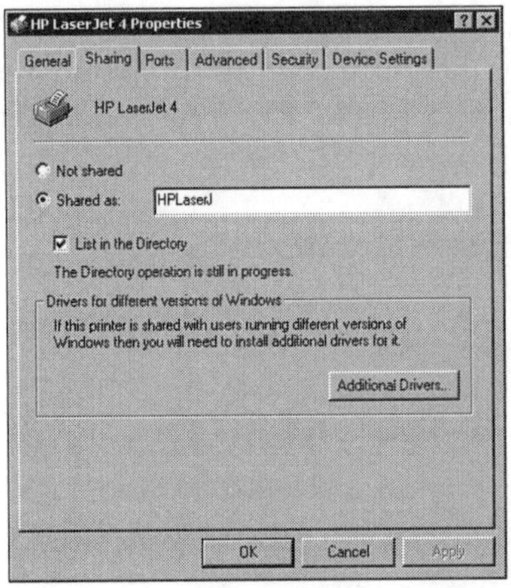

Figure 25.11
Use the Printer Properties dialog box to prevent the printer from being listed in the directory.

You also can move the printer to any other OU or container in the directory by selecting the printer object and then right-clicking and selecting Move. You then determine the location within the current domain to move the object to.

ADDING PRINTERS TO THE DIRECTORY FROM NON–WINDOWS 2000 PRINT SERVERS

You can add printers to your Active Directory if they are not connected to a Windows 2000 print server. This is useful during a migration or even when printers are attached to Novell NetWare print servers. Another scenario is when you need to publish printers from another Windows 2000 forest to your directory for access.

This is accomplished one of two ways. The first is by using Active Directory Users and Computers:

1. Right-click whichever OU or domain you want to create the printer in and select New, Printer. A dialog box appears similar to the one shown in Figure 25.12.

2. Type the UNC pathname to the printer you want to be published to the directory.

Figure 25.12
Enter the complete path of your printer to create a new printer object.

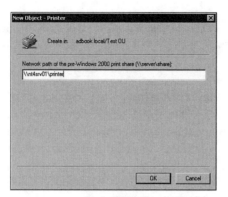

> **Tip**
>
> Ensure that the printer is currently shared and online; otherwise, the Add Printer function will fail.

> **Note**
>
> The printer cannot be a printer that has been shared on a Windows 2000 operating system in the same forest because the Add Printer function is available only for non–Windows 2000 printers. When sharing printers on a Windows 2000 computer, the printer is automatically published to the directory.

The second method involves using a Visual Basic script file—`pubprn.vbs`. This file is located in the `%systemroot%\system32` directory and is intended to be run from the command prompt by typing **cscript pubprn.vbs** and then the appropriate parameters, which are as follows:

```
pubprn.vbs \\servername\printer DS path to publish object
```

The following is an example:

```
cscript pubprn.vbs \\fs1\laser1 "LDAP://OU=Printers,DC=fis,DC=local"
```

This script essentially performs the same task as using Active Directory Users and Computers to add a non–Windows 2000 printer to the directory. For some, being able to perform this function from a command line provides a greater feeling of control. If you are interested in learning more about the script itself, you can use Notepad or your favorite text editor to view the script.

COMPUTER OBJECTS

Computer objects represent physical computers that are members of the domain. The computers can be either servers or workstations and also can be either Windows 2000 computers or pre–Windows 2000. However, this does not include Windows 9x. Four ways exist to add a new computer object to the directory.

Ch

25

Note

Windows 9x does not have the capability to join a domain. It can use resources in a domain but is not capable of being a member of a domain.

CREATING COMPUTER OBJECTS

The first method is to use the Active Directory Users and Computers snap-in to create the object. Similar to creating any other object (an exception being a Windows 2000 printer), you right-click the OU in which you want to create the new object and select New, Computer. The New Object - Computer dialog box appears (see Figure 25.13).

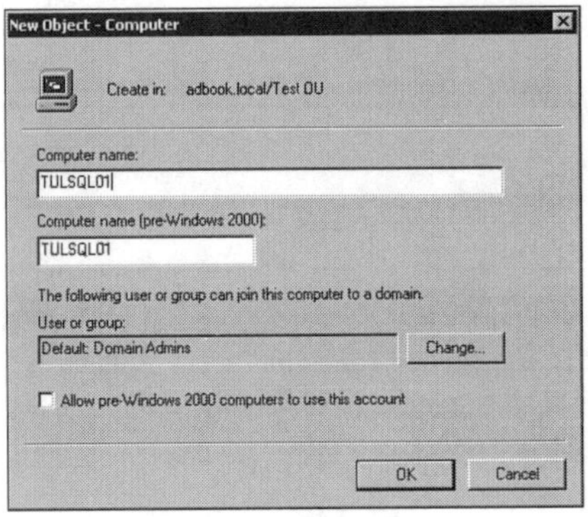

Figure 25.13
You can create a new computer object simply by using Active Directory Users and Computers.

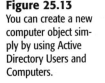

The Windows 2000 computer name can be up to 64 characters in length, whereas the pre–Windows 2000 name can be only 15 characters. Additionally, you should consider DNS when naming computers. DNS allows for characters A–Z, a–z, 0–9, and a hyphen.

By default, a user can add only 10 computer accounts to the domain, whereas members of the Domain Admins group can join any number of computers to the domain. However, you can change this to enable users to join their computers to the domain without having to give out the Administrator password.

Note

To assign someone the permission to add more than 10 computer accounts to a domain, you must use the Delegation Control Wizard to assign him the Create Computer Accounts right on the domain or on a particular OU.

For pre–Windows 2000 machines to use this object, you must select the Allow Pre-Windows 2000 Computers to Use This Account check box.

Figure 25.14 shows the next screen if you have remote installation services (RIS) installed in your domain. Managed computer accounts are for prestaging computers in the directory for the use of RIS.

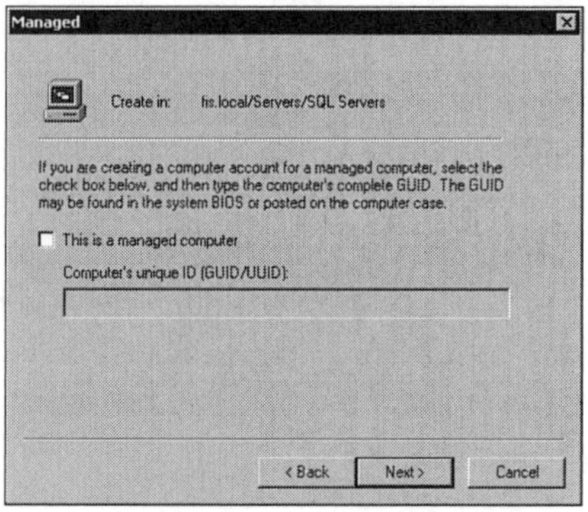

Figure 25.14
The Managed dialog box enables you to specify which accounts will use RIS for installation.

RIS is a Windows 2000 service that enables administrators to install an "image" of a Windows 2000 Professional install to a computer that supports the PXE standard. By prestaging accounts in the directory, you are able to place computers in the appropriate OU without any extra effort. RIS, in combination with Software Installation GPOs, can fully automate a workstation installation.

At the end of the process of creating a new computer, you will see a summary screen. Click Finish; the account will then be created in the appropriate location.

CREATING A COMPUTER OBJECT USING VBSCRIPT

Another method of creating computer objects in Active Directory is by using the ADSI object model and either VBScript or Jscript. This example uses VBScript. You can type the sample script to create computer accounts into Notepad or the text editor of your choice. The script is as follows:

```
Dim objDN
Dim objComputer

Set objDN=GetObject("LDAP://ou=Servers;DC=fis,DC=local")
Set objComputer=objDN.Create("computer","cn=WKS01")
objComputer.Put "samAccountName","WKS01"
objComputer.SetInfo

objComputer.Put "Description","This is a test workstation"
objComputer.SetInfo
```

Note

The Windows Scripting Host enables multiple scripting languages to be used for writing scripts. The most prevalent are Visual Basic Script (VBScript) and Java Script (JScript). Administrators who might already be familiar with Visual Basic or even BASIC will find that VBScript has many familiar aspects. Some administrators who have had experience with other computer programming languages, such as C or C++, will find JScript more familiar. In terms of performance, there is no real advantage to either language when interfacing with the scripting host.

CH

25

The GetObject statement specifies where in the directory to start. It also could be used for modifying the computer account or even deleting the object.

The Create method tells VBS to create an object with a class of computer; then you can give its DN entry for a name. If you were to leave off the cn=, VBS would report an error stating that the server is unwilling to perform the operation.

Notice that the samAccountName attribute is set prior to calling the first SetInfo method. This is the pre–Windows 2000 name for the computer account. This requirement is also true for creating user accounts.

→ **See** Chapter 30, "Scripting the Active Directory," **p. 515**

CREATING A COMPUTER OBJECT USING NET COMMANDS

Another method of creating computer accounts is using the NET command. This is not a new feature to Windows 2000; it is present in NT 4. The use of this command is straightforward:

```
NET COMPUTER \\computername /add
```

You also can remove an account from the domain by using the /del switch instead of the /add switch.

CREATING A COMPUTER OBJECT BY JOINING A DOMAIN

The more common method of adding a computer to the domain is during the installation of a computer, by making it a member of the domain. Figure 25.15 shows the dialog box that enables you to change the domain membership of any member server or workstation.

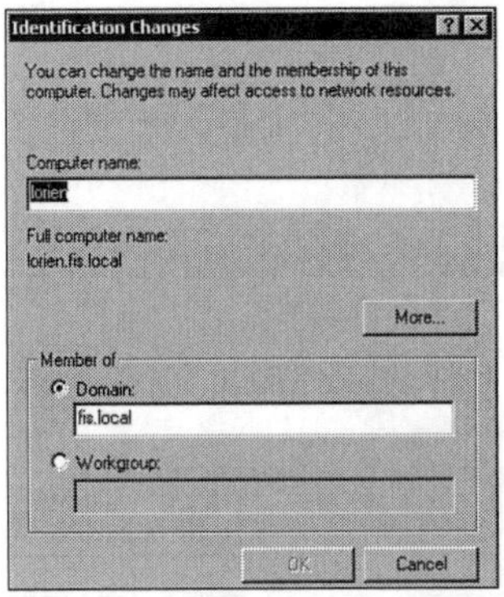

Figure 25.15
Changing domain membership.

> **Note**
>
> You are not able to change the membership of a domain controller without first demoting it to a member server by running dcpromo.

COMPUTER OBJECT PROPERTIES

At this point, you will tour each computer object property tab to get a better look at some of the features added by Windows 2000.

Figure 25.16 shows the General tab from the properties of my test domain controller, SAURON. You can edit the description, as well as enable this server or workstation for delegation. You also are able to see the role of this machine.

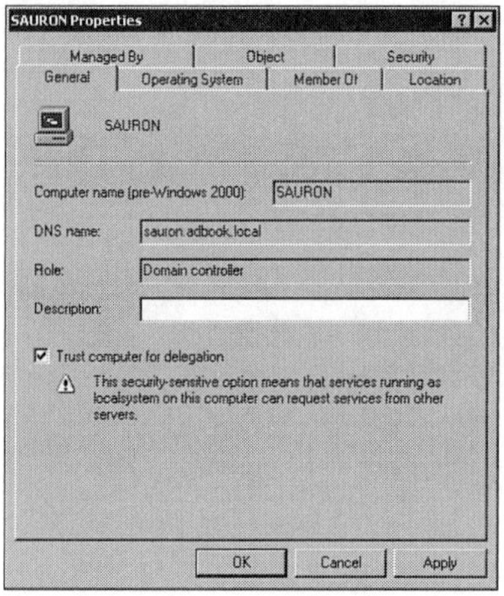

Figure 25.16
The General tab of the Properties page provides the name and role of the computer account.

The Operating System tab is one of my favorites because it enables me to determine which OS and which service pack level machines are in my network without having to touch each one (see Figure 25.17).

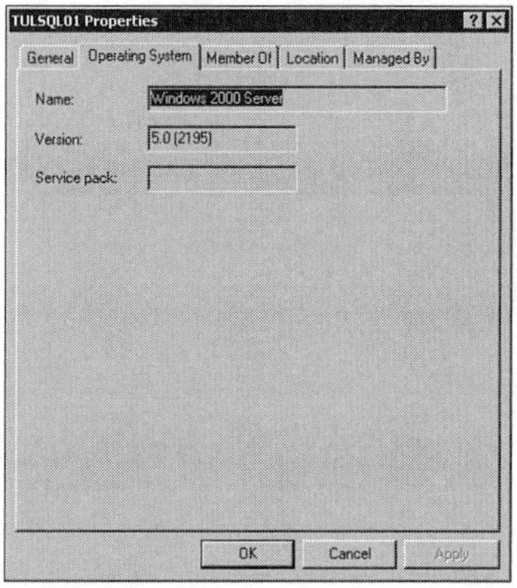

Figure 25.17
The Operating System tab provides useful information even if you are not sitting at the computer.

Because Windows 2000 enables computer objects to now be security principals, you can place computers into groups (see Figure 25.18).

CH
25

Figure 25.18
You can add a computer to a group using the Member Of tab.

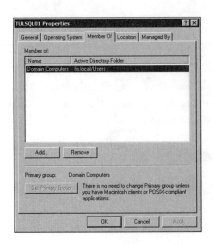

For implementation of group policies specific to an OU, you can filter the implementation of the GPO by assigning deny permissions on the apply group policy to the computer object.

As with printers, you can specify a location for a particular computer object (see Figure 25.19). You must assign locations to computer objects to fully take advantage of the Printer Location feature.

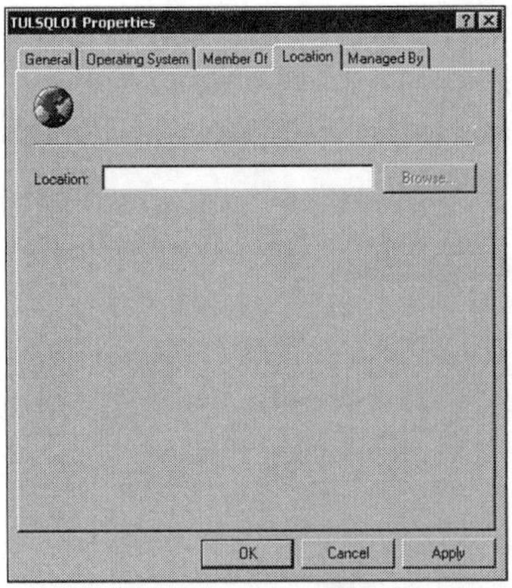

Figure 25.19
Use the Location tab to work together the printer location service.

You can use the Managed By tab to provide information about who is responsible for a particular machine (see Figure 25.20). This does not assign any unique permission to the user selected. This tab simply provides a GUI so a user or another administrator can find the contact information for the person to contact when a problem with a particular machine arises.

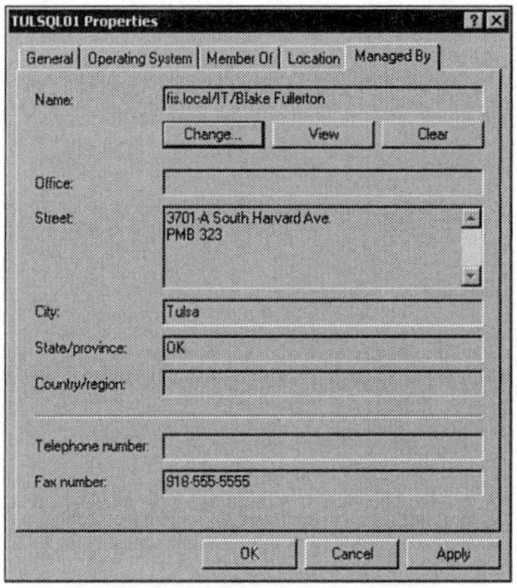

Figure 25.20
You can find information about who is responsible for a given machine by viewing the Managed By tab.

SUMMARY

This chapter looked at publishing three objects to Active Directory. Publishing objects is not necessarily the greatest feature for Active Directory; instead, the capability to search for these objects is one of the items that makes Active Directory such a compelling directory service. This facilitates users being able to find the resources they need in a much more efficient manner than browsing the network.

TROUBLESHOOTING

CANNOT CONNECT TO SHARED FOLDERS

I am unable to connect to a shared folder after publishing to the Active Directory.

This most likely is an issue with NetBIOS having been disabled over TCP/IP. To connect to a share using a UNC, NetBIOS must be enabled.

CANNOT CREATE PRINTERS

I'm not able to create a printer object in the directory using Active Directory Users and Computers.

You can create printer objects in the directory using the Active Directory Users and Computers snap-in only for printers that are not attached to a Windows 2000 computer.

CHAPTER 26

CONTAINERS AND ORGANIZATIONAL UNITS

In this chapter

ORGANIZATIONAL UNITS

Organizational units (OUs) are objects that exist within Active Directory as containers, meaning they can contain other objects, such as users, computers, or even other OUs. They serve to help administrators organize and administer the directory. When Active Directory is first installed, only one OU exists by default—Domain Controllers. Figure 26.1 shows the default view of a fresh Active Directory installation.

> **Tip**
>
> If you upgrade your network from NT to Windows 2000 Active Directory, all your users will, by default, end up in the Users Container. In addition, your computers will be in the Computers Container. To reap the benefit of the hierarchical Active Directory, you must move the users and computers to organizational units.

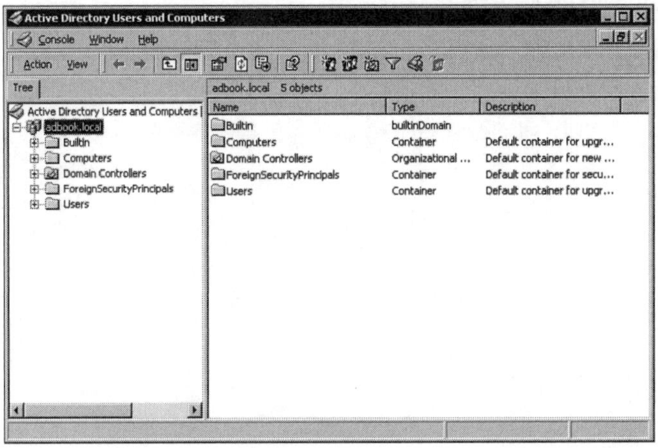

Figure 26.1
The Domain Controllers OU has an added graphic to its folder icon to indicate it is more than a simple container.

This section focuses on creating and managing OUs.

CREATING AN OU

To create an OU, right-click the level at which you want to create the OU and select New, Organizational Unit. Then, type the name; you now have a new organizational unit.

You need at least read, list contents, and create organizational unit object rights before you can create an OU. For example, if you wanted to create an OU under the Domain Controllers OU, you would have to have the previously mentioned rights on the Domain Controllers OU.

→ **See** "Security Components of the Active Directory," **p. 312**

You can create multiple levels of organizational units if you want (see Figure 26.2).

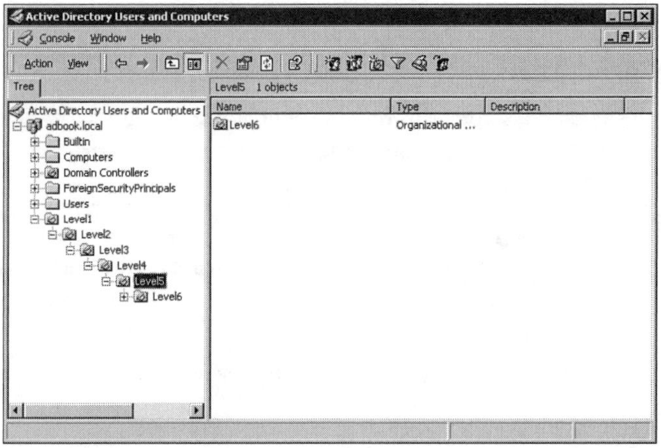

Figure 26.2
The extended hierarchy of the OU provides a graphical representation of how all the folders are contained within one another.

Having a deep OU structure is not always necessary or even desired. Usually, an OU structure more than six organizational units deep is not necessary. User logon and group policies can be adversely affected with a deep OU structure. The deep OU structure in itself does not primarily cause performance degradation. If, however, each of the organizational units has a group policy attached to it, the logon process can become slower.

→ For more information on group policy and performance, **see** "Choosing Where to Assign Group Policy," **p. 339**

Organizational units can be created at any level within the AD structure, except within containers. You can visually identify an OU from a container based on the icon used to represent an OU. The icon is a folder with a partially opened phone book (at least it looks like a phone book).

→ **See** "Containers," **p. 465**

Note

It is important to note that, in this documentation and others, any object that can contain another object is described as a *container*. This includes organizational units. Here we will refer to items such as the default Users Container with an uppercase "C" and the concept of a generic container object with a lowercase "c".

Another method of creating an OU is to use ADSI. This is similar to creating users or any other object in the directory, with the only main difference being the object class. The following code snippet is all that is necessary to create a new OU called Marketing at the root of the domain, fis.local:

```
'bind to the LDAP server
Set objDN=GetObject("LDAP://DC=fis,DC=local")

'create the Organizational Unit
Set objOU=objDN.Create "organizationalUnit", "ou=Marketing"

'use the setinfo method to write the new object
ObjOU.SetInfo
```

CH
26

→ For more information on ADSI scripting, **see** "Using ADSI with WSH," **p. 516**

DESIGN CONSIDERATIONS

Although this book does not focus on designing an Active Directory implementation, we should discuss some issues concerning the creation of an OU structure.

Tip

If you are upgrading from an NT multiple-domain model, you can "collapse" your domains into one domain with multiple organizational units. This enables a simpler single-domain structure.

→ For more information on collapsing domains, **see** "movetree," **p. 504**

First, you must assess how you want to delegate administration. This is the first consideration when designing your OU structure. Because users are not exposed to the OU structure, you don't have to make it easy to understand from a user perspective. Instead, focus on what works in your organization. When creating the OU structure, three variations seem to fit most organizations. As with most designs, this is just what seems to fit at this time. Every organization is different and therefore could have other ways to design its OU structure. However, it seems that most are a combination of the following three design methods:

■ Geographic topology of the organization

■ Business units

■ Organizational roles

The first design methodology is to base the OU structure on the geographic topology of the organization. Figure 26.3 shows such a structure.

Figure 26.3
Naming the organizational units after specific U.S. states maps the OU structure by physical location.

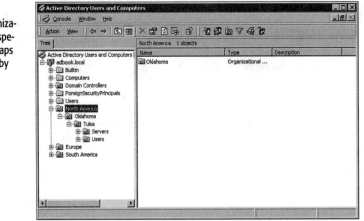

You could then delegate administration for the administrator at each location.

The second design methodology is to base the OU structure on the business units. This is focused more on the divisions of a company than the actual locations. Figure 26.4 shows an example.

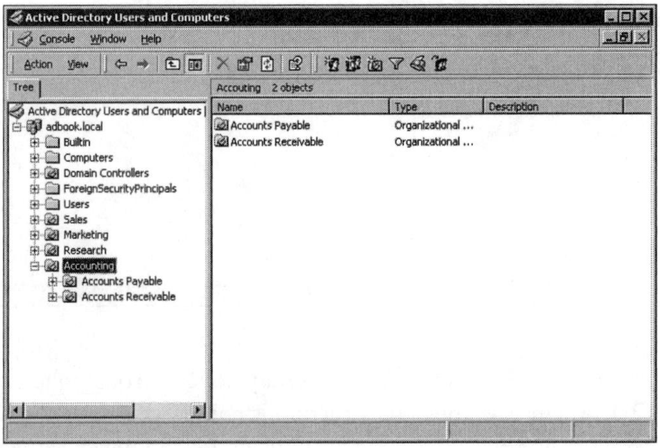

Figure 26.4
Naming the organizational units by their functions as business units also adds to the overall design organization.

The third approach is to base it on roles. With this design, you create an OU structure based on the types of objects to be managed. For example, an Exchange Servers OU could be created, and then all your exchange servers could be in this OU. Figure 26.5 shows such a structure.

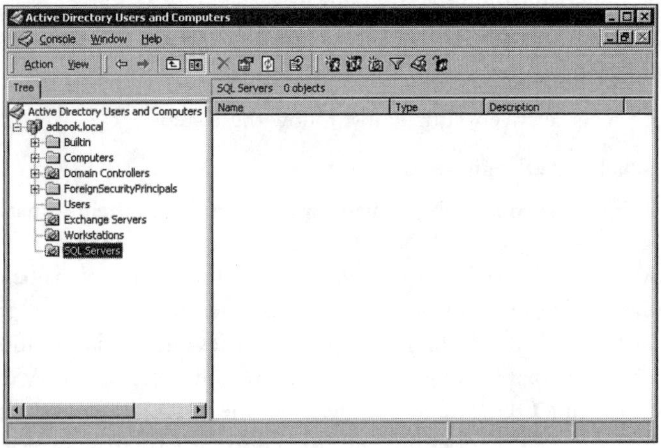

Figure 26.5
Naming OU structures by roles, such as Exchange Servers, helps identify the organizations at a glance.

CH
26

One other variation exists, which really is nothing more than a combination of the previous design methodologies. You could create a structure similar to what is shown in Figure 26.6 and essentially have a little of each design methodology.

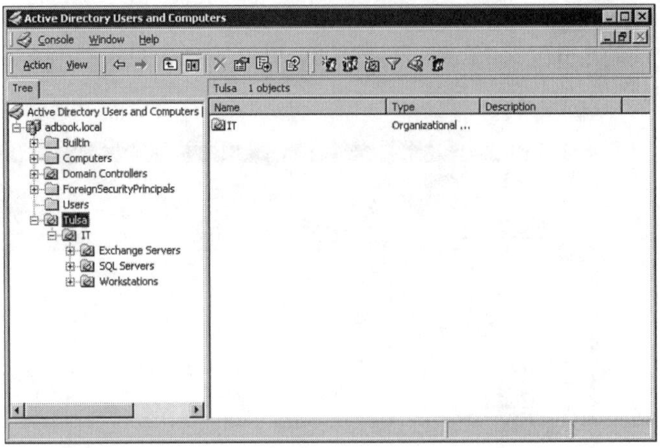

Figure 26.6
Using mixed naming conventions can ease the overall organization of the domain, but be sure you plan everything out before you begin mapping.

Another design consideration is the use of group policy. Group policy, by default, flows down the OU structure. If your OU structure is not planned carefully with this in mind, assigning group policy can be much more difficult. Group policy is the preferred methodology for managing everything from desktops to password restrictions and, as such, is a huge subject. See Chapter 20, "Group Policy," for more information.

MOVING AN OU

You can move an OU anywhere within the domain. When you select an OU to move, all the objects contained within that OU move as well. This is a great feature because as organizations continue to change, the Active Directory can adapt to the changes without a complete network redesign.

Moving an OU is relatively simple; just follow these steps:

1. Right-click the OU and select Move.

2. Select either the root of the domain or another OU as the destination. Click OK.

When moving an OU, you must consider some of the ramifications before actually conducting the move. Most of the issues you should consider have to do with group policies and policy inheritance. When dealing with group policies and the implication of moving an OU, you must consider what GPO is set at the new parent object and how this will affect the move of the existing OU. The nice thing about the way the OU is structured is that it is very portable and the user does not get exposed to the OU structure.

Tip

You also can move organizational units across domains in the same forest with the move-tree tool from the Windows 2000 Support Tools.

DELETING AN OU

Removing an OU from the directory is easier than moving one: You just click the OU you want to delete and press the Delete key. Remember, however, that when you delete a container, all the objects within that container are deleted as well.

Caution

If you accidentally delete an OU, the only way to recover it and its contents is through an authoritative restore. See Chapter 28, "Backup and Restore," for information on how to perform an authoritative restore.

Deleting an OU might have ramifications that aren't obvious. If computer accounts are located within an OU prior to deletion and you have forgotten to move them, the computer accounts are deleted along with the OU. Now, you might be thinking that this is no big deal. But consider this: The computer accounts have a unique SID that is associated with them. If you attempt to log on to the domain from one of the workstations, you are unable because the account no longer is a member of the domain. To rejoin the domain, you must perform the following steps at the machine that has been removed from the domain:

1. Log on to the computer with a local account having administrative permissions.
2. Right-click My Computer and select Properties.
3. Select the Network Identification tab and click Properties.
4. Click the option button next to Workgroup in the Member of Area and type a name for a workgroup.
5. You receive a message stating that the computer was removed from the domain, but the computer account was unable to be deleted. This is as expected, because the computer account no longer exists in the domain. Click OK.
6. You then receive a dialog box that welcomes you to the workgroup. Click OK, and then click OK in the System Properties dialog box.
7. Reboot the computer.
8. After logging on to the computer again, perform steps 2–4, but this time click the option button next to Domain and type the name of the domain you want to join.
9. You must present a username and password that has rights to add a workstation to the domain.
10. Close the System Properties dialog box by clicking OK on the Welcome to the Domain message. Then, click OK in the System Properties dialog box.
11. Reboot the machine; this computer should now be back in the domain.

After rejoining the domain, you can move the computer account like any other object into the correct OU.

CH
26

Tip

When a Windows 2000 computer first joins the domain, it is placed, by default, in the Computers Container. For this computer to process a group policy other than the one assigned at the domain level, it must be moved to an OU.

Caution

Deleting an OU does not delete the group policy associated with the OU. A group policy can always be deleted from the Policies Container inside the System Container in the Active Directory Users and Computers MMC Snap-in.

Deleting organizational units has other ramifications that must be considered because of the distributed directory structure of Active Directory. When an object is deleted from AD, it is actually marked with a Tombstone for 60 days. Just performing a restore of the OU will not bring it back. To permanently restore a deleted OU, you must perform an authoritative restore.

Figure 26.7 shows a sample configuration of two domain controllers in separate sites but a part of the same domain, fis.local. As discussed earlier, both DCs contain the same data as far as AD is concerned. This is where the challenge exists when deleting an OU or any container.

Figure 26.7
TULDC01 and DFWDC01 are in two different states and are connected to one another via the fis.local network.

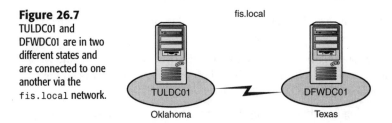

fis.local

TULDC01 — DFWDC01

Oklahoma   Texas

Figure 26.8 shows a sample OU structure for the fis.local domain. An administrator in Tulsa decides that the Training OU is no longer needed, so he deletes the OU while connected to the DC—TULDC01. (To connect to a particular DC, right-click the Active Directory Users and Computers node in the Active Directory Users and Computers snap-in and select Connect to Domain Controller.) The Training OU is marked for deletion.

→ **See** "Deleted Objects," p. 261

Before replication can be completed, an administrator in Dallas decides to move the user object Cameron Blake from the Sales OU to the Training OU. If the MMC Snap-in, Active Directory Users and Computers, is currently focused on DFWDC01, the operation completes successfully. This is possible because each DC in a domain has a complete copy of the directory.

Figure 26.8
This representation of the OU structure for `fis.local` shows how anyone using the `fis.local` drive can manipulate any part of the entire structure from any location.

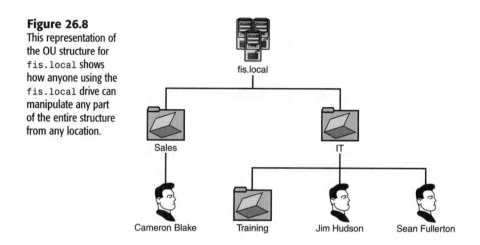

After replication does occur, the user object is moved to the LostAndFound Container because the Training OU has been marked for deletion. The user is still able to log on but does not receive any special GPO that you might have set because the object would be capable of receiving GPOs only from the site and domain level.

→ See "Introduction to Group Policy," **p. 334**

This is one of the unique aspects of Active Directory that requires foresight to manage.

OU DESIGN CONSIDERATIONS

When considering how to create your OU structure for your domain, you should consider a variety of issues before settling on any one design.

The primary considerations are administration and inheritance. In Active Directory, you can delegate the administration of an OU to a user or group by giving him or them the full-control permission to an OU and allowing the permissions to inherit to child objects. If you plan your OU structure properly—with both group policy and permissions inheritance in mind—you can give a user or group permissions at a point in the OU structure, and they can manage virtually anything below them in the OU hierarchy.

The best rule of thumb is to group users and computers together by what they need and what they do. If the salespeople all need the same desktop, applications, and logon scripts, this is a natural starting point for planning organizational units.

CONTAINERS

Containers as a class of objects are unique. Even though an OU is a container, the class of object is `organizationalUnit`. The easiest way to distinguish an OU from a container is by the icon in Active Directory Users and Computers. The icon for a container object looks like a folder with no other features, whereas an OU has a folder icon with a open book.

CH

26

By default, six containers are created in every domain: Builtin, Computers, ForeignSecurityPrincipals, LostAndFound, System, and Users.

Tip

> The LostAndFound and System Containers are not visible in the Active Directory Users and Computers MMC Snap-in unless you turn on Advanced Features from the View menu.

The Builtin container holds the default local groups that are the same on every Windows 2000 system. The SIDs on the specific accounts are the same on every Windows 2000 domain as well. In addition, you can't change any of the accounts in the Builtin container. The groups that are found in this container are as follows:

- Account Operators
- Administrators
- Backup Operators
- Guests
- Pre-Windows 2000 Compatible Access
- Print Operators
- Replicator
- Server Operators
- Users

The Users Container is specifically designed for holding user and group accounts that are created from down-level management tools, such as User Manager for Domains, or more specifically, tools that use the SAM API. It also serves as a container for user and group accounts following an upgrade from NT 4 or NT 3.51.

The Computers Container holds computer accounts for the domain following an upgrade from NT 4 or NT 3.51. This container—just like the Users Container—also acts as a container for computer accounts created by using the SAM API.

LostAndFound, on the other hand, holds accounts that have been misplaced. Essentially, this occurs when an account is being created in a container on one DC while that same container is being deleted on another DC in the domain.

The System Container holds a wide variety of information that pertains to the domain. For more details on this container, see Chapter 11, "Domains, Trees, and Forests."

The ForeignSecurityPrincipals Container holds proxy objects for principal accounts from NT 4 or NT 3.51 trusted domains, as well as from Windows 2000 domains that are a part of a separate forest. For an account to appear in this container, it must have been added to Windows 2000 groups for access to resources in the domain.

CREATING CONTAINER OBJECTS

No method exists in the Active Directory Users and Computers snap-in for creating a container object by default. You can, however, still create them.

First, you can create a container object with ADSI by specifying the class of object:

```
'bind to the LDAP server
Set objDN=GetObject("LDAP://DC=fis,DC=local")

'create the container
Set objOU=objDN.Create "container", "cn=TrashContainer"

'write the change to the Active Directory database
ObjOU.SetInfo
```

→ **See** "Using ADSI with WSH," **p. 516**

This code creates a container at the root of the domain called TrashContainer. Note the difference between this code and the code used to create an OU—the class of the object and the DN.

Using script, you can create a container anywhere in the domain, even as a child of an OU. In addition, you can create accounts in these containers. However, you would not be able to implement GPO on any object inside a container.

DELETING CONTAINER OBJECTS

Deleting container objects is as simple as any other object. You simply either select the container and press the Delete key or right-click the object and select Delete.

SUMMARY

Organizational units are a major enabling feature of Windows 2000 Active Directory. They enable delegation of authority, to a large extent group policy, and the single-domain model.

Planning organizational units is probably the most time-consuming process, unlike creating them, which is operationally very simple. A good OU design takes into account security and group policy inheritance as well as administrative delegation.

TROUBLESHOOTING

ORGANIZATIONAL UNIT CHANGES

I have moved users to a new OU, but when they log on they do not see any difference.

OU membership is largely invisible to users. If they are moved from one OU to another, they will see the difference only in group policy, if any exists. Their placement in the Active Directory hierarchy, however, should not be visible to them.

GROUP POLICY AND ORGANIZATIONAL UNITS

I have moved users into a new OU, but they are not processing part of the group policy for their new OU.

Make sure that the portions of group policy you are missing are not in the computer section of group policy. Both the user and the computer must be in the OU to process both sections of group policy.

DELEGATION OF CONTROL WIZARD

I have used the Delegation of Control Wizard to delegate control of an OU to a user. However, she can only create users and groups in the OU.

By default, using the Delegation of Control Wizard does not give a user the permissions necessary to create new organizational units. An easy way to assign the permissions necessary to do this is to grant the user or group full control to the OU and set the permissions to apply to This Object and All Child Objects.

MOVING AND CREATING USERS

I have moved user Joe into a new OU. Now I want to create a new user Joe in another OU, but the Active Directory Users and Computers MMC Snap-in won't let me.

The user principal name of any user must be unique. Placing a user in a different OU changes his LDAP distinguished name, but not his UPN.

CHAPTER **27**

ACTIVE DIRECTORY DATABASE OPTIMIZATION

In this chapter

INTRODUCTION TO THE ACTIVE DIRECTORY DATABASE

Active Directory uses a fault-tolerant transactional database for storing objects, the schema, and configuration information. You can divide the database into two main parts: the directory database and the transaction logs.

As an administrator, you will need to know how to prepare for the storage of the directory (sizing), how to maintain the database, and how the database operates.

UNDERSTANDING TRANSACTIONAL DATABASES

The Active Directory database is *transactional*. This means two things. First, it means that every modification to the database is written first to a page in memory and then to the log file and is finally committed to the database. Second, every transaction is *atomic*. This means that either the entire modification is written or none of it is written. This prevents partial modifications from being applied to an object. A *modification* to the Active Directory database is defined as a single attribute being changed.

The transactional attributes of Active Directory enable you to recover from a loss of power to the server without encountering partially modified objects. Because it is written to a separate transaction log, the database and transaction log can be compared at startup, and any committed transactions can then be written to the AD database.

ACTIVE DIRECTORY DATABASE STRUCTURE

The directory database is divided into six tables (see Table 27.1).

TABLE 27.1   THE DIRECTORY DATABASE TABLES

Table	Description
System Table	This table is created by the ESE and contains information about the DSA-defined tables and indices.
Link Table	The Link table contains information about linked attributes. Linked attributes are references to other objects in the directory.
Data Table	This table holds the actual objects—in other words, users, groups, computers, sites, servers, and so on. This is the main table for Active Directory.
Hidden Table	This table contains bootstrap information that is used by the directory system agent (DSA)—specifically, the distinguished name tag (DNT) of the NTDSA object. This, in turn, is used to retrieve the local DSA object from the Data table.
Security Descriptor Propagation Table (SDPropTable)	Any time someone modifies an SD, the DSA queues an SD propagation from that point down, and it uses this table to ensure that the queue of pending propagations persists across reboots. As propagations are completed, they are removed from the front of the queue.
MsysDefrag1 Table	This table is used in the defrag process.

The distinguished name tag (DNT) is a 4-byte DWORD value. A DWORD is a 32-bit unsigned integer. It serves as the row ID for each object in the Data table and is incremented each time a new object is created in the directory database. Every object in the directory is stored as a row.

This is where you run into a limitation with the number of objects that can be stored in Active Directory. As mentioned in earlier chapters, the global catalog (GC) contains a copy of every object in the forest. This would, in effect, limit the directory to 4 billion objects.

The database is managed by the extensible storage engine (ESE), which is implemented in the ESENT.DLL file. The ESE is the only piece that directly manipulates the database. Figure 27.1 shows a portion of the layers and interfaces that interact with the database.

Figure 27.1
The Active Directory database is managed by various layers.

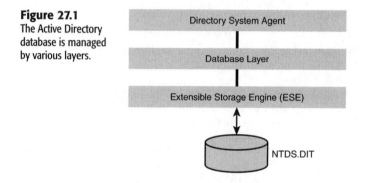

The database layer provides a layer between applications and the directory database. This interface is not directly exposed. Instead, most of the directory access calls are made from the directory system agent (DSA). The DSA is what provides the API calls that enable other application developers to write applications that communicate with the directory. Whether you are using Visual Basic Script, Visual Basic, or C++, the API calls are exposed via the DSA.

→ **See** "Using ADSI with WSH," **p. 516**

DATABASE FILES

The database files for Active Directory are the real meat behind AD. As an administrator, you are abstracted from the Active Directory database during normal operation. However, like any database, the AD database can require direct, file-level care and feeding.

A good knowledge of the architecture of the database makes caring for it much easier and more effective. It also enables performance-tuning the database by allowing the administrator to know which files to place on what kind of drive subsystem.

Knowing which files are crucial to the proper performance of Active Directory also enables planning for fault tolerance. Although simply creating multiple domain controllers per domain implies some fault tolerance, you also can place the database and its log on mirrored or RAID disk subsystems.

THE ACTIVE DIRECTORY DATABASE FILE

The actual database file for the directory is `ntds.dit`, and by default, it is stored in `%systemroot%\NTDS`. However, during the installation of Active Directory, you can choose where you want to place the database file.

> **Note**
> When installing Active Directory, you can place the database files on either FAT, FAT32, or NTFS partitions. The only portion of the Active Directory installation that requires NTFS is the `sysvol` folder.

If you were to search your hard drive for `ntds.dit`, you would actually find two files. The version located in `%systemroot%\system32`, referred to as the distribution copy, is the file the system uses during `dcpromo` to initialize the installation of Active Directory.

The other copy is the database copy and the actual Active Directory database for this domain controller (DC). This copy contains all the objects for the domain that the DC is hosting and the configuration naming context for the forest.

When viewing the size of the database in Explorer, you see the file size at the time the database was first opened. For example, if the server has been online for 23 days and at the beginning of those 23 days the database was 100MB, Explorer reports 100MB regardless of the number of objects that have been added to the directory. To correctly view the database size, you must shut down and restart the server.

Some advantages to the way the directory functions are that the database allocates space only for those attributes that have a value. For example, a user object has approximately 213 attributes, only 8 of which are mandatory attributes. Therefore, when a user account is initially created, it takes up approximately 4,366 bytes, assuming it is populating only the mandatory attributes. This results, in my opinion, in a much more efficient use of database storage.

The database is limited to 16 terabytes at the present time. This is inherited, not from a limitation of Active Directory, but from the limitation of PCs to handle a partition greater than 16TB. A variety of tests have been performed to determine the number of objects that can be stored in the directory; the largest I have seen to date is 40 million per domain. This number reflects only current tests and not actual limitations. I have personally tested 1.8 million objects in a domain. It took a considerable amount of time to create that many objects, but the wonders of VBScript made it possible.

If you are operating in mixed mode, you must consider the fact that any number of accounts above 40,000 will reach the limit of the NT 4.0 SAM. However, a much more realistic number is approximately 25,000–30,000 security principals (users, groups, and computers). NT 4.0 has performance issues with SAMs that have reached numbers larger than those stated here. While in mixed mode, the domain controllers are still replicating to any NT 4.0 BDCs in the domain. In some organizations, this is a very real factor when considering how to migrate to Windows 2000 and Active Directory.

> **Note**
>
> Every Windows 2000 Active Directory domain is in mixed mode by default. The sole indicator of whether a domain can be converted to native mode is the presence or absence of NT backup domain controllers. After all the NT BDCs (if any) are upgraded or gone, you can convert the domain to native mode by right-clicking the domain in the Active Directory Users and Computers MMC Snap-in and choosing Properties. The Change Mode button can then be clicked to make the one-way trip to native mode.

TRANSACTION LOG FILES

By default, the transaction logs are stored in the same directory in which the database file is kept. However, this should be one of the first things you change. You can improve performance and reliability by moving the log files to a separate physical disk.

The transaction logs are used for recovery purposes only. LSASS.EXE is the process that handles updates to the directory by first writing any changes to memory and then writing them to the log file. As this is occurring, the next write is to the database from memory (not the log files).

These log files are 10,485,760 bytes in size, or approximately 10MB. If the log files ever are of any other size, a problem with the log file will occur. The current log file is always EDB.LOG. *Current* means the log that is receiving transactions from LSASS.EXE.

Active Directory uses circular logging by default for the transaction logs. *Circular logging* means that the database engine writes changes to the current transaction log, and after it fills that log with transactions, it subsequently creates a new EDB.LOG and renames the filled log to a hexadecimal numbered file—for example, EDB00001.LOG. This is partly why Active Directory supports only normal backups and not incremental or differential.

To turn off circular logging, you must edit the Registry key HKEY_LOCAL_MACHINE\ CurrentControlSet\Services\NTDS\Parameters\CircularLogging and change the value to 0. However, because Active Directory does not support incremental or differential backups, no reason exists to turn this off.

These log files are kept only until all the transactions have been committed to the database. After the log files are no longer needed, the garbage collection process deletes the log file. Log files are flagged as unneeded after all transactions in that log file have been reflected in the database. The database engine maintains a record of which transactions have been committed to the database by what are known as *checkpoint* files, which are discussed later in this chapter, in the section "Checkpoint Files." However, you always will have the current log file at the very minimum.

The garbage collection process is responsible for removing "tombstoned" objects and unnecessary log files from the directory, and it performs an online defragmentation of the directory database. This process runs 15 minutes after the DC boots and then every 12 hours by default. To change this interval, you must use ADSI Edit to manipulate the interval as described in the following steps. This example assumes that the forest root domain is `fis.local`:

1. Open ADSI Edit. This tool is part of the Support Tools from the Windows 2000 CD.

2. If necessary, right-click the ADSI Edit node and choose Connect To. Then, connect to the Configuration Container naming context.

3. Click the cross next to Configuration Container to open the node.

4. Open the `CN=Configuration,DC=fis,DC=local` node.

5. Open the `CN=Services` node.

6. Open the `CN=WindowsNT` node

7. Right-click the `CN=Directory Service` node and choose Properties.

8. Make sure that the Optional or Both option is selected in the Select Which Properties to View drop-down list.

9. In the Select a Property to View drop-down list, choose garbageCollPeriod.

10. By default this is undefined, which means that the default of 12 hours will be used. To modify it, insert a value and click Set.

> **Note**
>
> Setting the garbage collection interval to more than 1/3 of the tombstone lifetime for deleted objects is impossible. If you attempt to do so, the system will use the lower value.

→ For more information on tombstone lifetime, **see** "Authoritative Restore," **p. 490**

The online defragmentation does not reduce the size of the database file itself. Instead, space is made available inside the database through the removal of deleted objects, which therefore presents more space for objects in the directory database.

If the database is halted for any reason other than a clean shutdown, the directory performs recovery operations upon reboot. The database engine replays any log files that contain uncommitted transactions and therefore places the directory back into a consistent state.

CHECKPOINT FILES

Checkpoint files are used to determine which transactions have been committed to the database. The file, edb.chk, is located in the same directory as the database file—%systemroot%\ntds. The checkpoint file contains pointers to which transactions have been committed to the database and which ones have not. As each transaction is committed to the database, the pointer or checkpoint is moved to the next uncommitted transaction.

If the system experiences a failure that causes the system to shut down—such as a power loss—then when the directory restarts, it will be capable of picking up where it left off.

Because each transaction is written to both memory and the transaction logs, the directory is capable of maintaining a consistent database. This checkpointing process enables the directory to recover much more quickly than if it had to read each transaction log as it started.

RESERVE LOG FILES

Active Directory maintains two reserve log files for the singular purpose of reserving disk space in the event that the system runs out of space on the disk. RES1.LOG and RES2.LOG are each 10MB in size and therefore reserve 20MB of hard disk space.

For example, say the hard drive that contains the transaction log files has run out of space. At this point, Active Directory is no longer capable of writing information to the logs and now must write transactions to RES1.LOG and RES2.LOG. The system event log reports Event ID 2013 when the hard drive is full. Active Directory no longer accepts updates and subsequently shuts down. You also receive Event ID 1393, informing you that the directory is no longer capable of receiving updates (see Figure 27.2). Here's the code:

```
Event ID: 1393
   Attempts to update the Directory Service database are failing with error 112.
   Since Windows will be unable to log on users while this condition persists,
   the Netlogon service is being paused. Check to make sure that adequate free
   disk space is available on the drives where the directory database and log
   files reside.
   Event ID 2013:
   The D: disk is nearing Capacity. You may need to delete some files.
```

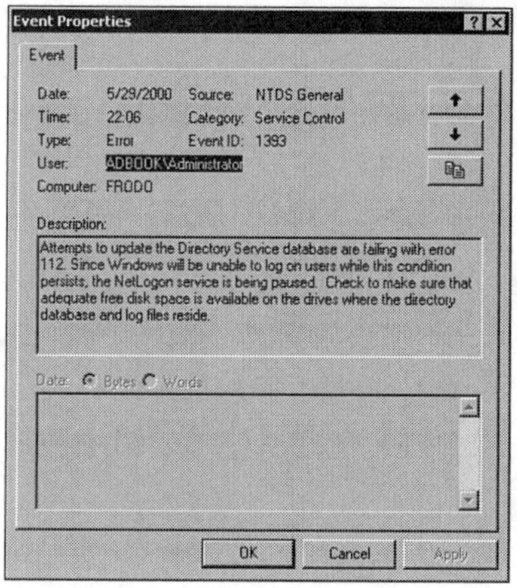

Figure 27.2
Active Directory is no longer capable of receiving updates because of a lack of disk space.

PATCH FILES

Patch files are used during the course of backing up the directory database. When the backup software is reading the database, any pending modifications are written to ntds.pat. This file is used temporarily while AD backup is occurring, and when the database is ready to receive changes, the changes are written from the patch file to the database. For more information on Active Directory backup and patch files, see "System State," p. 486.

DATABASE MAINTENANCE

The Active Directory database automatically performs most of the maintenance necessary for proper operation. Old transaction logs are deleted every 12 hours; the transaction logs and database are compared and recovered every time Active Directory starts; and the database is defragmented automatically. However, inevitably, you will at times need to care directly for the database files.

DEFRAGMENTATION

A database that experiences any amount of write operations, including deletions, will at some time or another become fragmented. This can have an ill effect on performance. To resolve this issue, Microsoft has implemented a defragmentation process for the directory database.

You must familiarize yourself with two types of defragmenting processes to manage Active Directory: online and offline.

ONLINE DEFRAGMENTATION

During the garbage collection process that occurs every 12 hours, the database engine performs an online defrag. Event IDs 700 and 701 are recorded in the directory service event log on the DC. Figures 27.3 and 27.4 show the details of the online defrag that is reported.

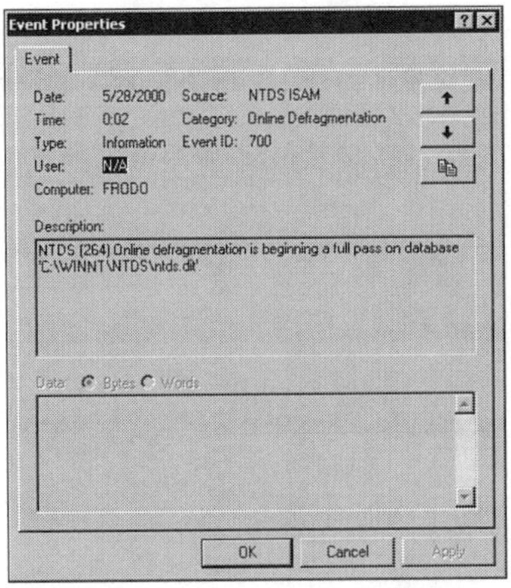

Figure 27.3
The online defrag begins to process the database.

The *online* defrag essentially just rearranges the information in the database to allow room for more objects. It does not, however, reduce the size of the database file itself. This must be done through an offline defrag.

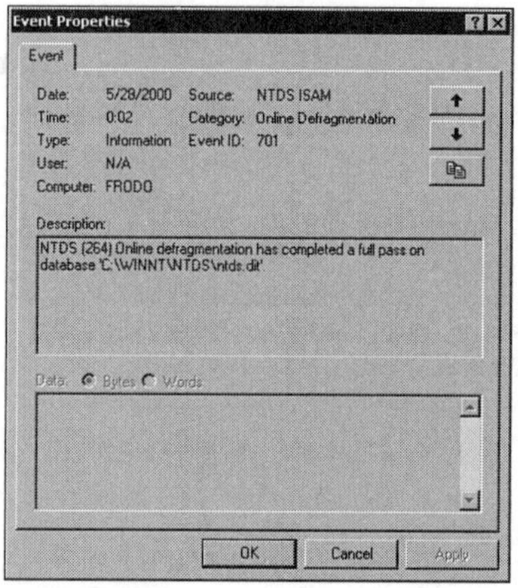

Figure 27.4
The online defrag has successfully completed.

OFFLINE DEFRAGMENTATION

To reduce the amount of space the `ntds.dit` file occupies on the hard disk, you must perform an offline defrag. This is not something that is normally performed, nor should it be. The only times this becomes necessary are when the directory has received an abnormal amount of delete operations, such as electing to no longer operate as a global catalog server.

The *offline* defrag creates a copy of the current database to perform the operation against. Therefore, it is important that you ensure that you have enough space to create another copy of the database.

The following are the steps to perform an offline defrag:

1. Reboot the DC in directory services restore mode.
2. Run `ntdsutil` and type **files**.
3. Type **compact to *path to tempdb***. The path must be a folder that has enough hard drive space to hold the compacted copy of `ntds.dit`.
4. After the defrag is complete, copy the new compacted `ntds.dit` to the original location, `%systemroot%\NTDS`. Then, delete all the files with a `.log` extension.
5. Reboot the DC.

OTHER MAINTENANCE TASKS

NTDSUtil has numerous options that can assist you in maintaining your database. You can do everything from ensuring the integrity of the database files to moving the database files. So understanding this utility is a very important part of successfully maintaining your Active Directory database. The basic interface to NTDSUtil appears in Listing 27.1.

CH
27

LISTING 27.1 BASIC NTDSUTIL INTERFACE

```
G:\WINNT\NTDS>ntdsutil
ntdsutil: help

?                           - Print this help information
Authoritative restore       - Authoritatively restore the DIT database
Domain management           - Prepare for new domain creation
Files                       - Manage NTDS database files
Help                        - Print this help information
IPDeny List                 - Manage LDAP IP Deny List
LDAP policies               - Manage LDAP protocol policies
Metadata cleanup            - Clean up objects of
➥ decommissioned servers
Popups %s                   - (en/dis)able popups with "on" or "off"
Quit                        - Quit the utility
Roles                       - Manage NTDS role owner tokens
Security account management - Manage Security Account Database
➥ - Duplicate SID Cleanup
Semantic database analysis  - Semantic Checker

ntdsutil:
```

LOCATING THE DATABASE FILES

Before being able to move the files, you need to know where they are. This can be accomplished by using ntdsutil.

Perform these steps to locate the database files:

1. Reboot the DC into directory services restore mode.

2. Run ntdsutil at a command prompt.

3. Type **files**.

4. Type **info**. This displays the location of the files, as shown in Listing 27.2.

LISTING 27.2 FILE LOCATIONS

```
ntdsutil: files
file maintenance: info
Drive Information:
    C:\ NTFS (Fixed Drive ) free(5.7 Gb) total(7.6 Gb)
    E:\ FAT (Network Drive) free(88.8 Mb) total(95.7 Mb)
DS Path Information:
    Database : C:\WINNT\NTDS\ntds.dit - 54.1 Mb
    Backup dir : C:\WINNT\NTDS\dsadata.bak
    Working dir: C:\WINNT\NTDS
    Log dir : C:\WINNT\NTDS - 40.1 Mb total
        res2.log - 10.0 Mb
        res1.log - 10.0 Mb
        REPAIR.TXT - 0.0 Kb
        ntds.pat - 16.0 Kb
        edb0000A.log - 10.0 Mb
        edb.log - 10.0 Mb
```

The simplest method to locate the database and log files is to search the system for `ntds.dit` and any of the log files—for example, `edb.log`. The default location is `%systemroot%\NTDS`. However, it is preferable on larger databases to separate the files on different disks. I recommend the following configuration, shown in Table 27.2.

TABLE 27.2   DRIVE CONFIGURATIONS

Drive	Filesystem	Format
`C:\`	NTFS	`%systemroot%pagefile.sys`
`D:\`	FAT (Mirror)	Active Directory log files
`E:\`	NTFS (RAID 5)	Active Directory database `sysvol`

MOVING DATABASE FILES

Moving the database files requires a little more effort than just moving the files with Explorer. You need to move the files with NTDSUtil. Use these steps to move the directory database file:

1. Reboot the DC into directory services restore mode.
2. Run `ntdsutil` at a command prompt.
3. Type **files** and press Enter.
4. Type **Move DB to E:\NTDS**. (This moves the database to a directory called NTDS on the E: drive.)

> **Tip**
>
> If the path you are using includes a space, be sure to wrap the path in quotes—for example,
> `move db to "e:\database folder"`.

5. Type **quit** and reboot the DC into normal mode. Listing 27.3 shows this process.

> **Note**
>
> Although Listing 27.3 shows a lot of textual activity, it is important to note that from the `"move db to e:\ntds"` command to the `quit` commands near the end the output is system generated. The console neither requires nor accepts input during this period.

CH
27

LISTING 27.3   MOVING THE ACTIVE DIRECTORY DATABASE FILES

```
G:\WINNT\NTDS>ntdsutil
ntdsutil: files
file maintenance: move db to e:\ntds
Opening database [Current].

G:\WINNT\NTDS>REM - ***********************************************
```

LISTING 27.3 CONTINUED

```
G:\WINNT\NTDS>REM - Script to move DS DB file

G:\WINNT\NTDS>REM - **********************************************

G:\WINNT\NTDS>e:

E:\>cd \

E:\>mkdir "ntds"
A subdirectory or file ntds already exists.

E:\>cd "ntds"

E:\ntds>move "G:\WINNT\NTDS\ntds.dit" "e:\ntds\ntds.dit"

E:\ntds>G:\WINNT\system32\ntdsutil.exe files
➥"set path DB \"e:\ntds\ntds.dit\"" quit quit
G:\WINNT\system32\ntdsutil.exe: files
file maintenance: set path DB "e:\ntds\ntds.dit"
file maintenance: quit
G:\WINNT\system32\ntdsutil.exe: quit

E:\ntds>G:\WINNT\system32\ntdsutil.exe files
➥"set path backup \"e:\ntds\DSADATA.BAK\"" quit quit
G:\WINNT\system32\ntdsutil.exe: files
file maintenance: set path backup "e:\ntds\DSADATA.BAK"
file maintenance: quit
G:\WINNT\system32\ntdsutil.exe: quit

E:\ntds>G:\WINNT\system32\ntdsutil.exe files
➥"set path working dir \"e:\ntds\"" quit quit
G:\WINNT\system32\ntdsutil.exe: files
file maintenance: set path working dir "e:\ntds"
file maintenance: quit
G:\WINNT\system32\ntdsutil.exe: quit

E:\ntds>G:\WINNT\system32\ntdsutil.exe files info quit quit
G:\WINNT\system32\ntdsutil.exe: files
file maintenance: info

Drive Information:

        C:\ FAT (Fixed Drive ) free(636.6 Mb) total(1.9 Gb)
        D:\ FAT (Fixed Drive ) free(574.1 Mb) total(1.6 Gb)
        E:\ FAT (Fixed Drive ) free(1.9 Gb) total(1.9 Gb)
        G:\ NTFS (Fixed Drive ) free(1.7 Gb) total(3.9 Gb)
        H:\ NTFS (Fixed Drive ) free(4.2 Gb) total(8.4 Gb)

DS Path Information:

        Database   : e:\ntds\ntds.dit - 12.1 Mb
        Backup dir : e:\ntds\DSADATA.BAK
        Working dir: e:\ntds
```

LISTING 27.3   CONTINUED

```
        Log dir    : G:\WINNT\NTDS - 40.0 Mb total
                        res2.log - 10.0 Mb
                        res1.log - 10.0 Mb
                        edb00009.log - 10.0 Mb
                        edb.log - 10.0 Mb
file maintenance: quit
G:\WINNT\system32\ntdsutil.exe: quit

E:\ntds>REM - *********************************************

E:\ntds>REM - Please make a backup immediately else restore

E:\ntds>REM - will not retain the new file location.

E:\ntds>REM - *********************************************
Opening database [Current].
If move database was successful,
 please make a backup immediately else restore
 will not retain the new file location.


file maintenance: quit
ntdsutil: quit

G:\WINNT\NTDS>
```

Follow these steps to move the directory log files:

1. Reboot the DC into directory services restore mode.

2. Run ntdsutil at a command prompt.

3. Type **files** and press Enter.

4. Type **Move logs to D:\NTDSLogs**. (This moves the log files to a directory called NTDSLogs on the D: drive.)

5. Type **quit** and reboot the DC into normal mode.

If you have lost the directory database or the logs and have restored to a separate drive that has a different drive letter from the original location, you can just change the paths for the database or logs.

> **Tip**
>
> Remember that, to use the files command section of NTDSUtil, you must have booted to Active Directory restore mode. An override is available: "set SAFEBOOT_OPTION= DSREPAIR". Its use is not recommended, however. When Active Directory is running, these are open files. The function of Active Directory restore mode is to boot with these files closed and inactive.

CH
27

Follow these steps to change the database path:

1. Reboot the DC into directory services restore mode.

2. Run ntdsutil at a command prompt.

3. Type **files** and press Enter.

4. Type **set path db e:\winnt\ntds\ntds.dit**. This process is illustrated in Listing 27.4.

> **Caution**
>
> Note that with this path command, the path includes the filename. Some of the other path commands just want the path to the folder. If you do not specify the fully qualified path-name of the file here, Active Directory will not start.

5. Options also are available to set the log path, backup path, and working directory.

LISTING 27.4   RESETTING THE DATABASE PATH USING ntdsutil

```
C:\WINNT\NTDS>ntdsutil
ntdsutil: files
file maintenance: set path db e:\winnt\ntds\ntds.dit
file maintenance: quit
ntdsutil: quit
C:\WINNT\NTDS>
```

> **Caution**
>
> If you encounter problems after moving the database files, make sure the administrator and system have full control to the root of the volume the database is on, all the folders from the root to the files, and the files themselves.

REPAIRING THE DATABASE

With NTDSUtil you have the ability to run a repair of the database if you can't start Active Directory. This will result in loss of data, and unfortunately it will be random. The only scenario in which this is likely to be necessary is when only one DC exists in the domain or forest. No other reason to perform a repair seems to exist. If other DCs do exist in the domain, you can just reinstall Active Directory and let replication handle updating the "new" DC.

> **Caution**
>
> Having only one DC per domain borders on malpractice. Implementing fault tolerance by using multiple domain controllers per domain is very important.

Follow these steps to repair the database:

1. Reboot the DC into directory services restore mode.

2. Run ntdsutil at a command prompt.

3. Type **files** and press Enter.

4. Type **repair** and press Enter.

The repair process creates a temporary database, so you need to ensure you have enough space to create the copy. A log is written to `repair.txt` by default for you to receive any details of the repair. The time necessary to complete the operation varies widely, but 2GB per hour is a good rule of thumb.

After the repair process completes, you *must* delete the log files for this database.

SOFT RECOVERY

The soft recovery option enables you to replay the log files following a failure of some kind. However, this is not really necessary because the database engine will replay the logs after an unclean shutdown.

This is an automatic function, similar to those implemented in other industrial-strength databases. Essentially, the logs and the database are read for completed transactions that need to be rolled forward and uncommitted transactions that need to be rolled back.

SUMMARY

In the best of all possible worlds, you will never have to manually care for Active Directory database files. However, you can use the `ntdsutil` tool to check, repair, and move these files. Additionally, a good knowledge of the files will assist you in troubleshooting Active Directory and performance tuning.

TROUBLESHOOTING

BOOTING ERRORS

When I boot the DC, I get an error message (#0xc00002e1) stating Active Directory cannot be started.

Check permissions on the `ntds.dit` and `edb.log`. Make sure the system and the administrator have full control. Use the `ntdsutil/files/info` command to ensure that AD thinks the files are where they really are.

MOVING FILES

I cannot move the files with the Explorer or the move command.

Unless the DC is booted to Active Directory restore mode, many of the files in \winnt\ntds are open files and therefore cannot be moved, renamed, or deleted. If you want to move the database to a new drive for whatever reason, reboot in Active Directory restore mode and use the `move files` command from `ntdsutil`.

UNSUCCESSFUL FIX ATTEMPTS

I have tried using `ntdsutil` *to fix the database files and have been unsuccessful.*

Assuming the corruption is local to this copy of Active Directory, use `dcpromo` to demote the DC. This erases the files. Then, reboot and promote the server back to a domain controller. This causes it to use replication mechanisms to re-create Active Directory and all the database files locally.

CHAPTER **28**

BACKUP AND RESTORE

In this chapter

ACTIVE DIRECTORY BACKUP

Backups are the most important aspect of an administrator's job and hence are the reason for this chapter. When deciding on whether or not to back up, the choice is always to back up and the frequency is always daily. This chapter looks at a variety of methods for backing up Active Directory and all the data required to get your system back to the state it was in before any disaster that might have occurred.

When asked what to back up, the easiest answer is usually everything. However, this chapter specifically discusses backing up your directory and all the dependent information that is necessary to recover your directory.

You are unable to back up just Active Directory. Active Directory is dependent on an assortment of other functions working properly before it can be in a pristine state. Therefore, to perform a backup, you must back up what is know as the system state data.

SYSTEM STATE

System state data is the phrase used to represent the Active Directory information that is backed up when using the Microsoft Backup tool or other third-party tools. More specifically, this includes

- **Active Directory**—This includes the following files:
    - `ntds.dit`
    - `res1.log`
    - `res2.log`
    - `edb.chk`
    - `edb*.log`

→ For more details about these files, **see** "Active Directory Database Optimization," **p. 469**

- **Boot files**—This includes boot files and all system files that are protected by Windows File Protection (WFP). This is all SYS, DLL, EXE, TTF, FON, and OCX files that are installed from the Windows 2000 CD.

> **Note**
>
> WFP is a new feature in Windows 2000 that protects system files by using file signatures stored in a catalog. During a backup of the system state, the catalog is backed up as well. The catalog is located at `%SystemRoot%\System32\catroot\{F750E6C3-38EE-11D1-85E5-00C04FC295EE}`. If a system file is modified by another installation of software, WFP checks the signature. If the signature is proven to be invalid, the file is replaced from either the `dllcache` folder or the original media. The default location for the folder is `%SystemRoot%\System32\dllcache`. In addition, the folder is a protected folder, so you must enable viewing protected operating system files in Folder Options.

- **Component Services Class Registration Database**—The components themselves are backed up during a normal file backup, but the Component Services Database is backed up as a part of the system state.

- **Registry**—In addition to backing up the Registry, a copy of the Registry is placed in `%SystemRoot%\Repair\Regback`.

- **sysvol**—sysvol is composed of the domain scripts and the group policy template files. It also contains any Windows 9x and NT 4.0 system policies, as well as the `NETLOGON` share, the SysVol share, and user logon and logoff scripts.

- **Performance counters**—The configuration information for performance counters is the specifics of what is backed up during the system state backup.

- **Certificate Services**—The database that contains information vital to the restoration of the X.509 certificates, as well as configuration information, is backed up. This is done only if Certificate Services is installed.

- **Cluster Service**—The quorum resource logs is the only piece that gets backed up.

- **DNS**—The zone data that is Active Directory–integrated is backed up.

To perform a backup of the system state data, the user performing the backup must be either a member of the Backup Operator group or an administrator.

In addition to backing up the system state data, you might want to include all the protected system files. This is enabled through the advanced options just before beginning a backup. Figure 28.1 shows the correct option.

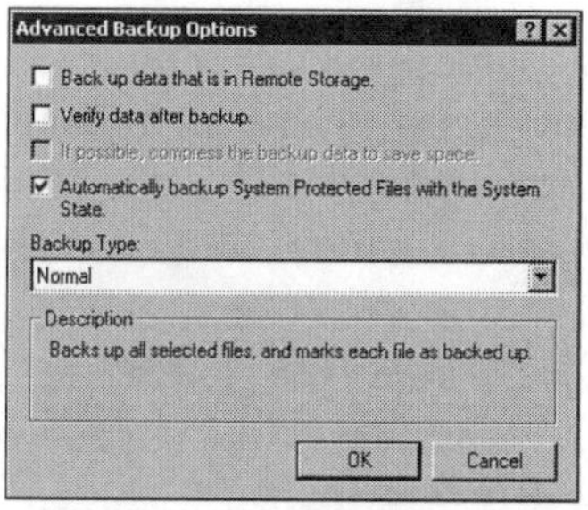

Figure 28.1
Select Automatically Backup System Protected Files with the System State.

> **Tip**
>
> The system state data backup can be performed only on a local server.

Follow these steps to turn on the option to automatically back up system protected files:

1. Determine which files you want to back up, and select the appropriate files and folders.
2. Click Start Backup.
3. Click Advanced.
4. Select Automatically Backup System Protected Files with the System State.
5. Click OK, and then Start Backup.

CH
28

A backup only performs a normal backup of Active Directory. The backup is performed while the DC is online; therefore, no downtime occurs. A normal backup results in the log files being flushed and the database being backed up, which is why it's the fastest method of restore.

During the backup of Active Directory, no changes are written to the directory per say. Instead, they are stored in patch files. However, the directory does continue to stream data to the tape while changes are still occurring. Therefore, to get a complete backup, patch files are created. The logs are marked as nonwritable, and as transactions occur that need to be written to sections of the directory database that has already been backed up, those are written to the patch files. If the transaction can be written to a section of the directory database that has not been backed up yet, the transaction gets written to the directory database. After all the transactions have been written to the directory database and the database has been backed up, the backup process flushes the log files and writes the patch file to the tape media.

MICROSOFT WINDOWS BACKUP TOOL

Microsoft includes with Windows 2000 a pretty robust backup tool created by Veritas. Some of you might be familiar with Veritas and will recognize the interface as being similar to Veritas's own backup software, BackUpExec.

Notice in Figure 28.2 that the system state information is displayed as an option along with the drives and the Exchange Server. On my demo machine, I am running Exchange 2000, and the Windows Backup tool is further extended to include support for backing up Exchange.

Figure 28.2
Microsoft Windows Backup provides a tool that enables backups and restores of the Active Directory.

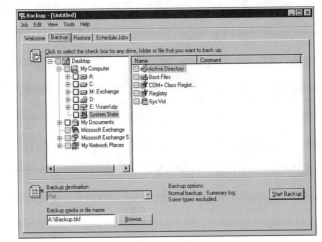

You can back up data to a variety of locations ranging from tape to actually floppies or hard disk.

A major enhancement to Backup is the capability to schedule backups. However, it does suffer from one major issue—you can back up data only on the local DC. Therefore, to get a complete backup of Active Directory, you must back up every DC in the enterprise or select another backup product, such as BackUpExec from Veritas.

RESTORING ACTIVE DIRECTORY

Getting a backup of Active Directory is not complicated, but it is a process that must be performed. In addition, as an administrator you must be prepared to recover the directory if something happens. This could range from a catastrophic failure of a hard drive with the NTDS.dit file to someone deleting an object from the directory that should not have been deleted. The time to understand how to perform a restore is not when you have someone standing over your shoulder wanting to know how long it is going to take to get the network back online. So let's look at a variety of restore scenarios and how to get your data back.

The simplest way to restore a single DC is to reinstall Windows 2000 and then enable replication to return that DC to the current state. This works as long as the only thing that occurred was a failure on that DC, which did not result in a loss of data. On the other hand, if you did lose data and want to restore the directory back to a state prior to the failure or loss, you must restore from a backup.

RESTORING FROM A BACKUP

When restoring from a backup, you should be familiar with three types of restores: non-authoritative, authoritative, and primary.

NON-AUTHORITATIVE RESTORE

A *non-authoritative* restore returns the DC to the state it was in before the failure. If an object has been deleted on another DC between the time of failure and time of restore, that object is still deleted on the restored DC. This process is handled through the normal replication cycles.

To perform a non-authoritative restore, the directory needs to be offline. This is accomplished by booting the system into directory services restore mode, which puts the server into safe mode and takes the directory offline. Safe mode starts only the minimum number of services necessary to start the operating system, such as the mouse, keyboard, CD-ROM, Logical Disk Manager, VGA, Event Log, Plug-and-Play, and RPC.

When you enter safe mode, you are presented with a logon that authenticates you against a local SAM (the local security account database). This password was assigned when you ran dcpromo. After you have successfully logged on, you see a dialog box that describes the safe mode. For more information on dcpromo and the Active Directory Installation Wizard, see "Promoting a Server to Domain Controller," p. 15.

CH
28

Here are the steps to perform a non-authoritative restore:

1. Reboot the server into directory services restore mode by pressing F8 at the Starting Windows screen and selecting Directory Services Restore Mode (Windows 2000 domain controllers only).

2. Start the Backup tool and click the Restore tab (or you can use the Restore Wizard).

3. You must select to either restore the files to the original location or to an alternative location.

> **Note**
> If you elect to restore to an alternative location, Active Directory, the Component Services Registration Database, and the Certificate Services Database will not be restored. Restoring to an alternative location restores only the boot files, SysVol directory files, and Registry files.

If you select Original Location, you receive a warning stating that restoring the system state will always overwrite the current system state.

4. Click Start Restore. Click OK and the restore will begin.

5. After the restore process has completed, view the log file to see whether any errors occurred. The log files are located in the local profile of the user performing the backup—for example, `c:\Document and Settings\administrator\Local Settings\Microsoft\Windows NT\NTBackup\data`.

6. Reboot the machine. Windows 2000 verifies the consistency of the directory database and reindexes the files.

That's it; you've performed a non-authoritative restore. Your directory will now be in a state in which it can receive any changes that might have occurred while it was offline.

AUTHORITATIVE RESTORE

When determining which type of restore you need to perform, ask yourself whether you need to recover a specific object from the directory or whether you just need to restore a DC. If the answer is that you need to restore a specific object, you will need to perform an authoritative restore.

An *authoritative* restore is useful when an object is accidentally deleted from the directory. In the normal course of events, when an object is deleted from the directory, a tombstone is set on the object. By default, tombstones have a lifetime of 60 days. The tombstone is replicated throughout the enterprise to enable DCs to remove the object that has been marked for deletion. The object is subsequently moved to the Deleted Objects Container in the domain. The distinguished name (DN) of the object is then changed by appending the GUID of the object to its original DN. For example, say you have a user object with the following DN:

`CN=Blake Fullerton,OU=IT,DC=adbook,DC=local`

If you delete Blake's user account from the directory, the object is moved to the Deleted Objects Container and its DN now reads as follows:

```
CN=Blake Fullerton\DEL:eb4e8852-5228-4e88-b2e1-c0ad25d0bef0,
➥CN=Deleted Objects,DC=adbook,DC=local
```

> **Note**
>
> The Deleted Objects Container is a hidden container. You can use the Active Directory Administration Tool to bind to the directory and perform LDAP queries to find all deleted objects.

As you can tell, it is a tad bit different now. The GUID for the user has been appended to the object and an attribute—isDeleted—has been set to TRUE. This is what marks this object as having been tombstoned.

Every 12 hours a process known as *garbage collection* runs, looking for expired tombstones. At that time, the object is deleted from the directory. You can change the interval that garbage collection runs by editing the garbageCollPeriod attribute.

> **Note**
>
> The garbage collection process runs only after 12 hours of continuous operation. If the machine is shut down anywhere within that 12-hour time period, the process does not execute.

Follow these steps to modify the garbage collection interval:

1. Start ADSI Edit.

2. Navigate to CN=Directory Service, CN=Windows NT,CN=Services,CN=Configuration, DC=*domain*,dc=*domainsuffix*, as shown in Figure 28.3.

Figure 28.3
Editing the garbage collection interval attribute.

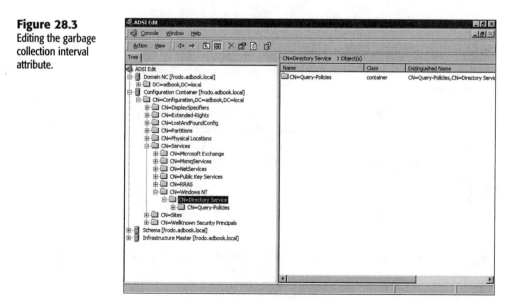

CH
28

3. Right-click the CN=Directory Service node and select Properties.

4. In the combo box, select which properties to view, and ensure that Optional is selected.

5. Select garbageCollPeriod in Select a Property to View (see Figure 28.4).

Figure 28.4
Selecting
garbageCollPeriod
enables you to
change the attribute.

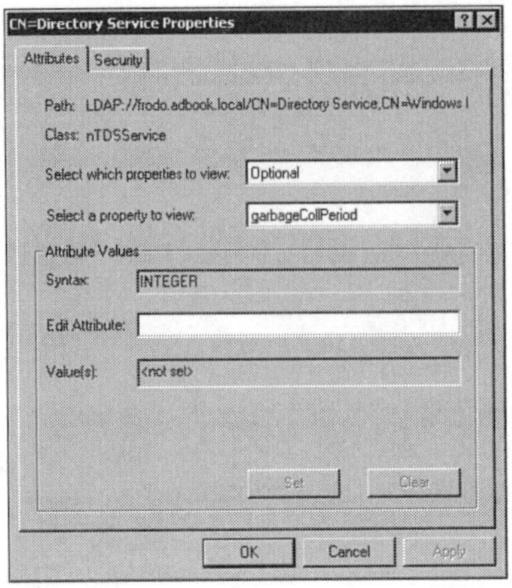

6. Type the new value in the Edit Attribute field. This value needs to be at least 1 hour because this is the minimum. The maximum value is one-third of the tombstone life-time value.

Now an object has been deleted, and you need to get it back. In jumps the authoritative restore process. With this type of restore, you are essentially telling the directory that this particular DC is "authoritative" for this particular node of the directory.

To perform an authoritative restore, you must first follow the steps outlined in performing a non-authoritative restore—except do not reboot the server just yet. Before you reboot, you need to run NTDSUtil to authoritatively restore the object.

You must decide how much information you need to restore. You can choose to do one of the following:

■ **Restore the entire database**—This marks this replica as authoritative. It also, in effect, forces replication with all other replicas on the enterprise, which results in the directory being restored back to the state backed up on the media. The command to mark the entire database as authoritative is restore database.

Note You cannot authoritatively restore the schema. Only the domain and the configuration NC can be authoritatively restored.

■ **Restore only a particular subtree of the directory**—This is useful if you need to restore an OU with the children objects or restore a single object, such as a user or group. The command to mark only a particular node of the database authoritative is `restore subtree ou=IT,dc=adbook,dc=local`.

You must refer to the distinguished name of the object you want to restore.

Caution

Be careful when typing the DN of the object you want to restore. The restore subtree restores the object and any children objects. This is helpful if it is what you intended, but if you wanted to restore only a user, use the DN for the user—for example, `cn=Fred,ou=IT,dc-adbook,dc=local`.

In addition, you also can correct a previously corrupt authoritative restore. By default, the USN for either a subtree or an entire database restore gets increased by 100,000. You can change this number if you need to correct a previously incorrect authoritative restore. This is accomplished by using either of these two commands:

```
Restore database verinc 250,000
Restore subtree ou=IT,dc=adbook,dc=local verinc 250,000
```

Note

Use this option only if you need to replace an earlier mistaken authoritative restore.

You also must run NTDSUtil to perform an authoritative restore of a single-user account. To do so, follow these steps:

1. Type **ntdsutil** at a command prompt.
2. Type **authoritative restore**.
3. Type **Restore subtree cn=Bob,cn=users,dc=adbook,dc=local**.
4. Click OK when asked whether you want to perform an authoritative restore.
5. If the restore was successful, you will see a message stating `Authoritative Restore completed successfully`, as shown in Figure 28.5.

When you perform an authoritative restore of the directory, you also should perform an authoritative restore of SysVol. Due to the nature of the contents stored in SysVol—group policy templates, scripts, and file replication information—it is important to restore the SysVol alongside an authoritative restore of the directory. For more information on the SysVol share, see "Group Policy Template," p. 408.

You authoritatively restore SysVol by following these steps:

1. Restore the system state data to an alternative location. When you restore system state data to an alternative location, it restores only SysVol and the Registry.
2. Authoritatively restore the directory as described previously.
3. Reboot the server and do *not* enter safe mode.
4. Copy sysvol from the alternative location to the original location.

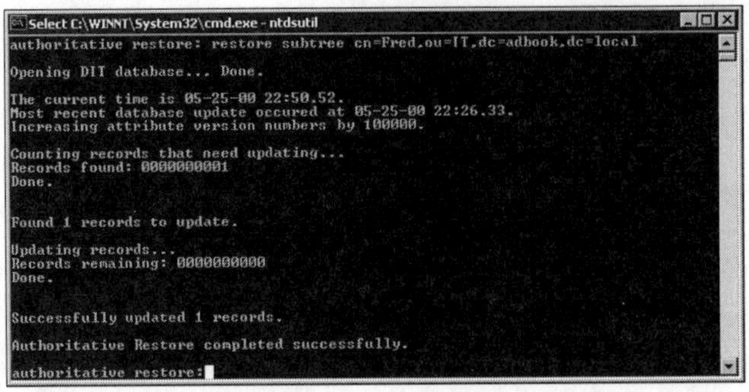

Figure 28.5
A successful authoritative restore.

PRIMARY RESTORE

Another type of restore is known as a *primary* restore. This is necessary when you have lost every DC in your enterprise. If that happens, you should perform a primary restore on the first DC and then perform only a non-authoritative restore for the remaining DCs.

The steps are the same as performing a non-authoritative restore, but after you click Start Restore in step 4, click the Advanced button and select When Restoring Replicated Data Sets, Mark the Restored Data as the Primary Data for All Replicas (see Figure 28.6).

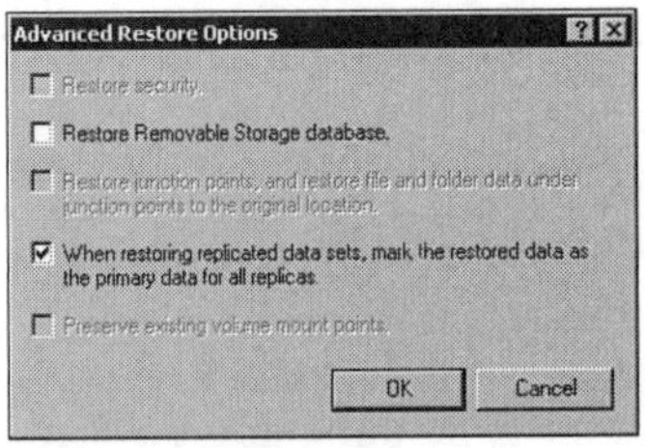

Figure 28.6
Advanced options to perform a primary restore.

ADDITIONAL CONCEPTS

Some additional details should be considered that you might find helpful when planning your disaster recovery operations.

OFFLINE BACKUP

You can perform an offline backup of the Active Directory. You only need to either boot into directory services restore mode and copy the NTDS.dit file to an alternative location or use the recovery console to make a copy of the file. Performing an offline backup is possible because, during a smooth shutdown, the transactions are committed to the database. For more information on the recovery console, see the "Troubleshooting" section, later in this chapter.

DETERMINING THE DATE OF THE LAST FULL BACKUP

To properly determine the date of the last backup, you must use NTDSUtil. This provides a correct date to determine the age of the last backup, which helps you determine whether you will have to deal with the backup that's older than 60 days. You must be in directory services restore mode to use the File command in NTDSUtil. You can see a great deal of information about the directory database by dumping the header of the database. After typing **file**, type **Header**.

IMPACT OF THE TOMBSTONE LIFETIME ON RESTORES

The backup API does not allow any restore of a backup set that is older than the tombstone lifetime value; it does this to prevent the introduction of orphaned objects in the directory. The default value for tombstone lifetime is 60 days. This setting can be changed by editing the tombstone attribute on CN=Directory Service, CN=Windows NT,CN=Services, CN=Configuration,DC=*domain*,dc=*domainsuffix*.

If a restore is allowed that is older than the tombstone lifetime, the restored copy of Active Directory could contain deleted objects for which the fact of their deletion would not be replicated into the restored replica. This could lead to objects that exist on one replica of Active Directory that do not exist on other replicas.

COMPUTER MEMBERSHIP AND TRUSTS

When performing an authoritative restore, be careful to ensure that computer memberships in the domain and trusts are not adversely affected. You can restore objects that have different trust relationship passwords and computer account passwords, subsequently causing communication between these computers and domains to cease.

This occurs when you restore objects that reside in the domain naming context. Because these passwords are changed every seven days by default, if you restore a backup that is greater than seven days old, you risk disrupting communications and even potentially prohibiting member workstations or servers from communicating with a domain controller for their domain. To avoid potential issues, authoritatively restore only those specific objects that you need instead of the entire domain naming context—for example, dc=adbook,dc=local.

SUMMARY

Backing up your system is one of the most vital tasks you can ever perform in your role as a network administrator; however, it is also one of the most least understood. You must not only perform your backups, but you also must prepare and document the restore process. You definitely do not want to wait to perform your first restore until your boss is standing over your shoulder waiting for the system to be brought back online. Back up daily and perform a test restore at least once a month to keep your sanity and your job.

CH
28

TROUBLESHOOTING

AUTHORITATIVE RESTORE AND TRUSTS

I had to restore my directory, and I think my trusts are disrupted.

When you have performed an authoritative restore of the directory, you must be aware of the implications with regard to computer trusts and domain trusts. The trusts are disrupted if you have restored an object from a backup more than seven days old. By default, the passwords used by the system to establish and maintain the trust are automatically changed every seven days. As a result, the trust can be broken. To correct this problem, you must restore the trust, which can be accomplished by right-clicking the object in Active Directory Users and Computers and selecting Reset Account.

BOOTING THE DOMAIN CONTROLLER

I need to boot my DC but am unable to because of a renamed, moved, or deleted file.

The Windows 2000 Recover Console can be used to copy, rename, and delete files on FAT, FAT32, and NTFS partitions. It also can set services to stop or start the next time Windows 2000 boots.

Perform the following steps to boot Windows 2000 using the recovery console:

1. Place the Windows 2000 CD in the CD-ROM drive and boot from the CD.
2. At the Setup Notification screen, press Enter.
3. At the Welcome to Setup screen, press R to repair the installation.
4. At the Windows 2000 Repair Options screen, press C to enter the recovery console.
5. At the recovery console prompt, you are asked to choose which copy of Windows you want to repair. Type the number of the copy and press Enter.
6. Type the password to the Administrator account and press Enter. If this is a DC, you will need the Active Directory restore mode password.

After you have authenticated to the console, you are dropped off at the recovery console prompt. From here you can delete, rename, and copy files. You can access only the `%systemroot%` and `%windir%` folder and subfolders. However, you can copy files from a floppy or CD to these folders. You can use `fixboot` and `fixmbr` to repair the boot sector or master boot record. You also can use the `help` command to get a listing of available commands. The Windows 2000 online help has a complete listing of commands and their syntax.

Tip   The Recovery Console functionality can be used on a Windows NT computer, too.

CHAPTER 29

MIGRATING FROM NT TO ACTIVE DIRECTORY

In this chapter

UPGRADING AND MIGRATING

Because few of us will be starting our Windows 2000 Active Directory implementations from scratch, it seems appropriate to discuss how to get there from here. Obviously, this was an issue that Microsoft has given a lot of thought to, because a variety of tools are now available to move from NT to Active Directory. `ldifde`, `movetree`, and `netdom` are all powerful tools that can be used in the domain migration and consolidation process.

This chapter discusses several upgrade scenarios. None are better or worse than others, but each has its place. In your environment, you likely will choose a combination approach. The following is a list of scenarios covered here:

- **Upgrade in Place**—An upgrade in place is basically loading the Windows 2000 CD into the CD-ROM drive on your Windows NT primary domain controller and typing **winnt32.exe**. Your computer settings for the domain controller, as well as users, groups, security settings, and passwords will be maintained.

- **Consolidation by Moving Objects**—Regardless of how you get here, you can use tools to move objects from one domain to another, and in a limited fashion from one forest to another. In the section "Consolidation by Moving Objects," you will see how to move Active Directory objects from one domain to another to consolidate your domain structure.

- **Migration with FastLane**—You can migrate objects from an existing NT domain to a Windows 2000 Active Directory. This chapter uses FastLane DM to do this.

UPGRADE IN PLACE

As the name implies, an *upgrade in place* assumes that currently a good implementation of an NT domain structure exists, complete with users, groups, and computers. It also assumes that a security infrastructure is in place, with access control lists set on NTFS filesystem objects that restrict access to portions of the filesystem to the appropriate users. The goal of an upgrade in place is to preserve this structure, while also moving it to Active Directory.

If your current domain structure does not require collapsing or reorganization, an upgrade in place is as simple as upgrading your PDC, upgrading your BDCs one at a time, and then converting the domain to native mode as soon as the last NT BDC is upgraded to Windows 2000.

Many shops with only a handful of domains will find an upgrade in place to be the best path. You should consider collapsing or reorganizing your domains only when the current domain structure either is so complex as to be unwieldy or no longer meets your needs.

PLANNING

Planning for an upgrade differs from planning from scratch in only one respect. If you start from scratch, you have nothing to lose. Here, with an existing NT domain, it pays to be paranoid.

FAILOVER PLANNING

With failover planning, you are asking yourself, "What could go wrong?" It might pay to put the most detail-oriented person on your team in charge of this planning. A very workmanlike attention to detail will pay big benefits here.

Plan for what NASA calls *cascading failures*. Many disasters are the result of several small, innocuous failures that happen simultaneously. The following list covers some disasters to plan for:

- **Plan for WAN outages**—Do you have redundant WAN links? If you are upgrading an NT BDC, a synchronization event will occur during the upgrade process. Will your backup links be capable of handling the traffic?

- **Plan for application issues**—Have you disabled virus checkers and the like, which might object to the upgrade at an inopportune time? Have you checked your applications that might run on your BDCs to see whether they function well with Windows 2000?

- **Plan for hardware failures**—This might be the first time you have rebooted this server in six months. What if a drive or controller or NIC goes bad? One of my favorite aphorisms is "The chance of the toast falling butter side down is directly proportional to the cost of the carpet." Right now the carpet is very expensive.

- **Plan the upgrade order**—You must upgrade the PDC first. Then, you will need to upgrade the BDCs one at a time. The order can be based on geography, politics, or a variety of other factors. I would upgrade a BDC that was physically near me first, after the PDC, so that I would have a high level of physical control over the process. If you have upgrades that you need to perform over the phone with a junior network administrator in Antarctica, I would save that for last.

You must have backups of your domain controllers (DCs), and you must have an offline BDC that represents a good copy of your NT accounts database. But most importantly, you need the answer to this question: "What do I plan to do if this really falls apart?" More than your career is on the line here. If people can't do their jobs on Monday morning because you did not prepare for the worst, you've failed miserably.

Now, having prepped you with all this gloom and doom, I have never had an NT–to–Active Directory upgrade croak. The process is intensely stable. As professionals, however, we must ensure that we have our belts and suspenders firmly fastened.

Caution

Back up everything. Back up your PDC. Back up more than one BDC. More importantly, identify or create a backup domain controller, synchronize it with the NT domain using Server Manager, and then take it offline. I mean take it down, turn it off, and put a piece of duct tape over the power switch. You want at least one functioning copy of the NT accounts database that has not participated in the upgrade process at all.

Note

Planning for Active Directory namespace, database, and SysVol locations and planning for domain placement within the tree are no different in an upgrade from what they are with a new installation. The same decisions *must* be carefully made in advance.

→ **See** "Decisions, Decisions," **p. 12**
→ **See** "Namespaces," **p. 92**

PREPPING THE PDC FOR UPGRADE

In most cases, checking the PDC for viruses and then disabling virus checkers, screensavers, and so on is best. These can impact any upgrade at the most inopportune times. Any third-party disk utilities in use should be closely checked for compatibility with Windows 2000. Losing contact with the filesystem the first time you boot the upgraded DC to Windows 2000 is inconvenient. You must either have an NTFS filesystem or identify a partition to convert. Active Directory DCs require one partition to be NTFS to support the File Replication Service for the sysvol folder.

→ **See** "sysvol," **p. 28**

PERFORMING THE OS UPGRADE

After you havedetermined where you are going and what you are going to do if things go badly, it is time to kick off the upgrade. Load the CD, find your installation key, change to the i386 folder, and execute winnt32.exe. The actual upgrade process for the operating system is fairly simple. In a nutshell, the OS upgrade resembles an unattended install. You will be prompted for a few items, such as the installation key and whether to upgrade a filesystem to NTFS 5.0. The system then automatically reboots and goes through the character mode and then the GUI mode of setup without user intervention. The real work starts when the system boots for the first time.

RUNNING dcpromo

After the system boots and you are logged on, the Active Directory Installation Wizard, dcpromo, runs automatically. You do not have to complete the dcpromo now. You can cancel out of it. Every time you log on, however, you will be prompted to complete the Active Directory upgrade process by finishing the Active Directory Installation Wizard. You might have several reasons for not upgrading the Active Directory immediately. You might want to add a new disk subsystem to host the Active Directory database; you might want to run the server for 24 hours to perform testing of the server before committing to the Active Directory upgrade; or you might have a specific time set aside for the Active Directory upgrade process versus the Windows 2000 upgrade. The dcpromo process is covered in much detail in Chapter 2, "Installing Active Directory." The only difference you will notice in the dcpromo process is that the first screen in the upgrade wizard is worded somewhat differently (shown in Figure 29.1) than if you were firing up dcpromo on a new box.

Figure 29.1
When you log on to your DC for the first time, the dcpromo Active Directory Installation Wizard runs automatically.

When dcpromo completes, you are prompted to reboot. The reboot process takes longer than normal because some of the conversion and setup is taking place during the boot process. After you reboot and log on again, you have an upgraded, mixed mode Windows 2000 Active Directory domain.

TESTING THE UPGRADE

The best way to test the new Active Directory is to log on as a normal user and test whether you can still see files normal users could before, and not see files they couldn't. Users, groups, passwords, and security settings should have survived intact.

WHERE ARE YOU NOW?

As you upgrade your DCs to Windows 2000 and Active Directory, your NT and 98 clients will still be able to log on. They will still be able to print and use files on the servers. Although an optional Active Directory client for Windows 9x and NT exists, which enables users to take advantage of sites (so they can log on to a DC near them) and upgrades them to LanMan authentication V2, the best client for an Active Directory is a Windows 2000 computer. You can upgrade your workstations and member servers in any order—before or after moving to Active Directory—but to take advantage of the myriad advantages that Active Directory offers, you must be running Windows 2000 on the client.

> **Caution**
>
> Although the dsclient.exe file in the \clients\win9x folder has a Windows 95/98 client for use with Active Directory, this is not designed for use with Windows Me. Knowledge Base article Q276472 describes a workaround for this.

IMPORTANT CONSIDERATIONS WHEN UPGRADING NT DOMAINS

In the previous section, I made much of the fact that except for the need to protect your current NT domain investment, planning and implementing an Active Directory for an upgrade differs only slightly from a new install. Both should be approached with much planning and testing. However, some operational differences do exist, which are worth noting here. Most of these deal with the opportunity you have to restructure your domains before, during, and after the upgrade process.

STRUCTURAL MODIFICATIONS

You can modify your domain structure when you run the dcpromo Active Directory Installation Wizard. You can merge an NT domain that had no previous trust relationships with the Active Directory forest and still maintain your users, groups, and security settings. This is done by choosing to become a part of an Active Directory forest when you run the dcpromo wizard. When you are prompted to choose the Active Directory forest and tree structure, you can choose to join an existing AD forest or tree. If you do so, all the transitive Kerberos trusts to the new forest are set up for you, and existing NT trusts to other NT domains (if any) are preserved. Although this does not merge your domain into another domain, it does merge your domain into the forest.

SECURITY ISSUES DURING THE UPGRADE

The section "Running dcpromo" previously noted that dcpromo runs immediately after startup. Note that you did *not* have to press Ctrl+Alt+Del to log on. When the system boots for the first time, it performs an autologon as the local administrative account. You must be careful if you are doing this remotely through some kind of remote control tool or are walking someone else through it over the phone because, if the system is unattended (for whatever reason) by highly trusted personnel and is rebooted remotely, when the system comes up, the first user to access the console will be in charge.

You also can cancel the dcpromo process and check out the system as a whole. You can log on and off and reboot. Every time you cause a logon event, dcpromo runs. If you log off and try to log on again, you must choose the administrator in your old domain account from the Domain drop-down box, because (as far as I can tell) the account that is used for autologon has a password that is unavailable to us. Also, let me make one final note: If you reboot the server before you run dcpromo, every time you reboot, the autologon process will occur and expose the previously noted possible security breach.

CHECKING THE UPGRADE

After you haveupgraded Active Directory, try to log on as various users from various computers and make sure that simple connectivity is still in place. Check the event log for errors and ensure that the DNS is running and has records for the new SRV records. Don't forget to re-enable your virus software and any other background software you have in place, such as automatic backups.

CONSOLIDATION BY MOVING OBJECTS

Many larger shops have, over the last few years, created very complex domain structures. For some, it was simply because of a lack of centralized planning. Windows NT, because of its trust management structure, encouraged companies to create trusts between domains to facilitate cross-domain permissions. The effect of this was that various groups in the company created domains and then joined together over a period of time without a larger plan. I have seen NT domain structures that looked like a football play gone bad. For others, this occurred because of scalability. Windows NT did not recommend domains with more than 40,000 objects. But Active Directory scales to millions of objects.

You can consolidate your domains when you upgrade your NT domains to Active Directory. To consolidate or modify your domain structure, you must be able to move Active Directory objects from one place to another. This can be simple or complex, depending on the source and target containers.

MOVING OBJECTS INSIDE A DOMAIN

Moving Active Directory objects from one container to another—usually an organizational unit (OU)—inside a domain is a simple, GUI-driven process. In this chapter's example, you have two users—Vivian and Venus—who you want to move from the sales OU to the mfg OU. To do so, simply right-click the objects and choose Move, as shown in Figure 29.2.

Figure 29.2
Using the Move feature of the Active Directory Users and Computers MMC Snap-in to move users.

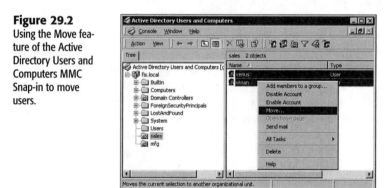

After you click Move, you see the screen shown in Figure 29.3. Simply choose the target container and click OK. Your objects will move almost instantly.

This is a very fast operation. I have moved 2,000 users at a time with this tool in less than 2 minutes on a dual processor P450 with 512MB of RAM and a SCSI disk.

MOVING OBJECTS BETWEEN DOMAINS OR TREES

Several tools in the Windows 2000 support tools can move objects between domains. This is an important capability because you can use these tools to collapse Windows 2000 Active Directory domain trees from a complex structure to a simpler one.

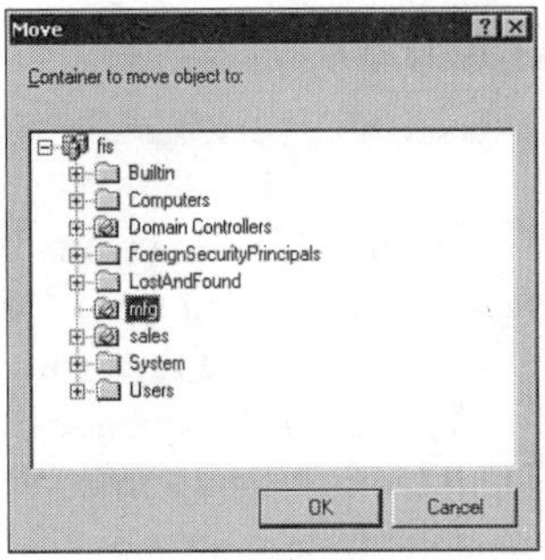

Figure 29.3
Choosing the target of
the move operation.

`movetree`

You can use the `movetree` command to move user objects, groups, and organizational units between domains in the same forest.

In this example, you have a parent domain, `fis.local`, and a child domain, `sales.fis.local`. You want to leverage the fact that you can collapse child domains into organizational units in AD, so you will move the users and then group objects in the child domain into an OU of the same name in the `fis.local` domain.

`movetree` excels at moving users, universal groups, and organizational units from one domain to another in the same forest. It cannot, however, move computer objects, populated domain local groups, or populated global groups. Instead, you can use `netdom.exe` to move computer objects from one domain to another. Additionally, if the source and target domains are native mode domains, you can convert your domain local and global groups to universal groups, move them, and then change them back to domain local and global groups. There is one caveat to the group approach, however. Universal groups are replicated to the global catalog (GC). This can cause an enormous amount of GC replication to occur. A less invasive methodology is to use ADSI to read the membership of the groups you are interested in maintaining, empty the groups, `movetree` the groups to the target domain, and then use ADSI to repopulate the groups.

A `movetree` EXAMPLE

The following command prepares to move the OU `insidesalesOU` in the `sales.fis.local` domain to the `salesOU` OU in the `fis.local` domain. It also takes the users and universal groups in the OU. This assumes that the `salesOU` OU already exists in `fis.local`, but the `insidesalesOU` OU underneath `salesOU` does not. This command does need to be entered on one line.

Note   Many times, commands must be all on one line, even though they are somewhat lengthy. I have had good results from creating a batch file that contains the code and executing the batch file. Then, if I have made a typo, it is easier to fix.

Here is the command:

```
C:\>    movetree /check /s silver.sales.fis.local /d gold.fis.local /sdn
➥ou=insidesalesOU,dc=sales,dc=fis,dc=local /ddn ou=insidesalesOU,
➥ou=salesOU,dc=fis,dc=local /verbose
```

The /check parameter simply does what its name implies. It checks the source and destination servers, denoted by the /s and /d parameters, and the source and destination distinguished names, denoted by the /sdn and /ddn parameters, and makes sure everything is in a row. The /verbose parameter causes a lot more information to be echoed to the screen. Although it's optional, I highly recommend using /verbose. movetree.err, movetree.log, and movetree.chk are created with information about the end result of the command.

After you have checked the movetree operation and are sure this is what you want, you can simply change the /check to /start, causing the operation to execute and complete.

> **Note**
>
> When you move organizational units from one domain to another using movetree, the permissions on files that existed before the move will still exist. This is good. Another thing that is preserved are connections to any group policy objects that were linked to the OU before the move. If you plan to remove the child domain as part of your consolidation strategy, you should re-create the group policy in the target domain and remove the old links to the group policy in the child domain.

netdom

One of the things netdom can be used for is moving computer objects from one domain to another. This is a fast and painless tool. The following example moves the computer account from the sales.fis.local domain to the fis.local domain:

```
C:\>netdom move /d:fis.local stone /ud:fis\administrator /pd:password
```

The /d: parameter sets the target domain, whereas stone is the computer name. /ud: is the account that has the permissions to move the account, and /pd: sets the password.

MOVING OBJECTS BETWEEN FORESTS

This chapter is explicitly about upgrading from NT domains to Active Directory. However, because moving objects from one place to another is many times an integral part of a domain migration, I wanted to give you a look at some of the technologies involved.

At least two ways exist to move objects between forests: ldifde.exe and the FastLane DM/Manager. You use FastLane in the next section to collapse an NT domain into a Windows 2000 forest, but this section briefly looks at using ldifde.

ldifde.exe

ldifde's main strength is bulk exporting and importing of Active Directory objects. The syntax for this tool is documented in the Windows 2000 Online Help.

The ldif in ldifde stands for Lightweight Directory Interchange Format and is documented in RFC 2849, which can be obtained from www.ietf.org. ldifde can read an Active Directory and write the contents out to a text file or read an `ldif` text file and copy the contents into an Active Directory. In the following example, you use `ldifde` to move several users in an OU from one forest to another. To create the `ldif` output file, you simply execute the following code:

```
ldifde -f sales.ldf -d "ou=sales,dc=abc,dc=local" -p subtree -r
➥"(objectcategory=cn=person,cn=schema,cn=configuration,dc=abc,dc=local)"
```

First, let's have a look at the syntax. The `-f sales` parameter sets the output file, whereas `-d "ou=sales,dc=abc,dc=local"` sets the LDAP name of the container you will search. `-r "(objectcategory=cn=person,cn=schema,cn=configuration,dc=abc,dc=local)"` sets a filter for the object class you are looking for—in this case, it's users.

> **Note**
>
> All the `ldifde` code examples assume that you are logged in as administrator at the console of a computer that is a member of the current domain. You can use the `-s` and `-b` parameters to bind to a particular server if you are not logged on as described.

If you plan to use the `.ldf` file to import your objects into a new directory, you must use search and replace to replace instances of the old domain name with the new target domain name. This can be done with Notepad or through scripting.

Listing 29.1 shows a partial output file created by the `ldifde` command after you have performed a search and replace to update the domain name. This is the information that is exported for your first user, `fred`. As you can see from the output, some information comes across, but not all of it does. The amount of information generated by the tool is in direct proportion to the number of attributes set on the object. For example, if you do not have the email address of the user set in Active Directory, an entry for it won't exist in the `ldif` file, empty or otherwise.

LISTING 29.1   SAMPLE `ldifde` OUTPUT FILE (`sales.ldf`)

```
dn: CN=fred,OU=sales,DC=fis,DC=local
changetype: add
accountExpires: 0
adminCount: 1
cn: fred
codePage: 0
countryCode: 0
distinguishedName: CN=fred,OU=sales,DC=fis,DC=local
instanceType: 4
name: fred
objectCategory: CN=Person,CN=Schema,CN=Configuration,DC=fis,DC=local
objectClass: user
sAMAccountName: fred
sn: smith
userAccountControl: 512
uSNChanged: 152865
uSNCreated: 152864
whenChanged: 20000621175632.0Z
whenCreated: 20000621175632.0Z
```

After you have the `.ldf` output file, importing it is trivial. The following is the command necessary to import the file into your current Active Directory:

```
C:\>ldifde -i -f sales.ldf
```

The `-i` parameter sets the `ldifde` tool to import mode rather than the default of export mode.

`ldifde.exe` uses the aforementioned `ldif` format to read and write its information. A similar tool is `csvde.exe`. `csvde` does essentially the same job as `ldifde`, but because its output is a comma-separated value file, the information from your AD can easily be moved into a database for perusal. Combining this feature with the Data Transformation Services of SQL Server enables you to pull the contents of the AD into a SQL database. This could be used to generate interesting statistics on your users, computers, and so on.

Although most of the object attributes can be moved, it is important to note that `ldifde` does not move permissions. Another tool that can be used to migrate users between forests is FastLane DM/Manager.

FASTLANE

FastLane Technologies Incorporated has a product called FastLane DM/Manager that is a migration administrator's dream. Although in the previous sections of this chapter you have looked at some very well-architectured tools to enable moving objects between domains and trees, this tool provides an enormous amount of power and is very easy to use.

I want to make clear that this book does not attempt to document every feature of FastLane DM/Manager. The capabilities exposed by this product fill several books that come with the product. In this section, however, you use the Migration Wizard to migrate users from an NT 4 domain into a Windows 2000 OU. FastLane DM/Manager can not only copy or move computers, global groups, and users from an NT domain to the Active Directory, but it also enables precollapsing domains before upgrading to Active Directory by moving or copying objects from one domain to another. It also can copy objects from one forest to another if the source and target domains are connected by external trusts.

Installing DM/Manager is well documented in the books that come with the product. In short, you will need the software and the activation keys. For further information on this process, see www.fastlane.com.

After the product is installed, you can load the DM/Manager interface from the FastLane DM Suite folder from the Start, Programs menu (see Figure 29.4).

By default, because you are logged on as `administrator@fis.local`, the Source and Target domain windows show the `fis.local` domain. To see the domain you want to migrate from, you must use Add/Remove Domains from the Edit menu (see Figure 29.5).

You can use the Refresh Domains button to update the domain list in the Available Domains window. To add domains to the Source and Target domain windows, simply select the domains you want in the Available Domains window and click the > button. Obviously, if you don't want certain domains currently in the Source and Target domain windows, select them in the Domains and Forests window and click the < button. Because you are interested in the Domain9 domain, add it. Then, click OK to return to the main DM/Manager screen.

Figure 29.4
The FastLane Manager interface.

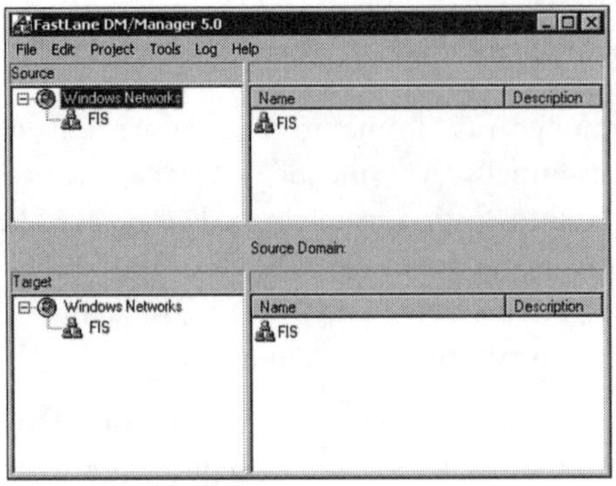

Figure 29.5
Selecting the source and target domains.

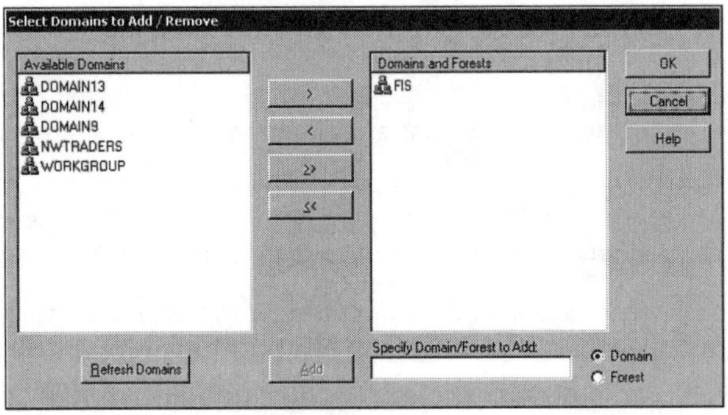

You can double-click each domain and peruse its users, global groups, local groups, and computers (see Figure 29.6).

Figure 29.6
Using FastLane DM to browse NT and Active Directory domains.

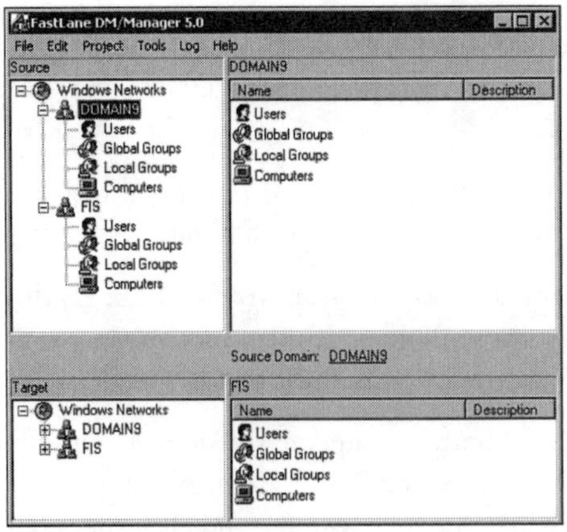

As mentioned earlier, this tool offers several ways to migrate users, global groups, and computers, including drag and drop. In this section, however, you use the Migration Wizard by choosing the Project Manager option from the Project menu. The Project Manager screen appears in Figure 29.7.

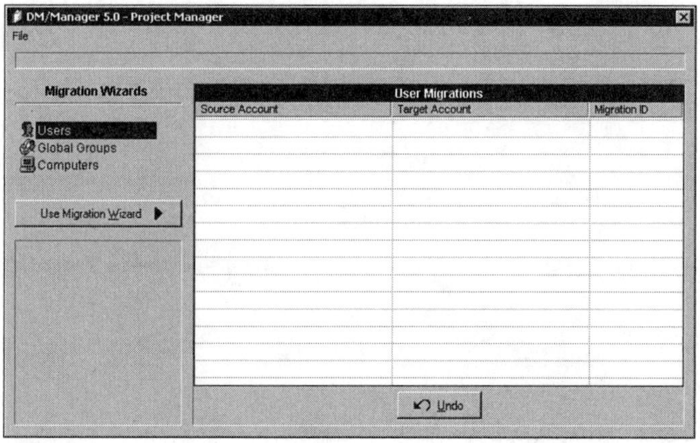

Figure 29.7
The Project Manager screen is where you begin your migration.

Before you can use the Use Migration Wizard button on the Project Manager page, you must use the New option on the File menu to create a new project or the Open option to open an existing project. After you have done so, you can select Users, Global Groups, or Computers; then, click the Use Migration Wizard button. This loads the User Migration Wizard welcome screen.

Click Next. The FastLane Mapping Technology screen enables you to use a FastLane Migration Mapping Technology (MMT) file. This enables you to use delimited data to populate Windows NT or 2000 domains. You do not need to, so click Next.

Figure 29.8 shows the Source and Target Location screen. After you have used the Select Source Domain and Select Target Domain buttons to choose to migrate from the Windows NT domain, `Domain9`, to the Active Directory domain `fis`, click Next.

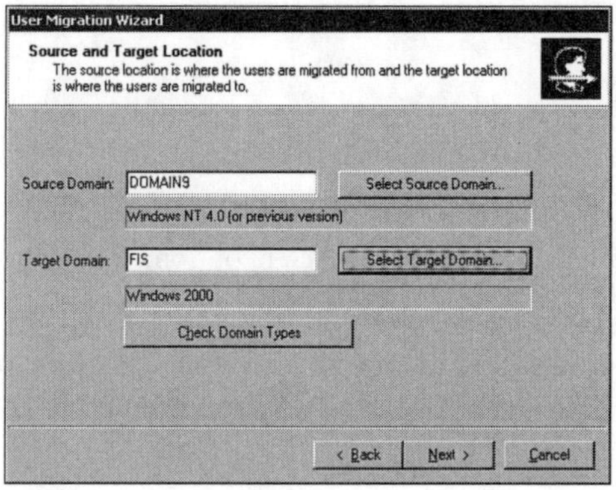

Figure 29.8
You can use the Source and Target Location page to set where your users will migrate to.

Because your target domain is an Active Directory domain, you next see the Target OU screen shown in Figure 29.9. Choose to copy the source objects into the mfg OU. If you do not choose a target OU, the users will be placed in the Users container in Active Directory.

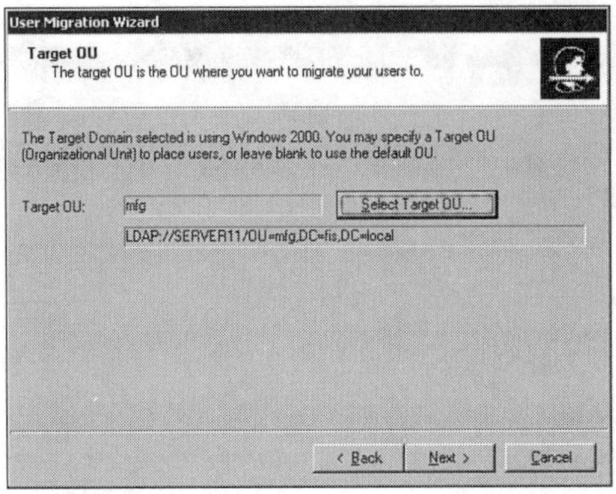

Figure 29.9
Use the Target OU page to choose where in Active Directory to place migrated users.

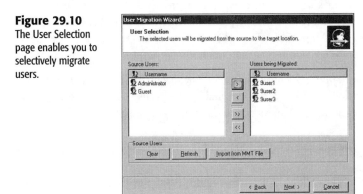

In Figure 29.10, click the Refresh button to populate the Source Users window. Then, select the users you want to copy and click the > button to move them to the Users Being Migrated window.

Figure 29.10
The User Selection page enables you to selectively migrate users.

The Attribute Selection screen enables you to copy common user attributes from the NT domain to your Active Directory. Choose the attributes you want and click Next.

Figure 29.11 shows the Set Password screen, where you can choose how to set passwords for the new account. Choose the Random Characters option; then, click Next.

In the Name Duplication screen, you can set automatic options either to rename, delete, or merge the accounts, or to prompt you in the event of a name conflict (see Figure 29.12). In a domain migration, this can be a frequent occurrence and should be the subject of some planning. Accept the default and click Next.

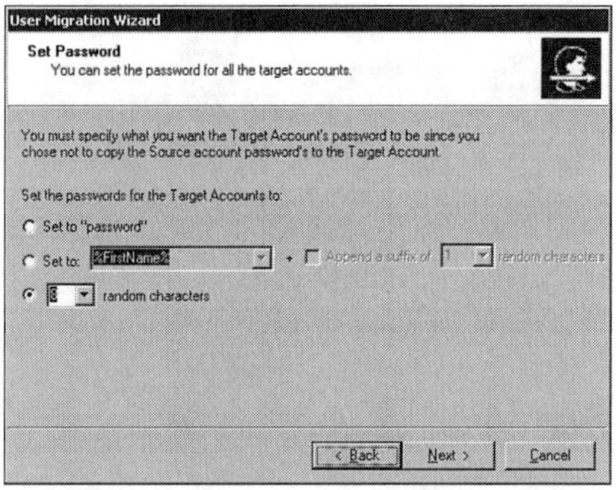

Figure 29.11
Because the user's original password does not migrate with the account, use the Set Password page to control how you will create passwords for the migrated users.

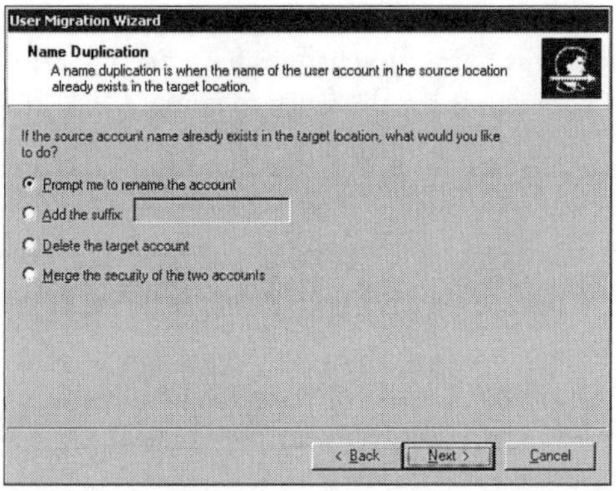

Figure 29.12
Name collisions are inevitable. Use this page to set the rules for dealing with accounts that have the same name.

The Target Account Settings page, shown in Figure 29.13, enables you to set security on your user objects (including password options), set the account expiration, and disable the account. Disabling the account can be useful if you are copying a large number of user objects and want to "turn them on" selectively. Because you chose random passwords in the Set Password screen, you must select the User Must Change Password check box here. This forces the user to change the password to something that makes sense to him. Very complex passwords are a great security tool, but they are difficult to remember. Additionally, in some situations, users compensate by writing the password on the bottom of their keyboards or using sticky notes on the backs of their monitors. You must choose what is best for your situation. Even if you allow or force your users to change passwords, you can still set some rules on how long and complex those passwords should be by using group policy.

In the Source Account Settings screen, you can choose to expire the source accounts if you want. You might want to use the accounts in tandem for a time until you are confident that all the permissions issues have been resolved. This page lets you make that decision en masse.

When you click Next, you see the FastLane Mapping Technology screen. Depending on your migration load, it might take a few seconds for the mapping file to be created. If you click the Edit MMT Mapping File button, you can view and save the MMT Mapping file. This file could be reused to script the actual migration if you choose not to migrate at this time.

Figure 29.13
You can modify a variety of security settings for your migrated accounts with the Target Account Settings page.

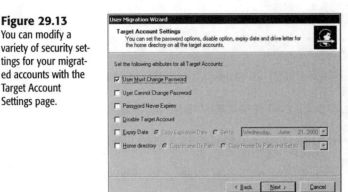

When you click Next, you finally see the Completing the User Migration Wizard screen. It is important to note that up to this point, no changes have been made or committed. You have simply set options and commands for the work to come. Click Finish.

The Pre-Process Migration Status screen is one step away from the final migration (see Figure 29.14). At this point, two files—wizard.mmt and wizard.hdr—have been created with all the information you have set. You could choose to close out the wizard now and perform the actual migration at a later time. The MMT files then could be used to automate the migration process.

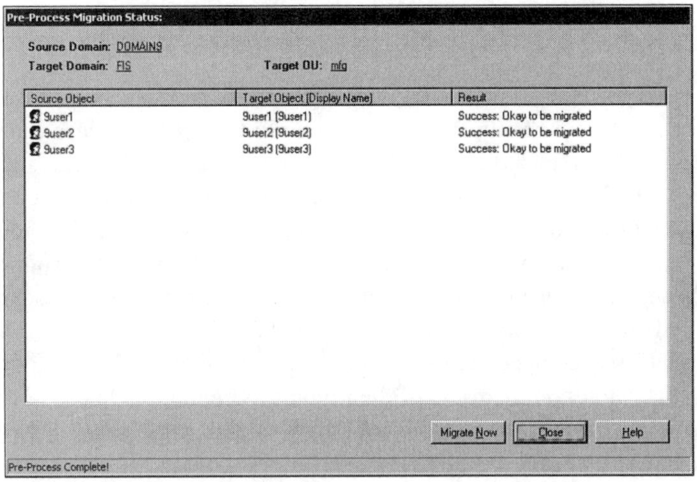

Figure 29.14
Clicking the Migrate Now button on the Pre-Process Migration Status screen commits the migration.

When you click Migrate Now, you see several screens at once. Let's look at each one in turn.

The Step Two of a Successful Migration dialog box reminds you that, for the new accounts to retain their access to files on computers from the source domain, you must update the computers. This can be done from DM/Manager.

The result column of your Pre-Process Migration Status screen has been updated to reflect the successful migration of the users.

Perhaps the most important bit of information here is the Notepad file that is automatically loaded and displayed. Guard and save this file carefully because it contains the new account/ random password pairs you just migrated. You can use this file to give your users their new passwords and also to check and ensure that the properties you chose were implemented properly. A partial listing of the file appears in Listing 29.2. The report generated by the migration process should be secured because it contains your new username/password pairs.

LISTING 29.2 MIGRATION PROCESS REPORT

```
User Migration Report
- - - - - - - - - - - - - - - - - - - -


Date.........: 6/22/2000 12:49:05 AM
Migration Type: NT4 -> Win 2000
Source Domain.: DOMAIN9
Target Domain.: FIS
Target OU.....: mfg
- - - - - - - - - - - - - - - - - - - - - - - - - - - - - - - - - - - - - - - - - - - - - - - - - - - - - - - -

-Migrating user 9user1 to 9user1 (9user1) ... (1/3)
    -Full Name              :
    -Password               :Kd>0Q+40
    -Password Properties    :MUST-CHANGE-PASSWORD
    -RAS Settings           :Dialin Permission Granted... No Call Back
    -Logon Hours            :5-22|5-22|5-22|5-22|5-22|5-22|5-22
```

When you close the current window, you are returned to the Project Manager screen. From this screen, you can choose to undo a user after the migration by using the Undo button. When you close this screen, you see the default DM/Manager Screen.

SUMMARY

Domain upgrades and migrations are planning-intensive projects. They require a very real investment in planning and knowledge of the source and destination domains. Both Microsoft and third parties provide a number of tools to ease this sometimes onerous process.

The upgrade should be planned with long-term goals in mind. Some companies will want to simplify their domain structures as a part of the upgrade process. The scalability of Windows 2000 and Active Directory encourages fewer domains. Several tools that are part of the Windows 2000 product, such as movetree, ldifde, and netdom, enable you to move or copy users and computers from one domain to another.

FastLane and other third-party companies make a variety of robust tools that simplify the planning and implementation of domain upgrades and consolidations both before and after the actual upgrade from NT to Windows 2000 and Active Directory take place.

TROUBLESHOOTING

CAN'T MOVE USERS

When I try to move users from one domain to another with movetree, *the operation fails.*

Don't forget to turn on verbose logging with the /verbose parameter. This creates .err, .log, and .chk files that are useful for troubleshooting the problem.

OBJECTS CAN'T BE DISPLAYED AFTER MIGRATION

When I migrate more than 2,000 users into an OU in Active Directory, the Active Directory Users and Computers MMC Snap-in complains that it can't display all the objects in the OU.

Choose View, Filter Options in the MMC and set the Maximum Number of Items Displayed Per Folder to whatever number is convenient.

UPDATES ARE FAILING

I have upgraded my domain to Active Directory and converted immediately to native mode. Now my NT BDCs are not receiving updates to the domain, such as new users.

An Active Directory domain should not be converted to native mode until all NT BDCs are upgraded to Windows 2000. When the domain is converted to native mode, all Netlogon replication stops. Netlogon replication is the basis for NT domain replication. To fix this, you must upgrade your NT BDCs to Windows 2000 and Active Directory immediately. The newly upgraded DCs will then catch up on changes made to the domain since the conversion to native mode.

CHAPTER 30

SCRIPTING THE ACTIVE DIRECTORY

In this chapter

THE ACTIVE DIRECTORY SERVICES INTERFACE

The Active Directory Services Interface (ADSI) is a COM-based interface to the power of the Windows 2000 Active Directory. Because you are using the exact same COM DLLs with ADSI scripts that you use with the Active Directory Users and Computers tool, there is practically no limit to the functionality exposed with ADSI.

This chapter looks at ADSI scripting with the goal of automating some mundane administrator tasks. Then, you use the `iadstools.dll` found in the support tools to build some troubleshooting tools for replication and group policy.

This is not a programming book. You will find that the code examples used to illustrate ADSI make much more sense if you have a basic scripting or development background. If you have never written code, I must warn you up front that it can be an addictive experience. After you have automated a procedure that used to take five minutes of drudgery into three seconds of code, you will be hooked. Windows 2000 exposes a very rich scripting interface through WSH that can automate virtually anything.

> **Note**
>
> You can use the ADSI COM interface from both Visual Basic and Visual C++. However, this book uses a subset of Visual Basic—VBScript. You will use VBScript in both WSH and ASP.

WINDOWS SCRIPT HOST

Windows Script Host (WSH) is a scripting host that supports both VBScript and JScript. Using WSH, you can write logon and logoff scripts for users, write startup and shutdown scripts for computers, and access COM DLLs. The capability to touch COM makes WSH perfect for your needs in this chapter. Also, you might or might not own Visual Basic, but if you own Windows 2000, you have a copy of WSH already installed—by default—on every Windows 2000 computer in your enterprise. WSH and VBScript also are covered briefly in Chapter 26, "Containers and Organizational Units," with logon scripts. You can create these scripts in Notepad, save them with a `.vbs` extension, and run them from the command line by executing the filename.

USING ADSI WITH WSH

In the next few pages, you will take a very hands-on approach to learning the basics of ADSI. This is hardly an exhaustive approach. Therefore, if you want more information, you can find an enormous amount available by searching for ADSI at `msdn.microsoft.com`, including the downloadable Microsoft Active Directory SDK.

In this chapter's ADSI examples, you will create a user, add users to groups, move objects, and enumerate the properties of an object. After you have seen how to script these actions, adapting them to ease your workload will be trivial. For example, the code to create a user could easily be adapted to read a text file to mass create users from another operating system.

CREATING A USER

In the first example, you create a user. This is a fairly straightforward process that demonstrates the basics of much of ADSI programming. Listing 30.1 shows a simple script to create a user in a specified context and assign a password. Let's step through this example to view and apply the basic concepts of ADSI scripts.

LISTING 30.1   CREATING AN ACTIVE DIRECTORY USER WITH ADSI

```
'set error handling
on error resume next

'enable command line arguments
set objargs=wscript.arguments
username=objargs(0)
contextpath=objargs(1)
pwd=objargs(2)

'bind to LDAP server
set context=getobject("LDAP://" & contextpath)

'set up the creation and schema type
set usr=context.create("user", "CN=" & username)

'set mandatory attributes for user object
usr.put "samaccountname",username
usr.put "useraccountcontrol","0020"

'commit the change
usr.setinfo

'error handling and feedback
if err.number=0 then
    usr.setpassword(pwd)
    wscript.echo "created user: cn=" & username & "," & contextpath
else
    wscript.echo err.number, err.description
end if
```

The first two sections are not really ADSI programming but simply the code necessary to use command-line parameters with your scripts and an error-handling directive. `on error resume next` enables your script to continue if it encounters errors. This also enables your error-handling code to run because otherwise the script would simply exit with a VBScript error. Because some scripts can encounter real errors and still accomplish work, this is critical.

Note

Be careful about setting error handling when debugging your code. If you have `on error resume next` set, your code might run, fail, and never return an error. You can turn this command on and off selectively during the debugging process by commenting it out with a single quote (`'`). Make sure it is a single quote and not an apostrophe. An apostrophe causes the VBScript runtime to terminate with an error.

CH
30

The `'enable command line arguments` section sets up your code to use parameters input at the command line. Even though you could use input boxes with your scripts, because this is designed to be a command-line tool, you should use the `arguments` property of the `wscript` object. This enables you to execute the following command and create a user named `Mike` in the Sales organizational unit (OU) of the `fis.local` domain and set his password to `qwerty`:

```
C:\>createuser mike ou=sales,dc=fis,dc=local qwerty
```

The first event of virtually any ADSI operation is binding to the AD. Several ways to do this exist, including methods that work with NT domains and Novell NDS. However, in this chapter, you will focus on binding to an LDAP server on whichever domain controller (DC) the DNS service returns to you. The `contextpath` variable in the `'bind to LDAP server` section of Listing 30.1 is your LDAP path to the container in which you want to create your user. The previous command has set this to the Sales OU of `fis.local`.

The `'set up the creation and schema type` section of the code tells ADSI that you are going to create a user. The `create` method prepares AD to create an object of a given type and name. The type must be a valid class in the schema. The previous example has used class `user`, but the code easily could be modified to create an instance of class `computer` or `group`.

In the `'set mandatory attributes for user object` section, you supply values that must be present to create the user successfully. Many attributes can be set on a user object, and because the schema is extensible, you could add more. The only two that are required in this scenario are `cn` and `samaccountname`. Because you set the `cn` in your `createobject` call, you have to set only one other attribute, `samaccountname`, with the `put` method. However, because the default behavior is for ADSI to create the user with a disabled account, the second `put` method sets the `useraccountcontrol` to `0020`, which enables the account.

Although the `create` method has been used, the addition is not persisted to the AD until you call `setinfo`. Then, your object is written to the database. This code appears in the `'commit the change` section of Listing 30.1.

> **Note**
>
> If you are curious about what is happening under the hood with any of these examples, run the code snippets on a workstation or member server and use Network Monitor to capture the packets during code execution. You will quickly see that what you are basically doing is using COM and VBScript to manipulate LDAP. Because LDAP is responsible for finding, adding, changing, and deleting objects in the AD and it sends many of its commands in clear text over the network, there is much that can be learned here.

This last section of code, `'error handling and feedback`, simply checks to see that no errors occurred, sets the password to the third command-line parameter, and then echoes a message box with the information that the object was created. If an error has occurred, the error number is sent in a message box, too. The `Success` output message from the previous command appears in Figure 30.1.

Figure 30.1
The user has been
successfully created.

MANIPULATING GROUPS WITH ADSI

Another common administrative task is adding users to groups. Although a perfectly good
GUI interface is available for this in Active Directory Users and Computers, you also can do
this from ADSI.

This example takes a slightly different slant on binding to the Active Directory. The example takes three or more command-line parameters. The first is the OU; the second is the
group name; and the third through *n*th parameters are existing users to add to the group.
For example, the following command adds the users kiley, abby, logan, landon, and allysa
to the group Consultants in the Sales OU of the current domain:

```
C:\>add2group3 sales consultants kiley abby logan landon allysa
```

The code for the utility appears in Listing 30.2. Just like before, we'll look at the code one
section at a time to understand how the utility works.

CH

30

LISTING 30.2   USING ADSI TO CREATE A GROUP

```
'set up error handling
on error resume next

'set command line arguments
set objargs=wscript.arguments

'serverless bind to root DSA Specific Entry
set root=getobject("LDAP://rootDSE")

'get default naming context
domainpath=root.get("DefaultNamingContext")

'get context for operation
set ou=getobject("LDAP://ou=" & objargs(0) & "," & domainpath)

'get group to add to
set grp=ou.getobject("group", "cn=" & objargs(1))

'iterate through list of users and add to group
for ctr=2 to (objargs.count-1)
  set usr=ou.getobject("user", "cn=" & objargs(ctr))
  grp.add usr.adspath
next
```

As before, the 'set up error handling section simply enables you to recover from errors.
In this utility, it is particularly useful because even if you misspell a user's name or list a user
who is already a member of the group, the other users will still be successfully added. Note
that no other error handling exists in this code, so if you want feedback on success or failure,
you must add the appropriate code.

As before, the 'set command line arguments section enables you to specify the users and so on at the command line.

Proper binding to the AD is probably the most critical component of ADSI binding. The 'serverless bind to root DSA Specific Entry (DSE) code shows one way to do this. If you don't bind or bind to the wrong context, the code will not run. Binding to the AD is conceptually the same as opening a connection to a SQL database. When you connect to a SQL Server, you connect to the target server and database before you start selecting or modifying data. The AD database is no different. Here, however, you should avoid connecting to a specific server. It is the function of the SRV records in the DNS infrastructure to return an LDAP server "near" you to bind to and execute the LDAP commands.

Here you bind to the rootDSE, which holds information about the LDAP server that you need to continue your operation.

> **Note**
>
> Although you see no evidence of security in these examples, you will need to be logged on with credentials sufficient to perform these operations.

The 'get default naming context code gets the default LDAP naming context. This is one reason why more binding code exists in this example than the previous one; however, the command-line parameters are simpler. The defaultnamingcontext is the LDAP distinguished name of the domain of which this server is a member.

The 'get context for operation code sets the organizational unit of which the group and users are members.

The next code section, 'get group to add to, sets the group to which you will add users. Notice that the call to getobject is different here from what it was in the getobject call to rootDSE. If you call getobject without specifying the schema class name (in this instance it's group), getobject returns the first object in the container with that name.

Because you have written the utility to accept one or more users to add to the group, you do not know in advance how many users are on the command line. However, in the 'iterate through list of users and add to group section, you can use the count property of the arguments collection to find that. The reason you use count-1 is that arguments collection is zero based—in other words, the first argument is 0, the second argument is 1, and so on.

Because you have done all the work of binding to the AD up front and have created your objects, all you have to do now is iterate through the list of users and pass the adspath property of the user object to the add method of the group object.

MOVING OBJECTS

After you understand the previous examples, the next one becomes very simple. Just like the code to add users to a group, moving objects from one container to another inside a domain is mostly an exercise in binding to an LDAP server and then executing one or more methods of the ADSI library and passing parameters from the command line.

The code in Listing 30.3 is straightforward. You bind to LDAP, set where the object is, and set where it is going. In this example, you will use your ADSI code to move a computer object from the Computers Container to the mfg OU. This same code can, with different command-line parameters, move users, groups, printers, and so on. It can even move organizational units from one place in the tree to another with its child objects intact. In addition, the objects retain their original group membership and permissions.

LISTING 30.3   MOVING ACTIVE DIRECTORY OBJECTS WITH ADSI

```
'cn, sourceou, targetou
set objargs=wscript.arguments
set root=getobject("LDAP://rootDSE")
domainpath=root.get("DefaultNamingContext")

'where we are moving to....
set target=getobject("LDAP://" & objargs(2) & "," & domainpath)

'where we are moving from....
set newobj=target.movehere("LDAP://" & objargs(0) & "," &
➥objargs(1) & "," & domainpath, objargs(0))
```

Note

> If you are writing these in Notepad, make sure that word wrap is turned off and that each of your commands does not wrap. For example, the last two lines of the code in Listing 30.3 are long enough that they might wrap. If your code is saved with the lines wrapped, your application will crash.
>
> Also, be sure to set the screen buffer width properties of the command prompt window in which you are testing the command to wider than the default of 80 characters. This can be done by opening the command prompt and pressing Alt+spacebar and choosing Properties/Layout.

The 'cn, sourceou, targetou section of the code does exactly what it did in the previous example—it binds to the LDAP server.

Here is where it gets interesting. To set the target container, whether it's a container or OU, you simply call the getobject method and pass it the LDAP path of your target container. This is shown in the 'where you are moving to... section of the code.

The movehere method enables you to move or rename objects within the domain. The method takes two parameters: the LDAP path of the object to be moved and the LDAP relative distinguished name (RDN) of the object. The 'where we are moving from... code accomplishes this.

When you run the command shown here, the computer server12 is moved from the Computers Container to the mfg organizational unit:

```
C:\>moveit cn=server12 cn=computers ou=mfg
```

LISTING AND VIEWING PROPERTIES

The final ADSI script enables you to view many of the populated attributes for an object. Shown in Listing 30.4, it simply binds to the target object in the AD, reads the attributes of the object, and then writes the attribute name and values to the screen.

Because some of the attributes are multivalued, you might see some listed twice. In this example, you'll look at a user object that is a member of several groups, so the `memberof` attribute is displayed more than once with various values. The number of attributes displayed also is directly proportional to the number of attributes populated.

Generally, the AD does not set aside space in the database for attributes of objects that are not populated. Therefore, if you do not have the telephone number attribute populated for an object, a perusal of that object does not return a telephone number attribute, populated or not.

> **Note**
>
> In this section, I will use the terms *property* and *attribute* to mean essentially the same thing. What this section does is create an object in memory that holds the values of the attributes of the AD object in the database. When you read the attributes of the AD object and assign them to your instance of an ADSI object in memory, you then refer to the values as *properties* of the COM object you have created.

In this example, you use three objects: `propertylist`, `propertyentry`, and `propertyvalue`. The list is the list of the attributes; you will have one entry per attribute and one value per value stored in the attributes.

LISTING 30.4   VIEWING ACTIVE DIRECTORY PROPERTIES WITH ADSI

```
'set up error handling and arguments
on error resume next
set objargs=wscript.arguments

'bind to target
set iplist=getobject("LDAP://" & objargs(0))

'load or refresh the property cache
iplist.getinfo

'loop through properties
for ctr=0 to (iplist.propertycount-1)

'create propertyEntry object for each property
set ipropEntry=iplist.item(ctr)

'read the value(s) of each property entry
for each val in ipropEntry.values

  'create a propertyValue object for each value
  set ipropVal=val
```

LISTING 30.4   CONTINUED

```
    'write out each property/value pair
wscript.stdout.writeline ipropEntry.name & ": "
➥& ipropVal.getobjectproperty(ipropEntry.adstype)
  next
next
```

The first section of code does exactly what it has done in the previous examples. The `on error resume next` command is critical here, however, because many objects will have attributes whose datatype does not echo well to a text screen. With proper error handling, the value is simply skipped; without it, the script terminates with an error.

By now, binding to an LDAP server should be old hat. The difference in the `'bind to target` section is that you are interested in only one object. Therefore, you are using one command-line parameter, which is the LDAP distinguished name (DN) of the object in which you are interested.

The call to `getinfo` in the `'load or refresh the property cache` section populates the client-side property cache for your `propertylist` object. After you call this method, any manipulation or discovery of properties in the property cache takes place on your local version until you either call `getinfo` again to refresh the cache from the database or call `setinfo` to update the database with the values in memory.

The `propertycount` property of your `propertylist` object is a zero-based count of the number of available properties for your object. For example, if the `propertycount` is 42, they are numbered 0–41. This `for...next` statement in `'loop through properties` simply lets you iterate through each one.

The `'create propertyEntry object for each property` code enables you to create a property entry object for each property in the property list. The `item` method can be used with the name of the property rather than the ordinal number, but because you have used the `propertycount` property to get the total number of properties, you should use the number.

Because each `propertyEntry` can have one or more values, you should use the values collection to iterate through the list. The code shown in the `'read the value(s) of each property entry` section does this for you.

For each value in the values collection, you create a `propertyValue` object to manipulate. This enables you to get its name, datatype, and value. This is located in the `'create a propertyValue object for each value` section.

The first thing you must note about the `'write out each property/value pair` section of code is that the first line has nothing to do with ADSI. Because you want command-line output for a command-line tool, you use the `writeline` method to send a CR/LF terminated string to `stdout`. `stdout` in this instance means the command prompt. For this to work, however, you must call the script at the command line with `cscript` rather than just typing the name of the script. Listing 30.5 demonstrates this. If you forget and simply use the script name, the script will simply terminate with an error. You also must specify the extension .vbs on the command line. See the WSH documentation for more information.

You are using the name property of the propertyEntry object to show the name of the property. The getobjectproperty method reads the property values of the object in the property cache. It requires one input parameter—the adstype, or datatype, of the value.

LISTING 30.5   CALLING YOUR SCRIPT WITH cscript RATHER THAN THE DEFAULT wscript INTERPRETER

```
C:\>cscript showprops.vbs cn=alix,ou=mfg,dc=fis,dc=local
Microsoft (R) Windows Script Host Version 5.1 for Windows
Copyright (C) Microsoft Corporation 1996-1999. All rights reserved.

memberOf: CN=mgrs,OU=mfg,DC=fis,DC=local
memberOf: CN=consultants,OU=sales,DC=fis,DC=local
badPwdCount: 0
codePage: 0
cn: alix
countryCode: 0
displayName: alix
givenName: alix
instanceType: 4
logonCount: 0
distinguishedName: CN=alix,OU=mfg,DC=fis,DC=local
objectCategory: CN=Person,CN=Schema,CN=Configuration,DC=fis,DC=local
objectClass: top
objectClass: person
objectClass: organizationalPerson
objectClass: user
primaryGroupID: 513
name: alix
sAMAccountName: alix
sAMAccountType: 805306368
telephoneNumber: 555-1234
userAccountControl: 512
userPrincipalName: alix@fis.local
whenChanged: 6/24/2000 7:41:30 PM
whenCreated: 6/24/2000 7:39:56 PM
```

---

iadstools

If you install the support tools from the \support\tools folder of the Windows 2000 CD and then look in \program files\support tools on your local hard drive, you will find, among other things, two very interesting files. They are iadstools.dll and iadstools.doc. The DLL hosts the functionality exposed by another support tool: replmon.exe, the Active Directory Replication Monitor.

This one DLL exposes an enormous amount of functionality. In this section on Active Directory scripting, you use iadstools.dll to build a troubleshooting tool for group policy and an Active Server Page (ASP) to list troubleshooting information about replication.

Similar to the previous section, this is hardly an attempt to exhaustively document the capabilities of this COM object; instead, it simply gives you a glimpse of its power and use. `iadstools.doc` is a very detailed look at the properties and methods of the `iadstools` COM object.

Note

> The previous section on ADSI assumed only that you were logged on at the console of a Windows 2000 computer as a user with sufficient Active Directory credentials to perform the task. For these scripts to work, `iadstools.dll` must be registered. This is done automatically when the support tools are installed or manually by copying the DLL and executing `regsvr32 iadstools.dll`.

CH
30

CHECKING GROUP POLICY VERSIONS

The code in this section checks the version numbers for the Group Policy Container and group policy template. The container is the information about the group policy in Active Directory, and the template is the filesystem objects that actually do the work of a group policy. Because you use AD replication to replicate the container and the file replication service to replicate the template, these can be out of sync. If that happens, group policy can be applied somewhat irregularly. This tool simply identifies any group policy objects for a given container and looks to see whether the version numbers match. If they do, all is well and it exits with a success message. If, on the other hand, some group policies are out of sync, it identifies them by name and returns the respective version numbers. Listing 30.6 shows how to check group policy versions programmatically.

LISTING 30.6   CHECKING GROUP POLICY VERSIONS WITH `iadstools`

```
'instantiate the object
set dcf = createobject("IADSTools.DCFunctions")

'set up arguments and variables
set oArgs = wscript.arguments
Dim numGpos
Dim ctr
dim flag

'get number of group policies for container
numGpos = dcf.GetGPOs(CStr(oArgs(0)), CStr(oArgs(1)), 0)

'iterate through group policies
For ctr = 1 To numGpos

'compare version numbers
  if dcf.GPOSysVolVersion(ctr) <> dcf.GPOVersion(ctr) then

    'if they don't match echo version status and set flag
wscript.echo dcf.gponame(ctr) & " has a gpoversion of " & dcf.gpoversion(ctr)
➥& " and a sysvol version of " & dcf.gposysvolversion(ctr)
      flag=1
  end if
```

LISTING 30.6   CONTINUED

```
Next

'echo success
if flag=0 then wscript.echo "all gpos are in sync"
```

Caution   Pay very close attention to wrapping on this script. Every command must be on its own line regardless of length.

Before you can use the properties and methods of iadstools, you must instantiate the object. This is shown in the 'instantiate the object section of the code. The createobject function uses the programmatic identifier (IADSTools.DCfunctions) to find the GUID of the object in the Registry, load it into memory, and get an instance of the object.

The arguments again enable you to pass command-line arguments or parameters to the code. Explicitly declaring the variables in the 'set up arguments and variables section is not necessary in VBScript, but it is a good habit. You have no reason to set the datatype for the variables because VBScript supports only variant datatypes.

The getgpos function shown in 'get number of group policies for container returns the number of gpos for the container and also enumerates the group policies. This enables you to use other methods that require getgpos to be run first, before they can be used. Notice that this example uses the cstr function to convert the arguments to string datatypes before it passes them to the getgpos function. This is required if you are using VBScript. The arguments are the name of the OU and the LDAP DN of the domain.

The 'iterate through group policies line simply enables you to run through the group policies one a time. Here, you are checking the version of the group policy template (sysvolversion) versus the container (gpoversion) in the 'compare version numbers section.

Next, you simply use the properties of the group policy to echo the name, and respective versions if they do not match. Because the flag has not explicitly had its value set, it is (by default) 0. Setting it to 1 even once in this loop causes the success message not to show. This is accomplished by the 'if they don't match echo version status and set flag section.

If all the version numbers match, you can exit with a success message. You use wscript.echo in the 'echo success example, but you also could use writeline to send the output to the command line. The following code shows the command-line use of the script, and Figure 30.2 shows the success message box:

```
C:\>gpocheck sales dc=fis,dc=local
```

REPLICATION STATUS

Replication is the heart of Active Directory. Because AD uses a multimaster replication model, objects can be created, deleted, or modified on any domain controller for the object's domain. Replication is the process of copying those changes from one DC to another. Many great tools are available in the support tools and Resource Kit to view and troubleshoot replication. The tool you'll build here, however, is a simple reporting tool you could use to check the replication status of a DC on demand or to modify the code to have it email you the result on a scheduled basis.

Figure 30.2
The success message tells you that your group policy versions match on this server.

The code appears in Listing 30.7 and is fairly straightforward. You instantiate the object, use the getdirectpartners method to retrieve the information, and then iterate through some interesting properties for each replication partner.

LISTING 30.7   PROGRAMMATICALLY DISPLAYING REPLICATION STATUS FOR A DOMAIN CONTROLLER

```
'create arguments collection
set oargs = wscript.arguments

'instantiate dcfunctions
Set objIADS=CreateObject("IADSTools.DCFunctions")

'read information from dc and populate properties
prtNrs=objIADS.GetDirectPartners(CStr(oargs(0)), CStr(oargs(1)))

'iterate through interesting properties
For ctr=1 to prtNrs
    wscript.stdout.writeline"DirectPartnerGuid: " &
    ➥objIADS.DirectPartnerGuid(ctr)
    wscript.stdout.writeline"DirectPartnerHighOU: " &
    ➥objIADS.DirectPartnerHighOU(ctr)
    wscript.stdout.writeline"DirectPartnerHighPU: " &
    ➥objIADS.DirectPartnerHighPU(ctr)
    wscript.stdout.writeline"DirectPartnerLastAttemptTime: "
& objIADS.DirectPartnerLastAttemptTime(ctr)
    wscript.stdout.writeline"DirectPartnerLastSuccessTime: " &
objIADS.DirectPartnerLastSuccessTime(ctr)
    wscript.stdout.writeline"DirectPartnerName: " &
    ➥objIADS.DirectPartnerName(ctr)
    wscript.stdout.writeline"DirectPartnerNumberFailures: " &
objIADS.DirectPartnerNumberFailures(ctr)
    wscript.stdout.writeline"DirectPartnerObjectGUID: " &
    ➥objIADS.DirectPartnerObjectGUID(ctr)
    wscript.stdout.writeline
Next
```

Again, the 'create arguments collection code simply enables you to use command-line parameters.

The 'instantiate dcfunctions code instantiates and connects you to the DLL.

Here, you use the getdirectpartners function to load the information to create the prtNrs object and load it with information about your replication partners in the 'read information from dc and populate properties code. If you do not call this function, the rest of the code will not work. The two required parameters are the server name (expressed in NetBIOS or DNS format) and the naming context for replication (expressed in LDAP format). See Listing 30.8 for an example.

All these properties (and more: see iadstools.doc) shown in 'iterate through interesting properties are populated when you call getdirectpartners. These properties can give you immediate feedback on the health of the replication topology and process for a given domain controller.

Listing 30.8 shows the execution of this script. Note the use of cscript and the errors reported with the second replication partner. This kind of information, gathered in a timely manner, is effective in proactively dealing with replication issues.

LISTING 30.8   USING YOUR SCRIPT, replcheck.vbs, TO CHECK REPLICATION STATUS

```
C:\>cscript replcheck.vbs server11.fis.local dc=fis,dc=local
Microsoft (R) Windows Script Host Version 5.1 for Windows
Copyright (C) Microsoft Corporation 1996-1999. All rights reserved.

DirectPartnerGuid: F687F628-538B-4251-9464-16BE5D1C30E4
DirectPartnerHighOU: 23743
DirectPartnerHighPU: 23743
DirectPartnerLastAttemptTime: 6/24/2000 6:18:52 PM
DirectPartnerLastSuccessTime: 6/24/2000 6:18:52 PM
DirectPartnerName: Default-First-Site-Name\DC1
DirectPartnerNumberFailures: 0
DirectPartnerObjectGUID: 5452748A-79FD-4C7E-B6B7-DC73A4D0A20B

DirectPartnerGuid: D18806C3-5CEB-4A9F-ABF1-3B5F1AF59523
DirectPartnerHighOU: 17947
DirectPartnerHighPU: 17947
DirectPartnerLastAttemptTime: 6/24/2000 6:08:28 PM
DirectPartnerLastSuccessTime: 6/23/2000 11:11:08 PM
DirectPartnerName: **DELETED SERVER #2
DirectPartnerNumberFailures: 23
DirectPartnerObjectGUID: 06BD0EBA-01BB-4D12-9886-2C268132A4DF
```

SUMMARY

The main reason you should use Active Directory scripting is because it's fun. Okay, seriously. There is virtually nothing you can't do to AD with ADSI and iadstools. From automating repetitive tasks to remotely viewing AD statistics, the possibilities are endless.

After you have seen the capabilities and have amassed a library of scripts, you will find that many things can be done to ease your administrative burden. You can use ADSI to look for certain properties, modify group membership en masse, and script the creation of reports on the health and status of your Active Directory.

TROUBLESHOOTING

RUNNING SCRIPTS ON NT

When I run my scripts from an NT computer, they don't work.

Although most ADSI scripts do not have to be run on the DC, you must be on a Windows 2000 computer to run them because the scripts are using locally registered COM Dynamic Link Libraries to do their work.

SCRIPTS RUN ONLY ON SOME COMPUTERS

My scripts run from some computers and not from others.

These scripts require the same resources that the other Active Directory tools require. DNS, LDAP, and Kerberos must be in place. Check whether the Active Directory Users and Computers MMC Snap-in works. If that won't run locally, you don't have a scripting problem; you have an Active Directory problem.

HEXADECIMAL ERROR MESSAGES

I am getting a hexadecimal error message and I can't find any help for this message.

Use the search feature of msdn.Microsoft.com; many COM error messages can be found there. Also try Support and the Knowledgebase at search.Microsoft.com/us/ SearchMS25.asp. I have found answers to COM problems I was having that had nothing to do with code and everything to do with issues such as permissions.

CHAPTER 31

CONCLUSION

In this chapter

ACTIVE DIRECTORY SUMMARY

Active Directory is an ambitious project. It is the work of thousands of coders and testers and the product of millions of man hours. The current versions of Windows 2000 and Active Directory provide a scalable, highly available network infrastructure. In this chapter you get a glimpse of the future, and we discuss where to go for more Active Directory information.

THE FUTURE

I don't know who said it, but they were right: "It's the Internet, stupid." Globally available networks will define information technology for the foreseeable future. This is one of the reasons Windows 2000 and Active Directory are built on standard protocols.

WHISTLER

Rumor has it that the project name for the next version of Windows is Whistler. Whistler probably will be an evolutionary change from Windows 2000, and the next version—Blackcomb—will fully integrate some of the massive changes that are envisioned with the .NET initiative. Although it is a little early in the game to be making hard predictions about this product, documents available on Microsoft's Web site lay out some specifications for Whistler.

HEADLESS SERVERS

A *headless* server sounds very much like a server appliance. This implementation would not require a monitor, keyboard, or mouse.

MSMQ 5.1

The new version of MSMQ, the message queuing functionality that debuted in the NT 4.0 Option Pack, would take on added capabilities, such as the capability to reference queues by URLs.

NETWORKING CHANGES

Rumor has it that NetBEUI and DLC protocols will be dropped from Whistler, whereas IPV6 will be added.

APPLICATION DIRECTORY PARTITIONS

Application Directory Partitions will allow more support for storing dynamic application data in Active Directory. Currently, storing dynamic application data is discouraged because it creates unnecessary Active Directory replication. Application Directory Partitions, however, will enable the developer and administrator to control the scope of replication and the placement of specific replicas of the Active Directory database.

IMPROVED SUPPORT FOR WIRELESS LANs

Wireless technology has been used at Microsoft for some time now and is increasingly becoming part of corporate landscapes. Wireless support will be better supported in Whistler.

DYNAMIC OBJECTS

Dynamic objects exist in the Active Directory for a specified lifetime and then are automatically deleted.

DYNAMIC AUXILIARY CLASSES

Dynamic Auxiliary Classes will enable additional classes to be used to define individual objects rather than entire classes.

VIRTUAL LIST VIEWS AND ATTRIBUTE SCOPED QUERIES

Both of these features enable administrators to more finely tune searches for Active Directory objects. Virtual List Views enable ranges to be set when returning a list of objects from a query, rather than just all the objects that meet a certain criteria. Attribute Scoped Queries allow searches against the contents of a multivalued attribute of a specific object.

CH
31

UNIVERSAL PLUG-AND-PLAY

This is Plug-and-Play over the wire for any networked object. It enables Whistler to find and control networked objects. A COM+ API supports scripting to find remote objects and control them from a central location.

NEW WINSOCK 2 APIs

This will ease and speed the creation of WinSock 2 applications. WinSock is an API for creating TCP/IP-based applications.

WINDOWS MEDIA RIGHTS MANAGER

This supports the creation and delivery of secure online media. This will protect the rights of the creator from unauthorized use and reproduction of the media.

.NET

.NET is currently a specification for a highly interconnected, distributed environment. The technologies implemented here would include the standard COM+ services, as well as SQL Server, Exchange, Biztalk, IIS, and such Internet protocols as Extensible Markup Language (XML) and Simple Object Access Protocol (SOAP). XML and SOAP already are being integrated into Windows 2000 now, but will become more feature-rich as time passes.

One of the key concepts behind .NET is the use of Web Services. Because the data is being interchanged in an XML format, we are no longer as concerned with where the data is stored. .NET provides an application infrastructure that can be developed against by Windows-centric developers and others.

AppCenter

AppCenter is a version of Windows 2000 designed to be used in server farms. The goal here is to provide application-level load balancing across an array of servers. This would provide the capability to add and subtract servers from a site based on need.

Biztalk Server

Biztalk Server will accept documents of varying type—such as Electronic Data Interchange, XML, and ASCII text—and will transform them into other formats (generally XML) and then route them to their destinations. Biztalk Server is designed to enable the interchange of information from disparate sources and make them usable to other information systems.

SQL Server 2000

SQL Server 2000 provides a robust, scalable database engine, along with native support for XML to enable cross-platform data querying and modification.

Host Integration Server 2000

The reality of many corporate networks today is that much of the companies' information is still on mainframes. Host Integration Server 2000 enables PC-based systems to more actively access that information and gives developers increased programmatic access to host-based systems.

Internet Security and Acceleration Server 2000

This product provides firewall and caching support for corporate internetworks.

64-Bit Windows

The current version of Windows 2000 is designed to run on 32-bit, Intel-based processors. Microsoft currently is working on a new version of Windows 2000 that is specifically designed to run on a 64-bit processor. Among other things, this will enable the capability to address much more RAM than currently possible.

Blackcomb

Blackcomb is the current code name for the version of Windows that will fully implement the .NET vision Microsoft has for the future. This is (currently) slated for release sometime in 2002.

WHERE TO GO FROM HERE...

We hope you have enjoyed the book. Like virtually any other data source, it is finite. Microsoft provides a multitude of Web-based sources for more information, and you can also find useful tools on the CD.

ONLINE HELP

Don't overlook the basics. The Online Help that ships with Windows 2000 has a wealth of information and is an enormous improvement over previous versions. You can access the Online Help by clicking Start, Help.

SUPPORT TOOLS

Don't forget the support tools. They are on the Windows 2000 CD in the `support\tools` folder. Although most of the functionality here is from the tools themselves, don't overlook the documentation that comes with the tools.

RESOURCE KITS

This is a massive source of knowledge. Although separately purchased products, they are pound for pound worth every dollar. Again, much of the value is in the tools, but the Books Online for the Resource Kits are knowledgeable, authoritative, and well written. Some of the contents of the Resource Kits can be accessed online at `www.microsoft.com/windows2000/library/resources/reskit`.

msnews.microsoft.com

This publicly available NNTP server has hundreds of open public forums that are visited by people all over the world. You usually can find much enlightenment in these newsgroups, and learning to search them can become quite an art.

www.microsoft.com

The Microsoft Web site, similar to its sister, `msdn.microsoft.com`, can be daunting because of its sheer size, but an amazing amount of information is found here. White papers written by the people who are creating the product are a marvelous tool for learning a product. The search engine can be put to excellent use to find Knowledge Base articles and white papers.

This is a very dynamic resource and should not be overlooked when searching for information about Windows 2000.

www.microsoft.com/windows2000

This is a great entry point for looking for free information about Windows 2000. From here, you can read online articles and download white papers.

CH
31

KNOWLEDGE BASE

Go to www.microsoft.com and choose Search/Search Microsoft.com. Deselect every check box except Support and the Knowledge Base. Then, type some keywords in the text box and click Search. Generally, you will get inundated with information.

WHITE PAPERS

White papers are free sources of information about a specific subject. Many times portions of the Resource Kit are developed from the white papers that are developed with the product. Try www.microsoft.com/windows2000/library/default.asp. This site is a great place to start looking for white papers.

TECHNET

TechNet is available online at www.microsoft.com/technet or as a CD subscription. Unless you have a very fast Internet connection, I suggest you get the CD subscription simply for speed and use the online version for information that has been added in the last few weeks.

SEMINARONLINE

These are audiovisual technical seminars that can be viewed over the Web at www.microsoft.com/seminar/1033. Many times these are copies of talks delivered at TechEd or other tech meetings and are a marvelous source of free training. The faster your connection, the more you are going to like this feature. Some of this content is included with the TechNet CD subscription.

MICROSOFT OFFICIAL CURRICULUM

MOC is training material on virtually any Microsoft product that is delivered by Microsoft-certified trainers at a Microsoft-certified technical education center. This material is specifically designed to address real-world issues and includes a large hands-on lab component. To find information on classes or a training center near you, go to www.microsoft.com/trainingandservices and click Training.

msdn.microsoft.com

Although directed primarily toward developers, this site contains some of the most detailed architectural information I have ever seen about Windows 2000 and Active Directory. Here again, the Search feature is almost mandatory because of the amount of information presented.

TECHED

Once a year, usually in May or June, Microsoft throws a week-long in-depth series of technical seminars called TechEd. These are held in the United States and abroad. Some seminars focus on development, as well as administrative issues. At the time of this writing, TechEd 2001 will be held June 17–21, 2001, in Atlanta, Georgia.

THE END

We hope this book is of use to you. We firmly believe that the lion's share of corporate networks for the foreseeable future will be built on Windows 2000 and Active Directory.

Information technology is a constantly changing field. You already know this; otherwise, you wouldn't be reading this book. A knowledge of the fundamentals of Active Directory will be good for your career and your company's network infrastructure.

CH
31

INDEX

Q - R

X - Z